Promises to Keep

Stopping by Woods on a Snowy Evening

Whose woods these are I think I know.
His house is in the village though;
He will not see me stopping here
To watch his woods fill up with snow.

My little horse must think it queer
To stop without a farmhouse near
Between the woods and frozen lake
The darkest evening of the year.

He gives his harness bells a shake
To ask if there is some mistake.
The only other sound's the sweep
Of easy wind and downy flake.

The woods are lovely, dark and deep,
But I have promises to keep,
And miles to go before I sleep,
And miles to go before I sleep.

—Robert Frost, 1923

Promises to Keep

The United States Since World War II

THIRD EDITION

Paul S. Boyer

University of Wisconsin–Madison

Houghton Mifflin Company   **Boston**   **New York**

Publisher: Charles Hartford
Senior Sponsoring Editor: Sally Constable
Development Editor: Lisa Kalner Williams
Senior Project Editor: Christina M. Horn
Editorial Assistant: Michelle O'Berg
Senior Art and Design Coordinator: Jill Haber
Senior Photo Editor: Jennifer Meyer Dare
Senior Composition Buyer: Sarah Ambrose
Senior Manufacturing Coordinator: Marie Barnes
Senior Marketing Manager: Sandra McGuire

Cover image: Working mother Jennie Magill shopping with her children at the supermarket, 1956. Time Life Pictures/Getty Images.

Credits appear on page 544.

Printed in the U.S.A.

Library of Congress Catalog Card Number: 2004108453

ISBN: 0-618-43383-X

23456789-QF-09 08 07 06 05

Contents

CHAPTER **6**

The Cold War Heats Up: From *Sputnik* to Vietnam   160

CHAPTER **7**

The Liberal Hour   185

CHAPTER **8**

The Civil-Rights Movement at Flood Tide   214

PART THREE   The Loss of Innocence   241

CHAPTER **9**

Radicalization: Black Power, the New Left, and the Counterculture   244

CHAPTER **10**

Out of Control: War in Vietnam, Protest at Home   263

CHAPTER **11**

1968 and the Nixon Years   291

CHAPTER 15

America at the Turn of the Century: Prosperity, Scandal, a Changing Society   425

CHAPTER 16

A Sea of Troubles, Glimmers of Promise, as a New Century Dawns   479

Charts and Graphs

Maps

Preface

Promises to Keep seeks to make sense of a cycle of American history that continues to shape the world in which we live, even though its beginnings now seem remote. The initial impetus behind the book was personal: this work covers a span of U.S. history that I myself experienced. Researching *Promises to Keep* helped me understand more about a period still vividly present in my own memory. Indeed, I frequently found that my recollections were imprecise and distorted, and needed to be checked against the historical record and current scholarship! I hope this effort at self-education will prove useful to others as well, including those whose memories begin well after 1945.

No work of history—and especially none dealing with contemporary events—can claim to be the final word. Yet enough time has now passed that some of the major contours and fault lines of the past six decades of American history are coming into focus. Thus, although the book includes essential factual coverage, it is also selective and interpretive, interweaving four principal themes.

The first is the pervasive impact of world events. For nearly fifty years, the superpower struggle known as the Cold War touched all facets of U.S. history, from nuclear strategy and international relations to the domestic economy and culture. Despite the Cold War's end, external events have continued to shape American history, especially in the form of a deadly cycle of terrorist attacks related to conflicts in the Middle East, culminating in the shocking attacks of September 11, 2001, and their aftermath.

A second theme is the sweeping effect of social protests and activist movements by many diverse groups—including African Americans, women, environmentalists, persons with disabilities, cultural conservatives, religious evangelicals, and others—that by the early twenty-first century had given rise to a society radically different from the America of 1945.

Third, *Promises to Keep* pays close attention to an interconnected set of economic, demographic, and technological changes, including the rise of a service-based economy, changes in the nature of work, an increasingly global economy, a growing Hispanic and Asian population, the surging growth of the Sun Belt, and, not least, the computer and information-technology revolutions that have transformed the way Americans communicate and entertain themselves.

Finally, the book documents the sweeping political changes of these decades. *Promises to Keep* takes politics seriously. Old-fashioned political history declined after 1960 as many students and young scholars dismissed it as sterile and boring. But we are now gaining an enlarged understanding of politics as the arena where vital issues are defined, debated, and (sometimes) resolved. Ongoing political wrangles over budget deficits, health care, education reform, welfare policy, and national security, for example, are one way Americans decide what kind of society they wish to live in and want their children to inherit.

The structure and style of *Promises to Keep* reflect my commitment to narrative history. The first histories were heroic tales and epics, initially transmitted orally and then written down, and historians abandon these roots at their peril. Although I offer analysis and interpretation and discuss broad themes and trends, I do so within a narrative framework grounded in human action and in a story unfolding over time. Reflecting this approach, the chapters are organized chronologically within four major sections that reflect key historical turning points.

Part One, "The American Century," focuses on the aftermath of World War II—the years when the optimism of victory dissipated amidst the U.S.-Soviet confrontation; a new political generation defined a post–New Deal public agenda; and citizens spooked by depression, war, and fresh global menaces sought the security of 1950s-style material abundance, mass culture, and suburban living.

Part Two, "Dissent, Terror, Reform," considers another side of the 1950s and carries the story forward to the mid-1960s. While the Cold War ground on, bringing moments of frightening confrontation and home-front fears of subversion and nuclear menace, a surge of reform inspired by the southern civil-rights struggle crested in 1964–65 with a wave of legislation that represented the high-water mark of postwar liberalism.

Part Three, "The Loss of Innocence," explores the breakdown of this liberal consensus. The late sixties and early seventies saw turmoil and white backlash on the racial front, conflicts over the Vietnam War, and a wrenching political crisis summed up in a single word: Watergate.

Part Four, "Setbacks, Achievements, New Dangers," brings the narrative to the present. As Americans in the seventies coped with the triple traumas of defeat in Vietnam, presidential malfeasance, and runaway inflation, they struggled to chart new directions in public policy and social action. While this reorientation brought feminism and environmentalism to the fore, it also spawned a conservative reaction that propelled Ronald Reagan to the White House in 1980, followed by George Bush senior in 1988.

Democrat Bill Clinton, elected president in 1992 on a middle-of-the-road platform, confronted a changing national demographic profile summed up in the phrase "the browning of America": a booming but volatile economy; the spread of personal computers and new electronic communications technologies; a continued political and cultural shift to the right; and policy issues as diverse as health care, welfare, campaign-finance reform, and tobacco-industry regulation. Internationally, Americans confronted a post–Cold War world that brought both promise and new forms of menace. Hijacked airplanes and other terrorist attacks in the 1980s and 1990s kept Americans on edge, and the catastrophic attack of September 2001 escalated the edginess to near panic. Our story concludes with the early years of the twenty-first century, which brought a sharp and painful recession, corporate scandals, and a presidential administration led by George W. Bush that intensified the conservative trend of recent years, responding to the interests of corporate America and the religious right. The Bush administration's response to the challenge of 9/11, at home and abroad, profoundly shaped American public life and political discourse as the nation moved further into a new century.

But structure and thematic generalizations, although essential if we are to make sense of history, are no substitute for attention to the gritty reality of the past. Through the book's sixteen chapters flow the juices of living history: the heroism of civil-rights marchers; the charisma and shocking deaths of John and Robert

Kennedy and Martin Luther King, Jr.; the vitriolic rhetoric of George Wallace; the boldness of feminists who challenged entrenched gender stereotypes; the passionate voices of writers such as Rachel Carson, Ralph Nader, and Michael Harrington who changed the way Americans perceived their society; the media wizardry of actor-turned-politician Ronald Reagan; the talented but flawed Bill Clinton; the boyish computer tycoon Bill Gates; the colorful revival preachers and televangelists; the blue-collar workers coping with disruptive economic changes; the marchers and activists who revitalized the nation's reform tradition; the Americans who served and died in Vietnam and Iraq and the Americans who protested those wars; the cultural conservatives and Christian evangelicals who struggled to put their concerns on the national agenda. History is made not only in Washington, D.C., or in corporate boardrooms but also at the grassroots all across the land—a fact I have tried to keep constantly in mind while writing *Promises to Keep*.

This, then, is not an authoritative, predigested, take-it-or-leave-it version of recent U.S. history, but simply one perspective on that history presented in a way that I hope will stimulate discussion and reflection. The text, the charts and photographs, the "In Perspective" essays, and the bibliographies at the end of each chapter are all intended to encourage readers to probe facets of the story more deeply and to reach their own conclusions.

No historian works in a vacuum, and certainly not one who rashly attempts an interpretive overview of six decades of American history. In addition to my own research in the sources, I have profited from the books and essays of scores of historians and journalists who have written about specific movements and events. These works are acknowledged in the chapter bibliographies, but I also wish to thank their authors here. Without the wealth of specialized scholarship now in print on the postwar period, the writing of this book would have been vastly more daunting.

This third edition of *Promises to Keep* assesses the central public issues and key domestic and international developments of the years since the contested 2000 presidential election. It also also offers fresh interpretive perspectives on earlier events and trends. New findings and analytic insights based on the most recently published scholarship or newly released documents are incorporated throughout the book. Several new "In Perspective" essays place important topics in a broader historical framework. The prose has been tightened and sharpened to incorporate new material without significantly adding to the length.

I am grateful to the scholars who reviewed the third edition: Richard G. Davies, University of Nevada, Reno; Thomas W. Devine, California State University, Northridge; Ignacio M. Garcia, Brigham Young University; Erik C. Maiershofer, MiraCosta College; and Sayuri Shimizu, Michigan State University. The finished product is much stronger because of their unsparing but constructive criticism.

I am pleased to express my warm appreciation to the superb and supportive editorial team at Houghton Mifflin's College Division, especially Sally Constable, Christina Horn, Christina Lembo, and Lisa Kalner Williams, who helped shepherd this third edition of *Promises to Keep* through the editorial and production labyrinth. Bruce Carson provided invaluable help in the selection of photographs. Jean Woy has been consistently supportive of the project. And a nostalgic salute to Leah Strauss and Janet Young, who played crucial roles in bringing the second edition to fruition, and to Jim Miller, Sylvia Mallory, Lauren Johnson, and others who were "present at the creation" when the first edition was planned, written, and brought into existence. Ann Boyer's perceptive comments and eagle eye for typos improved Chapter 16.

Finally, I take pleasure in acknowledging the friendship and sustained intellectual stimulation of my colleagues in the University of Wisconsin–Madison history department and at the Institute for Research in the Humanities, housed in the Washburn Observatory overlooking Lake Mendota on the Madison campus. This fine old structure, built when Rutherford B. Hayes occupied the White House, provided not only an ideal workplace but also a living architectural link with the past as *Promises to Keep* was researched and written.

P. B.

PART ONE

The American Century

This book is the story of three generations of Americans. The first came of age during the Great Depression, fought in World War II or worked in home-front defense plants, and in 1945 looked forward to a future of peace, security, and prosperity. The second generation—the baby boomers—grew up in the affluent yet anxiety-ridden 1950s and reached maturity in the turbulent 1960s. The baby boomers' children, the third generation, will lead the United States in the early twenty-first century. To tell the story of these three generations is to write the history of the United States over the past half-century.

Part One focuses on the generation shaped by World War II and the early postwar years. The events and trends of that era molded the diplomacy, the politics, the economic and social agenda—even the cultural climate—of the next fifty years. The vast upheavals of 1941–45 also set the stage for the Cold War. This confrontation would split the wartime Grand Alliance, pitting the Soviet Union (and China, after 1949) against the United States and its Western European allies. World War II had scarcely ended before the new all-consuming confrontation began to influence U.S. foreign policy and military planning. Initially focused on Europe and the Middle East, the Cold War soon spread to Asia and elsewhere, including the United States itself. As fear of communism seized the nation, opportunistic politicians stoked suspicions of domestic subversion and disloyalty. Intellectuals who had criticized capitalism in the depression-ridden 1930s now hailed America as humanity's last best hope against totalitarianism. These thinkers deplored the vulgarity and conformity of middle-class culture but rarely challenged the postwar order in more fundamental ways.

World War II ended the Great Depression, revived the tarnished reputation of big business, and stimulated an economic boom. Military technological developments and production innovations gave rise to a postwar cornucopia of consumer products that enabled millions of Americans to enjoy unprecedented affluence. Construction techniques devised to house war workers made possible the suburbs that burgeoned in the late 1940s and the 1950s. Television, which would revolutionize U.S. politics, marketing, and mass culture, burst on the scene just after the war.

Fought against racist regimes abroad, World War II also revealed the irony of racism at home, most notably in the internment of thousands of Japanese Americans in remote detention camps in the West. Yet the global conflict also stimulated social changes that ultimately would defy entrenched gender, racial, and ethnic hierarchies. Women poured into war plants, thousands of African Americans migrated to cities, and Mexicans immigrated in great numbers to work in agriculture and in urban jobs. These demographic trends fostered social movements that would transform America in the decades ahead.

Finally, the war and the early Cold War years engendered a cultural mood that would resonate for decades. The conflict and the sweeping victory in 1945 stimulated national unity and encouraged feelings of national omnipotence summed up in the phrase "the American Century," coined in 1941 by magazine mogul Henry Luce. To some extent, this spirit of unity and high resolve spilled over into the immediate postwar years, as Washington mobilized public opinion against the new adversary based in Moscow. The stark rhetorical polarities of the early Cold War—polarities that pitted the "Free World" against the dark menace of a global communist conspiracy—enhanced the sense of destiny and mission that had long undergirded the national self-image. Booming prosperity whipped up further optimism about American capitalism, as well as pride in the American way of life.

But beneath the surface, currents of fear and uneasiness eddied. The nuclear arms race—the war's grimmest legacy—yielded nightmares of global annihilation. And beyond the well-tended suburbs lay a very different America of rural poverty and inner-city slums. The political process occasionally addressed the racial discrimination and economic disparities plaguing American society, but this early postwar generation more often swept such matters under the carpet. The Fair Deal, President Harry Truman's domestic reform program of 1948–49, may have set the political agenda for the next generation, but at the time most of Truman's program languished.

As the Democrats' long hold on the White House loosened in the early 1950s before a resurgent Republicanism led by war hero Dwight Eisenhower, the impetus for reform slackened. Dissenters—most notably African Americans no longer willing to tolerate second-class citizenship—would challenge the status quo more insistently as the decade wore on. Nevertheless, for a brief postwar moment, all seemed bright in America, and the future shone with promise. To a prospering and powerful nation, the "American Century" was not journalistic hyperbole but unvarnished truth.

CHAPTER

Crucible of Change: World War II and the Forging of Modern America

FEW AMERICAN ENTERTAINERS of the 1940s enjoyed greater popularity than the singer Kate Smith, famous for her soaring rendition of "God Bless America." Thus, when CBS radio executives planned "War Bond Day" for September 21, 1943, they invited Miss Smith to host it. From 8 A.M. until well past midnight she tirelessly urged listeners to buy bonds, raising nearly $40 million in support of the war. The overwhelming success of "War Bond Day," thanks in part to the promptings of a popular-culture celebrity, symbolizes the national mood during World War II. During these years, the American people, reinforced by official propaganda and media publicity, stood united to a degree rarely seen either before or since. Social tensions and partisan conflicts simmered beneath the surface, but the widely shared goal of defeating the United States' enemies muted these differences.

For those who lived through it, World War II remains etched in memory, one of those events by which people mark the stages of their lives and define their generation. For historians, the war presents multiple layers of significance that go beyond the conflict itself and the immediate objectives for which it was fought. Any serious effort to understand modern America must circle back to World War II.

The Grand Alliance, Globalist Dreams, Big Power Realities

World War II spawned a tangle of postwar issues. This great conflict brought together an alliance of nations committed to the defeat of Germany, Italy, and Japan, the so-called Axis powers ruled by militaristic, expansionist dictatorships. The United States, Great Britain, and the Soviet Union led the coalition that ultimately defeated the Axis powers, and some policymakers hoped that this "Grand Alliance" among the "Big Three" would continue after the war. But the Grand Alliance, forged in opposition to a common foe rather than from a broad range of common interests, proved highly unstable. Although the U.S.-British coalition held firm and became part of a larger postwar Atlantic alliance linking the United States with Western Europe, the Soviet Union soon moved from the status of ally to that of deeply mistrusted adversary.

As for the Axis powers, ironically, World War II laid the groundwork for the eventual emergence of Germany and Japan as world economic giants and major trading competitors. Their industrial infrastructure shattered by bombs, both nations built new factories and the latest equipment from scratch after the war. This retooling depended, in part, on massive aid supplied by the United States, the nation that had defeated them militarily.

During the war itself, some visionaries hoped that out of the struggle would emerge a harmonious new global system based on internationalist principles. This dream, eloquently articulated by Woodrow Wilson during World War I, had survived the disillusionments of the interwar years and remained alive in the early 1940s. Republican Wendell Willkie's *One World* (1943), a wartime bestseller, fervently preached postwar global cooperation. The United Nations Charter, adopted at a fifty-nation conference in San Francisco in June 1945, seemed a step toward realizing this lofty vision.

Some opinion molders envisioned the new international order as a Pax Americana, or peace imposed by America. As early as 1941, writing in his *Life* magazine, publisher Henry R. Luce had hailed the advent of the "American Century." U.S. goods and popular culture already dominated the globe, proclaimed Luce; now the task was to spread American values: democracy, capitalism, philanthropy, and benevolence. "We must undertake now to be the Good Samaritan of the entire world," Luce grandly asserted. Physically untouched by the war, its industrial infrastructure intact and powerful, a seemingly omnipotent United States could well contemplate establishing a benign world order—the American way of life writ large.

But World War II had unleashed forces that would shatter the Grand Alliance, overwhelm the fledgling United Nations, and mock Henry Luce's rose-tinted scenario. The conflict left Europe prostrate and intensified nationalist stirrings in onetime colonial regions of Asia and Africa. Moreover, it set the stage for confrontation between the United States and the Soviet Union.

Soviet dictator Joseph Stalin held a very different view of the postwar world from the one envisioned by the Pax Americana theorists. Certainly Stalin had gone to war against Hitler in the early summer of 1941, thereby joining the Grand Alliance. But earlier, in August 1939, Hitler and Stalin had signed a nonaggression pact dividing Poland between them. The Nazi-Soviet Pact had collapsed in June 1941, however, when the German *Wehrmacht* (army), rumbling across a 2,000-mile front, attacked the Soviet Union. The U.S.S.R. suffered ghastly losses in repelling Hitler's forces. One campaign alone—the terrible German siege of Stalingrad in 1942–43—cost a million casualties on both sides. The Soviets' experience in what they called the "Great Patriotic War" deepened an already strong determination to maintain absolute security around the perimeter of their vast but unstable empire.

By the summer of 1945, Soviet armed might stood unrivaled on much of the Eurasian land mass. That stark military fact would soon translate into political realities. Repelling the Nazi invaders, the Soviet army had swept across Eastern Europe and thrust deep into Germany in the war's final months. Stalin set out to build a buffer zone of Soviet-controlled satellite states in this region. Marxist-Leninist ideology, with its prediction of inevitable world revolution, neatly dovetailed with Russian concerns about border security. Stalin also sought a sphere of influence in Eastern Europe to match what he saw as Anglo-American dominance in Western Europe. Even as the war wound down, shrewd observers detected the contours of a new conflict in the diametrically opposed worldviews of the two emerging superpowers.

During the war, a series of Big Power conferences and pronouncements had glossed over these differences. At the final meeting of the wartime Big Three leaders, held at the Crimean resort of Yalta early in 1945, Stalin, President Franklin D. Roosevelt, and British prime minister Winston Churchill laid plans for pursuing the war in the Pacific and set the course for the early postwar era. Stalin agreed to join the planned United Nations after extracting a pledge from Roosevelt and Churchill to admit two Soviet republics, Ukraine and Byelorussia, as full UN members. The Soviet leader secretly pledged to declare war on Japan within "two or three months" of Germany's surrender, in return for an occupation zone in Korea and other concessions. The Americans viewed Stalin's promise as highly important, because Japan, although battered in the Pacific island campaign and running low on war materiel and fuel, still had more than 4 million troops under arms.

The shadow of Poland hung over Yalta. Germany's invasion of that nation in 1939 had triggered the war, and the Western powers felt a moral obligation to protect Poland's postwar interests. Furthermore, a large Polish American community in the United States remained vitally interested in the homeland. Nevertheless, Roosevelt and Churchill were in a weak bargaining position, given the Soviets' physical hold on Poland. On the key question of Poland's postwar boundaries, Stalin demanded a slice of the eastern portion of the country. More important, to weaken hated Germany, he proposed moving Poland's western boundary so as to incorporate large chunks of eastern Germany. Playing a weak hand, Roosevelt and Churchill proposed deferring the Polish-border issue to a postwar "peace conference," which never convened. After the war, Stalin unilaterally rearranged Poland's borders as he had proposed at Yalta. In another Yalta agreement that proved meaningless, Stalin offered promises of free elections in postwar Eastern Europe. In reality, he imposed pro-Soviet regimes throughout the occupied lands where his armies held sway.

Yalta would play a key role in American domestic politics when in the 1950s, Republicans charged that President Roosevelt had "given away" Eastern Europe to Stalin. In fact, the realities of Soviet military control of Eastern Europe, hopes that the United Nations might indeed function as a force for peace and world order, and FDR's eagerness to secure Stalin's entry into the war against Japan all shaped the terms of the Yalta settlement. But the tenacious myth of a "great betrayal" at Yalta would for years be used by Republicans to portray Democrats as naive dupes, if not traitors, in their dealings with the Soviet Union.

Popular misconceptions of the wartime alliance helped shape Americans' postwar attitudes toward the Soviets. Behind the scenes, this coalition of wartime convenience crackled with tension, as Stalin made territorial demands and urgently called on the Allies to open a western front against the Nazis, a move that the Allies delayed until 1944. Despite Stalin's cooperation with the West against Germany, his brutal regime in many ways mirrored Hitler's. Indeed, as we have seen,

Stalin and Hitler in 1939 had cynically sliced up Poland between them. In 1940 Soviet forces had massacred twenty thousand Polish officers and subsequently blamed the Nazis for the crime.

Most Americans, however, remained largely unaware of these tensions. The media and official Washington pronouncements generally presented the Soviet Union as a heroic ally in a struggle for common ideals. One poster depicted a row of cannons bearing the flags of the United States, the Soviet Union, and the other Allies with the caption "UNITED We Will Win." Hollywood movies such as *Mission to Moscow* (1943), *North Star* (1943), and *Song of Russia* (1944), produced with the Roosevelt administration's blessing, offered idealized images of the brave Russian people struggling against the Nazi invaders. *Life* magazine portrayed pipe-puffing "Uncle Joe Stalin" as a benevolent, beloved leader.

Such propaganda encouraged the popular assumption that Soviet-American cooperation would endure into the postwar era. Yet within months of the war's end, as conflicts and power rivalries took shape, U.S. leaders began publicly to portray the Soviet Union in menacing terms. Americans soon came to view the Soviet Union with a deep hostility that was a mirror image of the simplistic and rose-tinted perceptions fostered during the war. Thus, as the war years' unrealistic expectations eroded under harsh postwar realities, disillusionment set in and a stark, black-and-white worldview emerged that would characterize Cold War America. In this, as in many other ways, World War II continued to influence events long after hostilities had ceased.

High Resolve and National Unity

Most of America's twentieth-century wars were far from universally popular. In 1917, a minority of socialists, pacifists, and some German Americans bitterly opposed President Woodrow Wilson's call for war. The Korean War (1950–53) initially won broad support, but many citizens soon turned against the frustrating, stalemated conflict. The Vietnam War proved deeply divisive in the 1960s, as did the Iraq War of 2003 and its fustrating aftermath.

World War II was different; it stirred near-universal feelings of patriotism and common purpose, and for good reason. Although the conflict actually started when Germany invaded Poland on September 1, 1939, for Americans it began on December 7, 1941, with Japan's sneak attack on the U.S. Pacific fleet at Pearl Harbor, which killed 2,400 U.S. servicemen. In his war message, President Roosevelt described December 7 as "a date which will live in infamy," and, indeed, "Remember Pearl Harbor" became a driving slogan of the war. Unlike the murky justifications offered for some other wars, the issues in 1941–45 seemed crystal clear: to avenge Pearl Harbor and to defeat the dictators and militarists in Germany, Italy, and Japan who threatened the world with their racism, totalitarianism, and brute strength. With enemies like these, the war took on overtones of a religious crusade. Americans "in their righteous might," Roosevelt proclaimed after Pearl Harbor, "will win through to . . . inevitable triumph." One top general, George C. Patton, reportedly assured a group of army chaplains that he went to church "every goddam Sunday."

Some fifty thousand young men from Quaker, Mennonite, or other historic peace churches refused to bear arms for reasons of conscience. Most accepted non-combat roles in the military or were assigned to homefront Civilian Public Service (CPS) camps. A few went to prison. This history would be remembered during the Vietnam War, when antiwar sentiment ran high. But most young men responded willingly when drafted, or enlisted voluntarily.

If GIs at the front felt less enthusiasm than propagandists suggested, most nevertheless believed that they were fighting for a just cause and performing a necessary job. Families that sent a son or daughter into the service proudly displayed a blue star in their window. Those who received the dreaded War Department telegram that began "I regret to inform you . . ." substituted a gold star. Millions purchased war bonds, contributed to paper drives, and planted victory gardens. War workers shared in the sense of national purpose. As one recalled, Pearl Harbor brought "an immediate change in people's attitude toward their work—their sense of urgency, their dedication, their team work." Children chalked caricatures of Hitler and Japan's wartime military leader Hideki Tojo on walls and turned in pencil stubs so the graphite could be recycled as a lubricant. Gleefully, they passed along anti-German, anti-Japanese jokes overheard from adults. (The German *Messerschmidt* fighter, they told each other, savoring the naughty word, was a "mess o' shit.") When Japan formally surrendered on August 14, 1945, the nation erupted in celebration. Even toddlers sensed the excitement; one man recalled decades later: "I remember leading a parade of kids around our summer house, me with a potato masher."

To be sure, the war spirit was carefully orchestrated. The government's Office of War Information (OWI) ground out propaganda posters, magazine ads, and radio spots and worked with Hollywood studios to ensure that wartime movies promoted patriotism and reinforced U.S. war aims. Director Frank Capra's *Why We Fight* series offered troops the OWI version of the nation's objectives and the heinous nature of the enemy. By controlling the flow of photographs from the front, particularly images of U.S. dead, the OWI further molded popular perceptions of the conflict. The OWI also fostered myths of American GIs' wisecracking under fire, such as the one about the survivors of a bloody U.S. assault in the Pacific who supposedly radioed the jaunty message: "Send us more Japs."

The Office of Censorship (OC) monitored the nation's media for anything that might weaken morale or undermine support for the war. Although it stressed voluntary compliance rather than legal prosecution, the OC did have the power of the federal government behind it. Another government agency, the Office of Civilian Defense (OCD), offered an idealized version of the home-front mood. A 1942 OCD pamphlet reported, "The kids still play baseball in the corner lot—but they knock off early to weed the victory garden, cart scrap paper to the salvage center, carry home the groceries that used to be delivered." These manipulative techniques, however heavy-handed, had their desired effect: a nation already well aware of the stakes of the conflict solidified its support for the war.

Influential mass-culture organs—from movies, ads, cartoons, and popular songs to novels, essays, newspaper editorials, and political speeches—contributed to the martial mood. The Association of Music Educators did its bit in 1943 by preparing a version of "The Star-Spangled Banner" that was pitched in A-flat, and thus easier to sing. The heroes of children's radio shows like *The Green Hornet* and *Captain Midnight* pursued enemy spies and saboteurs. *Dick Tracy* fans who promised to save scarce wartime commodities had their names inscribed on the show's "Victory Honor Roll." Over a million youthful listeners to *Jack Armstrong, All-American Boy* joined his "Write-a-Fighter Corps," pledging to write a soldier once a month. Even comic-strip characters, including the hero of "Terry and the Pirates," marched off to war. Of the major male comic-strip characters, only Superman and Li'l Abner (Al Capp's stereotypical southern hayseed) failed to don a U.S. military uniform. (Superman, of course, already had a uniform in which to fight for "truth, justice, and the American way.") War reporters such as Ernie Pyle and battlefront cartoonists such as Bill Mauldin might underscore the grimmer aspects of war, but they never questioned the righteousness of the war itself. War bond drives raised $186 billion. School kids bought war stamps that could be converted to bonds. The actress Lana Turner raised over $5 million by offering a kiss to everyone who bought a $50,000 bond.

Only rarely in 1941–45 did an American writer suggest that even a just war could involve official hypocrisy, routinized slaughter, and the denial of the essential humanity of those labeled "the enemy." Among the few who acknowledged this side of the story was the poet Randall Jarrell, whose 1945 poem "Losses" began:

> In bombers named for girls, we burned
> The cities we had learned about in school—
> Till our lives wore out; our bodies lay among
> The people we had killed and never seen.
> When we lasted long enough they gave us medals.
> When we died they said "Our casualties were low."

A few pacifists and religious leaders protested the Allies' terror-bombing of cities, a practice initiated by the Nazis that spread more widely as the war ground on. (In fact, the firebombing of Tokyo by an armada of U.S. B-29s on the night of March 10–11, 1945, killed more civilians than later died in the atomic bombing of Hiroshima.) The political writer Dwight Macdonald, anticipating a theme later expanded by opponents of the Vietnam War, warned of the anonymity of mass slaughter by modern technological means. In *Politics,* his one-man journal of opinion, Macdonald wrote in 1944:

> One of the things which makes it possible for a modern civilian to participate in war without more psychological resistance . . . is the fact that the murderous aspect of war is depersonalized. Most of the killing is done at such long range that the killers have no sense of the physical effects of their attack. . . . [I]t is one thing to know that one *may* be responsible for the death and mutilation of invisible people ten miles away or five miles down, and another to cut a man's throat with one's own hands.

But such reflections were rare as the nation mobilized for the struggle against totalitarianism.

Despite propaganda campaigns that channeled patriotism in specific directions, Americans' overwhelming support for the war was genuine. At the most elemental level, Americans saw the war as a fight for a perhaps semi-mythic but cherished way of life that the Axis powers threatened. Lumps swelled in throats when Kate Smith sang "God Bless America"; when Humphrey Bogart gave up Ingrid Bergman to Paul Henreid, a courageous Czech Resistance leader, in *Casablanca* (1943); when Bing Crosby crooned "I'm Dreaming of a White Christmas," the hit song of 1942; or when the hero of Nevil Shute's *Pied Piper* (1942) spirited a group of children out of France ahead of the advancing Nazis. A California girl later reminisced, recalling her family's victory garden, "[W]e all wanted to do our part for the war. You got caught up in the mesmerising spirit of patriotism."

Anticipating a major cultural theme of the 1950s, the propagandists of 1941–45 defined American war aims in terms of community life and family togetherness. One war-bond poster featured a little girl with a message written in a childish hand: "Please help bring my Daddy home." The war's most famous visual images, initially published as *Saturday Evening Post* covers, were Norman Rockwell's illustrations of the "Four Freedoms" enunciated by President Roosevelt in 1941. In Rockwell's version, a family Thanksgiving dinner embodied "Freedom from Want," a mom and dad lovingly looking at their sleeping children represented "Freedom from Fear," a man having his say at a New England town meeting stood for "Freedom of Speech," and parishioners in a little church portrayed "Freedom of Worship."

In contrast to the Vietnam era, World War II veterans came back as heroes. The Servicemen's Readjustment Act of 1944, popularly known as the GI Bill of Rights, gave veterans hiring preference, tuition and other educational benefits, and loan guarantees to purchase homes, farms, or small businesses. The measure staved off postwar unemployment and eased veterans' reentry into the labor force, although often displacing women workers. Driving college enrollments to record highs, the act hastened the growth of a college-trained middle class in postwar America. Finally, the program contributed to a surge of suburban housing construction.

Just as wartime unity and idealism affected Cold War attitudes toward the Soviet Union, so, too, did they influence the postwar domestic political climate. As the sense of common purpose gave way to political dissent and ideological differences—normal ferment in a democracy—some Americans responded by charging dissenters with disloyalty and even subversion. The climate of the war years thus contributed to the postwar drive for conformity, as patriots tried to impose on the nation the consensus and dedication to a common purpose that characterized the war era. As early as 1944, while the war still raged, the Republican vice-presidential candidate, Senator John W. Bricker of Ohio, ominously previewed the postwar air of suspicion when he warned that sinister and divisive forces were "worming their way into our national life."

The American Economy Goes to War

The war finally broke the back of the Great Depression and laid the foundation for sustained postwar economic growth. After Pearl Harbor, surging military spending and war production fueled an economic boom, and by June 1942, more than $100 billion in military contracts had poured out of Washington. By 1943–44, with war production in full swing, joblessness almost vanished. The Works Progress Administration (WPA), the New Deal's principal relief agency, distributed its final checks early in 1943.

The war brought unprecedented affluence for millions of Americans. From 1939 to 1945, average real wages for all employees (adjusted for inflation) increased 44 percent, and the gross national product soared from $90 billion to $212 billion. Farmers prospered as crop production rose by 50 percent and farm income by 200 percent in the period. Reviving prosperity stimulated an upturn in the birthrate. The 1943 birthrate, although below that of the fecund 1950s, was still more than 20 percent higher than the mid-1930s rate. Despite the absence of many males at the front, the "postwar baby boom" actually began during the war itself.

The heavy government spending of 1941–45 appeared to validate the theories of British economist John Maynard Keynes, who argued that to fight a depression, a government should stimulate consumer demand and buying power through massive spending, even if large budget deficits resulted in the short run. FDR, distrustful of unbalanced budgets, had rejected Keynesianism during the 1930s, but the war-induced spending of the early 1940s produced precisely the economic result that Keynes had predicted, although by means of military spending rather than government-encouraged consumer buying.

With the military absorbing much of the nation's industrial and agricultural production, numerous consumer goods and basic foodstuffs fell in short supply (coffee, sugar, butter, and meat) or disappeared entirely (new cars, household

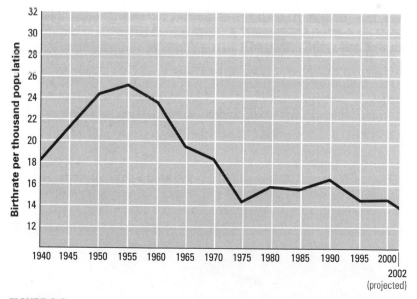

FIGURE 1.1

Birthrate, 1940–2002

SOURCE: National Center for Health Statistics, U.S. Department of Health and Human Services, in *Statistical Abstract of the United States, 1997* and *World Almanac, 2004.*

appliances). Many citizens, now benefiting from rising wages, apparently saw no contradiction between patriotic support for the war and turning to the black market to acquire and hoard scarce goods, thereby circumventing wartime rationing.

When the war began, a British observer, D. W. Brogan, predicted that the U.S. war effort, like the rest of American life, would be mechanized, and that victory would depend on the nation's "colossal business enterprises, often wastefully run in detail, but winning by their mere scale." Brogan was right. The war drove industrial production to new levels. Factories ran twenty-four hours a day, pouring out planes, tanks, jeeps, guns, and the vast array of support materials, from shoes to typewriters, needed by the military. The Ford bomber plant at Willow Run, Michigan, with a main building covering sixty-seven acres, employed more than forty thousand workers. One awed observer called it "a sort of Grand Canyon of the mechanized world." By 1944, total annual U.S. aircraft production reached a staggering 96,318. Dam builder Henry J. Kaiser, turning to ship construction during the war, cut the manufacturing time for a cargo carrier from 355 days to 14. Securing government loans to cover start-up costs, Kaiser by 1943 held $3 billion in war contracts and controlled 30 percent of U.S. shipbuilding. Even occasional embar-

The Homefront Mobilizes, August 1943. A war worker at the Electric Boat Company in Groton, Connecticut, helps construct the hull of a U.S. Navy submarine. *(Photo by Lt. Comdr. Charles Fenno Jacobs, AP/Wide World Photos)*

rassments such as a ship that sank at the launching dock left intact Kaiser's reputation as a wizard of wartime production.*

Some feared that the Depression would come roaring back once the war ended, but in fact the groundwork was being laid for a postwar boom. Mass-production and prefabrication techniques perfected in wartime would soon be converted to peacetime purposes, and the accumulated savings and pent-up purchasing impulses of war workers would fuel a monumental postwar buying binge. Wartime productivity feats had ideological consequences as well, for the corporate contribution to victory reshaped popular attitudes toward business. After the 1929 stock-market crash, the reputation of businessmen had plummeted, and in 1936 President Roosevelt had denounced them as "malefactors of great wealth." As war approached, however, Washington portrayed giant corporations as partners in a common cause. A wartime Senate committee admiringly noted, "The hand that signs the war contract is the hand that shapes the future." Congress granted war industries tax breaks and exemption from antitrust laws. Many corporate executives served in Washington as unpaid administrators of wartime agencies. Factories proudly flew the "Army and Navy 'E'" banner (a War Department commendation), and a heavy gloss of patriotism overlay corporate advertising. Indeed, some business ads did not mention a product at all but simply featured public-service messages urging Americans to buy bonds. "War Bonds Mean Bullets in the Bellies of Nazi Hordes," proclaimed one ad sponsored by a New York City banking association.

Businesses showed remarkable ingenuity in linking their products to the war effort. By building bottling plants wherever GIs went, the Coca-Cola Company cultivated a taste for Coke among the troops and developed a worldwide market. The Parker Pen Company boosted sales of its ink 800 percent with an ad campaign reminding Americans of their patriotic duty to write long and frequent letters to lonely GIs overseas. Tobacco companies hooked a new generation of smokers by distributing free cigarettes to soldiers, including those in military hospitals. As John Morton Blum notes in *V Was for Victory* (1976), Philip K. Wrigley persuaded the government to include his Wrigley's chewing gum in the "K-Rations" (food packs) distributed to servicemen in combat and urged war plant managers to give each worker five sticks daily to combat boredom, fatigue, nervous tension, and an insidious condition known as "false thirst."

The war influenced corporate attitudes toward government as well. In the 1930s, many corporate leaders had vehemently attacked the New Deal and the proliferation of regulatory agencies. Now the mood shifted. As FDR appointed businessmen to Washington posts and the shower of military contracts demonstrated the profitable possibilities in business-government cooperation, antigovernment hostility faded. In *America Unlimited* (1944), Eric Johnston of the U.S. Chamber of Commerce sought to solidify the heightened prestige of business and to reinforce corporate leaders' newly positive attitude toward government. "[C]redit for the most astounding production job in all human history," declared Johnston, "must go primarily to American capitalism." Calling for an end to the

---

*Kaiser also pioneered an employee medical plan that would later provide a model for health-care plans nationwide, another example of World War II's long historical reach.

feud between corporate America and the Roosevelt administration, Johnston urged forward-looking capitalists to accept the new reality of greater federal regulation. Such conciliatory views decisively influenced postwar political thought. President Dwight Eisenhower's espousal of "moderate Republicanism" in the 1950s rested on the premise of cooperation between government and enlightened leaders from all sectors of society, including business. Thanks in part to memories of the wartime experience, this view won many adherents.

Organized labor, which had thrived in the later New Deal years, experienced further growth but also setbacks during the war. To head off strikes that could hurt war production and to control inflationary wage increases, the Roosevelt administration limited hourly wage raises during the war to no more than the rise in the cost of living. (Thanks to overtime hours at time-and-a-half pay, however, many war workers took home fat paychecks.) To enforce the labor unions' wartime "no-strike" pledge, the National War Labor Board (NWLB) focused on settling disputes by arbitration. In 1943 conservatives in Congress passed, over Roosevelt's veto, the Smith-Connally Anti-Strike Act. This law forbade political contributions by labor unions and expanded the president's powers to take over war plants threatened by labor disputes. When the nation's rail workers threatened a strike late in 1943, the U.S. Army at FDR's direction briefly seized the railroads. In another example of the war's aftereffects, these measures anticipated the Taft-Hartley Act of 1947, which further restricted labor unions.

Despite these constraints, the surge in wartime employment proved a boon to the labor movement. From 1941 to 1945, union membership soared from about 10.5 million to nearly 15 million. By the latter year, nearly 36 percent of the labor force was unionized, an all-time high. Moreover, the NWLB was generally prounion, for example, by approving contracts that required union membership, or at least the payment of union dues, as a condition of employment. The labor movement came of age during World War II, as the principle of collective bargaining gained wide acceptance. At the same time, the wartime boom and the favorable climate toward unions diluted the militance of the 1930s and led to a bureaucratization of the labor movement that would prove costly after the war.

Government and Politics in the War Years

The role of the federal government, already vastly enlarged in the New Deal era, expanded still more in 1941–45 as wartime agencies mobilized the economy and the American people for total war. The War Production Board oversaw resource allocation and industrial output. The National War Labor Board arbitrated labor disputes in defense industries. The Office of Price Administration (OPA) touched every American with its rent controls in cities with war plants and its price controls and ration coupons for butter, sugar, coffee, meat, tires, gasoline, and other products. Although merchants, landlords, and many consumers grumbled at the OPA's bureaucracy, it achieved its goal: From mid-1943 to mid-1945, consumer prices rose by less than 2 percent. These and other agencies brought home to Main Street the reality of Washington's expanded regulatory role. As one New Dealer observed in 1943, "The most important change wrought by the war has been the greatly increased participation of Government in our economic life." Even FDR's Republican predecessor, Herbert Hoover, declared in 1942, "To win total war, President Roosevelt must have many dictatorial economic powers. There must be no hesitation in giving them to him."

Overall, the ranks of civilian federal employees more than tripled from 1940 to 1945, growing from a little more than 1 million to nearly 3.4 million. The giant Pentagon building, erected in 1942 to house the War Department, symbolized the expansion of the executive branch. Celebrated as the world's largest office building, the Pentagon featured 17.5 miles of corridors.* This wartime growth of the federal government accelerated a long-term trend that would continue in the decades to come.

Wartime politics cast a long shadow on postwar political history. In 1940 President Roosevelt had won an unprecedented third term, defeating Republican candidate Wendell Willkie. As Roosevelt shifted roles from, as he put it, "Dr. New Deal" to "Dr. Win-the-War," his popularity remained high. In 1944, despite undisclosed failing health, he ran for a fourth term against New York governor Thomas E. Dewey and again won, garnering 53.4 percent of the vote. Despite voter frustration with wartime regulation and Republican attacks on the administration's alleged radicalism and socialistic tendencies, the Rooseveltian magic and well-coordinated Democratic efforts to retain the Solid South while wooing blacks, union members, and big-city ethnics—all key components of the New Deal coalition—paid off. Roosevelt's wartime role as commander-in-chief, along with favorable news from the front, also served him well at the polls.

Nevertheless, the conservative shift already evident in the late 1930s and in the 1940 election was accelerating. In the midterm election of 1942, Republicans gained nine Senate and forty-four House seats. Farmers led the defection from the New Deal coalition. Their goal, however, was not to reduce the government's role in the economy but to enlarge it. Specifically, they wanted increased federal price supports for agricultural commodities. When the administration tried to fight inflation by capping escalating agricultural price supports, the farmers, especially the larger agribusinesses represented by the American Farm Bureau Federation, struck back at the polls.

Interpreting the 1942 election as a repudiation of the New Deal, a conservative coalition of Republicans and southern Democrats in Congress in 1943 passed the Smith-Connally Anti-Strike Act and slashed the funding of many New Deal agencies. That same year, the House Un-American Activities Committee, which in the 1950s would stoke the flames of a domestic Red Scare, issued a list of administration officials it considered dangerously radical. (HUAC, created by Congress in 1938 to investigate fascist groups in America, quickly became a vehicle for attacking alleged radicals and communists in New Deal agencies.) Observed the liberal *New Republic,* "The New Deal is being abandoned. . . . A new crowd is preparing to take over." The conservative coalition that solidified after the 1942 election would hold sway in Congress for years to come. In short, the shift to the right that would profoundly influence American politics in later decades had gathered steam in the war years.

---

*The construction of the Pentagon was supervised by General Leslie R. Groves, later director of the Manhattan Project, the research effort that developed the atomic bomb.

The Republican Party, although united in its desire to unseat Roosevelt, otherwise suffered from deep internal divisions. Across a broad swath of states from Ohio to Colorado, conservative GOP members denounced the New Deal and adopted isolationist stances in foreign policy. Influential legislators such as Senator Robert A. Taft of Ohio, son of former president William Howard Taft, led this wing of the party. The Republican Party's eastern, New York–based wing, by contrast, was more internationalist in outlook and marginally more receptive to the fundamental contours of the welfare state. Thomas E. Dewey, for example, elected governor of New York in 1942 after winning fame as a racket-busting district attorney, accepted various New Deal programs, including social security. The 1940 Republican presidential candidate, Wendell Willkie, although a native of Indiana and a power-company executive, embodied this internationalist, somewhat more liberal wing of the Republican Party. (His 1943 book, *One World,* written after a world tour undertaken with Roosevelt's blessing, underscored his global vision.) Midwestern conservatives deplored the maverick Willkie, and his campaign for the 1944 Republican presidential nomination had already failed before his death from a heart attack that fall. Yet despite Republican right-wingers' strength in the party, they could not control it, and the 1944 presidential nomination went to Dewey. Senator Taft and other archconservatives mistrusted Dewey, whom Taft called "arrogant and bossy." The New Yorker's skill at building alliances—he named Ohio's conservative senator John Bricker as his running mate, for example—brought the party a degree of unity. But Dewey's stiff manner alienated voters (one critic quipped that he was the only man who could strut sitting down), and he lost the election to FDR. These divisions in Republican rank would continue long into the postwar era.

Roosevelt's 1944 decision to change running mates also helped the Democrats to hold the White House until 1952. Vice President Henry Wallace would have continued happily in that post, but his unabashed liberalism had antagonized the party's conservative wing, and Roosevelt dropped him. In choosing Senator Harry S Truman of Missouri from a large field of prospects, Roosevelt unwittingly bequeathed his final legacy to the American people. A protégé of Kansas City's corrupt Democratic political machine, Truman had won respect as an honest, hardworking senator but enjoyed little national reputation. "Who the hell is Harry Truman?" exploded a top navy official upon learning of the nomination.

The importance of Roosevelt's choice became apparent on April 12, 1945, when the vacationing sixty-three-year-old president died of a massive cerebral stroke. The administration and the media had largely concealed Roosevelt's worsening health, so the news came as a profound shock. The radio networks broke into regular programming for the bulletin; newspapers unfurled their blackest headlines; in the Solomon Islands halfway around the world, a U.S. Navy patrol boat received the message in Morse code beamed from a nearby island: "Y-E-S-T-E-R-D-A-Y P-R-E-S-I-D-E-N-T R-O-O-S-E-V-E-L-T D-I-E-D." On the eve of victory, the wartime leader had fallen. As the nation mourned, Truman assumed the presidency. The news of Roosevelt's death, he told reporters, made him feel as if "the moon, the stars, and all the planets had fallen on me." Over the next seven years, however, Truman would prove a far more capable chief executive than most would have predicted in April 1945.

A People in Wartime

World War II generated population movements, social changes, and ethnic tensions that deeply influenced postwar American life. Continuing a long-term trend, urbanization gained momentum. As war plants posted "Help Wanted" signs, workers flocked to the cities. An estimated 15 million Americans moved during the war to take advantage of job opportunities. Indiana farm girls, for example, ventured to Dayton, Ohio, to work as secretaries at Wright-Patterson Air Force Base. Cities in the mid-Atlantic region burgeoned, as did southeastern coastal regions that were home to shipyards and naval bases. The industrial belt around Detroit hummed as auto companies converted to war production. The West Coast, especially California, with its sprawling shipyards and aircraft plants, saw explosive growth. California's population spurted by 3.7 million in the 1940s. Many newcomers would remain in the cities, or more typically move to the suburbs, once the war ended. Indeed, the migration to the suburbs that reached flood tide in the 1950s was already well under way during the war.

Population movements on such a scale produced severe housing shortages and overcrowding, with families doubling up in beds or even sleeping in garages. Some landlords devised the "hot bunk" system, renting the same bed to three different tenants working successive eight-hour shifts. In 1942 Roosevelt set up the Federal Housing Agency to respond to this shortage. By the war's end, a combination of federal and private construction had built more than 1.8 million new housing units. Construction firms such as Abraham Levitt and Sons of Long Island developed prefabrication techniques that would make possible the boom in suburban housing construction in the postwar period.

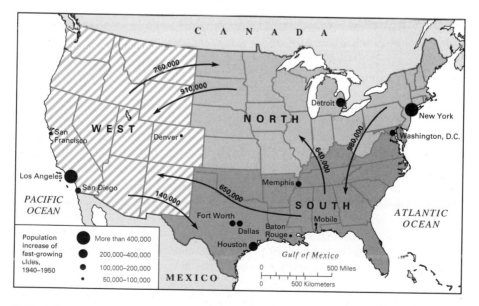

MAP 1.1

Internal Migration in the United States During World War II

For the nation's African American population, the war brought changes heavy with implications for the future. Although the military services remained segregated, for some of the 1 million blacks in uniform,* the experience provided a glimpse of European societies less rigidly racist than the United States. Moreover, military service in some cases gave blacks training in skills transferable to the postwar civilian labor market. Continuing a migration under way for decades, blacks joined the trek to the cities, seeking jobs in the booming war plants. By 1945 African Americans composed 9 percent of the labor force in war production.

Many of these workers relocated in northern factory centers. Detroit's black population grew from fewer than 150,000 in 1940 to more than 350,000 in 1950. Others moved to the new industrial cities of the South, such as the shipbuilding center of Mobile on Alabama's Gulf coast. In 1944 black workers in a Mobile shipyard set a yard record for the speed with which they built a merchant ship. Even in the war emergency, however, some major employers initially confined African Americans to low-paying jobs or excluded them altogether. The giant Douglas Aircraft plant in Los Angeles, for example, had an overwhelmingly white work force.

The surge in the urban black population sparked social tensions that sometimes erupted in violence. Unrest tore at America's cities during World War II, as it would later in the 1960s. Three days of racial conflict in Detroit during the hot summer of 1943, triggered by rumors that whites had pushed a black woman and her baby into a lake in a city park, left twenty-five blacks and nine whites dead before federal troops could quell the violence. Thurgood Marshall, the chief counsel of the National Association for the Advancement of Colored People (NAACP), bitterly criticized the Detroit police for using excessive force against blacks. The police handled the riot and previous racial incidents like "the Nazi gestapo," he declared. A racial explosion in Harlem that same summer, set off by stories of racist abuse of African American soldiers, caused five deaths, hundreds of injuries, and the looting and burning of white-owned shops and businesses. Ignoring the obvious, a secret 1943 report to President Roosevelt by J. Edgar Hoover, director of the Federal Bureau of Investigation (FBI), blamed the pervasive "unrest and dissatisfaction" in black America on "Foreign-Inspired Agitation."

But the war also prepared the way for the civil-rights activism that would sweep America in the 1950s and 1960s. The paradox of a nation's fighting tyranny abroad while tolerating racism at home did not escape African Americans. Lillian Smith, a white Georgia writer who toured the South in the summer of 1942, commented on "a quiet . . . resentment, running like a deep stream through [young blacks'] minds and hearts." A white Virginia newspaper editor wrote of Virginia's African Americans, "The war and its slogans have roused . . . hopes, aspirations and desires which they formerly did not entertain, except in the rarest instances." NAACP membership soared. At its 1942 convention, the NAACP denounced segregation and discrimination against black voters and called for a "double victory": over America's enemies abroad and over racism at home. In *What the Negro Wants*

---

*Blacks made up 16 percent of the total armed forces, higher than their proportion (10 percent) of the population as a whole.

(1944), a group of prominent African American leaders set forth an uncompromising agenda for the postwar civil-rights struggle.

Anticipating tactics that civil-rights demonstrators of the 1960s would employ, black students at Howard University entered a segregated Washington, D.C., restaurant in 1944 while others marched outside with signs bearing the emotion-laden slogan: "We Die Together. Let's Eat Together." The Congress of Racial Equality (CORE), a biracial organization founded in 1942, organized similar demonstrations at segregated theaters and restaurants in a number of cities.

The Roosevelt administration and the courts responded to this rising discontent. In 1941 FDR issued Executive Order 8802, which barred racial discrimination in defense plants and created the Fair Employment Practices Committee (FEPC) to investigate discrimination in the defense industry and labor unions. The president's immediate goal was to avert a massive protest march in Washington, D.C., threatened by A. Philip Randolph, head of the Brotherhood of Sleeping Car Porters. In a 1944 decision that sent shivers of apprehension through the white South, the U.S. Supreme Court declared the Texas Democratic Party's all-white primary unconstitutional.

Government propagandists worked hard to build African American support for the war despite racism and segregation in the military and at home. The OWI featured upbeat stories about black achievers, and played down racial tensions and conflict. The popular black boxer Joe Louis, an army volunteer, spoke at bond rallies, entertained the troops with boxing demonstrations, and was featured in propaganda posters targeting black America (see Laura Rebecca Sklaroff, "Constructing G.I. Joe Louis," *Journal of American History,* December 2002).

But these few gestures against domestic racism were primarily cosmetic. The FEPC, beset by a minuscule budget, bureaucratic infighting, and hostility from racists, accomplished little. One bigoted southern journalist ridiculed it as "dat cummittee fer de perteckshun of Rastus & Sambo." Because sustaining war production outranked racial justice in Washington's and the nation's priorities, the FEPC could use only moral suasion to combat racial discrimination in war plants. Although the war raised the consciousness of black America and brought a few steps toward equality, the great struggles for civil rights lay in the future.

For Hispanic Americans, too, the years 1941–45 brought fresh reminders of the ugly reality of prejudice. When an undertaker in Three Rivers, Texas, refused to bury Felix Longoria, a Mexican American war hero, young congressman Lyndon B. Johnson arranged for his burial in Arlington National Cemetery with full military honors. Despite urgent labor needs, war plants discriminated against Mexican Americans and denied them promotions. Of ten thousand employees at giant Kelley Air Base in Texas in 1944, for example, not one Mexican American held a post above the level of laborer or mechanic's assistant. The vast Los Angeles Shipbuilding and Dry Dock Company employed only three hundred Chicanos among its twelve thousand workers. When Mexican American war workers in Hanford, Washington, protested their exclusion from the dormitory occupied by other workers, the FBI investigated them.

Mexican Americans played a key role, however, in western agriculture, where labor needs intensified after the internment of Japanese Americans (see page 21). Many Mexicans entered the United States under the so-called *braceros* ("helping arms") agreement negotiated by the U.S. and Mexican governments in 1942. For the United States, the program met urgent farm needs; for Mexico, it alleviated the desperate poverty of a rapidly growing population.* The *braceros* contracts guaranteed temporary agricultural workers a minimum wage of thirty cents per hour and exemption from the draft. Under the agreement, 220,000 Mexicans entered the United States between 1942 and 1947, laboring in Texas cotton fields, California truck farms, and Northwest sugar-beet fields. Some 67,000 *braceros* worked on U.S. railroads as well. These laborers often endured racism and discrimination, graphically illustrated by signs reading "No Mexicans. White Trade Only," posted in saloons and pool halls in Washington and Oregon. Texas cotton growers, too, unhappy with the protections and wage guarantees of the *braceros* program, pressured Washington to leave the border open, in violation of the 1942 agreement. Thus, many thousands more Mexicans flooded north to work in the agricultural harvest as undocumented laborers.

The Chicano population of West Coast cities grew rapidly amid the wartime employment boom. By 1942 Los Angeles' Mexican population stood at more than three hundred thousand. Anti-Mexican prejudice intensified with this growth and erupted in the so-called Sleepy Lagoon case. In August 1942, after a young Mexican American died in a Los Angeles gang fight, twenty-three male Chicanos were arrested and charged with the murder. Tried before an openly prejudiced judge in a hostile climate fanned by sensational press stories, three of them were convicted of first-degree murder and nine of second-degree murder. A defense committee gained a reversal of the convictions on appeal, but the case exacerbated anti-Mexican feeling. The Los Angeles Police Department, with only 22 Mexican American officers in a force of 2,547, systematically harassed the Mexican American community.

Hostility also broke out in the Los Angeles "zoot suit" riots of 1943. During the war, some young men, including Mexican Americans, favored a flamboyant outfit that featured widely draped trousers pegged at the ankle, a broad-rimmed hat, a long double-breasted jacket, and a long gold watch chain. The popularity of this so-called zoot suit with Mexican American street gangs, or *pachucos,* led the Los Angeles City Council to outlaw the clothes, but with little success. In June 1943, sailors on leave in Los Angeles rampaged against zoot suiters for their alleged lack of patriotism, beating them and pulling off their garb. These flashes of racism and urban ethnic conflict in wartime warned of social tensions that would erupt repeatedly in succeeding decades.

The war touched the nation's Native American communities as well. Many Indians served in the military. The U.S. Signal Corps used Navajo-speaking "code talkers" to radio secret messages among U.S. command centers in the Pacific. Some Iroquois resisted the draft, however, claiming treaty rights that barred the U.S. government from drafting them. As with other groups, the wartime experiences of Indians heightened group awareness and activist energies that would find expression in the postwar years.

The persistence of racist attitudes in wartime emerged starkly in anti-Japanese propaganda. In ads, political cartoons, and animated cartoons produced by the Disney organization, the "Japs" figured as grotesque, buck-toothed caricatures, subhuman primates, or even insects. "Probably in all our history," wrote historian

---

*From 1940 to 1950, Mexico's population swelled by 16.5 million, some 30 percent.

Allan Nevins in 1946, "no foe has been so detested as were the Japanese." (The Japanese, in equally crude racist propaganda, portrayed Americans as greedy, predatory monsters.) In later years, when Japanese automobiles, TVs, and other products flooded the American market, echoes of this wartime anti-Japanese propaganda would reverberate.

Racist attitudes toward the Japanese were echoed in the treatment of the West Coast's Japanese American population, consisting of some 47,000 Issei (foreign-born aliens) and 80,000 Nisei (Japanese Americans born in the United States and thus U.S. citizens). This minority had long faced hostility, sometimes rooted in economic rivalry, and after Pearl Harbor, it broke into the open. Powerful groups in California demanded the detention of all Japanese Americans, citizens and aliens alike, for the duration of the war. California's attorney general, Earl Warren (later chief justice of the Supreme Court), told a congressional committee early in 1942 that "something should be done and done immediately" about the threat of sabotage by Japanese Americans. Warren invoked dire images of another Pearl Harbor, this time in California. That no evidence of sabotage or planning for sabotage had been uncovered, he explained, proved the diabolical cleverness of the potential perpetrators. Japanese American leaders protested. One Japanese American asked, "Is citizenship such a light and transient thing that [it] . . . can be torn from us in times of war?"

But their pleas fell on deaf ears. In February 1942, President Roosevelt authorized the army to designate any area a military zone from which persons might be excluded. Under this order, the War Relocation Authority (WRA) rounded up 110,000 Japanese Americans in California, Oregon, and Washington and sent them to primitive detention camps hastily built in remote parts of the West. In many cases, the internees' property was confiscated and sold. One young internee recalled that her house was ransacked by investigators, who took "everything we had, all the old Japanese suitcases filled with parents' old kimonos, my parents' past life. . . . Everything." Seeking to maintain morale under trying conditions, the internees held religious services, conducted schools, and organized baseball teams and Boy Scout troops. Some talented artists recorded camp life in watercolors and oil paintings. Nevertheless, such activities could not erase the emotional distress that internees suffered at being held in the camps virtually as prisoners. In April 1943, a guard at a Utah internment camp shot and killed a sixty-three-year-old internee when he approached the camp fence.

The constitutionality of the Japanese American internment was upheld by the U.S. Supreme Court in the 1944 case *Korematsu* v. *United States*. The WRA gradually released internees who could prove their loyalty (by enlisting in the military, for example) or who were willing to take jobs elsewhere in the country, but as late as 1945 nearly twenty thousand remained in custody. Only years later, in 1988, would Congress at last partially redress the injustice by compensating surviving internees.

As a side effect of internment, parental authority in Japanese American families weakened, a phenomenon occurring throughout American society in the war years. One young internee, Ben Yorita, later recalled:

> [In Japanese American families] the father was the traditional breadwinner and in total command of the family. But after going into the camps, fathers were no

longer the breadwinners; the young sons and daughters were. Most of them couldn't even communicate in English, so all the burdens fell on the second generation. . . . Consequently there was a big turnover of responsibility and authority. . . . When we returned to the cities after the war, it was the second generation again that had to make the decisions and do all the negotiating with landlords, attorneys, and the like.

For all the nation's minorities, the experiences of wartime, whether military service, geographic mobility, expanded job opportunities, or bigotry and discrimination, would shape peacetime attitudes. As historian John Dower has observed, "The war set whole new worlds of racial thinking in motion."

Although racism stained America's home-front record during World War II, the Nazi foe far more openly pursued a deadly program aimed at wiping out European Jewry. German persecution of the Jews, which during the war became genocide, met with a somewhat ambiguous response in the United States. Many Jewish scholars, scientists, psychiatrists, artists, writers, and musicians escaping Nazism found a haven in the United States, where they would profoundly influence postwar American cultural life. But anti-Semitism and anti-immigrant sentiments also influenced the U.S. reaction to the crisis. While Roosevelt and other national leaders routinely condemned Nazi anti-Semitism, proposals to admit large numbers of Jewish refugees faced legislative roadblocks, bureaucratic stonewalling, and public opposition as expressed in opinion polls. As word of the magnitude of the Holocaust filtered out of wartime Europe, the story received only muted and fragmentary coverage in the American press. Military planners vetoed proposals to bomb the death camps at Auschwitz and elsewhere, or even the railroads leading to the camps. The best way to help the Jews, they argued, was to win the war.

Only after the war, as accounts and photographs of the death camps, gas chambers, crematory ovens, mountains of corpses, and emaciated survivors received wide publicity, did the Holocaust's full horror penetrate the American consciousness. In 1940 the American author John Dos Passos had written that the only hope of preserving a sense of humanity as the tide of atrocities mounted lay in "the frail web of understanding of one person for the pain of another." During the years when the Nazis and their collaborators systematically tried to exterminate Europe's Jews, that web of understanding, tragically, failed to develop in America.

Finally, American women experienced profound, if sometimes short-lived, changes in their lives during the war. Some 60,000 volunteered as military nurses, serving in army hospitals and dispensaries and aboard naval ships. Nearly 300,000 women, black and white, became army nurses or went directly into the military, serving in noncombat roles in the female branches of the Army Air Corps (WACS), Navy (WAVES), Coast Guard (SPARS), and Marine Corps Women's Reserve. The number of women government workers, mostly in clerical positions, also increased sharply. After initial reluctance, war-plant managers hired armies of women to replace male workers, now at the front. During the Great Depression of the 1930s, government policy and popular attitudes had strongly opposed working women because so many men lacked jobs. In wartime, views changed markedly. "Longing won't bring him back sooner . . . GET A WAR JOB!" one government poster exhorted women. With the War Department's urging employers to draw upon "the vast resources of womanpower," the female labor force jumped from 14.6 million in 1941 to 19.4 million in 1944. In some plants, including the giant Boeing aircraft factory in Seattle, women composed half the work force. A particularly high rate of married women, many of them servicemen's wives, went to work; by 1945, 25 percent of married women held jobs outside the home.

Women encountered resentment from male coworkers and the stereotype that they were suited only for simple, repetitious tasks, and few rose to managerial ranks. But in general, a highly favorable public response prevailed. To encourage women to join the work force, the mass magazines featured photos and cover art of strong-armed women assembling warplanes, stitching parachutes, or working in munitions plants. "Rosie the Riveter," a muscular, confident female worker pictured in a Norman Rockwell *Saturday Evening Post* cover in 1943, also became the subject of a popular song of the day. A photo of an eighteen-year-old California airplane-plant employee, Norma Jean Dougherty, adorned a *Yank* magazine article on women war workers. Later she would win fame as Marilyn Monroe.

But one must not exaggerate the change. The increase in women workers reflected a gradual, long-term trend associated with industrialization. The upsurge of female employment in 1942–45 represented not an awakening of feminism but a response to the war emergency. Government propaganda and the media made clear that traditional notions of women's roles remained intact and treated females' entrance into the work force as strictly temporary. Indeed, wartime concerns about the divorce rate, extramarital sex, child neglect, and juvenile delinquency testify to the uneasiness that the notion of working women aroused. As one worried commentator observed: "The hand that holds the pneumatic riveter cannot rock the cradle at the same time." The federal government belatedly funded daycare centers for the children of working mothers in 1943 but met a mere 10 percent of the need. In Seattle, for example, only seven publicly funded and three private facilities, accommodating a total of 350 children, served the city's 75,000 working women. In some cases, working mothers themselves opposed government daycare facilities as a form of welfare and left children with friends and relatives instead.

How did these millions of new women workers assess their situation? In wartime surveys, many described their jobs as more interesting than housework, and a majority, especially older women with grown children, consistently expressed a desire to continue working. But most admitted that they probably would return to the home when peace came. "My husband wants a wife, not a career woman," said a female naval worker in Washington State. Whatever their wish, women workers had little choice about keeping their jobs: They were fired in droves as veterans returned. Daycare centers closed, and the media's celebration of working women abruptly fell silent. But even during the heyday of domesticity in the 1950s, many women who had found employment during the war would remain in the labor force or return to work. Memories of the war years, when barriers to female employment had temporarily fallen, remained vivid, a precedent for the dramatic changes to come.

On several fronts, then, a war that united the nation against a foreign foe also exposed fissures in American society and darker realities about American attitudes. The racism, prejudice, and mixed messages about the role of women that surfaced during the war—along with the great capacity of millions for self-sacrifice in a common cause—would help to sculpt the nation's social agenda after peace returned.

IN PERSPECTIVE

Women and War

[Note: These "In Perspective" features will trace the shifting historical impact of certain major themes through the entire time span of this study, from World War II to the beginning of the twenty-first century.]

The high level of participation by women in World War II—as members of female military branches, as nurses and volunteers in service organizations, and as workers in war plants—was not unique. Although war is sometimes considered the quintessential male experience, women have participated in important ways in every American war, and their status has been affected, in turn, by each of these wars.

During the American Revolution, a few women disguised as men, including Deborah Sampson of Massachusetts, actually participated in combat. Others accompanied their husbands to camp and performed domestic duties for the troops, such as laundry and food preparation. Women in Philadelphia, Boston, and other cities organized to support the patriot cause, from boycotting English tea and fabrics before the war to knitting scarves and stockings for the often threadbare Continental army during the war itself. After the war, the prevailing ideology that stressed women's maternal and domestic role took on a political dimension, sometimes called "republican motherhood," as women were urged to instill in their children the republican values on which the new nation was founded. Beyond all this, thousands of women managed farms, stores, print shops, and other enterprises, replacing their absent husbands.

In the Civil War, some 3,200 women served as nurses in Union and Confederate military hospitals. Clara Barton, who later founded the American Red Cross, organized a service that rushed medical supplies to Antietam and other battles. Mary Ann Bickerdyke, a widow from Galesburg, Illinois, operating on her own, moved from one battle to another, nursing the Union wounded. Chicago's Mary Livermore and many other women helped organize "sanitary fairs" in northern cities that raised thousands of dollars to provide food, medicine, and sanitary supplies to Union troops. White women north and south managed farms and plantations while their menfolk fought. "I find myself every day doing something I never did before," wrote a Virginia woman.

Despite women's key role, the Civil War's aftermath set back the women's-rights movement. The Fourteenth Amendment (1868), granting freedmen the vote, for the first time injected the word *male* into the Constitution. Susan B. Anthony and other women's-rights leaders tried to use the goodwill generated by women's wartime service, as well as the precedent offered by the enfranchisement of former slaves, to push their agenda, but this effort failed. A New York newspaper called the effort to link black suffrage and woman suffrage "nonsense and tomfoolery."

During World War I, women again played a significant role as nurses and volunteers with organizations such as the Red Cross and the YMCA. As they would later do in World War II, women also took home-front jobs vacated by men, and—again as in World War II—most were displaced when the war ended.

But in contrast to the Civil War, World War I helped the woman-suffrage cause. Suffrage leaders like Carrie Chapman Catt, head of the National American Woman Suffrage Association, and Harriot Stanton Blatch, daughter of the women's-rights pioneer Elizabeth Cady Stanton, supported the war and held government positions during the conflict. In turn, they urged President Wilson to endorse the woman-suffrage cause. A more militant group, the Congressional Union, led by Alice Paul, picketed the White House with signs denouncing Wilson for supporting democracy abroad while opposing woman suffrage at home. Some were jailed for chaining themselves to the White House fence. When they refused to eat, prison officials force-fed them. Thanks to the war, the suffrage movement gained momentum. The Nineteenth Amendment, granting women the vote, was ratified in 1920.

Other leading feminists deplored this strategy, however, arguing that women should promote peace, not become cheerleaders for war. Settlement-house leader Jane Addams strove to keep America out of the war, and when that effort failed in 1917 she focused her energies on supplying food to war refugees. Addams later described these trying years in her book *Peace and Bread in Time of War* (1922).

Women were fully integrated into the military in 1948 (though in noncombat roles). An estimated 7,500 servicewomen saw duty in the Vietnam War as nurses, physical therapists, air-traffic controllers, language and intelligence specialists, and other professionals. Women also served in Vietnam in civilian capacities with the Red Cross, the USO (United Service Organizations), the CIA, and the Agency for International Development. The Vietnam Women's Memorial, dedicated in 1993 near the Vietnam Veterans Memorial in Washington, D.C., commemorates all women who served in Vietnam. Other young women were drawn into the 1960s antiwar movement, and this experience (including being discriminated against by young male activists) led many of them into the revived women's movement of the 1970s.

By the late 1990s some 200,000 women were on active duty in the military, with another 225,000 in the reserves. Many served in the Persian Gulf and Iraq Wars. In short, women's participation in World War II was only one episode in a long history of involvement in the nation's conflicts from the Revolutionary War onward.

Technology, Oil, and the Atomic Bomb

War-spawned technological innovations played their part, too, in shaping post-war America. The Office of Scientific Research and Development (OSRD), set up in 1941, sponsored studies on defense-related projects. The computer emerged from wartime research aimed at improving Great Britain's antiaircraft defenses against the German *Luftwaffe*. These early calculating machines were massive. The Mark I, completed in 1944 by Harvard physicist Howard Aiken, stretched 50 feet in length, stood 8 feet high, and required 765,299 separate parts. Another prototype computer, the ENIAC (Electronic Numerical Integrator and Calculator), built by John Mauchly and John Eckert, Jr., at the University of Pennsylvania, boasted eighteen thousand vacuum tubes. These wartime behemoths laid the groundwork for a revolution that in future years would transform information processing and revolutionize American life.

Many aeronautical advances, including helicopters and jet propulsion, date from World War II. U.S. pilots tested the first jet planes in 1942. Radar, developed in the 1930s as a technology for tracking distant objects by electromagnetic waves, was perfected in World War II by scientists at the Massachusetts Institute of Technology and elsewhere with OSRD funding. Asserts historian Robert Buderi: "Atomic bombs only ended the war, radar won it." After the war, radar figured in the development of transistors and magnetic resonance imaging and led to advances in astronomy, aircraft navigation, and weather forecasting.

The German V-2 rockets that fell on British cities evolved after the war into intercontinental missiles and space-launch vehicles. Synthetic rubber filled in for the scarce real article in automobile tires and other products. Synthetic fabrics such as nylon, introduced by the Du Pont Corporation in 1938, did duty as wartime substitutes for silk and other natural fabrics in short supply. Department stores that advertised "nylons" during the war faced deluges of eager buyers. In the postwar years, a shimmering array of synthetic fabrics would find many varied uses.

The war, ironically, also produced notable advances in the saving of human lives. Research on blood-plasma technology and on antibacterial sulfa drugs progressed rapidly. Production of penicillin, discovered in England in 1929, moved to America when the war began. Funded by the War Production Board, researchers developed new techniques for vastly increasing the output of this lifesaving antibiotic. Wartime research led to the development of other substances of value to peacetime medicine, including streptomycin, another key antibiotic. The insecticide DDT, developed in the 1930s, first received wide use during the war to protect GIs from typhus, malaria, and other insect-borne diseases.

The role of science and technology in ensuring victory over the nation's enemies solidified a protechnology mindset that in later decades would come under heavy criticism. In particular, the government's large-scale funding of research would generate ambivalence in the future, especially for its environmental implications. DDT, hailed as a lifesaver during the war, later would spark controversy as an ecological menace. During the war, however, compelling military objectives overrode all other considerations.

Of the war's technological aspects, none held more portents for the future than the struggle for oil. Indeed, oil oozes its way through the history of World War II.

Japan's efforts to reduce its dependence on Western oil spurred the expansionist policies in Asia that led President Roosevelt in July 1941 to freeze all Japanese funds in the United States and in effect to embargo oil exports to Japan. The Japanese attack on Pearl Harbor would have been even more catastrophic had the Japanese also destroyed the 4.5 million barrels of oil stored there in surface tanks.

During the initial stages of the war, Japan met its energy needs by seizing British and Dutch refineries in Borneo and Sumatra. But as U.S. forces advanced across the Pacific and sank more and more Japanese tankers en route to the home islands, Japan's oil reserves dwindled to practically nothing, crippling its war-making capacity. Toward the end, Japan resorted to desperate measures to save fuel, sending pilots on *kamikaze* suicide missions against U.S. ships carrying just enough gasoline to reach their targets.

Hitler frantically sought fuel for his war machine, too. He invaded the Soviet Union in part to capture a vast Soviet oil refinery in the Caucasus and to prevent the Soviets from seizing the rich oilfield in Romania, a German ally. Hitler also channeled enormous resources into developing synthetic fuels. But fuel shortages ultimately doomed Germany just as they did Japan. Stalin's counteroffensive denied Hitler the oilfields he desperately needed, and Allied bombing slashed the synthetic-fuel output of the German chemical giant I. G. Farben. The Nazi's North African campaign faltered for want of gasoline, and by the end of the war, the German armies had run dry. In the spring of 1945, German military vehicles in Italy were being towed by oxen.

For the Allies, too, oil was critical. U.S. oil shipments to Great Britain under the wartime Lend Lease program helped the British to repel the Nazi *Luftwaffe* during the 1941 Battle of Britain. Once the United States entered the war, Interior Secretary Harold Ickes, doubling as petroleum administrator, stimulated domestic oil exploration and vastly expanded production. Two major pipelines, the "Big Inch" and the "Little Inch," built in 1943–44, carried gasoline and other petroleum products from the Southwest to the East Coast. Strict rationing, coupled with tire shortages, a moratorium on auto production, and a 35-mile-per-hour speed limit, cut civilian oil and gasoline consumption by 30 percent. By such means, the United States met nearly 90 percent of the Allies' wartime oil needs.

Meanwhile, the shape of the future emerged on another front when U.S. geologists on a government mission in 1943 conservatively assessed the oil potential of Saudi Arabia and other Middle East nations at 25 billion barrels. "The oil in this region," the mission reported, "is the greatest single prize in all history." A behind-the-scenes struggle unfolded between the United States and Great Britain for control of this find. Early in 1945, following Yalta, President Roosevelt met with King Ibn Saud of Saudi Arabia for a conference that included intense discussions of oil.*

In August 1944, meanwhile, the United States and Great Britain signed the Anglo-American Petroleum Agreement creating an eight-member International Petroleum Commission (IPC) charged with shaping postwar oil policy, allocating

---

*The American president and the Mideast monarch got along famously. When Ibn Saud, who limped severely from old war injuries, admired Roosevelt's wheelchair, Roosevelt promptly gave him a duplicate, which the Saudi ruler thereafter highly prized.

quotas, and recommending production levels. When U.S. oilmen rebelled, fearing that the new agency would meddle in U.S. oil production and pricing, the agreement was revised to deny the IPC any authority over the American oil industry. The postwar American economic boom would roar forward on a tide of oil, untrammeled by limits or restraints.

Oil, then, was never far from the mind of any world leader during World War II and by 1945 had emerged as a key issue in postwar diplomacy. The war demonstrated the industrialized world's utter dependence on this limited resource and showed that, in an emergency, America could radically cut its consumption. The conflict also made crystal clear the Middle East's critical role in postwar geopolitics. Through all the world upheavals from the 1940s to the present, the central role of oil would remain a constant.

Of all the scientific breakthroughs of World War II, none had a more immediate impact on the consciousness of ordinary citizens than the atomic bomb. In August 1939, a few weeks before Hitler invaded Poland and plunged Europe into war, Albert Einstein, a world-famous émigré German Jewish physicist, sent President Roosevelt a message sketching the implications of current work in his field. Einstein wrote the letter at the initiative of Leo Szilard, a refugee Hungarian physicist worried about German research in atomic energy. Recent research by Szilard and the Italian physicist Enrico Fermi, wrote Einstein,

> leads me to expect that the element uranium may be turned into a new and important source of energy in the immediate future. . . . This new phenomenon would also lead to the construction of bombs, and it is conceivable—though much less certain—that extremely powerful bombs of a new type may thus be constructed.

Heeding Einstein's suggestion that the government support further research, Roosevelt approved a modest grant. The army took over the project in 1942 and code-named it the Manhattan Project. In 1943, bomb construction began at Los Alamos, New Mexico, under the direction of physicist J. Robert Oppenheimer. Other major sites were at Oak Ridge, Tennessee; Hanford, Washington; and the University of Chicago. All told, some 150,000 workers at thirty-seven sites in nineteen states worked on the project, although only a handful knew its ultimate objective. The Danish physicist Niels Bohr had predicted that an atomic bomb could not be built "without turning the whole country into a factory," and in some respects his prophecy proved true.

Before dawn on July 16, 1945, a group of scientists huddling in the darkness at the Alamogordo Bombing Range in New Mexico detonated the world's first atomic bomb. Physicist Philip Morrison, watching from ten miles away, later wrote, "You felt the morning had come, although it was still night, because there your face felt the glow of this daylight—this desert sun in the midst of night." A few minutes after the blast (code-named Trinity), test director Kenneth Bainbridge approached Oppenheimer, shook his hand, and said, "Oppie, now we're all sons of bitches."

The Alamogordo test that propelled humankind into a new era also presented Roosevelt's successor, President Truman, with a fateful decision. Eager to end the war with a crushing display of U.S. might, Truman ordered use of the atomic bomb against Japan as soon as technically possible and without explicit warning.* Leo Szilard and other Manhattan Project scientists proposed a demonstration, but neither the president nor Secretary of War Henry Stimson appear to have considered this option.

A U.S. B-29, the *Enola Gay*, dropped an atomic bomb, nicknamed "Little Boy," utilizing uranium-235, on Hiroshima on August 6, destroying the city and killing upward of a hundred thousand people instantaneously. The second, "Fat Man," a plutonium bomb, was dropped on Nagasaki on August 9, leaving more than forty thousand dead. Tens of thousands more in both cities would eventually die of radiation sickness. As promised, Russia entered the war on August 8.

On August 14, Japan offered to surrender if Emperor Hirohito could retain his throne. Despite their earlier "unconditional surrender" demand, the Allies accepted this condition. World War II was over. The news flash set off frantic celebrations. Crowds swarmed the streets, horns honked, whistles blared. Photographers captured scenes of delirious joy.

The Atomic-Bomb Decision: The Ongoing Debate

President Truman and Secretary of War Stimson would later assert that the atomic bomb offered the only sure alternative to a land invasion of Japan that might have cost thousands of American lives. Indeed, War Department contingency plans called for an invasion of Japan's southernmost island late in 1945 and of the main island, Honshu, early in 1946 if the war continued. Thousands of GIs never doubted that Truman's decision spared them from death on Japanese soil.

But other factors likely figured in Truman's decision. Although some Japanese military leaders were prepared to fight on, a new Japanese government that came to power in April 1945 soon began maneuvering to end the war on the Allied terms, and Washington knew of this. (U.S. and British cryptologists had broken the Japanese diplomatic code, and all official communications out of Tokyo were monitored.) In spring 1945, U.S. intelligence officials advised that the promised Russian declaration of war, coupled with Allied signals that Hirohito could remain a figurehead leader of postwar Japan, would probably lead to Japan's surrender. At the Potsdam Conference, when Stalin renewed his pledge to declare war on Japan by mid-August (and before Truman learned of the atomic bomb test in New Mexico), Truman noted exultantly in a hasty diary jotting: "[Stalin] will be in Jap War on August 15 . . . Fini Japs when that comes about."

A postwar U.S. Strategic Bombing Survey went even further, concluding in 1946 that Japan would have surrendered "certainly prior to 31 December 1945, and in all probability prior to 1 November 1945 . . . even if the atomic bombs had not been dropped, even if Russia had not entered the war, and even if no invasion had been planned or contemplated."

---

*In the July 1945 Potsdam Declaration, the Allied leaders had vaguely threatened Japan with "prompt and utter destruction" if they did not surrender.

Hiroshima, September 1945. A survivor pushes his possessions along a path amid the rubble of what had been a bustling city. Images such as this offered Americans a grim preview of what a future atomic war might bring. *(UPI-Corbis/Bettmann)*

It was probably not, then, the nightmare of a bloody land invasion months in the future that loomed large in Truman's mind as he made his decision to drop the atomic bomb but rather the precise means by which Japan's imminent surrender would be achieved. If Japan's surrender were seen as a response to the Soviet declaration of war, Stalin would have won a propaganda victory and a substantial claim to a role in postwar Japan. But if the U.S. atomic bomb appeared to be the major factor in Japan's capitulation, America would hold the upper hand in postwar Japan—indeed, in the entire postwar world. British Prime Minister Winston Churchill later described U.S. leaders' thinking in late July 1945: "It was now no longer necessary for the Russians to come into the Japanese war; the new explosive alone was sufficient to settle the matter."*

Truman himself firmly rejected all such speculation and always insisted that he made up his mind quickly and without the slightest qualm: "Let there be no mistake about it," he wrote, "I regarded the bomb as a military weapon and never had any doubt that it should be used."

The atomic bomb gave the final push to a Japanese government already on the verge of surrender, but at a terrible cost: two cities destroyed; countless thou-

---

*The Manhattan Project's enormous cost may have been another influence. How could Truman justify to Congress and to U.S. taxpayers spending $2 billion on a weapon and then not using it?

sands of civilians dead; and a horrendous weapon unleashed on the world, under circumstances that vastly complicated efforts at international control. Within a few years, the United States and the Soviet Union would become locked in a dangerous nuclear arms race, and nuclear weaponry would spread to other nations as well.

Conclusion

The final chapter of World War II, then, also served as the opening chapter of the nuclear age. Americans swiftly realized that their world had changed forever. Dreams of a technological utopia formed one strand of the nation's initial response to the atomic bomb. President Truman hailed atomic energy as "the greatest achievement of organized science in history" and stressed its peacetime promise. Magazine writers and radio commentators conjured up visions of atomic cars, atomic power too cheap to meter, atomic agriculture that would solve the world's food problems, and atomic medicine that would conquer death itself. But Americans soon recognized that the force that had demolished two Japanese cities could be turned against themselves. Radio newscasters compared Hiroshima with U.S. cities of similar size, such as New Haven and Denver; newspapers printed maps of their own communities overlaid by concentric circles showing the pattern of devastation at Hiroshima. The life expectancy of the human species, commented the *Washington Post* on August 26, 1945, had "dwindled immeasurably in the course of two brief weeks." Fears deepened with the realization that atomic bombs could be attached to the long-range rockets developed by Nazi scientists during the war.

Even President Truman, in private diary jottings, expressed grave misgivings about the new weapon. After the Alamogordo test, he called the atomic bomb "the most terrible thing ever discovered" and resorted to apocalyptic biblical imagery: "It may be the fire destruction prophesied . . . after Noah and his fabulous Ark." Fear of nuclear holocaust sank deep into the American consciousness in August 1945, where it would linger for decades, rising and falling with the ebb and flow of Cold War hostilities.

For some Americans, sober second thoughts tempered the joy of victory. At a cost of 405,000 dead and 672,000 wounded, the United States had contributed its share to the defeat of powerful foes. But what kind of world would peace bring? What would life be like in the postwar United States? With a mixed sense of their nation's vast power and sudden vulnerability, Americans faced the postwar age.

Despite America's losses, the war touched it less heavily than some other nations. Historians conservatively estimate that the conflict cost the lives of some 17 million soldiers and 20 million civilians, plus millions more who were injured or made refugees. Germany lost more than 3 million soldiers, Japan and China around 2 million each. The Soviet Union suffered the heaviest casualties, including the death of more than 6 million soldiers and as many as 20 million civilians; the precise number will never be known. After the war, Stalin would say that Great Britain paid for the war in time, the United States in materials, and the Soviet Union in blood. The war brought massive physical devastation and shattered the industrial infrastructure of Germany, the Soviet Union, Japan, and other nations.

By contrast, the United States in 1945—its factories intact, its economy booming, and its occupying armies triumphant in Western Europe and Asia—stood at the pinnacle of world power. What would it do with that power?

"The past is never dead. It's not even past"—so observes a character in William Faulkner's 1948 novel *Intruder in the Dust*. This observation certainly applies to World War II. In countless ways, the history of the United States since 1945 has its roots in the years 1941–45. Nearly every important strand of early postwar American history—the booming prosperity, the Cold War, the civil-rights revolution, the nuclear arms race, the cultural conservatism and business-oriented government of the Eisenhower years, the rise of computers, the space program, even social trends such as suburbanization, the growth of the middle class, and the climbing birthrate—can be understood only if one pays careful attention to World War II.

Later generations of Americans would often assess their own era from the perspective of World War II. During the conflict-ridden 1960s, many would nostalgically recall the early 1940s as a time when Americans had stood united. They contrasted the murky and divisive Vietnam engagement with the moral clarity of what came to be called 'the Good War." The 1990s brought a flood of books and movies about the war. Stephen Ambrose's *D-Day* (1994) and Stephen Spielberg's 1998 film *Saving Private Ryan* evoked the fortitude of the nearly 200,000 American, British, and Canadian troops who invaded France's Normandy coast on June 6, 1944, under the command of General Dwight D. Eisenhower, despite the operation's chaos, confusion, and tremendous cost in human life. TV news anchor Tom Brokaw honored the nation's aging World War II veterans in his 1998 book *The Greatest Generation*. Were today's Americans capable of comparable heroism and self-sacrifice, such works seemed to ask.

The deadly terrorist attacks of September 11, 2001, invited comparisons to Pearl Harbor and triggered a wave of World War II nostalgia, including a revival of Kate Smith's anthem, "God Bless America." The sixtieth anniversary observances of D-Day in 2004 evoked yet another wave of tributes to aging veterans. Even as the ranks of those who actually participated in or even remembered World War II grew thinner, it remained vividly alive in the nation's collective consciousness.

When Franklin Roosevelt led the nation into war on December 8, 1941, he little realized how profound would be the long-range consequences of the conflict whose end he did not live to see.

SELECTED READINGS

The War, Wartime Diplomacy, and the Holocaust

Edward M. Bennett, *Franklin D. Roosevelt and the Search for Victory: American-Soviet Relations, 1939–1945* (1990); Joanne Bourke, *The Second World War: A People's History* (2002); Russell D. Buhite, *Decision at Yalta* (1986); Steven Casey, *Cautious Crusade: Franklin D. Roosevelt. American Public Opinion, and the War Against Nazi Germany* (2001); Patrick J. Hearden, *Architects of Globalism: Building a New World Order During World War II* (2002); John Keegan, *The Second World War* (1990); Warren Kimball, *The Juggler: Franklin Roosevelt as Wartime Statesman* (1991); Robert James Maddox, *The United States and World*

War II (1992); Eric Markusen and David Kopf, *The Holocaust and Strategic Bombing: Genocide and Total War in the Twentieth Century* (1995); J. Robert Moskin, *Mr. Truman's War: The Final Victory, World War II, and the Birth of the Postwar World* (1996); Verne Newton, ed., *FDR and the Holocaust* (1996); Emily S. Rosenberg, *A Date Which Will Live: Pearl Harbor in American Memory* (2003); Peter Schrijvers, *The G.I. War Against Japan: American Soldiers in Asia and the Pacific in World War II* (2002); Michael S. Sherry, *The Rise of American Air Power* (1987) and *In the Shadow of War: The United States Since the 1930s* (1995); E. B. Sledge, *With the Old Breed at Peleliu and Okinawa* (1990); David Wyman, *The Abandonment of the Jews: America and the Holocaust, 1941–1945* (1984); Daniel Yergin, *The Prize: The Epic Quest for Oil, Money, and Power* (1991).

Domestic Social Trends During World War II

Amy Bentley, *Eating for Victory: Food Rationing and the Politics of Domesticity* (1998); John Costello, *Virtue Under Fire: How World War II Changed Our Social and Sexual Attitudes* (1985); John W. Jeffries, *Wartime America: The World War II Homefront* (1996); David M. Kennedy, *Freedom From Fear: The American People in Depression and War, 1929–1945* (1999); Kenneth Paul O'Brien and Lynn Hudson Parsons, eds., *The Home-Front War: World War II and American Society* (1995); William L. O'Neill, *A Democracy at War: America's Fight at Home and Abroad in World War II* (1993); Kathleen E. R. Smith, *God Bless America: Tin Pan Alley Goes to War* (2003); Kevin Starr, *Embattled Dream: California in War and Peace, 1940–1950* (2002); William M. Tuttle, *Daddy's Gone to War: The Second World War in the Lives of America's Children* (1993).

Women, Minority Groups, Internment of Japanese Americans

Allan Berube, *Coming Out Under Fire: The History of Gay Men and Women in World War Two* (1990); Dominic J. Capeci, *The Harlem Riot of 1943* (1977); Richard M. Dalfiume, *Desegregation of the United States Armed Forces: Fighting on Two Fronts, 1939–1953* (1969); Clete Daniel, *Chicano Workers and the Politics of Fairness: The Fair Employment Practices Committee in the Southwest, 1941–1945* (1991); Roger Daniels, *Concentration Camps USA: Japanese Americans and World War II* (1981); Mario T. Garcia, *Mexican-Americans: Leadership, Ideology, and Identity, 1930–1960* (1989); Robert A. Hill, ed., *The FBI's RA CON: Racial Conditions in the United States During World War II* (1995); Maureen Honey, *Creating Rosie the Riveter: Class, Gender, and Propaganda During World War II* (1984); Andrew Edmund Kersten, *Race, Jobs, and the War: The FEPC in the Midwest, 1941–1946* (2001); Daniel Kryder, *Divided Arsenal: Race and the American State During World War II* (2000); Kristine C. Kuramitsu, "Internment and Identity in Japanese American Art," *American Quarterly*, December 1995; Ruth Milkman, *Gender at Work: The Dynamics of Job Discrimination by Sex During World War II* (1987); Gary Y. Okihiro, *Whispered Silences: Japanese Americans and World War II* (1996); Margaret Paton-Walsh, *Our War, Too: American Women Against the Axis* (2002); Merl E. Reed, *Seedtime for the Modern Civil Rights Movement: The President's Committee on Fair Employment Practices, 1941–1946* (1991), Greg Robinson, *By Order of the President: FDR and the Internment of Japanese Americans* (2001); Laura Rebecca Sklaroff, "Constructing G.I. Joe Louis: Cultural Solutions to the 'Negro Problem' During World War II," *Journal of American History*, December 2002; Ronald Takaki, *Double Victory: A Multicultural History of America in World War II* (2000); Kenneth William Townsend, *World War II and the American Indian* (2000).

Cultural Trends and Wartime Propaganda

Jeanine Basinger, *The World War II Combat Film: Anatomy of a Genre* (1986); Michael E. Birdwell, *Celluloid Soldiers: The Warner Bros. Campaign Against Nazism* (1999); John Morton Blum, *V Was for Victory: Politics and American Culture During World War II* (1976); John Dower, *War Without Mercy: Race and Power in the Pacific War* (1986); Lewis A. Erenberg and Susan E. Hirsch, eds., *The War in American Culture: Society and Consciousness During World War II* (1996); William S. Graebner, *The Age of Doubt: American Thought and Culture in the 1940s* (1991); Gerd Horton, *Radio Goes to War: The Cultural Politics of Propaganda During World War II* (2001); Clayton R. Koppes and Gregory D. Black, *Hollywood Goes to War: How Politics, Profits and Propaganda Shaped World War II Movies* (1987); Clayton D. Laurie, *The Propaganda Warriors: America's Crusade Against Nazi Germany* (1996); Mark H. Leff, "The Politics of Sacrifice on the American Home Front in World War II," *Journal of American History*, March 1991; George H. Roeder, Jr., *The Censored War: American Visual Experience During World War II* (1993); Leila J. Rupp, *Mobilizing Women for War: German and American Propaganda, 1939–1945* (1978); Lawrence R. Samuel, *Pledging Allegiance: American Identity and the Bond Drive of World War II* (1997); Holly Cowan Shulman, *The Voice of America: Propaganda and Democracy, 1941–1945* (1990); Michael Sweeney, *Secrets of Victory: The Office of Censorship and the American Press and Radio in World Warr II* (2001); Studs Terkel, *"The Good War": An Oral History of World War II* (1984); Alan M. Winkler, *The Politics of Propaganda: The Office of War Information, 1942–1945* (1978); Robert B. Westbrook, "Fighting for the American Family: Private Interests and Political Obligation in World War II," in Richard Wightman Fox and T. J. Jackson Lears, eds., *The Power of Culture: Critical Essays in American History* (1993).

The War's Impact on the Economy, Labor, and Technology; the Atomic Bomb

Stephen Adams, *Mr. Kaiser Goes to War* (1998); Gar Alperovitz, *The Decision to Use the Atomic Bomb and the Architecture of an American Myth* (1995); Robert Buderi, *The Invention that Changed the World* [radar] (1996); Charles D. Chamberlain, *Victory at Home: Manpower and Race in the American South During World War II* (2003); Gerard H. Clarfield and William M. Wiecek, *Nuclear America: Military and Civilian Power in the United States, 1940–1980* (1984); James W. Cortada, *The Computer in the United States: From Laboratory to Market, 1930–1960* (1993); Greg Herken, *Cardinal Choices: Presidential Science Advising from the Atomic Bomb to SDI* (rev. ed., 2000), and *Brotherhood of the Bomb: The Tangled Lives and Loyalties of Robert Oppenheimer, Ernest Lawrence, and Edward Teller* (2002); Richard G. Hewlett and Oscar E. Anderson, Jr., *The New World, 1939–1946* [atomic-bomb project] (1972); Michael J. Hogan, ed., *Hiroshima in American Memory* (1996); Gregory Michael Hooks, *Forging the Military-Industrial Complex: World War II's Battle of the Potomoc* (1991); Paul A. C. Koistenen, *The Military-Industrial Complex: A Historical Perspective* (1980); Nelson Lichtenstein, *Labor's War at Home: The CIO in World War II* (1982); Richard Rhodes, *The Making of the Atomic Bomb* (1986); Martin Sherwin, *A World Destroyed: Hiroshima and Its Legacies* (3rd ed., 2003); J. Samuel Walker, *Prompt and Utter Destruction: Truman and the Use of Atomic Bombs Against Japan* (1997).

2

"Not Since Rome and Carthage": Into the Cold War

EARLY IN 1945, as Germany's defeat was near, staff at the American embassy in Moscow seemed more worried than joyous. Conflict simmered between Washington and Moscow over several issues, including Stalin's apparent unwillingness to honor his Yalta pledge to permit free elections in Poland. On March 8, the young daughter of the U.S. ambassador to the Soviet Union wrote to her sister back home, "The war is going wonderfully well. . . . But the news is slightly dampened here by our gallant allies who at the moment are being most bastard-like."

The climate in Washington mirrored the dark mood at the embassy in Moscow. Throughout the war, President Roosevelt had uneasily hoped for postwar cooperation with the Soviets, but he fully understood a somber wartime warning given him by diplomat William C. Bullitt: "To win the peace at the close of this war will be at least as difficult as to win the war." By March 1945, FDR's hopes had faded: "We can't do business with Stalin," wrote the president. "He has broken every one of the promises he made at Yalta." Worries about the future, rooted in disturbing Soviet actions, soon rippled across America. C. L. Sulzberger of the *New York Times* wrote shortly after Japan's surrender: "The most important political development during the last ten years of localized and finally global warfare has been the emergence of [the Soviet Union] as the greatest dynamic and diplomatic force on the vast Eurasian land mass."

In many respects, of course, America in 1945 had reason for exuberant confidence. Triumphant in war, it stood at the pinnacle of power. The war had so expanded U.S. productive capacity that by 1945 the United States accounted for 60 percent of the world's industrial output. However, America faced not only friction with the Soviet Union but also rancorous domestic politics, the task of converting to a peacetime economy, and the complex challenges posed by the atomic bomb. Facing these demanding issues was an untested new president, Harry Truman. Treasury Secretary Henry Morgenthau, Jr., offered a cautious early assessment: "[Truman] has a lot of nervous energy, and seems to be inclined to make very quick decisions. But, after all, he is a politician, and what is going on in his head only time will tell."

The peace that Americans had longed for brought new worries and crises. A series of confrontations with the Soviet Union produced a well-grounded conviction, transmitted from Washington and the media to the grassroots, that Moscow's course profoundly threatened U.S. national-security interests. From this belief arose the long political, economic, and military struggle that pundits soon would label the Cold War.

Roots of the Cold War

The conflict that erupted after World War II between the Soviet Union and the West, most notably the United States, had deep roots in ideology and history. A belief in the New World's divine commission to redeem and uplift humanity had influenced American thought since the days of the Puritans. Gradually secularized, this sense of mission had, by Woodrow Wilson's day, evolved into a vision of spreading democracy and a liberal capitalist order around the globe.

World War II, which left the United States powerful and physically unscathed, deepened this sense of America's global destiny. As Dean Acheson, a leading diplomat of the era, put it: "In the final analysis, the United States [is] the locomotive at the head of mankind, and the rest of the world is the caboose." For corporate America, from bankers and industrialists to moviemakers, farmers, soft-drink bottlers, coffee marketers, and banana importers, the war's end meant a renewed quest for foreign markets, raw materials, and investment opportunities. America's Cold War history, in short, is not only a story of U.S. responses to Soviet provocations; it is also a story of how U.S. statesmen, politicians, military leaders, and captains of business and finance took positive actions to assert America's political and economic dominance of the postwar world.

In Russia, meanwhile, a succession of autocratic tsars and an elaborate centralized bureaucracy had ruled a growing empire of many peoples and languages. As in America, many Russians viewed their nation as specially favored by God. Memories of 1812, when Russia had heroically thrown back Napoleon's invading armies, evoked patriotic pride. Along with expansionist tendencies, however, Russia also suffered from a backward economy and chronic feelings of insecurity. These problems worsened in the nineteenth and early twentieth centuries under a series of reactionary tsars.

When Europe plunged into war in 1914, Russia under Tsar Nicholas II joined the Allies and declared war on Germany. But after the Bolshevik Revolution of 1917, the communist rulers of the new Soviet Union signed a separate peace with Germany and proclaimed their primary goal: the overthrow of world capitalism. In 1918 President Woodrow Wilson ordered some ten thousand U.S. troops to the Soviet Union as part of an Allied force that remained until 1920. Although its initial aim was to protect Allied war materiel and prevent Germany from occupying Russia's Baltic ports, this force also aided Russian groups seeking to overthrow the new Bolshevik regime. Soviet propagandists would long recall these events as proof of the capitalist powers' hostile intentions.

Between World Wars I and II, official Washington, along with most Americans, viewed the Soviet regime, with its announced enmity to capitalism, as a threat to U.S. security. The United States did not even recognize the Soviet Union diplomatically until 1933.

This hostility diminished during World War II, when the two nations joined forces against Nazi Germany. President Roosevelt, although cautiously hoping for postwar accord, never forgot that "a dictatorship as absolute as any ... in the world" ruled in Moscow. He hid from the Soviets the war's supreme secret, the Manhattan Project. (Stalin learned of it anyway through espionage and began his own atomic program.) British prime minister Winston Churchill never doubted Stalin's duplicity and urged Roosevelt to beware of the Soviet dictator.

The Soviet Union's postwar outlook reflected its ghastly wartime losses: more than 6 million soldiers dead and 14 million injured. The toll in the Battle of Stalingrad alone exceeded U.S. combat casualties for the entire war. Massive civilian deaths and physical destruction deepened the Soviets' concern with border security and roused a grim determination that their wartime enemies (not only Germany but nearby Finland, Hungary, Romania, and Bulgaria) would never again pose a threat. As U.S. ambassador W. Averell Harriman cabled the State Department early in 1945, "The overriding consideration in Soviet foreign policy is ... 'security' as Moscow sees it." As Soviet forces rumbled across Eastern Europe and into Germany, Moscow, despite Western protests, was determined to establish a buffer zone in the territories it was occupying.

World War II roused other tensions as well. As the Red Army had battled the invading Nazis, Stalin had implored his Western partners to open a second front that would compel Hitler to divert some forces westward. When the United States and Great Britain waited until June 1944 to do so, the delay deepened the Soviet dictator's suspicions of their intentions.

Despite the signs of trouble ahead, many Americans invested great faith in a new world organization, the United Nations. After World War I, the United States had refused to join the League of Nations, but now it would make amends. The Senate quickly ratified the UN Charter adopted at the San Francisco conference of June 1945. Secretary of State James F. Byrnes, addressing the UN in January 1946, pledged America's "wholehearted cooperation."

Internationalist dreams withered, however, as relations with Russia soured. The first conflict focused on Eastern Europe. Americans—many with ancestral roots in this region—had long supported the aspirations of Eastern Europeans for independence and freedom from domination by powerful neighbors. As the war in Europe ended, U.S., British, and other Western leaders committed themselves to independence for the nations of Eastern Europe and criticized Stalin's moves to impose Soviet control on the region. To Moscow, the United States and Great Britain, with their atomic bombs, seemed poised to pursue their own form of economic if not military expansion: the quest for raw materials and new markets that, according to Marxist doctrine, capitalism needed to survive. Soviet control of Eastern Europe, Stalin insisted, would be a counterweight to America's overwhelming economic and military superiority.

Attention initially centered on Poland. The Allies had an emotional investment in restoring freedom to that unhappy country, which Stalin and Hitler had callously divided between them in 1939 and which had suffered first under the Nazis and then under the advancing Red Army. Soviet troops had deliberately halted on the outskirts of Warsaw in August 1944 as an uprising by Polish insurgents engulfed the city, allowing the Nazis to kill many thousands of Poles and raze the city before retreating. Throughout the war, a Polish government-in-exile had functioned in London. When Roosevelt and Churchill insisted at Yalta that Stalin permit free elections in Poland, he retorted, "The Prime Minister has said that for Great Britain the question of Poland is a question of honor. For Russia it is not only a question of honor, but of security. . . . During the last thirty years our German enemy has passed through this corridor twice." Despite vague pledges of free elections, Stalin soon set up a pro-Soviet puppet government in Warsaw.

Tightening his grip in Eastern Europe, Stalin also installed a puppet government in Romania and reoccupied Latvia, Estonia, and Lithuania, Baltic nations he had annexed in 1940 and then lost to Hitler's armies. In mid-1945, foreshadowing his famous "Iron Curtain" speech of 1946 (see page 40), Churchill criticized Stalin for building an "iron fence" across Europe. Moscow tolerated a degree of political autonomy in Hungary and Czechoslovakia until 1948, but the prospects for freedom in Eastern Europe looked bleak in 1945–46.

Crucial to understanding the early Cold War is the fact that the Soviet Union was a one-party state ruled by one man, Joseph Stalin. Born Josif Visarionovich Dzhugashvili in 1879, the son of a Georgian shoemaker, he studied for the priesthood but in his mid-twenties became a communist and took the name *Stalin* ("Man of Steel"). He rose in the party and entered the cabinet after the 1917 revolution. After the death in 1924 of V. I. Lenin, the Soviet Union's first leader, Stalin soon gained supreme power. In the Moscow purge trials of the later 1930s, he ruthlessly eliminated former comrades and potential rivals. Millions of peasants died under Stalin's program of forced collectivization. Nevertheless, as the symbol of resistance against the German invaders, Stalin achieved almost mythic status during World War II. After 1945, a cult of personality, promoted by a vast propaganda machine, grew up around him. Despite his power, paranoid fears assailed him before his death in 1953. "He saw enemies everywhere," his daughter later wrote. This, then, was the ruler and the state that Western leaders confronted in the early Cold War years. Soviet foreign policy cannot be separated from Stalin's absolutist rule. As diplomatic historian Robert H. Ferrell has written, "Stalin almost needed a foreign enemy in order to tighten his control upon the Russian people."

While Karl Marx's prediction of communism's inevitable triumph lent a certain rhetorical coherence to Moscow's postwar strategy, balance-of-power calculations, territorial ambitions, and security fears took top priority. Stalin's postwar course, although cautiously pursued, followed a long tradition of Russian imperialism, but an imperialism whose limits and objectives now seemed menacingly imprecise. Gripped by suspicions and obsessed with secrecy, Stalin seemed unable to delimit Russia's legitimate security concerns. Imposing near-absolute rule across much of Eastern Europe, he also sought to expand Soviet influence in Western Europe and elsewhere, alarming leaders in Washington and other Western capitals.

In Washington, the challenge of dealing with Stalin while juggling domestic ideological pressures and corporate interests fell to President Truman, a novice in foreign policy. After twelve years of FDR's patrician speech, aristocratic manner, and larger-than-life image, Truman's flat Missouri twang and lack of charisma came as a rude jolt. "I look just like any other fifty people you meet in the street," he

The Big Three. President Truman with Prime Minister Winston Churchill and Premier Joseph Stalin, July 1945. Barely three months after becoming president, Truman traveled to the Berlin suburb of Potsdam for the last of the Allied leaders' wartime conferences. The smiles and handshakes masked deepening differences. *(Imperial War Museum.)*

once observed. A farm lad whose poor eyesight had excluded him from boyhood games and from West Point, Truman had served in World War I and operated a Kansas City men's store before winning election as a county executive in 1922. His political rise, including election to the U.S. Senate in 1934, had hardly been meteoric. An avid reader of American history, he had won respect, but only modest public visibility, as chair of a Senate committee investigating waste in military contracts. Now he was a world leader.

Cocky, self-assured, and inclined to snap judgments, Truman quickly decided that Stalin understood only force and blunt language. Soviet expansionism, coupled with Truman's short temper, led to volatile early encounters. Outraged by Stalin's failure to hold free elections in Poland, Truman in April 1945, a few days after becoming president, delivered such a tongue-lashing to visiting Soviet foreign minister V. I. Molotov that, according to Truman, Molotov sputtered, "I have never been talked to like that in my life!" Truman allegedly retorted, "Carry out your agreements and you won't get talked to like that."

Stalin responded with equal vehemence, pushing forward with the imposition of a pro-Soviet communist regime on the Poles despite his earlier promises. "Poland borders . . . the Soviet Union," he cabled Truman sarcastically, "[which] cannot be said of Great Britain and the United States." Stalin's stonewalling on Poland convinced Truman that an equally tough Western response was necessary.

A few Washington voices, including Secretary of War Henry Stimson and Army Chief of Staff George C. Marshall, urged a patient search for common interests with the Soviets. Soviet security concerns made Stalin's actions understandable, argued Stimson. This minority view, however, largely vanished from Truman's inner circle when Stimson retired in September 1945 and when Marshall left Washington in November on an extended mission to China.

1946: Eastern Europe, Iran, Atomic Energy

In 1946 the dispute over Poland widened into a conflict involving Eastern Europe, the Middle East, and the United Nations. *Pravda,* Stalin's propaganda voice, grew virulently anti-American, and from the White House to Main Street, American hostility toward the Soviets deepened. Early in the year, *Time* published a map portraying "Communist Contagion" as a global epidemic. Iran, Turkey, and China were already "infected," warned *Time;* Saudi Arabia, Egypt, Afghanistan, and India had been "exposed" and might sicken at any moment.

Two speeches underscored the widening chasm. On February 9, 1946, Stalin belligerently blamed the capitalist nations for World War II and reaffirmed Moscow's determination to lead the struggle against Western imperialism. The war-weary Soviet people, Stalin announced, must achieve new feats of military production. The speech reverberated through Western capitals. Supreme Court Justice William O. Douglas, a New Deal liberal, called it "the Declaration of World War III." A month later, on March 5, 1946, Great Britain's wartime prime minister, Winston Churchill, traveled to Fulton, Missouri—Truman's home state—to speak at tiny Westminster College. With Truman applauding behind him, Churchill bluntly warned of ominous developments:

> From Stettin in the Baltic to Trieste in the Adriatic, an iron curtain has descended across the continent. Behind that line lie all the capitals of the ancient states of central and eastern Europe. Warsaw, Berlin, Prague, Vienna, Budapest, Belgrade, Bucharest, and Sofia, all the famous cities and the populations around them lie in the Soviet sphere and all are subject . . . to a very high and increasing measure of control from Moscow.

The Soviets did not want war, advised Churchill; "What they desire is the fruits of war and the indefinite expansion of their power and doctrines." The response, he insisted, had to be unflinching resistance: "There is nothing [the Russians] admire so much as strength, and there is nothing for which they have less respect than military weakness." Eager to continue London's wartime partnership with Washington, especially on atomic matters, Churchill called for Anglo-American cooperation to resist this latest threat to Western civilization.

Americans revered Churchill, and they took his warning seriously. Moreover, events lent his claims credence: Stalin had unleashed his blast only weeks earlier; much of Eastern Europe did lie under Moscow's heel; and, as we shall see, a crisis mood hung over Iran and the Middle East.

In response to threatening events and to Churchill's eloquence, a new ideological consensus coalesced across the United States. Republican senator Arthur Vandenberg of Michigan, head of the Senate Foreign Relations Committee and once a well-known isolationist, wrote in May 1946, "I am more than ever convinced that communism is on the march . . . world-wide . . . which only America can stop."

One prominent dissenter from this view was Truman's secretary of commerce, Henry Wallace, a New Dealer who had served President Roosevelt as secretary of agriculture and then as vice president. In a July 1946 memo to Truman, Wallace deplored "the irrational fear of Russia . . . being built up in the American people by certain individuals and publications." That September he made the same argument in a speech at New York's Madison Square Garden, triggering a blowup in the administration. Secretary of State Byrnes cabled Truman from Paris: "You and I spent fifteen months building a bipartisan [Soviet] policy. . . . Wallace destroyed it in a day." Truman had approved Wallace's speech after a quick reading, but faced with Byrnes's fury, he demanded Wallace's resignation.

Amid belligerent speechmaking and wrangling over Eastern Europe, conflict flared in Iran, a familiar cockpit of Big Power rivalry. Russia had long coveted the warm-water ports of the Mediterranean and the Persian Gulf. By the 1930s, oil-rich Iran, a gateway to the Persian Gulf, had become a special focus of Soviet interest. During World War II, the British and Russians had occupied Iran jointly, agreeing to withdraw six months after Germany's defeat. But Soviet troops remained into 1946, well beyond the six-month deadline, while Stalin pressured Tehran to permit joint Soviet-Iranian oil exploration in northern Iran.

The Soviet presence in Iran posed strategic worries for the West (including Western oil interests) and deepened Truman's distrust of Stalin. "I'm tired of babying the Soviets," he complained in January 1946 to James Byrnes, who sent Moscow a note demanding immediate Soviet withdrawal. The administration also brought the matter before the fledgling UN Security Council. By May, having extracted from Tehran a pledge of an oil exploration treaty, the Soviets had departed. (No longer menaced by Soviet troops, Iran's parliament rejected the proposed treaty.)

As the Russians withdrew, Western oil companies moved in. In September 1947, two major U.S. oil companies, in partnership with a British company, signed a twenty-year agreement to drill and market Iranian oil. The next year, following up on FDR's 1945 meeting with King Ibn Saud (see Chapter 1), a consortium of four U.S. oil companies organized as Aramco (Arab-American Oil Company) concluded an oil agreement with Saudi Arabia. At the same time, the American-owned Gulf Oil Company, in partnership with Royal Dutch Shell, arranged to refine and market Kuwaiti oil. (The oil output of Iran's neighbor Iraq remained under British control, as it had been for years.) The corporate structure was in place for a massive flow of oil from the Middle East to the United States, Western Europe, and elsewhere in the noncommunist world. The Iran crisis thus not only played a role in the early Cold War but also figured in the continued jockeying among the industrialized powers for the region's most precious resource.

Issues related to the atomic bomb molded postwar diplomacy as well. Indeed, by no coincidence, the Cold War's beginnings coincided with the United States' four-year atomic monopoly (1945–49). From the moment of the Alamogordo test, President Truman had understood that the atomic bomb had implications not only for the circumstances of Japan's surrender (see Chapter 1), but also for postwar Soviet-American relations. When the news from Alamogordo reached Truman at the Potsdam Conference in July 1945, he was, according to Secretary of War Stimson, "tremendously pepped up," showing an "entirely new feeling of confidence" in his dealings with Stalin. At conferences late in 1945 in London and Moscow, Secretary of State Byrnes tried to use U.S. atomic supremacy to influence Soviet behavior in Eastern Europe and elsewhere, but with disappointing results. Henry Stimson, troubled by this heavy-handed atomic diplomacy, wrote to Truman:

> [O]ur . . . relations with Russia . . . [are] virtually dominated by the problem of the atomic bomb. . . . These relations may be perhaps irretrievably embittered by the way in which we approach the solution of the bomb with Russia. For if we fail to approach them now . . . , having this weapon rather ostentatiously on our hip, . . . their distrust of our purposes and motives will increase.

In fact, the atomic bomb's vast destructive power diminished its value in diplomatic negotiations. As the Soviets menaced Iran and Eastern Europe in late 1945, an adviser tried to lift Truman's spirits by commenting, "Mr. President, you have an atomic bomb up your sleeve." Truman replied, "Yes, but I'm not sure it can ever be used."

Still, the bomb did have symbolic importance for balance-of-power politics. Soon after Hiroshima, Stalin directed Soviet scientists, "Provide us with atomic weapons in the shortest possible time. . . . The equilibrium has been destroyed. . . . [A Russian atomic bomb] will remove a great danger from us." The U.S. atomic bomb, coupled with Byrnes's veiled atomic threats, fed the fear of encirclement already prevalent in Moscow. The bomb, wrote Ambassador Harriman late in 1945, had "revived [the Soviets'] feeling of insecurity. . . . The Russian people have been aroused to feel that they must again face an antagonistic world. American imperialism is included as a threat."

A combination of idealism and suspicion of Soviet intentions drove Washington's abortive efforts for the international control of atomic energy. Early in 1946, a State Department committee chaired by Undersecretary of State Dean Acheson and including David Lilienthal, head of the Tennessee Valley Authority, unveiled a plan for UN control of atomic energy. The Acheson-Lilienthal plan won praise in the American press, although a few critics saw it as a formula for a continued U.S. atomic monopoly. Under the proposal, the United States reserved the right to build and stockpile atomic bombs until a control plan acceptable to Washington was fully in place. Doubts about U.S. intentions intensified when Truman named the fiercely anti-Soviet Bernard Baruch to conduct the atomic energy negotiations at the UN.

Baruch's plan (a toughened version of the Acheson-Lilienthal plan) proposed an international atomic development authority to license and supervise the mining of uranium and the manufacture of fissionable material. Nations would be encouraged to explore the atom's peaceful uses but forbidden to make nuclear weapons. Any nation violating this ban would face "condign [appropriate] punishment" under UN authority.

The Soviet Union's UN delegate, Andrei Gromyko, rejected the plan as a scheme to serve U.S. interests. As hopes for international control of atomic energy faded, some U.S. military planners were quietly pleased, viewing the bomb as America's "winning weapon" in the emerging conflict with the U.S.S.R. The World

War II hero General Dwight Eisenhower cautioned Baruch against any plan that limited America's capacity to build atomic bombs, which he saw as "a deterrent . . . to aggression in the world."

In the summer of 1946, during the UN debate, the United States conducted a series of atomic tests at Bikini Atoll in the Pacific. (A French swimwear designer named one scanty number "the Bikini.") The Soviets denounced the tests as further proof of America's determination to maintain atomic supremacy.

Later that year, in a memo to Truman, presidential adviser Clark Clifford warned against disarmament negotiations "as long as the possibility of Soviet aggression exists" and called for an urgent military buildup, including readiness for "atomic and biological warfare." Truman heeded this advice, which came from other quarters as well. By 1949, before the Soviets had exploded a single nuclear weapon, the U.S. possessed about 150 atomic bombs and a growing number of nuclear-capable bombers.

As 1946 ended, with memories of victory celebrations still vivid, the Cold War already loomed large. The first half of the 1940s had witnessed history's bloodiest war; as the second half unfolded, a still more horrendous conflict seemed all too possible.

1947: The Truman Doctrine, Containment, and the Marshall Plan

The year 1947 brought influential statements of America's Cold War purposes as well as major initiatives aimed at blunting Soviet influence in postwar Europe. The first of the policy pronouncements, the Truman Doctrine, emerged from a crisis in Greece. An insurgency backed by Marshall Josip Broz Tito, the communist ruler of neighboring Yugoslavia, and by the pro-Soviet puppet regimes of Albania and Bulgaria was battling Greece's corrupt, right-wing monarchy. Great Britain, with historic interests in the region, had restored Greece's monarchy in 1944 after expelling German and other occupation forces. But in February 1947, the economically strapped British informed Washington that they could no longer finance the Greek government's fight. The Soviet Union, while backing the Greek insurgents, was also pressuring Turkey to share control of the Dardanelles strait, the vital waterway linking the Black Sea and the Mediterranean. Russia had long sought access to the Mediterranean for its Black Sea fleet, and Stalin, too, pursued this goal.

U.S. and British strategists agreed that the Russians must be kept out of the Mediterranean and that Greece and Turkey must be held in the Western camp. President Truman favored military and economic aid to the two nations, but congressional approval was uncertain. Opponents raised various objections. Leftists such as Henry Wallace, now a private citizen, denounced the administration's bellicose tone toward the Soviet Union. Greece and Turkey, they pointed out, hardly shone as beacons of freedom and democracy. Even stronger opposition came from conservatives. Republican senator Robert Taft of Ohio warned against new global involvements. Some fiscal conservatives deplored the cost; others predicted that aid to Greece and Turkey would lead to deeper foreign entanglements. Senator Walter George of Georgia, a Democratic elder statesman, cautioned against starting down a road whose end no one could predict.

IN PERSPECTIVE

Presidential Persuasion on Foreign-Policy Issues

When President Truman in 1947 asked Congress to invest millions of dollars to buttress Greece and Turkey against feared Soviet expansionism, he joined a long line of presidents who sought with varied success to win backing for major foreign-policy initiatives from an often reluctant nation. The Constitution puts the president in charge of foreign affairs, but it also sets up an elaborate system of governmental checks and balances, so presidents from George Washington on have had to struggle to exercise that power.

In 1846, President James K. Polk called for war with Mexico because (among other reasons) the Mexicans had shed "American blood on American soil." In fact, the circumstances were highly ambiguous: The bloodshed had occurred during a U.S. Army foray into territory that was in fact claimed by Mexico. Antiwar Whig congressmen, including Abraham Lincoln, challenged Polk's claims. Lincoln, for example, introduced his "spot resolutions" insisting that Polk identify the precise spot on which American blood had been shed "on American soil." But expansionist sentiment prevailed, and the war came.

President William McKinley, by contrast, only reluctantly backed war with Spain in 1898. Pressured by tabloid newspapers like William Randolph Hearst's *New York World* that trumpeted Spain's misdeeds in Cuba, McKinley eventually called for war. Most Americans rallied behind what promised to be a quick and one-sided contest (one U.S. statesman declared it a "splendid little war"). But influential opponents, including the philosopher William James and the steel magnate Andrew Carnegie, denounced the war and challenged McKinley's justifications. The controversy deepened when the Spanish-American War evolved into a bloody, drawn-out campaign to suppress an independence movement in the Philippines. McKinley's justification for this action—reached, he said, after an anguished night of prayer—was that the Filipinos, left on their own, would soon fall prey to European imperial rivalries, and thus it was in the interests of "our little brown brothers" to be under the benign oversight of Christian

America. But despite McKinley's rationale, the fighting in the Philippines stirred congressional opposition. Senate hearings publicized shocking atrocities committed by U.S. soldiers in the Philippines.

President Woodrow Wilson's eloquent summons to war in April 1917 anticipated Truman's 1947 call for aid to Greece and Turkey. Wilson, too, framed the issue in cosmic terms: This would be a war to defend American ideals, make the world safe for democracy, elevate the conduct of international relations, and create a new world order based on justice, not brute power. Americans embraced the war on gusts of Wilsonian rhetoric, but such exalted idealism could not possibly be sustained, and by 1919 a reaction had set in. Congress repudiated Wilson's beloved League of Nations, and Wilson left the White House in 1921 broken and embittered. President Franklin Roosevelt trod a careful line from the late 1930s through 1941 as he tried to maneuver a reluctant Congress and nation into supporting U.S. efforts to resist Hitler and aid a beleaguered Great Britain. Isolationist and pacifist sentiment was strong, and Roosevelt faced bitter opposition at every step. FDR's task eased immeasurably after December 7, 1941. With the Japanese surprise attack on Pearl Harbor, an outraged Congress and nation rallied behind Roosevelt's call for war. The force of that outrage, and the sense that the nation's cause was righteous, sustained U.S. support for the war, and for Roosevelt as war leader, up to the moment of FDR's death in April 1945, and on to the final victory that August.

When North Korea invaded South Korea in 1950, President Truman initially enjoyed strong support as he portrayed the invasion as a test of U.S. will that had to be bravely met. Americans also backed Truman's plan to fight under the United Nations flag in a multinational "police action" authorized by UN resolutions rather than by a congressional declaration of war. As the Korean War dragged on, however, support for Truman eroded. By 1952 the war had become deeply unpopular, and Truman's defense of it was no longer sufficient to rally national support.

Vietnam, of course, offers the classic instance of a president's failure to rally the nation behind a foreign war. Initially, Johnson and his advisers marshaled support for the war with apparent success. The 1964 Gulf of Tonkin Resolution, passed overwhelmingly by Congress after a supposed attack on U.S. Navy ships by North Vietnamese gunboats, provided Johnson with the congressional support he wanted for an expanded war. But Johnson's escalation of the war in early 1965 brought the first ominous stirrings of opposition. Initially Congress and most Americans supported the war, but the support was reluctant and uneasy, and as the war dragged on, it steadily eroded. Johnson never succeeded in finding a coherent and persuasive rationale for the war that would rally undivided support for the expenditure of American life and treasure. Like Wilson, he, too, left office under a cloud, successful domestically but a failure in his role as shaper of the nation's foreign policy.

Given this mixed record, Truman's ability early in 1947 to rally a war-weary nation for yet another major foreign-policy initiative, and the administration's campaign for the Marshall Plan a few months later, must count as notable successes in the long history of presidential efforts to exert leadership in shaping America's relations with the rest of the world.

At a White House meeting of congressional leaders, Dean Acheson presented the administration's case in somber and sweeping terms. Greece and Turkey, he intoned, were part of a larger drama: "Like apples in a barrel infected by . . . one rotten one, the corruption of Greece would infect Iran and all to the East . . . , Africa . . . , Italy, and France." "Not since Rome and Carthage," he concluded, had there been "such a polarization of power on this earth." Senator Vandenberg, now fully convinced that only America could halt communism's worldwide march, urged Truman to follow Acheson's lead and "scare hell out of the country" to ensure congressional support for his aid request.

Adopting Vandenberg's advice, Truman addressed Congress on March 12, 1947. Requesting $400 million in aid to Greece and Turkey, he couched the issue in apocalyptic terms. The world, he pronounced, must choose between two ways of life: democracy and freedom or totalitarianism and oppression. The United States and the Soviet Union, he implied, exemplified these two opposed philosophies. Wherever this struggle erupted, the president declared, America must "support free peoples who are resisting attempted subjugation by armed minorities or by outside pressures." Giving Truman a standing ovation, both houses of Congress passed the aid bill by solid majorities. Public opinion polls backed the aid request, and Truman's poll ratings shot up. Democrat Sam Rayburn of Texas, the House minority leader, declared: "People who love liberty . . . want us to . . . lead the world. . . . If we do not accept our responsibility [and] . . . extend a helping hand to people . . . who do not want to be smothered by communism, . . . [then] God help this world."

Labeled the Truman Doctrine, this aid program succeeded. Soviet pressure on Turkey eased, and by 1949 the authoritarian Greek government, with U.S. help (and Tito's defection from the Soviet camp), had quashed the insurgents. Equally important, the Truman Doctrine, in its melding of the specific realities of the situation in Greece and Turkey into a sweeping scenario of cataclysmic world conflict, hastened a process by which Americans came to view every confrontation with Soviet power as part of an all-encompassing, primarily ideological global struggle.

The most influential summation of early Cold War thinking was an essay, "The Sources of Soviet Conduct," in the July 1947 issue of the journal *Foreign Affairs*. The author, initially identified only as "X," was George Kennan, director of the State Department's policy-planning staff. Early in 1946, Kennan, then a diplomat in Moscow, had sent to Washington a secret "Long Telegram" summarizing his views of Soviet foreign policy and U.S.-Soviet relations. Amid such ominous developments as the Iran crisis, Moscow's actions in Eastern Europe, and Stalin's bombastic talk of communism's inevitable triumph, Kennan's telegram attracted notice. It particularly impressed navy secretary James V. Forrestal, who in 1947 became the nation's first secretary of defense.* An early and passionate Cold Warrior, Forrestal publicized Kennan's telegram and supported his transfer from Moscow to the State Department.

Kennan's *Foreign Affairs* article, written at Forrestal's urging, proved highly influential in shaping opinion about the Soviet Union and the nature of the Cold War. Soviet rhetoric, Kennan suggested, arose from "a traditional and instinctive

---

*Prior to 1947, the Department of Defense was known as the War Department, and the cabinet officer who ran it bore the title secretary of war.

Russian sense of insecurity." For historical and ideological reasons, he argued, the Soviets were waging "a patient but deadly struggle" to expand their influence and crush all rivals. The U.S. objective must be "a long-term, patient, but firm and vigilant containment of Russian expansive tendencies." Echoing nineteenth-century prophecies of America's manifest destiny, Kennan said that Americans should be grateful to "a Providence which, by providing [them] with this implacable challenge, has made their . . . security as a nation dependent on their pulling themselves together and accepting the responsibilities of moral and political leadership that history plainly intended them to bear."

In practical terms, Kennan's "containment" doctrine, which soon became official administration policy, meant the deployment of U.S. economic and military resources to prevent Moscow from expanding Russian power beyond its historic Eurasian base. (A traditional balance-of-power strategist, Kennan accepted spheres of influence so long as they kept within bounds.) In many respects, Kennan offered a prudent, long-term response to the threat posed by an insecure, ideologically driven nation ruled by an unpredictable dictator. As head of the policy-planning staff until 1949, Kennan applied his strategic vision to specific areas of U.S.-Soviet confrontation.

However, to Kennan's dismay, some Cold Warriors, at least in their public pronouncements, ignored his emphasis on the cautious side of Soviet behavior and his call for patience and restraint in dealings with the Soviets. Instead, they embraced apocalyptic scenarios of Moscow's lust for "world domination." James Forrestal, for example, became dangerously obsessed with the global communist menace, finding revolutionary conspiracies everywhere and offering nightmarish visions of "Russians swarming over Europe."* Forrestal's lurid anticommunism demonstrated how Kennan's limited, cautious doctrine could mutate into a far more aggressive formulation of the nation's Cold War mission.

As Washington debated containment doctrine, Western Europe struggled with runaway inflation, crippled industry, and near-famine conditions. A fierce winter in 1946–47 deepened the suffering. Train cars froze to the tracks; government workers shivered in frigid offices; misery was everywhere. The Truman administration responded with the most important initiative of the early Cold War era: the European Recovery Plan, more commonly known as the Marshall Plan.

The political situation looked equally alarming. European Marxist parties seemed poised to exploit the crisis, perhaps with the goal of dragging the whole region into the Soviet orbit. The powerful French Communist Party, for example, was doggedly loyal to Moscow. A *New York Times* reporter, writing from Paris in February 1947, found "the old strongholds of democracy in Europe . . . battered and shaken." "[I]f freedom . . . is to survive," he warned, "it's up to the United States to save it." Although few U.S. strategists seriously feared a Soviet invasion of Western Europe, they did worry that desperate people, especially in France and Italy, might vote communist regimes into power.

Against this backdrop, Secretary of State George C. Marshall, in a June 1947 commencement address at Harvard University, offered Europe a program of

---

*Forrestal's demons eventually destroyed him; he committed suicide in May 1949.

massive U.S. economic assistance.* While appealing to Americans' humanitarian impulse to alleviate hunger and poverty, and denying that the plan was "directed . . . against any country," Marshall made clear the program's larger geopolitical goal: "the revival of a working economy . . . to permit the emergence of political and social conditions in which free institutions can exist."

Beyond economic and social recovery lay a still larger objective: the creation of a strong and united Europe, allied with the United States, that could stand firm against Soviet pressures. To further this aim (and to facilitate the inclusion of Germany in the aid program), the architects of the Marshall Plan insisted that aid not be distributed on a piecemeal, nation-by-nation basis but collectively as part of a unified recovery strategy drafted collaboratively by the European nations themselves. In effect, the Marshall Plan envisioned an American-style liberal capitalist order in Europe, where consumer abundance, economic integration, and a federative political system would dilute the national conflicts that had so often torn apart Europe in the past and inoculate the masses against radical appeals from the Right or Left.

Marshall's proposal set off feverish political activity. In Washington, despite some grumbling about the cost and complaints from the Left about the "Martial Plan's" anti-Soviet subtext, Congress by 1951 had funded $13 billion in Marshall Plan aid. In Europe, the plan stimulated economic cooperation with profound long-term significance. In July 1947, sixteen European foreign ministers gathered in Paris to draft the European Recovery Plan. From these beginnings evolved the European Coal and Steel Community (1952), the European Economic Community or Common Market (1958), and the European Union (1991), with a parliament, a judicial system, a common currency (the Euro), and, by 2003, the draft of a constitution. The Marshall Plan launched this historic development.

Mainly for propaganda reasons, the Truman administration initially invited the Soviet Union and Eastern European nations to participate in the Marshall Plan, with no real expectation that they would accept. Somewhat to Washington's surprise, Poland and Czechoslovakia tried to join the 1947 Paris talks. Stalin objected, however. U.S. plans for revitalizing Western Europe challenged his hopes of expanded influence in the region, and the prospect of a thriving Germany touched an always raw nerve. The Soviets denounced the inclusion of Germany in the Marshall Plan (and U.S. promotion of Japanese economic recovery) as a U.S. plot to restore the wartime enemies as major powers, only this time "subordinated to [the] interest of American capital." Stalin angrily ordered Poland and Czechoslovakia to leave the Paris talks, further underscoring Europe's deepening division.

In September 1947, the Soviet diplomat Andrei Vyshinsky blasted the Marshall Plan for bypassing the United Nations, "split[ting] Europe into two camps," denying European nations the right of economic self-determination, and subordinating Western Europe to "the interest of American monopolies . . . [seeking] an accelerated export of commodities and capital to Europe." Although Vyshinsky's hostile analysis reflected his Marxist assumptions, he had a point. Along with its other purposes, the plan did benefit American business by enabling Europe to buy U.S. goods. This

---

*Marshall, a career army officer who had served as army chief of staff during World War II, had replaced James Byrnes as secretary of state earlier in 1947.

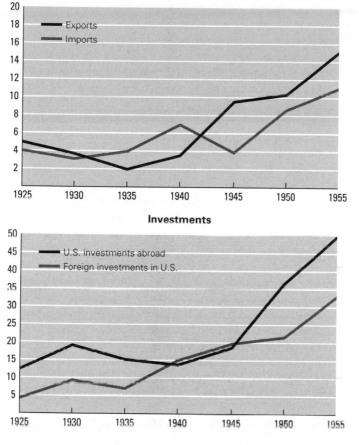

FIGURE 2.1

U.S. Foreign Trade and Investments, 1925–1955

SOURCE: Adapted from *Historical Statistics of the United States* (Washington, D.C., 1975), pp. 537, 542, 564.

goal was candidly acknowledged by one of the plan's key architects, William L. Clayton, undersecretary of state for economic affairs and a millionaire Mississippi cotton investor. "Let us admit right off," said Clayton in 1947, "our objective has as its background the needs and interests of the people of the United States. We need markets—big markets—in which to buy and sell." Indeed, millions of dollars in Marshall Plan aid returned in the form of orders for U.S. farm commodities and manufactured goods. As the journal *Foreign Affairs* observed in a fiftieth-anniversary retrospective in June 1997: "[The Marshall Plan] was neither naive nor devoid of self-interest. . . . [T]his was clearly a policy to benefit the United States."

Overall, U.S. merchandise exports jumped from $9.5 billion to $15 billion between 1946 and 1952, thanks in large part to the Marshall Plan. These years also saw growing corporate investment abroad as U.S. businesses pursued foreign markets and built factories and distribution facilities overseas. By 1950 foreign investment by U.S. corporations approached $12 billion. A decade later it would total some $32 billion.

Recent assessments of the Marshall Plan, while granting its importance, offer a more nuanced view than some earlier studies. Michael Hogan's *The Marshall Plan* (1987) sees its significance less in the aid provided than in its role in pushing Europe toward a U.S.-style corporatist model of business/government/labor cooperation that had emerged in America during the New Deal. John Killick's *The United States and European Reconstruction* (1997) argues that Europe was already on the road to recovery by 1947 but was hampered by war-damaged and outdated factories, harbors, mines, refineries, power grids, and transportation systems. By providing grants that allowed European governments to buy urgently needed food, fertilizer, coal, farm equipment, and other basic necessities from America, he contends, the Marshall Plan enabled these governments to channel more resources to modernizing their industrial infrastructure, thereby speeding long-term recovery.

The Marshall Plan was part of a larger American effort to rebuild a world financial structure shattered by depression and war, and to ease an acute postwar dollar shortage in the industrialized world. In 1944, a twenty-eight-nation monetary conference in Bretton Woods, New Hampshire, had laid the groundwork for two important agencies: the International Bank for Reconstruction and Development, or World Bank, and the International Monetary Fund (IMF). The World Bank arranged long-term loans to help poor nations develop their transportation, health, and educational infrastructure. The IMF promoted trade, monetary cooperation, and exchange-rate stability among the world's industrialized nations. The Soviet Union, despite repeated invitations, refused to join. (In 1992, after the Cold War's end, Russia and other former Soviet republics would at last become members.) This new monetary system, coupled with the Marshall Plan and private investment by U.S. corporations, helped to rebuild Europe's economy and improved living conditions for millions. It also served the interests of American business by stimulating foreign trade and creating the framework for the eventual emergence of a multinational corporate order.

These initiatives, and especially the Marshall Plan, also forestalled the economic stagnation that would have provided fertile breeding ground for social unrest and communist gains. As such, they represented another front in the Cold War. As early as 1950, Western European production was 25 percent above prewar levels. The twenty-five years after 1948 saw the highest rates of economic growth in Europe's history. West Germans spoke of the *Wirtschaftwunder* (economic miracle) in their country.

At home, meanwhile, the Cold War intensified long-standing rivalries among the military services. The air force, in particular, feared being marginalized. This jockeying for resources and power influenced and sometimes distorted early postwar military planning, as each service promoted strategies and weapons systems that served its interests. To address these problems, the National Security Act of July 1947 combined the separate army and navy departments, together with a newly independent air force, into the cabinet-level Department of Defense headed by a civilian secretary. This legislation also unified the military services under the Joint Chiefs of Staff. Interservice struggles persisted, but the military now functioned with a higher degree of coordination.

The National Security Act also created a new strategic planning body, the National Security Council (NSC), to advise the president, and it set up the Central Intelligence Agency (CIA) to carry on the espionage operations of the wartime Office of Strategic Services (OSS). These reforms hastened the shift of foreign-policy formation from the State Department to the White House, a development that by the late 1960s and early 1970s would enable President Richard Nixon and National Security Adviser Henry Kissinger to ignore the secretary of state as they took sweeping foreign-policy initiatives.

By 1947 the wartime Grand Alliance lay in ruins. That August, Charles E. Bohlen, a Soviet specialist in the State Department, gloomily assessed the new world order and sketched a scenario for U.S. foreign policy:

> Instead of unity among the great powers . . . , there is complete disunity between the Soviet Union and [its] satellites . . . and the rest of the world. . . . Faced with this disagreeable fact, . . . the United States . . . must reexamine its major policy objectives. . . . [T]he non-Soviet world . . . [must] draw closer together politically, economically, financially, and, in the last analysis, militarily. . . . Only in this way can a free and non-Soviet world hope to survive.

In the months ahead, the policy reorientation that Bohlen advised would proceed with breathtaking speed.

1948–1949: The Prague Coup, the Berlin Airlift, and NATO

Moscow's grip on Eastern Europe tightened in February 1948, when Czech and Slovak communists overthrew Prague's fragile coalition government and installed a pro-Soviet regime. Soon after, Czechoslovakia's foreign minister Jan Masaryk, a national hero, died in a plunge from a foreign-ministry window. The country's new rulers called it suicide, but many suspected murder. The Prague coup alarmed Western Europe; in Washington, it seemed further proof of Stalin's treachery.

The sense of crisis deepened that summer, with Germany now the focus. At the war's end, the Allies had divided Germany into four occupation zones: the Soviets in the mainly agricultural east; the British, French, and Americans in the more populous and industrialized west. These supposedly temporary divisions rapidly hardened as Moscow clamped down on eastern Germany and the Western powers combined their zones into one. As West Germany's economy revived, thanks in part to Marshall Plan aid, the Allies laid plans to convert the region into an independent nation linked to the West.

Stalin, determined to stop this process, took Berlin hostage. Although the former German capital lay deep in the Soviet zone, the four powers governed it jointly and kept it open to access from the West. But on June 24, 1948, as the Western occupiers prepared to integrate Berlin into the West German economy through currency reform, the Soviets abruptly blocked all highway routes to the city. This action posed a major dilemma for President Truman: To smash through the Red Army's barricades could bring war, yet to abandon Berlin would make a mockery of the containment doctrine and weaken Truman's chances in the upcoming presidential election.

The Berlin Airlift, 1948. A group of Berliners watches as a C-47 cargo plane lands at Tempelhof Airfield, transporting vital supplies to the beleaguered city. *(Time Life Pictures/ Getty Images)*

In a brilliant stroke, Truman ordered the U.S. Air Force to maintain a lifeline to Berlin. For the next 321 days, an armada of U.S. and British aircraft flew around the clock into Berlin's Templehof Airport, ferrying food and other necessities of life into the beleaguered city. Conceding defeat in May 1949, the Soviets reopened land access to Berlin. Within days, a new constitution launched the Federal Republic of Germany as a parliamentary democracy. In October, Soviet authorities set up the German Democratic Republic in the east.

The Prague coup and the Berlin crisis, heightening European fears of an imminent military showdown, hastened plans for a Western military alliance. After the communist takeover in Czechoslovakia, British foreign secretary Ernest Bevin warned Washington of an encroaching "Soviet tide" and urged a military alliance to defend "Western civilization." With twenty-five Soviet-led divisions in Central Europe facing twelve underequipped divisions in Western Europe, these fears seemed well grounded.

Working behind the scenes, the Truman administration built bipartisan support for an alliance. In June 1948, Congress adopted, 64 to 4, a resolution approving, in principle, security alliances with other nations. In April 1949, a treaty-signing cere-

MAP 2.1
Cold War Europe, 1950

mony in Washington launched the North Atlantic Treaty Organization (NATO) joining the United States, Canada, and ten nations of Western Europe in a mutual defense arrangement: Article 5 of the treaty declared that an attack on any member would be an attack on all.* The Senate ratified the treaty in July, and in September—the Soviets having exploded an atomic bomb in the interim—Congress voted $1.5 billion in military aid for Western Europe.

The historic U.S. opposition to peacetime foreign alliances, dating to the 1780s, had fallen victim to the Cold War. A key step in America's postwar emergence on the world stage, NATO for four decades would symbolize Western resolve

---

*After the September 11, 2001, terrorist attack on the World Trade Center and the Pentagon, NATO invoked Article 5 and declared that the attack on the United States was an attack on all NATO members. NATO subsequently cooperated in the U.S. response, including the assault on terrorist groups centered in Afghanistan. See Chapter 16.

in the Cold War. Like the Marshall Plan, it was intended in part to shore up European unity against the Soviet threat. As Dean Acheson observed, "[Without] the continuing association and support of the United States . . . free Europe would split apart." When the Cold War ended, as we shall see, NATO faced deep strains.

President Truman signaled a still greater expansion of America's global commitments in his January 1949 State of the Union message, announcing a major program of U.S. aid to poor nations. Like the Marshall Plan, this Point Four program (it was the fourth item in the foreign-policy section of Truman's address) combined humanitarian, anticommunist, and business objectives. By the early 1970s, the Agency for International Development (AID), set up to distribute aid under the Point Four program, had channeled over $100 billion to nations in Latin America, Asia, Africa, and the Middle East to promote economic development and political stability, and so forestall the spread of communism. Point Four assistance also promoted U.S. exports and foreign investment. Indeed, some Point Four aid agreements required the recipients to use the money to purchase U.S. manufactured goods or farm commodities.

The close of 1949 found Cold War hostilities deeply entrenched. In Moscow, fears of atomic blackmail and encirclement by "capitalist imperialism" were almost palpable. In the United States, the conviction that the Soviets harbored a grand design for world conquest had, for many, become an article of faith. "There is only one language [the Soviets] understand, force," declared Truman in 1949. George Kennan, leaving the State Department for private life, blasted the administration's neglect of diplomacy, its "preoccupation with military affairs," and its rhetorical excesses and "flamboyant anti-communism" as it sought support for its foreign-policy initiatives.

Kennan's critics insisted that the scary scenario of a worldwide death struggle with communism presented in Churchill's Iron Curtain address, in the Truman Doctrine, and in countless apocalyptic speeches and editorials accurately reflected postwar realities. The Soviet Union *was* a brutal dictatorship, they pointed out; its military forces *did* prop up pro-Soviet regimes across Eastern Europe; and Mao Zedong's triumph in China in 1949 (see page 55) seemed further proof of communism's global march.

Nevertheless, Kennan had a point. The black-and-white worldview of many early Cold War ideologists obscured the fact that numerous states of the so-called Free World—Greece, Spain, Iran, South Africa, military dictatorships in Latin America, and authoritarian regimes in the Middle East, for example—fell far short of the democratic ideal. Furthermore, leading nations of the Western Alliance still held colonies in Africa and Asia. Even in the United States, racial discrimination against African Americans still prevailed, as Soviet propagandists loved to point out.

More important, the Truman administration's exclusive focus on the ideological differences between the two systems, to the neglect of strategic and economic considerations, made it hard for diplomats to address specific, limited issues. The endless insistence on the Soviets' alleged master plan of world domination obscured in a fog of verbiage the diplomatic processes by which concrete issues might have been addressed.

In its internal strategic assessments, the administration understood that "the communist world" was not monolithic. (This had become clear in 1948 when Marshall Tito, Yugoslavia's communist ruler, broke with Moscow.) Still, many early Cold Warriors proved better at lurid portrayals of the communist menace than at the art of negotiation. Wrote Dean Acheson in 1947: "[I]t is a mistake to believe that you can, at any time, sit down with the Russians and solve questions. . . . [T]hat is [not] the way that our problems are going to be worked." How would differences over specific issues be resolved other than by negotiation? Acheson provided no answer.

Thus the nation that had invented pragmatism succumbed to a rigidly ideological mindset suspicious of negotiation and compromise. Some Cold War rhetoric resembled theological pronouncements more than diplomatic exchange. The Truman administration's effort to build support for its national-security program by simplistic representations of world realities succeeded in its immediate purpose, but it impeded the long-term goal of easing tensions and finding areas of common interest. With Soviet diplomacy equally hamstrung by Marxist ideology and a dictator gripped by suspicion and paranoia, the conflict wore on.

Deeper into the Cold War: China, the H-Bomb, Korea

The initial Cold War confrontations arose in Europe and the Middle East. By 1949, Asia loomed large as well. Late that year, after a long civil war, communists came to power in China. Since the late 1920s, communists under Mao Zedong (Mao Tsetung) had battled the pro-Western government of Jiang Jieshi (Chiang Kai-shek). During World War II both sides had focused on expelling the Japanese invaders, but full-scale civil war had resumed in 1945.

Jiang's regime was corrupt, inefficient, and unpopular. Rampant inflation further eroded its support. Meanwhile, communist organizers, heeding Mao's advice to move among the people like fish in a stream, built a base among China's peasantry—80 percent of the population. With the communist victory in 1949, Jiang and his remaining troops and supporters withdrew to the offshore island of Taiwan and established a regime that for the next quarter-century the United States would recognize as China's legitimate government.

Mao's triumph sent shock waves across the United States. America's long and somewhat paternalistic interest in China, a legacy of the early New England China trade, had intensified with the activities of Christian missionaries to China. (Henry Luce, whose *Time* and *Life* magazines championed Jiang's cause, was the son of missionaries to China.) China's sufferings under Japanese aggression in the 1930s had touched American sympathies.

In the civil war, the United States had backed Jiang Jieshi's regime. President Roosevelt, envisioning a noncommunist China as a counterweight to Japan in postwar Asia, had superficially treated Jiang as an equal during wartime meetings of the so-called Big Four. As Jiang's power crumbled, however, Washington's ties to him became a liability. U.S. support for Jiang, a State Department Asian specialist predicted, would bring "only trouble, trouble, trouble." The victorious Mao Zedong established a new government, the People's Republic of China, and early in 1950 signed a trade and mutual-assistance treaty with the Soviet Union.

To the casual observer, the Eurasian landmass from Germany's Elbe River to the China Sea seemed one vast domain of communist power. In reality, as Washington officials well knew, deep differences rooted in history and geography divided Moscow and Beijing. Stalin and Mao distrusted one another, and the Soviet leader had given Mao virtually no help in the Chinese civil war. Even as he negotiated the 1950 treaty, Stalin had maneuvered to extend Moscow's influence in Manchuria and Mongolia, long-time objects of Russian imperialist ambition. But for most Americans, "the world communist conspiracy" seemed all too real. U.S. politics blazed with accusations over who had "lost" China.

On September 3, 1949, as climactic events convulsed China, Russia tested an atomic bomb. The United States' brief reign as the only nuclear power had ended. "This is now a different world," Senator Vandenberg wrote gloomily. The Soviet test triggered an intense debate in the Truman administration. Some advisers, led by the physicist Edward Teller, advocated a crash program to build the hydrogen bomb, an awesome weapon a thousand times more powerful than the atomic bomb. Opponents included David Lilienthal, head of the Atomic Energy Commission (AEC), and most of the AEC's scientific advisory committee, chaired by J. Robert Oppenheimer, director of the wartime Los Alamos project. These critics argued for a new effort at international control of atomic energy. But Truman rejected their advice and in January 1950 ordered full-scale research on the hydrogen bomb. In a poll, 78 percent of Americans endorsed Truman's decision. The post-Hiroshima terror of atomic war and support for international control had been replaced by a grim determination to maintain U.S. nuclear supremacy.*

The ominous developments of 1949 gave rise to NSC-68, a strategic planning document drafted by the National Security Council. The principal author was Paul Nitze, a hardliner who had replaced George Kennan in the State Department's policy-planning office. Discerning a Soviet master plan for global domination, NSC-68 envisioned "an indefinite period of tension and danger." "The Kremlin is inescapably militant," the document declared;

> it possesses and is possessed by a worldwide revolutionary movement, . . . it is the inheritor of Russian imperialism and . . . it is a totalitarian dictatorship. Persistent crisis, conflict and expansion are the essence of the Kremlin's militancy. . . . [The American people] in the ascendancy of their strength stand in their deepest peril.

A few months later, as the Korean War raged, President Truman approved NSC-68 as official U.S. policy.

Portraying the Cold War as an all-consuming global struggle, NSC-68 downplayed divisions within the communist camp, strategies for reaching accommodation with the Soviets, and world trends that did not fit its stark bipolar model. Foreseeing indefinite military confrontation between two nuclear-armed superpowers, the document called for massive military spending to build up America's conventional and nuclear arsenal and to rearm NATO. It offered few hints for constructive steps Washington might take to reduce hostilities.

The communist victory in China, which helped inspire NSC-68, also focused U.S. attention on Asia. In Indochina, the French were fighting to maintain their colonial power against a nationalist insurgency led by the communist Ho Chi Minh. Ho had courted U.S. support, but the Truman administration, eager to bring

---

*The United States exploded its first hydrogen device in November 1952, and the Soviet Union soon followed suit. By the mid-1950s, both sides were testing full-scale hydrogen bombs. For discussion of the nuclear arms race in the 1950s, see Chapter 4.

France into NATO, had rejected his overtures. In May 1950, Dean Acheson, George Marshall's successor as secretary of state, announced a small program of U.S. aid to the French in Indochina. This little-noted action started a process that fifteen years later would find the United States fighting a full-scale war in Vietnam.

It was Korea, not Vietnam, that soon dominated U.S. headlines. In 1945, ending forty years of Japanese rule, the United States and the Soviet Union had jointly occupied Korea, with the 38th parallel demarking the two occupation zones. Both powers had withdrawn most of their troops by 1949, but, as in Germany, each still dominated its respective sector. In 1948, with U.S. support, South Korea's president Syngman Rhee proclaimed the Republic of Korea, with its capital in Seoul. In the north, the Soviets set up their own client government in Pyongyang, headed by Kim Il Sung. Each regime was armed by its respective sponsor, and each claimed sovereignty over all Korea. The stage was set for confrontation.

Late in 1949, according to the memoirs of Nikita Khrushchev, later premier of the Soviet Union, Stalin approved Kim Il Sung's request to invade South Korea. Recent scholarship based on Soviet archives makes clear Stalin's central role in planning North Korea's invasion and the ensuing war. Stalin may have hoped that Pyongyang could win control over all Korea and provide a counterweight not only to the United States and Japan but also to Mao's China. Ambiguous statements by U.S. leaders may have encouraged Kim and Stalin. In a January 1950 speech, Secretary of State Acheson defined the U.S. defense perimeter in Asia in a way that excluded South Korea.* In May, Texas senator Tom Connally, chair of the Senate Foreign Relations Committee, similarly appeared to dismiss Korea as of little strategic importance. America's rapid postwar demobilization and subsequent emphasis on nuclear rather than conventional weaponry probably figured in Kim Il Sung's calculations as well.

On June 25, 1950, Soviet-armed North Korean troops stormed across the 38th parallel. Capturing Seoul and pushing southward, they soon pinned the South Korean defenders and a few U.S. troops within a small defensive perimeter around the port of Pusan. President Truman responded by ordering full-scale U.S. military action to expel the invaders. Korea was the Greece of Asia, he argued—a further test of America's will to contain Soviet-sponsored communist aggression. The United States also rushed the case to the UN Security Council. With the Soviet delegate absent, the council passed U.S. resolutions calling on member nations to aid South Korea. The conflict was thus fought under UN auspices, and the Truman administration dubbed it a "police action" rather than a war. Congress never formally declared war, as required by the Constitution, underscoring the expansion of executive power in these years. Under whatever flag, American, Korean, and eventually Chinese troops did most of the fighting, and Korean civilians suffered the heaviest casualties.

General Douglas MacArthur, the World War II hero who later headed the U.S. occupation of postwar Japan, commanded the UN forces in Korea. On September 15, 1950, MacArthur led a daring amphibious landing behind the enemy

---

*The defense of parts of Asia outside this perimeter, asserted Acheson, rested with "the entire civilized world," acting through the United Nations.

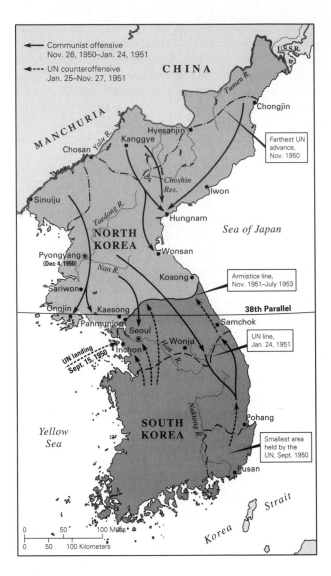

MAP 2.2
The Korean War, 1950–1953

lines at Inchon. Simultaneously breaking out of the Pusan perimeter, MacArthur's forces swept across the 38th parallel and by late October had captured Pyongyang and were nearing the Yalu River separating Korea and the Chinese province of Manchuria. When China warned MacArthur against approaching the Yalu River, he dismissed this statement as "hot air" and promised to have "the boys home by Christmas." He also made the tactical error of dividing his strongest forces, with a weaker South Korean contingent in the middle.

Up to a point, the administration supported MacArthur's aggressive actions. Some in Washington now saw the possibility not merely of repelling the invaders

Korea, Winter 1950. U.S. marines retreating from North Korea's Changjin Reservoir after Chinese communist forces entered the war in massive numbers. *(UPI/Corbis-Bettmann)*

but of overthrowing Kim Il Sung and creating a united and noncommunist Korea. Secretary of State Acheson, for example, viewed all of Korea as "a stage to show the world what Western Democracy can do to help the underprivileged countries of the world."

On November 26, thirty-three Chinese divisions poured across the Yalu. Once more, the North Koreans, now massively reinforced by the Chinese, drove down the peninsula. Viewing the Korean fighting as a prelude to a larger struggle against communism in Asia, MacArthur urgently asked permission to widen the war by bombing Chinese bases in Manchuria and "unleashing" Jiang Jieshi from his base on Taiwan for an invasion of the Chinese mainland.

President Truman and his military advisers rejected the general's request. With the Sino-Soviet alliance still in force, they feared that MacArthur's aggressive plan would trigger all-out war. Further, Washington strategists argued, a wider war in Asia would weaken the U.S. ability to respond to hostile Soviet moves in Europe. Truman also vetoed using atomic bombs in Korea, a course favored by about half the American public in opinion polls. He did, however, toy with the idea of giving the Soviets a nuclear ultimatum. In December 1950, an alarmed British prime minister Clement Atlee flew to Washington, fearful that using nuclear weapons in

Korea might provoke Moscow to attack Western Europe and even to drop atomic bombs on Great Britain.

MacArthur, meanwhile, pushed his proposals in media interviews and wrote a prominent Republican congressman complaining of the restraints imposed on him by the White House. "Here in Asia . . . the communist conspirators have elected to make their play for global conquest," MacArthur stormed. "Here we fight Europe's war with arms while the diplomats there fight it with words." In war, he summed up, "there is no substitute for victory." *Time* magazine and leading Republicans endorsed MacArthur's call for a wider war.

Furious over MacArthur's insubordination, Truman stripped him of his command on April 10, 1951. The aging general returned to a tumultuous welcome that reflected not only enthusiasm for a war hero but also the frustrations of the Korean stalemate and an apparently endless Cold War struggle. Sixty-six percent of Americans initially opposed Truman's firing of MacArthur. As New York City gave the general a ticker-tape parade, fans booed Truman when he threw out the first ball on opening day of the baseball season at Washington's Griffith Stadium.* A *Chicago Tribune* cartoon portrayed Truman as a boy in short pants, gazing up enviously at the larger-than-life profile of a heroic MacArthur.

In an emotional address to a joint session of Congress, MacArthur ended with the lines of a barracks ballad: "Old soldiers never die, they just fade away." His congressional fans held hearings to air his views, but Truman countered with General Omar Bradley, chairman of the Joint Chiefs of Staff, who testified that MacArthur's strategy would "involve us in the wrong war, at the wrong place, at the wrong time, and with the wrong enemy." As Americans reflected further on the issues at stake, the general faded away, as he predicted.

In Korea, armistice talks began in July 1951. The fighting dragged on until 1953, however, by which time it had taken the lives of 54,000 Americans and some 3,000 soldiers from other nations who fought under the UN command. Even this heavy toll paled in comparison to the estimated deaths of up to 100,000 South Korean soldiers, 500,000 North Korean troops, and a million Chinese. From 2 to 3 million Korean civilians died from bombing or from the war's side effects, including lack of food, shelter, heat, and medicine. Although North Korea, abetted by Stalin, started the war, writes historian William Stueck, it was MacArthur's menacing of China's borders and his threats of a wider war that "escalat[ed] the battle to the brink of Armageddon." The U.S. defense budget, fueled by the Korean War and by the military buildup outlined in NSC-68, surged to $50 billion in 1953, up sharply from the 1946–49 levels of about $13 billion annually.

In *Truman and Korea: The Political Culture of the Early Cold War* (1999), historian Paul Pierpaoli, Jr., sees the Korean War as a Cold War watershed, enabling the Truman administration to implement the military agenda of NSC-68; stimulating war mobilization based on World War II precedents; and, in effect, laying the groundwork for a militarization of U.S. politics, society, and economic activity.

Despite Korea, Cold War strategists never lost sight of Europe. In 1950, the administration proposed to rearm West Germany within a NATO framework. The

---

*In 1951 the nation's capital still had a big-league baseball team, the Washington Senators.

aim was less to repel a Soviet invasion, which few expected, than to ensure West Germany's integration into the European community. To overcome the protests of Great Britain, France, and other NATO members with vivid war memories, Truman in December 1950 named General Dwight Eisenhower to command NATO's newly integrated command structure. Truman also pledged four more U.S. divisions for Europe, to join the two already there.

The NATO ministers in December 1950 agreed in principle to include German troops in a joint defense force. Not until 1955, however, over die-hard French resistance, did West Germany formally join NATO. In March 1952, the Soviet Union called for a conference to discuss German reunification. Whether this was a propaganda ploy or a serious proposal aimed at preventing West German rearmament may never be known; Dean Acheson rejected the proposal out of hand.

Prospects for peace looked grim as the 1950s dawned. As more U.S. troops poured into Europe, NATO strategy contemplated a nuclear response if the Soviets attacked. NATO expanded eastward, adding Greece and Turkey in 1952. Turkey, on the Soviet Union's border, bristled with U.S.-supplied air power, including 180 F-47 fighter planes and 30 B-26 bombers.

U.S. policy toward Russia, still somewhat open to debate in the late 1940s, rigidified after Korea. As Republicans exploited the communist issue domestically, the administration took an increasingly hard line toward the Soviets. A similar intransigence gripped Moscow, where the aging, fear-ridden Stalin still ruled. George Kennan, appointed ambassador to the Soviet Union in 1952, was appalled by the vitriolic anti-Americanism he found. He would later write, "I began to ask myself whether . . . we had not contributed . . . by the overmilitarization of our policies and statements—to a belief in Moscow that it was war we were after." The Soviet Union bore heavy responsibility for the dismal state of U.S. Soviet relations, but Kennan's reflections on America's share of responsibility merit consideration. However one apportions the blame, the wartime allies had become bitter enemies.

Conclusion

While the Cold War was in full swing, historians tended to differ sharply over its origins. Some placed the blame entirely on Moscow; others, glossing over Soviet actions, pointed their finger at the United States. Some, from a Marxist perspective, portrayed America's Cold War policies as dictated solely by capitalism's global search for raw materials, markets, and investment opportunities.

By the late 1980s, as Cold War tensions eased, more nuanced assessments emerged. In *The Long Peace: Inquiries into the History of the Cold War* (1987), historian John Lewis Gaddis, although far from uncritical of U.S. Cold War policy, stressed the stability of U.S.-Soviet relations through their long confrontation. "[Despite] all the conceivable reasons for having had a major war in the past four decades," he observed, "there has not in fact been one. . . . The Cold War, with all of its rivalries, anxieties, and unquestionable dangers, has produced the longest period of stability in relations among the great powers . . . in this century." To be sure, this "long peace" saw bloody conflicts in Korea and Vietnam; the terrifying Cuban missile crisis (see Chapter 6); a nuclear-weapons proliferation whose long-term effects still plague us; and festering unrest, poverty, and disease in parts of the world largely ignored as Cold War preoccupations gripped Washington. Still, Gaddis's point merits recognition.

In *A Preponderance of Power: National Security, the Truman Administration, and the Cold War* (1992), Melvyn Leffler credited Washington diplomacy for Western Europe's recovery and the emergence of Germany and Japan as pro-Western democracies, and for containment of the Soviet Union's expansionist impulses. Rejecting the caricature of U.S. policymakers as warmongering imperialists or capitalist stooges, Leffler portrays them for the most part as prudent, responsible leaders intent on protecting America's legitimate security interests as Moscow worked to extend its sphere of influence by a variety of means short of war.

But Leffler, like George Kennan, also finds misjudgments and lost opportunities in U.S. postwar policy, including a tendency to denigrate diplomacy, to exaggerate both Moscow's lust for conquest and the danger of all-out Soviet attack, and to downplay the caution that often characterized Soviet policy. He also argues that Truman-era policymakers paid insufficient attention to the indigenous sources of the social unrest, anticolonialism, and nationalism seething in many parts of the world. The tendency to view all local conflicts through a Cold War lens, he suggests, ultimately led to America's disastrous intervention in Vietnam.

More critical still is historian Arnold Offner. In *Another Such Victory: President Truman and the Cold War, 1945–1953* (2002), Offner contends that the Truman administration, by militarizing the conflict with the Soviets and pursuing it with such implacable intensity, foreclosed any possibility of limited agreements or negotiated settlements. Truman, he writes bluntly, was a "parochial nationalist who lacked the leadership to move the U.S. away from conflict and toward détente"; embracing a simplistic black-and-white worldview, Truman "abandon[ed] diplomacy as a means to deal with the Soviets." (The popular writer David McCullough offered a very different view in his warmly admiring and Pulitzer Prize–winning 1992 biography, *Truman.*)

Although historians continue to analyze the Cold War's origins, few question the degree to which the conflict became all-consuming for both sides, or the risks it posed. That the Cold War arose just as nuclear weapons entered the world sharply heightened those risks. Indeed, the existence of the ultimate weapon may have encouraged both sides' tendency to identify the Cold War adversary as the ultimate enemy.

Yet the fear of nuclear holocaust may, in fact, have helped to prevent the Cold War from turning hot. John Lewis Gaddis, for one, sees "the nuclear deterrent" as the reason the Cold War never escalated into actual war between the United States and the Soviet Union. "[T]he development of nuclear weapons," Gaddis concludes, " . . . had, on balance, a stabilizing effect on the postwar international system."

Whatever its deterrent effect, the threat of nuclear war terrified many Americans in these years. In 1947, U.S. Air Force general H. H. ("Hap") Arnold warned that the combination of atomic bombs and guided missiles (another legacy of World War II) had made the United States more vulnerable than ever before in its history. "Without warning," wrote Arnold, nuclear-armed missiles could "pass over all . . . 'lines of defense' and . . . deliver devastating blows at our population centers and our industrial, economic, or governmental heart." Such somber warnings profoundly influenced Cold War American thought and culture.

Even apart from nuclear weapons, the early 1950s saw an unprecedented U.S. arms buildup. This "enormously expanded military establishment, beyond anything we had ever contemplated in time of peace," wrote military historian Walter Millis in 1951, had called forth "a huge and apparently permanent armament industry now wholly dependent . . . on government contracts." Yet, Millis reflected, the Truman administration seemed unsure about the long-term objectives of its militarized strategy or how the Cold War might be ended.

Nuclear fear and the rise of a vast peacetime military establishment were only two of the many ways by which the Cold War seeped into the fabric of U.S. society and into the everyday existence of this generation of Americans. As he left office in 1953, President Truman observed: "I suppose . . . history will remember my term . . . as the years when the 'cold war' began to overshadow our lives." Chapter 3 looks at the American home front in the early postwar years, as Cold War anxieties shaped not only U.S. foreign relations but the domestic scene as well.

SELECTED READINGS

The Early Cold War: General Studies

Terry H. Anderson, *The United States, Great Britain, and the Cold War, 1944–1947* (1981); James Chace, *Acheson: The Secretary of State Who Created the American World* (1998); Richard Crockatt, *The Fifty Years War: The United States and the Soviet Union in World Politics, 1941–1991* (1995); Thomas H. Etzold and John L. Gaddis, eds., *Containment: Documents on American Policy and Strategy, 1945–1950* (1978); John L. Gaddis, *The United States and the Origins of the Cold War, 1941–1947* (1972), *Strategies of Containment: A Critical Appraisal of Postwar American National Security Policy* (1982), *The Long Peace: Inquiries into the History of the Cold War* (1987), and *We Now Know: Rethinking Cold War History* (1997); James L. Gormly, *The Collapse of the Grand Alliance, 1945–1948* (1987); Allen Hunter, ed., *Rethinking the Cold* War (1998); Walter LaFeber, *America, Russia, and the Cold War, 1945–1984* (1985); Melvyn Leffler, *A Preponderance of Power: National Security, the Truman Administration, and the Cold War* (1992); Melvyn Leffler and David S. Painter, eds., *The Origins of the Cold War: An International History* (1994); Arnold Offner, *Another Such Victory: President Truman and the Cold War, 1945–1953* (2002); Martin Walker, *The Cold War: A History* (1994); Daniel Yergin, *Shattered Peace: The Origins of the Cold War and the National Security State* (1977).

Nuclear Policy; Postwar Diplomacy in Europe and the Middle East

Michael J. Cohen, *Truman and Israel* (1990); Lawrence Freedman, *The Evolution of Nuclear Strategy* (1981); James F. Good, *The United States and Iran, 1946–1951* (1989); Fraser J. Harbutt, *The Iron Curtain: Churchill, America, and the Origins of the Cold War* (1986); Gregg Herken, *The Winning Weapon: The Atomic Bomb in the Cold War, 1945–1950* (1980); Michael Hogan, *The Marshall Plan* (1987); Timothy P. Ireland, *Creating the Entangling Alliance: The Origins of NATO* (1981); John Killick, *The United States and European Reconstruction, 1945–1960* (1997); Jon V. Kofas, *Intervention and Underdevelopment: Greece During the Cold War* (1989); Bruce R. Kuniholm, *The Origins of the Cold War in the Near East* (1980);

Alan Milward, *The Reconstruction of Western Europe, 1945–1951* (1984); Steven M. Neuse, *David E. Lilienthal: The Journey of an American Liberal* (1996); David S. Painter, *Oil and the American Century: The Political Economy of U.S. Foreign Oil Policy, 1941–1954* (1986); Robert A. Pollard, *Economic Security and the Origins of the Cold War, 1945–1950* (1985); David Alan Rosenberg, "American Atomic Strategy and the Hydrogen Bomb Decision," *Journal of American History* (June 1979); Martin Schain, ed., *The Marshall Plan: Fifty Years After* (2001); Georg Schild, *Bretton Woods and Dumbarton Oaks: American Economic and Political Postwar Planning in the Summer of 1944* (1995); Avi Shlaim, *The United States and the Berlin Blockade* (1983); Lawrence L. Wittner, *American Intervention in Greece, 1943–1949* (1982).

The Korean War and the Cold War in Asia

Russell D. Buhite, *Soviet-American Relations in Asia, 1945–1954* (1982); Ronald J. Caridi, *The Korean War and American Politics: The Republican Party as a Case Study* (1969); Bruce Cumings, *Child of Conflict: The Korean-American Relationship, 1943–1953* (1983); Roger Dingman, "Atomic Diplomacy During the Korean War," *International Security* (Winter 1988–89); John W. Dower, *Embracing Defeat: Japan in the Wake of World War II* (1999); June Grasso, *Harry Truman's Two-China Policy* (1987); Jon Halliday and Bruce Cumings, *Korea: The Unknown War* (1988); Gary Hess, *The U.S. Emergence as a Southeast Asian Power* (1986); Geoffrey Perret, *Old Soldiers Never Die: The Life of Douglas MacArthur* (1996); Paul G. Pierpaoli, Jr., *Truman and Korea: The Political Culture of the Early Cold War* (1999); Andrew J. Rotter, *The Path to Vietnam: Origins of the American Commitment to Southeast Asia* (1987); William W. Stueck, Jr., *The Road to Confrontation: American Policy Toward China and Korea, 1947–1950* (1981) and *The Korean War: An International History* (1995); Kathryn Weathersby, "From the Russian Archives: New Findings on the Korean War," *Cold War International History Project Bulletin* [Woodrow Wilson International Center for Scholars], Fall 1993; Odd Arne Westad, *Cold War and Revolution: Soviet-American Rivalry and the Origins of the Chinese Civil War, 1944–1946* (1993).

CHAPTER

3

Uneasiness at Dawn: Domestic Trends in the Early Postwar Years

NEW YORK CITY, September 1945. As the writer James Agee watched a victory parade, his pleasure was edged with apprehension: "The whole city has . . . [the] warmth of thousands of . . . homecomings," he wrote a friend. But immediately he added, "God, what most of the homecomers, and those they come home to, are in for!"

Agee had reason to worry. Even as they welcomed the peace, Americans eyed the future nervously. The mushroom cloud that had risen over New Mexico in July 1945 seemed to hover over the entire culture as Americans contemplated the atomic era and worsening relations with the Soviet Union. "The Age of Anxiety," a 1948 poem by W. H. Auden, summed up at least a part of the postwar mood. Less apocalyptic sources of concern also shadowed the victory celebrations. As military production declined, would hard times return? In fact, demobilization proceeded smoothly. The economy absorbed the returning veterans as industry switched promptly to peacetime production. These years launched an economic boom that with periodic setbacks would last for several decades.

Nevertheless, as peace returned, so did the political cleavages of the 1930s. Truman and his liberal supporters sought to expand the New Deal, but conservatives in both parties doggedly hacked away at its "socialistic" excesses, and business groups gained a greater voice in policy debates. Although Truman won an upset electoral victory in 1948, disputes over the postwar domestic order raged on.

The war had brought many changes. Women had donned uniforms or worked in war plants. African Americans had served in the military or moved northward and cityward to seek work. Mexican workers had immigrated to the United States in great numbers. Poverty and economic inequities pervaded America. Yet the early postwar era generally failed to address the social and political implications of these developments. President Truman's reform program, offered in the 1948 campaign, made little headway. Indeed, the late 1940s brought a conservative turn in U.S. politics and social thought. In celebrating the good life of suburbia and an idealized domesticity, the mass culture, including television, the newest medium, sought to contain the forces of social change. Just as Cold War fears drove U.S. foreign policy, so, too, did the anticommunist struggle influence domestic politics and culture. In its most extreme manifestation, the national obsession with the communist menace led to the so-called Red Scare, an almost hysterical campaign to expose and silence all those suspected of disloyalty, subversion, or a communist taint.

Demobilization and the Limits of Liberalism at Home

Fears of a new depression as military contracts dried up and veterans reentered the labor market were widespread in August 1945. A bleak movie about veterans' problems, sardonically titled *The Best Years of Our Lives,* won the Academy Award for best picture of 1946. In fact, demobilization proceeded rapidly as industries re-tooled to meet pent-up demands for consumer goods. "From tanks to Cadillacs in two months," boasted General Motors. Unemployment remained mostly under 4 percent from 1946 to 1952. Helping these figures were the millions of veterans who, taking advantage of the GI Bill's educational benefits, enrolled in school rather than entering the labor market.* Many women workers, fired to make room for veterans, chose not to seek other employment. Other women left the workplace voluntarily for the domestic sphere. The female labor force fell from 35.8 million in 1945 to 30.8 million in 1946; not until 1956 would it regain its 1945 level.

Demobilization was not *entirely* painless. Housing shortages and inflation plagued postwar America. Addressing the latter issue, Truman in June 1946 asked Congress to extend the authority of the wartime Office of Price Administration (OPA), which had controlled prices and rents. But conservative legislators, hostile to this reminder of wartime regulations, radically cut the OPA's powers, and prices shot up. A Tulsa grocer advised customers not to buy his shrimp, so outrageous was the cost. By the end of 1946, price controls on all but a few items had ended, and inflation had set in. Coffee prices rose by 54 percent from 1945 to 1947; the cost of meat nearly doubled. In 1947 the overall inflation rate stood at 14.6 percent.

Galloping inflation sparked a rash of strikes for higher wages. In late 1945 and early 1946, nearly five thousand walkouts idled some 4.6 million workers. President Truman reacted firmly to stoppages that threatened the national welfare. When railway workers struck early in 1946, he told the union leaders, "If you think I'm going to sit here and let you tie up this whole country, you're crazy as hell." As Truman prepared to ask Congress for powers to resolve the crisis, the strike collapsed. When four hundred thousand coal miners belonging to John L. Lewis's United Mineworkers union walked out on April 1, 1946, Truman ordered the army to seize the mines. Lewis finally called off the strike late in 1947, after a long court battle. Truman took these conflicts as personal challenges; when the miners went back to work, he wrote his mother, "Well, John L. had to fold up. He couldn't take the gaff. No bully can."

Amid labor unrest and consumer anger over high prices, the Republicans adopted a simple slogan for the 1946 midterm elections: "Had enough? Vote Republican." The strategy worked: Republicans won control of both houses of Congress for the first time since 1928. Among the newcomers, reported *Time* magazine, were

---

*By 1956, 7.8 million veterans had attended college or technical schools with federal support.

Joseph McCarthy of Wisconsin, elected on the slogan "Washington Needs a Tail-Gunner"; a "dark, lank, Quaker attorney" from California, Richard M. Nixon; and a Democrat, "boyish, raw-boned, Harvard-bred" John Kennedy of Massachusetts.

The strains of demobilization intensified the ongoing debate over America's political course. FDR's New Deal had sketched the outlines of a welfare state. The 1930s' legacy to postwar America was a federal government committed to maintaining prosperity, regulating capitalism, protecting workers' rights, and ensuring the general well-being through social security and other measures. Liberals hope to expand these reforms to include other objectives, such as full employment and universal health insurance. Others, in both parties, accepted the basic New Deal reforms but believed that the nation needed breathing space. They urged consolidation, not more reform. At first, Truman shared this view. "I don't want any experiments," he told an adviser in 1945. "The American people want a rest." Steering a middle course, the president and his advisers also kept their eye on a more mundane goal: electoral victory in 1948.

Further right on the political spectrum gathered those who hated the New Deal for undermining individualism and free enterprise. Down with government regulation and welfare programs, they urged; up with laissez faire. This camp much admired the émigré Austrian economist Friedrich Hayek, whose *The Road to Serfdom* (1944) portrayed the welfare state as a step down the slippery slope to socialism and tyranny. Hayek's work propelled a resurgent conservative ideology that would gain strength over the years.

The reputation of corporate America, tarnished in the 1930s, had improved during the war, and business groups such as the National Association of Manufacturers and the U.S. Chamber of Commerce sought to use this new prestige to influence domestic policy. As one business leader wrote in 1944, corporations in the postwar era should work to "rid the economy of injurious or unnecessary regulation" and to create a political climate "in which a private enterprise system can flourish." The Advertising Council, an association of ad agencies and corporate advertisers that published public-service ads in support of the war effort, led this campaign, supplementing its ads for driver safety and charitable giving with pitches aimed at "selling" the free-enterprise system and the "economic miracle" of modern capitalism.

For a while after the war, advocates of expanding the New Deal appeared to hold the political high ground. In September 1945, President Truman, despite his worries about "experiments," proposed several reform measures, including expanded social security, public housing, and a federal commission to combat racism in employment. But much of Truman's program languished in a Congress veering rightward. One exception, the Employment Act of 1946, which passed with bipartisan support, committed the government to a policy of "maximum employment, production, and purchasing power." To this end, it required the president to submit an annual economic report to Congress, with recommendations for promoting economic growth. It also created a presidential Council of Economic Advisers (CEA) to help shape economic policy.

The legislative history of the Employment Act of 1946 illustrated the business community's mounting influence. The initial drafts had a distinctly "New Dealish" tone, reflecting the ideas of the British economist John Maynard Keynes, calling for government spending on health, education, and public works to promote full employment. Business lobbyists blunted this activist thrust, however, and in its final form, the bill called for tax cuts to stimulate investment and business-government cooperation in achieving economic growth.

The Employment Act of 1946 also reveals the multiplying links between foreign affairs and domestic policy. At the 1944 Bretton Woods Conference (see Chapter 2), the British had insisted that if the dollar were to become the world's monetary standard, Washington must ensure economic stability at home. This pressure from abroad proved a major impetus behind the passage of the 1946 legislation committing the government to an expanded economic role.

The Atomic Energy Act of 1946 further highlights the political crosscurrents of the period. The law mandated public control of atomic energy under a civilian Atomic Energy Commission (AEC) and called for research on peaceful uses of the atom. Truman named David Lilienthal, head of the New Deal's Tennessee Valley Authority (TVA), as the AEC's first chairman, strengthening the act's link to the liberal tradition. In reality, the AEC mainly supplied nuclear weapons to the military. While publicly touting the atom's peacetime benefits, Lilienthal privately despaired over his agency's focus on bomb making. Deeply discouraged, he resigned in 1950.

Although basic New Deal measures such as social security remained in place, many Republicans and southern Democrats loathed other reforms of the Franklin Roosevelt era. Business leaders and their political allies had long chafed at the expansion of union power under the 1935 Wagner Act. This law, they insisted, went too far in protecting union rights. Behind the scenes, corporate lawyers worked with conservatives in Congress to craft a new labor law. The resulting Taft-Hartley Act of 1947,* passed over Truman's veto, outlawed the provision in many union contracts that hiring must be done through a union hall (the so-called "closed shop") and permitted states to pass laws allowing the hiring of nonunion workers in unionized plants (the "open shop"). It also permitted employers to sue unions on various grounds and authorized federal injunctions against strikes that jeopardized public health or safety. Finally, reflecting the Cold War climate, the law required union leaders to swear that they were not communists.

The Taft-Hartley Act symbolized the conservative climate of late 1940s America. It directly undercut union leaders eager to make organized labor a forceful voice in shaping public policy. One bitter union official complained, "When you think of [the Taft-Hartley Act] as merely a combination of individual provisions, you are losing entirely the full impact of the program, the sinister conspiracy that has been hatched." Encouraging the probusiness mood was the nation's general prosperity as a postwar economic boom gained momentum.

Boom Times

At an August 1945 meeting of marketing experts to plan postwar selling strategies, a Du Pont executive offered a bright vision of coming prosperity as U.S. business met the "great backlog of unfilled wants" after fifteen years of consumer depriva-

---

*Named for its sponsors, Senator Robert Taft of Ohio and Representative Fred Hartley of New Jersey, the bill's official title was the Labor-Management Relations Act.

tion. Marketers, he said, must stimulate consumer demand and "see to it that Americans are never satisfied . . . ; a satisfied people is a stagnant people." If they did their job well, he predicted, the postwar era would bring "an upward spiral of productivity, raising the standard of living, increasing the national income, [and] making more jobs." To a remarkable degree, this rosy vision was realized.

These years of Cold War, conflict in Korea, and sometimes bitter political controversy also brought an economic boom of impressive proportions. By late 1948, unemployment stood at an amazingly low 2 percent. The gross national product, after hitting a wartime peak of $211 billion, surged to $346 billion by 1952. Their savings accounts bulging with wartime earnings, Americans went on a buying spree. *Holiday* magazine, founded in 1946 to capitalize on the wanderlust of newly affluent Americans, typified the new culture of consumption. *Holiday,* proclaimed the editors, was "dedicated to the pursuit of happiness."

As consumer spending exploded, businesses expanded and retooled to meet the demand. The goods that gushed from U.S. factories in 1950 included 6.2 million refrigerators, 14.6 million radios, and 6.2 million automobiles. Nearly 5 million new housing units sprang up between 1945 and 1950. Corporate America prospered as never before. By 1952 the nation boasted fifty-nine companies with more than $1 billion in assets.

The military demands of the Korean War cut civilian output somewhat, but overall the conflict stimulated the economy. Adding to the prosperity caused by the defense buildup, U.S. exports of military hardware reached $2.1 billion by 1952, translating into jobs and profits for defense industries. As we saw in Chapter 2, nonmilitary foreign aid also drove exports of farm commodities and industrial goods. To sustain the economic boom during the Korean War, the government permitted corporations to depreciate capital investment in five years rather than the usual twenty-five, spurring plant construction and modernization.

A baby boom fueled postwar prosperity. From a 1930s low of fewer than twenty births per thousand population, the U.S. birthrate climbed during and after the war to more than twenty-five per thousand in 1947.* Home building thrived, along with school construction and sales of baby food, diapers, strollers, and play equipment. Fueled by pent-up demand, a surging birthrate, plentiful energy and raw materials, and well-established corporate systems for producing, advertising, and distributing goods, the economy took off.

Not all was bright. Inflation remained a problem through 1948, and surged again in 1951 during the Korean War. Nor did all Americans share in the boom. As we shall see in Chapter 4, millions lived in poverty, especially the rural poor, migrant workers, inner-city minorities, and Native Americans. In 1950 over a third of U.S. families earned under $3,000 annually (about $22,400 in current dollars). For families at the lower end of the income scale, the new cars and appliances in showrooms, department stores, and magazine ads remained distant dreams. This underside of the economic picture, however, attracted little notice as the consumer boom roared on.

A parade of new products, from ballpoint pens and televisions to transistor radios and Polaroid cameras, contributed to the boom. In 1947 a small company in

---

*By contrast, the 2000 birthrate was 14.8 per thousand.

Rochester, New York, bought the rights to a machine that could reproduce print copy by means of a recently patented process called "xerography." Soon the company would become the Xerox Corporation. Photocopying machines, spreading from corporate offices, government bureaus, and academia into the larger society, launched a revolution in print communications.

Computer technology, spurred by wartime antiaircraft research (see page 26), also burgeoned. In 1946 University of Pennsylvania engineers formed a company to produce and market a computer they called UNIVAC (Universal Automatic Computer), one of which became the first government computer, delivered to the Census Bureau in 1951. International Business Machines (IBM) marketed its first computer in 1953.

The full-scale computer age still lay ahead, but its theoretical and technical foundations were in place by the early fifties. Norbert Weiner of the Massachusetts Institute of Technology, who had set forth key theoretical elements of the modern computer as early as 1940, speculated on its social implications in *Cybernetics* (1947) and *The Human Uses of Human Beings* (1950). Although conceding the new technology's promise, Weiner remained apprehensive. As computers took over routine production functions, he warned, "the average human being . . . [will have] nothing to sell that is worth anyone's money to buy." Weiner also foresaw a time when the computer's data-processing capacity would vastly extend the power of governments, the military, and corporate giants.

Of all the new products, none better captured the postwar sense of promise than plastic, which exploded into the consumer marketplace after World War II. A "National Plastics Exposition" in New York City in 1946 drew thousands of excited visitors. Around the same time, Earl Tupper introduced his line of plastic kitchen and household products. Marketed through suburban house parties, "Tupperware" became an icon of postwar culture. By the end of the 1950s, plastic production surpassed 6 billion pounds annually. Almost everything, it seemed, could be made of plastic, from furniture, countertops, and luggage to toys, shower curtains, raincoats, garden hoses, lawn ornaments, and Christmas trees. Cultural critics deplored the flow of plastic oozing lavalike across America, but by the mid-fifties, writes historian Jeffrey Meikle, plastic products "had penetrated so far into . . . everyday life that their presence could not be denied no matter how many people considered them second-rate substitutes or a sad commentary on modern times."

Beyond "Rosie the Riveter": Women in Early Postwar America

For American women, the postwar era brought uncertainty as cultural and social forces buttressed the status quo in the face of incipient pressures for change. At first glance, postwar employment data suggest major changes in women's lives. The drop in female employment immediately after the war soon reversed itself. By 1950, 29 percent of U.S. women held jobs, below the wartime peak but higher than in 1940. Women who entered the labor force in this period—especially middle-class married women—seemed more interested in contributing to the family income than in pursuing feminist goals or breaking new ground professionally. Discriminatory

hiring practices and subtle cultural pressures channeled most of them into traditional "women's jobs" as secretaries, salesclerks, librarians, nurses, or teachers.

Isolated efforts to better women's lot through legislation fared badly. When the
Senate in 1946 killed a proposed constitutional amendment guaranteeing equal
rights for women, the *New York Times* intoned approvingly, "Motherhood cannot
be amended." That same year, an equal-pay bill for women workers failed in the
Senate. Longing for stability after years of upheaval, most men and many women
firmly embraced traditional gender roles.

Writers reinforced this impulse, urging women to accept the domestic role that
nature intended. Dr. Benjamin Spock's best-selling *Baby and Child Care* (1946) assumed the mother's presence at home. In a 1950 *Atlantic Monthly* article, "Women
Aren't Men," the female author exclaimed, "God protect us from the efficient go-
getter business woman whose feminine instincts have been completely stifled." In
Modern Woman: The Lost Sex (1947), Freudian analyst Marynia Farnham and sociologist Ferdinand Lundberg warned that women who resisted the domestic and maternal roles would suffer emotional and social difficulties.

The mass culture drove home the message. In the 1950 film *All About Eve,* Ann
Baxter played a coldly ambitious career woman whose charming manner masked
her ruthless drive to succeed—hardly an admirable role model. While Tennessee
Williams's play *A Streetcar Named Desire* (1947) and Mickey Spillane's murder mys-
teries such as *I, the Jury* (1947) featured violent, macho protagonists, the mass media

Mixed Messages. During World War II, government propaganda urged women to take
jobs in industry. By the 1950s, the culture pressured women to believe they could find
fulfillment in housework, which might include vacuuming their toaster. (*Left: National
Archives, AP/Wide World Photos; Right: © Bettmann/CORBIS*)

increasingly domesticated the American woman. Predictably, this theme pervaded the *Ladies Home Journal* and other leading women's magazines.

The day of the WACS, the WAVES, "Rosie the Riveter," and "Wonder Woman," a comic-book character created in 1941, seemed remote by the late 1940s. The idealized domesticity that pervaded the culture had roots in a nine-teenth-century view of gender roles sometimes called "the cult of true woman-hood," but its more immediate source lay in a widespread reaction to the unsettling changes in women's roles during World War II. Just as anticommunist crusaders responded to global threats by trying to enforce political conformity at home, so the celebrators of the domestic ideal coped with shifting gender roles by seeking to reimpose the imagined stability and clear-cut gender distinctions of an earlier era.

African Americans and the Liberal Agenda

For organized labor, militancy declined in the postwar era as the gains of the 1930s eroded. For African Americans, the situation was reversed. Their grievances largely ignored during the New Deal, many blacks emerged from the war deter-mined to force the nation to honor its egalitarian pretensions. The growing politi-cal clout of northern blacks, the surge of black activism during World War II, court challenges to segregation by the National Association for the Advancement of Col-ored People (NAACP), and Cold War propaganda calculations all combined to gave racial issues high priority in the Truman years.

The logic of America's wartime struggle against fascism also helped put race on the postwar agenda as well. As the Swedish economist Gunnar Myrdal wrote in *An American Dilemma: The Negro Problem and American Democracy* (1944): "This war is an ideological war fought in defense of democracy.... Fascism and nazism are based on a racial superiority dogma.... In fighting [them], America had to stand before the whole world in favor of racial tolerance and ... equality." Further, Myrdal predicted, the United States would confront the issue even more directly in the internationalist climate of the postwar era: "America has now joined the world and is tremendously dependent upon the support and good-will of other countries.... The treatment of the Negro is America's greatest and most conspicuous scandal.... For the colored people all over the world, whose rising influence is axiomatic, this scandal is salt in their wounds."

As the Cold War intensified, American racism did indeed prove a major embar-rassment. With Washington and Moscow mounting rival propaganda campaigns around the globe, notes historian Mary L. Dudziak, U.S. racial practices moved "from the streets of America to the newsstands of the world" (*Cold War Civil Rights: Race and the Image of American Democracy* [2000]). When U.S. hotels and restaurants re-fused service to dark-skinned diplomats from developing nations, the insults received worldwide publicity. Racial segregation, declared the African American leader A. Philip Randolph, was "the greatest single propaganda and political weapon in the hands of Russia and International Communism today." As Cold War considerations propelled race onto President Truman's agenda, the interconnection between domes-tic and international issues in the early postwar era again became evident.

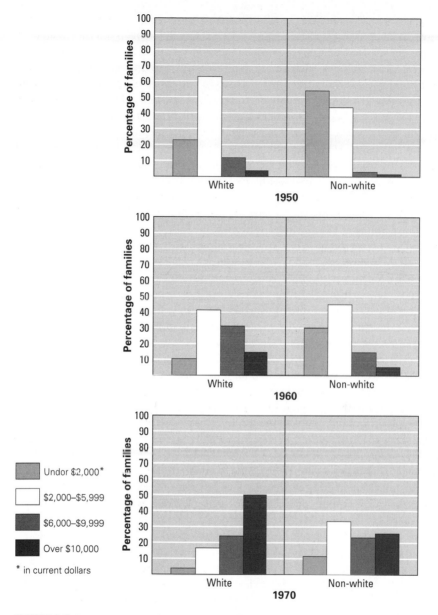

FIGURE 3.1

Family Income by Race, 1950–1970

Source: Adapted from *Statistical Abstract of the United States,* 1974 (Washington, D.C., 1973), p. 382.

For Truman, civil rights posed a dilemma both personally and politically. The grandchild of slaveowners, he grew up in an era of blatant and pervasive racism. While a Missouri senator, he had supported a federal antilynching bill while privately assuring southern colleagues that he did so only because of blacks' voting power in Kansas City and St. Louis. But Truman grew during his White House years. His sense of decency recognized injustice when it was made plain to him. As a politician, Truman realized that the Democratic coalition included northern liberals and blacks as well as southern whites who clung to racial segregation. As president, he had to deal with powerful southern Democrats in Congress, but he also realized that racism represented a painful liability in America's efforts to win allies abroad.

Amid these contradictory impulses and calculations, Truman cautiously embraced the black cause. Late in 1946, after heavy Democratic losses in that year's midterm elections, he set up the presidential Committee on Civil Rights, dominated by liberal activists. Its 1947 report, *To Secure These Rights,* called for vigorous action against racism, including an end to school segregation. That year Truman delivered a strong address to the NAACP, and early in 1948 (an election year) he sent Congress a civil-rights message proposing a federal antilynching law and a permanent Fair Employment Practices Commission patterned on FDR's temporary wartime agency. Southern Democrats buried Truman's proposals, but the message placed racial issues squarely on the national agenda.

Truman's major civil-rights achievement came in July 1948, when he ordered an end to racial segregation in the military. Although not fully implemented until the Korean War, this order directly challenged deeply embedded patterns of institutionalized racism. The *Chicago Defender,* a black newspaper, compared it to Abraham Lincoln's Emancipation Proclamation.

With a broad-based civil-rights movement still in the future, attention focused instead on individual black achievers: diplomat Ralph Bunche, boxer Sugar Ray Robinson, and baseball player Jackie Robinson, who broke the major-league color barrier in 1947. In 1949, playing for the Brooklyn Dodgers, Robinson led the National League in batting and was the league's most valuable player. After years of segregation in the Negro League, black baseball stars could now compete on the same fields with whites.

Despite Truman's actions and notable individual achievements, racism held a seemingly unbreakable grip on America. Jackie Robinson stayed in segregated hotels when the Dodgers traveled. Black jazz musicians, however famous, faced the humiliation of racial segregation. In 1946 a security guard pistol-whipped bandleader Cab Calloway as he tried to enter Kansas City's all-white Pla-Mor Ballroom. Despite gradual gains, blacks lagged far behind the white majority economically and educationally. In 1950, when some 39 percent of white families earned annual incomes under $3,000, the figure for black families was 77 percent. Black high-school graduates attended college in the early 1950s at less than half the rate of whites.

Postwar antiradical obsessions discouraged racial protest. African American leaders such as Paul Robeson and W. E. B. Du Bois, because of their ties to the Communist Party, were ostracized even by black organizations like the NAACP. The absence of grassroots civil-rights activism also reflected the NAACP's preference for litigation rather than marches and protests. In 1947, when two small civil-rights organizations, the Fellowship of Reconciliation and the Congress of Racial Equality (CORE), organized an interracial "Journey of Reconciliation" to protest segregated interstate buses operating in the South, the NAACP stood aside.

Washington's efforts to protect America's image abroad against well-founded charges of racism included not only positive actions, but also the denial of visas to

Robeson, Du Bois, and other outspoken critics. Instead, as "cultural ambassadors" abroad, the government preferred black performers who advocated accommodation rather than confrontation, or sidestepped the whole issue. In *The Cold War and the Color Line: American Race Relations in the Global Arena* (2001), Thomas Borstelmann argues that the administration tread a fine line on race in these years, proposing cautious measures against the more blatant manifestations of racism in America while trying not to alienate powerful southern white Democrats, European powers that still held colonies in Asia and Africa, and openly white-supremacist nations such as South Africa.

Yet changes were astir. As Truman's election-year attention to civil rights made plain, blacks' political clout was growing. Even in the South, bastion of white supremacy, where election boards used various devices to bar blacks, the number of African American voters rose from 250,000 to more than 1 million between 1940 and 1950. The NAACP's patient legal approach, if undramatic, showed signs of paying off. In three landmark cases of 1950—all argued by NAACP lawyer Thurgood Marshall—the Supreme Court outlawed segregated railroad dining cars and narrowed the scope of *Plessy* v. *Ferguson,* the 1896 decision permitting segregated schools and other public facilities. Although *Plessy* was not actually overturned until 1954, these decisions did weaken segregation's legal underpinnings. As the NAACP observed, "Some might call these [rulings] mere straws in the wind, but they do indicate the direction in which the wind is blowing."

Many of these gains resulted from dedicated effort at the local level. In Houston, for example, Lulu B. White, a black schoolteacher, resolutely battled the city's pervasive racism. Named head of the local NAACP in 1943, she built it up to twelve thousand members, making it the second largest branch in the nation, after Detroit. When the Supreme Court struck down Texas's all-white primary in 1944, White campaigned for black voter registration. The civil-rights movement that surged to national visibility in the later 1950s arose from years of dogged grassroots efforts by such people as Lulu White.

While black discontent mounted and pressure for change intensified, most white Americans remained oblivious. As journalist John Gunther wrote in 1947, the fact that America was 10 percent black was "known to everybody and ignored by almost everybody—except maybe the ten percent."

A Growing Mexican American Community Faces Postwar Challenges

The postwar years saw a continued influx of Mexican immigrants, both legal and illegal. Through the influence of agribusiness owners, the wartime *braceros* program—which admitted Mexicans for low-paid seasonal farm labor, mainly in California and Texas—was renewed after the war, bringing in some three hundred thousand Mexicans annually. (The program ended in 1964, amid mounting evidence of exploitation of workers.) Many *braceros* remained in the United States legally, either by securing temporary work permits ("green cards") or by marrying Mexican American women who were U.S. citizens. Many thousands of poor Mexicans also crossed the border illegally each year, seeking work. These *mojados,* or "wetbacks," often performed the unskilled and low-paid—but essential—labor that other workers scorned. Under "Operation Wetback," a major program launched by the Immigration and Naturalization Service (INS) in 1954, over 1 million illegal immigrants were arrested and returned to Mexico.

This influx of newcomers profoundly affected the Mexican American community. It reinforced the Spanish language and Mexican culture in the barrios (urban Mexican American neighborhoods) and also produced tension between the new arrivals and second- or third-generation Mexican Americans. The flow of newcomers represented a large pool of unskilled workers desperate for even low-wage jobs. Although some Mexican Americans became entrepreneurs, professionals, or skilled workers, most labored at unskilled or semiskilled jobs. The median level of schooling for Mexican Americans in the 1950s was 8.1 years, well below the national median. Even though the more overt manifestations of hostility were fading, Mexican American and Latin American immigrants faced subtle forms of prejudice and discrimination.

In the postwar years, Mexican Americans began to address these problems. In East Los Angeles (the nation's largest concentration of Mexican Americans), the Community Service Organization focused on civil-rights and police-abuse issues, promoted community improvement projects, and in 1949 elected the first Mexican American to the Los Angeles city council. The Associación Nacional México Americana (National Mexican American Association), founded in Albuquerque, New Mexico, in 1949 by left-wing labor union leaders, sought a similar role in the larger Mexican American community, but it was weakened by attacks on it as a communist front.

Mexican American women in Texas and California, writes historian Vicki L. Ruiz, negotiated the tensions between their traditional culture and the greater openness of Anglo life: "[S]tanding at the cultural crossroads, [they] blended their options and created their own paths" (*From Out of the Shadows: Mexican Women in Twentieth-Century America* [1998]). These *Mexicanas* selectively embraced U.S. consumer culture, resisted the traditional chaperones at dances, and protested bad conditions in the workplace. One *Mexicana*, Luisa Moreno, organized the first national civil-rights gathering of Hispanic immigrants, El Congreso de Pueblos de Habla Española (Congress of Spanish-Speaking Peoples) as early as 1939.

The Cold War at Home and the 1948 Election

The Cold War had a chilling effect on home-front politics. The 1946 dismissal of Commerce Secretary Henry Wallace (see Chapter 2) signaled a more general stifling of dissident opinion. Politicians and conservative groups responded to the drumfire of warnings about the Red menace by raising the specter of domestic disloyalty. The socialist leader Norman Thomas, visiting California in 1947, expressed shock at the "hysterical anticommunism" he found.

To be sure, fears of subversion had a basis in fact. The tiny American Communist Party did promote Moscow's interests, and the Soviets, like most nations, did conduct espionage. In March 1945, OSS security officials found three hundred secret government documents, including OSS reports, in the office of a left-wing

Anticommunism in Los Angeles, July 1950. Autoworkers attack a fellow employee for refusing to tell them whether he is a communist. *(AP/Wide World Photos)*

journal of Asian affairs, *Amerasia*. One file bore the cryptic label "'A' Bomb." Six persons were arrested on espionage charges, but the government dropped the case, raising suspicions of a cover-up. In 1946 Canadian authorities uncovered a Soviet spy ring. And in 1948, amid newspaper stories about a "Beautiful Blonde Spy Queen," the House Un-American Activities Committee (HUAC) questioned Elizabeth Bentley, a former government employee who had confessed to the Federal Bureau of Investigation (FBI) that during the war she had transmitted secret documents to a Soviet agent who was then her lover.

But the spreading hysteria about domestic subversion went far beyond specific security lapses. In fact, it was a predictable byproduct of the fear of communism that the Truman administration, J. Edgar Hoover's FBI, and media voices such as Henry Luce's *Life* and *Time* magazines fanned to build support for the Cold War. As *Life* put it, "The fellow traveler [communist sympathizer] is everywhere, in Hollywood, on college faculties, in government bureaus, in publishing companies, even on the editorial staffs of eminently capitalist journals." Conservatives who cried "communist subversion" to attack dissidents of all kinds and politicians who hammered at the same theme for partisan purposes simply exploited fears already being fanned by many sources, including the White House.

In March 1947, Truman launched the domestic corollary of his global anticommunist struggle: a federal loyalty-review program. By 1952 the FBI had investigated some twenty thousand government employees, of whom about four hundred were fired and twenty-five hundred resigned "voluntarily." Although Truman warned against "witch hunts," his loyalty program invited abuse. Persons accused of subversive associations or sympathies could appeal, but they could neither examine the material in their FBI files nor confront their anonymous accusers. The attorney general compiled a list of "subversive" organizations. Some of these had expired years before, but even past membership drew suspicion. Employees faced questions about their opinion of Henry Wallace or the Truman Doctrine, or whether they owned recordings by Paul Robeson. Civil-rights activists and homosexuals (considered vulnerable to blackmail) endured special scrutiny. Following Washington's lead, local groups launched their own loyalty-review programs. Although the postwar Red Scare crested in the McCarthyite witch hunts of the early 1950s, the Truman administration's loyalty program nurtured it.

Meanwhile, as the 1948 election neared, Truman's chances looked bleak. The Republicans, having won control of Congress in 1946, exuded confidence. Inflation fed voter discontent. Henry Wallace, running for president on a third-party Progressive ticket, posed a threat from the Left. In 1947, according to a diary entry recently discovered in the Truman Library, the president suggested to General Eisenhower that he, Eisenhower, head the 1948 Democratic ticket, with Truman as the vice-presidential nominee!

Compounding Truman's troubles, the Democratic convention in Philadelphia that nominated him also triggered a party split. Following a plan adopted by administration strategists and big-city Democratic leaders, the convention featured a ringing civil-rights speech by the young mayor of Minneapolis, Hubert Humphrey, who urged the party "to walk out of the shadow of states' rights and into the sunlight of human rights." Prodded by northern liberals, the convention adopted a strong civil-rights plank—not part of the White House game plan. When protesting southern delegates found their microphones dead, the Mississippi and Alabama delegations angrily walked out.

Soon after, six thousand cheering whites in Birmingham, Alabama, formed the States' Rights Democratic Party (known as the Dixiecrats) and nominated South Carolina governor Strom Thurmond for president. Elected governor in 1946 on a mildly progressive platform, Thurmond sensed the potency of the "states rights" issue for Deep South whites fearful of the region's large black population, and he jumped aboard an essentially white-racist movement. Truman's prospects appeared doomed. "Send up a bottle of embalming fluid," a roomful of convention delegates in Philadelphia told room service. "If we're going to hold a wake, we might as well do it right."

The confident Republicans again nominated New York governor Thomas Dewey, who had run well against Roosevelt in 1944 and appeared certain to win this time. "How long is Dewey going to tolerate Truman's interference in the government?" mused one reporter as the campaign unfolded. Dewey's running mate, California governor Earl Warren, strengthened the ticket in the West.

But Truman's adviser Clark Clifford, in a 1947 memo, had devised a potent three-part campaign strategy. It involved energizing key elements of the old Roosevelt coalition, notably blacks, union members, and New Deal liberals; deflecting anger over inflation and other problems from the White House to Congress; and exploiting the anticommunist theme. The "battle with the Kremlin," Clifford noted, offered Truman "considerable political advantage."

Truman was receptive. He had initially distanced himself from the New Deal legacy, but the Republican gains in 1946 had been a wake-up call. Implementing Clifford's plan, Truman in 1948 peppered Congress with reform proposals, including repeal of the Taft-Hartley Act, a housing bill, and a civil-rights program. Most of these proposals predictably died, but they positioned Truman as a reformer in the FDR tradition and Congress as reactionary and deaf to social issues. Truman called a special session of Congress in July, supposedly to enable the Republicans to pass all the measures promised in their platform. As Truman anticipated, this session accomplished little.

The president undertook a grueling national campaign by rail, traveling 22,000 miles and delivering 271 speeches. He lambasted the "gluttons of privilege," the "economic tapeworms of big business," and, above all, "the do-nothing Eightieth Congress," shrewdly shifting attention from the bland Dewey to the Republican Congress. The drama of the Berlin airlift that summer helped Truman as well. The crowds grew larger and the shouts of "Give 'em hell, Harry" more exuberant. Dewey, meanwhile, spoke in vague generalities. ("Your future is still ahead of you," he informed one audience.) With his stiff manner, mechanical smile, and trim black mustache, Dewey reminded one commentator of "the little man on top of the wedding cake." But still the polls predicted a Dewey landslide. The vast illusion continued into the early balloting. The *Chicago Tribune,* in an instantly famous election-night headline, proclaimed "DEWEY DEFEATS TRUMAN."

The polling had stopped too soon, missing a last-minute swing to Truman. In a stunning upset, Truman amassed 24.2 million votes to Dewey's 22 million, and the Democrats regained both houses of Congress. The next day, a Kentucky store offered portraits of Truman with the sign "Were $1.98, Now $10.00."

Accounts of the 1948 campaign understandably focus on Truman's feisty personality, but his victory also owed much to a brilliant campaign strategy. Targeting key voting blocs and demonizing the Republican Congress, Truman ran as a battler against communism abroad and reaction at home. "The issue . . . in this campaign," he told voters in Rock Island, Illinois, "is the people against the special interests." In contrast to Dewey, Truman talked about matters important to millions of voters, including, historian Donald McCoy writes, "housing, federal aid to education, health care, higher minimum wage and Social Security benefits, flood control, public power, civil rights, labor, conservation, agriculture, and regulation of business, among others."

The splinter parties fared poorly. Most voters rejected Wallace's attacks on Truman's foreign policy and objected to the Communist Party's role in his campaign. Wallace, who garnered just over a million votes, may even have helped Truman by validating the president's anticommunist credentials; deflecting Republican redbaiting; and solidifying the support of the noncommunist Left, as represented by the organization Americans for Democratic Action (see page 89). Not only did the racist States' Rights Party show little appeal beyond its southern base, but the Democrats' civil-rights plank that triggered the Dixiecrat revolt also produced a tidal wave of northern black votes for Truman. Thurmond, however, with 1.7 million votes, carried

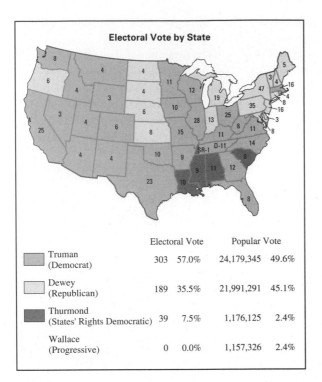

MAP 3.1
Presidential Election of 1948

four Deep South states, portending the region's eventual shift to the Republican Party—a move Thurmond himself made in 1964.

Truman did well among farmers, urban ethnics, and union members irked by the Taft-Hartley Act. Although weakened, the New Deal coalition still held. Having emerged from Roosevelt's shadow to win the presidency on his own, Harry Truman stood at the pinnacle of his career. His final White House years, however, would bring mostly frustration and setbacks.

The Fair Deal and the Red Scare

While pursuing the Cold War abroad, the Truman administration struggled to chart a domestic agenda in an increasingly venomous political climate. In his January 1949 State of the Union address, Truman proposed a far-reaching domestic program soon labeled the Fair Deal. The president again urged repeal of the Taft-Hartley Act and recommended broader social security coverage, an increase in the minimum wage from forty to seventy-five cents an hour, and development programs for the nation's river systems modeled on the TVA. He proposed aid to education, a cabinet-level department of welfare, expanded public housing, and—most ambitious of all—a national health-insurance system. To finance all this, and to combat inflation, the president recommended a $4 billion tax increase. (The health program would be funded by federal money plus contributions from employers and employees.) On the civil-rights front, Truman again called for a Fair Employment Practices Commission (FEPC) and, in later messages, federal laws against lynching and the poll tax, a stratagem used to exclude black voters in the South.

A laundry list of advanced liberal thinking on domestic issues, the Fair Deal assumed an expansive economy and an array of federal initiatives to promote the public welfare, combat racial discrimination, maintain prosperity, and ensure fair play in the marketplace. Coming at a time of growing conservatism and retreat from reform, most of the Fair Deal got nowhere. Lacking the broad support that FDR had initially rallied behind the New Deal, Truman's program faced strong legislative opposition. The president's party nominally controlled Congress, but in practice a coalition of Republicans and conservative Democrats held sway. Furthermore, Truman was unwilling to weaken bipartisan support for his foreign policy, especially after the Korean War began in June 1950, by pushing his domestic program. When conservative Democrats opposed his Fair Deal proposals, he took no steps to curb their power. Truman's health-insurance plan met a firestorm of opposition from the American Medical Association (AMA), which denounced it as "socialized medicine." Fearful of federal regulation and physicians' income loss, the AMA posted billboards that showed a worried doctor at a patient's bedside and warned, KEEP THE GOVERNMENT OUT OF THIS PICTURE.

Truman's farm program also ran into trouble—from farmers. The New Deal's strategy for raising farm income had included buying and storing the unsold surplus of basic commodities. By the late 1940s a glut of wheat, corn, and other commodities choked government warehouses. To cope with this headache, the administration in 1949 proposed to stop buying farm surpluses, allow the total output to be sold on the open market at lower prices, and then pay farmers cash subsidies to cover their losses. Labor and consumer groups welcomed this plan for its promise of lower food prices, but the Farm Bureau Federation, the voice of the largest farmers, charged that the scheme would cut farm income. When the Marshall Plan and other foreign-aid programs depleted the overflowing farm surpluses, the administration quietly shelved its complicated farm plan, again demonstrating the Cold War's influence on domestic politics.

The president's civil-rights program was blocked by southern Democrats, joined by conservative Republicans. Even a bill to grant self-government to the heavily black District of Columbia failed. The only governmental progress on civil rights came through executive action. Truman integrated the military (as we have seen), named several African Americans to midlevel federal posts, and in 1951 moved to deny government contracts to firms practicing racial discrimination.

Congress did pass a few of Truman's Fair Deal proposals. The National Housing Act of 1949, supported by the construction industry, authorized federal subsidies for eight hundred thousand low-income housing units. But the postwar housing shortage had eased, and only half that number were built. In 1950 Congress raised the minimum wage and expanded the coverage of social security, a program whose retirement benefits appealed to a broad spectrum of middle-class and working-class Americans. Despite its meager results, however, the Fair Deal remains historically significant. In putting civil rights, education, welfare policy,

IN PERSPECTIVE

The National-Security State

It was in the early Cold War that Congress, fearful of communist subversion at home and abroad, created what came to be called the national-security state. In 1947 Congress transformed the wartime Office of Strategic Services into the Central Intelligence Agency (CIA) and set up the high-level National Security Council to advise the president on security matters. The Internal Security Act of 1950 restricted the civil rights of communists and alleged "fellow-travelers." In these years, too, the Justice Department's Federal Bureau of Investigation, headed since 1924 by J. Edgar Hoover, expanded its national-security role, gathering files on individuals and organizations stigmatized as subversive or disloyal. There were 890 FBI agents in 1940 and 10,000 by 1970.

Initially, the public paid little heed to these agencies' activities. When security operations did impinge on Americans' awareness, the response was generally favorable. *The FBI in Peace and War,* a popular radio show of the 1950s, presented Hoover's agency in a heroic light, as did the 1959 movie *The FBI Story.* Tourists flocked to FBI headquarters in Washington, where exciting exhibits showed how the G-men had cracked tough cases.

The heyday of the national-security state came in the 1950s and 1960s. The CIA, operating largely outside congressional oversight, plotted assassinations, overthrew hostile governments, and conducted clandestine operations all over the world. It promoted anticommunism by secretly funding Radio Free Europe, the Congress of Cultural Freedom, and other front organizations. In addition, CIA money financed activities of the National Student Association, the largest student organization in the 1960s. At home, the FBI pursued its antiradical activities, even conducting illegal break-ins and tapping telephones to spy on what it considered extremist groups. Reflecting Hoover's hostility to the civil-rights movement, the FBI, with the approval of Attorney General Robert Kennedy, tapped the telephones and hotel rooms of Martin

Luther King, Jr., in 1963. America's national-security apparatus, created to protect U.S. freedom, began to threaten that freedom.

The CIA's botched Bay of Pigs invasion of Cuba in 1961 had stimulated some criticism of national-security agencies, but far harsher attacks came in the mid-1970s in the wake of the Watergate scandal. In 1974 the *New York Times* reported that the CIA, although legally banned from domestic activities, had assembled dossiers on thousands of American citizens and organizations. In 1976 President Ford's attorney general, Edward Levi, revealed that J. Edgar Hoover, who had died in 1972, had secretly kept derogatory files on presidents and legislators as a way of protecting his vast power. Responding to the shifting mood, Congress expanded the 1966 Freedom of Information Act ensuring citizens' access to their government files and restricted the CIA's power to carry out clandestine operations.

But abuses continued. The National Security Council became the focus of controversy in 1986–1987 with revelations that staffer Oliver North, operating out of the White House, had funneled millions of dollars to a CIA-backed army fighting Nicaragua's leftist government. Congress had explicitly banned such funding. Much evidence linked CIA director William Casey to these illegalities, but Casey died before his role could be fully explored.

In 1986, Congress at last reined in the FBI, requiring that all future FBI directors be approved by Congress and limited to ten-year terms. (Hoover had enjoyed a forty-eight-year tenure.) At the same time, historians and journalists began to chip away at the FBI's carefully burnished image. Books such as Athan Theoharis and John Stuart Cox's *The Boss* (1988) and Curt Gentry's *J. Edgar Hoover: The Man and the Secrets* (1991) revealed shocking details about the FBI and its director. As Americans requested their FBI files under the Freedom of Information Act, the scope of the agency's snooping emerged. Even Walt Disney was exposed as an FBI informant. (Disney gave FBI agents free admission to Disneyland, and Hoover permitted Disney to film an episode of TV's *Mickey Mouse Club* at FBI headquarters after Disney assured him that the show would portray the FBI in a laudatory light.) Questions about the FBI's shadowy relations with a succession of presidential administrations from Roosevelt's to Nixon's remain unanswered.

The end of the Cold War further eroded the national-security state, as the CIA struggled to redefine its role in a political culture no longer obsessed by the Soviet menace. In 1993, fending off calls for deep cuts in the agency's budget, CIA director R. James Woolsey portrayed the post–Cold War world as a jungle in which a dragon had been killed but where deadly snakes still abounded. Reflecting the shift from military to economic issues, the agency turned its sleuthing skills to ferreting out the positions of America's economic rivals in sensitive trade negotiations.

The period from the mid-1970s through the 1990s, in short, proved trying for the national-security state. Having enjoyed high public esteem earlier as leaders in the crusade against communism abroad and subversion at home, these agencies now confronted an uphill battle to reshape their mission and rebuild their tarnished reputations.

and health care on the table, Truman raised issues that would occupy the nation for decades to come.

As Truman's second term wore on, charges of corruption beset his administration. Journalist I. F. Stone described the president's cronies as "the kind of men one was accustomed to meet in county courthouses . . . big-bellied, good natured guys who knew a lot of dirty jokes [and] spent as little time in their office as possible." GOP orators denounced the "mess in Washington," especially targeting the Internal Revenue Service and the Reconstruction Finance Corporation (RFC), a New Deal agency that lent large sums to banks and corporations. The "mess" also included "five percenters"—officials who took payoffs for helping favored corporations secure government contracts.

The scandals mirrored postwar consumer society. One Truman aide allegedly accepted no fewer than seven freezers, which he gave to friends, including Mrs. Truman; a White House secretary received a mink coat from a corporation seeking an RFC loan; the Lustron Corporation got millions in RFC funds, never repaid, to build pastel-tinted prefabricated houses. Although not personally implicated in wrongdoing, Truman drew criticism for his lax judgment in friends and advisers. But while his opinion ratings fell and anti-Truman jokes spread, the president remained in good spirits, perhaps sensing that his historical reputation would outdistance his sagging opinion-poll ratings.

Charges of disloyalty and subversion, rooted in the anticommunist preoccupations of the era, increasingly poisoned national politics. In January 1949, further displaying its toughness on domestic radicals, the administration put on trial eleven Communist Party leaders. They were tried under the 1940 Alien Registration Act (also known as the Smith Act), which made it illegal to advocate the forcible overthrow of the government. The eleven were convicted in a decision upheld by the Supreme Court in 1951.

Along with the Elizabeth Bentley case (see page 77), two other highly publicized spy cases surfaced in these years. The first began in August 1948 when ex-communist Whittaker Chambers, an editor at *Time,* told HUAC that as a spy for the Soviets in the 1930s he had received secret government documents from Alger Hiss, then a State Department official. With a flair for drama, Chambers hid microfilms of the documents in a hollowed-out pumpkin on his Maryland farm. Hiss, urbane and self-assured, denied the charges. But as Congressman Richard Nixon doggedly pursued the case, HUAC investigators traced a typewriter once owned by Hiss and found that it matched the typing on Chambers's documents. Convicted of perjury (the statute of limitation on treason having expired), Hiss served five years in prison.

The second of these espionage cases began in England in 1950 when Klaus Fuchs, an émigré German physicist who had worked on the wartime atomic-bomb project at Los Alamos, was arrested as a Soviet spy. Fuchs fingered David Greenglass, a serviceman who had worked in the Los Alamos machine shop. Greenglass in turn charged that his sister and brother-in-law, Ethel and Julius Rosenberg, had recruited him for Soviet espionage. The Rosenbergs were arrested, convicted of spying for the Soviets, and sentenced to death. Despite worldwide protests, they went to the electric chair in New York's Sing Sing prison on Friday, June 19, 1953. (The presiding judge, Irving R. Kaufman, moved the time of execution to late afternoon from

Alger Hiss Testifies, 1948. As spectators crowd the room, Alger Hiss appears before the House Un-American Activities Committee to answer charges leveled against him by Whittaker Chambers. (© *Bettmann/CORBIS*)

the traditional 11 P.M. so the Rosenbergs, who were Jewish, would not be killed on the Sabbath.) Although other Americans have since been convicted of far more serious espionage charges, none has been executed.

The Hiss and Rosenberg cases long stirred impassioned debate. Recent scholarship suggests that all three were guilty, but that the Rosenbergs to some extent were victims of Cold War hysteria. For example, prosecutors appear to have sought the death sentence for Ethel Rosenberg, despite her minor role, hoping—in vain, as it turned out—that Julius Rosenberg would name other spies to save his wife. In a 1971 novel about the Rosenberg case, *The Book of Daniel*, E. L. Doctorow linked the shrill anticommunism of the time to the passions of World War II: "Enemies must continue to be found. The mind and heart cannot be demobilized as quickly as the platoon. . . . [L]ike a fiery furnace at white heat, it takes a considerable time to cool."

The Hiss and Rosenberg cases worsened an already rancorous political climate. From 1945 to 1952, HUAC conducted some eighty probes of atomic scientists, black activists, Hollywood writers, and others. Ten directors and screenwriters who refused to discuss their political beliefs or to implicate others before the committee went to prison. In 1951 the chair of HUAC, J. Parnell Thomas, convicted of fraud, found himself in the same federal prison with Ring Lardner, Jr., one of the "Hollywood Ten." One day as Thomas worked in the prison chicken yard while Lardner cut grass with a sickle nearby, Thomas called out: "Hey Lardner, I see you've got part of your old communist emblem. Where's the hammer to go with the sickle?" Lardner replied, "I see you're up to your old tricks, Congressman, shoveling chicken shit."

HUAC's circuslike investigations, some based on FBI files that included rumor, gossip, and material gathered by illegal wiretaps, left a trail of shattered reputations and careers. When a former State Department official committed suicide by leaping from a building, a HUAC committee member announced that HUAC had been investigating him and added jovially, "We will give out the other names as they jump out of windows."

The fearful climate underlay two laws passed over Truman's veto. The Internal Security Act of 1950 required communist and "communist-front" organizations to register with the government. The Immigration Act of 1952 set up procedures to keep out "subversives" and mandated the deportation of immigrants, even those who had become citizens, who belonged to suspect organizations. Echoing the wartime confinement of Japanese Americans, the law provided for the imprisonment of suspected security risks in the event of a national emergency.

Of the politicians who capitalized on the communist scare, none gained greater notoriety than Senator Joseph McCarthy of Wisconsin. At a Lincoln Day speech in West Virginia in February 1950, McCarthy, waving a piece of paper, claimed to have a list of 205 communists in the State Department. (In what would become a typical pattern, McCarthy eventually reduced the number to 1.) Refusing to release his "list," he hedged on whether he meant actual communists or vaguely defined "policy risks." But the public took notice, and for nearly five years McCarthy basked in the limelight as the media reported his endless accusations and sensational "revelations." In a rambling four-hour Senate speech fueled by swigs from a bottle of "cough medicine," McCarthy in May 1950 smeared the reputation of Owen Lattimore, an Asian scholar and occasional State Department adviser. "Ask almost any schoolchild who the architect of our Far Eastern policy is," McCarthy declared inanely at one point, "and he will say 'Owen Lattimore.'"

Like many Asian specialists, Lattimore had viewed Mao Zedong's revolution as a complex phenomenon rooted in China's history and politics, not simply a manifestation of a "world communist conspiracy" controlled from the Kremlin. No evidence supported McCarthy's claims that Lattimore was "the top Russian spy in America." At worst, Lattimore was "guilty" of having written naively upbeat assessments of the Soviet system in the 1930s and the war years. But his challenge to Cold War simplifications in his view of China made him vulnerable. By their smear tactics, McCarthy and those who echoed his charges blighted the careers of a generation of Asian specialists whose wisdom would be sorely missed.

A Senate committee chaired by Millard Tydings of Maryland found McCarthy's charges "a fraud and a hoax," but to little avail. When McCarthy campaigned against several Democratic senators in the 1950 elections and four of them lost, including Tydings, the potency of the "communist issue" became chillingly clear. At first, Republican leaders, looking to the 1952 elections, embraced McCarthy. Senator Taft advised, "Keep talking. . . . [I]f one case doesn't work out, proceed with another." McCarthy, invariably lugging a briefcase crammed with "documents," became a fixture on the lecture circuit.

"McCarthyism," however, was not the creation of a lone senator. Many others, from Congress to small-town America, joined in the frantic search for subversives.

Senators from both parties joined in. Pat McCarran, a Nevada Democrat and chair of the Senate Internal Security Subcommittee, although less publicity-mad than McCarthy, grimly pursued security risks. Blacklists circulated by shadowy organizations called for boycotts of suspected actors and performers; one notorious list was called *Red Channels*.

An American Legion post in Syracuse set up its own Un-American Activities Committee. To a blitz of media attention, legionnaires in Mosinee, Wisconsin, in 1950 dramatized the Red menace by staging a one-day "communist takeover" of the town. Pennsylvania's governor warned in 1951 that the Cold War's frontlines might soon be "our familiar backyards, the Turnpike, our suburbs and cities." As paranoia spread, authorities ringed the Pittsburgh airport with antiaircraft artillery.

Teachers, ministers, librarians, radio commentators, TV performers, and labor organizers faced charges of disloyalty. Methodist bishop G. Bromley Oxnam, folksinger Pete Seeger, playwright Arthur Miller, and actors Charlie Chaplin, John Garfield, and Zero Mostel ranked among the targets. Some three hundred New York City schoolteachers were fired as security risks. A University of Michigan mathematician went to jail for six months for refusing to tell HUAC whether he was a communist. Witnesses before investigative committees who invoked their constitutional right to remain silent were smeared as "Fifth Amendment Communists."

As politicians, patriotic groups, and right-wing radio broadcasters fanned the anticommunist flames, labor unions, film studios, school boards, professional societies, and even the American Civil Liberties Union purged alleged radicals and affirmed their patriotism. Universities imposed loyalty oaths. The president of the American Historical Association declared in 1949: "Total war, whether . . . hot or cold, enlists everyone and calls upon everyone to assume his part. The historian is no freer from this obligation than the physicist." A widely adopted high-school U.S. history textbook contributed to the climate of suspicion: "Unquestioning [Communist] party members are found everywhere," it warned. "Everywhere they are willing to engage in spying, sabotage, and the promotion of unrest on orders from Moscow."

By late 1954 McCarthy was discredited, done in by his own excesses (see Chapter 4). But in the early fifties, he reigned as one of the most powerful and feared men in America. Primarily an opportunist, he cared about little beyond tomorrow's headlines. But the fears and suspicions that he and others rubbed raw represented the early Cold War's principal domestic legacy. Soviet espionage was a reality, but the peddlers of hysteria and ideological conformity exploited that reality to smear reputations and pollute the political climate. As it championed "cultural freedom" abroad, America seemed in danger of denying it at home.

All Aboard the Freedom Train: Rallying Against Communism

While the Red Scare pushed anticommunism to a paranoid extreme, much of early postwar culture mobilized behind the stark ideological polarities of the early Cold War. A red, white, and blue "Freedom Train," its gleaming engine named "The Spirit of 1776," toured America in the late 1940s, bearing replicas of the Declaration of Independence, the Constitution, and other icons of American liberty.

Hollywood, having glorified the heroic Soviet people during the war, quickly shifted gears after 1945. *Red Danube* (1949) chronicled Eastern Europe's fall to Soviet imperialism. In *I Married a Communist* (1950) and *My Son John* (1952), horrified patriots discover the communist taint in their own families. *Big Jim McClain* (1952) starred John Wayne as a HUAC investigator tracking communists in Hawaii.

The art world, too, reflected Cold War preoccupations. When abstract-expressionist artist Jackson Pollock began to drip paint on canvas to produce his swirling "action paintings" in the late 1940s, *Life* magazine promoted him as evidence of America's rise to artistic supremacy, paralleling its military and economic dominance, and as proof of U.S. cultural freedom in contrast to the repression behind the Iron Curtain.

Political intellectuals who rejected Frederick Hayek's repudiation of liberalism nevertheless called for a toughened anticommunist liberalism purged of the supposed naiveté of the 1930s Left. The critic Lionel Trilling in his 1947 novel *The Middle of the Journey* and the 1950 collection of essays *The Liberal Imagination,* repudiated Marxism and criticized liberals' faith in reform and their optimism about human nature. Although he viewed all political systems as morally suspect, Trilling insisted that an open and democratic society was far preferable to an absolutist one (such as Stalinist Russia), whatever the latter's ideological pretensions.

In *The Vital Center* (1949), historian Arthur Schlesinger, Jr., offered a chastened liberalism—sternly anticommunist yet committed to the New Deal's social-welfare agenda—as the fighting faith that could fortify America against totalitarianism of the Right or Left. Schlesinger carefully distinguished his anticommunism from HUAC's redbaiting, yet his own discussion of communism was fairly monolithic. The Soviet Union could never be negotiated with, only defeated, Schlesinger implied, if not in war then through the West's superior "technological dynamism." Like NSC-68, *The Vital Center* largely ignored legitimate Russian security interests and world realities that did not fit Schlesinger's analytical framework.

The Protestant theologian Reinhold Niebuhr, a professor at New York's Union Theological Seminary, profoundly influenced these Cold War intellectuals. Drawn to the reform-minded Social Gospel in the 1920s, Niebuhr had embraced Marxism in the early 1930s. But disillusionment soon set in, and in a stream of books and essays, he exhorted Americans to get over their sentimental optimism and to recognize the power calculations that underlie international relations and the sinfulness inherent in the behavior of all nations and social groups.

Communists were especially fearsome, Niebuhr warned in *The Irony of American History* (1952), because in their absolutist zeal they tried to achieve by force the social ideals that Western liberals only fitfully pursued. Indeed, Niebuhr found communism more sinister than Nazism, because its gloss of idealism masked its evil. Although skeptical of American political thought, Niebuhr, like Trilling, argued that the United States, with its freedom of expression and relatively open politics, offered greater promise of a reasonably just social order than did communist ideology.

Niebuhr translated these generalities into avid support for the Cold War. Not content with swallowing Eastern Europe, he predicted in 1946, the Soviets would try to "extend their power over the whole of Europe." To avoid war, he advised, a nation must be ready to wage it. He praised the apocalyptic tone of the Truman Doctrine. That Greece and Turkey had repressive and undemocratic governments was irrelevant, he insisted: "What is at stake is not the internal structure of these nations, but [stopping] . . . the communist tide."

Niebuhr's message resonated powerfully. Popularized versions appeared in *Time, Life,* and *Reader's Digest.* One journalist called him "the official Establishment theologian." His world-weary visage on a *Time* cover in 1948 seemed to personify the desperate nature of the Cold War struggle. Under Niebuhr's influence, anticommunism became the one absolute for Cold War liberals otherwise wary of absolutist thinking. In 1947 Niebuhr, Schlesinger, and others founded Americans for Democratic Action (ADA) to rally anticommunist liberals. In 1948, the ADA endorsed Truman and denounced Henry Wallace's Progressive Party as a communist front.

These liberal intellectuals formulated their anticommunist dogma when Joseph Stalin ruled the Soviet Union, when Moscow held Eastern Europe in an iron grip, and as communists came to power in China. The breakup of the Sino-Soviet alliance and Moscow's somewhat more moderate stance after Stalin died in 1953 all lay ahead. Their worldview thus merits respect. But to a degree they served as ideological cheerleaders for the Cold War in its period of maximum rhetorical excess. Their broad generalizations about communist ideology tended to ignore the Soviet Union's actual history and legitimate interests and to blur the nuances of specific issues. The logic of their position encouraged an unquestioning embrace of "the West" and of the Truman administration's version of Cold War issues. The oversimplification became even cruder as their message was packaged for mass consumption. When the *New York Times Magazine* in April 1948 published an article by Schlesinger entitled "Not Left, Not Right, But a Vital Center," the magazine's cover illustration, reminiscent of 1930s propaganda posters, pictured the armies of "the Left" and "the Right" retreating in disarray as a giant fist bearing a flaming torch smashes a wedge between them.

Cold War liberals generally dismissed the conservatives at the other end of the ideological spectrum. In *The Liberal Imagination,* Trilling insisted that the Right had no ideas, only "irritable mental gestures which seek to resemble ideas." Even as he wrote, however, a conservative ideological resurgence could be discerned, not only in the popularity of Hayek's *Road to Serfdom* but elsewhere. The era brought a stream of confessional literature from disillusioned Marxists who had moved rightward, including the 1950 anthology *The God That Failed* and Whittaker Chambers's *Witness* (1952). In *The Struggle for the World* (1947), the ex-communist James Burnham issued a bloodcurdling call for a no-holds-barred crusade against communism. Unless America used its atomic monopoly to create a "World Empire," he declared, the Soviets would soon rule the earth. In 1951, the young conservative William F. Buckley, Jr., entered the polemical wars with *God and Man at Yale,* a caustic attack on the secular rot eating away at his alma mater. Soon Buckley would found a magazine, the *National Review,* to challenge Marxists, socialists, and liberals alike. Although different in many ways, these early Cold War liberals and conservatives shared a relentless preoccupation with communism that linked them more closely than either camp cared to acknowledge.

While Schlesinger and his ADA colleagues succeeded wonderfully well in cementing the Cold War consensus on international issues, their social-welfare domestic agenda stirred less enthusiasm. White, middle-class Americans, including many business leaders, may have come to terms with the New Deal, but they were in no mood for further reforms such as those espoused by Left-liberal intellectuals and embodied in Truman's Fair Deal. Embracing an aggressive, confrontational foreign policy, Middle America sought a politics of stability at home.

Diversion and Doubt: Early Postwar Literature and Popular Culture

Early postwar popular culture reflected the ambivalence of a nation powerful and prospering yet beset by Cold War anxiety, nuclear fears, unsettling social changes, and a jittery preoccupation with subversion. Movies like *The Sands of Iwo Jima* (1949), starring John Wayne and featuring the famous flag raising over Mount Suribachi, evoked the patriotism and unity of the war years. The popular 1954 TV documentary *Victory at Sea,* with a rousing musical score by Richard Rodgers, celebrated the navy's role in the war in carefully edited highlights. But uneasiness about the atomic bomb shadowed Americans' satisfaction about the triumph of 1945. John Hersey's *Hiroshima* (1946), initially published in the *New Yorker* magazine, offered a horrifying account of what a single atomic bomb could do to a major city. In the 1951 film *The Day the Earth Stood Still,* highly evolved aliens arrive in a spaceship and command earthlings to stop their foolish quarrels before they self-destruct. Mass magazines such as *Reader's Digest* and *Life* offered not only warnings of the communist menace but also lurid scenarios of a nuclear World War III and scary images of mushroom clouds from nuclear tests in Nevada and the South Pacific.

A few Hollywood movies and TV series presented a heavy-handed anticommunist message, but the mass culture more frequently offered escape than overt propaganda. Indeed, the quest for distraction from the alarms and threats of the real world was a shaping force in the popular culture of the early postwar years. A series of lighthearted Broadway musicals—*Guys and Dolls* (1949), *South Pacific* (1950), *The King and I* (1951)—with their movie and record spinoffs, epitomize the trend.

While radio newscasters brought word of disturbing developments abroad, America's radio stations, whose numbers nearly tripled from 1945 to 1950, offered escapist fare in many forms. In the late 1940s, millions of housewives tuned in daily for teary soap operas such as *Stella Dallas* and *When a Girl Marries.* World issues rarely intruded into these sagas of romance and domestic crisis. To adolescents, radio continued to offer a series of mostly male role models and stereotypes: *Sergeant Preston of the Yukon; Jack Armstrong, All-American Boy;* or *The Lone Ranger* with his faithful Indian companion, Tonto. The whole family gathered for the evening comedy shows of vaudeville veterans such as Jack Benny and the husband-and-wife team George Burns and Gracie Allen.

Radio's preeminence soon ended, however. The first commercial television broadcast dated from 1939, when NBC televised Franklin Roosevelt's opening of the New York World's Fair. Soon after the war, small-screen TV sets attracted fascinated crowds to store windows even when transmitting only a greenish test pattern. By 1952, amid the postwar economic boom, more than a third of U.S. households had television. Corporate spending on TV advertising surged from $171 million in 1950 to $454 million by 1952; by mid-decade it would surpass $1 billion.

Early TV shows often copied radio programming. *Faraway Hill,* the first TV soap opera, debuted in 1946, as did two durable variety shows: Ed Sullivan's *Toast of the Town* and *Arthur Godfrey's Talent Scouts.* Some shows, such as *The Life of Riley* and *The Lone Ranger,* moved directly from radio to TV. Live drama began in 1947 with *Kraft Television Theater;* that year also launched the popular children's show *Howdy Doody.* One mother remarked, "The hours between play and bed used to be . . . hectic. . . . Now I know where the children are. The television set is the best nurse in the world."

At first, local channels did their own programming with homegrown talent—an Atlanta station spotlighted "Morgus, the Crazy Weatherman"—but television soon went national. NBC put together the first television network in 1949. CBS, under hard-driving William Paley, soon bested NBC in the ratings. Paley perfected the concept of "audience flow," luring the fans of one show to stay tuned for the next.

Although Hollywood and TV eventually formed a profitable alliance, movie moguls initially feared the new medium, and with good reason: Movie attendance fell by 14 percent between 1946 and 1949. The mention of television in movie-industry circles, the *New York Times* reported in 1949, "evokes only icy silence." Politicians, on the other hand, loved TV, trimming their long-winded speeches to fit its demands. Planners of the 1948 Democratic convention warned delegates to behave, for they would now be seen as well as heard. When television covered Truman's 1949 inaugural, *Time* magazine exclaimed: "Ten million televiewers from the Atlantic coast to the Mississippi felt that they had truly been there with Washington's cheering thousands."

Some held high hopes for the new medium's cultural promise. A media executive in 1945 proclaimed: "[T]elevision . . . is going to make every city, town, and village in the United States a more democratic, more progressive, more closely knit community." For a time, well-written dramatic shows like *Playhouse 90* and light-classical musical programs such as *The Voice of Firestone* seemed to fulfill such hopes.

But advertisers' demands for ever-larger audiences quickly doomed such quality fare, and TV devoted itself mainly to offering undemanding diversion. Scriptwriters for *Men Against Crime,* which premiered in 1949, were instructed, "[W]e retain audience interest best when our story is concerned with murder. Therefore . . . somebody must be murdered, preferably early, with the threat of more violence to come." (The cigarette-company sponsor of *Men Against Crime* also insisted that no actor ever cough on the show.) Hand wringing over the medium's banality replaced the early enthusiasm; comedian Fred Allen called TV "chewing gum for the eyes." Television did sometimes give viewers a window on the world—live coverage of the UN debates when the Korean War broke out, for example—but as the Cold War grew more dangerous, escapism predominated.

The marketing of goods drove the entertainment media, hastening the emergence of a standardized mass culture organized around consumerism. As in the rest of corporate America, large companies dominated. Three networks—CBS, NBC, and ABC—controlled early TV; *Life, Collier's, Saturday Evening Post,* and *Reader's Digest* ruled the magazine world; and five major studios produced nearly all U.S. movies. Along with corporate consolidation and pressure from advertisers, powerful institutions and interest groups also pushed the mass culture toward the bland

and noncontroversial. The Catholic Church's Legion of Decency and Hollywood's own Production Code Authority monitored movie morals. (The Legion of Decency condemned the 1953 film *The Moon Is Blue* because the word *virgin* appeared in the script.) The Cold War climate of intellectual conformity intensified what one critic called the movies' "retreat into apathy" and "ideological fatigue." A mass culture driven by market calculations and a quest for the lowest-common-denominator level of entertainment had little time for innovation, creativity, or the thoughtful exploration of public issues.

Beneath the culture's escapist surface, however, eddied currents of apprehension and sharp social criticism. A rash of "flying saucer" sightings began in 1947. (Soviet diplomat Andrei Gromyko, in a rare flash of humor, quipped that they came from his nation's discus throwers practicing for the Olympics.) Postwar movies of the "film noir" genre, such as *He Walked by Night* (1949), featured menacing dangers lurking in familiar settings. The mystified hero of one such film complained, "I'm backed up in a dark corner and I don't know who's hitting me!"

The nervousness revealed in these movies affected American religion as well. Young people flocked to the Saturday-night rallies of a newly founded evangelical Protestant movement, Youth for Christ. Evangelist Billy Graham rocketed to fame on the strength of a 1949 Los Angeles tent revival just as the Soviet Union exploded its first atomic bomb. "An arms race unprecedented in the history of the world is driving us madly toward destruction!" Graham thundered. "Time is desperately short. . . . [P]repare to meet thy God!" Other religious leaders offered less apocalyptic remedies for nuclear worries. In *A Guide to Confident Living* (1948) and other books, the Reverend Norman Vincent Peale advised anxious Americans to "say confidently to yourself: 'Through God's help and the application of simple techniques, I will be free from fear.' Believe that—practice it, and it will be so." Pharmaceuticals offered a chemical means to the same end; the year that witnessed the advent of hydrogen-bomb research, the outbreak of the Korean War, and the onset of Senator McCarthy's anticommunist rampage (1950) also brought the first commercially available tranquilizer, called Miltown.

While popular culture offered its mix of diversion, escape, and foreboding, a few writers questioned the upbeat images of American life and probed the social problems lurking beneath the surface. (In most of these works, interestingly, women are either absent or ineffectual background figures.) Norman Mailer's cynical war novel *The Naked and the Dead* (1948) offered a view of the coarse and brutalized behavior of men in combat very different from the wartime propaganda images. Arthur Miller's play *Death of a Salesman* (1949) searingly portrayed a bewildered loser caught up in fantasies of success pathetically at odds with the realities of his life. Nelson Algren's *Man with the Golden Arm* (1949) looked at drug addiction, gambling, and crime in Chicago's inner city. Kurt Vonnegut's *Player Piano* (1952) presented a bleak fantasy of a totally automated society ruled by the masters of the machines. The novel's influences included Vonnegut's unhappy experience as an employee of the General Electric Company and earlier dystopian novels such as Aldous Huxley's *Brave New World* (1932).

Laura Hobson's *Gentlemen's Agreement* (1946), written in the shadow of the Holocaust, whose horror emerged in shocking photographs of the Nazi death camps, exposed anti-Semitism in American society. Hobson began her novel in

1944 when a Mississippi congressman called the gossip columnist and radio personality Walter Winchell "the little Kike" on the House floor and not a single legislator rebuked him. Both as a novel and a 1947 movie starring Gregory Peck, *Gentlemen's Agreement* spotlighted a hitherto-neglected social issue.

J. D. Salinger's coming-of-age novel *The Catcher in the Rye (1951)* viewed middle-class pretenses through the eyes of seventeen-year-old Holden Caulfield. An atomic-age Huck Finn, Holden clings to his innocence—trying, for example, to erase "Fuck You" graffiti so his kid sister won't see it—in a cynical and hypocritical adult world. *Catcher* captured the historical moment when the wartime sense of unity and purpose had dissolved into postwar rancor and confusion. In his youthful naiveté, Holden judges a "phony" society troubled by Cold War obsessions, nuclear angst, and growing evidence of social problems at home—a society that finds escape in the mass culture and determinedly insists that all is well because the economy is booming. Huck heads west at the end of Mark Twain's novel; Holden, after a nervous breakdown, narrates his story from a psychiatric institution.

Ralph Ellison's *Invisible Man* (1952) explored the theme of race in America from a black perspective. In a succession of often surreal episodes of great imaginative power, the action moves from the early-twentieth-century rural South to the urban North of World War II. The nameless narrator seeks his identity ("When I discover who I am, I'll be free") and probes the states of consciousness of a fictional African American male living as an outsider in a society that is simultaneously racist and blind to his existence. He joins "The Brotherhood," a fictionalized Communist Party, but finds that it, too, exploits him. Apart from this abortive experience, *Invisible Man* avoided politics and any hint of collective protest against a racist social order. "This is not an attack upon white society," Ellison insisted. "[The protagonist] must assert and achieve his own humanity." Indeed, most of these early postwar literary works proved more effective at probing the darker undercurrents of American life than at suggesting, within their fictional framework, possible strategies of change.

Postwar social critics, too, employed the neutral vocabulary of psychology and sociology rather than of political action. In his best-selling book *The Lonely Crowd* (1950), sociologist David Riesman looked at the psychological effects of mass society and consumer abundance. Exploring changes in "the American character" (that is, the white, middle-class character), Riesman discerned a progression from "inner directedness" to "other directedness." Modern Americans, he claimed, lacked a firm sense of self and thus placed a high premium on social acceptance and "fitting in." *The Lonely Crowd,* as we shall see, opened a floodgate of books lamenting the conformism and insipidity of 1950s America.

Conclusion

What underlying themes emerge from the events and trends chronicled in the last two chapters? First, of course, these years gave rise to the Cold War. President Truman's handling of the early postwar differences with the Soviets and his presentation of the issues to the American people set a course that would influence U.S. history for decades. But many voices contributed to the molding of Cold War ideology, from

Washington politicians to theologians, historians, literary critics, magazine editors, and moviemakers. In their sweeping rhetorical portrayals of the communist menace, the ideologists of 1945–52 introduced enduring themes into American public discourse. Domestically, the administration's apocalyptic drumbeat of warnings of a global communist conspiracy masterminded from the Kremlin led to a panicky search to ferret out subversion and disloyalty—the Red Scare.

The nuclear arms race dates from these years as well. Like a row of falling dominos, Truman's fateful decision to drop atomic bombs on Japan, the failure of the postwar international-control effort, the 1949 Russian A-bomb test, and the president's subsequent decision to build the hydrogen bomb launched a proliferation of nuclear weapons that for decades would stoke fears of annihilation and that remains a matter of urgent concern today.

The postwar economic boom had a dramatic impact on American life and politics, as the U.S. economy achieved new levels of consumer abundance. Corporate America, taking the credit, moved to translate economic achievement into political influence, accelerating a conservative political turn that Truman's come-from-behind victory in 1948 would only temporarily slow. The rhetoric of "business-government partnership" that would pervade the politics of the 1950s took shape in this period. Organized labor, on the other hand, highly influential in the 1930s, found itself increasingly marginalized in public-policy debates.

Despite the postwar boom, surging college enrollments, and the upward mobility of young families moving to the burgeoning suburbs, millions remained outside looking in. Within the African American community, growing political clout and rising frustration with second-class citizenship produced rising levels of protest and activism. The Truman administration, meanwhile, sought to counter adverse publicity about America's discriminatory racial practices in nations whose allegiance it sought to win. Nevertheless, engrained patterns of institutionalized racism persisted. A growing Hispanic population, many at the bottom of the economic ladder, also began to organize against subtle forms of discrimination. And despite the culture's insistent celebration of domesticity, the constraints that early postwar society imposed on women in its quest for stability would ultimately prove unsustainable. The elements of future social conflict and protest, in short, were already evident in the late 1940s and early 1950s.

While redbaiters flung their charges of "subversion" and "disloyalty," novelists, playwrights, and social thinkers criticized the hypocrisies and evasions of postwar America. The society portrayed by Hobson, Salinger, Ellison, Arthur Miller, and the others was not the America of the TV shows, the mass magazines, and the glossy ads. The alienation of an articulate minority of writers and intellectuals would intensify as the 1950s wore on.

The Truman years thus marked an uneasy transition from fifteen years of depression and war to an era of economic abundance and a superficially upbeat popular culture tempered by Cold War fears, nuclear menace, political and ideological conflicts, and half-acknowledged social problems and inequities. The apprehension that James Agee had felt as he watched the victory celebrators in September 1945 proved all too well founded.

By 1952 war memories were fading; Americans no longer self-consciously perceived themselves as living in a "postwar" era. As the ever-feisty Harry Truman rounded off a remarkable political career, the voters elected a new president—a war hero known more for his generalship than for his political views. The Eisenhower era was about to dawn.

SELECTED READINGS

Demobilization and Early Postwar Politics

Jack S. Ballard, *The Shock of Peace: Military and Economic Demobilization After World War II* (1983); William C. Berman, *The Politics of Civil Rights in the Truman Administration* (1970); Gary A. Donaldson, *Truman Defeats Dewey* (1998); Robert Donovan, *Conflict and Crisis* (1977) and *Tumultuous Years* (1982) [on the Truman presidency]; Andrew Dunar, *The Truman Scandals and the Politics of Morality* (1984); Robert H. Ferrell, *Harry S. Truman and the Modern American Presidency* (1983); Kari Frederickson, *The Dixiecrat Revolt and the End of the Solid South, 1932–1968* (2001); Alonzo L. Hamby, *Beyond the New Deal: Harry S. Truman and American Liberalism* (1973); Zachary Karabell, *The Last Campaign: How Harry Truman Won the 1948 Election* (2000); Michael J. Lacey, ed., *The Truman Presidency* (1989), Part I, "Domestic Politics and Issues"; Donald McCoy, *The Presidency of Harry S. Truman* (1984); Monte S. Poen, *Harry S. Truman Versus the Medical Lobby: The Genesis of Medicare* (1979); Irwin Ross, *The Loneliest Campaign* [1948] (1968); Sean J. Savage, *Truman and the Democratic Party* (1997); Alice Kimball Smith, *A Peril and a Hope: The Scientists' Movement in America* (1965); Athan Theoharis, *The Truman Presidency: The Origins of the Imperial Presidency and the National Security State* (1979).

African Americans, Hispanics, and Women in Early Cold War America

Thomas Borstelmann, *The Cold War and the Color Line: American Race Relations in the Global Arena* (2001), Albert Camarillo, *Chicanos in California* (1984); Mary L. Dudziak, *Cold War Civil Rights: Race and the Image of American Democracy* (2000); Mario T. García, *Mexican-Americans: Leadership, Ideology and Identity, 1930–1960* (1989); Susan Hartman, *The Homefront and Beyond* [women in the war and early postwar era] (1984); Stephen Lawson, *Running for Freedom: Civil Rights and Black Politics in America Since 1941* (1977); Azza Salama Layton, *International Politics and Civil Rights Policies in the United States, 1941–1950* (2000); Merline Pitre, *In Struggle Against Jim Crow: Lulu B. White and the NAACP, 1900–1957* (1999); Vicki L. Ruiz, *From Out of the Shadows: Mexican Women in Twentieth-Century America* (1998); Leila J. Rupp and Verta Taylor, *Survival in the Doldrums: The American Women's Rights Movement, 1945 to the 1960s* (1987); Julian Samora, *Los Mojados: The Wetback Story* (1971); Penny Von Eschen, *Race Against Empire: Black Americans and Anti-Colonialism, 1937–1957* (1997).

Postwar Society, Economy, Labor, and Popular Culture

Erik Barnouw, *Tube of Plenty* [television] (1982); Paul Boyer, *By the Bomb's Early Light: American Thought and Culture at the Dawn of the Atomic Age* (1985); Mary Ann Doane, *The Desire to Desire: The Woman's Film of the 1940s* (1987); Elizabeth A. Fones-Wolf, *Selling Free Enterprise: The Business Assault on Labor and Liberalism, 1945–60* (1994); Carol George, *God's Salesman: Norman Vincent Peale and the Power of Positive Thinking* (1993);

James A. Gross, *Broken Promise: The Subversion of U.S. Labor Relations Policy, 1947–1998* (1995); Wendy Kozol, Life *'s America: Family and Nation in Postwar Photojournalism* (1994); Nelson Lichtenstein, "From Corporatism to Collective Bargaining: Organized Labor and the Eclipse of Social Democracy in the Postwar Era," in Steve Fraser and Gary Gerstle, eds., *The Rise and Fall of the New Deal Order, 1930–1980* (1989); Martin E. Marty, *Modern American Religion, Vol. 3 [1941–1960]* (1996); Lary May, ed., *Recasting America: Culture and Politics in the Age of the Cold War* (1989); Jeffrey L. Meikle, *American Plastic: A Cultural History* (1995); Geoffrey Perrett, *A Dream of Greatness: The American People, 1945–1963* (1979); Allan M. Winkler, *Life Under a Cloud: American Anxiety About the Atom* (1993).

Red Scare, Anticommunism, Intellectuals in the Early Cold War

Nancy E. Bernhard, *U.S. Television News and Cold War Propaganda, 1947–1960* (1999); H. W. Brands, *The Devil We Knew: Americans and the Cold War* (1993); Virginia Carmichael, *Framing History: The Rosenberg Story and the Cold War* (1993); David Caute, *The Great Fear: The Anti-Communist Purges Under Truman and Eisenhower* (1978); K. A. Cuordileone, "'Politics in an Age of Anxiety': Cold War Political Culture and the Crisis in American Masculinity, 1949–1960," *Journal of American History* (September 2000); Sigmund Diamond, *Compromised Campus: The Collaboration of Universities with the Intelligence Community, 1945–1955* (1988); Bernard F. Dick, *Radical Innocence: A Critical Study of the Hollywood Ten* (1988); John Ehrman, *The Rise of Neoconservatism: Intellectuals and Foreign Affairs, 1945–1994* (1995); Richard Wightman Fox, *Reinhold Niebuhr: A Biography* (1985); Richard M. Fried, *Nightmare in Red: The McCarthy Era in Perspective* (1990); William S. Graebner, *The Age of Doubt: American Thought and Culture in the 1940s* (1991); M. J. Heale, *McCarthy's Americans: Red Scare Politics in State and Nation, 1935–1965* (1998); Philip Jenkins, *The Cold War at Home: The Red Scare in Pennsylvania, 1945–1960* (1999); David K. Johnson, *The Lavender Scare: The Cold War Persecution of Gays and Lesbians in the Federal Government* (2004); Mary McAuliffe, *Crisis of the Left: Cold-War Politics and American Liberals, 1947–1954* (1978); George H. Nash, *The Conservative Intellectual Movement in America Since 1945* (1976); William L. O'Neill, *A Better World: The Great Schism: Stalinism and the Intellectuals* (1982); David M. Oshinsky, *A Conspiracy So Immense: The World of Joe McCarthy* (1983); Richard Gid Powers, *Not Without Honor: The History of American Anticommunism* (1995); Ronald Radosh and Joyce Milton, *The Rosenberg File* (1983); Natalie Robins, *Alien Ink: The FBI's War on Freedom of Expression* (1992); Ellen W. Schrecker, *No Ivory Tower: McCarthyism and the Universities* (1986) and *The Age of McCarthyism: A Brief History with Documents* (1994); Athan Theoharis, *Seeds of Repression: Harry S Truman and the Origins of McCarthyism* (1971); Allen Weinstein, *Perjury: The Hiss-Chambers Case* (1978); John Kenneth White, *Still Seeing Red: How the Cold War Shapes the New American Politics* (1997); Stephen J. Whitfield, *The Culture of the Cold War* (1991).

CHAPTER

4

Modern Republicanism and Suburban Togetherness in the 1950s

IN THE 1955 movie *Strategic Air Command,* World War II air force ace Dutch Holland is recalled to active duty. Dutch (James Stewart) grumbles at first; he and his pregnant wife, Sally (June Allyson), have just redecorated their home and are settling into cozy domesticity. But when a giant bomber flies overhead, Dutch recalls the lure of the skies and gladly joins the new Strategic Air Command (SAC). Sally gamely supports Dutch as he defends the nation. "Anything you do is fine with me," she assures him, "just as long as you don't leave me behind."

The movie reflected several realities of the 1950s: SAC embodied the new emphasis on nuclear readiness in U.S. defense policy; SAC's complex organizational hierarchy, into which Dutch smoothly fits, paralleled that of corporate America; and Sally's loyal support of her husband echoed the idealization of domesticity at a time of rising birthrates and migration to the suburbs. Indeed, the movie repeatedly equates real-life families with the SAC "family" of pilots and crews and "the new family of nuclear weapons" that the bombers are designed to deliver.

As the public flocked to view *Strategic Air Command,* both the Cold War and the postwar economic boom surged on. Americans, prosperous yet worried about communism and nuclear war, had little patience with social critics or political dissidents. Ready enough to endorse Washington's pursuit of the Cold War overseas, people turned away from public concerns at home. The media presented the burgeoning suburbs as a microcosm of an affluent America, downplaying such social problems as poverty and ignoring the citizens excluded from the charmed circle of economic abundance. In the White House, a new president, Dwight D. Eisenhower, mirrored the nation's cautious, conservative, inward-turning mood.

The Politics of Moderation

Dwight Eisenhower, in Paris as supreme commander of NATO forces, faced a stream of visitors in 1951 and early 1952 as top Republicans shuttled in to implore him to run for president. He seemed a sure winner, although few knew anything about his politics. Indeed, as we have seen, Harry Truman, who had decided not to be a candidate in 1952, had earlier urged him to run as a Democrat.

Born in Texas in 1890, Eisenhower had graduated from West Point and won fame during World War II as commander of the North African invasion in 1943 and the Normandy landing in 1944. After serving for a time as president of Columbia University, he had returned to Europe to head NATO's military forces. Americans weary of the Korean War and of Truman administration scandals saw in Ike a refreshing political outsider and delighted in his easy smile and avuncular manner.

The Republican Party Eisenhower considered joining remained divided. The party's eastern, moderate, internationalist wing mistrusted the more conservative and isolationist midwestern wing, headed by Ohio's senator Robert Taft. If Taft won the 1952 party nomination, they feared, he would either lose the election (the more likely prospect) or win and turn the party sharply to the right. Behind Taft, too, loomed Senator Joseph McCarthy. For the moment, McCarthy served GOP interests by attacking Democrats, but a strong Republican was needed in the White House to curb his excesses. All of these reasons—plus the overriding desire

They Liked Ike. Although he was no silver-tongued orator, Dwight Eisenhower's infectious grin and status as a World War II military hero drew adoring throngs during the 1952 presidential campaign. *(Joe Scherschel/Life Magazine, © Timepix–Getty Images)*

to regain the White House—led moderate Republicans to woo Eisenhower. As Thomas Dewey put it, "We must look around for someone of great popularity . . . [who can] lead us back to safe . . . paths."

Ending the suspense early in 1952, Eisenhower proclaimed himself a Republican and threw his hat in the ring. He won several state primaries, but Taft loyalists controlled other states' delegations. However, Eisenhower's floor managers at the GOP convention in Chicago won a battle over disputed delegates, and the general gained a first-ballot nomination. As his running mate, Eisenhower tapped Senator Richard Nixon of California, known for his dogged pursuit of accused spy Alger Hiss.

The Democrats nominated Illinois governor Adlai Stevenson. Stevenson's witty speeches charmed liberals, but given his aloof manner and Eisenhower's appeal, plus the Republicans' potent themes—Korea, China, communism, and corruption (summed up in the formula K_1C_3)—few oddsmakers bet on him. As Eisenhower campaigned, large and enthusiastic crowds, invoking his nickname, chanted "I like Ike."

Two campaign incidents illuminated Senator McCarthy's continuing power and Richard Nixon's political style, both of which would pose dilemmas for Eisenhower. In McCarthy's home state of Wisconsin, Eisenhower dropped from a prepared speech a passage implicitly criticizing the senator for his attacks on General George Marshall. Marshall had been Eisenhower's superior in World War II, yet Ike dared not challenge McCarthy's smear even of his old comrade-in-arms.

When the press revealed a secret Nixon fund set up by rich California businessmen, Eisenhower declined to defend his running mate, the first of many indications

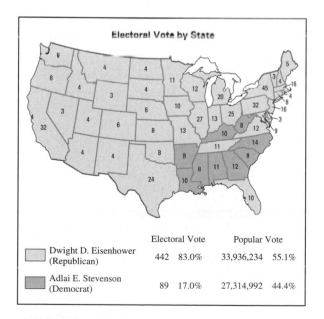

Electoral Vote by State

	Electoral Vote	Popular Vote
Dwight D. Eisenhower (Republican)	442 83.0%	33,936,234 55.1%
Adlai E. Stevenson (Democrat)	89 17.0%	27,314,992 44.4%

MAP 4.1

Presidential Election of 1952

that Ike neither liked nor trusted Nixon. Demonstrating the political clout of the new medium of television, Nixon fought back with a cloying TV speech that included a teary reference to his daughters' little dog, Checkers, another campaign gift. An outpouring of support ensured Nixon's place on the ticket and a long run in U.S. politics. Connoisseurs of political demagoguery still cherish "the Checkers speech."

That November, Eisenhower garnered 55 percent of the vote. Foreshadowing later Republican successes, he even did well in the once solidly Democratic South, winning 49 percent of the vote and carrying Virginia, Florida, Tennessee, Texas, and Oklahoma. He would win again in 1956, once more over Stevenson, and extend his presidency to two terms.

Hardly a sophisticated thinker, Eisenhower was on firmer ground on foreign affairs than on domestic issues. Nevertheless, he possessed a well-formulated set of political views. He deplored, for example, the politicizing of class differences. All Americans shared "areas of common interest," he believed, and the political process should promote these commonalities. In this cooperative process, he urged public-spirited business leaders to play a key role.

The "drift toward statism" troubled him as well. Like many conservatives, he chafed at the growth of the federal government and the consequent weakening of both the private sphere and the power of the states. But he was no knee-jerk enemy of "big government" or cheerleader for laissez faire. Like Theodore Roosevelt, Eisenhower believed that capitalism should be moderated by regulatory laws and a concern for social welfare, and he advocated a government strong enough to pro-

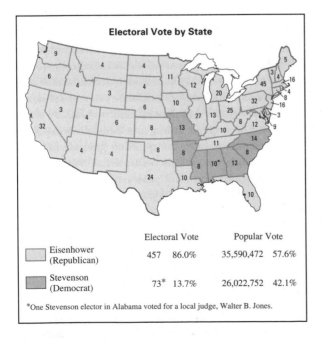

MAP 4.2

Presidential Election of 1956

mote the national interest, including economic growth, productivity, and foreign trade. The Republican Party must be "progressive," he insisted, "or it is sunk." His outlook reflected that of the more sophisticated corporate leaders of these years. Rejecting the backward-looking politics of people like Taft who still fought the New Deal, this corporate elite accepted the main outlines of FDR's reforms, including social security, the rights of organized labor, and a regulatory role for government in the economy. A partnership of government, business, and "responsible" labor leaders, they argued, could lead the country in progressive paths.

Yet Eisenhower Republicans also believed that the New Dealers had pushed America too far in a "socialistic" direction. Their self-assigned mission was to trim the "excesses" of the 1930s while administering New Deal programs and agencies in a conservative fashion. Accordingly, Eisenhower always balanced his concern for the general welfare with calls for governmental and fiscal restraint. Avoid extremes, he advised Republicans, and hew to the center of the road "where the traction is best and where you can bring the most people along with you." To Eisenhower's admirers, his moderation provided a needed respite after the traumas of depression and war. His liberal critics, a small band in the 1950s, charged that his cautious approach to politics muffled fundamental social issues in the bland rhetoric of cooperation and shared interests.

Eisenhower's popularity briefly propelled his party to majority status. The Republicans narrowly won both houses of Congress in 1952, but in the 1954 midterm election, despite general prosperity, the end of the Korean War, and McCarthyite attacks on Democrats' disloyalty, the Democrats regained control of both houses and retained it for the rest of the decade. To Eisenhower, this proved that the GOP must purge its reactionary elements and broaden its base.

In Congress, Ike thus faced not only a core of reactionary Republicans but also a powerful band of Democrats led after 1954 by two wily Texans, House speaker Sam Rayburn and Senate majority leader Lyndon Johnson. The decade's legislation thus emerged from complex three-way negotiation among the White House, various stripes of congressional Republicans, and congressional Democrats.

Several measures reflected the Republican belief that twenty years of Democratic rule had concentrated too much power in Washington, and testified to Eisenhower's suspicions of excessive federal power. In 1953, reversing the policy of the Truman administration, Eisenhower transferred control of offshore oil rights, and the lucrative tax revenues they generated, from the federal government to the states. This change opened the door to private drilling and pleased U.S. oil companies. In 1954 the administration supported a private power company's challenge to the Tennessee Valley Authority, a New Deal showpiece.* Finally, in 1955 the Federal Power Commission rejected congressional calls for a TVA-like public-power project on Idaho's Snake River and instead authorized privately financed hydroelectric dams.

Venting their hostility to FDR and the New Deal, conservative Republicans in Congress killed the Reconstruction Finance Corporation (RFC), a once powerful

---

*Eisenhower later reversed himself on this issue when evidence surfaced of legal improprieties by the private-power interests.

New Deal agency. (Ironically, the RFC actually dated from 1932, when the Republican Herbert Hoover was still president.) They changed the name of Boulder Dam to Hoover Dam and in 1954 nearly passed a constitutional amendment that would have restricted the president's treatymaking powers and subjected presidential "executive agreements" with foreign nations to the same Senate ratification the Constitution required for treaties. The amendment, provoked by Roosevelt's alleged "giveaway" of Eastern Europe to Stalin at Yalta, fell one vote short of the necessary two-thirds majority in the Senate.

In other respects, the Eisenhower administration lived up to its progressive claims. For this purpose, Eisenhower relied on the Democratic leadership in Congress, especially Lyndon Johnson. The wheeling-dealing Texan dominated the Senate, and no important legislation passed without his approval. Most notably, Johnson played a critical role in passage of the Civil Rights Act of 1957 (see pages 154–155). Eisenhower admired Johnson, whom he privately called "the best Democrat of them all," and welcomed his cooperation.

Of course, Johnson never lost sight of his party's interest in building its own liberal record. On housing and school construction bills, for example, the Democrats voted more money than Eisenhower requested. However, except for election time, Johnson, with his House counterpart Sam Rayburn, worked so closely with the White House that more partisan Democrats criticized them. Later, when Johnson as president became indelibly identified with the Vietnam War, his legislative record in the 1950s sank into undeserved obscurity.

This cooperation between the White House and Congress led to the creation of the Department of Health, Education and Welfare; an increase in the minimum wage; and the extension of social security to more than 7 million farmers and other self-employed workers. In 1954, with White House support, Congress approved construction of the Saint Lawrence Seaway, which gave oceangoing freighters access to Great Lakes ports. That year Eisenhower signed a bill that expanded the Truman housing program. This and later measures funded "slum clearance" and "urban renewal" (projects that would later prove controversial) and guaranteed housing loans and low-cost mortgages to Korean War veterans.

Eisenhower's belief that government should promote economic growth helped sustain the prosperity of the 1950s. Federal outlays for housing, highways, and, above all, defense yielded many thousands of jobs. The Saint Lawrence Seaway Project stimulated the economies of the Northeast and the Great Lakes.

The Eisenhower era's most enduring monument, a vast highway program, rivaled the New Deal's public-works projects. The Federal Highway Act (1956) allocated more than $30 billion for a 41,000-mile interstate-highway system. Soon ribbons of concrete and asphalt were slicing through prairies, cornfields, and congested urban districts. The program stimulated the economy and eventually enabled motorists to drive cross-country without encountering a stop sign or traffic light. A key rationale for the interstate system once again illustrated the Cold War's effect on domestic policy: the new highways would provide escape from cities in a nuclear war.

The highway program spawned what historian Kenneth Jackson calls the 1950s "drive-in culture." Motels proliferated, and fast-food franchises mushroomed along the new interstates, offering identical fare to travelers nationwide. In 1954 salesman Ray Kroc bought a locally popular hamburger restaurant from the

McDonald brothers of San Bernardino, California. Soon McDonald's golden arches would rise across America.

The automobile had dominated U.S. transportation policy for decades, and the highway planners ignored mass-transit alternatives. Only later would the downside of the program become apparent: air pollution, a degraded landscape, profligate gasoline consumption, heightened racial and class divisions, the withering of small towns bypassed by the interstates, and—ironically—increased automobile congestion. Countless poor but vibrant city neighborhoods were ripped apart by a tangle of overpasses, concrete pylons, and access ramps. The entire program, concludes historian Tom Lewis in *Divided Highway: Building the Interstate Highways* (1997), reflected not only the nation's technological prowess but also its "impetuousness and shortsightedness."

The interstate program, a gold mine for the construction industry, illustrates how Eisenhower's policies, in this case with bipartisan support, nurtured a probusiness climate in Washington. Ike's cabinet, drawn mainly from the corporate world, revealed this orientation as well. A much-quoted comment by Secretary of Defense Charles E. Wilson summed up the prevalent view. Asked about possible conflict of interest between his public duties and his former role as head of GM, Wilson replied, "I have always assumed that what was good for the United States was good for General Motors, and vice versa."

Meanwhile, Senator Joseph McCarthy, bored by such mundane topics as housing or highways, continued to exploit the national obsession with communism. Even Eisenhower was blind to the Red danger, McCarthy hinted. In 1953 McCarthy warned of communist infiltration of the U.S. Army, focusing on an obscure left-wing army dentist. During the so called Army McCarthy hearings, televised live in 1954, a riveted nation watched as McCarthy badgered witnesses, including a rather timid secretary of the army.

As in the Truman era, McCarthy and other witch-hunters continued to ruin reputations and trample constitutional rights. Citizens were pressured not only to "confess" their own radical pasts but also to implicate others. Filmmaker Elia Kazan, hauled before the House Un-American Activities Committee, agreed to "name names." In his next movie, *On the Waterfront* (1954), Kazan justified his action by making a hero of a dockworker (Marlon Brando) who informs on the mobsters, including his own brother, who control his union. "I'm glad what I done—you hear me?—glad what I done!" Brando stridently insists. To Kazan's death in 2003 at ninety-four, many in Hollywood never forgave him, while others viewed him as a hero.

McCarthy, a Roman Catholic, won influential Catholic support. The Knights of Columbus, a large Catholic fraternal organization, strongly backed him. New York's Francis Cardinal Spellman asserted: "[McCarthy] is against communism and he . . . is doing something about it. He is making America aware of the dangers."

Under McCarthyite pressure, the State Department in 1953 ordered books or artwork by "Communists, fellow travelers, etc." removed from United States Information Agency libraries abroad. Eisenhower condemned "bookburners," but when asked whether he meant McCarthy, he backed off. Consistently avoiding challenging McCarthy, the president in 1953 even agreed to Senator Taft's demand that McCarthy, in effect, be given a veto over all diplomatic nominations. This concession came after a bruising Senate battle over the White House's nominee as ambassador to

IN PERSPECTIVE

Highways and America's
Car Culture

The Federal Highway Act of 1956 defined the decade. It set off a surge of highway construction that reshaped American life and brought Americans' long love affair with the automobile to its pinnacle of besotted infatuation. In fact, however, transportation issues had loomed large in American history from the beginning. The National Road (1811–38), stretching westward from Maryland to Illinois, was one of the new nation's major public-works projects, linking the coast and the interior. President Jackson's 1830 veto of federal support for a Kentucky road project favored by his political rival Henry Clay enlivened the politics of the era. The *Charles River Bridge Case* (1837), involving two rival bridges in Boston, produced a notable Supreme Court decision defining the rights of publicly chartered corporations.

After 1900, highway-construction issues became interconnected with the automobile. The first automobiles were playthings of the rich, but thanks to Henry Ford and mass production, they soon came within reach of the masses. The automobile's rural cousin the tractor transformed U.S. agriculture, and its big brother the truck revolutionized transportation. Popular culture embraced the automobile. "Come away with me, Lucille, in my merry Oldsmobile," went a pop song of 1906. George F. Babbitt, the conformist hero of Sinclair Lewis's 1922 novel *Babbitt,* idolizes his new car with its array of gadgets. Laurel and Hardy starred in a 1924 comedy about a traffic jam—an experience familiar to many moviegoers.

The first wave of interstate highway construction in the automobile era was a series of two-lane roads stretching westward to the Pacific. Most famous of all was Route 66 linking St. Louis and Los Angeles, featured in John Steinbeck's Depression-era classic *The Grapes of Wrath.* "You'll get your kicks, on Route 66," went a popular song of 1946.

"Futurama," the General Motors exhibit at the 1939 New York World's Fair, previewed America's postwar car culture. Visitors watched mesmerized as a miniature landscape unfolded, crisscrossed by ribbons of limited-access highways with gracefully curving ramps and cloverleafs, carrying thousands of cars smoothly and effortlessly, with no accidents, stop signs, or traffic jams. A brilliant piece of corporate propaganda, "Futurama" helped convince Americans that the future of transportation lay with the automobile, not with light-rail systems or mass transit. This propaganda subtly appealed to something deep in the American soul that cherished freedom and individuality and resisted constraint. Of course, the cars were mass-produced, and the dream highways were crowded with drivers all headed in the same direction, but the illusion of freedom remained. Mass transit was for conformist societies; the car and the open road embodied America.

With the coming of peace in 1945, the nation set about translating "Futurama" from dream to reality. By the 1950s, the magazines and TV commercials were full of alluring ads for Chevrolets, Mercurys, and Plymouths. "See the USA in your Chevrolet," warbled singer Dinah Shore on her TV show. The introduction of new models brought moments of high drama, heightened by Detroit hype. The models usually differed only superficially from their predecessors, but the excitement remained. In 1958 came the Pontiac Bonneville Custom Sport Coupe, with "Tri-Power Engine," three "two-barrel carburetors," and a body design that—like the Russian *Sputnik* launched the year before—seemed poised for space travel.

With the car culture came the postwar wave of interstate highway construction, anticipated in the 1930s by Pennsylvania's "Super Highway," modeled on Adolph Hitler's Autobahn. Drivers loved the new high-speed highways, as did the construction companies that built them and the trucking companies that relied on them. Civil-defense experts emphasized their value for quick evacuation in a nuclear war.

U.S. business embraced the interstate highways as well. Holiday resorts and theme parks catered to car-driving vacationers. Standardized chains of motels (an American coinage, dating from 1925) replaced the spartan, unpredictable tourist cabins of the 1930s. The fast-food chains grew up with the automobile and the new highway systems. A&W Root Beer and White Castle hamburger stands started it all in the 1920s and the 1930s. But it was in the 1950s, the heyday of America's love affair with the automobile, that the fast-food franchises soon to spread around the world— Howard Johnson, McDonald's, Burger King, Kentucky Fried Chicken, and the others— became icons of the American road.

Like most romances, this one eventually cooled. After the 1950s came the second thoughts. Not only did highways eat up thousands of acres of farmland, but their voracious space demands and spaghetti-like interchanges destroyed hundreds of urban neighborhoods—usually the poorest and politically weakest. As the public mood changed, some highway projects were abandoned, leaving interstates dead-ending in cornfields and access ramps soaring off to nowhere. With the 1970s energy crisis, Detroit's gas-guzzlers gave way to smaller, more energy-efficient cars, often Japanese imports. Environmental awareness intensified, and automobile emissions faced strict regulation. Mass transit and electric cars stirred new interest. But if the romance with the automobile had lost its glow, few spoke of divorce. In the car ads, highway projects, and glittery dealer showrooms of the 1950s, the careful observer would have seen the shape of the future.

the Soviet Union, whom McCarthy, typically, found soft on communism. In a diary entry, Eisenhower rationalized his policy of silence: "Nothing will be so effective in combatting [McCarthy] . . . as to ignore him. This he cannot stand."

The McCarthyite taint infected the administration itself. In 1953 Eisenhower revoked the safeguards built into President Truman's internal-security program, making it easier to fire radicals or suspected "security risks." Indeed, both parties played the politics of anticommunism. In 1954, congressional Democrats passed the Communist Control Act. Toughening earlier legislation, this law limited the legal rights of "Communist-infiltrated" organizations and required them to register with the government. All the same, Vice President Nixon that fall accused Democrats of being "blind to the Communist conspiracy."

Fame offered no protection against the spreading paranoia. In 1954 Eisenhower approved the Atomic Energy Commission's decision to cancel the security clearance of physicist J. Robert Oppenheimer. This action, ostensibly based on old charges that Oppenheimer had had communist friends in the 1930s, in reality grew out of his opposition to the H-bomb. "The impossible search for 'absolute security' is incompatible with a free and healthy society," journalist I. F. Stone wrote of the Oppenheimer case. "If this is to be national policy, why should anyone be trusted?"

The miasma of suspicion prevented the vigorous debate over the precise nature of the Soviet threat that might have moderated the rhetorical excesses, and left in place the Cold War oversimplifications that had solidified in the late 1940s and early 1950s. Leading Democrats, terrified of the "soft on communism" label, outdid each other in denouncing the Soviet Union. Even liberal senator Hubert Humphrey endorsed the Communist Control Act. Robert Kennedy, brother of the future Democratic president John F. Kennedy, served on Senator McCarthy's staff.

But the four-year McCarthy show was wearing thin. On TV, the Wisconsin senator came across as a barroom bully. Joseph Welch, a lawyer in the Army-McCarthy hearings, shrewdly heightened this impression. When McCarthy implied that one of Welch's assistants was a communist, Welch burst out, "At long last, Senator, have you no decency?" A damning 1954 TV documentary on McCarthy by CBS newsman Edward R. Murrow hastened the senator's decline while underscoring TV's growing influence.

As an anti-McCarthy slogan put it, key Republican senators concluded that "Joe Must Go." A motion to censure him, introduced by GOP senator Ralph Flanders of Vermont, passed in December 1954 by a 67–22 vote. McCarthy, predictably, accused his foes of communist sympathies, but he was finished. Drinking heavily, he died in 1957.

What of Eisenhower's overall domestic record? Although leery of federal power, he endorsed measures that buttressed and even extended the New Deal reforms. Some of his measures benefited corporate interests, but others, such as the extension of social security, responded to the needs of a broader spectrum of the population. Construction workers prospered thanks to public housing and highway projects. Urban-renewal projects, which often bulldozed run-down but still viable housing to make way for bleak high-rise apartments for low-income residents, would later prove controversial, but at the time were generally viewed as a good idea.

Ike's reputation has evolved over the years. At first, historians echoed 1950s critics such as I. F. Stone, who saw him as an amiable cipher "who enjoys his bridge and his golf, . . . [leaving a] political vacuum in the White House." Accustomed to the military chain of command, he often seemed unsure of himself in the rough-and-tumble political arena. His rambling answers to reporters' questions confirmed skeptics' doubts. At one press conference he observed: "Great Britain has a hard row to hoe to keep its economic head above water." Eisenhower also slowed noticeably during his two terms, partly as a result of a heart attack in 1955 and intestinal surgery in 1956. An aide noted privately in 1958, "He can sprint a few yards, but he tires quickly. . . . [M]omentarily fascinated by individual pieces of the international jigsaw puzzle, he does not seem to be able to see what the [completed] picture would look like."

Eventually, however, a more nuanced picture emerged. Eisenhower's letters and diaries and his associates' memoirs reveal a thoughtful pragmatist who actively, if unobtrusively, pursued his political goals. One historian has described his administration as "the hidden hand presidency." Ike's talent for compromise and staff coordination served him well as both general and president. But he was no bloodless manager. Behind the easy smile lay a temper capable of explosive rages and barracks-room language. And the puzzling verbal gridlock was often deliberate. When his press secretary worried about how he would handle a complex issue in a news conference, Ike responded slyly: "Don't worry, I'll just confuse them."

Eisenhower, nearly mute during McCarthy's rampages, also responded reluctantly and hesitantly to the most profound public issue of the day: racism and civil rights. As we shall see in Chapter 5, the politics of moderation proved ill-adapted to an issue that involved fundamental matters of justice and human dignity.

1953–1956: Nuclear Strategy and Global Containment

Fulfilling a campaign pledge, Eisenhower flew to Korea soon after the election to prod the cease-fire talks. He also dropped hints to China of his readiness to use nuclear weapons in Korea. In July 1953, negotiators signed a cease-fire that restored the line between North and South Korea close to the 38th parallel, where it had stood when hostilities began in 1950.

In shaping its strategic policy, the Eisenhower administration faced a dilemma. The key planning document of the Truman years, NSC-68, had called for a broad military buildup to prepare for everything from local conflict to nuclear war. The resulting expansion, coupled with Korean War costs, nearly quadrupled military spending from 1950 to 1953 and produced a whopping budget deficit.

Eisenhower's belief in limited government and balanced budgets tempered his enthusiasm for military spending. Whereas the armed services called for ever larger defense budgets, the budget balancers—led by Treasury Secretary George Humphrey, the Council of Economic Advisers, and Eisenhower himself—warned that runaway deficits could undermine the United States from within as surely as communist expansion abroad. The deterrent threat of nuclear weapons offered a way to resolve the dilemma. Far cheaper than large armies and a full arsenal of conventional weaponry, nuclear armaments promised, in the blunt phrase of Defense Secretary Wilson, to give America "more bang for the buck." An NSC document approved by Eisenhower in October 1953 declared that in the event of war "the United States will consider nuclear weapons to be as available for use as other munitions." In the future, warned Secretary of State John Foster Dulles in January 1954, U.S. defenses would "depend primarily upon a great capacity to retaliate, instantly, by means and at places of our own choosing." The policy was summed up in the phrase "massive retaliation."

To be effective as a deterrent, the massive-retaliation doctrine had to be believable. Dulles observed in a 1953 NSC meeting, "Somehow or other we must . . . remove the taboo from the use of these [nuclear] weapons." To increase the credibility of its threat, the United States stepped up construction of hydrogen bombs and planes capable of delivering them. By 1956, SAC possessed an armada of 1,400 such aircraft. The Soviets, in contrast, had no more than 150 strategic bombers.

The air force invested heavily in computer technology to enhance its nuclear-age capabilities. In 1954, researchers at the Massachusetts Institute of Technology working under military contract began development of a computerized air defense and war-fighting system, called SAGE (Semi-Automatic Ground Environment). Operational by 1958 and fully deployed by 1963, SAGE involved giant IBM computers, an elaborate infrastructure, and the largest computer programs written up to that time. Computer science, destined to play so important a role in American life, got a major boost from 1950s' military planning.

This so-called New Look defense policy (a term borrowed from the fashion world), coupled with the end of the Korean War, enabled Eisenhower to slash defense spending by some 20 percent by 1955 and to produce a budget surplus in 1956. The cuts were imposed selectively, however; while army appropriations fell, the air-force budget soared.

While ethicists and religious leaders attacked massive-retaliation doctrine on moral grounds, analysts at think tanks such as California's RAND Corporation charged that it lacked credibility. Was the United States really prepared to obliterate Moscow or Vladivostok in response to a localized Soviet move anywhere in the world? Furthermore, the strategy assumed decisive U.S. nuclear superiority, but Moscow was balancing the scales. The Soviets tested a hydrogen device in 1953, and air shows in Moscow in 1954 and 1955 featured overflights by strategic bombers capable of delivering nuclear bombs to North America. (The Soviets apparently flew the same ten planes repeatedly over Red Square, awing U.S. observers.) In Eisenhower's second term, as we shall see in Chapter 6, the nuclear balance of terror would grow more precarious still.

The Eisenhower administration's public pronouncements continued to focus on the ideological sources of Soviet behavior and the apocalyptic nature of the Cold War conflict. As Eisenhower warned in his first inaugural address, "Forces of good and evil are massed and armed and opposed as rarely before in history." Indeed, under Eisenhower and especially Secretary of State Dulles, U.S. Cold War policy, while essentially continuous with that of the Truman years, became even more ideologically charged. A devout Presbyterian and Wall Street lawyer, Dulles brought to diplomacy a rigid moralism; a starkly black-and-white view of the "vast, monolithic system" of "world communism"; and a passion for encircling the Soviet Union with a network of treaties and military alliances. By 1960, the United States was treaty-bound to defend no fewer than forty-three different nations against "communist aggression." The secretary of state delivered sanctimonious harangues that even his supporters found tedious. "Dull, duller, Dulles," went one Washington joke. Even Eisenhower occasionally lost patience, calling Dulles in a 1958 diary entry "a sort of international prosecuting attorney."

A shrewd negotiator behind closed doors, Dulles also had a penchant for scary public rhetoric. In 1956 he boasted of his readiness to go to "the brink of war" to defeat communism. Rejecting George Kennan's containment doctrine, he insisted that the United States must aggressively roll back communism on all fronts. To this end, he asserted America's readiness to help Eastern Europeans throw off Soviet rule. "You can count on us," he assured them in 1953 on a Radio Free Europe broadcast.

In practice, U.S. policy toward Eastern Europe proved cautious. When Soviet and East German troops in 1953 put down uprisings in East Berlin and elsewhere in East Germany, the United States did nothing. Similarly, when Russian tanks crushed an anti-Soviet revolt in Hungary in 1956, the United States verbally supported the insurgents but did not intervene. Dulles's rhetoric gradually grew more muted, particularly with reference to Eastern Europe, where the nuclear stalemate and Soviet conventional military might limited U.S. options. After the Hungarian incident, President Eisenhower explicitly disavowed any interest in stirring rebellion in Russia's European satellites.

The death of Joseph Stalin in 1953 and the rise of Nikita Khrushchev to power in Moscow further moderated U.S. posturing. Khrushchev was no democrat, but neither was he another Stalin. He softened some brutal features of Stalinist rule and in 1956, at a Communist Party congress, emotionally denounced the "crimes of the Stalin era." These changes encouraged a more temperate U.S. stance.

Eisenhower even saw merit in a Big Power *summit*—a term coined by Winston Churchill in 1953—despite Dulles's doubts. In 1955 he and Khrushchev, with their British and French counterparts, met in Geneva for the first top-level conference of the wartime allies since 1945. Such issues as European disarmament and German reunification remained unsettled, and Khrushchev rejected Eisenhower's proposal that the two sides permit aerial surveillance of each other's territories. (When the Soviets spurned this idea, Eisenhower authorized a CIA plan for high-altitude photographic spying on the Soviet Union, a decision that would return to plague him.) But the nebulous "Spirit of Geneva" did suggest an easing of Cold War tensions. Ignoring advice by Dulles that he maintain an "austere countenance" in all photographs taken at Geneva, Ike repeatedly flashed his famous grin. In 1956 the Soviets contributed to the thaw by proclaiming a policy of "peaceful coexistence" with the capitalist world.

Although the power balance in Europe somewhat stabilized, a series of regional conflicts kept Cold War antagonisms raw. These situations had complex origins, but Washington viewed them as aspects of the U.S.-Soviet struggle. This tendency is evident, for example, in U.S. policy toward the oil-rich Middle East. The formation of the new nation of Israel with U.S. backing in 1948 had produced a tide of Palestinian refugees and angered Arab countries opposed to a Jewish state. Vowing destruction, the Arab countries launched a war against the fledgling nation.

The Eisenhower administration, like its predecessor, backed Israel diplomatically and economically, in part as a bastion against Soviet penetration in the Middle East. At the same time, Washington worked to weld the divided Arab nations into an anticommunist alliance. In 1955, pursuing his strategy of encircling the Soviet Union with military treaties, Dulles stage-managed the Baghdad Pact, a mutual-defense treaty linking Turkey, Pakistan, Iran, and Iraq. Although Washington did not officially join the pact (to avoid antagonizing Iraq's rival Egypt), it cooperated with the members on security matters. Furious over U.S.-Iraqi military cooperation, Egyptian leader Gamal Abdel Nasser late in 1955 allied with Moscow and stockpiled Soviet arms for the struggle against Israel. The crisis worsened in 1956, when Dulles, angered by Nasser's actions, abruptly canceled promised U.S. aid for the construction of the Aswan Dam on the Nile, a big Egyptian development project. In retaliation, Nasser nationalized the Anglo-French-owned Suez Canal.

This sparked another war in the Middle East. In October 1956, as Soviet tanks rumbled through Budapest, Israel, France, and Great Britain attacked Egypt. The Israeli army rolled across the Sinai Peninsula, while the British and French bombed Egyptian military targets and seized the canal in a paratroop assault. But the Cold War superpowers quickly squelched this imperialistic venture. The Soviet

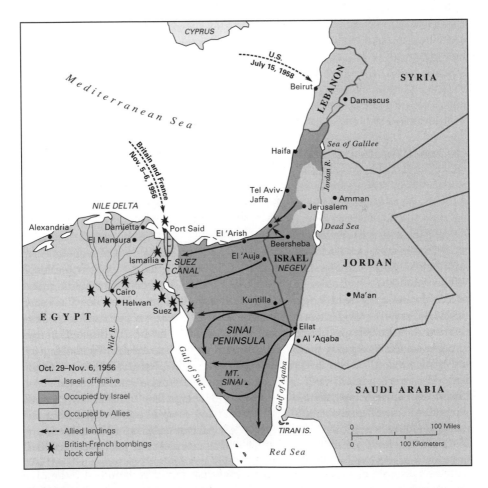

MAP 4.3
The Suez Crisis, 1956

Union threatened to come to Egypt's defense and, borrowing Dulles's "massive retaliation" threat, hinted at nuclear attacks on Paris and London. The Eisenhower administration, unwilling to be sucked into war by its allies and concerned about the flow of oil, opposed the British-French-Israeli action. A cease-fire soon followed, and the invading forces pulled back. The episode led to a rift among the NATO allies, but a larger war had been avoided.

Instead of direct military intervention, the Eisenhower administration more often pursued its goals through alliances, foreign aid, and clandestine action. The CIA under Allen Dulles, brother of the secretary of state, expanded its role beyond intelligence gathering to secret political activities, including the overthrow of foreign governments. Events in Iran and Guatemala illustrate the pattern.

After the Soviets withdrew from Iran in 1946 (see page 41), the British-owned Anglo-Iranian Oil Company controlled the country's vast oil resources. But by 1951 Mohammed Mossadegh, a nationalistic premier given to fits of weeping, dominated Iranian politics. As part of his program, Mossadegh nationalized the Anglo-Iranian Oil Company. When the United States rejected his aid requests, Mossadegh turned to Russia. This galvanized Washington. A 1953 coup, planned, financed, and orchestrated by the CIA, overthrew Mossadegh and gave full power to Iran's monarch, Shah Reza Pahlavi, who until his own overthrow in 1979 would remain a staunch U.S. ally and brutally repress all dissident activity in Iran.

The Iran coup illustrates how anticommunism could mesh with more practical U.S. interests, in this case, the need to preserve the flow of oil. As Eisenhower noted in his diary, the United States had to keep the oil-producing regions "under the control of people who are friendly to us . . . [or]suffer the most disastrous and doleful consequences."

A similar mix of anticommunism and hard-nosed economic calculations shaped U.S. policy toward Guatemala, a nation dominated by the United Fruit Company, a U.S. corporation with close links to the administration. John Foster Dulles's former law firm represented United Fruit, the assistant secretary of state for Latin American affairs owned a large block of stock in the company, and the husband of Eisenhower's personal secretary headed the firm's public-relations department. In the early 1950s, United Fruit was less concerned with bananas and avocados than with Guatemala's leftist president, Jacob Arbenz Guzmán. Promoting land reform in a country where 2 percent of the people owned 70 percent of the land, Arbenz appropriated more than two hundred thousand undeveloped acres held by United Fruit, at a price that the corporation considered unfair.

When a small shipment of arms from Czechoslovakia reached Guatemala in May 1954, John Foster Dulles warned that the country could become an outpost of communist power. The Senate, by a 69–1 vote, denounced "Soviet interference" in Guatemala. The CIA, meanwhile, working with United Fruit, organized an anti-Arbenz coup. In June, the conspirators overthrew Arbenz and installed a military regime headed by the CIA's handpicked man, Carlos Castillo Armas, who restored the appropriated lands to United Fruit and abandoned efforts to tax the corporation's profits. "Tell me what to do, and I will do it," Armas told Vice President Nixon. U.S. aid poured into Guatemala, and in 1956 the two nations signed a military pact. In the judgment of historian Stephen Streeter, the CIA-led coup "bequeathed to Guatemala human tragedy, economic dependence, and political disorder."

In 1956, when the Senate rejected a proposal to tighten oversight of the CIA, Senator Richard Russell of Georgia declared, "If there is one agency of the Government in which we must take some matters on faith without a constant examination of its methods and sources . . . [it] is the Central Intelligence Agency." This see-no-evil, hear-no-evil attitude would haunt the nation in future years.

The CIA, with the State Department and other agencies, also helped fund a U.S. propaganda offensive aimed at discrediting communism, destabilizing the Soviet sphere, and (as one official put it) "selling the American way of life." The CIA set up clandestine operations in Eastern Europe and secretly funded magazines, student groups, and organizations such as the Congress for Cultural Freedom. Radio Free Europe beamed behind the Iron Curtain.

Along with the covert operations, the government sold "the American way of life" by more open means as well. The United States Information Agency, set up in 1953, broadcast the Voice of America and operated libraries abroad. Congress in 1954 appropriated $5 million to send U.S. artists and musicians abroad as "cultural ambassadors." The Jose Limon dance troupe toured Latin America. The George Gershwin musical *Porgy and Bess* proved a big hit. The State Department sent black jazz musicians abroad (some called them "jambassadors") to counter charges of U.S. racism—although, as historian Penny Von Eschen has noted, some candidly criticized conditions back home. A lavish U.S. exhibit at the 1958 Brussels world fair showed off American arts, architecture, popular culture, and consumer goods. (A part of the exhibit called "Unfinished Work" gingerly hinted at racial discrimination and other social problems.) In 1959 the Soviets even permitted an exhibit of American consumer products in Moscow. Stalin had once jeered that "America's primary weapons . . . are stockings, cigarettes, and other merchandise," but in fact the lure of U.S. consumer goods and popular culture proved a potent weapon in the cultural Cold War.

The strident Cold War propaganda campaign continued to affect home-front culture as well, not only heightening fears of subversion, but also encouraging a heavy emphasis on patriotism. Veterans' groups sponsored "rededication weeks" when schoolchildren avowed their love of country. *Reader's Digest* and other magazines luridly warned of the communist menace and called for patriotic affirmation and ideological unity against the alien foe.

Deepening Entanglements in Asia

The Cold War unfolded in a world also torn by resistance to European colonialism. The resulting complexities and ambiguities emerged starkly in Vietnam, where the Vietnamese Communist Party under Ho Chi Minh led the fight against the French colonial power and its puppet government in Saigon. The United States, facing a choice between anticommunism and anticolonialism, supported the colonial power against nationalists who were also communists. By 1954 Washington was paying 80 percent of the cost of France's war against the Vietminh, the military arm of the Vietnamese Communist Party.

Early in 1954, when the Vietminh besieged a large French garrison at Dienbienphu in northern Vietnam, the French urgently requested U.S. military intervention. In Washington, the chairman of the Joint Chiefs of Staff proposed an air strike by sixty B-29s, including the dropping of three atomic bombs. Eisenhower wisely vetoed this operation, however, and the French garrison surrendered.

That July, the French and the Vietminh signed an armistice in Geneva that temporarily divided Vietnam at the 17th parallel, gave Ho Chi Minh control of the north, and called for Vietnam-wide elections in 1956. Ho's negotiators left Geneva confident that all of Vietnam would soon be theirs. The United States, however, did not sign this agreement. In fact, Washington had already decided on a major effort to foil Ho Chi Minh's plans. Drawing an analogy to a row of dominoes, Eisenhower argued that if Vietnam fell to communism, the rest of Southeast Asia would inevitably follow.

The administration realized, as Eisenhower conceded in his memoirs, that the popular Ho Chi Minh would win a free election. Seeking an alternative leader, Washington pushed aside France's puppet emperor and replaced him with Ngo Dinh Diem, a Vietnamese nationalist and devout Roman Catholic. Senator John Kennedy, Francis Cardinal Spellman, and the CIA's top agent in Vietnam all voiced confidence that Diem could rally Vietnam against communism. U.S. aid flowed to South Vietnam, and U.S. military advisers arrived in February 1955. Energetic, idealistic Americans would surely succeed where the French had failed!

Meanwhile, Dulles in 1954 set up yet another military alliance, the Southeast Asia Treaty Organization (SEATO). Under this agreement, the United States pledged to defend Australia, New Zealand, Thailand, Pakistan, and the Philippines against communist aggression. The treaty also extended U.S. military protection to Vietnam, Laos, and Cambodia, thus providing a legalistic basis for U.S. intervention in Vietnam.

Elsewhere in Asia, relations with the People's Republic of China (PRC) remained frigid. When China's foreign minister, Zhou Enlai (Chou En-lai), offered to shake hands with John Foster Dulles at the 1954 Geneva Conference, Dulles rebuffed him. Washington continued to recognize the nationalist regime of Jiang Jieshi on Taiwan as China's legitimate government. Eisenhower in 1953 ordered the U.S. 7th fleet out of the straits of Taiwan, supposedly unleashing Jiang to renew the war against the PRC. Privately Eisenhower and Dulles hoped for an eventual Sino-Soviet split and considered strategies for promoting such a break. But in the face of a powerful pro-Jiang "China Lobby" in Congress and the press, including the magazine publisher Henry Luce, Eisenhower publicly remained unbendingly hostile toward Beijing.

In late 1954, when the PRC began shelling two nationalist-held islands off China's coast, Washington signed a vaguely worded treaty with Jiang pledging to resist any PRC attack on Taiwan and at least some of the disputed islands. Both houses of Congress passed resolutions authorizing Eisenhower to defend Taiwan and certain disputed islands by any means necessary. For a time, war between the United States and China—perhaps even the nuclear "massive retaliation" invoked by Dulles—over a few tiny islands seemed possible. In a 1955 memo to Eisenhower, Dulles saw "at least an even chance that the United States will have to go to war." When the PRC made conciliatory gestures, announcing its shelling schedule in advance, for example, the crisis eased. But the deep freeze in U.S.-Chinese relations continued.

Overall, Eisenhower's first-term foreign-policy record was mixed. He ended the Korean War and showed restraint in the Suez crisis; additionally, U.S.-Soviet relations improved somewhat. Yet his public inflexibility toward China set a pattern that would continue for two decades, and fateful decisions he made in 1954 laid the groundwork for the Vietnam War. Guided by the image of a globe divided between good and evil that Eisenhower evoked in his first inaugural address, his administration lavished attention on issues that fit its Cold War mindset but largely ignored the upsurge of nationalism as well as the poverty, illiteracy, disease, and overpopulation that plagued much of the world, planting the seeds of future problems.

Moreover, although Eisenhower's New Look defense policy held down military spending, it accelerated the nuclear arms race and increased the risk of a full-scale nuclear response in a variety of Cold War confrontations. These years also saw the expansion of the CIA, with its far-flung clandestine operations. Thus, despite Eisenhower's loathing of statism, the Cold War's home-front ramifications included a significant extension of government power.

The weakening of Congress's role as a check on the executive branch under Cold War pressures emerged not only in its failure to monitor the CIA but also in a readiness to approve almost any action that could be linked to the struggle against communism. The 1955 resolution giving Eisenhower a free military hand against the Chinese in the offshore-islands dispute, strongly supported by Senator Lyndon Johnson, uncannily anticipated the 1964 Gulf of Tonkin resolution (see page 266) that would give Johnson as president a virtual blank check in Vietnam.

The Eisenhower-Dulles team infused Truman's anti-Soviet policy with a quasi-religious fervor and extended it globally. Yet Eisenhower at crucial junctures refrained from the military or even nuclear response that some urged. This restraint averted open hostilities. In Eisenhower's second term, however, a series of crises (discussed in Chapter 6) would wither the hopeful spirit of the mid-fifties and further fuel the Cold War.

Presidents also shape the larger national discourse on issues of war and peace, and here, too, Eisenhower compiled a mixed record. Following the logic of the massive-retaliation deterrence strategy, he occasionally spoke of city-destroying nuclear bombs as simply another weapon. Asked in 1955 whether he would use atomic bombs in a potential war with China, he replied, "I see no reason why they shouldn't be used just exactly as you would use a bullet or anything." While such comments were intended to make the deterrent threat more credible, they left America's allies and even officials of Eisenhower's administration, not to mention millions of ordinary people worldwide, deeply fearful of America's nuclear intentions at times of crisis.

On the other hand, Eisenhower understood war's human toll and the social cost of military spending. A career soldier, he had been reared in a small Mennonite-related pacifist church, the Brethren in Christ, whose values remained close to him. For the cost of one modern bomber, he noted in a 1953 speech, the nation could build thirty schools or two hospitals. "Every gun made, every warship that is launched, every rocket fired," he asserted, "signifies . . . a theft from those who hunger and are not fed, those who are cold and are not clothed."

In his 1960 farewell address he deplored the wastefulness of the arms race and warned of the growing influence, "economic, political, and even spiritual," of the nation's "military-industrial complex." This phrase referred to the vast sector of the U.S. economy, including defense industries, labor unions, think tanks, and university-based research programs, that relied heavily on Pentagon contracts. To be sure, Eisenhower presided over a major nuclear buildup, unsavory CIA operations, and the burgeoning military-industrial complex he so deplored. Still, the irony remains: This war leader and Cold War president left as his best-remembered legacy somber warnings of an increasingly militarized American society.

The Economic Boom Rolls On

As the administration pursued the Cold War, the economic boom continued. President Eisenhower saw a close link between these two realities. "[A] prosperous and happy America," he believed, demonstrated the superiority of the free-enterprise system over Russia's state-run economy. The thriving economy provided an upbeat accompaniment to 1950s politics and culture. In *People of Plenty* (1954), historian David Potter even argued that America's material well-being explained much of U.S. history and "the American character." Economist Walt Rostow's *The Stages of Economic Growth* (1960) contended that the United States had reached the ultimate stage: "high mass consumption." With 75 percent of adult Americans owning automobiles and 87 percent of households boasting TV sets, Rostow's analysis seemed justified.

Not all was rosy. Mild recessions slowed growth in 1953–54 (owing in part to defense-spending cuts after the Korean War), 1957–58, and 1960–61. In the 1957–58 slowdown, triggered by plant overexpansion and a drop in exports, unemployment rose to 7.5 percent. Wrote one Democratic wag, "Eisenhower is my shepherd, I am in want. He leadeth me through still factories. He restoreth my doubt in the Republican Party." Ike's popularity fell below 60 percent for the first and only time, and the Democrats won big in the 1958 midterm elections.

And poverty persisted, particularly among older citizens, inner-city blacks, small farmers, displaced New England millworkers, female-headed households, rural southerners both white and black, and the nation's growing Hispanic population. A 1957 study found that nearly one in four American were living below the government's poverty line. And while overall wealth increased, its distribution remained very uneven. In 1950 the bottom one-fifth of American families received only 4 percent of the total national income, whereas the top fifth garnered 43 percent. Ten years later, these figures remained practically unchanged.

But despite recessions, large sectors of poverty, and uneven income distribution, prosperity in the 1950s was real and widespread. Encouraged by federal spending and growth-promoting measures, the GNP increased 25 percent from 1953 to 1961. Stock prices in 1954 at last regained their pre-1929 level. General Motors's 1955 profit exceeded $1 billion, a first for a U.S. corporation. Joblessness in the 1950s averaged a modest 4.6 percent, and when Ike left office, a record 73 million Americans held jobs, up from 66.5 million eight years earlier. Per-capita income, in constant dollars, grew by about 10 percent from 1952 to 1960. By 1960, on the basis of income levels, demographers defined 60 percent of Americans as "middle class." And unlike other boom times, income kept pace with prices: Inflation averaged only 1.5 percent annually in the 1950s. Catering to a newly affluent clientele seeking leisure-time diversion, Walt Disney opened a Disneyland theme park in Anaheim, California, in 1955. An instant success, it eventually spawned an even larger version in Florida, Walt Disney World.

Home construction boomed as Americans snapped up suburban tract houses. Many such buyers, new to the middle class, spent freely on household goods, from bedroom sets, dishwashers, and freezers to power mowers and lawn furniture. The rising birthrate stimulated sales of products for infants and children, as well as school construction. Suburban families needed transportation, and auto sales soared. Car models changed yearly amid great hoopla, and two-car households became common. To entice buyers, the typical 1950s auto flashed some 180 separate pieces of chrome or stainless steel "brightwork."

New products, from ballpoint pens to electric knives, poured into the marketplace. The postwar vogue for plastic continued. The number of TV sets zoomed from 1 million in 1950 to 50 million in 1960. Trix, the world's first multicolored breakfast cereal, made its debut. Westinghouse introduced all-color refrigerators in 1956. Chemical companies offered a rainbow of synthetic fabrics with such futuristic names as Orlon, Dacron, and Acrilan.

Advertising, a $12-billion-a-year industry by 1960, fueled the boom. TV screens and the pages of *Life, Collier's,* and the *Saturday Evening Post* glittered with

Nixon Visits the Magic Kingdom. Vice President Richard Nixon with his family at the grand opening of Disneyland in Anaheim, California, 1955. *(AP/Wide World Photos)*

ads. "Home Means More with a Carpet on the Floor," proclaimed the Carpet Institute. "Be Happy, Go Lucky," chirped the makers of Lucky Strike cigarettes. "I Dreamed I Went Shopping in My Maidenform Bra" launched a series of fantasy ads in which women cavorted in public in their brassieres.

The first credit card, Diner's Club, debuted in 1950; American Express cards soon followed. When Sears, Roebuck offered its credit card, 10 million customers signed up. Signaling a long-term trend, aggregate consumer debt neared $200 billion by 1960.

The glorification of American business, rooted in the war years, continued in the 1950s. "The . . . chemical industry has transformed American life," gushed *Life* in 1953. "It has scrubbed the modern world with detergents, doctored it with synthetic drugs, dressed it in synthetic textiles, cushioned it with synthetic rubber and adorned it from head to toe with gaudy plastic." What the media trumpeted, scholars echoed. Economist John Kenneth Galbraith, in titling his 1958 book *The Affluent Society,* also named the era. Although critical of the way Americans expended their abundance, Galbraith did not question its reality. For him, as for many other social scientists in the 1950s, poverty scarcely existed. The typical American, Galbraith wrote, enjoyed a level of material well-being "in which not even the rich rejoiced a century ago."

America's global economic situation looked bright as well. U.S. exports—mainly machinery, cars and trucks, grain, metals, and manufactured goods—nearly doubled during the decade, reaching just under $20 billion by 1960. Imports rose also, but most of what Americans bought still bore the "Made in the USA" label. In contrast to the massive trade deficits of future decades, the United States enjoyed a trade surplus of nearly $5 billion in 1960.

The rise of the multinational corporations accelerated in the 1950s, as U.S. companies built plants and distribution centers near their foreign markets. As early as 1951, twenty-three General Motors factories in seven foreign countries were producing 176,000 vehicles annually. By 1960 the value of such corporate investment abroad stood at nearly three times the 1950 level. This trend, actively encouraged by various federal agencies, meshed neatly with Cold War ideology. As U.S. corporations brought jobs and consumer goods to a waiting world, government leaders calculated, the lure of communism would surely evaporate.

The globalization of American capital emerged with particular clarity in the Middle East, as the postwar boom floated on a tide of oil. The United States in 1953 for the first time imported more oil than it exported. As access to Middle Eastern petroleum fields grew more vital, U.S. companies muscled aside the British firms that dominated the region. In 1950 a consortium of U.S. oil companies built a thousand-mile pipeline from Saudi Arabia to Lebanon, from which tankers shipped oil to European refineries. These developments required vast investments in the Middle East and in European production and distribution facilities. By 1960, thanks to favorable U.S. tax laws and other government policies, five of the world's seven largest oil companies (quaintly nicknamed the Seven Sisters) were American owned. Ironically, the centralized structure of oil production and distribution developed by U.S. and other Western oil companies in the 1950s would be imitated by the oil-producing nations themselves when they set up their own cartel, the Organization of Petroleum Exporting Countries (OPEC), in 1960.

Along with an abundance of consumer goods, the postwar economy was also characterized by deeper structural changes. Business consolidation, a long-term trend, continued. In 1960 the top 5 percent of U.S. corporations earned nearly 90 percent of all corporate income. The ranks of the self-employed dwindled from 26 percent of the work force in 1940 to 11 percent in 1960. With fewer individual entrepreneurs and small businesses, the American economy increasingly featured giant conglomerates that controlled an ever-larger share of the market.

Other economic changes hinted at trouble ahead. For example, although Detroit still dominated U.S. auto sales, the popularity of the cheap and fuel-efficient German-made Volkswagen, nicknamed the "Bug" or the "Beetle" for its rounded body, foretold the day when car buyers would increasingly turn to foreign imports. In another portentous shift, the number of industrial workers dropped from 39 to 36 percent of the labor force in the fifties, while the ranks of professional and service workers crept up from 40 to 46 percent. GM alone employed about one hundred thousand salaried white-collar workers by the mid-1950s. Efficiencies made possible by automation and the increasing use of computers by large corporations account for part of this shift, but it was a troubling omen nevertheless. With only 6 percent of the world's population, the United States in the 1950s produced about half the globe's manufactured goods, yet the trend of labor statistics suggested that this dominance might not last. The long decline in the farm population continued as well, as mechanization and the rise of agribusinesses rendered the family farm an endangered species.

The growth of the "professional and service workers" census category attracted the notice of social observers. As early as 1951, in his study *White Collar,* sociologist C. Wright Mills speculated about the social effects of the rise of a new class that shuffled paper rather than tilled the soil or ran machines. A society shaped by the farm, frontier, and factory, wrote Mills, was evolving into "a great salesroom, an enormous file, an incorporated brain, a new universe of management and manipulation." People reared on the ideology of free enterprise and individual opportunity, Mills gloomily speculated, faced monotonous working lives molded by the demands of impersonal corporate, institutional, or governmental bureaucracies.

Even the decade's feats of productivity and consumption look different from a later perspective. To a generation worried about the environment and dwindling resources, the soaring statistics on energy use and raw-materials consumption cited so pridefully at the time suggest a heedless disregard for the future. When *Life* in the 1950s gloated over the groaning shelves of U.S. supermarkets or photographed a family posed with mountains of goods representing the typical middle-class family's annual consumption, it all seemed wonderfully reassuring. In retrospect, these images evoke a society wallowing in abundance, oblivious to the earth's finite resources, the ecological costs of unchecked consumption, and the chasm separating the world's rich and poor societies.

The prosperity and expansive mood of the 1950s, combined with rapid growth in the West, underlay the emergence of Las Vegas as a gambling and pleasure resort. A dusty Nevada railroad town in 1940, Las Vegas prospered in World War II, thanks to nearby Nellis Air Force Base. The gangster Meyer Lansky saw the possibilities, and assigned Benjamin "Bugsy" Siegel to build a fancy casino in Vegas. Siegel erected the Flamingo, and Hollywood stars turned out for the grand opening on New Year's Eve 1946. (Disputes broke out, and Siegel was gunned down in 1947.) As more casinos sprang up, visitors arrived by plane and eventually via Interstate 15 from southern California to gamble and enjoy the entertainment. Emulating Paris, the Dunes casino first featured topless show-girls in 1957. Meyer Lansky's vision proved prophetic. By the 1990s Las Vegas was awash in spectacular resort hotels; Atlantic City had copied its garish grandeur; twenty-four states had licensed casinos or lotteries; and Indian-run casinos were proliferating.

A few observers criticized the decade's materialism and consumerist binge on aesthetic grounds—one journalist complained that "the loudest sound in the land has been the oink-and-grunt of private hoggishness"—but praise for capitalism more typically replaced the criticism of the 1930s. Columbia University professor Adolph A. Berle, who in the 1930s had warned against corporate power, now exulted that the U.S. economy had "left every other system in recorded history far behind" as a mechanism for bringing material goods and leisure-time pleasure to the masses. *Life* summed up the prevailing mood by quoting a steelworker: "In the 1930s I worried about how I could eat. Now I'm worrying about where to park." Such cheery assessments resonated powerfully with the millions for whom the 1950s brought unprecedented prosperity.

The determinedly upbeat tone of this economic and social commentary was clearly linked to Cold War fears and anxieties about subversion. With Americans longing to enjoy the good life that the marketers promised, the menace of communism seemed especially intolerable. The conviction that America, having survived depression and war, at last stood on the threshold of a millennium of material abundance reinforced the prevalent Cold War image of a people threatened by evil forces bent on destroying all they held dear.

The prosperity of the fifties also forms the background of the cultural and social conflicts explored in Chapter 5. As millions of middle-class or would-be middle-class citizens pursued their versions of the American dream, they resented those who questioned that dream. To upwardly mobile white citizens, cultural critics, youthful rebels, and civil-rights protesters seemed unwelcome naysayers amid the abundance and optimism suffusing the decade's burgeoning consumer culture.

Suburban Living and Family Togetherness

As in the movie *Strategic Air Command,* the family loomed large in 1950s American culture. Postwar America longed for stability and traditional values, and no institution better embodied these virtues than the nuclear family. The focus on the family was rooted in the statistics recording marriage and birthrates. As the Depression-ridden 1930s and the disrupted 1940s faded, young people rushed to the altar. The median age at first marriage for both men and women dropped nearly a full year between 1947 and 1957, and these young couples produced children in record numbers. The upturn in the birthrate that began during World War II accelerated in the 1950s. After hovering at around eighteen per thousand during the 1930s, the birthrate stood at more than twenty-five per thousand through most of the 1950s, a spurt of nearly 40 percent. This legendary "baby boom" generation would profoundly influence U.S. history. As children in the 1950s, they fueled the economic boom. In the 1960s, many rallied and marched to protest racism and the Vietnam War. In the seventies and eighties, many would become Yuppies—affluent young urban professionals. In the 1990s and beyond, baby boomers would snap up books about menopause and experiment with Viagra, the pill to enhance male sexual function. As the twenty-first century wears on, the toddlers of 1955 will swamp the nation's health-care facilities and retirement homes and (some economists warn) bankrupt the social-security system.

As marriage and birthrates soared, suburban growth exploded. Of course, throughout history, people have left cities to settle on the outskirts. A cuneiform letter written in 539 B.C. boasted, "Our property . . . is so close to Babylon that we enjoy all the advantages of the city, and yet when we come home we are away from all the noise and dust." But suburban growth, a U.S. social trend throughout the early twentieth century, proceeded at an especially sizzling pace in the 1950s. Aided in many cases by low-cost government loans for veterans, young couples and many older families flocked to the single-family housing developments that sprang up around America's cities. From 1950 to 1960, the suburban population surged from 21 million to 37 million. As whites abandoned the cities, low-income or discriminatory real-estate policies forced most blacks and Hispanics to remain behind, a development that exacerbated racial and ethnic tensions.

The explosive growth of suburbia also laid the groundwork for future environmental problems, as historian Adam Rome documents in *The Bulldozer in the Countryside* (2001). Developers converted vast tracts of open land to mass housing, disrupting the ecology of entire regions. Water demands and septic tanks further stressed the environment; household appliances and air conditioners consumed massive amounts of electricity. But with energy prices at an all-time low, these problems remained latent, only to surface when inner-city riots erupted in the 1960s and a full-scale environmental movement arose in the 1970s.

The suburban developers used techniques pioneered by Abraham Levitt and Sons, who in the late 1940s had transformed Long Island potato farms into Levittown, a community of seventeen thousand houses. Similar projects followed in Pennsylvania and New Jersey. The Levitts standardized every stage of the process, from laying out streets and hooking up utilities to pouring concrete-slab foundations and erecting as many as thirty houses a day from components assembled elsewhere. Thanks to mass-production wizardry and nonunion labor, the Levitts sold their standard two-bedroom house for less than $8,000. Not all suburban houses were that cheap, but easy credit made these dwellings accessible to millions. The year 1955 alone saw 1.65 million new housing starts. Farmland and rolling hills on the outskirts of the nation's cities sprouted rows of tract houses. If the gaunt-eyed sharecropper was the iconic visual image of the 1930s, the suburban housing development became the central symbol of the 1950s.

The more capacious of the new suburban residences were called "ranch houses," but despite the evocation of the Old West, the design, as historian Clifford Clark has pointed out, originated in postwar California, the fastest-growing state in these years. "Picture windows" showcased the possessions within and opened the family to neigh-

Welcome to Suburbia! Hundreds of would-be buyers turned out in 1951 to view the model homes planned for Levittown in Bucks County, Pennsylvania. By 1958, this development boasted more than 17,000 nearly identical houses. *(Temple University Libraries, Urban Archives, Philadelphia, Pennsylvania)*

bors' scrutiny. The layout expressed the occupants' aspirations, with not one but two bathrooms, the second attached to the "master bedroom," and two-car garages sheltering what one writer called the "insolent chariots" that were another icon of the decade. Family togetherness found expression in designs that combined kitchen, dining room, and living room into one large space, plunging occupants and visitors alike into a swirl of family activity. In larger houses, a separate "family room" provided space for TV, pool table, board games, and other leisure pursuits.

As we shall see, critics deplored the suburbs for their alleged conformity and cultural aridity. The naysayers often overstated their case, but the new suburban communities were quite homogeneous economically, racially, and demographically. The Levittowners' newsletter noted: "Our lives are held closely together because most of us are within the same age bracket, in similar income groups, live in almost identical houses, and have common problems." Cut off from the extended families and social networks of the small town or the urban immigrant enclave, the new suburbanites turned for emotional support to the nuclear family and sometimes to their new neighbors, uprooted like themselves. The conformity and stifling family togetherness that some observers lamented in the 1950s often stemmed from feelings of isolation and disorientation.

While the critics carped, the suburbs soared. For millions, suburban life was a dream come true. "Houses are for people, not critics," declared Abraham Levitt's son William. "We who produce lots of houses do what is possible—no more—and the people for whom we do it think it's pretty good." When asked, suburbanites denied that they were mindless conformists. Objected one, "We're not peas in a pod. I thought it would be like that, especially because incomes are nearly the same. But it's amazing how different and varied people are."

Suburbia loomed large in the cultural discourse of the fifties. For some, it proved the vitality of the U.S. free-enterprise system; for a vocal minority, it summed up all that they disliked about Eisenhower's America. The truth lay somewhere in between. Suburbia was not utopia, but neither was it the social disaster conjured up by some. The suburbs and their accompanying network of highways unquestionably promoted a degree of homogeneity among the middle class (a category that included many upwardly mobile blue-collar workers) and cut off millions of whites from the poor and minorities of the inner cities. Yet it also provided affordable, safe, and pleasant housing and a crucial boost up the ladder for these same millions. For them, as historian Warren Susman has put it, a house in the suburbs symbolized "the world of new possibilities" in postwar America.

Advertisers zeroed in on the suburban market of young marrieds and their growing families. As *Life* pointed out in 1959, affluent suburban teenagers, possessing camera, sports gear, portable radio, 45-RPM record player, bulging clothes closet, and ample funds for movies, concerts, and drive-in restaurant visits, were "big-time consumer[s]." The ads' images of young parents and excited children hovering worshipfully around the new Chevrolet, Zenith TV set, or Kelvinator refrigerator conveyed a potent unspoken message: Consumption itself gave life meaning. Benjamin Franklin had once urged frugality: "A penny saved is a penny earned." In an era of abundance, advertisers proclaimed, consumption became almost obligatory, and everyone had a right to share the bounty.

Advertisers offered endless variations on a single image: the young, white, middle-class nuclear family in a new suburban house, tending the weed-free lawn, or gliding along in a shiny new car. Blacks, Hispanics, and Asian Americans; manual laborers; urban apartment dwellers; and single-parent or multigenerational families rarely appeared. To people who vaguely fit the image, the ads confirmed their vision of America. Those on the outside also hungered for the good life portrayed in the ads, but they knew firsthand about the diversity, discrimination, and deprivation that the ads ignored.

The movies reinforced this fantasy of the United States as one big suburb. Despite undercurrents of menace, most movies offered upbeat fare. Five of the ten films awarded the best-picture Oscar in the 1950s were lighthearted musicals or escapist epics, including *An American in Paris* (1951), *Around the World in Eighty Days* (1956), and *Ben Hur* (1959). *Bedtime for Bonzo* (1951), featuring Ronald Reagan and Diana Lynn as the long-suffering "parents" of a chimpanzee, typified the 1950s frothy domestic comedy. *Room for One More* (1952), a celebration of domesticity, starred Cary Grant and Betsy Drake as a kindly couple who can't resist adopting children to add to their ever-growing family.

Walt Disney, technologically brilliant and politically conservative, upheld traditional values in his 1950s animated films. In *The Lady and the Tramp* (1956), a mongrel street dog and his dainty pedigreed mate achieve a canine version of suburban do-mesticity. *Sleeping Beauty* (1959), based on the fairy tale of the dreaming young woman awakened by a handsome prince, combined familiar ideas of romantic love and gen-der stereotypes with the promise of upward mobility. Disneyland theme parks, mean-while, offered visitors a mythic version of America as the ideal and untroubled society, past, present, and future, beginning with a nostalgic stroll down "Main Street U.S.A." and ending with the technological utopia of "Tomorrowland U.S.A."

TV producers loved suburbia. Shows like *Ozzie and Harriet, Father Knows Best,* and *Leave It to Beaver* offered an idealized image of middle-class family life and gen-der roles: supportive, apron-clad wives and mothers, benign fathers who material-ize at dinnertime to resolve the day's petty crises, wisecracking kids who get into amusing scrapes but who ultimately recognize their parents' authority. In the im-mensely popular *I Love Lucy* show (1951–57), starring Lucille Ball, Lucy invariably met disaster when she sought a job or pursued interests beyond the home. (She never stopped trying, however, revealing the underlying tension in the cult of do-mesticity.) Her bandleader husband, played by Desi Arnaz, Ball's real-life spouse, treated her like a lovable but irresponsible child. Reality and make-believe blended when the producers incorporated Ball's pregnancy and the birth of her child into the show. (Ball and Arnaz later divorced, off camera.) Only a few shows—such as *Our Miss Brooks,* with Eve Arden as a tart-tongued, unmarried schoolteacher, and *The Honeymooners,* with Jackie Gleason and Audrey Meadows as a childless working-class couple living in a bleak apartment—resisted gender stereotypes or hinted at the world beyond suburbia.

The "America" portrayed in 1950s mass culture masked the full reality: The na-tion was not all white, and few teenagers fit the bland stereotype of the TV sitcoms. The labor force did not consist entirely of white-collar workers, and not all women were happy housewives. Still, the idealized image captured part of fifties social real-ity and affected the way Americans at the time and since perceived the decade.

Suburbs also influenced 1950s religious life. Church membership soared from 64 million in 1940 to 114 million in 1960. Many of the newly devout were doubtless sincere in their faith, but other factors played a part as well. Church membership of-fered a way to overcome isolation and to embrace community norms. Indeed, as churchgoing increased, specific theological belief seemed to fade for some. As a vogue for mergers swept liberal Protestantism, the media celebrated the virtue of "belief" for its own sake, regardless of content. The Advertising Council's "Religion in American Life" series of public-service messages ignored theological details and instead stressed the family closeness and sense of belonging that church attendance provided. One church advertised in 1955, "Lots of acquaintances, not many friends? . . . Meet future friends in church next Sunday."

Religion's social utility emerged in *The Organization Man* (1956), William H. Whyte's study of a white-collar Chicago suburb. Most residents, Whyte found, con-sidered a church's ability to provide a sense of community more important than its creed. "This is the basic need . . . , to belong to to a group," one minister told him; "when young people see how many other people are going to church regularly, they feel they ought to."

Churchgoing also highlighted the contrast between America and the officially atheistic Soviet Union. "Against the force of Communism," *Life* observed, "we still have faith that the force of Christendom, arrayed with the other great religions of the world, will prevail." The staunchly anticommunist Catholic bishop Fulton J. Sheen became a TV celebrity of the 1950s for his show *Life Is Worth Living.* (Accepting an award, Sheen modestly thanked his writers, "Matthew, Mark, Luke, and John.") Reinhold Niebuhr remained influential as he dissected Cold War issues in a series of books and essays. In a slap at the atheistic adversary Soviet Union, Congress added "under God" to the Pledge of Allegiance and "In God We Trust" to the nation's coinage in 1954.

Like much else about the 1950s, the religious reality was complex. Despite the bland suburban "social religion" of mainstream Protestantism, traditional evangelicalism remained strong. "Youth for Christ" rallies continued to draw young people. Billy Graham's fame grew as he spread his evangelical message worldwide through revival crusades, films, books, television, and the *Hour of Decision* radio program. The faith healer Oral Roberts attracted throngs to his evangelistic tent, and Charles E. Fuller's *Old Fashioned Revival Hour,* broadcast from Long Beach, California, reached a vast weekly radio audience. Evangelical and Pentecostal churches such as the Assemblies of God grew rapidly. Membership in Southern Baptist churches increased by 2.7 million in the decade. The National Association of Evangelicals provided an organizational haven for conservative Protestant denominations. Underestimated at the time, evangelicalism would surge to prominence in the 1970s.

Middle-Class Women in 1950s America

Suburban culture and the rites of family togetherness had obvious implications for middle-class women, as 1950s mass media celebrated domesticity. Marketers adapted to the cultural scene. Young wives uncertain of their kitchen skills could rely on prepared cake mixes, Swanson's frozen TV dinners (introduced in 1953), or *Betty Crocker's Picture Cook Book* (1950). Offering the suburban wife a kind of surrogate mother or grandmother, General Mills Corporation gave "Betty Crocker" a makeover in the mid-fifties, graying her hair and endowing her with a more mature look. Another iconic fifties female, Mamie Eisenhower, with her perky bangs, benign if rather vague smile, and matronly "New Look" fashions, hovering charmingly in the background while her husband led the Free World, epitomized one version of the decade's feminine ideal.

A product that directly targeted suburban housewives was Tupperware, a line of sealed plastic food containers invented by Earl Silas Tupper in the 1940s. After 1951, under a self-taught marketing genius named Brownie Wise, Tupperware was sold exclusively through home-based "Tupperware parties." By 1954, sales topped $25 million. For homebound women, Tupperware parties provided social contacts, entrepreneurial experience, and extra income. The annual Tupperware "Jubilees" at the corporate headquarters in Florida, with costume parties and awards of fur coats, new cars, and trips to Europe to top saleswomen, provided excitement and diversion for many suburban housewives. Brownie Wise became in 1954 the first woman to appear on the cover of *Business Week* magazine.

The domestic role for women was endlessly reinforced. In *A Man Called Peter* (1953), Catherine Marshall eulogized her recently deceased husband, the minister Peter Marshall, and regretted the rebelliousness that she had felt in his shadow. Adlai Stevenson, refurbishing an argument mossy with age, advised the 1955 graduates of Smith College, an all-women's school, to embrace "the humble role of housewife" and introduce their busy husbands to the finer things of life. "Keeping your man straight on the difference between Botticelli and Chianti," he suggested, should be challenge enough for any woman.

The same gender stereotypes pervaded the popular culture. In *The French Line* (1954), a feisty, independent Jane Russell is literally carried away in the final scene by a Frenchman with whom she has had a shipboard romance. The 1954 musical *Seven Brides for Seven Brothers* offered a pop-culture version of the Roman myth of the rape of the Sabine women, a tale of forcible abduction and male power. In 1950s ads, women invariably played subordinate roles. Ads for Mr. Clean, a household cleanser, featured a brawny superman performing tough chores for grateful housewives.

Similar sexist assumptions pervaded the business world. In a 1951 study, William H. Whyte found that most corporate executives viewed the ideal wife as one who put her husband's career first; conversed wittily at parties while avoiding controversial topics; soothed and satisfied her man at night; and ran the household efficiently, never distracting her husband with domestic worries. Most business wives accepted this role, Whyte insisted, having concluded that "nurturing the male ego" was "a form of therapy made increasingly necessary by the corporation way of life."

These stereotypes distorted the actual situation of many women. The rise in female employment of the late 1940s continued in the 1950s, and by 1960, some 40 percent of American women held jobs. Even in this heyday of culturally promoted domesticity, millions of these working women were also wives and mothers. By mid-decade, one-quarter of all mothers with young children were wage earners as well.

Largely confined to specific job categories and paid less than men for the same or comparable work, employed women continued to face discrimination. Few held political office, rose to the executive ranks in business, or became doctors, lawyers, or professors. Even a strong-willed and talented woman such as playwright Clare Booth Luce, who served as U.S. ambassador to Italy in the 1950s, owed her influence to her husband, the publisher Henry Luce. African American, Hispanic, and other minority women faced dual discrimination, that of gender and race.

The rise in female employment was not accompanied by an organized women's movement, and social observers downplayed its long-term significance. *Harper's* magazine editor Frederick Lewis Allen, for example, compared "the strident suffragettes" of earlier days with the married working women of the 1950s whose only goal, he claimed, was "the double paycheck that makes it possible to buy a TV set, a car, or in many cases simply to make ends meet." Once these needs were met, Allen implied, women would return to the kitchen, and the natural order would be restored.

Indeed, many housewives professed to find their lives fulfilling. As one told a psychologist in 1955, "[Marriage has given me] my place in life. I feel I am doing exactly as I am fitted—with an occasional spurt of independence growing less all the time." And many women *did* work for practical economic reasons. The cultural climate of the 1950s did not encourage feminist theorizing or challenges to gender stereotypes. But profound changes lay ahead, and the working women of the 1950s laid the groundwork.

Conclusion

Working women represented only one of many groups that did not fit the 1950s picture of America as a prosperous, lily-white suburb populated by happy nuclear families led by hardworking dads and contented, homebody moms. The stereotype never offered more than a blurred approximation of one slice of 1950s social reality, and forces astir in America would soon undermine it further. Nevertheless, it wielded enormous power. As historian Elaine Tyler May argues, this image intersected in complex ways with Cold War ideology. Policymakers' obsession with containing communism abroad paralleled a compulsion to contain threatening social pressures at home with an ideology of domesticity, consumption, and clear gender roles. The conviction that "the American way of life" faced heavy ideological assault from abroad intensified pressures to defend the status quo at home, with suburbia as a key ideological battleground. As homebuilder William Levitt put it, "No man who owns his own house and lot can be a Communist. He has too much to do."

Richard Nixon's famed 1959 "kitchen debate" with Nikita Khrushchev at the U.S. exhibit in Moscow, conducted as the two leaders gazed earnestly at automatic dishwashers and boxes of laundry detergent, epitomized the interconnectedness of global anticommunism and the home-front ideology of domesticity. The essential meaning of America, it seemed, resided in the suburban kitchen and its panoply of appliances and consumer products. One of capitalism's finest achievements, boasted Nixon, was to ease women's domestic labor. Khrushchev, by contrast, insisted that Soviet women were valued as workers, not just as housewives. Ridiculing U.S. kitchen technology, the Soviet leader jeered, "Don't you have a machine that puts food into the mouth and pushes it down?"

Like Nixon in Moscow, many cultural voices insisted in the 1950s that the American social order approached perfection. "Looking ahead 10 years, 25 years, there is nothing to hold us back," exulted *Life* in 1954. But *Life's* crystal ball was clouded. The twenty-five-year time frame that the magazine evoked in 1954 in fact would bring civil-rights struggles, urban riots, bitter protests against an unpopular war, a resurgent women's movement, and deep worries about economic decline and limited resources. Indeed, already in the 1950s powerful currents of anxiety, unease, and protest roiled beneath the deceptively placid surface of American life.

SELECTED READINGS

Politics in the Eisenhower Era

Charles C. Alexander, *Holding the Line: The Eisenhower Era, 1952–1961* (1975); Craig Allen, *Eisenhower and the Mass Media: Peace, Prosperity and Prime-Time TV* (1993); Stephen E. Ambrose, *Eisenhower: The President* (2 vols., 1983–84); Jeff Broadwater, *Eisenhower and the AntiCommunist Crusade* (1992) and *Adlai Stevenson and American Politics* (1994); Blanche Wiesen Cook, *The Declassified Eisenhower: A Divided Legacy* (1981); Fred L. Greenstein, *The Hidden-Hand Presidency: Eisenhower as Leader* (1982); Robert Griffith, "Dwight D. Eisenhower and the Corporate Commonwealth," *American Historical Review* (February 1982); Robert P. Newan, *Owen Lattimore and the "Loss" of China* (1992); Herbert Parmet, *Eisenhower and the American Crusades* (1972); Gary W. Reichard, *Politics as Usual: The Age of Truman and Eisenhower* (1988); David W. Reinhard, *The Republican Right Since 1945* (1983). On McCarthy and the Red Scare, see Chapter 3 bibliography.

Foreign Policy and Nuclear Strategy in the 1950s

James R. Arnold, *The First Domino: Eisenhower, the Military, and America's Intervention in Vietnam* (1991); Scott D. Breckinridge, *The CIA and the Cold War: A Memoir* (1993); Nick Cullather, *Secret History: The CIA's Classified Account of Its Operations in Guatemala, 1952–1954* (1999); Saki Dockrill, *Eisenhower's New Look National Security Policy* (1996); Richard M. Fried, *The Russians Are Coming! The Russians Are Coming! Pageantry and Patriotism in Cold War America* (1998); Norman Graebner, ed., *The National Security: Its Theory and Practice, 1945–1960* (1986); Robert H. Haddow, *Pavilions of Plenty: Exhibiting American Culture Abroad in the 1950s* (1997); George C. Herring, *America's Longest War: The United States and Vietnam* (3rd ed., 1996); Walter L. Hixson, *Parting the Curtain. Propaganda, Culture, and the Cold War, 1945–1961* (1997); Richard H. Immerman, *The CIA in Guatemala: The Foreign Policy of Intervention* (1982) and *John Foster Dulles: Piety, Pragmatism, and Power in U.S. Foreign Policy* (1999); Burton Kaufman, *The Arab Middle East and the United States* (1996); Stephen Kinzer, *All the Shah's Men: An American Coup and the Roots of Middle East Terror* (2003); Richard A. Melanson and David Mayers, eds., *Reevaluating Eisenhower: American Foreign Policy in the 1950s* (1987); Gregory Mitrovich, *Undermining the Kremlin: America's Strategy to Subvert the Soviet Bloc, 1947–1956* (2000); William B. Pickett, *Dwight David Eisenhower and American Power* (1995); Ronald E. Powaski, *March to Armageddon: The United States and the Nuclear Arms Race, 1939 to the Present* (1987); Andrew Rotter, *The Path to Vietnam: Origins of the American Commitment to South East Asia* (1987); Frances Stonor Saunders, *The Cultural Cold War: The CIA and the World of Arts and Letters* (1999); Penny Von Eschen, *Race Against Empire: Black Americans and Anti-Colonialism, 1937–1957* (1997).

Economic and Social Trends in the 1950s

John F. Bauman, *Public Housing, Race, and Renewal: Urban Planning in Philadelphia, 1920–1974* (1987); Clifford E. Clark, Jr., "Ranch-House Suburbia: Ideals and Realities," in Lary May, ed., *Recasting America: Culture and Politics in the Age of the Cold War* (1989); Claudia Dale Goldin, *The Great Compression: The Wage Structure in the United States at Mid-Century* (1991); Delores Hayden, *Redesigning the American Dream* (1984); Thomas Hine, *Populuxe* [1950s popular culture and product design] (1998); Kenneth T. Jackson,

Crabgrass Frontier: The Suburbanization of the United States (1985); Landon Y. Jones, *Great Expectations: America and the Baby Boom Generation* (1980); Tom Lewis, *Divided Highways: Building the Interstate Highways, Transforming American Life* (1997); Elaine Tyler May, *Homeward Bound: American Families in the Cold War Era* (1988); Douglas T. Miller and Marion Nowak, *The Fifties: The Way We Really Were* (1977); William L. O'Neill, *American High: The Years of Confidence, 1945–1960* (1986); Richard Polenberg, *One Nation Divisible: Class, Race, and Ethnicity in the United States Since 1938* (1981); Adam Rome, *The Bulldozer in the Countryside: Suburban Sprawl and the Rise of American Environmentalism* (2001); Stephen Watts, *The Magic Kingdom: Walt Disney and the American Way of Life* (1997).

Women in the Fifties

Wini Breines, *Young, White and Miserable: Growing Up Female in the Fifties* (1992); Alison J. Clarke, *Tupperware: The Promise of Plastic in 1950s America* (2001); Ruth Schwartz Cowan, *More Work for Mother: The Ironies of Household Technology from the Open Hearth to the Microwave* (1983); Benita Eisler, *Private Lives: Men and Women of the Fifties* (1986); Cynthia Harrison, *On Account of Sex: The Politics of Women's Issues, 1945–1968* (1988); Brett Harvey, ed., *The Fifties: A Women's Oral History* (1993); Eugenia Kaledin, *Mothers and More: American Women in the 1950s* (1984); Susan Estabrook Kennedy, *If All We Did Was to Weep at Home: A History of White Working-Class Women in America* (1979); Leila Rupp and Verta Taylor, *Survival in the Doldrums: The American Women's Rights Movement, 1945 to the 1960s* (1990).

Mass Culture and Popular Religion

Glenn T. Altschuler and David I. Grossvogel, *Changing Channels: America in T.V. Guide* (1992); James L. Baughman, *The Republic of Mass Culture: Journalism, Filmmaking and Broadcasting in America Since 1941* (2d ed., 1997); Peter Biskind, *Seeing Is Believing: How Hollywood Taught Us to Stop Worrying and Love the Fifties* (1983); William Boddy, *Fifties Television: The Industry and Its Critics* (1990); Stephanie Coontz, *The Way We Never Were: American Families and the Nostalgia Trap* (1992); Richard O. Davies, *The Maverick Spirit: Building the New Nevada* (1998); Carol V. R. George, *God's Salesman: Norman Vincent Peale and the Power of Positive Thinking* (1993); James Hudnut-Beumler, *Looking for God in the Suburbs: The Religion of the American Dream and Its Critics, 1945–1965* (1994); Stefan Kanfer, *Ball of Fire: The Tumultuous Life and Comic Art of Lucille Ball* (2003); George Lipsitz, *Class and Culture in Cold War America* (1981) and *Time Passages: Collective Memory and American Popular Culture* (1990); David Marc, *Democratic Vistas: Television in American Culture* (1984); Karal Ann Marling, *As Seen on TV: The Visual Culture of Everyday Life in the 1950s* (1994); William Martin, *A Prophet with Honor: The Billy Graham Story* (1991); Martin E. Marty, *Modern American Religion, Vol. 3 [1941–1960]* (1996); Nora Sayre, *Running Time: Films of the Cold War* (1982); Joanne P. Sharp, *Condensing the Cold War: Reader's Digest and American Identity* (2000); Lynn Spiegel, *Make Room for TV: Television and the Family Ideal in Postwar America* (1992); Robert Wuthnow, *The Restructuring of American Religion: Society and Faith Since World War II* (1988).

PART TWO

Dissent, Terror, Reform

From some perspectives, the United States in the mid-1950s radiated confidence. Ike presided benignly in the White House, the Cold War consensus enjoyed broad support, and the media offered reassuring images of an affluent society typified by TV sitcoms' cheery white suburban families.

But no society, and certainly not Eisenhower's America, is wholly homogeneous or uncomplicated. America in the 1950s concealed more turbulence and tension than a casual observer might have guessed. This darker, more ambiguous side of the picture emerged with growing starkness as the decade wore on, coming to the light most graphically in the popular culture. Anxieties about nuclear war, alien menace, and social-conformist pressures all surfaced intriguingly in the Hollywood films of the fifties. As the baby-boom generation reached adolescence, the bland world of pop music found itself shaken and rattled by rock-and-roll. Indeed, the gyrating Elvis Presley and other new rock-and-roll icons won a fanatically loyal following among the young. The Beats sounded a jarring, assertive new note in the decade's literature. And social critics, although they stepped gingerly around fundamental issues of social injustice and class inequities in capitalist America, offered sharp-edged critiques of middle-class conformity and mass-culture insipidity.

Regarding race, the Supreme Court in 1954 thrust a profoundly important issue onto the national agenda by outlawing segregation in public schools. This ruling, reflecting years of legal effort by the National Association for the Advancement of Colored People (NAACP) and other groups, launched a civil-rights movement that would transform America. In 1955–56, African Americans in Montgomery, Alabama, organized a successful, yearlong boycott of the city's segregated buses that radically challenged the political passivity of the decade. From the Montgomery movement emerged Martin Luther King, Jr., who raised a powerful moral voice against racism and on behalf of Americans' common humanity.

As the nation confronted the ugly reality of racism, a new menace materialized: radioactive fallout from U.S. and Soviet nuclear tests that posed alarming environmental and health hazards. Further roiling the political waters, citizens organized campaigns to ban nuclear testing and rein in the nuclear arms race. Moviemakers, television producers, and science-fiction writers explored the not-so-hidden terror of nuclear holocaust underlying the surface optimism of the fifties.

A further shock came in 1957 when the Soviet Union launched its space satellite, *Sputnik*. Sharply eroding the sense of invincibility in which Americans had gloried since World War II, *Sputnik* unleashed an orgy of self-doubt. Continued Cold War jousting only worsened the national attack of the jitters. Despite a partial thaw in East-West relations after Stalin's death in 1953, tensions remained high as the fifties ended.

This intensifying sense of unease contributed to the Democratic victory of 1960 that put John F. Kennedy into the White House. The "Eisenhower generation" that had led the nation during World War II now yielded to the generation that had been only in their twenties during the war. JFK, however, pursued the Cold War as relentlessly as had his predecessors. His activist, liberal foreign policy espoused economic development, social programs, and nation building as strategies for winning over the Third World. Convinced that the United States must stand firm against the Soviets, Kennedy set out to prove his toughness to the Kremlin leaders. In this spirit he presided over an expanded military budget, a nuclear-weapons buildup, an abortive invasion of Castro's Cuba, and a terrifying missile crisis. He also edged cautiously toward a deeper engagement in Vietnam. In contrast to these aggressive strategies, however, Kennedy's foreign-policy legacy also included the Peace Corps and the 1963 limited nuclear-test ban treaty.

At home, Kennedy brought the cool, pragmatic, and liberal outlook of his generation to domestic policy. In the later 1950s, congressional Democrats led by liberals such as Senator Hubert Humphrey and Senate majority leader Lyndon Johnson had helped the Eisenhower administration to pass a landmark civil-rights bill over conservative opposition. In the early sixties, with the Democrats now in control of both the White House and the Congress, the momentum for reform gained strength. President Kennedy proposed various measures but did not live to see many of them enacted. His successor, Lyndon Johnson, used the nation's grief over Kennedy's assassination and his own political genius to push through Congress a remarkable array of reforms, from civil-rights legislation to antipoverty, education, and urban measures to environmental-protection laws. The result was a surge of reform matched in the twentieth century only in the Progressive era and in Franklin D. Roosevelt's New Deal. In 1964, Johnson won one of the great landslide victories of U.S. political history.

The years 1964–65 represented the high-water mark of postwar liberalism. The civil-rights campaign lay at the heart of the reformist wave that crested in the mid-1960s. Since its beginnings in the 1950s, the movement had broadened and deepened into a full-scale assault on the South's deeply entrenched racial caste system. The moment of liberal ascendancy would prove brief. The electorate veered rightward as early as the 1966 midterm election, and by the later 1960s a troubled economy, racial divisions, and civil turmoil over the war in Vietnam had shattered the fragile consensus over which Johnson had presided in the bright noonday of his presidency.

CHAPTER

The Other Side of the Picture Window: Outsiders, Dissidents, and Critics in the 1950s

THE YEAR IS 1954, and in movie houses and drive-ins across America, wide-eyed audiences are watching *Them!* an early entrant in a deluge of "mutant" movies. The film depicts a family—father, mother, and daughter—vacationing in New Mexico. But even before the action begins, disaster has struck: Monstrous creatures have ripped apart the family's camper and brutally murdered the parents, leaving the daughter so traumatized that she cannot speak except to scream, *"THEM!!!"* Soon we learn that the killers are giant ants, hatched from the radioactive soil of the atomic-bomb test site at Alamogordo. The army finally exterminates the last of the loathsome mutants in the Los Angeles storm sewers.

In its bizarre fashion, *Them!* epitomized a central paradox of the 1950s. Americans should have been happy and confident. A booming economy, cheap suburban housing, and abundant consumer products placed the good life within reach of millions. Hollywood, television, and mass magazines provided diversion. But an undercurrent of anxiety reflected in movies, youthful rebelliousness, cultural criticism, fear of nuclear tests, and stirrings of civil-rights protest all belied the upbeat mood. The United States in the 1950s was neither as trouble-free nor as homogenous as a quick visit to suburbia or a glance at television might have suggested.

Prosperity's byproducts—rampant materialism, a standardized mass culture, and the growth of a desk-bound white-collar class—troubled dissident artists, writers, and intellectuals. Was a nation noted for its individualism becoming timid and conformist? Alexis de Tocqueville had raised the question in the 1830s, and it resurfaced in the 1950s. Others pointed to the persistence of want in a time of general prosperity. In 1959 economist Robert Lampman of the University of Wisconsin estimated the size of America's underclass at a dismaying 32 million. Journalist Michael Harrington published several articles in small-circulation magazines in the 1950s with titles such as "Our Fifty Million Poor." At the time, these reports attracted little notice. The poor, including many blacks, Indians, and a swelling tide of Hispanic newcomers, as well as many whites, struggled in rural regions and inner cities, but the realities of poverty and economic inequities remained on the periphery of the nation's consciousness. Globally, nuclear fears and Cold War anxieties added to the somber undercurrents that eddied beneath the more upbeat surface mood.

With two notable exceptions—the movement to halt nuclear testing and an emerging civil-rights campaign—protest impulses stood little chance against the conservative, stand-pat outlook expressed in Eisenhower's two electoral victories. Suburban complacency and Cold War ideological conformity were too powerful. And despite the rising tempo of civil-rights activism in the South, white America had yet to confront racism as a *national* issue.

In contrast to the 1930s or the 1960s, reform currents flowed sluggishly in Eisenhower's America. Rather than coalescing into a single movement, discontent with the status quo found a variety of outlets, from the writings of critics and novelists to the world of jazz and folk-music clubs, drive-in theaters, coffee houses, rock-and-roll concerts, antinuclear marches, and southern black churches.

Films of the Fifties: Undercurrents of Menace

The Hollywood dream factory both shaped and reflected American hopes and fears in the 1950s. The decade's films mirrored the ambivalent public mood, some offering escapist fare and endorsing conventional social values, others revealing— sometimes unintentionally—the anxieties of the era.

Looking for moneymakers, producers crafted movies with broad audience appeal. Many films of the decade therefore can be interpreted in various ways. In Howard Hawks's *The Thing* (1951), for example, the alien blob buried in the Arctic ice may represent communist subversion, repressed sexuality, modern science—or simply an alien blob. The popular western *High Noon* (1952) invites a similar array of interpretations. As badman Frank Miller rides into town to kill marshal Will Kane (Gary Cooper), who had sent him to prison years before, Kane expects the townspeople to rally to his aid. But they are a cowardly lot and abandon Will to confront Miller and his two brothers alone. Once the Miller boys lie dead in the street, the townspeople rush out to congratulate Kane, but he disgustedly throws his badge in the dust and rides out of town.

High Noon's director and scriptwriter, opponents of McCarthyism, intended the film as a critique of those cowed into silence by McCarthy's demagoguery. Did moviegoers catch this political message, or did they view the film as a traditional western extolling individualism, a classic American theme? Kane's Quaker bride (Grace Kelly) is portrayed as naive for trying to persuade him to avoid the showdown. Thus, the film could also be read as a Cold War tract preaching the inevitability of a nuclear "shootout" with the Russians.

Despite the ambiguity in many 1950s movies, an underlying pattern emerges. Typically, a menace lurks beneath a tranquil surface. Many begin with cheerful, everyday scenes in an ordinary community, followed by mounting tension as weird events shatter the routine. The giant ants of *Them!* spawned a lurid progeny of shrinking men, towering women, creatures from black lagoons, and prehistoric monsters jolted from their long slumber.

The Invasion of the Body Snatchers (1956) is particularly terrifying because the monsters appear in human guise. As the movie opens, Dr. Miles Bennell (Kevin McCarthy) gradually realizes that all is not well in his California town. People look the same, but they are different. As Miles's girlfriend Becky says of her Uncle Ira, "There's something missing. Always when he talked to me there was a certain look in his eyes. Now it's gone. There's no emotion." Uncle Ira is actually a clone, hatched from a pod brought by space aliens intent on creating a race of zombies who will carry out their evil schemes.

Like many 1950s movies, *The Invasion of the Body Snatchers* played upon multiple anxieties. Most obvious is the Cold War obsession with subversion, the suspicion of alien ideologies, the fear that one's neighbor might be a traitor. Unlike the stereotypical "redskins" of countless westerns or the "Japs" of World War II propaganda, the communists *looked* like everyone else, yet they threatened everything Americans held dear.

As pod people take over the town, Becky and Miles flee for their lives. Finally Becky herself falls victim to the aliens. In the film's original ending, Miles stares wild-eyed at the camera and screams, "You're next!" In the ending actually released, a police official telephones Washington and shouts, "Get me the FBI!" Even so paranoid a film as *The Invasion of the Body Snatchers* had to offer assurance of *some* center of stability and authority.

Invasion of the Body Snatchers (1956). Filmed in Sierra Madre, California, and drenched in Cold War paranoia, this film features space aliens who assume human form and conspire to take over America, one citizen at a time. *(PHOTOFEST)*

Other movies exposed the fragility of the middle-class family ideal. In William Wyler's *The Desperate Hours* (1955), an escaped convict terrorizes a suburban family. In the 1958 potboiler *I Married a Monster from Outer Space,* a middle-class housewife discovers that her model husband is not what he seems. Whatever the specific threat in these films, the pervasive mood is one of danger hovering just out of sight. In *The Thing,* the scientist who wants to communicate with the mysterious blob rather than destroy it is portrayed as dangerously naive. As he approaches it, calling out, "I am your friend," the malicious creature zaps him. This sense of encroaching horror—of amorphous but deadly forces that cannot be understood or negotiated with, only destroyed—captured a powerful undercurrent in the national mood.

Rebellious Youth

Movies of the fifties often featured angry, alienated teenagers very different from the cheery juveniles of the TV sitcoms. In *Rebel Without a Cause* (1955), James Dean, Natalie Wood, and Sal Mineo play a trio of disturbed youths from affluent homes who are frustrated with their privileged lives and hell-bent on trouble. Dean's character races hot rods and pretends to be tough. Actually, he is unsure of his masculinity because his father sometimes wears an apron and helps with the housework. Natalie Wood's character, troubled by her father's inability to deal with her budding sexuality, has turned to promiscuity.

Rebel Without a Cause pictured a suburbia awash in psychopathology. The social order as a whole is affirmed, however, and by the end, Dean and Wood have fallen in love (with Mineo as a kind of surrogate child) and have begun to accept middle-class values. This fundamentally conservative film idealizes Dean's juvenile-court officer and other therapeutic experts.

Blackboard Jungle (1955) offered a look at inner city schools, a subject rarely examined in the 1950s. After scenes of violence and mayhem at North Manual High, accompanied by a rock-and-roll soundtrack, an idealistic teacher (Glenn Ford) wins over his tough class and even persuades a black student (Sidney Poitier) to apply to college. Not only is the ending optimistic, but the movie insists that schools like North Manual are rare. When Ford visits a suburban high school, a teacher takes him to an assembly where rows of well-groomed youths are fervently singing the national anthem. "For every school like [North Manual] there are thousands like this one," he says reassuringly.

Other films were more threatening. In *The Wild One (1953),* based on an actual incident, Marlon Brando and Lee Marvin play the leaders of rival motorcycle gangs that invade a California town. When a waitress asks Brando what he's rebelling against, he sneers, "What have you got?" An opening message made the movie's point frighteningly clear: "This is a shocking story. It could never take place in most American towns—but it did in this one. It is a public challenge not to let it happen again."

The discontent of many 1950s youth found expression above all in music. The early-fifties pop-music scene was numbingly bland, with singers such as Perry Como and Pat Boone crooning insipid love ballads. Rock-and-roll and its first superstar, Elvis Presley, defied all that. Born in 1935 in Mississippi, Elvis was a nineteen-year-old truck driver when he recorded demo tapes for Sun Records, a small

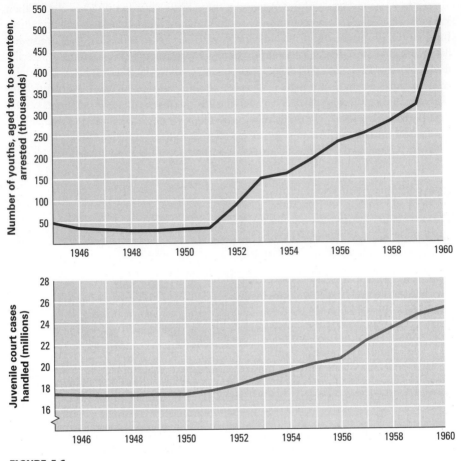

FIGURE 5.1

Youth Arrests and Juvenile Court Cases, 1945–1960

SOURCE: *Historical Statistics of the United States: Colonial Times to 1970,* U.S. Department of Commerce, Bureau of the Census.

Memphis label, in 1954. He crafted his singing style from black rhythm and blues (R&B) singers such as Robert Johnson of Mississippi, popular with African Americans but largely unknown to whites. Elvis blended R&B with country music and the gospel songs of his boyhood Assemblies of God church. Teenagers across America responded rapturously to his rocking version of such R&B standards as "That's All Right Mama."

The new star enthralled screaming audiences, his records sold by the millions, and youth-oriented radio stations programmed hours of rock-and-roll. Elvis's "Heartbreak Hotel" topped the charts in 1956. Songs such as "I'm All Shook Up" and "Don't Be Cruel" sustained his popularity. Male fans adopted his glistening pompadour hairstyle. As the crooners gave way to the shouts, moans, percussive beat, and raw eroticism of rock-and-roll, teenage dances became loud, rocking affairs, very different from the sedate, chaperoned events of a few years earlier.

Bill Haley and the Comets won fame with "Rock Around the Clock," heard on the soundtrack of *Blackboard Jungle*. Out of Georgia burst the black R&B singer Little Richard (Richard Wayne Penniman) with such hits as "Tutti Frutti" (1955) and "Long Tall Sally" (1956). Chuck Berry, from a poor black neighborhood in St. Louis, was a reform-school veteran when he started an R&B band in 1953. His first big hit, "Maybelline," came in 1955. In Texas, teenager Charles "Buddy" Holly assembled a band and soon achieved stardom; in the barrio of East Los Angeles, Ritchie Valens (shortened from Valenzuela) headed a popular Chicano rock-and-roll group. (Holly and Valens both perished in the same plane crash in 1959.)

Much of adult America recoiled from this multiethnic explosion of raucous music. Church leaders denounced rock-and-roll as indecent and attacked Elvis's suggestive hip thrusting that earned him the nickname Elvis the Pelvis. In a 1955 Florida concert, police insisted that he sing without moving his midsection. Wrote one worried parent, "The gangster of tomorrow is the Elvis Presley type of today."

Indeed, fears of "juvenile delinquency," comparable to a later generation's concern about drugs, swept America. Movies like *Rock All Night* (1957) and *High School Hellcats* (1958) fed the fantasy of an entire generation sliding into anarchy. Stories of rebellious youth filled the newspapers. A U.S. Senate subcommittee investigating the problem in 1959 called a parade of expert witnesses and received a flood of mail from concerned parents.

Leonard Bernstein elevated gang warfare to the status of Shakespearean tragedy in his 1957 musical, *West Side Story,* but anxieties about the younger generation continued. These fears had some basis in fact. Statistics on youthful arrests, for everything from vandalism to murder, rose sharply in the fifties. In New York City, they more than tripled. But the "juvenile delinquency" hysteria also expressed more intangible concerns about the emerging teenage subculture, often linked to broader Cold War fears. Communism abroad and moral rot at home, many believed, were somehow connected. As the head of the Chicago Crime Prevention Bureau put it, "The obscene material that is flooding the Nation today is another cunning device of our enemies, deliberately calculated to destroy the decency and morality which are the bulwarks of society." The communists' alleged skill at "brainwashing" the innocent into accepting their doctrines thus dovetailed with fears about the power of the mass media to sabotage parental authority and to peddle alternative cultural values to the young.

Radio disc jockeys struck frightened elders as demonic Pied Pipers luring children away from their parents' influence. DJ Alan Freed, using the name Moondog, popularized rock-and-roll on his radio shows, first in Cleveland and then in New York City. In 1955 a Buffalo DJ caused a traffic jam by broadcasting from atop a large downtown billboard. He urged youthful drivers in the cars below to blow their horns if they liked "Rock Around the Clock," the song that he was playing. Hundreds obeyed, creating a deafening cacophony. The DJ spent six hours in jail.

In the 1960s, generational conflict would erupt in campus protests and street marches. In the 1950s, it took the form of angry quarrels over music, dress, and hairstyles. In 1957, a Texas school board banned from high schools "tight blue jeans worn low, or ducktail haircuts," citing the link between "undisciplined dress and undisciplined behavior." The rock revolution's response to such pronouncements was summed up in the title of one hit song: "Yakkety Yak."

This distinct youth culture had its roots in larger social changes. With postwar young people remaining in school, the American high school became a cultural bazaar where youth of diverse backgrounds shared tastes and fads. As early as 1950, a White House Conference on Children noted with alarm that "the standards of the lowest class" were infecting "the boys and girls of other social groups." With the economy booming, many high-school students held part-time jobs, boosting their buying power and reducing their dependence on their parents. Many had access to a family car or even owned one of their own. Hot rods, congregated at drive-in hamburger shops or other oases, became a symbol of teenage autonomy. Rock-and-roll gave youth a way to protest the blandness of 1950s mass culture. Although the decade's cultural ferment did not evolve into a politically conscious counterculture, it created a distinctive adversarial style among the baby boomers that in the 1960s would take an overtly political turn.

Historian Michael T. Bertrand, in *Race, Rock, and Elvis* (2000), sees a connection between the rock-and-roll craze and the rising tempo of civil-rights protests. Elvis and other white rock-and-roll stars hardly rank as civil-rights heroes, but their admiration for (and liberal borrowing from) black musical styles, as well as the interracial popularity of rock-and-roll and the ethnic diversity of the performers, Bertrand argues, offered a pop-culture challenge to the South's ideology of strict racial separation and helped prepare the way for the more explicit assault on racial segregation that soon spread across the South.

Ironically, this youth subculture rested on the same affluence that underlay the middle-class suburban culture that it challenged. The phenomenon spread via the radios and 45-RPM record players in countless teenagers' bedrooms. Indeed, corporate America profited hugely as it supplied the records, movies, fashions, and reading matter by which the younger generation defined itself. In a further irony, the dominant culture partially absorbed and tamed rock-and-roll and youthful unrest. As early as 1956, Elvis signed a movie contract and appeared (from the waist up) on Ed Sullivan's TV variety show. His movies and albums of the late fifties and early sixties proved bland and forgettable. The mass-entertainment industry neutralized Presley's iconoclastic energy and turned him into a conventional romantic idol. (Much of the blame lies with Presley's manager, a Dutch fugitive from justice named Andries van Kuijk who in America became a carnival pitchman under the name Colonel Tom Parker.) Toward the end of Presley's life (he died in 1977), even an admirer observed, "Elvis transcends his talent to the point of dispensing with it altogether." Distancing himself from the musical and cultural revolution of the 1960s that he helped spawn, Presley even volunteered his services as an FBI informant; J. Edgar Hoover tactfully declined the offer.

As the mainstream culture co-opted rock-and-roll, middle-class fears of a rebellious younger generation temporarily faded. By 1959 a movie such as *Teenagers from Outer Space* could celebrate suburban togetherness as perceived by a time traveler from the future who has no family. In *Blue Denim* (1959), teenage rebel Brandon De Wilde (touted as the successor to James Dean, who had died in an auto crash in 1955) sees his error and joins his family for dinner as his father says a prayer. But society's ability to absorb youthful dissent would be tested again in the late 1960s, with the stakes incomparably higher.

Cultural Resistance: The Arts and Social Criticism in Cold War America

Some artists and social critics also expressed doubts about Eisenhower's America. But in contrast to the Depression-ridden 1930s and the politicized 1960s, the dissidents of the 1950s avoided politics. They focused on the psychological and cultural toll of affluence, not on poverty, economic inequities, or the unequal distribution of power across the lines of class, race, and gender. Rather than proposing structural changes in society, they urged individuals to seek a more authentic existence in a materialistic, conformist age. The existentialist credo of French intellectuals Jean-Paul Sartre and Albert Camus, with its focus on individuals' search for meaning in a meaningless universe, enjoyed a vogue on U.S. college campuses.

In the realm of jazz, the culture dynamics of the postwar era encouraged the decline of swing and the rise of bebop. Swing, popular in the 1930s and the war years, had evolved from its African American roots to reach a mass audience through the big bands of Benny Goodman, Tommy Dorsey, and others. Bebop, featuring long, introspective solos, was promoted by small jazz ensembles. Whereas swing offered jazz adaptations of familiar melodies, bebop involved complex improvisation. Demanding the listener's full concentration, bebop arose outside a music industry that had diluted the authentic jazz tradition. Tense and edgy, bebop expressed the anxious underside of the fifties. Bebop musicians, spurning the suburban middle class, shared their highly personal vision with small audiences of rapt fans in smoky jazz clubs.

White musicians had dominated swing; bebop's high priests were African American, including trumpeter Dizzy Gillespie, pianist Thelonious Monk, and saxophonists Charlie Parker and Lester Young. Although bebop musicians avoided politics, they saw their music as an expression of black consciousness and thus politically significant. Bebop promoted social change, Gillespie later wrote: "We didn't . . . make speeches or say 'Let's play eight bars of protest.' We just played our music. . . . The music proclaimed our identity."

In the visual arts, abstract expressionism remained the most vital movement of the 1950s. Like bebop, this movement prized individual expression rather than overt social or political commentary. Jackson Pollock's career illustrates the shift. Pollack began in the late 1930s as a protégé of Thomas Hart Benton, who had portrayed workers and farmers in realistic canvases and murals. After World War II, however, Pollack began to drip and swirl paints directly onto large canvases stretched on the floor. Initially, the new style aroused ridicule, but like the beboppers, abstract expressionists such as Pollack, Robert Motherwell, and Mark Rothko viewed their innovations as a response to the postwar world. "Modern art to me is nothing more than the expression of . . . the age that we're living in," Pollack commented in 1950. "The modern painter cannot express this age, the airplane, the atom bomb, the radio, in the old forms. . . . Each age finds its own technique."

But like rock-and-roll, bebop and abstract expressionism experienced the dominant culture's capacity to absorb even mildly subversive cultural manifestations. Musicians such as Gillespie and artists like Pollack may have been troubled by racism and nuclear dangers, but the government and the media promoted their art as weapons in the ideological Cold War. Gillespie, for example, gave concerts in Europe for the State Department, implicitly countering allegations of racism in

IN PERSPECTIVE

The Mass-Culture Debate

The culture critics of the 1950s drew on a long tradition in American thought. A century earlier, writer Nathaniel Hawthorne had attacked the fickle, novel-devouring public for slighting him in favor of a "damn'd mob of scribbling women." Movies, radio, and television gave the critics a succession of new targets.

Postwar mass-culture critics fell into three broad camps. Conservatives such as Dwight Macdonald dismissed popular culture as *kitsch*—German for "rubbish." The avidity with which the vulgar hordes consumed it, they declared, proved the low state of American culture and the need to defend elite standards. This dismissive view often, although not always, reflected a deeper bias against democracy itself.

Marxists treated mass culture as another form of capitalist exploitation, a view most fully articulated at the University of Frankfurt's Institute for Social Research, founded in 1923. With Hitler's rise in the 1930s, the leaders of the Frankfurt school fled to America, where, traumatized by European fascism, they cast a critical eye on U.S. mass culture. In *The Eclipse of Reason* (1947), Max Horkheimer probed the mass media's totalitarian potential. Theodor Adorno, writing in the 1950s, portrayed television as a weapon of class manipulation, numbing the masses to their own alienation. Horkheimer and Adorno charged in a coauthored essay that radio and the movies left "no room for imagination or reflection on the part of the audience. . . . [T]hey react automatically [and] fall helpless victims to what is offered them." The Italian Marxist Antonio Gramsci, who died in a fascist prison in 1937, elaborated his theory of cultural hegemony in a series of influential essays in the 1920s and 1930s. Elites employ mass culture, Gramsci argued, to achieve hegemonic control, thereby persuading the rest of society willingly to embrace the existing social order, with all its inequities, as wholly desirable and "natural."

America and underscoring Western cultural freedom at a time when Moscow forbade jazz and kept classical composers like Dmitri Shostakovitch on a tight rein. An abstract-expressionist exhibit toured Europe in the 1950s with a State Department subsidy, in pointed contrast to the communist world's heavy-handed "socialist realism." *Life* magazine promoted abstract expressionism as proof of the Free World's cultural openness.

Others, including the Canadian medievalist Marshall McLuhan, viewed mass culture more positively. In *Understanding Media* (1964) and other works, McLuhan hailed the new electronic media, especially TV, as a quantum leap in human communications as profound as that introduced by Gutenberg. McLuhan's aphorism, "The medium is the message," summed up his belief that the technology of television itself, apart from program content, would change the world by transforming human perception of reality. In place of the linear medium of print, television's ceaseless flow of images would bring the world into the living room with compelling immediacy.

As the mass-culture debate wore on into the 1980s and 1990s, all three viewpoints found adherents. In *The Closing of the American Mind* (1987), the elitist Alan Bloom railed against rock music as "junk food for the soul" that ruins the young for serious intellectual pursuits. Bloom placed his hope in an elite who would carry on the great traditions of Western civilization. The religious Right, meanwhile, like earlier moral reformers, attacked the media for promulgating sex and violence. The American Family Asssociation of Tupelo, Mississippi, for example, founded by the Reverend Donald Wildmon, organized boycotts of the sponsors of television programs that it considered indecent or immoral. The radical critique of mass culture continued to find champions as well. Historian T. J. Jackson Lears, in "The Concept of Cultural Hegemony" (*American Historical Review*, June 1985), restated the Gramscian view of mass culture as a means by which capitalist elites market goods, mute class tensions, and in general legitimate the status quo.

Other mass-culture observers remained more upbeat. In *The Global Village* (1989), Marshall McLuhan envisioned a world united electronically—an image that would resurface in President Bill Clinton's dream of America linked by an "electronic highway." A more positive outlook emerged, too, in historian Lawrence Levine's studies of popular culture. Rejecting the view that moviegoers, radio listeners, and TV viewers are an inert mass that can be manipulated at will, Levine in *The Unpredictable Past: Explorations in American Cultural History* (1993) emphasized the active role of mass-culture consumers. They not only choose which movies and television shows to watch, but they imaginatively adapt these products to their own purposes. Indeed, in a 1992 *American Historical Review* essay, Levine portrayed mass culture as an arena of dynamic interaction between producers and consumers that creates a kind of TV-age folk culture. He cited research documenting how listeners and viewers continually criticize and comment on radio and TV programs rather than passively absorbing them. In a sharp rebuttal, Jackson Lears rejected this view as a romantically sentimental view of America's "culture industry."

This was hardly the last word. The mass-culture debate that flared so vigorously in the 1950s shows no signs of abating. And as the controversy rolls on, so does American mass culture, playing an ever-larger global role.

Yet the Cold War's cultural ramifications could cut both ways. While Washington promoted some artists and writers, radicals and leftists suffered. Folksinger Pete Seeger, an unabashed leftist and Cold War critic, found his career stymied. The black singer Paul Robeson, long identified with communist causes, left the country in 1958.

On the literary front, some writers continued to cast a jaundiced eye on the suburbs and material abundance. John Cheever's *The Wapshot Chronicle* (1957) dissected the lives of New Englanders cut off from their ancestral roots. Cheever's short stories in the *New Yorker,* peopled with white-collar workers who commute from boring jobs in New York City to bland Connecticut suburbs, evoked alienation in the midst of prosperity.

John Updike's *Rabbit Run* (1960) features Harry "Rabbit" Angstrom, a young family man and former high-school basketball star who senses that his best years are already behind him. "He feels underwater," Updike wrote, "caught in chains of transparent slime." Bored by his job as a vacuum-cleaner salesman, lacking inner resources, and clueless about the larger social sources of his malaise, Harry turns to extramarital affairs to stave off despair.

Philip Roth's *Goodbye Columbus* (1959), a collection of stories about urban middle-class Jewish life, conveyed the same claustrophobia that pervades the stories of Cheever and Updike. In Saul Bellow's *Henderson the Rain King* (1959), the protagonist abandons wife, family, and a stifling daily routine to immerse himself in African tribal culture.

A few writers commented more directly on the political and cultural realities of the 1950s. Arthur Miller's *The Crucible* (1953), a play about Salem witchcraft, was widely and correctly seen as an attack on McCarthyism. In Ray Bradbury's science-fiction story *Fahrenheit 451* (1953), which projected the Cold War, McCarthyism, and mass culture trends into the future, the state has outlawed books and controls television, broadcasting propaganda and mindless entertainment through giant living-room wall screens. Only a handful of dissidents, who recite the classics to each other in remote hideaways, preserve humanity's cultural heritage.

While some writers criticized 1950s culture implicitly, the Beats challenged it frontally.* The Beat movement began after World War II when Allen Ginsberg, a Columbia University undergraduate, befriended Jack Kerouac, a college dropout of working-class origins. The movement coalesced in 1955 at San Francisco's City Lights Bookstore when Ginsberg read *Howl,* a hallucinatory, drug-influenced poem portraying America as a ravenous beast sacrificing its young on the altars of commerce and technology. Kerouac's *On the Road* (1957), a sprawling autobiographical novel, recounts the adventures of two young men, one based on Kerouac himself and the other on Neil Cassady, a fringe figure in the Beat movement, as they crisscross the country by car and bus.

With *Howl* and *On the Road,* the Beat movement streaked like a Fourth of July rocket across the grey skies of Eisenhower's America. Young people and others dissatisfied with the blandness of the mass media welcomed its outrageousness. *On the Road* sold half a million copies, and *Howl* became a campus favorite, its cachet heightened by efforts to suppress it as obscene. Like the satirical songs of Tom Lehrer and the mordant humor of coffee-house comics Lenny Bruce and Mort Sahl, the Beats appealed to Americans seeking alternatives to banality. Like Elvis and other rock-and-roll stars, Ginsberg, Kerouac, and lesser Beats became cultural heroes of the disaffected. Asked at a poetry reading what his work meant, Ginsberg responded, "Nakedness," and proceeded to remove all his clothes.

---

*The origin of the term *Beat* is unclear. Jack Kerouac, asserting the movement's fundamentally religious impetus, claimed that it was short for "beatitude."

In a decade that idolized family life and domesticity, the Beats cultivated spontaneity, fleeting relationships, and casual sex. *On the Road,* which begins with the breakup of the narrator's marriage, is a classic tale of footloose males seeking freedom and wary of commitment. In the male-centered and often homoerotic world of the Beats, women provided diversion but otherwise played little role. Rejecting middle-class conformity, the Beats idealized outsiders—criminals, addicts, inner-city blacks, the truckers whose sixteen-wheelers rumble through the night. In the opening lines of *Howl,* Ginsberg wrote:

> I saw the best minds of my generation destroyed by madness, starving
>   hysterical naked,
> dragging themselves through the negro streets at dawn looking for an angry fix

Novelist Norman Mailer shared the Beats' fascination with the underclass. In his essay "The White Negro" (1957), Mailer romanticized the dangerous world of "hipsters"—criminals, juvenile delinquents, streetwise blacks—as an alternative to white middle-class America.

Anticipating a 1970s' vogue for Eastern religions, the Beats referred knowingly to *Satori, Karma,* and Zen Buddhism. But for all their cultural exoticism, they were solidly in the American grain. Ginsberg's summons to "return to nature and . . . revolt against the machine" echoed Ralph Waldo Emerson and Henry David Thoreau. Kerouac's *On the Road* evoked Huck Finn's preference for freedom over civilization and Walt Whitman's exuberant patriotism. Looking eastward from San Francisco Bay, Kerouac's narrator exults in "the great raw bulge and bulk of my American continent."

Predictably, the mass media soon took up and exploited the Beats. *Life* featured the movement, and Kerouac recited his work on TV. Like Elvis, the bearded "Beatnik" became a stereotypical symbol of social and sexual menace. A 1950s potboiler, *Pads Are for Passion,* bore the alarming caption "Anita Was a Virgin—Till the Hipsters Got Hold of Her."

The Beat movement, like rock-and-roll, anticipated the politicized counterculture of the 1960s. Indeed, Ginsberg would become a campus guru in the sixties and beyond. Kerouac, however, like Presley, denounced the radicals of the 1960s. But however they viewed their progeny, the Beats played a seminal role as fomenters of cultural change.

Cultural critics offered their own dissections of postwar America. William H. Whyte in *The Organization Man* criticized the corporate business world for breeding conformity. Dwight Macdonald, in essays reprinted in *Against the American Grain* (1962), criticized both the profit-driven mass media and what he called the "midcult" for debasing cultural standards. Macdonald lambasted the Revised Standard Version of the Bible (1952), for example, for reducing the majestic English of the King James Bible to the level of prose produced by a committee.

Historian Daniel Boorstin in *The Image* (1961) criticized the mass culture for inducing Americans to settle for secondhand experience. People listened to Muzak instead of going to concerts, bought art posters instead of visiting museums, and skimmed *Reader's Digest* condensed books instead of reading the original works. Like Bradbury, Boorstin feared a world of brain-dead citizens passively accepting the version of reality spoon-fed to them by the state or by the mass media.

The journalist Vance Packard added his voice to the critics of 1950s culture in several best-selling books. *The Hidden Persuaders* (1957) exposed manipulative advertising; *The Status Seekers* (1959) deplored social climbing through the accumulation of high-status products; and *The Waste Makers* (1960) lamented that Americans were forgetting the virtue of frugality in the orgy of consumption.

The jacket blurb of John Keats's *The Crack in the Picture Window* (1956), a muckraking attack on suburban conformity, reads like a caricature of 1950s cultural criticism:

> Even while you read this, whole square miles of identical boxes are spreading like gangrene. . . . In any one of these new neighborhoods you can be sure all other houses will be precisely like yours, inhabited by people whose age, income, number of children, problems, habits, conversation, dress, possessions, and perhaps even blood types are precisely like yours.

Many of these critics had come of age in the 1930s, when FDR's New Deal had won the allegiance of many; others, looking to the Soviet Union as a model, had embraced Marxism. By the 1950s, however, the New Deal was history, Depression-era misery had yielded to prosperity, and a history of youthful radicalism had become a matter of embarrassment rather than pride. Sociologist Daniel Bell, himself an ex-radical, summed up the 1950s in the title of his 1960 book about postwar America: *The End of Ideology*.

Prosperity, the weakness of organized labor, and the stifling effects of McCarthyism all served to mute political debate. So, too, did a Cold War consensus that celebrated America as the last bulwark against the Red menace. Whatever its flaws, U.S. democracy was demonstrably superior to totalitarianism. The capitalist system might be dominated by vast corporations and faceless managers, but it was preferable to the state-run Iron Curtain economies. The ethic of consumption and endless growth could be faulted for encouraging materialistic excess, but it moderated the class conflict that Marxism thrived on. Such observations, while true enough, did not encourage trenchant political debate or radical social criticism. Historian Christopher Lasch, a baby boomer, later complained that his generation "lacked a political education."

In this climate, most intellectuals adopted the safe course of criticizing aspects of American cultural life but not challenging society's basic structure or ideological premises. One observer wrote in 1957, "Almost all the problems that were once called 'political' now belong to a different context, psychological, sociological, and cultural." Sharing the prevailing view that U.S. capitalism had ensured abundance for all and that the remaining pockets of poverty would quickly vanish, critics such as Whyte, Packard, Macdonald, and Boorstin concentrated their observations on the managerial elite and the newly affluent middle class, largely ignoring the poor, the blue-collar workers, and the blacks and Hispanics in the inner cities.

They also paid scant attention to the economic system that underlay the cultural trends they deplored. Focused on matters of aesthetics, psychology, and individual behavior, Whyte, Packard, Macdonald, Boorstin, and others said little about the distribution of power and economic opportunity, or the underlying structure and operation of the capitalist system, in postwar America. Nor did these critics suggest any solution for the problems they identified. Like 1950s novelists, they aimed not to mobilize collective action but to heighten individual sensibility. The jacket blurb for *The Crack in the Picture Window* ended breathlessly, "The shaken reader puts down the book, stares for a moment, and then screams, 'Somebody do something!'" In fact, such a response was alien to the mood of the fifties, when cultural criticism rarely led to action. When radical activists of the 1960s criticized the capitalist system and called for resistance (see Chapter 9), they dismissed the 1950s intellectuals who, in their view, had offered the bark of cultural criticism without the bite of political action.

The 1960s protesters did, however, admire one 1950s thinker, the sociologist C. Wright Mills, a product of Depression-era Texas and the University of Wisconsin, where a tradition of radical social thought survived Mills's *White Collar*, as we have seen, examined middle-class discontent. But unlike other critics who made similar points, he linked his insights to a structural analysis of the political and economic order. The impotence felt by mid-level white-collar workers was well founded, he insisted, since they had little voice in the political or corporate decisions that shaped their lives. In a phrase evocative of the 1930s, Mills called them "sharecroppers in the dustbowl of business."

Mills extended his argument in *The Power Elite* (1956). Power in contemporary America, he argued, lay in the hands of shifting but basically stable and interlocking corporate, political, and military elites. Mills went on to explore the social and cultural institutions—family, schools, clubs—by which these elites perpetuated themselves. Liberal theorists who celebrated the health of American democracy, argued Mills, ignored the ease with which voters could be manipulated. Mills rejected the theory advanced by economist John Kenneth Galbraith in *American Capitalism* (1951) that competing and countervailing interest groups divided power among them. This argument, he protested, obscured the concentration of power at the top and the convergence of interest among "the Ones Who Decide." Mills's analysis anticipated President Eisenhower's 1961 warning about the military-industrial complex, but his polemical style and unconventional ways (he rode a motorcycle to work and built his own house) heightened his vulnerability to criticism. In a decade when most intellectuals avoided radical analysis or calls to action, however, Mills's impassioned, readable books expressed what most Americans knew in their bones: that some groups and individuals wielded great power and influence, while most did not. His belated influence among 1960s radicals came posthumously, however. Mills died of a heart attack in 1962, at forty-five.

Despite the diminished social activism of the Eisenhower years, two issues did stir organized protest: the nuclear threat and racial discrimination. Each would continue to loom large long after the fifties had become a memory.

Fallout Fears and Test-Ban Activism

The fear of a nuclear World War III that had gripped America after Hiroshima revived in a different form in the mid-1950s as scientists reported deadly radioactive fallout from hydrogen-bomb tests conducted in the South Pacific. The U.S. test series of 1954 set off the first alarm, spreading radioactive ash over a vast area and causing illness and death to a Japanese fishing crew. In 1955 radioactive rain fell on Chicago, and meteorologists reported high-level radioactive clouds spreading over North America. Medical specialists warned of the health hazards of fallout, particularly to children, including leukemia, bone cancer, and long-term genetic damage. Despite efforts by the Eisenhower administration to downplay the danger, a full-blown fallout scare gripped the nation. Even the conservative *Saturday Evening Post* magazine ran a feature called "Fallout: The Silent Killer."

The mutant movies churned out by Hollywood in these years usually blamed the scary creatures on nuclear blasts. A 1954 rock-and-roll song by Bill Haley and the Comets, "Thirteen Women (and Only One Man in Town)," offered a male fantasy of endless sex in the aftermath of an H-bomb attack. Tom Lehrer, popular on college campuses, extracted black humor from the prospect of nuclear annihilation with such songs as "We'll All Go Together When We Go." *Mad* magazine, a favorite with teenagers, fantasized a post-nuclear-war Hit Parade of songs that young lovers would sing as they "walk down moonlit lanes arm in arm in arm."

Novels like Nevil Shute's *On the Beach* (1957) and Walter Miller's *A Canticle for Leibowitz* (1959) imagined apocalyptic scenarios of human extinction. In Mordecai Roshwald's *Level 7* (1959), the inhabitants of a vast underground shelter die, level by level, as radiation seeps deeper into the earth. The last survivors create a new religion in which strontium-90 becomes the ultimate embodiment of evil.

Even on television, rarely a bearer of bad news in the fifties, the science-fiction series *Outer Limits* and Rod Serling's *Twilight Zone* offered post-nuclear-war plots or explored the psychological effect of atomic terror. In one *Outer Limits* episode, bees that have been genetically enhanced by radioactive fallout decide to infiltrate the human race. They transmute their queen into a young female humanoid who gets a job in the home of a suburban couple and sets out to seduce the weak-willed husband. But the wife grows suspicious when she sees the newcomer in the yard one night pollinating flowers. As a swarm of bees stings the wife to death, the bee-woman offers herself seductively to the distraught husband. In his revulsion he kills her, foiling, for the moment, insect-world challenges to middle-class propriety. Laden with multiple cultural messages, this episode reflected not only fallout fears but also uneasiness about threats to suburban domesticity posed by the youth culture's brazen sexuality.

The federal government, ironically, intensified nuclear anxiety with a civil-defense program of school drills, propaganda films, and a fallout-shelter campaign. In a 1956 civil-defense test in Washington, thousands of federal workers scattered to relocation centers, and President Eisenhower was helicoptered to an underground command post in Maryland. In 1959, *Life* persuaded a newlywed couple to honeymoon in an underground shelter, publishing photographs of them kissing as they descended for two weeks of subterranean bliss. "Fallout can be fun," quipped *Life*. Schoolchildren crouched under desks in nuclear-war drills and watched civil-defense films such as *Duck and Cover,* in which Burt the Turtle explained what to do when the nuclear flash came. In a rare manifestation of feminist activism in this decade, women's organizations pressured the Federal Civil Defense Administration to add a women's advisory board to help formulate and publicize civil-defense advice.

From the fallout scare arose a national movement to stop nuclear tests. When Adlai Stevenson called for a test ban in the 1956 presidential campaign, the Republicans accused him of aiding the enemy, but the issue would not fade. Groups with names like the Council for a Livable World and the Committee for a Sane Nuclear Policy (SANE) took up the cause. One memorable SANE ad featured baby doctor

Atomic-Age Domesticity. In this posed *Life* magazine photo of 1961, family members embody gender stereotypes as they await the end: Dad ready to dig through the rubble, Mom with kitchen gear, son in charge of flashlight and radio, and daughters with blankets and board games. *(Dmitri Kessel/Life Magazine, © Timepix-Getty Images)*

Benjamin Spock gazing with furrowed brow at a little girl under the caption DR. SPOCK IS WORRIED. In New York, antinuclear activists were jailed for refusing to go into shelters during a civil-defense drill. In the early 1960s, the test-ban movement attracted thousands of college students. An antinuclear group called Women's Strike for Peace organized marches in several big cities. Often led by religious pacifists or veteran peace activists, these movements attracted thousands of ordinary citizens as well.

Responding to scientific warnings and world opinion, the superpowers halted nuclear testing in 1958. This moratorium broke down in 1961 as the Soviets and then the United States resumed testing. But in 1963, after the Cuban missile crisis (see Chapter 6), the two nations plus Great Britain signed a treaty banning atmospheric (but not underground) tests. The test-ban movement, a rare instance of political engagement in a mostly passive decade, thus partially achieved its objective.

Controversy surrounding radioactive fallout and its consequences continued for decades. A five-year study by the Department of Health and Human Services, made public in 2003 under congressional pressure, calculated that fallout from all atomic tests in the 1950s probably caused at least fifteen thousand U.S. cancer deaths and an additional twenty thousand nonfatal cancers.

Brown and Beyond: The Civil-Rights Movement in Eisenhower's America

Even more dramatic evidence of reviving political activism was the drive for racial justice that gathered momentum as the decade wore on. Focused initially on segregation in the South, this movement gradually broadened in scope, launching a revolution in race relations whose full implications continue to unfold. This chapter looks at the early stages of the drive for racial justice; Chapter 8 explores the changes that overtook this effort in the late 1950s and beyond, propelling it in more radical directions.

Across the South, and in parts of the North as well, blacks attended segregated schools as the fifties began, a practice upheld in 1896 by the U.S. Supreme Court in *Plessy* v. *Ferguson*. The high court in *Plessy* had specified that the facilities provided for blacks and whites must be equal, thus providing the legal rationale for the South's so-called separate but equal public-school system. In reality, funding for black education rarely matched that for whites, and the facilities provided for black students were often appallingly inferior.

Segregated schools formed only one piece in a vast mosaic of institutionalized racism. Although some of its cruder and more brutal manifestations had faded by midcentury, prejudice and discrimination infected every national institution from schools and churches to the media and the workplace. Wherever one looked in early postwar America, blacks were treated as second-class citizens.

A convergence of social and ideological trends challenged this pervasive reality. World War II had changed the lives of many blacks. Thousands served in the military or flocked to the North and West, where they took jobs in war plants, joined labor unions, and swelled the voting ranks. The narrator of *Invisible Man*,

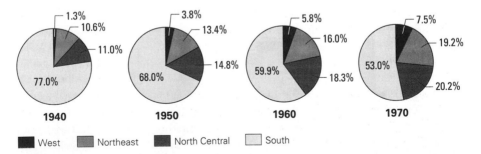

FIGURE 5.2

Regional Distribution of the Black Population, 1940–1970

NOTE: The Northeast consists of New England and the Middle Atlantic states of New York, Pennsylvania, and New Jersey. The North Central region consists of the Great Lakes states along with Missouri, Kansas, Iowa, Nebraska, and the Dakotas. The South is made up of all states south of the Mason-Dixon line (including the border states of Delaware, West Virginia, and Kentucky) and extends as far west as Texas and Oklahoma. The remaining states are in the West.

SOURCE: *The Negro Almanac: A Reference Work on the African American,* 5th ed. (Detroit: Gale Research Inc., 1989).

Ralph Ellison's meditation on the modern African American experience, comes North during the war to find work. (Ellison, writing on the symbolic as well as the realistic plane, gives his narrator a job at the Liberty Paint Company, a factory that specializes in an eye-dazzling paint called Optic White. The few drops of black added to each batch totally disappear.)

At the same time, industrialization and urbanization strained the South's racial caste system. As blacks poured into southern cities and factories, and as the urban black middle class grew, segregation proved increasingly difficult to enforce. In the civil-rights activism that would soon sweep the South, white corporate and financial leaders, worried that protests would threaten the region's economy, often worked quietly to moderate the more extreme and degrading forms of racial segregation. The affluence of the 1950s played a role as well, increasing the urban black work force, adding to the ranks of middle-class black churches and colleges, and fattening contributions to civil-rights organizations. The mass media—especially television—spotlighted civil-rights protests and violent white resistance in southern communities that might otherwise have gone unnoticed. Even rock-and-roll, with its blurring of racial lines, played a role.

At the ideological level, long-entrenched racial beliefs no longer commanded unthinking assent. Hitler's racism and the Holocaust discredited a once semi-respectable body of racial thought that had long undergirded the southern caste system and American racism in general. Gunnar Myrdal's *An American Dilemma* of 1944, discussed in Chapter 3, accelerated this change in the intellectual climate.

As we have seen, Cold War realities further undermined ingrained patterns of racism. As Washington denounced Moscow's human-rights record and courted allies in Asia and Africa, the reality of racism at home became highly embarrassing. The worldwide revolutionary upsurge against colonialism stirred U.S. blacks as well. Thus economic, demographic, cultural, ideological, and strategic trends converged to erode the foundations of racial segregation.

The immediate impetus for change came from the National Association for the Advancement of Colored People (NAACP), which had long mounted court challenges to racism, including segregated schools. As early as 1938, the Supreme Court had ordered the University of Missouri Law School to admit a black applicant on the grounds that because Missouri had no law school for blacks, the separate-but-equal standard obviously could not be met. Supreme Court decisions in 1950, in cases brought by the NAACP (see page 75), had further eroded *Plessy* v. *Ferguson.* Particularly important were *McLaurin* v. *Oklahoma State Regents* and *Sweatt* v. *Painter,* in which the high court outlawed segregated professional schools not fully equal to those open to whites.

The years of painstaking legal work paid off on May 17, 1954, when a unanimous Supreme Court under Chief Justice Earl Warren, in the case of *Brown* v. *Board of Education of Topeka,* ruled that racially segregated public schools violated the constitutional principle of equal treatment for all. The NAACP brief, presented by Thurgood Marshall (later the first black Supreme Court justice), cited studies showing the effects of segregation on children. The psychologist Kenneth Clark, for example, had found that black children, when presented with otherwise identical brown-skinned and white-skinned dolls, usually chose the white doll. "The fact that young Negro children would prefer to be white," he wrote, "reflects their knowledge that society prefers white people."

Citing the work of Clark, Myrdal, and others, the justices declared:

> [S]egregation of children in public schools solely on the basis of race, even though the physical facilities . . . may be equal, deprive[s] the children of the minority group of equal educational opportunities . . . [and] generates a feeling of inferiority . . . that may [never] be undone. . . . [I]n the field of public education the doctrine of "separate but equal" has no place. Separate educational facilities are inherently unequal.

Although the Court declared in a follow-up ruling of 1955 that school segregation should end "with all deliberate speed" and instructed the federal courts to ensure "a prompt and reasonable start toward full compliance," southern white segregationists organized a campaign of massive resistance. White "Citizens' Councils"—more "respectable" versions of the Ku Klux Klan—sprang up to fight integration. Early in 1956, echoing the states-rights battles of the pre–Civil War era, the Virginia legislature proclaimed the right of a state to "interpose its sovereignty" to preserve segregation. That March, one hundred southern members of Congress announced their intent to use "all lawful means" to overthrow the *Brown* decision. Opponents of court-ordered integration like the influential Richmond, Virginia, newspaper editor James J. Kilpatrick claimed that the issue was states rights, not segregation, but everyone understood that the *Brown* decision struck at the roots of the South's pervasive system of racial separation and white supremacy. When Clinton, Tennessee, integrated its high school, segregationist mobs shouted "Kill the niggers!" at the black students. Soon after, a dynamite blast demolished the school.

President Eisenhower at first remained aloof from the controversy. Privately critical of the *Brown* decision, he later described his choice of Earl Warren as chief justice as "the biggest damnfool mistake I ever made." Citing Prohibition as an example, Eisenhower insisted to friends that deep-seated social mores could not be changed by court rulings. Political calculations also underlay Ike's silence. He had won four southern states in 1952, and Republican strategy assumed growing white support in the once solidly Democratic South.

Instead of using his enormous prestige to help white America come to terms with its racist history, Eisenhower held back, tacitly encouraging those fighting to preserve white supremacy. The cabinet rarely discussed civil rights, and White House meetings with black leaders were rare and tense. When the one black in the Eisenhower White House, E. Frederick Morrow, a foreign affairs specialist, alerted Eisenhower to rising racial tensions, Ike replied, "Oh Fred, you're an alarmist." When pressed, Eisenhower claimed that his was the path of moderation, as though racism and opposition to racism were equally deplorable extremist positions.

Eisenhower did concede that the law must be obeyed. In a press conference after the *Brown* decision, he said: "The Supreme Court has spoken. . . . I am sworn to uphold the constitutional processes in this country; and I will obey." It was this commitment to the rule of law, not support for integration, that finally forced Eisenhower to take a decisive stand.

The flashpoint came in Little Rock, Arkansas, a moderate city whose school board, in cooperation with local black leaders, had worked out a plan for gradual

"Tsk Tsk — Somebody Should Do Something About That"

---from Herblock: A Cartoonist's Life (Times Books, 1998)

Raging Crisis, Hesitant Response. In 1956 *Washington Post* cartoonist Herbert Block criticized President Eisenhower's failure to act decisively as massive resistance to the Supreme Court's school-integration order raged across the South. *("Tsk Tsk—Somebody Should Do Something About That," from* Herblock: A Cartoonist's Life *[Times Books, 1998])*

integration. But the politics of race intervened. When Alabama's George Wallace lost a gubernatorial primary campaign to an outspoken segregationist in 1958, he commented, "They out-segged me that time, but they'll never do it again." Arkansas governor Orval Faubus, hitherto a moderate on racial issues, had taken the same demagogic low road in winning a third term in 1956. As school opening approached in September 1957, Faubus called out the Arkansas National Guard to prevent nine black students from enrolling at Little Rock's all-white Central High School. In a radio talk the night before the fall term began, Faubus peddled alarmist rumors about caravans of white racists converging on Little Rock from all over the South. If the integration of Central High went forward, he intoned, "blood will flow in the streets."

After Faubus's speech, black leaders decided to delay the black teenagers' enrollment, fearful for their safety. However, one of the nine, Elizabeth Eckford, did not get the word. Showing up at Central High the next morning, she encountered ranks of stony-faced Arkansas national guardsmen blocking her way and a screaming, spitting mob. "Lynch her! Lynch her!" they shouted. "No nigger bitch is going to get into our school. Get out of here!" Shielded by two sympathetic whites, she barely escaped. After a meeting with President Eisenhower, Faubus grudgingly obeyed a federal court order to withdraw the state national guard, but when the black students again tried to enroll, segregationist mobs once more blocked their way.

At last, Eisenhower acted. In a nationally televised address, he denounced the Little Rock mob as "disgraceful" and vowed to enforce the law. Responding to a request for help from Little Rock's mayor, he ordered a thousand U.S. paratroopers to the city and federalized the Arkansas National Guard. Protected by federal troops, the black students enrolled. When racists bombed the home of one student, Carlotta Walls, she went to school as usual. "Nothing has changed," she told reporters. Although local school boards resisted integration and the white Citizens' Councils opened white-only private schools across the South, school segregation slowly eroded in the later 1950s and the 1960s under the pressure of court orders and media publicity.

The sociological and psychological research cited by the Supreme Court in *Brown* v. *Board of Education* was not universally accepted at the time, and it later came into even greater question. In *Forced Justice: School Desegregation and the Law* (1995), for example, David J. Armor marshaled social-science studies challenging the argument that self-esteem and academic performance are linked to segregated or integrated education. Similarly, the process of school integration proved far more complex, and its social benefits more elusive, than the Supreme Court assumed in 1954. Faced with court-ordered integration, many whites simply moved, so that school desegregation, ironically, may have furthered de facto housing segregation. What has remained unchallenged, however, is the recognition that officially sanctioned, legally enforced racial segregation has no place in a society claiming to embrace principles of democracy and equality. The Warren Court grasped that essential fact, and acted accordingly. Despite the resistance and the slow progress, writes historian Waldo E. Martin, Jr., the *Brown* decision remains monumentally important "as both a historical watershed and powerful cultural symbol" of an unfolding black freedom struggle.

Meanwhile, the revolution spread from the courts to the streets and churches, as years of suppressed anger and aspirations for equality burst forth. Attention soon focused on Montgomery, Alabama, the self-proclaimed "cradle of the Confederacy." As in much of the South, Montgomery had a segregated public transit system: Blacks sat in the back of the bus, whites in the front. When a bus filled, blacks had to yield their seats to whites on demand. On December 1, 1955, Rosa Parks, secretary of the state NAACP and a long-time activist, after a day's work as a department-store seamstress, refused the driver's order to give up her seat to a white man. "I felt it was just something I had to do," Parks would later recall of a simple act of defiance that challenged an entire structure of racial injustice. With Parks's arrest, the state NAACP led by E. D. Nixon, a railroad porter, proposed that Montgomery's blacks organize a bus boycott, a technique that had been briefly tried in 1953 in Baton Rouge, Louisiana. Volunteers stayed up all night preparing leaflets announcing the boycott.

The boycott planners recruited the Reverend Martin Luther King, Jr., the newly appointed, twenty-six-year-old pastor of a middle-class black Baptist church in Montgomery. King, the son and namesake of a prominent Atlanta minister, had just received his Ph.D. in theology from Boston University. His influences included not only Christian thought but also Henry David Thoreau, who had gone to jail rather than pay taxes to support the Mexican War, and Mohandas Gandhi, whose nonviolent tactics had helped to end British rule in India.

The Reality of Segregation. Dr. Charles Atkins, a psychiatrist, with his wife Hannah and their sons in Oklahoma City's railway station, 1955. Hannah Atkins later served in the Oklahoma legislature and as assistant director of the Oklahoma Department of Human Services. *(AP/Wide World Photos)*

From the first, King underscored the ethical issues at stake and appealed to conscience. For him, nonviolence did not mean passive acquiescence in oppression. Rather, he argued, protesters must dramatize patterns of racism and generate a "creative tension" between the principle of equality and the fact of injustice. Heir to a rich tradition of black pulpit oratory, King would ultimately win a vast following of blacks and whites. Not only charismatic but also a skillful tactician, he knew how to translate principles into actions.

King and his associates set three goals for the bus boycott: courteous treatment of blacks, more black drivers, and seating on a first-come, first-served basis. (In this cautious early stage of the civil-rights movement, the boycott leaders did not initially challenge the custom that relegated blacks to the rear of the bus.) For nearly a year, by walking or sharing rides, blacks stayed off the buses. "I'm not walking for myself," reflected one boycotter, "I'm walking for my children and my grandchildren." A bomb shattered the front of King's house in January 1956, and in February he and the other boycott leaders briefly went to jail, but they held firm. In weekly mass meetings at his church, King and others placed the boycott in a broader context. As

King promised his followers in December 1955, "When the history books are written . . . , somebody will have to say, 'There lived a race of people . . . who had the marvelous courage to stand up for their rights and thereby they injected a new meaning into the being of history and of civilization.' And we are going to do that."

At last, in November 1956, a federal court threw out all state and local laws upholding segregated buses in Alabama. Beyond the legal victory, the Montgomery boycott had energized the black community and replaced resignation with hope. When an auto caravan of white racists prowled through Montgomery's black neighborhood the night after the court ruling, expecting to inspire terror, a crowd of blacks trailed it exuberantly through the streets. Rather than huddling in the dark, as in the past, the residents flung up their shades and left their lights blazing.

For Martin Luther King, Jr., the Montgomery bus boycott launched a career that would propel him to world fame and end with an assassin's bullet. But in 1956, all that lay ahead. Moving back to Atlanta to become copastor of his father's church, King with other black ministers in 1957 started the Southern Christian Leadership Conference (SCLC) to guide the growing movement. In *Stride Toward Freedom* (1958), he told the story of the bus boycott and provided a blueprint for similar actions elsewhere.

Black writers helped shape the new consciousness spreading among African Americans. Although Ellison's *Invisible Man* was concerned less with immediate political action than with heightened individual consciousness, he, like jazz artist Dizzy Gillespie, viewed his work as a step on the path to liberation. Any work by a black writer or artist, he insisted, inevitably represented a political act. "The consciousness of a race is the gift of its individuals," observes the narrator. "We create the race by creating ourselves."

James Baldwin, born in Harlem in 1924, commented on the civil-rights movement in a series of essays collected in *Notes of a Native Son* (1955) and *Nobody Knows My Name* (1961). Baldwin pondered the role of black intellectuals and writers in the freedom struggle and explored how racism penetrated the nation's institutions and the consciousness of whites and blacks alike. Echoing psychologist Kenneth Clark, he lamented racism's effects on the self-image of black children, "taught from the moment their eyes open on the world that their color was a badge of inferiority."

The Montgomery bus boycott also drew upon a long tradition of African American protest. In the 1930s, black activists in Harlem had organized boycotts of white-owned businesses that refused to hire black salespersons. Various southern communities had witnessed black activism against segregated institutions well before World War II. But Montgomery was unique in scope and visibility, and it propelled black protest to unprecedented new levels.

The surge of civil-rights activism posed problems for both major political parties. Republicans sought to enlarge their traditional appeal to black voters while retaining their base in the white South. The Democratic Party was torn between its northern and southern wings. The former included a strong black and white-liberal component but also many conservative white ethnics. The lily-white southern wing was overwhelmingly segregationist, with a few liberals on racial and other issues, mostly on university campuses.

Out of this political minefield emerged the Civil Rights Act of 1957, the first such federal law since the 1870s. Attorney General Herbert Brownell had convinced Eisenhower that by introducing a civil-rights bill, Republicans could further split the

Democratic Party and lure back northern blacks who had been voting Democratic since the New Deal. Blacks, Brownell calculated, held the balance of power in seven states and sixty congressional districts. The administration's bill, introduced in the election year 1956, passed the House but was bottled up in the Senate Judiciary Committee by chairman James Eastland of Mississippi, a rabid segregationist.

Senate majority leader Lyndon Johnson opposed the 1956 bill, aware of the risks it posed for the Democrats. But when Eisenhower again sent Congress a civil-rights bill in 1957, Johnson, eager for the 1960 Democratic presidential nomination and seeking to shed his regional image, cajoled his fellow southern Democrats to support it.

The compromise bill that emerged, although watered down by southern legislators, did establish important precedents. The measure focused entirely on voting rights. Although only part of the larger struggle, this issue was vital, since the disfranchisement of southern blacks by a variety of subterfuges posed a massive roadblock to the civil-rights cause. The new law authorized the attorney general to seek court injunctions to stop electoral officials from interfering with any citizen's voting rights. It created a civil-rights division within the Justice Department and a new federal agency, the U.S. Civil Rights Commission, to monitor racial issues. A follow-up measure, the Civil Rights Act of 1960, authorized federal courts to appoint referees to ensure local compliance with the voting-rights laws.

Important as it was, this early phase of the civil-rights movement illustrated the limits of the nation's understanding of racism's grip. Liberal whites and even the middle-class leaders of the NAACP saw the problem as primarily a legal one involving segregation and voting rights in the South. If the more blatant forms of legalized racism were outlawed and Americans of goodwill united against southern segregation and and its racist defenders like Faubus and Wallace, they believed, the problem would ease.

Some evidence encouraged this reassuring view, including the Supreme Court's unanimity in the *Brown* decision, the bipartisan support for the 1957 Civil Rights Act, and the successful Montgomery bus boycott. These examples suggested that moderate steps focused on ending officially enforced racial segregation in public facilities in the South would accommodate the grievances of African Americans, without undue social turmoil. In the next decade, this comfortable assumption would shatter as new strategies, leaders, and issues radically transformed the fight for racial equality.

Beyond Suburbia: Hispanics and Native Americans in Eisenhower's America

As African Americans mobilized to protest segregation, other groups, too, faced difficult times outside the charmed circle of the good life in suburbia. The influx of Hispanics continued through the 1950s, including many from Puerto Rico. As U.S. citizens, Puerto Ricans are free to come to the United States at will, and many thousands did after World War II, settling in East Coast cities that welcomed them as a source of cheap labor. By 1960, New York City's Puerto Rican population, concentrated in East Harlem, stood at nearly a million. Thousands more settled in Hartford, Philadelphia, Jersey City, and other urban centers. Entering a new environment at the bottom of the ladder, the newcomers often endured crowded, substandard housing and inadequate health care, police protection, and schooling.

Eager to work, the men labored at unskilled jobs that were nevertheless essential to urban life, while women managed their families or found jobs as domestics, garment workers, or in other low-paying positions. Hispanic kids picked up English rapidly, but language barriers and discrimination persisted. In the crowded barrios, the shiny cars, household appliances, suburban homes, and consumer goods glimpsed in store windows, magazine ads, movies, and TV commercials seemed part of another America.

But East Harlem and other Puerto Rican enclaves also sheltered a strong culture of close-knit families, vibrant street life, Catholic mass and religious festivals, and Caribbean music and cuisine. Puerto Ricans embraced the national sport, baseball. Roberto Clemente, a hero beloved by Hispanics and Anglos alike, was a Puerto Rican who began with the Pittsburgh Pirates in 1955 and went on to win four National League batting championships and twelve Golden Glove awards for his fielding prowess. Clemente died in a plane crash in 1972 on a mission to aid Nicaraguan earthquake victims. Despite the positive aspects, however, most Puerto Ricans, as well as other Hispanics, lived in hard-pressed communities grappling with poverty, youth gangs, and a median income only about two-thirds that of non-Hispanic whites.

Immigration from Mexico further swelled the ranks of Hispanic Americans. Although concentrated in the Southwest and Pacific Coast, Mexican newcomers ranged widely in the search for work. As irrigation systems brought more acreage into cultivation in the arid West, the demand for seasonal agricultural workers increased. By 1959 some 450,000 Mexicans were arriving annually under the federal *bracero* program. Though required to return to Mexico after the harvest season, many *braceros* and their families remained in the United States. Mexicans lacking proper documentation were deported, especially in times of recession, but the ceaseless flow of new arrivals more than balanced the deportees. As urban job opportunities increased, many Mexican Americans headed for the burgeoning *barrios* of Los Angeles and other cities of the West. By 1960, some three-quarters of all Mexican Americans resided in cities, adding a distinctive Hispanic note to urban life. Hispanic organizations continued to battle discrimination, and in 1954 the U.S. Supreme Court, underscoring the concern for the civil rights for minorities evident in the *Brown* decision, barred the exclusion of Mexican Americans from juries.

Hispanic Americans gradually gained political clout, as the career of Henry Gonzales dramatically illustrates. Earning a law degree in 1943, Gonzales was elected to the city council of San Antonio, Texas, in 1953. Three years later he won a seat in the Texas senate, where on one occasion he filibustered for thirty hours against bills designed to preserve racial segregation in Texas schools. In 1961 Gonzales won a special election to the U.S. Congress, where he served for thirty-seven years. At his death in 2000, a San Antonio newspaper eulogized his long political career as "a voice for the downtrodden and racial minorities."

As with Hispanic Americans, urbanization also occurred among the nation's oldest ethnic group, the 256,000 Indians (according to the 1960 census) whose ancestors had arrived thousands of years before the first Europeans. Many Indians had left their reservations during World War II, serving in the military or seeking work, but the process was accelerated by government policy in the 1950s. In the 1930s, New Deal Indian policy and programs had encouraged tribal life on the reservations. But enthusiasm for this approach had faded, and by 1950 many reservations were plagued by poverty, alcoholism, social problems, and unemployment rates of 70 percent or higher. Partially to address this situation, and out of a desire to end the "segregation" of Native Americans, Congress in 1953 passed a Termination Resolution that defined a new policy goal: "to free Indians from federal control . . . and subject them to the same laws and privileges [as other citizens] as rapidly as possible." Under this law, Congress by 1960 had terminated treaties with sixty-one tribal groups from Wisconsin to Oregon, cutting off all economic assistance and services. To encourage Indians to move to cities, where job opportunities would theoretically be better and assimilation more likely, the government paid moving expenses and provided temporary housing and job assistance to Indians who agreed to leave the reservations. Some sixty thousand did so, but the adjustment proved difficult. Entering the urban labor market posed challenges, and social problems associated with poverty, educational deficiencies, and the loss of a support network were not easily overcome.

Economic interests as well as humanitarian concerns underlay the termination policy. Nearly half a million acres of "terminated" tribal land, some of it rich in timber or mineral resources, fell into corporate hands. Tribal leaders and the National Congress of American Indians, founded in 1944, protested termination, but to no avail. Nevertheless, anger over this policy stimulated Indian organizing and legal action, laying the groundwork for a wave of protest in the 1970s. In future decades Indian fortunes would improve and some treaty rights would be regained, but for many Native Americans the 1950s was a dark and difficult time.

Conclusion

The white, middle-class baby boomers who were children or teenagers in the 1950s later tended to bathe the decade in a glow of nostalgia. A 1970s comedy series set in the fifties was called *Happy Days*. A 1989 ad for a collection of 1950s' pop songs evoked those "warm, wonderful years, filled with magical memories." In some ways, the prosperous, comparatively tranquil decade does seem almost idyllic. The economy hummed, overall jobless rates remained low, and many young suburban couples looked confidently to the future.

Viewed more comprehensively, however, the "warm, wonderful" Eisenhower years take on a less rosy aura, shadowed by international tensions, nuclear fears, Red Scare paranoia, and the reality of economic want amid general prosperity. Most African Americans, Hispanics, and Indian peoples had little reason to look back on the fifties with nostalgia. As the Cold War narrowed political debate and cultural expression, the search for "subversives" intensified and dissident voices were marginalized. Nineteen-fifties conservatism stemmed not only from Cold War anticommunism but also from the economic boom and a longing for calm and stability after years of depression, war, and the stresses of postwar deconversion. Yet despite the conservative turn, few challenged the basic framework of welfare liberalism that was the New Deal's continuing legacy.

On the popular cultural front, television emerged as the dominant new medium. A potent instrument for marketing and entertaining, TV rarely offered a critical perspective on the consumerist culture it fostered or acknowledged the America beyond the affluent suburbs. Television occasionally riveted the nation's attention on public issues, but more often contributed to escapism and political apathy.

Yet this supposedly passive decade also spawned a campaign against nuclear testing, a historic Supreme Court school-desegregation ruling, an important if limited civil-rights act, and the moral drama of the Montgomery bus boycott. What finally impresses one most about the fifties is less its bland uniformity than its vibrant diversity. The decade of Dwight Eisenhower, John Foster Dulles, and Norman Vincent Peale also gave rise to C. Wright Mills, Allan Ginsberg, Jack Kerouac, Little Richard, Elvis Presley, Martin Luther King, Jr., Ralph Ellison, James Baldwin, and Henry Gonzales. Any ten-year period that can accommodate such a range of voices, viewpoints, and causes defies easy categorization.

SELECTED READINGS

Cultural Innovators and Rebels

Michael T. Bertrand, *Race, Rock, and Elvis* (2000); David Cochran, *America Noir: Underground Writers and Film Makers of the Postwar Era* (2000); Annette Cox, *Art-as-Politics: The Abstract Expressionist Avant-Garde and Society* (1982); Pete Daniel, *Lost Revolutions: The South in the 1950s* (2000); Joel Foreman, ed., *The Other Fifties: Interrogating Midcentury American Icons* (1997); Simon Frith, *Sound Effects: Youth, Leisure, and the Politics of Rock and Roll* (1981); James Gilbert, *A Cycle of Outrage: America's Reaction to the Juvenile Delinquent in the 1950s* (1986); John A. Jackson, *Big Beat Heat: Alan Freed and the Early Years of Rock and Roll* (1991); W. T. Lhamon, Jr., *Deliberate Speed: The Origins of a Cultural Style in the American 1950s* (1990); Bobbie Ann Mason, *Elvis* Presley (2003); Jane deHart Mathews, "Art and Politics in Cold War America," *American Historical Review* (October 1976); Alanna Nash, *The Colonel: Colonel Tom Parker and Elvis Presley* (2003); Maria Reidelbach, *Completely Mad: A History of the Comic Book and Magazine* (1991); David P. Szatmary, *Rockin' in Time: A Social History of Rock and Roll* (1991).

Literature and Social Thought in Eisenhower's America

William Chace, *Lionel Trilling: Criticism and Politics* (1980); Michael Davidson, *The San Francisco Renaissance: Poetics and Community at Mid-Century* (1989); Robert Booth Fowler, *Believing Skeptics: American Political Intellectuals, 1945–1964* (1978); Daniel Horowitz, *Vance Packard and American Social Criticism* (1994); Irving Louis Horowitz, *C. Wright Mills: American Utopian* (1983); Neil Jumonville, *Critical Crossings: The New York Intellectuals in Postwar America* (1991); George Lipsitz, *Class and Culture in Cold War America* (1981); Barry Miles, *Ginsberg: A Biography* (1989); Richard H. Pells, *The Liberal Mind in a Conservative Age: American Intellectuals in the 1940s and 1950s* (1984); Sanford Pinkser, *Jewish-American Fiction, 1917–1987* (1992); Thomas Hill Schaub, *American Fiction in the Cold War* (1991); John Tytell, *Naked Angels: The Lives and Literature of the Beat Generation* (1976); Alan M. Wald, *The New York Intellectuals* (1987); Stephen Whitfield, *The Culture of the Cold War* (1991).

Civil Defense, the Test-Ban Campaign, Segregation, and Civil Rights Protest

David L. Armor, *Forced Justice: School Desegregation and the Law* (1995); Taylor Branch, *Parting the Waters: America in the King Years, 1954–63* (1988); Robert Frederick Burk, *The Eisenhower Administration and Black Civil Rights* (1984); Robert Divine, *Blowing on the Wind: The Nuclear Test Ban Debate, 1954–1960* (1978); Charles W. Eagles, ed., *The Civil Rights Movement in America* (1986); David Garrow, *Bearing the Cross: Martin Luther King, Jr., and the Southern Christian Leadership Conference* (1986); Elizabeth Huckaby, *Crisis at Central High: Little Rock, 1957–1958* (1980); Gregory S. Jacobs, *Getting Around* Brown: *Desegregation, Development, and the Columbus* [Ohio] *Public Schools* (1998); Matthew D. Lassiter and Andrew B. Lewis, eds., *The Moderates' Dilemma: Massive Resistance to School Desegregation in Virginia* (1998); Susan Lyan, *Progressive Women in Conservative Times: Racial Justice, Peace and Feminism, 1945 to the 1960s* (1992); Waldo E. Martin, Jr., Brown v. Board of Education: *A Brief History with Documents* (1998); Laura McEnaney, *Civil Defense Begins at Home: Militarization Meets Everyday Life in the Fifties* (2000); Guy Oakes, *The Imaginary War: Civil Defense and American Cold War Culture* (1994); James T. Patterson, Brown v. Board of Education: *A Civil Rights Milestone and Its Troubled Legacy* (2001); Lucas A. Powe, Jr., *The Warren Court and American Politics* (2000); Howard L. Rosenberg, *Atomic Soldiers: American Victims of Nuclear Experiments* (1980); Jerome F. Shapiro, *Atomic Bomb Cinema* (2002); Harvard Sitkoff, *The Struggle for Black Equality, 1954–1992* (1992); Mark V. Tushnet, *Making Civil Rights Law: Thurgood Marshall and the Supreme Court, 1936–1961* (1994); Robert Weisbrot, *Freedom Bound: A History of America's Civil Rights Movement* (1990); Andreas Wenger, *Living with Peril: Eisenhower, Kennedy, and Nuclear Weapons* (1997); Lawrence S. Wittner, *Resisting the Bomb: 1954–1970* (1998).

The Other Americans In the Age of Suburbia

Rodolfo Acuña, *Occupied America: A History of Chicanos* (3rd ed., 1988); Donald Fixico, *Termination and Relocation: Federal Indian Policy, 1945–1960* (1986); Joshua B. Freeman, *Working-Class New York: Life and Labor Since World War II* (2000); Mario T. Garcia, *Mexican Americans: Leadership, Ideology, and Identity, 1930–1960* (1989); Leo Grebler, Joan W. Moore, and Ralph C. Guzman, *The Mexican American People* (1970); Douglas S. Massey, *American Apartheid: Segregation and the Making of the Underclass* (1993); James S. Olsen and Raymond Wilson, *Native Americans in the Twentieth Century* (1984); María Pérez y González, *Puerto Ricans in the United States* (2000); Clara E. Rodriguez, *Puerto Ricans: Born in the U.S.A.* (1991); Ricardo Romo, *East Los Angeles: History of a Barrio* (1983).

CHAPTER

The Cold War Heats Up:
From *Sputnik* to Vietnam

WASHINGTON, D.C., was cold and blanketed in snow on January 20, 1961, Inauguration Day, but the newly elected president, John Fitzgerald Kennedy, stood coatless and hatless, tousled hair blowing, as he took the oath of office from Chief Justice Earl Warren. An aged, frail Dwight Eisenhower huddled behind him. For a moment the flow of history seemed to pause, suspended between past and future. JFK's inaugural address, delivered in high-pitched, staccato bursts, offered a series of ringing assertions. The most memorable came near the end: "And so, my fellow Americans, ask not what your country can do for you; ask what you can do for your country." In the troubled and tragedy-ridden decade that lay ahead, Americans would have occasion to look back with mixed feelings at the high hopes many had felt on that blustery inauguration day.

Kennedy took office amid deepening global tensions. The late 1950s had seen worsening Cold War relations and rising fears that the United States was lagging militarily. Kennedy had played on these fears in the 1960 campaign, and as president he displayed a tough aggressiveness in the Caribbean, Europe, Africa, and Southeast Asia. In the 1962 Cuban missile crisis, the world came perilously close to nuclear war.

Nevertheless, the 1960s opened on an upbeat note. In March 1961, in one of his most popular actions, Kennedy created the Peace Corps. Young people by the thousands volunteered for two years of service in educational, agricultural, and technical assistance projects in developing countries. Under the energetic direction of Kennedy's brother-in-law Sargent Shriver, the Peace Corps captured the imagination of the young. By 1966 some fifteen thousand volunteers were working in nearly fifty countries. While some skeptics dismissed the program as Cold War propaganda, historian Elizabeth Cobbs Hoffman, in *All You Need Is Love: The Peace Corps and the Spirit of the 1960s* (1998), argues that volunteers made valuable contributions in the lands where they served and were changed in the process as they encountered cultures very different from their own.

The Peace Corps and the 1963 Test Ban Treaty halting atmospheric nuclear tests represented the best of the Kennedy legacy. Overall, however, Kennedy's record in international affairs remained inconclusive when his presidency ended tragically in November 1963, its major legacy an idealized image of the fallen leader and speculation about what might have been.

Cold War Alarms in the Late Fifties

Americans awoke to unsettling news on October 4, 1957: Russia had launched a 184-pound space satellite, called *Sputnik,* or "Little Traveler." A second satellite, launched a month later, carried a dog, the first living creature to leave Earth's atmosphere. The next May came *Sputnik III,* weighing nearly 3,000 pounds. More Soviet space probes followed, including one in 1959 that photographed the never-before-seen back side of the moon.

Initially, the Eisenhower administration had pooh-poohed the achievement as a stunt. But in reality, *Sputnik* and its successors jolted Americans' smug assumptions about U.S. scientific superiority and stimulated debate over U.S. public education. In *The American High School Today* (1959), former Harvard president James Conant found America woefully behind the Soviet Union in science, math, and foreign-language education.

In direct response to *Sputnik,* the National Defense Education Act (1958) appropriated $800 million for loans to college and university students and to the states to beef up science and foreign-language instruction. The measure once again illustrates the importance of Cold War calculations in shaping domestic policy. Whatever the motives, colleges and universities welcomed federal help in serving a crush of students. From 1952 to 1960, enrollment in America's institutions of higher learning surged from 2.1 million to 3.6 million.

Sputnik sent a still more chilling message: The Soviets now had the technology to deploy intercontinental ballistic missiles (ICBMs) that could whisk nuclear warheads to U.S. targets in minutes. Late in 1957, spooked by *Sputnik* and radioactive fallout, 64 percent of Americans cited the nuclear threat as the nation's top problem. Strategists, meanwhile, feared that the Soviets would use their edge in rocketry to push their broader foreign-policy goals. Policy analyst Herbert Dinerstein developed this point in a 1958 article in *Foreign Affairs:*

> If the Soviet Union should continue to gain technologically . . . [and] acquire . . . preponderant military strength, they would have policy alternatives even more attractive than the initiation of nuclear war. By flaunting presumably invincible strength, the Soviet Union could compel piecemeal capitulation of the democracies. This prospect must indeed seem glittering to the Soviet leaders.

As the Russians evened the nuclear balance, John Foster Dulles's doctrine of influencing Soviet behavior by the threat of massive retaliation lost credibility. Dulles himself, in a 1958 Pentagon speech, conceded as much. The United States clung to the massive-retaliation threat, but the policy's underlying assumptions began to crumble.

Although U.S. intelligence reported no evidence of an operational Soviet ICBM system, Congress, columnists, and Pentagon officials warned of a "missile gap" and called upon the United States to deploy an ICBM force. Eisenhower resisted, fearing the inflationary effect of uncontrolled military spending and confident that America's nuclear arsenal was strong enough to deter a Soviet attack.

Despite Eisenhower's reservations, the first U.S. ICBM, the Atlas, became operational in 1959. Indeed, by the end of his term, pushing the nuclear competition to new levels of menace, the president had authorized some eleven hundred nuclear missiles for deployment in the United States; European-based intermediate-range missiles; and nineteen nuclear-powered Polaris submarines, each carrying sixteen nuclear missiles. Despite Ike's cost-cutting efforts, by 1959 military spending had rebounded to Korean War levels, contributing to the largest peacetime budget deficit up to that time: $12.5 billion. Nevertheless, his emphasis on cost control had some effect: Military spending was a smaller percentage of the GNP in 1960 than in 1957.

In *Eisenhower and the Missile Gap* (1995), historian Peter J. Roman shows that intelligence estimates by the CIA and the military consistently inflated the Soviet Union's strength in missiles and delivery systems. These inflated estimates then became the basis of competing demands by the U.S. military services, leading to a proliferation of land-, sea-, and air-based nuclear delivery systems. Eisenhower tried to resist this process, but since he preferred working behind the scenes, he never effectively mobilized public opinion against the upwardly spiraling nuclear arms race.

Given the bipartisan support for the Cold War and the economic benefits of Pentagon contracts, the Democrats rarely challenged military spending levels in these years; indeed, in 1957 the liberal Americans for Democratic Action argued for *more* military spending, especially on conventional forces. Only a few mavericks criticized wasteful Pentagon procurement practices such as the "cost-plus" contracts that guaranteed a fixed profit regardless of cost overruns. The radical journalist I. F. Stone wrote in 1957, "How can there possibly be wise and adequate [funding] . . . of social welfare if the military are allowed a blank check?"

Although Stalin's death and the 1955 Geneva summit conference temporarily had eased U.S.-Soviet relations, the later 1950s brought fresh tensions. First, Moscow in 1957 agreed to assist the Chinese in building an atomic bomb. "The East wind is prevailing over the West wind . . . ," declared Chinese communist leader Mao Zedong. "The forces of socialism are overwhelmingly superior to the forces of imperialism."

A year later, in November 1958, Stalin's successor Nikita Khrushchev, seeking to force recognition of communist East Germany, set a six-month deadline after which, he insisted, the Western powers would have to deal directly with East Germany, not with Moscow, on matters relating to Berlin. When NATO rejected Khrushchev's ultimatum, another Berlin blockade seemed possible. But the mercurial Soviet leader, with a U.S. trip scheduled for 1959, allowed his deadline to pass. Racing through his American tour, Khrushchev met with Eisenhower and plied his heavy-handed folksiness on Hollywood stars and Iowa farmers. The two leaders scheduled another summit meeting for Paris in 1960. Soon Vice President Nixon visited Moscow and engaged in his impromptu "kitchen debate" with Khrushchev.

On the eve of the Paris summit, however, the Soviets shot down a U.S. U-2 spy plane and captured the pilot, Francis Gary Powers.* Washington initially

---

*Powers was tried in the Soviet Union and convicted of espionage but eventually was released. Ironically, he later died in a helicopter crash while employed as a radio traffic reporter.

claimed that a weather plane had wandered off course, but when the Soviets produced Powers, Eisenhower admitted responsibility for the flight, citing U.S. security needs. Khrushchev left Paris and stormed back to Moscow. Although a setback for détente, the incident solidified Eisenhower's popularity at home. Thousands turned out to welcome his return to Washington after the failed summit.

Soviet influence in the Middle East remained a concern as well. In 1957, following a speech by Eisenhower before a joint session of Congress, both houses passed a resolution that came to be called the Eisenhower Doctrine. It authorized the administration to provide economic and military aid and even to intervene militarily to defend any Middle East nation from "international communism." In the background loomed a vital resource: oil. From 1948 to 1972, Middle East oil production gushed from 1.1 million to 18.2 million barrels per day, and the region's proved reserves grew more than sixteenfold. As Middle East petroleum became increasingly important to the economies of the industrialized West and Japan, keeping the region in the Western camp became a keystone of U.S. foreign policy.

A major test of the Eisenhower Doctrine came in 1958 when Iraq, after a coup engineered by Egyptian leader Gamal Abdel Nasser, left the Baghdad Pact (see pages 109–110). Dreading similar coups elsewhere, Eisenhower ordered fifteen thousand marines to nearby Lebanon. British troops, meanwhile, landed in Jordan, whose pro-Western government faced threats by Nasser supporters. The troops soon withdrew as the immediate danger faded, but Washington's somewhat contradictory goals in the Middle East—to prevent Soviet penetration, secure the flow of Arab oil to the West, and maintain close ties with Israel—guaranteed that the United States would remain enmeshed in the affairs of this troubled and unstable region.

In Cuba, meanwhile, guerrilla leader Fidel Castro overthrew pro-U.S. dictator Fulgencio Batista in 1959. Castro initially received favorable U.S. press coverage, but relations with Washington soured as he allied with the Soviet Union, mounted a Marxist revolution, imprisoned opponents, expelled U.S. businesses (including organized-crime figures who ran the island's gambling casinos), and seized U.S.-owned oil refineries. After securing an anti-Castro resolution from the Organization of American States, the administration halted U.S. imports of Cuban sugar, vital to the island's economy. Secretly, Eisenhower approved a CIA plan for an anti-Castro invasion of Cuba in 1961.

Foreshadowing the 1960s, the later Eisenhower administration paid more attention to Southeast Asia. Having managed successful coups in Iran and Guatemala, the CIA in 1957 planned a similar operation to overthrow Indonesia's ruler, Sukarno, who was suspected of communist leanings. Sukarno maneuvered cleverly, however, and by 1959 Washington had shifted policy and was giving him aid.

In Vietnam, an increasingly autocratic Ngo Dinh Diem, a Catholic in a largely Buddhist country, ignored the political and economic reforms urged on him by Washington (see page 113). Declaring South Vietnam independent, he canceled the elections promised by the Geneva Accords. As anti-Diem military action intensified, so, too, did American involvement; by 1960, some seven hundred U.S. military advisers were in South Vietnam.

Campaign 1960: Variations on the Cold War Theme

The 1960 presidential race pitted Massachusetts senator John F. Kennedy against Vice President Richard Nixon. Kennedy, a Harvard graduate, was shaped from boyhood by his family's great wealth, Irish-Catholic roots, and immersion in politics going back to his maternal grandfather, a Boston saloon keeper who became mayor. Nixon was born in Whittier, California, to lower-middle-class Quaker parents who operated a small grocery store. He attended tiny Whittier College during the depths of the Depression, graduating in 1934.

Both men had served as naval officers in World War II, and both entered Congress in 1946. Whereas Kennedy's congressional years proved undistinguished, Nixon had achieved visibility for his dogged service on the House Un-American Activities Committee and had been tapped to run with Eisenhower in 1952. His vice-presidential years proved frustrating, as Eisenhower kept him at arm's length. Prodded at a press conference in 1960 to name a major policy decision that Nixon had participated in, Ike laughed and asked for a week to think about it.

Kennedy's father, Joseph P. Kennedy, had made a fortune in the stock market and in the movie business. He was appointed U.S. ambassador to Great Britain by President Roosevelt in 1938, but his isolationism and belief in the inevitability of a Nazi victory killed his political hopes, and he instead groomed his sons for high office. When his eldest son, Joseph, Jr., was killed in World War II, Joseph, Sr., turned to the next in line: John, a handsome, decorated navy veteran. Pressured by his father, John Kennedy ran for Congress in 1946. In 1952, still only thirty-four years old, he won election to the Senate. In 1953 he married Jacqueline Bouvier, a Rhode Island socialite twelve years his junior.

After a failed bid for the vice-presidential nomination in 1956, Kennedy in 1960 joined a crowded field seeking the Democratic presidential nomination. Senator Hubert Humphrey dropped out after Kennedy, aided by his father's fortune, won primary victories in Wisconsin and West Virginia. Senate majority leader Lyndon Johnson avoided the primaries and entered the race only five days before the party convention, where Kennedy won a first-ballot nomination. Despite animosity between the two ambitious men, Johnson accepted Kennedy's offer of the vice-presidential slot.

Launching what would become a tradition in presidential races, Kennedy and Nixon participated in four televised debates. In the first, Nixon, his makeup failing to mask his heavy five o'clock shadow, seemed awkward and sweaty. Kennedy, charismatic, smiling, and spewing facts like a machine-gun, dominated the event. His promises to bring fresh ideas and vigorous leadership to the White House and to "get America moving again" captured the public's attention. A recession that pushed joblessness to a postwar high in 1960 also helped Kennedy.

Democratic strategists targeted the critical African American vote. The Democratic platform included a strong civil-rights plank and promised presidential leadership on this front. On October 26, Kennedy phoned Coretta Scott King to express support for her husband Martin Luther King, Jr., in jail on a trumped-up traffic charge. Through the intervention of the candidate's younger brother, Robert F. Kennedy, King was released. While stopping short of a formal endorsement,

The First Family of Camelot. John F. Kennedy, Jacqueline Bouvier Kennedy, and daughter Caroline. The president's dashing good looks and his wife's cool sophistication underlay a carefully cultivated image that helped Kennedy win the presidency. *(AP/Wide World Photos)*

King praised Kennedy extravagantly. King's father, a Republican and prominent Baptist minister in Atlanta, switched his support to the Democratic candidate.

Playing on Cold War fears, Kennedy warned of a dangerous missile gap separating the United States and the Soviet Union, a gap that mysteriously vanished after the election. In the TV debate on foreign policy, the two candidates vied in portraying themselves as staunch Cold Warriors. Kennedy, however, argued that Eisenhower should have apologized for the U-2 flight to save the Paris summit. He also insisted that the small islands claimed by both the Chinese nationalists and the Chinese communists were not worth the risk of war with China (see page 113).

Kennedy's primary victory in overwhelmingly Protestant West Virginia helped to rebut the claim that a Catholic could not win, but concerns persisted. No Catholic had ever been elected president, and the only other one ever nominated, Governor Al Smith of New York in 1928, had lost resoundingly. When queried about the religion issue, Kennedy shot back, "Nobody asked if I was a Catholic when I joined the United States Navy. . . . Nobody asked my brother if he was a Catholic or a Protestant before he climbed into an American bomber to fly his last mission." When 150 prominent Protestants led by Reverend Norman Vincent Peale warned that a Catholic president would defer to the church hierarchy, Kennedy forcibly insisted that as president he would not allow Catholic doctrine or official pronouncements to dictate his decisions.

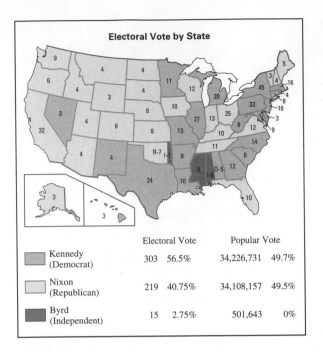

MAP 6.1
Presidential Election of 1960

In an extremely close election, Nixon carried all but four western states and won Tennessee, Kentucky, Virginia, and Florida in the South. Kennedy did well in the industrial belt and the big cities. Seventy percent of blacks voted Democratic, providing Kennedy's margin of victory in several key states. Illinois and Texas provided Kennedy's razor-thin 120,000-vote victory margin. Native-son Johnson helped the ticket in Texas, and in Illinois the Democratic machine run by Chicago mayor Richard J. Daley pushed hard for Kennedy. When Kennedy phoned Daley on election night, as Illinois teetered in the balance, the mayor promised him, "Mr. President, with a bit of luck and the help of a few close friends, you're going to carry Illinois." The Democrats retained control of both houses of Congress, although the Republicans gained twenty-one seats in the House.

Hispanic voters, especially Mexican Americans, played a key role in the election. Hispanic activist groups worked feverishly for Kennedy, founding "Viva Kennedy" clubs in the Southwest and elsewhere. Some 85 percent of Mexican American voters cast their ballots for Kennedy, contributing to his victory in the pivotal state of Texas. But as Ignacio M. García shows in *Viva Kennedy: Mexican Americans in Search of Camelot* (2000), Mexican American hopes that Kennedy would recognize their growing political clout and appoint more Hispanics to positions in government were dashed, leading some to embrace more radical strategies in the later 1960s.

For Richard Nixon, the 1960 defeat, followed by a loss in a California gubernatorial race two years later, was a bitter setback. "You won't have Nixon to kick around anymore," he told reporters after the 1962 defeat. His self-pitying prediction proved decidedly premature.

Kennedy, a boyish-looking forty-three, launched his presidency on a tide of popular support. Along with the call for service to the nation, his inaugural address invoked a "New Frontier" of social progress and underscored the theme of generational change:

> [T]he torch has been passed to a new generation of Americans—born in this century, tempered by war, disciplined by a hard and bitter peace, proud of our ancient heritage—and unwilling to witness or permit the slow undoing of those human rights . . . to which we are committed today at home and around the world.

The Cold War, Kennedy-Style

Shaped by an intensely competitive family and a hard-driving father whom he both admired and feared, Kennedy sought to prove his toughness to the Soviet adversary. America, he declared stridently in his inaugural address, would "pay any price, bear any burden, meet any hardship, support any friend, oppose any foes, . . . to assure the survival and success of liberty." Few expected that the nation would soon fulfill that grandiose pledge in the jungles and rice paddies of Vietnam.

The new president brought to the Cold War the outlook of Democratic liberals such as Harry Truman, Dean Acheson, and George Kennan, who had first committed the nation to the anticommunist cause. Cold War liberalism sprang from the belief, grounded in the reform activism of the New Deal, that through intelligent, planned effort the federal government could serve as an instrument of social betterment. Kennedy-style liberals such as White House speechwriter Arthur Schlesinger, Jr., a historian of the New Deal, applied this commitment globally. The United States under liberal leadership could pursue the Cold War more effectively than the Republicans, they believed, by working for democracy and social change worldwide to blunt communism's appeal. In the 1930s, Franklin Roosevelt had portrayed the fight against the Depression as a great national crusade, and liberal Cold Warriors infused the anticommunist cause with the same high rhetoric. As Undersecretary of Defense John McNaughton put it in a 1961 memo to the White House, "The United States needs a *Grand Objective*. . . . [W]e behave as if . . . our real objective is to sit by our pools and contemplate the spare tires around our middles."

The Kennedy administration also sensed new possibilities in foreign policy as old rivalries and border conflicts between Moscow and Beijing resurfaced. The CIA reported in 1963, "The U.S.S.R. and China are now two separate powers whose interests conflict on almost every issue." Washington did not fully exploit this division until the 1970s, but awareness of its possibilities influenced U.S. Cold War strategy from the early 1960s onward.

Kennedy's secretary of state, Dean Rusk, a soft-spoken political scientist and diplomat from Georgia, epitomized Cold War liberalism. As a progressive white southerner, Rusk had worked for civil rights. In the 1950s, as president of the Rockefeller Foundation, he had initiated health-care programs and other social reforms in the poor regions of the globe, which were coming to be called the Third

World. But Rusk was also a tough-minded Cold Warrior who had long urged a hard line toward communist China.

Quiet and self-effacing, Rusk often maintained a Buddha-like silence in meetings, allowing others to control the debate. On foreign-policy issues, Kennedy relied mainly on a team of advisers recruited from academia and corporate America, who prided themselves on being "hard-nosed realists." Secretary of Defense Robert McNamara, formerly president of Ford Motor Company, specialized in statistical analysis of policy options. Ridiculing McNamara's fondness for charts and graphs, Republican senator Barry Goldwater called him a computer with legs. National security adviser McGeorge Bundy had served as dean of Harvard College.

The grand strategist was Walt Rostow, a White House adviser who later headed the State Department's Policy Planning Staff. A professor of government at the Massachusetts Institute of Technology, Rostow was a facile synthesizer of big ideas. "Walt can write faster than I can read," Kennedy joked. His *Stages of Economic Growth: A Non-Communist Manifesto* (1960) argued that the United States could win the Cold War by supplying aid and technical assistance to turn Third World nations into modern industrial democracies. Rejecting the Eisenhower-Dulles policy of backing entrenched conservative regimes in Asia, Africa, and Latin America as long as they opposed communism, Rostow argued that the United States should support progressive, noncommunist forces in these countries to serve as agents of democratization and economic modernization. Too often, he warned, communists backed by Moscow presented themselves as the only force that could rescue the masses from poverty. In Rostow's view, an intelligent U.S. foreign policy could change all this by strengthening democratic alternatives. To achieve these goals, Rostow favored a highly interventionist U.S. role in the Third World.

This emphasis on social and economic development as a Cold War strategy had the added advantage of downplaying direct nuclear confrontation with the Soviets. Kennedy liberals differed from Republican Cold Warriors by deemphasizing nuclear weapons in strategic planning. Kennedy's favorite general, Maxwell Taylor, who became chairman of the Joint Chiefs of Staff in 1962, advocated supplementing nuclear weapons with a wide range of conventional armaments and strategies. Summing up the goal of Taylor's "flexible-response" doctrine in 1961, Kennedy declared: "We intend to have a wider choice than humiliation or all-out nuclear war."

Focusing initially on Latin America with its reactionary elites and deep social inequities, Kennedy in March 1961 announced the Alliance for Progress, which pledged $20 billion in foreign aid for the region. This aid, however, hinged on the recipients' committing themselves to radical social change, including reforms in their land-tenure and tax policies. The Alliance for Progress expressed the Rostow doctrine of encouraging fundamental reform in societies threatened by communist insurgency. As one U.S. official put it, "A revolution is inevitable in Latin America. If you don't do it peacefully, you'll end up with blood." Soon, however, the idealism of the Alliance for Progress was mocked by a debacle that, although not of Kennedy's doing, had consequences that fell at his doorstep.

Disaster at Bahía de Cochinos

Upon taking office, Kennedy learned from CIA director Allen Dulles of the plan to invade Cuba using anti-Castro Cuban refugees being trained in Guatemala. (The trainees joked that *CIA* stood for Cuban Invasion Authority.) With misgivings, Kennedy approved. The plan assumed that the Cuban masses would rise up and overthrow Castro. But when the sixteen hundred invaders landed on April 17, 1961, at Bahía de Cochinos (the Bay of Pigs), the local populace showed no interest in joining them. Castro, who often vacationed at Bay of Pigs, was popular in the region. Furthermore, the Escambray Mountains that the CIA planners had envisioned as a hiding place for the invaders lay *eighty miles* away through swamps and jungles.

In a disaster that delivered a sobering dash of reality to both the CIA and Kennedy, Castro's forces killed more than 100 invaders and captured 1,189. Eventually the administration ransomed them for $10 million in medical supplies. Even had the plan worked, the United States might have faced a protracted military occupation of Cuba evocative of the imperialistic days of the Spanish-American War.

Furious at his humiliation, Kennedy ordered the CIA to disrupt Cuba's economy and discredit its government. The agency responded with Project Mongoose, under which CIA operatives burned cane fields, blew up factories and power plants, and persuaded European industries to ship Castro defective equipment. CIA planners also devised harebrained schemes to lace Castro's cigars with poison, conceal underwater explosives in a giant clamshell near where he snorkeled, and even make his beard fall out by sprinkling depilatory powder into his shoes. In this campaign, the CIA recruited gangsters eager to regain control of their Havana operations. All this plotting helped lay the background for the 1962 Cuban missile crisis.

Meanwhile, China's nuclear-weapons program forged ahead. China did not test its first atomic bomb until October 1964, but Kennedy knew from intelligence sources of China's progress. The president hoped to exploit these circumstances to improve U.S.-Soviet relations, since Moscow and Beijing were now at odds, but initially this hope went unfulfilled. When Kennedy and Khrushchev met in Vienna in June 1961, the discussion, as so often in the past, centered on Germany. In an echo of the crises of 1948 and 1959, Khrushchev again used Berlin as a pawn in his larger strategy of forcing the West to accept the Soviet-backed East German regime. The continual flow of East German refugees seeking asylum in the West by way of Berlin posed another thorny problem for Moscow.

Amid this crisis atmosphere, the Vienna meeting fared badly. The sixty-seven-year-old Soviet leader treated the new president like an immature youth whom he could bully and intimidate. Kennedy left Vienna convinced that danger lay ahead. He called for increased military spending, tripled the draft call, activated thousands of reserves, and delivered a frightening TV address warning of possible nuclear war. Echoing John Foster Dulles's language of brinkmanship, Kennedy cautioned the Soviets not to make the mistake of assuming that the West was "too soft" to go to war. Once again, he declared, Berlin had become "the great testing place of Western courage and will."

As part of his war of nerves with Moscow, Kennedy urged a crash program of fallout-shelter construction. Civil-defense planning included a program called

NEAR (National Emergency Alarm Repeater) for installing alarms in every home and apartment. Nuclear fear, muted since 1958 when the superpowers had temporarily halted atmospheric tests, reawakened.

Khrushchev resolved the impasse with a retreat disguised as a bold initiative. On August 13, 1961, the Soviets erected a barrier across divided Berlin, blocking all movement between the two halves of the city, separating families, and thwarting would-be East German refugees. General Lucius Clay, Kennedy's representative in Berlin, advocated a military challenge to the Berlin Wall, but Kennedy rejected this advice. In fact, although the wall hardened the division of Europe, it ended the cycle of confrontation over Berlin. As Kennedy told an adviser, "This is [Khrushchev's] way out of his predicament. It's not a very nice solution, but a wall is a hell of a lot better than war." Visiting West Berlin in June 1963, Kennedy denounced the wall as proof of communism's failure and proclaimed to a cheering throng, "*Ich bin ein Berliner*" ("I am a Berliner"). This triumphal return to a city Kennedy had first visited as a GI just after World War II stands as a high point of his brief presidency.

The Cold War erupted also in Central Africa, where the former Belgian Congo, newly independent, was led by Prime Minister Patrice Lumumba, a popular nationalist leader who had received training in Moscow. Western leaders feared that Lumumba would halt the export to the West of copper, uranium, and other minerals from the southern province of Katanga. When Katanga's leader announced the province's independence, the United States supported the move. Lumumba's assassination in January 1961 was widely blamed on the CIA. As civil war erupted, the Kennedy administration, violating its own strategy of promoting democratic forces in Third World nations, gave aid and air support to Congo's right-wing president, Joseph Kasavubu, whom it viewed as a bulwark against Soviet expansion in Africa. These heavy-handed U.S. actions in a key African nation stirred ill will in states struggling against colonialism.

October 1962: To the Brink

Heightened Cold War tension turned to raw fear during the Cuban missile crisis of October 1962. The incident began when high-altitude photos by CIA spy planes confirmed earlier reports from a spy operating in Cuba: The Soviet Union had deployed in Cuba SS-4 intermediate-range ballistic missiles (IRBMs) designed to carry one- to three-megaton nuclear warheads.* With a range of 1,020 nautical miles, the SS-4s could reach targets in the eastern United States, including New York City and Washington, D.C., in eight minutes. Further, some of the missile sites were designed to house SS-5 missiles, which carried even larger warheads and had a range of more than 2,000 nautical miles. Whether the missiles in Cuba had actually been armed with nuclear warheads remained uncertain. Years later, when the Cold War was over, Russian military men would reveal that the U.S.S.R. had in-

---

*A megaton, the standard unit for measuring nuclear bombs, is the explosive force of one million tons of TNT. The bomb that destroyed Hiroshima in August 1945 had the explosive force of twenty thousand tons of TNT.

stalled nuclear weapons in Cuba and that the local Soviet commander had the authority to use them in the event of a U.S. invasion. Thus, the crisis was even graver, and the risks of nuclear war even higher, than Washington realized at the time.

Why did Khrushchev take this dangerous step? No evidence suggests that he planned an actual nuclear attack, but he surely sought to increase Moscow's bargaining power on a range of Cold War issues by achieving nuclear parity. Overall, despite Kennedy's talk in the 1960 campaign about a missile gap, the United States possessed many more nuclear missiles than the Soviets. As the Soviet ambassador to Cuba in 1962 later recalled, "[Khrushchev] was looking for any way to talk to the Americans equally." Furthermore, in July 1962 the Kennedy administration had deployed fifteen U.S. Jupiter missiles in Turkey, placing much of the Soviet Union within a few minutes' striking time. Finally, Fidel Castro, justifiably alarmed by the Bay of Pigs attack and by subsequent CIA plots against him, welcomed a stronger Soviet military presence.

To Khrushchev, putting SS-4s and SS-5s in Cuba offered a way to please Castro, counter the Jupiter missiles in Turkey, and partially redress the larger strategic imbalance. The Bay of Pigs fiasco and Khrushchev's poor impression of Kennedy in Vienna also may have encouraged him to believe that Kennedy would not dare challenge this provocation, especially in the midst of the 1962 midterm electoral campaign.

Khrushchev's move did not fundamentally alter the balance of power, but it gave the impression of a dramatic Soviet gain, and this Kennedy could not tolerate. The Cuban missile deployment, he told his advisers, "makes [the Russians] look like they're co-equal with us." In short, as historian Stephen Ambrose later observed, "The most serious crisis in the history of mankind . . . turned on a question of appearances. The world came close to total destruction over a matter of prestige."

Kennedy secretly assembled at the White House a team of advisers called the Executive Committee, or EXCOM. Some members—former secretary of state Dean Acheson; General Maxwell Taylor, chairman of the Joint Chiefs of Staff; and air force general Curtis LeMay—favored a preemptive air strike, followed by an invasion if necessary. Several top congressional Democrats also urged this course. Others, notably Undersecretary of State George Ball, advocated a blockade of Cuba, with the option of a military strike later. Kennedy, rejecting a surprise attack as too risky and too reminiscent of Japan's attack on Pearl Harbor in 1941, chose the blockade.

In a TV address on Monday evening, October 22, the president revealed the existence of the missiles in Cuba, demanded their withdrawal, and announced a naval blockade of Cuba to begin at 10 A.M. Tuesday. The next morning, when several Soviet ships turned back, tensions eased. Dean Rusk commented, "We're eyeball to eyeball and I think the other fellow just blinked." But fear ran high over the next few days as EXCOM—and the world—awaited the Soviet response. The Strategic Air Command moved to DEFCON 2, a high state of readiness. Presidential speechwriter Theodore Sorensen recalled, "Our little group seated around the Cabinet table in continuous session . . . felt nuclear war to be closer . . . than at any time in the nuclear age." Kennedy summoned his wife and children, who were traveling, back to the White House so that they could escape to a presidential nuclear shelter if necessary.

The Ironies of Civil Defense

Federal civil-defense preparations for nuclear attack shaped millions of Americans' Cold War experience. The civil-defense program of the 1950s (see Chapter 5) crested in the early 1960s as President Kennedy proved his toughness in dealing with the Russians by somberly warning the American people of the threat of nuclear war and calling for an urgent program of fallout-shelter construction.

Kennedy's 1961 warning was part of a long history of civil-defense activity that began in 1945 and lasted into the 1980s. In the first anxious months after Hiroshima, a variety of survival schemes were proposed, including vast underground complexes to which people could retreat in the event of attack. The Federal Civil Defense Administration (1950) put matters on a more systematic basis. The motives were complex. Of course, one motive was the desire to save lives should nuclear war come. But civil-defense preparation also made Washington's nuclear threat more credible: It signaled to the Russians that America would go to the nuclear brink and beyond if necessary. Further, civil-defense planners sought to reassure nervous Americans that nuclear war need not be a death warrant: With advance planning, it was survivable. An upbeat 1950 civil-defense handbook was titled *You Can Survive an Atomic Bomb.* It advised worried readers to rake the leaves away from their houses (to reduce fire risks in a nuclear attack); keep a full tank of gas in the car for quick evacuation; and always wear hats (for men) and long-sleeved blouses (for women), as protection from the atomic flash.

Civil defense planners in the 1950s sought to make civil defense a national priority. Radio stations broadcast practice nuclear alerts. Schoolchildren watched civil-defense films and hid under desks in nuclear-attack drills; some were issued metal name tags. In a 1956 federal civil-defense movie, *Operation Alert,* Manhattan is evacuated calmly and quickly before a hypothetical missile attack, with no confusion, panic, or traffic jams. Yellow "Fallout Shelter" signs appeared on public buildings, and metal drums containing emergency water were placed in the basements of designated buildings. (When empty, the instructions advised, the drums could double as emergency toilets.) The medical profession was mobilized. Physicians received training in how to treat nuclear-attack victims. Psychologists discussed strategies for counseling the distraught after the bombs fell. Entire cities organized emergency drills in which everyone was supposed to seek shelter when the alarm sounded. The federal government even held a drill in 1958 in which government workers retreated to fallout shelters and President Eisenhower was flown to a secret command center away from Washington.

The home fallout-shelter program was part of this larger effort. Some people constructed reinforced shelters in their basements. Others built backyard shelters and stocked them with emergency supplies. Theologians debated the morality of shooting outsiders who tried to break into one's family shelter in a nuclear emergency.

With the Limited Nuclear Test Ban Treaty of 1963 and the gradual easing of Cold War tensions, fear of nuclear war and the preoccupation with civil defense diminished. The Vietnam War, Watergate, and the 1970s energy crises focused attention on other matters.

But civil defense returned to center stage in the early 1980s, as the Reagan administration, pursuing its larger agenda of ideological and military confrontation with Moscow, aggressively pushed new civil-defense programs. The emphasis now was not on fallout shelters, but on "crisis relocation." Should nuclear war threaten, the plan went, city dwellers would evacuate to nearby rural areas and small towns, leaving the targeted cities empty when the missiles fell. Some questioned the practicality of crisis relocation. Given the typical rush-hour traffic jam, they wondered, what would happen when entire cities tried to evacuate simultaneously?

The skepticism about crisis relocation underscored a continuing irony and paradox of the entire civil-defense effort. The American people were never really convinced that civil defense offered genuine hope in the nuclear age, or that they would want to survive in a postnuclear world. Indeed, the main effect of the entire civil-defense effort seems not to have been to reassure the public, but to heighten nuclear fear by forcing Americans to confront a scary reality many would have preferred to ignore.

During the great waves of civil-defense activity, first in the fifties and early sixties, and again in the early eighties, critics dismissed and ridiculed the entire effort as deceptive and cynical. Science fiction stories like Walter Miller's *A Canticle for Leibowitz* (1954), movies such as *On the Beach* (1959), episodes on TV programs like *The Twilight Zone,* and TV specials such as *The Day After* (1984) offered a very different view of nuclear war than the reassuring pronouncements of civil-defense officials. Challenging the government's theme of safety through civil defense, antiwar activists presented an alternative message: that the best defense against nuclear war was to work for peace and nuclear disarmament, to make sure the attack never came.

By the late 1990s, as the Cold War receded into the past, so, too, did the era when fallout shelters, radio alerts, school drills, and Bert the Turtle were an everyday part of American life. Only those who had lived through the era were left with the memories of what it was like.

Tragically, the devastating terrorist bombings of September 11, 2001, followed by several deaths caused by anthrax-tainted letters (see Chapter 16), urgently revived civil-defense concerns. Unlike in the Cold War era, the fear now was less of a massive nuclear attack by an enemy state than of chemical, biological, or clandestine nuclear weapons deployed by shadowy terrorist groups against specific sites. Creating a Department of Homeland Security in 2003, the government guarded high-risk targets, issued color-coded warnings of the perceived threat level, tightened airport security and immigration procedures, and arrested or deported suspected individuals. Just as "civil defense" had begun to seem a quaint relic of the Cold War, the issue surged back to prominence and seemed likely to remain central for decades to come.

Millions of Americans waited as their fate hung in the balance. Through much of the Cold War, the nuclear threat loomed as a disturbing but somewhat abstract menace; in October 1962 it became starkly immediate, and low-level anxiety spiked into heart-throbbing terror.

Behind the scenes, Washington and Moscow were in urgent communication. On October 26, Khrushchev sent a rambling but conciliatory message conceding the horror of nuclear war and offering to remove the IRBMs in exchange for a U.S. pledge not to invade Cuba. A second message on the 27th took a harder line: The United States must also remove its missiles from Turkey. Again the Joint Chiefs and some EXCOM members clamored for an invasion. Still the president held back. At the suggestion of his brother, Attorney General Robert Kennedy, JFK answered Khrushchev's more accommodating first message and pledged not to invade Cuba if the missiles were withdrawn. Robert Kennedy secretly assured the Soviet ambassador that once the Cuban crisis was resolved, the administration would remove the Turkish missiles. With these promises, Khrushchev agreed to remove the IRBMs and Kennedy announced the news, to universal relief. Khrushchev kept his promise, and Kennedy lifted the blockade. A few months later the U.S. Jupiter missiles quietly disappeared from Turkey, as well as from Great Britain and Italy, to be replaced by seaborne missiles aboard Polaris submarines. Kennedy and Khrushchev had peered into the abyss and pulled back. Even for two such fiercely competitive Cold Warriors, the deadly logic of nuclear stalemate served as a powerful constraint.

Widely viewed as a victory for U.S. firmness and a triumph for Kennedy, the Cuban missile crisis also had unexpected ramifications. It undermined Khrushchev's position with his Kremlin colleagues, who saw him as having buckled under U.S. pressure, and within two years he had fallen from power. French leader Charles de Gaulle, convinced that in a crisis the United States would pursue its own interests without consulting NATO, accelerated France's nuclear-weapons research, ordered NATO's headquarters out of Paris, and eventually withdrew from NATO's military command structure.

Most important, the crisis underscored the risk of nuclear war. As economist John Kenneth Galbraith commented, "We were in luck. But success in lotteries is no argument for lotteries." After the crisis, Kennedy moderated his Cold War rhetoric and stepped up efforts to control the nuclear arms race. In 1961, confronted with a U.S. nuclear-weapons buildup, the Soviets had resumed nuclear testing, including a fifty-eight-megaton bomb, the equivalent of *three thousand* Hiroshima-type bombs. Kennedy ordered another round of U.S. tests, but he understood the fallout danger and genuinely desired a test ban. The prospect of a Chinese nuclear bomb continued to worry Kennedy as well. Indeed, he proposed a joint U.S.-Soviet military strike against China's nuclear facilities, an idea Khrushchev rejected.

Nuclear proliferation threatened in the Middle East as well. With Russia supplying military equipment to Egypt, the Kennedy administration, acting under the Eisenhower Doctrine, provided defensive missiles to Israel, beginning decades of close military cooperation between the two nations. Earlier, in 1958, fearful of attack by Egypt or other Arab states, Israel, with French assistance, had started a secret nuclear-weapons program at Dimona in the Negev desert. The United States learned of this project in 1960. Kennedy tried to negotiate a pledge by Egypt and Israel not to develop nuclear weapons, but Israel refused unless the United States would agree to a full-scale military alliance. Kennedy declined, and Israel proceeded with its nuclear-weapons program.

In an address in June 1963, Kennedy spoke of the "nuclear sword of Damocles" hanging over the Earth and exhorted world leaders to diminish the danger. "Our most basic common link," the president declared, "is the fact that we all inhabit this planet. We all breathe the same air. We all cherish our children's future. And we are all mortal." That August, the United States, the Soviet Union, and Great Britain signed a treaty banning nuclear testing in the atmosphere or under water. The Senate overwhelmingly ratified the treaty. Important as an environmental and public-health measure and as a gesture of goodwill, the Test Ban Treaty nevertheless did not halt the nuclear arms race or even nuclear testing. Underground testing continued under the treaty, and France and China carried on their atmospheric testing.

To reduce the risk of nuclear miscalculation, the United States and the Soviet Union also set up a telecommunications system, or hot line, between the White House and the Kremlin. (A cartoonist pictured a frustrated Khrushchev reaching Kennedy's daughter, Caroline, and sputtering in exasperation, "No, I don't want your *dolly,* I want your *daddy!*") In a further effort to improve relations, while also helping U.S. agriculture, Kennedy authorized wheat sales to the Soviet Union.

Nevertheless, Kennedy also initiated a nuclear buildup that by 1967 gave the United States 41 Polaris submarines armed with more than 650 missiles, 600 strategic bombers, and 1,000 intercontinental ballistic missiles (ICBMs)—a fivefold increase since 1960. The Soviet Union strove to keep pace. By 1967 even Defense Secretary McNamara conceded that the nuclear escalation had increased risks without strengthening U.S. security. Why did Kennedy authorize this expansion despite his administration's embrace of a flexible-response strategy stressing nonnuclear weaponry? Essentially, nuclear weapons had become the symbol of world power. Kennedy had no intention of launching a nuclear war, and he little expected the Soviets to start one. But in the post-Hiroshima world, a massive nuclear arsenal translated into superpower status. The Soviets naturally held the same view, and the nuclear arms race surged on.

Southeast Asia and Vietnam: Deeper into the Tunnel

Although the nuclear competition continued, more conventional patterns of conflict preoccupied Washington strategists, especially when they turned to Southeast Asia, a complex mosaic of poor and developing nations, many emerging from a colonial past, in which rival groups vied for dominance. Viewing this confusing reality through a Cold War lens, Kennedy-era policymakers saw new arenas of East-West confrontation that their predecessors had neglected. "If you don't pay attention to the periphery," Dean Rusk warned in 1961, in an updated version of Eisenhower's domino theory, " . . . the first thing you know the periphery is the center. . . . [W]hat happens in one place cannot help but affect what happens in another."

This shift in focus responded to changes in Soviet policy, which in these years oscillated between conciliation and belligerence. In their belligerent mode, the Soviets revealed a readiness to foment revolution in the Third World. In January 1961, just as Kennedy took office, Nikita Khrushchev made clear that Moscow, while still seeking peaceful coexistence with the West, would happily sponsor "wars of national liberation" in Africa, Latin America, and Southeast Asia. To contain this threat, Washington planners embraced Walt Rostow's emphasis on social and economic development. In September 1961, Congress created the Agency for International Development (AID) to coordinate all U.S. foreign-aid programs. Throughout the 1960s, AID funneled $47 billion to development programs world-

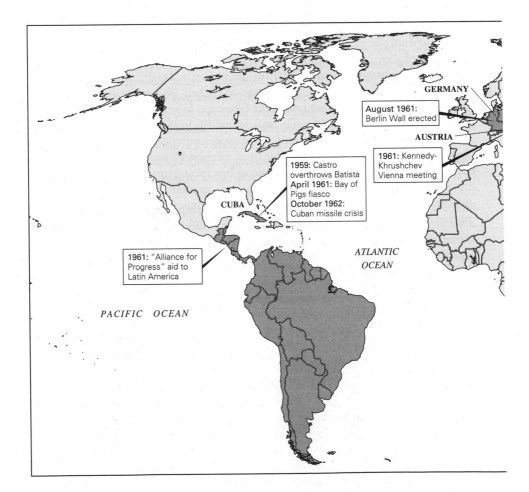

MAP 6.2
The Cold War Heats Up

wide. The Food for Peace program, another Kennedy initiative, had the dual function of easing hunger in poor nations while reducing U.S. farm surpluses.

But the liberal Cold Warriors saw the struggle in military as well as economic terms. Maxwell Taylor's flexible-response strategy included new techniques of counterinsurgency warfare designed to show Moscow, as Taylor argued, that sponsoring "wars of national liberation" would be "costly, dangerous, and doomed to failure." President Kennedy, a fan of Ian Fleming's debonair fictional hero James Bond, reveled in counterinsurgency planning. Even Walt Rostow had no qualms about supplementing social and economic development programs with military measures in the global power struggle with Moscow.

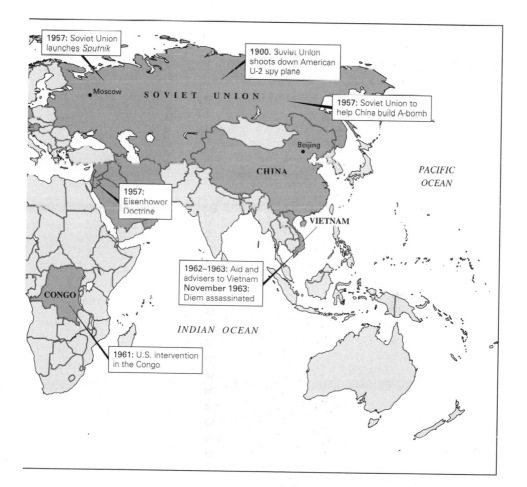

The shift of focus from Europe to the Third World did not diminish the tendency of Washington Cold Warriors to view the world in black-and-white terms. In an April 1961 speech to newspaper publishers, Kennedy described the struggle in phrases John Foster Dulles would have approved, updating the analysis to convey the new emphasis on developing regions. As the president declared, "We are opposed around the world by a monolithic and ruthless conspiracy that relies primarily on covert means for expanding its sphere of influence."

In Southeast Asia, attention initially focused on Laos, where a three-way civil war raged among a U.S.-supported right-wing general, a neutralist prince, and a Soviet-backed prince. Laos had little strategic significance, but much symbolic importance. As Kennedy told a columnist early in 1961, "We cannot and will not accept any visible humiliation over Laos." Victory was not worth full-scale war, however, and Kennedy opted for negotiation. At the 1962 Geneva Conference, the United States supported an agreement among the warring factions to call a truce and accept a neutral Laos.

This outcome encouraged Kennedy. Negotiations had staved off a possible communist takeover in Laos, and at least one small nation had been withdrawn from the arena of U.S.-Soviet conflict. In fact, the truce proved short-lived. As America became more deeply involved in Vietnam, the CIA trained and armed Laotian Hmongs, an indigenous upland people, to attack North Vietnamese supply routes along the Vietnamese-Laotian border. The result was renewed conflict in Laos. (After the Vietnam War, many Hmong would emigrate to the United States.)

In South Vietnam, conditions were deteriorating. As a senator, John Kennedy had supported the Eisenhower administration's handpicked ruler, Ngo Dinh Diem. But Diem's autocratic regime never won popular support. The Vietminh, the pro-communist force that remained in South Vietnam after the 1956 Geneva Accords, worsened the situation by systematically killing village leaders and local officials. In 1960 an anti-Diem coalition of communists and Buddhists (the latter made up 80 percent of the population) established the National Liberation Front (NLF) in South Vietnam, which, with its military arm, the Vietcong, began operations against Diem's forces.

The United States had pledged in the 1954 SEATO pact to defend South Vietnam against external aggression, and Kennedy determined to stand firm. In May 1961 he warned that the United States would not tolerate the military overthrow of the Diem regime. The United States must prove its resolve to the Soviets, he told a journalist, and the place to do so was Vietnam.

A series of key assumptions guided Kennedy's thought: that the Vietnam conflict was simply one front in a larger Cold War struggle; that the Vietnamese communist leader, Ho Chi Minh, was little more than a pliant tool of Moscow or Beijing; and that South Vietnam was a distinct nation subject to aggression from abroad (that is, from North Vietnam). Though simplistic and misguided, these assumptions would underlie U.S. policy in Vietnam for years.

Moreover, South Vietnam seemed the ideal laboratory to test the anti-insurgency strategies advocated by General Maxwell Taylor and the social-reform programs favored by Walt Rostow. While U.S. Green Berets, a counterinsurgency unit, advised the South Vietnamese army, U.S. civilian specialists introduced medical programs, technical aid, and economic and political reforms designed to win "the hearts and minds" of Vietnamese peasants. One reform measure, the Strategic Hamlet program, uprooted peasants from the lands of their ancestors and concentrated them in settlements supposedly secure from communist infiltration. The program only deepened the peasants' hatred of the Diem regime.

Administration leaders shared Kennedy's view of Vietnam as a vital Cold War battlefield. After touring South Vietnam early in 1961, Vice President Johnson advised, "The basic decision in Southeast Asia is here. We must decide whether to help these countries . . . or throw in the towel . . . and pull back our defense to San Francisco and a 'fortress America' concept." After visiting Saigon that fall, General Taylor, soon to be chairman of the Joint Chiefs of Staff, called for eight thousand U.S. combat troops, plus U.S. air support. As an area for military operations, Taylor declared, "[South Vietnam] is not . . . excessively difficult or unpleasant." Secretary of Defense McNamara, visiting in 1962, concluded that "every quantitative measurement we have shows we're winning this war."

A rare cautionary note came from Undersecretary of State George Ball, who warned Kennedy late in 1961, "Within five years we'll have three hundred thousand men in the paddies and jungles. . . . That was the French experience. Vietnam is the worst possible terrain both from a physical and political point of view." Kennedy replied, "George, I always thought you were one of the brightest guys in town, but you're just crazier than hell." In fact, within five years, U.S. troop strength in Vietnam would reach nearly four hundred thousand.

Amid the calls for escalation, Kennedy proceeded cautiously. He initially rejected General Taylor's recommendation for a modest infusion of combat units, sensing that the ante would inevitably rise. "It's like taking a drink," he reflected. "The effect wears off and you have to take another." Nevertheless, Kennedy continued to sip. He dreaded a 1964 presidential race dominated by Republican cries of "Who lost Vietnam?" as Democrats had earlier faced the taunt "Who lost China?" By mid-1962 Kennedy had increased the number of U.S. military "advisers" in Vietnam from seven hundred to twelve thousand. He added another five thousand in 1963. As casualties mounted, withdrawing became progressively more difficult.

In May 1963, a Buddhist monk in the ancient religious city of Hué burned himself to death to protest the Diem regime; in a macabre joke, Diem's sister-in-law, the powerful Madame Nhu, offered to "supply the mustard for the monks' next barbecue." But Diem's position eroded as Buddhist resistance grew. He also lost support in Washington because his rigid, family-based rule clashed with the administration's goal of promoting democracy and social reform in nations threatened by communism. Kennedy gave the green light for an anti-Diem coup in August, and on November 1, South Vietnamese military officers, in coordination with the U.S. embassy in Saigon, arrested Diem and his brother. While in custody, both were murdered.*

Kennedy's complicity in the anti-Diem coup hastened full-scale military involvement in Vietnam. The cabal of young military officers who took over South

---

*Ambassador Henry Cabot Lodge and other U.S. officials apparently did not anticipate Diem's assassination; they had advised the coup leaders to exile Diem and his family. On the other hand, neither the U.S. embassy nor the coup leaders had made any plans for such an evacuation.

Vietnam had little popular support and proved unable to govern effectively. As South Vietnam sank into chaos, the U.S. role increased. In a memo dictated on November 4 (available in an audio transcript on the Kennedy Library website), Kennedy regretted his cable approving a coup and said he "should never have given . . . consent to it" without more consultation.

Had Kennedy lived, what course might he have taken in Vietnam? Kennedy had little doubt that a combination of U.S. military might, counterinsurgency strategies, and nation building could contain communism anywhere. Had he survived, he would have been advised by the same hawks who determined Lyndon Johnson's course. Indeed, Kennedy's approval of a major buildup of U.S. "advisers" in Vietnam, as well as his role in the overthrow of the Diem regime, deepened America's involvement.

In one of his last comments on the war, Kennedy conceded that the United States could not control a civil war in a small, distant country. "In the final analysis," he mused, "it is their war." But, he added, a U.S. withdrawal "would mean a collapse not only of South Vietnam but [of] Southeast Asia. So we are going to stay there." The *New York Times,* a voice of the liberal establishment, agreed. Chiding Kennedy for his "it is their war" comment, the *Times* editorialized that Vietnam was "a war . . . we dare not lose." Had Kennedy lived, events in Vietnam would very likely have unfolded much as they did.

The Kennedy Cold War: A Summary

The six years from *Sputnik* in 1957 to the assassination of Diem in 1963 saw the management of the Cold War pass from moderate Republicans to liberal Democrats who defined the Cold War in terms that echoed the idealism and activism of the New Deal. The blend of anticommunist militance, social-reform zeal, and computer-based statistical analysis that one finds in New Frontiersmen such as Walt Rostow and Robert McNamara sums up Kennedy-style liberalism applied to world affairs.

This approach would come in for sharp attack in later years. In *The Kennedy Promise* (1973), British journalist Henry Fairlie deplored JFK's craving for empty displays of energy and his compulsive competitiveness. The Kennedy-era shift of focus from Western Europe to the murkier terrain of Third World struggles, Fairlie suggested, weakened Washington's Cold War leadership and led directly to the debacle in Vietnam that would shatter the liberal consensus. Garry Wills in *The Kennedy Imprisonment* (1982) argued that Kennedy's attraction to power struggles for their own sake, rooted in his father's influence, emerged in his campaign to destroy Castro, his alarmist response to Khrushchev's maneuvering over Berlin, and his views on Vietnam. The appeal that these traits held for liberals eager to move beyond Eisenhower's alleged inertia, Wills concluded, undermined the conduct of foreign policy.

Nuclear fears eased after the Cuban missile crisis, although the uneasy nuclear balance of terror hardly inspired long-term confidence as the United States and the Soviet Union piled up missiles and warheads. Still, with a rough nuclear balance in place and the Big Power confrontation in Europe stabilized, attention shifted to the Third World. From the days of President Truman's Point Four program, Washington strategists had recognized that developing nations represented an arena of Cold

War competition. In the later 1950s and early 1960s, this arena moved from the periphery to the center of strategists' thinking. When applied to South Vietnam, this shift had fateful consequences. After exploring domestic politics and social movements in the 1960s, we return to the unfolding Vietnam story in Chapter 10.

Tragedy in Dallas

On November 21, 1963, President Kennedy flew to Texas, a state he had barely carried in 1960, to patch up a quarrel among Texas Democrats that threatened his reelection hopes. Jackie Kennedy accompanied her husband, something she rarely did. At 12:30 P.M. on Friday, November 22, the presidential motorcade wound through Dallas. The Kennedys rode in the back of an open car, with Texas governor John Connally and his wife in front. Three shots rang out. The first bullet struck the president in the neck; the second tore a gaping hole in his head, killing him almost instantly.

The presidential car sped to Parkland Hospital, where priests administered last rites and Kennedy was pronounced dead. For the rest of their lives, Americans would remember where they heard the news. One young historian, working in Baltimore's public library, received word from a trembling librarian that the library was closing: President Kennedy had been shot.

Lyndon Johnson took the oath of office aboard Air Force One as the jet prepared to carry the dead and living presidents back to Washington. Jacqueline Kennedy, a coat covering her blood-spattered dress, looked on hollowly.

The nation mourned as the same horse-drawn caisson that had borne Abraham Lincoln's body in 1865 carried Kennedy's remains along Pennsylvania Avenue from the White House to the Capitol, followed by the closed black limousines carrying the bereaved family and the Johnsons. Armed Secret Service agents manned the rooftops of nearby government buildings. The burial took place in Arlington National Cemetery, the grave marked by a perpetual flame.

Within hours of the assassination, Dallas police had arrested Lee Harvey Oswald, a young ex-marine. Two days later, as police transferred Oswald to another prison, Dallas nightclub owner Jack Ruby shot and killed him. Oswald, with a record of mental instability and threats against public figures, had moved to the U.S.S.R., married a Russian woman, and belonged to a pro-Castro group, the Fair Play for Cuba Committee. To many, these circumstances hinted at a larger conspiracy.

To quell rumors, President Johnson appointed a blue-ribbon commission chaired by Chief Justice Earl Warren. After research by legal and forensic experts and interviews with 552 witnesses, the Warren Commission reported in September 1964 that Oswald had acted alone. But rumors of a conspiracy—by Cubans, by the Mafia, by Lyndon Johnson, by a right-wing cabal within the government—persisted. Critics at the time and later insisted that the political motive of reassuring the public, rather than the larger task of sifting all the evidence, had led the commission to assert an overly confident lone-assassin conclusion.

Later revelations of high-level conspiracies—from the Watergate cover-up to the Iran-contra affair—further encouraged those who doubted the official version of the assassination. By 1993, two thousand books had been written on Kennedy's

November 1963. In a tradition-shaped ritual, President Kennedy's flag-draped coffin leaves the White House. A press photographer captured the scene framed by the leafless trees of early winter and the starkly etched shadows of saluting soldiers. *(National Archives/Getty Images)*

death, many proposing various conspiracy theories. Oliver Stone's 1992 film *JFK* interspersed invented dialogue, fictional "witnesses," and imagined scenes with actual newsreel footage to portray an elaborate conspiracy involving Vice President Johnson, the FBI, the CIA, the Pentagon, defense contractors, and assorted other officials and agencies. In fact, no credible evidence has ever surfaced to disprove the Warren Commission report.

Conclusion

Popular in life, Kennedy assumed mythic proportions in death. Later, a reaction would set in. Historians would point out that for all the media hype, Kennedy's achievements proved modest. Countering the Peace Corps and the Test Ban Treaty was the strident Cold War rhetoric, the nuclear buildup, and the escalation in Vietnam. On the personal side, the Kennedy myth would be tarnished by revelations of his ruthless behavior, his use of amphetamines, and his compulsive promiscuity both before and during the White House years, including affairs with the actress Marilyn Monroe and the mistress of a Chicago mobster. Critics also questioned his concealment of serious physical ills, including a back condition that at times left him almost unable to walk and Addison's disease, a failure of adrenal function that required heavy cortisone medication.

The Kennedy myth had always revealed more about the needs and hopes of the American people than about Kennedy himself. Kennedy's wealth and surface charm brought him such easy success that he had little need to develop the more complex qualities that make for character. In *The Kennedy Persuasion: The Politics of Style Since JFK* (1995), Paul R. Henggeler finds Kennedy's political legacy generally negative, as post-Kennedy politicians substituted style for substance, to the debasement of American public life. For historian Thomas Reeves, the author of a highly critical biography of Kennedy, *A Question of Character* (1991), the lesson of his presidency was sobering: "In the early 1960s, we became involved in a sort of mindless worship of celebrity; it was a love affair largely with images. That could happen again. . . . And the target of our affection might be much worse than Jack Kennedy."

Nevertheless, after the mystique had faded, and in awareness of Kennedy's flaws, many still remembered the finer moments of his presidency. For a fleeting instant, the New Frontier—not as it was, perhaps, but as Americans wished it to be—offered the hope of bringing the American reality closer to the imagined ideal.

Kennedy's assassination was only one of a series of events that fragmented the liberal consensus. Rooted in the New Deal, World War II, and the early Cold War, this consensus underlay the Democratic Party's activist, reform minded approach to domestic problems and to global challenges. Lyndon Johnson, making shrewd political use of Kennedy's memory, sustained that consensus briefly during a remarkable season of reform in 1964–65. But the shining liberal hour that Kennedy had personified would ultimately lose its luster, darken, and pass into history.

SELECTED READINGS

Foreign Affairs and Defense Policy in the Later 1950s

Richard Aliano, *American Defense Policy from Eisenhower to Kennedy* (1975), Michael R. Beschloss, *Mayday: Eisenhower, Khrushchev, and the U-2 Affair* (1986); H. W. Brands, "The Age of Vulnerability: Eisenhower and the National Security State," *American Historical Review* (October 1989); Michael E. Brown, *Flying Blind: The Politics of the U.S. Strategic Bomber Program* (1992); Barbara B. Clowse, *Brainpower for the Cold War: The Sputnik Crisis and the National Defense Education Act of 1958* (1981); Lloyd C. Gardner, *Approaching Vietnam: From World War II Through Dienbienphu* (1988); Audrey R. Kahin and George McT. Kahin, *Subversion as Foreign Policy: The Secret Eisenhower and Dulles Debacle in Indonesia* (1995); Walter A. McDougall, *The Heavens and the Earth: A Political History of the Space Age* (1985); Donald Neff, *Warriors at Suez* (1981); Stephen G. Rabe, *Eisenhower and Latin America* (1988); Peter J. Roman, *Eisenhower and the Missile Gap* (1995); Patrick J. Walsh, *Echoes Among the Stars: A Short History of the U.S. Space Program* (2000); Richard E. Welch, Jr., *Responses to Revolution: The United States and the Cuban Revolution, 1959–1961* (1985). See also the Selected Readings for Chapter 4.

Kennedy, Nixon, and the 1960 Election

David Burner and Thomas R. West, *The Torch Is Passed: The Kennedy Brothers and American Liberalism* (1984); Ignacio M. García, *Viva Kennedy: Mexican Americans in Search of Camelot* (2000); Paul R. Henggeler, *The Kennedy Persuasion: The Politics of Style Since JFK* (1995);

Donald Lord, *John F. Kennedy: The Politics of Confrontation and Conciliation* (1977); Allen J. Matusow, *The Unraveling of America: A History of Liberalism in the 1960s* (1984), Chapter 1, "The Liberals, the Candidate, and the Election of 1960"; Richard M. Nixon, *Six Crises* (1962); Herbert S. Parmet, *JFK* (1981); Gerald Posner, *Case Closed: Lee Harvey Oswald and the Assassination of JFK* (1993); Thomas Reeves, *A Question of Character: The Life of John F. Kennedy in Image and Reality* (1991); Theodore White, *The Making of the President 1960* (1961); Garry Wills, *Nixon Agonistes* (1969) and *The Kennedy Imprisonment* (1983).

Kennedy and the Cold War

John C. Ausland, *Kennedy, Khrushchev, and the Berlin-Cuba Crisis* (1996); Warren Bass, *Support Any Friend: Kennedy's Middle East and the Making of the U.S.-Israel Alliance* (2003); Michael Beschloss, *The Crisis Years: Kennedy and Khrushchev, 1960–1963* (1990); Avner Cohen, *Israel and the Bomb* (1998); Robert Dallek, *An Unfinished Life: John F. Kennedy* (2003); Herbert Dinerstein, *The Making of a Missile Crisis: October 1962* (1976); William J. Duiker, *U.S. Containment Policy and the Conflict in Indochina* (1994); Henry Fairlie, *The Kennedy Promise* (1973); Lloyd Gardner and Ted Gittinger, eds., *Vietnam: The Early Decisions* (1997); John Girling, *America and the Third World* (1980); George Herring, *America's Longest War: The United States and Vietnam* (rev. ed., 1985); Trumbull Higgins, *The Perfect Failure: Kennedy, Eisenhower, and the Bay of Pigs* (1987); James W. Hilty, *Robert Kennedy: Brother Protector* (1997); Elizabeth Cobbs Hoffman, *All You Need Is Love: The Peace Corps and the Spirit of the 1960s* (1998); Robert Kennedy, *Thirteen Days* [Cuban missile crisis] (1969); Diane B. Kunz, ed., *The Diplomacy of the Crucial Decade* (1994); Walter LaFeber, *Inevitable Revolutions: The United States in Central America* (1985); Bruce Miroff, *Pragmatic Illusions: The Presidential Politics of John F Kennedy* (1976); John M. Newman, *JFK and Vietnam: Deception, Intrigue and the Struggle for Power* (1992); James S. Olson and Randy Roberts, *Where the Domino Fell: America and Vietnam, 1945 to 1995* (1996); Thomas G. Paterson, ed., *Kennedy's Quest for Victory: American Foreign Policy, 1961–1963* (1989) and "Bearing the Burden: A Critical Look at JFK's Foreign Policy," *Virginia Quarterly Review* (Spring 1978); Thomas G. Paterson and William J. Brophy, "October Missiles and November Elections: The Cuban Missile Crisis and American Politics, 1962," *Journal of American History* (June 1986); Glenn T. Seaborg, *Kennedy, Khrushchev, and the Test Ban* (1981); Roger Warner, *Back Fire: The CIA's Secret War in Laos and Its Link to the Vietnam War* (1995); Andreas Wenger, *Living with Peril: Eisenhower, Kennedy, and Nuclear Weapons* (1997); Francis X. Winters, *The Year of the Hare: America in Vietnam, January 25, 1963–February 15, 1964* [the overthrow and assassination of Ngo Dinh Diem] (1997); Peter Wyden, *Bay of Pigs* (1980).

CHAPTER

7

The Liberal Hour

IN OCTOBER 1967, Lady Bird Johnson, the wife of President Lyndon Johnson, received an honorary degree from Williams College in Williamstown, Massachusetts, and spoke on her favorite subject: the need to preserve America's natural beauty. The theme meshed perfectly with the setting: the autumn foliage of a picture-book New England college town. But the sylvan tranquility was shattered when hecklers protested a war raging in distant Vietnam. The scene was repeated the next day at Yale University in Connecticut. While an audience of eight hundred applauded Mrs. Johnson's speech inside the hall, an equal number of antiwar protesters milled outside, shouting and waving placards.

Her New England visit, wrote an aide, left the First Lady "very disheartened." During the preceding four years, she had emerged as a strong environmental advocate. Yet her audience seemed to be drifting away as the Vietnam War muscled its way into the public discourse. Soon, she feared, she would be unable to travel freely to promote the cause she deeply cared about.

Mrs. Johnson's dilemma reflected broader tensions within the administration and indeed in the nation. The Johnson years had begun on a note of high resolve, as the new president pushed an ambitious reform agenda. Four years later, the mood had soured. The protests that greeted Lady Bird Johnson soon would mushroom, forcing President Johnson out of the 1968 electoral campaign.

Vietnam alone caused Johnson's downfall. Thrust into the presidency by an assassin's bullets, Johnson seized the reins adroitly. After pushing Kennedy's stalled program through Congress, he went on to win passage of a far-reaching reform agenda. Johnson's domestic record surely places him among the great reform presidents. Having examined how the liberal tradition shaped U.S. foreign policy in the Kennedy years, we trace in this chapter liberalism's influence on domestic policy: the revival of reform energies in the late 1950s, the domestic initiatives of Kennedy's presidency, and the flood of reform legislation in 1964–65—the high noon of postwar liberalism. Chapter 8 focuses on the civil rights movement in the 1960s, from the confident early years to the controversies and loss of consensus at mid-decade. By 1968, the liberal consensus would collapse under the battering of domestic turmoil, the divisive war in Vietnam, and a renascent conservative movement.

Shaping a Liberal Agenda: The 1950s

Through much of the 1950s, the once-powerful trumpet of New Deal liberalism sounded only feebly. As liberal intellectuals rallied behind the Cold War, attention to domestic social and economic problems faded. The jobless and needy of the 1930s, wrote historian Richard Hofstadter reassuringly in 1955, "have in the course of the years . . . become homeowners, suburbanites, and solid citizens." In this climate, politics held only intermittent interest for intellectuals. To them, the provocative issues lay in the cultural arena. In 1957 Arthur Schlesinger, Jr., lamented, "[L]iberalism in America has not for thirty years been so homeless, baffled, irrelevant, and impotent as it is today."

Toward the end of the decade, however, some liberals began to question how America was expending its vast wealth. Inspired by John Kenneth Galbraith's *The Affluent Society* (1958), liberals called for increased investment in the nation's infrastructure and public sector—schools, housing, hospitals, cultural institutions, public works, and civic services—as a liberal agenda for the 1960s. Schlesinger's three-volume eulogy to the New Deal, *The Age of Roosevelt* (1957–60), presented Roosevelt's first term in glowing language calculated to inspire a new generation of liberals.*

Other liberals argued that even amid postwar abundance, the issues of the 1930s still lived. Leon Keyserling, chair of the Council of Economic Advisers under President Truman, vigorously rejected the widespread assumption that modern America enjoyed near-universal affluence. Despite the spread of middle-class suburbs, he insisted, the postwar boom had left millions of Americans behind. To fight poverty and want, Keyserling argued, liberals should work for government policies designed to promote economic growth. Further to the left, socialists criticized Cold War liberals who ignored domestic want and economic injustice while attacking the nation's cultural flaws. Amid all their cultural criticism, asked Irving Howe in the journal *Dissent* in 1955, why did liberals ignore the plight of southern sharecroppers, displaced New England textile workers, or New York's Puerto Rican immigrants? As a sign of rising ferment on the Left, the socialists' elder statesman, Norman Thomas, became increasingly popular on the college lecture circuit.

In short, the decade's end found the public increasingly receptive to liberals' calls for renewed governmental activism. The civil-rights movement spotlighted an urgent social issue in which government could play an important role. Globally, *Sputnik* and other events fed the growing conviction that America had lost direction. As media pundits anxiously debated "the national purpose," liberals' spirits rose. The election of a group of young, reform-minded Democrats to the Senate in 1956 and 1958 further roused liberals' hopes.

Liberals did not automatically rally to John Kennedy's candidacy for president, however. Many remained loyal to Adlai Stevenson or supported Hubert Humphrey, whose liberal credentials outshone Kennedy's. The Kennedy family had backed Senator Joseph McCarthy, and Kennedy's choice of Lyndon Johnson

---

*Significantly, perhaps, Schlesinger never continued his history into the years after 1936, when the New Deal stalled and ultimately failed to end the Great Depression.

from conservative Texas as his running mate further alienated liberals. As late as August 1960, Arthur Schlesinger, Jr., warned Kennedy that the liberal Americans for Democratic Action backed him only with the "utmost tepidity." But Kennedy avidly courted reformist intellectuals, and his campaign speeches stressed the liberal themes of economic growth and renewal of the public sector. "[T]he American people are tired of the drift in our national course . . . ," he asserted; "they are ready to move again."

Richard Nixon pointed to the 1950s economic boom and denied that the country had stagnated. At an Oregon shopping mall, Nixon declared, "If you think the United States has stood still, who built the largest shopping center in the world, the Lloyd Shopping Center right here?" But Nixon's gloating over a shopping mall simply confirmed liberals' complaint that the nation was mired in self-indulgent consumerism.

Despite their hesitations, liberals cautiously welcomed Kennedy's victory. Political scientist Michael Walzer found "an openness to new ideas probably unlike anything since the 1930s." Still, he noted, a vote for Kennedy was more an act of faith than an endorsement of a fully formed liberal agenda. Liberals thus watched nervously to see if events would justify their faith.

Sketching a Liberal Agenda: The Kennedy Years

Although civil-rights marches and Freedom Rides during the early sixties captured the nation's attention (see Chapter 8), President Kennedy turned his energies to other domestic economic and social issues. His approach, reflecting a liberal, social-activist orientation, yielded only mixed results. The most powerful figure in shaping economic policy was economist Walter Heller, chairman of the Council of Economic Advisers (CEA). Heller and the CEA argued that the government should use its full fiscal powers to fight recessions, control inflation, and stimulate economic growth. A disciple of John Maynard Keynes's activist model of government economic intervention, Heller was even prepared to accept federal budget deficits as a price of economic growth.

As a senator, Kennedy had generally opposed governmental intervention in the economy, but Heller converted him to Keynesian thinking: the promotion of economic growth through federal tax-and-spending policies. In the Truman era the CEA had pushed Keynesian strategies, but it was in 1961–63, when Kennedy made economic growth a top priority, that Keynesianism won broad acceptance in the White House. Guided by Heller, Kennedy fought the recession of 1960–61 with increased federal spending. At his request, Congress extended eligibility for unemployment compensation, raised the minimum wage, broadened social security benefits, and approved over $4 billion in long-term spending on federally financed housing. The Area Redevelopment Act authorized the secretary of labor to identify economically "distressed areas," making them eligible for federal aid. These programs (plus a 20 percent increase in military spending) accelerated the recovery that had started in early 1961.

Three measures of 1962 further stimulated the economy. The Trade Expansion Act granted the White House broad powers to cut tariffs on imported goods.

The Manpower Retraining Act provided some $435 million in matching grants to the states to retrain workers who had lost their jobs to automation. Finally, the Revenue Act of 1962 granted $1 billion in corporate tax breaks to stimulate investment in new machinery, factories, and equipment. Fueled by these stimulus measures, U.S. productivity (GNP) grew by an annual average of 5.3 percent from 1961 to 1964, significantly above the annual average of the 1950s. The unemployment rate, which stood at 6.7 percent in 1961, declined to 5.2 percent by 1964. But with recovery came rising prices, and by 1962 inflation loomed.

The administration's efforts to hold down the inflationary threat posed by price increases and union wage demands triggered a face-off with the steel industry. In March 1962, the administration helped avert a steel strike by persuading the steelworkers' union to accept a noninflationary contract. A few weeks later, however, the head of United States Steel coolly informed Kennedy of a $6-a-ton price increase. The other big steel companies quickly followed suit. This inflationary action infuriated the president. "My father always told me that all businessmen were sons-of-bitches," he fumed, "but I never believed it until now." When the Defense Department announced that no contracts would go to steel companies that raised their prices, the industry giants backed down.

The showdown with the steel industry, together with lawsuits against the General Electric Company for price fixing, turned most business leaders against Kennedy. In a 1962 survey of six thousand business executives, 52 percent rated the administration "strongly anti-business." In fact, the administration had compiled a probusiness record, with its tax-credit plan to promote investment; trade-reform bill; and support for a private communications-satellite corporation, a plan backed by the American Telephone and Telegraph Company (AT&T).

Despite some important initiatives, Kennedy's domestic record reflected more promise than achievement. Democrats controlled both houses of Congress, but a working alliance of Republicans and conservative southern Democrats stymied many of JFK's proposals. The Democratic congressional leadership, weakened by Lyndon Johnson's elevation to the vice presidency, eroded further in 1961 with the death of Sam Rayburn, the long-time Speaker of the House.

Of twenty-three bills that Kennedy submitted in his early months in office, only seven were enacted. The administration's health-care plan for the elderly, for example, roused the ire of the American Medical Association (AMA). Having battled Truman over this issue, the AMA now fought Kennedy's proposals. As key congressional Democrats also opposed the bill, it languished.

A White House proposal for federal aid to education met the same fate. Catholic leaders argued that such aid should go to parochial schools as well as to public schools, but Kennedy, unwilling to appear as yielding to church pressure, refused to concede this point. Southern legislators, meanwhile, saw the bill as a tactic to force integration, and some civil-rights leaders refused to support any bill that did not explicitly exclude segregated schools.

Other administration proposals, including medical-education assistance, immigration reform, help for migrant workers, federal aid to mass transit, and a department of urban and housing affairs, received an equally cool reception. Like President Truman, Kennedy placed many reform ideas on the national agenda but saw few of them translated into law.

In a rare domestic success, JFK did stimulate the space program. The technological race with the Soviets stirred the president's competitive juices, particularly when Moscow orbited a cosmonaut around the earth in 1961. Combining Cold War themes with familiar American images of bold pioneers pushing into the wilderness, the administration and the media built support for this multimillion-dollar scientific/technical project. Congress doubled the budget of the National Aeronautics and Space Administration (NASA) and approved a plan to put an American on the moon by 1970—a goal set by Kennedy in his inaugural address. In February 1962, astronaut John Glenn became the first American to orbit the earth. On July 20, 1969, beating Kennedy's deadline by five months, Neil Armstrong became the first human being to set foot on the moon. In a related 1962 program, Congress passed the Communications Satellite Act creating a private corporation to develop and operate a system of telecommunications satellites. The first Telstar satellite, orbited by AT&T in 1962 using a government-furnished rocket, proved the forerunner of a global system of instantaneous communications. The space program rebuilt confidence in U.S. technological know-how and, as satellites sent back breathtaking images of Earth, dramatized humanity's common fate. Some critics charged, however, that the billions spent on space research would be better channeled to urgent social needs.

The space program, the economic recovery, the successful outcome of the Cuban missile crisis, and Kennedy's continued popularity all aided the Democrats in the 1962 midterm elections. Reversing the usual midterm pattern, the Democrats increased their Senate margin by four seats and held their House losses to a minimum. In 1963, looking ahead to 1964, Kennedy pushed his domestic program enthusiastically, but again with scant results.

Kennedy's most innovative fiscal-policy initiative, which he would not live to see enacted, came early in 1963. Troubled by a dip in the economy's growth rate in mid-1962 and by hints of another recession, Walter Heller and the CEA urged a major tax cut to stimulate business investment and productivity. In August JFK announced that in January 1963 he would ask the new Congress for a $10 billion, two-year cut without a corresponding slash in spending. A tax cut would promote economic growth, he insisted, and the resulting boom would increase tax revenues despite lower rates. In 1981, when President Ronald Reagan argued, on precisely the same grounds, that a big tax cut would stimulate the economy and produce higher federal tax revenues, Democrats ridiculed "Reaganomics." Yet it was a liberal Democrat, John Kennedy, who first proposed to jump-start the economy by this means.

Powerful Democrats in Congress proved skeptical, however, and influential figures in the administration favored higher government spending rather than tax cuts as an economic stimulus. Some liberals criticized the proposed cut as unfairly tilted toward the well-to-do. Worse, the CEA soon projected deficits far higher than those anticipated earlier. The president nevertheless introduced the bill as promised in January 1963, although he spread the cut over three years rather than two. The measure finally passed the House in September 1963 but stalled in the Senate. The speech that JFK was scheduled to deliver on November 22, 1963, to a Dallas business group urged passage of his tax-cut bill.

Kennedy's domestic program stood largely unrealized at his death. He had sketched a new liberal agenda but never brought it to fruition. His major achievement

The Romance of Space. Astronaut John Glenn, the first American to orbit the globe, gives a thumbs-up before liftoff on February 20, 1962. Reflected in his suit is the face of back-up astronaut Scott Carpenter. *(Hulton Archive/Getty Images)*

centered on economic policy, especially his embrace of Keynesian principles. Thanks in part to JFK's initiatives, even a conservative president such as Richard Nixon later could assert, "We are all Keynesians now."

Kennedy's failure to cultivate relations with Congress, even during his years on Capitol Hill, had hampered his efforts. In this respect, his successor, a master of manipulating the levers of congressional power, would prove far more effective.

LBJ: The Making of a President

Lyndon Baines Johnson was born in 1908 in Stonewall, Texas, the eldest child of Sam and Rebecca Baines Johnson. Sam worked at various pursuits with little success and served several terms in the state legislature. Rebecca, whose grandfather had founded Baylor University, harbored great hopes for Lyndon; through her encouragement he graduated from Southwest Texas State Teachers' College in nearby San Marcos, where he excelled as a campus debater and student politician. After a stint of school-teaching, he took a job in Washington, D.C., in 1931 as clerk to a Texas congressman.

In 1935 Johnson became Texas director of the National Youth Administration, a New Deal agency. Two years later, he won a special election to Congress when the incumbent died in office. Johnson revered Franklin Roosevelt, whom he described as "like a daddy to me." For Johnson, the New Deal became the model of activist, reform government at its best. He styled himself "LBJ," in imitation of Roosevelt's "FDR." In 1948, after wartime service in the navy, he went to the Senate in an election so close that it earned him the derisive nickname "Landslide Lyndon." Ballot-box stuffing by Johnson operatives had put him over the top by eighty-seven votes.

In 1953, Johnson's Democratic colleagues chose him as minority leader; two years later he became majority leader. He worked closely with the Eisenhower administration while remaining a highly partisan Democrat. Indeed, as a central figure in shaping the Civil Rights Act of 1957, the 1958 National Defense Education Act, and other measures, he helped to set the liberal agenda in the era of the Cold War. He once summed up the art of political bargaining this way: "Before you do anything, your last thought ought to be 'I've got to live with the son-of-a-bitch.'" Surviving a near-fatal heart attack in 1955, Johnson sought the Democratic nomination in 1960 and grudgingly accepted Kennedy's offer of second place on the ticket.

A tall, physically imposing man with a fondness for earthy language and Scotch whisky, Johnson overwhelmed those from whom he wanted a favor; no one who experienced the "Johnson treatment" ever forgot it. He charmed, bullied, and made deals with a master's touch, wearing down opposition by the sheer force of his personality. Images of tornadoes and volcanoes came to mind when associates described his style. He often met with aides in his bedroom, while seated on the toilet, or even while swimming naked in the White House pool.

LBJ often resorted to crass manipulation. In 1965, eager to put his friend Abe Fortas on the Supreme Court, he persuaded Arthur Goldberg, a Kennedy appointee, to leave the Court, offering vague promises that went largely unfulfilled. Johnson's many petty slights toward Hubert Humphrey, his vice president from 1965 on, left Humphrey deeply embittered. After LBJ's death in 1973, journalist Robert Caro in a massive, multivolume biography portrayed him as virtually a monster of ego with "a genius for discerning a path to power, an utter ruthlessness in destroying obstacles in that path, and a seemingly bottomless capacity for deceit, deception and betrayal." Johnson's press secretary, George Reedy, similarly portrayed LBJ as selfish, insensitive, and exploitive. "There was no sense in which he could be described as a pleasant man," Reedy wrote.

These accounts capture part of the truth but fail to explain how Johnson managed, over a long career, to inspire loyalty in scores of people who willingly overlooked his faults. George Reedy provides one clue. Conceding all of Johnson's flaws, Reedy also noted that LBJ at times would "do something so magnificent that all of his nasty characteristics would fade. . . . He was a tremendous figure—a combination of complexities and simplicities that bewildered all observers."

Johnson's wife, Claudia, known from childhood as Lady Bird, was crucial to his career. A journalism graduate from the University of Texas, Mrs. Johnson promoted her husband's efforts while pursuing her own interests. With piercing eyes, jet-black hair, and a winning smile, Lady Bird Johnson had political instincts equal to her husband's and a commitment to public service that outmatched his. She managed his congressional office during his navy service and oversaw the family's financial interests in Texas, which eventually included real estate, ranch lands, and an Austin radio station and TV channel.

Johnson exhibited a quiet dignity in the traumatic days following Kennedy's assassination. Addressing Congress on November 26, 1963, he pledged to carry on

The Johnson Treatment. Energetic, domineering, calculating, and crude, Lyndon Johnson pursued his objectives with tireless intensity, and usually got his way. *(LBJ Library photo by Yoichi Okamoto)*

the slain president's agenda. Echoing JFK's inaugural exhortation "Let us begin," Johnson intoned in his Texas twang, "Let us contin-yah."

The Apex of a Liberal Agenda: The War on Poverty

Stressing continuity, Johnson asked the Kennedy cabinet and top advisers to stay on. Most did, although many resented him as a usurper. Johnson channeled the nation's grief into support for Kennedy's program. He pushed through a civil-rights bill that JFK had introduced (see Chapter 8) and the Kennedy tax-cut plan. A steady economic boom seemed to validate the wisdom of this pump-priming measure. Indeed, the GNP rose from $591 billion in 1963 to $977 billion in 1970.

Not content merely to complete the Kennedy agenda, however, Johnson sought a program that would bear his personal brand. He found it initially in the War on Poverty.

The Other America. President Johnson's ambitious War on Poverty reminded Americans of the persistence of want amidst abundance. Images such as this, of a poor family in Kentucky, reinforced the message. *(© Inge Morath/Magnum Photos, Inc.)*

Even liberal social thinkers of the 1950s had downplayed poverty. Galbraith in *The Affluent Society* saw it as a minor issue but hardly a "massive affliction." Michael Harrington's angry *The Other America: Poverty in the United States* (1962) challenged such perceptions. Harrington, a radical Catholic activist and socialist, documented the hardship in inner cities and rural backwaters and among the elderly, minorities, migrant laborers, and unskilled workers. Estimating the ranks of the poor at 40 to 50 million, Harrington argued that the problem was not simply isolated pockets of destitution, but a vast subculture of poverty. He urged readers "not [to] allow statistical quibbling to obscure the huge, enormous, and intolerable fact of poverty in America. For, when all is said and done, that fact is unmistakable, . . . and the truly human reaction can only be outrage."

Prodded by Harrington's work and by Walter Heller, John Kennedy had planned to showcase this issue in his 1964 legislative program. On November 19, 1963, he had authorized Heller to draft legislative proposals to fight poverty. President Johnson, meeting with Heller on November 23, endorsed this initiative. Knowing poverty from his own East Texas boyhood, he responded instinctively to the program.

Other factors underlay Johnson's sense of urgency. Black civil-rights activists were increasingly focusing on economic issues, and the movement was spreading from the South to the inner-city ghettos of the urban North (see Chapter 9). With more than 40 percent of African American families earning under $3,000 a year, an antipoverty program clearly would have major implications for black America and, Johnson hoped, quell the rising drumbeat of protest.

Similarly, unrest was stirring among the nation's growing Hispanic population—migrants from Mexico, Puerto Rico, Haiti, and elsewhere in Latin America who were eking out a living as migrant agricultural workers or in urban barrios, where they confronted joblessness, underemployment, poor living conditions, and inadequate public services. Early in 1963, for example, at a Mexican American protest rally in Crystal City, Texas, a crowd of several thousand cheered as activist José Angel Gutiérrez proclaimed: "They say there is no discrimination, but we have only to look around us to know the truth. We look at the schools, the houses we live in, the few opportunities, the dirt in the streets, and we know."

Legislators hesitant to appropriate massive funds to aid urban minorities, Johnson believed, might support a broadly focused "war on poverty." Americans understood calls for unity in times of crisis, and Johnson, as he would mention in his memoirs, used the rhetoric of war to "sound a call to arms which would stir people."

Cold War considerations also may have shaped Johnson's calculations. Improving the economic situation of the nation's poor would not only be good domestic policy, but also a demonstration to the world of America's ability and willingness to address its own social problems. Johnson's embrace of the antipoverty cause arose, too, from his exuberant personality. America was rich and resourceful enough, he believed, to uplift the poor without seriously inconveniencing the well-to-do. As he grandly put it, "We know what must be done, and this nation of abundance can surely afford it."

In January 1964, an election year, Johnson called on Congress to declare an "unconditional war on poverty. . . . [W]e shall not rest until that war is won. . . . We cannot afford to lose it." He proposed a battery of programs and approaches to attack poverty head-on and, in the remarkable political climate of 1964–65, he chalked up a striking string of successes.

The antipoverty package had taken shape in discussions late in 1963 at Johnson's Texas ranch by a team including Walter Heller and other top advisers. The program that emerged incorporated poverty-fighting ideas dating from the Truman and Eisenhower eras, Kennedy-era proposals, and programs initiated by private philanthropies such as the Rockefeller Brothers Fund and the Ford Foundation.

Johnson's omnibus antipoverty bill, the Economic Opportunity Act, passed in August 1964 after extensive hearings but with little critical scrutiny. As one Republican complained, criticizing the program seemed like "being in favor of poverty." Blunting southern opposition, Johnson had chosen a conservative congressman from Georgia as the bill's House floor manager. Still, many conservative Republicans and southern Democrats remained unconvinced, and the final vote was sharply divided: 226–185 in the House, 61–34 in the Senate.

The Economic Opportunity Act had ten major components. One section, expanding the 1962 Manpower Development and Training Act, focused on job training. Other sections created the Job Corps to teach marketable skills to unemployed inner-city youth, and Volunteers in Service to America (VISTA), a domestic parallel of the Peace Corps. The most innovative measure, Head Start, offered basic-skills training to preschool youngsters. The Upward Bound program helped gifted students from poor families to go to college. Other components funded public-works projects in poor areas and loans for small businesses and small farmers. The law created the Office of Economic Opportunity (OEO) as the command center of the antipoverty battle. To head OEO, Johnson chose Peace Corps director (and Kennedy in-law) R. Sargent Shriver.

Despite the program's ambitious scope, the first-year funding proved modest: only $500 million in new money (plus an additional $462 million from funds already budgeted). Later appropriations increased somewhat but then declined precipitously as Vietnam War costs skyrocketed. Antipoverty funding never really matched the sweeping goals, and dividing the funds among numerous programs further diminished their effect.

The assumptions underlying the War on Poverty were far from radical. Its framers never envisioned altering the nation's basic socioeconomic structure by redistributing wealth and power on a major scale. Nor did they propose direct income transfers—payments to bring all Americans up to a minimal income level. Instead, their strategy, implicit in the title Economic *Opportunity* Act, aimed to provide education, skills training, employment opportunities, and an aura of hope and motivation, so that all who wished a decent job could get one. Later criticism to the contrary, the aim was not welfare, but enabling the poor to become self-sufficient. In the phrase of the day, they favored a "hand up," not a "handout." As Johnson asserted on signing the bill, "The days of the dole in this country are numbered." This broad objective gave an underlying coherence to the War on Poverty's diverse programs.

The law's most controversial section was the Community Action Program (CAP), based on a Ford Foundation pilot project. It allocated $300 million for local antipoverty programs involving the "maximum feasible participation" of community members. The CAP initiative reflected the view of some analysts that social policy formulation had become top-heavy with experts and bureaucrats and needed grassroots input. As the OEO put it in 1965, the CAP program sought to empower the poor so they could challenge the more "politically effective sectors of society."

CAP advocates hoped that it would stimulate political activism, collective effort, and local initiatives by the poor themselves. And indeed, by 1966 more than a thousand CAPs were functioning in cities across the country. In many African American and Mexican American inner-city neighborhoods, locally run antipoverty programs funded by OEO provided an avenue of community activism and organizational experience. This proved particularly important in the rapidly growing Hispanic barrios, hitherto largely "invisible" in terms of political activism but increasingly alive with stirrings of protest. The Community Action Program encouraged political organization and community development in these settings. When used as intended, CAP funds went for legal services, medical clinics, educational services, and other needs identified by local community members and organizations.

But the program did not always work as planned. In Chicago, Mayor Daley's lieutenants simply commandeered CAP and operated it as an adjunct of the Daley machine. In some big-city ghettos, radical black activists dominated the CAPs. Often, however, local CAPs were led neither by the poor nor by machine politicians but by middle-class advocates skilled at the politics of poverty. These CAP activists typically decried the local power structure—city government, welfare agencies, school boards, the police, private charities—which they dismissed as more interested in keeping the poor pacified than in real reform. They formed tenant unions, used public funds to bail out demonstrators arrested in protest actions, and organized voter-registration campaigns aimed at throwing out elected city officials.

The OEO's apparent call to class conflict alarmed the establishment. Local Democratic officials groused that a Democratic-sponsored program was muscling them aside. Baltimore's mayor complained to President Johnson about CAP hotheads oblivious to "the problems and operations of local governments." When a CAP group in Washington, D.C., attacked local Democratic leaders, Johnson instructed his aide Bill Moyers: "For God's sake get on top of this and put a stop to it at once." But the turmoil persisted. At a 1966 Washington conference, Sargent Shriver was shouted off the stage and militants took the platform to denounce one aspect or another of the antipoverty program.

The Community Action Program became a prime target of critics of the War on Poverty. In *Maximum Feasible Misunderstanding* (1969), President Nixon's urban-affairs adviser, Daniel Moynihan, heaped scorn on the CAP initiative as the brainchild of liberals ignorant of the real world of politics and power. CAPs, he charged, were mainly functioning as a welfare program for the middle-class activists who ran them. Moynihan summed up a widely held view at the close of the 1960s, when the political climate had turned distinctly conservative. The War on Poverty, emphasizing expanded individual opportunity through job training and education, had been crafted to appeal to moderates, but the Community Action Programs, by encouraging collective action by the poor themselves, ultimately threatened the entire effort. As the 1964 election neared, however, few anticipated the intensity of the reaction that lay ahead.

Election 1964: Liberalism Triumphant

Riding a wave of liberal support for the War on Poverty and bathed in JFK's lingering aura, Johnson seemed a shoo-in for the 1964 Democratic nomination. At the party's Atlantic City convention, after a dispute over the makeup of the Mississippi delegation (see Chapter 8), Johnson won the nomination by acclamation. As his running mate, he chose Hubert Humphrey, the party's most outspoken champion of civil rights and New Deal–style liberalism.

LBJ dominated the proceedings. A journalist who covered the event for *Life* marveled:

> I had the feeling . . . that this was not a convention at all, [but] rather a party being thrown by the President in celebration of himself. The delegates, the visitors in the hall, the press, the television audience—we were all *his* guests. . . . Like a good host, or perhaps more correctly a good emperor, he thanked his subjects for coming, praised their little acts of fealty, and then said how things were going to be.

The Republicans, meanwhile, had moved sharply rightward. The party's moderate eastern wing failed to produce a candidate who had the appeal of an Eisenhower. With Richard Nixon biding his time, the party's right wing reasserted its power. Abetted by William Buckley's conservative journal, *National Review;* conservative radio commentators; and far-right organizations such as the John Birch Society, the Republican Right had steadily gained strength among conservatives disturbed by the welfare state and by the civil-rights movement and intent on escalating the global crusade against communism. As historian Lisa McGirr demonstrates in *Suburban Warriors: The Origins of the New American Right* (2001), a study of

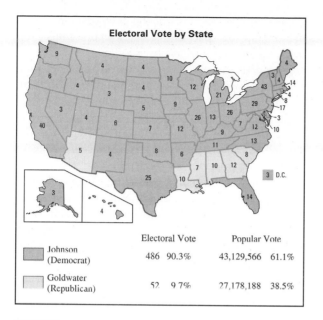

Electoral Vote by State

	Electoral Vote	Popular Vote
Johnson (Democrat)	486 90.3%	43,129,566 61.1%
Goldwater (Republican)	52 9.7%	27,178,188 38.5%

MAP 7.1
Presidential Election of 1964

Orange County, California, in the 1960s, white, middle-class, evangelical-Protestant suburbanites became increasingly conservative in these years and built a grassroots political movement to make their views heard. Although federal defense spending sustained the region's prosperity, an antigovernment ideology with both libertarian and intensely moralistic strands spawned hostility to liberal Democrats, who were denounced for allegedly promoting secularism, weakening traditional morality, and wasting citizens' tax dollars on hopelessly idealistic social programs.

The new conservative activists rallied around Senator Barry Goldwater of Arizona, an air force reservist and heir to a department-store fortune. Goldwater's 1960 book, *The Conscience of a Conservative,* though ghostwritten, summed up his creed: aggressive pursuit of the Cold War, untrammeled free enterprise, and a dismantling of character-sapping welfare programs. As a senator, Goldwater had praised Joe McCarthy, and now in 1964 he again hurled the "soft on communism" charge at the Democrats.

Defeating New York governor Nelson Rockefeller, the moderates' hope, in the crucial California primary, Goldwater handily won the nomination at the party convention in San Francisco. Welcoming the "extremist" label, he declared: "Extremism in the defense of liberty is no vice. Moderation in the pursuit of justice is no virtue." GOP campaign posters asserted of Goldwater, "In Your Heart You Know He's Right." Democrats retorted, "In Your Guts You Know He's Nuts."

Capitalizing on Goldwater's as-yet narrow appeal, LBJ cast his own campaign as a big tent and invited all Americans to gather inside. Downplaying divisive issues, he sought votes from business and labor, farmers and city dwellers, and all racial and ethnic constituencies. The key to political leadership, Johnson asserted, was "to make people aware . . . that they share a fundamental unity of interest, purpose and belief." This unity theme takes on special poignancy as one reflects on the polarization that would plague the end of Johnson's term.

Although the campaign highlighted domestic issues, Vietnam hovered ominously in the background. Whereas Goldwater advocated bombing North Vietnam and using tactical nuclear weapons on the battlefield, and even spoke cavalierly of "lobbing [a nuclear bomb] into the men's room of the Kremlin," LBJ posed as the peace candidate. He would not send American boys into any foreign war, he pledged. A Democratic TV commercial came close to predicting nuclear holocaust if Goldwater prevailed.

No longer the accidental president, Johnson scored a landslide victory. His role as Kennedy's heir and his advocacy of civil rights and domestic reform, together with fear of Goldwater, brought him 61 percent of the vote, more than even Franklin Roosevelt captured in 1936. The Democrats' margin in the House widened by thirty-eight seats and in the Senate by two seats. The southern political realignment continued, however: Of the six states that Goldwater carried, all but Arizona lay in the Deep South. He might have made even greater southern inroads had not Mrs. Johnson, evoking memories of Harry Truman in 1948, toured the region by rail on the "Lady Bird Special." But if some southern whites abandoned LBJ because of his identification with civil rights, black votes more than balanced the defections. Six million African Americans cast ballots in 1964—a third more than in 1960—and an astounding 94 percent voted for the Johnson-Humphrey ticket. Blacks provided the victory margin in Arkansas, Florida, Tennessee, and Virginia.

President Johnson Presses the Flesh. LBJ's War on Poverty and Great Society programs, together with his strong support for civil rights, seemed to assure him a stunningly successful presidency. Unfortunately, the Vietnam War would soon intervene. *(LBJ Library photo by Frank Wolfe)*

Despite Goldwater's loss, his candidacy energized the emerging conservative movement centered in the South and West but also stirring in the suburbs and even in white working-class neighborhoods nationwide. Suburban housewives in Orange County organized coffee klatches for Goldwater. College-age volunteers who belonged to Young Americans for Freedom (YAF), a conservative organization founded by William Buckley in 1960, rang doorbells and stuffed envelopes for Goldwater. Calling for a rollback of big government at home and more militant anticommunism abroad, YAF boasted fifty thousand members by 1970. Although overshadowed at the time by civil-rights marches, antiwar protests, and New Left manifestos, the conservatives mobilized by Goldwater were the shock troops of a movement that would grow steadily more powerful in the future.

Liberalism at High Tide: Johnson's Great Society

While promoting Kennedy's legislative program, the War on Poverty, and a civil-rights bill, President Johnson had also laid out a still more grandiose reform agenda. As early as May 1964, speaking at the University of Michigan, LBJ had limned an inspiring picture of America as a "Great Society." To waves of applause, he had poured out a cornucopia of social goals. Better schools, better health, better cities, safer highways, a more beautiful nation, support for the arts—Johnson's dream for America knew few bounds.

Fleshing out his Great Society vision early in 1965, Johnson proposed a list of reforms drawn from Truman's Fair Deal, earlier Kennedy proposals, and ideas current among social reformers. "Hurry, boys," he urged his aides. "Get that legislation up to the Hill. . . . Eighteen months from now, Ol' Landslide Lyndon will be lame-duck Lyndon." The heavily Democratic Congress passed a dizzying array of laws intended to improve American life. Congress increased funding for the antipoverty program and appropriated $1.1 billion for public-works projects, rural health centers, and other programs in the depressed Appalachian region.

The heart of the Great Society program lay in measures to improve cities, education, and health care. In his "Message on the Cities," Johnson observed:

> Within the borders of our urban centers can be found the most impressive examples of man's skill . . . as well as the worst examples of degradation and cruelty and misery. . . . The modern city can be the most ruthless enemy of the good life, or it can be its servant.

Congress responded. The Housing and Urban Development Act of 1965 offered reduced interest rates to builders of housing for the poor and elderly. It also allocated funds for urban beautification, health programs, recreation centers, repairs on inner-city housing, and a rent-supplement program for the poor. To avoid merely scattershot urban programs, this law mandated that all applications for federal aid to cities be approved by citywide or regional planning agencies. To administer the new programs, Congress created a new cabinet-level agency, the Department of Housing and Urban Development.

Attention to cities meant attention to transportation. The 1950s highway program, for all its benefits, had weakened public-transit systems, worsened urban

IN PERSPECTIVE

The Problem of Poverty
in the Land of Opportunity

Lyndon Johnson's War on Poverty was only the latest attempt to grapple with a problem that had long perplexed the nation. Americans with their egalitarian political ideology and their belief that hard work will bring success have always had difficulty coming to terms with the reality of poverty. In Early America, a mainly rural society of villages and small towns, poverty was largely an individual matter. If the poor person or family seemed needy through no fault of their own, such as illness, disability, or misfortune, neighbors or local magistrates would provide alms or supply funds to maintain a poor house. But if laziness, drunkenness, or vagrancy seemed to be the cause, the indigent could be jailed or ordered out of town.

With urbanization, and particularly the rise of the great industrial cities of the late nineteenth century, poverty became not a matter of a few individuals or families, but of huddled masses living in want. Entire sections of cities like New York and Boston became notorious for their concentrations of poverty.

Some churches, benevolent organizations, and kind-hearted individuals carried on the older tradition of providing alms to the poor, but the 1870s saw the rise of a new approach, called the Charity Organization movement. The key word was *organization.* Charity Organization societies in the major cities sought to replace the sentimental and random approach to charitable giving with what they considered a more rational and systematic strategy for dealing with poverty. This strategy was based on the familiar distinction between the "worthy" and the "unworthy" poor. The former were those whose poverty resulted from some external cause or misfortune, such as the family whose breadwinner was killed or injured on the job (a frequent occurrence in these years). Those in this category clearly merited temporary assistance if they did not have sufficient personal or family resources.

But the unworthy poor were another story. These were the people—often immigrants—who (in the view of the Charity Organization theorists) were lazy, had too many children, spent their money foolishly, consumed too much alcohol, or did not manage their finances wisely. For the unworthy poor, the Charity Organization societies pro-posed rigorous remedies. Careful records would be compiled about such people so that churches, well-meaning individuals, and do-good organizations could investigate their history when approached for a handout. Panhandling and door-to-door begging would be forbidden. Above all, poor families would be monitored by "Friendly Visitors"—usu-ally well-to-do female volunteers who would call on them regularly and instruct them in proper money management, the importance of sobriety, and the dangers of indulging in momentary pleasures rather than carefully budgeting family resources.

A related but even harsher view of the poor that flourished in the late nineteenth century (and still survives) was an ideology that applied Charles Darwin's evolutionary theory to society. According to this ideology, sometimes called Social Darwinism, and summed up in the phrase "survival of the fittest" (coined by the British sociologist Her-bert Spencer), those who were best adapted to thrive and prosper in the modern urban-industrial order would do so. Those unable to function efficiently in the new economic environment because of moral defects, physical or mental deficiencies, or flaws of character would fall by the wayside. This, in fact, was the path to social progress. Those well-meaning people who, through misplaced charitable impulses, helped the unfit to survive and reproduce simply drained resources from the striving, hardworking portion of the population and transferred it to the sluggish, worthless sector, thereby dragging down society as a whole.

Social Darwinism and the Charity Organization movement enjoyed their heyday in the 1880s. Both saw the root cause of poverty in individual and family dynamics. The 1890s, however, brought a harsh depression that threw millions out of work and blurred the distinction between the "worthy" and the "unworthy" poor. Soon a new generation of social workers and reformers began to look for the causes of poverty in the social order rather than in individual defects of character. Instead of preaching hard work, sobriety, and better household budgeting to individual families, they in-dicted a capitalist system that tolerated starvation wages, child labor, fetid and un-healthy slums, and dangerous working conditions. The photographer Charles Hine confronted middle-class America with images of pale, stunted children working in fac-tories, mines, and textile mills. The settlement-house leader Jane Addams in *Democracy and Social Ethics* (1902) made a compelling case that poverty was less a matter of indi-vidual flaws of character than of the social conditions prevailing in the new urban-industrial order. This view, which undermined the Charity Organization approach and the ideology of Social Darwinism, produced a wave of regulatory legislation in the early twentieth century aimed at improving slum conditions, making the workplace safer, and putting children in school rather than in factories. It had a powerful and long-lasting impact, influencing the New Deal social-welfare legislation of the 1930s and helping to shape the 1960s' War on Poverty launched by Lyndon Johnson, whose social thought was molded in the New Deal era.

But the debates continued, and by the 1980s, as the welfare rolls steadily in-creased, social observers began to speak of a "culture of poverty" dependent on pub-lic assistance and perpetuated from generation to generation. By the 1990s, as we shall see in Chapter 15, pressure grew for tougher welfare laws, and in the ongoing debate over poverty, the old themes of hard work and individual responsibility once more resonated powerfully.

traffic congestion, and destroyed inner-city neighborhoods. In 1964, conceding these problems, Congress granted some $375 million for urban mass-transit planning. In 1966 Congress allocated more funds for this purpose and created a new agency, the Department of Transportation, to administer them.

Another important urban-development measure, the Model Cities Act of 1966, granted $1.2 billion for slum clearance and renewal. The aim was to revitalize all aspects of inner-city life, from housing and schools to health care, job training, and recreation. The law provided funds for new model communities, reflecting the deep-rooted utopian strand in American social thought. To its supporters, this sweeping measure represented the Great Society vision at its loftiest.

Convening a White House Conference on Education in 1965, LBJ promised every child in America "the best education our nation can provide." In this spirit, the 1965 Elementary and Secondary Education Act (ESEA) directed over $1 billion for programs to aid "educationally deprived children." Much of this money went to schools in poor districts, but the bill also targeted bilingual education for Hispanic children and education of persons with disabilities. With this infusion of federal dollars, inner-city and rural schools and institutions serving children with special needs hired more teachers and aides and developed new programs. In 1966, under the adoring gaze of an aged former teacher, Johnson delivered an education speech in the Texas schoolhouse he had attended as a lad.

The Higher Education Act, also passed in 1965, created a federal scholarship and loan program for needy college students and provided library grants to colleges and universities. Public-education funding and policymaking, once exclusively a state and local matter, grew increasingly dependent on Washington. In 1965, federal spending on education topped $4 billion. Liberals hailed this trend as a national investment in the younger generation; conservatives worried that more federal dollars would mean more federal control.

The "big tent" motif of LBJ's 1964 electoral campaign found legislative expression in the Immigration Act of 1965. This measure eliminated the discriminatory quotas against certain national groups written into the nation's immigration law in 1924 and reaffirmed in the Immigration Act of 1952. The new law opened the door to an increased flow of immigrants from Asia and Latin America that would profoundly affect American life.

In a historic health-care achievement, Congress in 1965 enacted Johnson's Medicare bill providing health insurance for all Americans over age sixty-five. Initially funded with a $6.5 billion appropriation, Medicare's long-range funding came from increased social security payroll deductions. The plan covered most hospital expenses, diagnostic tests, home visits, and some nursing-home costs. To supply the additional personnel needed for this expanded health-care program, Congress voted funds for nursing schools, medical schools, and medical-student scholarships. Medicaid, a key section of the law little noticed at the time, provided grants to the states to cover medical care for the poor. The American Medical Association's dire warnings against "socialized medicine," potent in the conservative 1950s, proved less effective in the reform climate of 1965. LBJ signed the Medicare bill in Independence, Missouri, as a beaming eighty-one-year-old Harry Truman, who had proposed such a measure twenty years earlier, looked on.

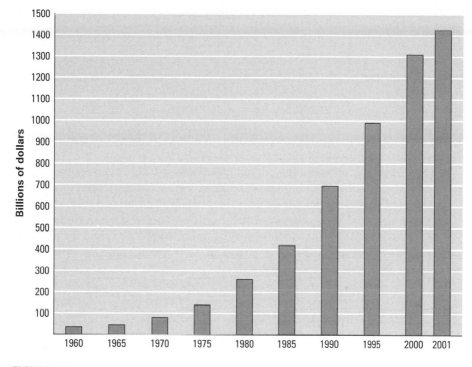

FIGURE 7.1

Total Spending on Health Care, 1960–2001

SOURCE: National Center for Health Statistics, U.S. Department of Health and Human Services, in *World Almanac, 2004*.

The influx of federal dollars generated explosive growth in the health-care and nursing-home industries. By the 1990s, soaring Medicare and Medicaid costs would exacerbate a staggering burden of public debt. In the optimistic summer of 1965, however, questions of long-range cost rarely shadowed liberal reformers' triumphant mood.

While President Johnson rallied the forces of liberalism, the Supreme Court contributed to the process by maintaining Chief Justice Earl Warren's activist course. A series of landmark rulings in the 1960s broke new ground in the areas of individual rights, electoral reform, and equal protection under the law.*

Seeking to give all citizens an equal voice at the polls, the Court in *Baker* v. *Carr* (1962) held that states must, "as nearly as practicable," maintain population balance in setting the bounds of congressional and state-legislature electoral districts. In *Gideon* v. *Wainwright* (1963), the Supreme Court extended the right of poor people to court-appointed counsel. In *Miranda* v. *Arizona* (1966), the justices mandated that all prisoners must be informed of their legal rights at the time of their arrest.

---

*Warren's closest allies in these endeavors were two FDR appointees, Hugo Black and William O. Douglas, and William J. Brennan, Jr., appointed by Dwight Eisenhower in 1956.

Expanding freedom of the press, the Court in *New York Times* v. *Sullivan* (1964) protected newspapers from libel suits by public officials except when actual malice could be proved. In 1966, the Court reversed a Massachusetts ban on John Cleland's erotic classic *Fanny Hill,* reaffirming a 1957 ruling *(Roth* v. *United States)* that only works "utterly without redeeming social value" could be denied First Amendment protection. In other personal-freedom cases, the Court banned organized classroom prayer in public schools as a violation of the constitutional prohibition against the establishment of religion (*Engel* v. *Vitale,* 1962), and it struck down a Connecticut law prohibiting the use of contraceptives or the distribution of contraceptive information (*Griswold* v. *Connecticut,* 1964).

These decisions reflected the outlook of an activist Court majority committed to democratic principles and to individual rights. When Warren retired in 1969, he left a harvest of decisions that for decades would make the Warren Court a target of both praise and attack. The activism that liberals applauded dismayed many conservatives, who deplored the Court's growing power and its penchant for plunging into highly contentious social issues that, in their view, were best dealt with through the legislative process.

The New Environmentalism

Environmental issues loomed large in Johnson's Great Society vision. "Once our national splendor is destroyed," the president cautioned, "it can never be recaptured." Indeed, he proclaimed, "The desire for beauty and the hunger for community" were the twin impulses driving his reformist campaign. Lady Bird Johnson and Interior Secretary Stewart Udall helped to translate that lofty goal into policy. Underlying their efforts was a growing national awareness that a century of industrialization had taken a dire toll: shrinking wilderness areas, vanishing wildlife species, health-threatening pollution, and a degradation of the visual landscape.

The environmentalism that emerged in the 1960s had deep roots. In the Progressive era, when some reformers had campaigned to conserve natural resources on the grounds of their economic utility, others had worked to preserve scenic beauty for its own sake. John Muir's Sierra Club, for example, lobbied to save California's Yosemite Valley and other wilderness areas. Still other Progressive-era reformers had battled factory pollution, tainted milk, and filthy slaughterhouses and had worked for urban beautification by establishing city parks and boulevards. After fading during the 1920s, environmental concerns had revived during the New Deal, only to diminish in the booming postwar years. Aldo Leopold's classic *Sand County Almanac* (1948), with its ecological focus and its call for "a new land ethic," at the time attracted little notice.

With liberalism's resurgence in the early 1960s, environmental concerns again found a voice. President Kennedy sent an environmentalist message to Congress in 1961 and in 1962 convened a White House conference on the subject. Kennedy and Udall pushed for more parks, especially along the crowded eastern seaboard. The Cape Cod National Seashore was one result. But it was Johnson who scored the major achievements. From 1963 to 1968, Congress at LBJ's initiative passed nearly three hundred measures relating to conservation, beautification, and pollution and appropriated some $12 billion for these purposes.

Environmentalists of the 1960s emphasized not only conserving natural resources but even more the aesthetic and social benefits of wilderness and natural beauty and the public-health hazards posed by pollution. These were not fringe issues, they insisted, but central to the quality of human life and social well-being.

Interior secretary Udall did much to foster this new environmental awareness. A friend of John Kennedy's from their days together in Congress, Udall played a central role in delivering Arizona to Kennedy at the 1960 Democratic convention. Appointed secretary of the interior, he crafted Kennedy's conservation message of 1961, planned the 1962 White House conference, and set forth his environmental views in an influential 1963 book, *The Quiet Crisis:*

> America today stands poised on a pinnacle of wealth and power, yet we live in a land of vanishing beauty, of increasing ugliness, of shrinking open space, and of an overall environment that is diminishing daily by pollution and noise and blight. This, in brief, is the quiet conservation crisis of the 1960s.

From the intersection of these personal and historical factors emerged a remarkable body of environmental law. The Wilderness Act of 1964 echoed Udall's warning that the nation's unspoiled areas were at risk from the advance of highways, tourism, and corporate exploitation. The culmination of a long campaign by the Sierra Club and the Wilderness Society, this law set aside over 9 million acres of national forest for preservation. The Wild and Scenic Rivers Act of 1968 protected sections of eight rivers from developers. The Endangered Species Act of 1966 for the first time set the protection of biodiversity as a national goal.

The 1960s environmentalists, like their Progressive-era predecessors, also battled the pollution of water, air, and land by the toxic byproducts of an urban-industrial society. An explosive bestseller, Rachel Carson's *Silent Spring* (1963), played a key role in this campaign. Just as Harrington's *The Other America* spotlighted poverty, so Carson's work thrust environmental pollution onto the national agenda.

A marine biologist with the U.S. Fish and Wildlife Service, Carson had grown alarmed by the environmental impact of DDT and other pesticides and herbicides pouring into the nation's water system and entering the food chain. Several magazines rejected her article on the subject because their food advertisers, particularly baby-food companies, worried that it would cause "unwarranted fear" among consumers. The *New Yorker* eventually serialized the work, and the book soon followed. Citing the mounting evidence of the ecological dangers of DDT and other chemicals, Carson concluded somberly:

> It is not my contention that chemical insecticides must never be used. I do contend that we have put poisonous . . . chemicals indiscriminately into the hands of persons largely or wholly ignorant of their potentials for harm . . . [and] subjected enormous numbers of people to contact with these poisons, without their consent and often without their knowledge.

The vogue for DDT and similar products, Carson warned, reflected a larger heedlessness of the environmental consequences of modern technology:

> The "control of nature" is a phrase conceived in arrogance. . . . The concepts and practices of . . . [the chemical eradication of unwanted insects] for the most part date from the Stone Age of science. It is our alarming misfortune that so primitive a science has armed itself with the most modern and terrible weapons, and that in turning them against the insects it has also turned them against the earth.

Pesticide manufacturers tried to discredit Carson, but her scientific credentials and scholarly documentation gave *Silent Spring* impressive credibility. Like Upton Sinclair's *The Jungle,* a 1906 exposé of Chicago packinghouses, *Silent Spring* shocked the nation, produced calls for stricter regulation, and became a key text of the emerging ecology movement.* The *Chicago Daily News* called Carson's work "one of the great and towering books of our time."

Responding to the furor, President Kennedy had appointed a scientific advisory committee on pesticides. President Johnson set up a Task Force on Environmental Pollution and prodded Congress to act. The Water Quality Act of 1965 authorized federal intervention if states failed to enforce water-quality standards for interstate rivers. The concern about pesticides, following a decade of publicity about radioactive fallout from nuclear tests, contributed to a larger awareness of environmental risks. Declared Johnson in 1965:

> Ours is a nation of affluence. But the technology that has permitted our affluence spews out vast quantities of wastes . . . that pollute our air, poison our waters, and even impair our ability to feed ourselves. At the same time, we have crowded together into dense metropolitan areas where concentration of wastes intensifies the problem.

The Clean Waters Restoration Act of 1966 authorized over $3.5 billion to clean up the nation's waterways and to halt further pollution by sewage or industrial waste. A series of clean-air laws culminating in the Air Quality Act of 1967 regulated a broad spectrum of atmospheric pollution sources, including coal-burning factories and automobile exhaust, and appropriated large sums for air-pollution abatement programs. Cumulatively, these laws identified environmental protection as a national issue requiring national action. Two major environmental disasters—the 1967 sinking of the giant oil tanker *Torrey Canyon* at the entrance to the English Channel that spilled thirty thousand tons of crude oil and damaged many miles of British and French coastline, and a 1969 oil drilling accident off Santa Barbara, California, that befouled beaches and devastated marine life—accelerated concern about pollution.

Environmental issues would loom still larger after Johnson left office. The National Environmental Policy Act of 1969 required federal agencies to file environmental-impact statements for all major activities or legislation they proposed. In 1970, Congress created the Environmental Protection Agency to enforce the growing body of federal environmental law. But the legislation and publicity of the Kennedy-Johnson years laid the groundwork for these later developments.

---

*The science of ecology views all plant and animal life within a given region, including human beings, as part of a single, complex, interdependent biological unit, or ecosystem.

Lady Bird Johnson inspired another major component of LBJ's environmental program: the campaign for national beautification. Although some ridiculed its advocates as "the daffodil and dogwood set," this reform, too, had deep roots. As early as 1791, Pierre L'Enfant had drafted a visionary plan for Washington, D.C. The turn-of-the-century City Beautiful movement had focused on urban beautification projects, including the completion of the L'Enfant plan.

Lady Bird Johnson built on this tradition. As early as the 1930s, she had promoted the movement to create roadside parks. During the White House years, she tirelessly pushed the beautification cause. The most influential presidential spouse between Eleanor Roosevelt and Nancy Reagan, she worked behind the scenes, lobbied the media, and gave dozens of speeches to spread the beautification gospel. At a 1965 White House Conference on Natural Beauty, Mrs. Johnson challenged the delegates: "Can a great democratic society generate . . . and execute great projects of beauty?" With LBJ's Great Society program at flood tide, that question could have but one answer.

Much of Lady Bird Johnson's campaign focused on Washington, D.C., as she sought not only to make the nation's capital more attractive for residents and visitors, but also to showcase Washington as a model for other communities. In 1965 she assembled a group of civic-minded Washingtonians to form the First Lady's Committee for a More Beautiful National Capital. Utilizing resources of the National Park Service, this committee transformed the city's appearance by planting trees and flowers, establishing parks, sprucing up Pennsylvania Avenue, and enacting other measures. Stewart Udall enthusiastically backed the First Lady's interest in Washington, recognizing its value in raising environmental awareness. (Once, when LBJ found Udall and Lady Bird crouched over a large set of plans for the renewal of Pennsylvania Avenue, he burst out in mock rage: "Udall, what in hell are you doing down there on the floor with my wife?")

Another of Mrs. Johnson's interests—and hence another item on LBJ's agenda—was highway beautification. Countless auto trips between Texas and Washington in the 1930s and 1940s had given her ample opportunity to observe the billboards and commercial clutter lining the nation's roadways. Through her efforts, Congress passed the Highway Beautification Act of 1965, despite opposition from the billboard lobby. The act banned or strictly regulated highway billboards outside commercial and industrial districts and required that roadside junkyards be concealed by fences. Proponents and opponents alike recognized Mrs. Johnson's key role. In the West billboards appeared demanding: "IMPEACH LADY BIRD JOHNSON."

The beautification campaign served the administration's interests at a time of growing divisiveness. As Mrs. Johnson emphasized in her speeches, beautification built consensus. At Yale in 1967, as antiwar protesters marched outside, she insisted almost plaintively that a concern for the environment was "one thing that we all share." Nevertheless, the divisions tearing at America's social fabric intruded even here. Young black activists in Washington, for example, attacked the elitist tinge of the First Lady's beautification campaign in the nation's capital. "How many rats can you kill with a tulip?" sneered one. Mrs. Johnson vigorously rejected the notion that her efforts solely concerned rich do-gooders, maintaining that "beauty cannot be reserved 'for nice neighborhoods only.'" Setting up a black-led committee to initiate projects in the city's African American districts, including vest-pocket parks and beautification efforts geared to schoolchildren and local residents, she took an avid interest in its work and visited neighborhoods that most government leaders rarely saw.

Lady Bird Johnson's efforts, like the War on Poverty and the Great Society reforms, ultimately faded in the face of rising controversy over Vietnam. At a 1966 National Youth Conference on Natural Beauty and Conservation, the First Lady urged the delegates to "consider making America's beauty a full-time vocation." By then, however, many young Americans found Lady Bird's home-front beautification campaign far less gripping than the war her husband was waging abroad.

The War on Poverty and the Great Society: A Retrospective View

With an awesome roster of reforms to his credit and more in the pipeline during 1964–65, LBJ's approval ratings hovered close to 70 percent. Indeed, a history of Johnson's domestic record written at the end of 1965, and including the civil-rights legislation discussed in the next chapter, would be a record of soaring aspirations and impressive achievement.

Yet by 1968 the spirit of reform had evaporated and a sharp backlash against some of Johnson's proudest achievements had set in. In that year, presidential candidate Richard Nixon declared, "For the past five years we have been deluged by government programs for the unemployed, programs for cities, programs for the poor, and we have reaped from these programs an ugly harvest of frustration, violence and failure." The OEO was already foundering when Nixon took office, and in 1974 he shut it down altogether. The political landscape altered so rapidly that Americans found it difficult to recall the reformist zeal of 1964–65.

What lay behind this wave of reform, and what was its long-term significance? Above all, why did it decline so rapidly? The causes are easiest to analyze. Kennedy's death, a series of books exposing problems in American life, and the idealism of the civil-rights movement encouraged a revival of liberal activism. Lyndon Johnson, with his New Deal background, political skills, and drive to build a memorable record, translated that mood into tangible achievement.

The long-term ramifications of LBJ's domestic record are less clear. Certainly the Civil Rights Act of 1964 and the Voting Rights Act of 1965, discussed in Chapter 8, left lasting legacies. Some Great Society measures—Medicare, aid to education, environmental legislation—had long-term significance. Yet, as often in politics, efforts to grapple with one set of issues only exacerbated others—including, as we have seen, soaring federal deficits related to the Medicare and Medicaid programs.

By some measures, the War on Poverty succeeded. The proportion of Americans below the federal poverty line fell from 20 percent in 1963 to 13 percent in 1968.* For African Americans, the statistics are even more impressive. In 1960 some 40 percent of blacks lived in poverty. By 1968, according to some data, this figure had been halved. In 1960 only 13 percent of black families had annual incomes over

---

*In 1964 the Council of Economic Advisers had set the poverty line at $3,000 annual income for a family of four—about one-half the median family income in America at the time.

$10,000; ten years later, the figure approached one-third. However, a booming economy contributed to these statistics as much as did the antipoverty program. The years of peak antipoverty spending also saw big federal outlays for the Vietnam War. The 1968–69 unemployment rate of about 3.4 percent, the lowest since the Korean War, reflected the increased draft calls, military spending, and war-related job opportunities as much as it did domestic economic policies. Similarly, another Vietnam byproduct, surging inflation, soon eroded many of the economic gains. All this complicates the task of isolating the effects of the War on Poverty.

LBJ's larger goal—poverty's eradication—remained a dream. The inequities and social ills that the antipoverty warriors set out to remedy, especially in the inner cities, proved more intractable than they had imagined. Despite the billions spent on social programs in 1964–67, inner-city joblessness, housing decay, educational problems, and social disorganization persisted. The unemployment rate among black males aged sixteen to twenty-four actually rose in the late 1960s, despite federal job-training programs. In later years, President Ronald Reagan would joke cynically, "We fought a war on poverty, and poverty won."

The same enthusiasm and boosterism that made Sargent Shriver an effective head of OEO inhibited critical self-scrutiny of the program. Like the reports from Vietnam touting enemy "body counts" and other statistics as proof that America was "winning" the war, the cheerleading for the War on Poverty tended to overstate its successes and sweep its failures under the rug.

Early evidence of a backlash came in the 1966 midterm election, when Republicans gained three Senate seats and forty-seven House seats. The electorate's conservative shift was accelerating. On the ideological plane, the old view that blamed the poor themselves for their plight found new advocates. In *The Unheavenly City* (1970), Edward Banfield argued that poverty stemmed from poor people's inability to grasp the concept of delayed gratification. The backlash was also connected with racial politics. As white America increasingly identified poverty as a problem of inner-city blacks and Hispanics, the antipoverty program came to be seen as simply a means of shoveling federal dollars to minorities. The racial backlash that would splinter the civil-rights movement in the later 1960s thus also helped shatter the liberal consensus that initially supported the War on Poverty.

In *The End of Liberalism* (1969), political scientist Theodore Lowi argued that despite Johnson's reverence for Franklin Roosevelt, his social agenda differed sharply from New Deal liberalism as embodied in the Social Security Act of 1935. Whereas social security clearly specified its operational rules and eligibility criteria, Lowi charged, the War on Poverty had a far looser structure, a "grab bag" of programs, and vaguely identified target groups. Rather than carefully pinpointing specific objects, he went on, the government merely threw money at the inner cities, letting local bodies referee the resulting free-for-all. Lowi also accused the antipoverty crusade of defining social problems, especially racial ones, in economic terms when in fact they had complex cultural and historical roots. The War on Poverty, he believed, drained the civil-rights movement of its momentum and moral authority. Lowi, a harbinger of "the emerging Republican majority" (the title of a 1969 book by Kevin Phillips), readily conceded that his real target was "the modern liberal state itself, its outmoded ideology, and its self-defeating policies." Johnson-style liberalism, he charged, was "sincere humanitarianism gone cockeyed."

The debate continued into the 1980s. In *The Unraveling of America* (1984), Allan J. Matusow attacked the War on Poverty from the left as a halfway palliative that offered superficial remedies without addressing underlying power realities. Only a radical redistribution of income and power, he argued, offered hope of eradicating want in capitalist America. The War on Poverty's epitaph, he concluded, should be "Declared But Never Fought." Although plausible on its own terms, Matusow's work gave little attention to the political realities of 1960s America, when the electorate's moderate-to-conservative tendencies put severe constraints on radical reform.

Charles Murray's *Losing Ground: American Social Policy, 1950–1980* (1984), a conservative critique, argued that by blaming poverty on social maladjustments that the government must correct, Johnson-era policymakers weakened the stigma associated with welfare. Despite LBJ's announced goal of ending welfare dependency, he suggested, 1960s social policy actually encouraged the poor to accept the dole as a way of life. New York City's welfare rolls did double between 1965 and 1975, with similar trends in other cities. By extending benefits to all whose income fell below a specified cutoff point, Murray contended, the War on Poverty and other well-intentioned programs reduced incentives to self-help.

The conservative critics paid scant attention to programs such as Head Start, the Job Corps, and Upward Bound that did encourage "middle-class" values of education, individual initiative, hard work, and personal responsibility. Further, if the problem was a growing dependence on federal largess, the poor were hardly alone. Defense industries boomed, and their employees enjoyed high wages as federal dollars showered down. Medicare retirement benefits constituted a vast new middle-class entitlement, and since physicians and nursing-home operators set their own fees, many profited vastly as Uncle Sam picked up the tab. Countless academics, lawyers, administrators, planners, builders, and "advocates for the poor" prospered from their participation in various War on Poverty programs. As we have seen, the funds designated to fight poverty often landed in the hands of the middle-class staffers who ran the agencies, programs, and centers.

Liberals—a dwindling breed—generally praised the War on Poverty, although they, too, criticized its scattershot approach and inflated rhetoric. They argued as well that the antipoverty campaign, for all the money spent, still suffered from underfunding. One called it "a classic instance of the American habit of substituting good intentions for cold hard cash." Finally, liberals and conservatives alike generally agreed that by raising expectations in the inner cities and then only partially following through, the War on Poverty left a legacy of bitterness.

Why did support for reform fade so rapidly? Urban riots offer one reason. Initially, inner-city unrest such as hit Birmingham in 1963 and Los Angeles in 1965 (see pages 226, 244) seemed to prove the urgency of antipoverty efforts. But as more cities erupted and the rhetoric of black radicals became more incendiary, skepticism about Johnson's programs intensified and the white middle class turned hostile. Not poverty but the poor now seemed the enemy.

LBJ launched his sweeping domestic reforms amid an economic boom, confident that the nation could divert large sums to social problems without paying higher taxes or jeopardizing middle-class living standards. "I'm sick of all the people who talk about the things we can't do," he burst out to a staff member. "Hell, we're the richest country in the world. . . . We can do it all, if we're not too greedy; that's our job: to persuade people to give a little so everyone can be better off." In the 1970s, as the boom faded and inflation worsened while spending on various entitlement programs soared,* expansiveness gave way to resentment. Johnson did little to combat inflation, wary of the politically risky tax increases and spending cuts needed to cool an overheated economy. The resulting economic slowdown and erosion of consumer buying power ate away at the liberal consensus. Richard Nixon exploited the shifting climate in the 1968 campaign when he championed not the poor but the middle class as the "Forgotten Americans."

Above all, the Great Society succumbed to the Vietnam War. From 1965 to 1973, when Washington spent about $15 billion combating poverty, funding for the war reached $120 billion. Vietnam diverted attention from home-front issues and undermined LBJ's moral authority as a champion of reform. In the summer of 1966, a Johnson aide traveled to New York City to discuss new domestic-policy initiatives with a group of liberal academics. In a later postmortem of the event, one of the participants, historian William Leuchtenburg, wrote: "Like Banquo's ghost, Vietnam was the unwelcome guest at the feast." As long as the war continued, he sadly concluded, "there is no hope at all for expanding the Great Society." The tough domestic challenges that Johnson set for the nation would have been daunting at best; after 1965, as he led the nation deeper into the Vietnam quagmire, they proved hopeless, and the reform consensus evaporated.

Conclusion

Yet much remains admirable in Johnson's domestic record. All the major issues that he tackled—racism, poverty, the cities, education, health care, the environment—stayed on the nation's agenda long after his presidency had ended. Thanks to him, the nation not only confronted these problems but for a time granted them priority, making the mid-1960s the most productive era in U.S. domestic reform since the New Deal. For liberals, the tragedy was not that the War on Poverty and the Great Society fell short, but that the impulse behind them faded so quickly. For conservatives, by contrast, the entire liberal project, with its reliance on federal activism, was misconceived. What America needed was not more government programs, they insisted, but a renewed commitment to free enterprise, individual responsibility, and private-sector voluntarism. For a generation to come, it would more often be the conservative perspective, not the liberal one, that would drive American politics.

Americans are still coming to terms with the crude, profane, arm-twisting Texan who figured so prominently in most of the great events that define the 1960s. As one struggles to understand how Lyndon Johnson could with equal fervor

---

*An entitlement benefit is one that the recipient is entitled to receive simply by virtue of being in a designated class of people: over age sixty-five or under a certain income level, for example.

espouse the rights of African Americans, the cause of the poor, educational and health reform, environmental protection and beautification, and a brutal and divisive war in Asia, one begins to understand not only Johnson but also American liberalism in the Cold War era.

SELECTED READINGS

The Liberal Agenda in the 1950s and the Kennedy Years

Irving Bernstein, *Promises Kept: John F. Kennedy's New Frontier* (1991); Robert Dallek, *Unfinished Life: John F. Kennedy* (2003); Wayne Flynt, *Dixie's Forgotten People: The South's Poor Whites* (1979); Patrick M. Garry, *Liberalism and American Identity* (1992); Robert A. Gorman, *Michael Harrington: Speaking American* (1995); Alonzo L. Hamby, *Liberalism and Its Challengers: From F.D.R. to Bush* (2d ed., 1992); Jim F. Heath, *John F. Kennedy and the Business Community* (1969); Maurice Isserman, *The Other American: The Life of Michael Harrington* (2000); James L. Kauffman, *Selling Outer Space: Kennedy, the Media, and Funding for Project Apollo, 1961–1963* (1994); Daniel Knapp and Kenneth Polk, *Scouting the War on Poverty: Social Reform Politics in the Kennedy Administration* (1971); Arthur Larson, *A Republican Looks at His Party* (1956); Robert Lekachman, *The Age of Keynes* (1968); Arthur M. Schlesinger, Jr., *A Thousand Days* (1965); Alan Shank, *Presidential Policy Leadership: Kennedy and Social Welfare* (1980).

The War on Poverty, the Great Society, and Their Conservative Critics

John A. Andrews, *Lyndon Johnson and the Great Society* (1998); Irving Bernstein, *Guns or Butter: The Presidency of Lyndon Johnson* (1996); Robert Caro, *The Years of Lyndon Johnson: The Path to Power (1982), Means of Ascent* (1990), and *Master of the Senate* (2002); Richard Cloward and Frances Fox Piven, *Poor People's Movements* (1978); Robert Dallek, *Lone Star Rising* (1991) and *Flawed Giant* (1998), a two-volume biography of Lyndon Johnson; Gareth Davies, *From Opportunity to Entitlement: The Transformation and Decline of Great Society Liberalism* (1996); Mark I. Gelfand, "The War on Poverty," in Robert A. Divine, ed., *The Johnson Years,* Vol. 1 (1987); Hugh Davis Graham, *The Uncertain Trumpet: Federal Education Policy in the Kennedy and Johnson Years* (1984); Robert H. Haveman, ed., *A Decade of Federal Antipoverty Programs* (1977); Lyndon Johnson, *The Vantage Point: Perspectives of the Presidency 1963–1969* (1971); Michael Katz, *The Undeserving Poor: From the War on Poverty to the War on Welfare* (1989); Theodore Marmor, *The Politics of Medicare* (1973); Alan Matusow, *The Unraveling of America: A History of Liberalism in the 1960s* (1984); Lisa McGirr, *Suburban Warriors: The Origins of the New American Right* (2001); Daniel Patrick Moynihan, *Maximum Feasible Misunderstanding* (1969); Charles Murray, *Losing Ground: American Social Policy, 1950–1980* (1984); James T. Patterson, *America's Struggle Against Poverty, 1900–1980* (1981); Rick Perlstein, *Before the Storm: Barry Goldwater and the Unmaking of the American Consensus* (2001); Kevin Phillips, *The Emerging Republican Majority* (1969); Frances Fox Piven and Richard A. Cloward, *Regulating the Poor: The Functions of Public Welfare* (1971); Diane Ravitch, *The Troubled Crusade: American Education, 1945–1980* (1983); Gregory L. Schneider, *Cadres for Conservatism: Young Americans for Freedom and the Rise of the Contemporary Right* (1999); Kent Schuparra, *Triumph of the Right: The Rise of the California Conservative Movement, 1945–1966* (1998); David Zarefsky, *President Johnson's War on Poverty: Rhetoric and History* (1986).

Environmentalism

Craig W. Allin, *The Politics of Wilderness Preservation* (1982); Jules Archer, *To Save the Earth: The American Environmental Movement* (1998); Thomas R. Dunlap, *DDT: Scientists, Citizens, and Public Policy* (1981); Robert Gottlieb, *Forcing the Spring: The Transformation of the American Environmental Movement* (1993); Lewis L. Gould, *Lady Bird Johnson: Our Environmental First Lady* (1999); Samuel P. Hays and Barbara D. Hays, *Beauty, Health, and Permanence: Environmental Politics in the United States, 1955–1985* (1987); Lady Bird Johnson, *A White House Diary* (1970); Linda J. Lear, *Rachel Carson: Witness for Nature* (1997); Martin V. Melosi, "Lyndon Johnson and Environmental Policy," in Robert A. Divine, ed., *The Johnson Years*, Vol. 2; Vera L. Norwood, "The Nature of Knowing: Rachel Carson and the American Environment," *Signs* (Summer 1987); Walter A. Rosenbaum, *The Politics of Environmental Concern* (1973); Victor B. Scheffer, *The Shaping of Environmentalism in America* (1991).

The Civil-Rights Movement at Flood Tide

ON MONDAY, FEBRUARY 1, 1960, four black freshmen from the North Carolina Agricultural and Technical College in Greensboro entered the local Woolworth's store, bought school supplies, and then sat down at the lunch counter and ordered coffee. When the white waitress uttered the familiar formula, "We don't serve Negroes here," they gave an unfamiliar response:

> We just beg to disagree with you. We've in fact already been served. . . . We wonder why you'd invite us in to serve us at one counter and deny service at another. If this is a private club or private concern, then we believe you ought to sell membership cards.

The four remained seated and waited—all day. Years later, one of the four, Franklin McCain, would look back on that Monday:

> If it's possible to know what it means to have your soul cleansed—I felt pretty clean at that time. . . . I felt as though I had gained my manhood. . . . Not Franklin McCain only as an individual, but I felt as though the manhood of a number of other black persons had been restored.

By Friday, more than three hundred protesters jammed the store and the nearby Kress's five-and-dime. The movement rapidly spread to Fisk University in Nashville, Atlanta University, and other black colleges and universities.

The sit-ins signaled fundamental changes in the civil-rights movement. From the early twentieth century to the 1950s, two organizations had spearheaded the cause: the National Association for the Advancement of Colored People (NAACP) and the National Urban League. Led by educated, middle-class blacks, both groups worked quietly through established channels. The NAACP fought discrimination in the courts; the Urban League promoted black employment by negotiations with corporate leaders. Neither encouraged mass demonstrations. These older organizations had significant achievements to their credit. The Supreme Court's 1954 *Brown* v. *Board of Education* decision outlawing school segregation, for example, culminated years of legal effort by the NAACP.

After the *Brown* decision, fresh currents of activism had energized black America, especially in the South. The Montgomery bus boycott of 1955–56 coupled the familiar strategy of litigation with new tactics of nonviolent mass action. From the

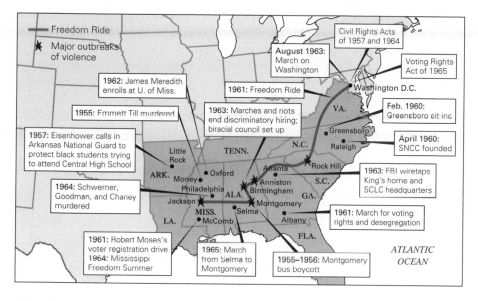

MAP 8.1

Key Events in the Civil-Rights Movement

Montgomery campaign had emerged a new leader, Dr. Martin Luther King, Jr.; a new organization, the Southern Christian Leadership Conference (SCLC); and the Civil Rights Act of 1957, with its focus on voting rights.

The NAACP, Urban League, and SCLC remained active in the 1960s, but after the sit-ins, a vigorous new organization, the Student Nonviolent Coordinating Committee (SNCC), won support from both white backers of the black cause and young African Americans. This proliferation of organizations generated tensions and rivalries, but it also yielded a creative array of strategies that produced results no single organization could have achieved. The 1960s saw a broadening of direct-action approaches that sometimes sparked violent confrontation.

The civil-rights movement that arose in the later 1950s and crested in the mid-1960s appalled most white southerners, for whom a racially segregated society seemed the natural order. Rooted in slavery, the South's racial caste system was buttressed by custom, law, disfranchisement, and, ultimately, the threat of violence. Through the first half of the twentieth century, two separate and unequal societies coexisted in the South. Strict segregation prevailed in schools, churches, courthouses, factories, residences, theaters, parks, even public restrooms. This caste system rested on ingrained white notions of racial superiority and a horror of the "mongrelization" that supposedly would result from lowering the racial barrier. Any who challenged this wall of separation faced swift retribution. In one brutal example, Mississippi vigilantes lynched a fourteen-year-old black visitor from the North, Emmett Till, in 1955. The boy allegedly had whistled at a white woman.

Northern blacks also faced prejudice, and de facto segregation existed throughout the nation. But the white South, for reasons embedded in its slave past, had translated racist thinking into a legally based caste system that relegated African Americans to second-class status. Accordingly, it was in the South that the civil-rights movement first took shape.

The "White South" was not a monolith. The Deep South clung to segregation more rigidly than did the border states. Better-educated and more cosmopolitan whites more readily recognized the inevitability of change. As we have seen, the region's business and professional elite often worked behind the scenes to ease racial tensions. Newspaper editors such as Ralph McGill of the *Atlanta Constitution* and Virginius Dabney of the *Richmond Times-Dispatch* spoke for this class by denouncing violence and by urging enlightened responses to the civil-rights campaign. Academic centers such as the University of North Carolina at Chapel Hill harbored eloquent critics of segregation. Georgia novelist Lillian Smith had explored southern racial taboos and the horror of lynching in her 1944 novel, *Strange Fruit*. On the legal front, some southern judges backed segregation, but others, especially at the federal level, supported the black struggle. Federal district judge Frank M. Johnson, Jr., of Alabama, for example, despite vilification by white racists, consistently upheld African Americans' constitutional rights. The revivalist Billy Graham, a son of the South, integrated his crusades and called racism "the most burning issue of modern times."

Nevertheless, the white South had an enormous investment in the prevailing system and in general saw any attacks on it, whether from local blacks or northern liberals, as a threat. Preserving the status quo seemed especially urgent to poorer, uneducated southern whites. So long as the racial caste system survived, such folk knew that they at least stood above blacks in the pecking order. Lower-class whites—and politicians and police officials who pandered to them—typically took the lead in opposing the black freedom struggle. Only a handful of white southerners resorted to actual physical violence to resist integration, but their actions reinforced the image of a white South united in murderous opposition to racial equality.

The intensity and scope of this new civil-rights activism caught Washington off guard. Presidents and congressional leaders accustomed to working with leaders such as Roy Wilkins of the NAACP; the Urban League's Whitney Young; and, more recently, Martin Luther King, Jr., waffled uneasily as grassroots activism sprang up across the South. John F. Kennedy courted black voters in 1960 but responded hesitantly to the rising demands for racial justice. As the demonstrations and the counterviolence intensified, however, the federal courts and Washington officialdom did extend decisive support at crucial junctures.

The civil-rights movement of the early 1960s did not unfold in an orderly fashion, one event at a time. Activists across the South simultaneously sought a variety of goals. And although Martin Luther King, Jr., and the SCLC played an important role, new leaders burst on the scene. As young activists pushed beyond the tactics that had worked in Montgomery, the SCLC, the NAACP, and the Urban League struggled to redefine their goals and tactics. Generational friction in white America arose over cultural issues; in black America it took the form of intense debates over how to conduct the freedom struggle.

Comprehending that struggle requires a multifocal approach that encompasses the strategies of competing organizations, the grassroots campaigns focused on specific local objectives, the responses of white southerners, and the national political stage, where all these pressures and counterpressures converged. From the movement that historian C. Vann Woodward has dubbed the "second Reconstruction," nothing less than a new society was painfully emerging.

1960–1962: Tactical Innovation, Political Hesitation

The sit-ins that began at Greensboro captured the imagination of young blacks. At an April 1960 conference at Shaw University in North Carolina, some three hundred student leaders from more than fifty black schools and colleges founded the Student Nonviolent Coordinating Committee (SNCC, pronounced "Snick"). White representatives from religious and student groups attended, but the movement was led by blacks. Ella Baker, SCLC's executive director, planned the conference and provided a modest grant to cover expenses. James M. Lawson, Jr., a divinity student at Vanderbilt University, drafted the statement of purpose. In a rousing address, Lawson criticized the NAACP and all "middle class conventional halfway efforts to deal with radical social evil." After initial hesitation, both the NAACP and the SCLC threw their prestige and support behind the new organization.

As the tempo of the sit-ins increased, so did white resistance. Governor Ernest Hollings of South Carolina, although not an extreme segregationist, warned that protesting black ministers and religious leaders would not be spared from legal reprisals. "Our law enforcement officers have their Bibles, too," Hollings observed. Sit in participants were assaulted, jailed, burned with lighted cigarettes, and scalded with hot coffee. Even some conservative black college administrators opposed the protests. But the demonstrators persisted, honing the strategy of nonresistance that so infuriated their opponents. From the sit-ins emerged the song that would become the movement's anthem: "We Shall Overcome," based on an old slave melody.

The Congress of Racial Equality (CORE), meanwhile, resumed the Freedom Rides that it had initiated shortly after World War II to test the Supreme Court's 1946 ruling barring racial segregation in buses and trains operating across state lines. In the 1960 case *Boynton* v. *Virginia,* the Supreme Court extended its 1946 ruling by outlawing segregated bus and train stations, airport terminals, and other facilities related to interstate transit. But the South widely ignored these decisions, and early in 1961, CORE director James Farmer announced another Freedom Ride to integrate bus-station facilities.

On May 4, 1961, biracial teams of CORE volunteers headed south from Washington, D.C., on Trailways and Greyhound buses. They integrated station facilities in Virginia without incident, but as they moved into the Deep South, white racists mobilized. In Rock Hill, South Carolina, young toughs clubbed twenty-one-year-old John Lewis, a Tennessee divinity student (and future congressman) as he entered the white waiting room. In Anniston, Alabama, a mob armed with clubs and metal bars beat the Freedom Riders, inflicting permanent brain damage on one. When the bus's slashed tires deflated a few miles out of Anniston, whites following in cars smashed the windows, threw a smoke bomb inside, and assaulted the occupants as they fled. A state trooper traveling on the bus in plain clothes at the order of the Alabama governor held the mob off with a pistol, preventing worse violence.

In Birmingham, Alabama, a thriving industrial city and hotbed of segregationist sentiment, the Freedom Riders endured attacks from a mob brandishing baseball bats and bicycle chains, with no police protection in sight. Birmingham's police commissioner, T. Eugene "Bull" Connor, spewed bigotry. A high-school dropout and former radio sports announcer, Connor over the next few years would become the symbol of rabble-rousing racism at its rawest.

Opposition only accelerated the movement's momentum as it rapidly expanded beyond bus stations and Woolworth lunch counters. As Ella Baker observed: "The current sit-ins are concerned with something much bigger than a hamburger or even a giant-sized Coke." James Lawson in a 1961 essay offered a radical analysis of American racism and of the movement's objectives:

> [I]f after over 300 years, segregation (slavery) is still a basic pattern rather than a peripheral custom, should we not question the American way of life which allows segregation so much structural support? . . .
>
> The sit-ins won concessions, not structural changes; the Freedom Rides won concessions, but not real changes.
>
> There will be no revolution until we see Negro faces in all positions that help to mold public opinion, help to shape policy for America.

As the movement grew, so did awareness that racism in America took many forms, including the structural racism in the North that contributed to the joblessness, poverty, and social problems of the urban black ghettos. But before the nation could confront these larger realities, officially enforced segregation had to be eradicated from its southern bastion. This was the work of the black activists of the 1950s and early 1960s, who, with white supporters, organized marches, Freedom Rides, sit-ins, and boycotts and, in some cases, suffered physical abuse, imprisonment, and even death.

The civil-rights movement echoed loudly in Washington. As a candidate in 1960, John Kennedy had praised the sit-ins and secured Martin Luther King's release from jail. Once in office, Kennedy set up the Equal Employment Opportunity Committee, headed by Vice President Johnson, to combat racial discrimination in the federal government and in firms with government contracts. With very few blacks in responsible federal positions, this effort paid off. In the administration's early days, joked Roy Wilkins of the NAACP, "everyone was scrambling around trying to find himself a Negro in order to keep the President off his neck."

Attorney General Robert Kennedy beefed up the Justice Department's anemic civil-rights division. Enforcing the Civil Rights Act of 1957, the department sued thirty-two southern electoral boards for denying voting rights to blacks. (The Eisenhower administration had filed only six such suits.) When Mississippi blacks who registered to vote faced economic reprisals, the Department of Agriculture, on JFK's orders, distributed surplus food to them. In 1962, Congress passed an administration-backed constitutional amendment banning poll taxes, long used in the South to bar black voters. It was ratified in 1964.

Nevertheless, President Kennedy's overall civil-rights record proved decidedly mixed. A practical politician above all, Kennedy viewed the civil-rights movement less as an occasion for moral leadership than as a political problem to be managed. His narrow 1960 electoral victory made him extremely solicitous of the lily-white southern Democratic Party and its powerful sachems in Congress. Despite urging by black leaders, Kennedy delayed introducing a civil-rights bill until mid-1963 and held back from outlawing racial discrimination in federally funded public housing until late 1962. As a candidate, he had pointed out that a president could effect the latter change "with the stroke of a pen." (Frustrated civil-rights advocates deluged the White House with pens.)

Under pressure from Mississippi's James Eastland, a notorious racist and chair of the Senate Judiciary Committee, Kennedy appointed to a Mississippi federal judgeship a segregationist who used every possible stratagem to thwart the civil-rights cause and on one occasion referred to litigants seeking voting rights as "a bunch of niggers . . . acting like a bunch of chimpanzees." Bowing to the tradition of senatorial privilege, Kennedy named other segregationists to the federal bench as well.

The administration's response to the 1961 Freedom Rides illustrates its ambivalence on civil-rights issues. Preoccupied with the Berlin crisis, Kennedy viewed the Freedom Rides as a distraction. "Tell them to call it off. Stop them," he told an aide. (He was also hampered by limited information. FBI director J. Edgar Hoover knew of Sheriff Bull Connor's willingness to allow attacks on the Freedom Riders in Birmingham, but he failed to pass along the information.)

Kennedy did telephone Alabama's governor, who promised to protect the Freedom Riders, a pledge he promptly broke. But Kennedy neither sent federal marshals nor spoke out publicly except to issue a general plea for law and order.

The Freedom Rides Turn Violent, May 1961. Two blood-spattered SNCC volunteers, John Lewis of Fisk University (*left*) and James Zwerg of Beloit College, after a white mob attacked the Freedom Riders in Montgomery, Alabama. In 1986, John Lewis was elected to Congress from Georgia. (*© Bettmann/CORBIS*)

Deprived of protection from the local police or from Washington, CORE volunteers left Birmingham by plane on May 17, ending this phase of the Freedom Rides.

But John Lewis, working with SNCC leaders, recruited volunteers to continue the Freedom Rides. Police arrested them at the Birmingham bus terminal, drove them to the Tennessee state line, and dropped them off beside the highway. Friends immediately drove them back to Birmingham, and on May 20 they set out on a Greyhound bus bound for Montgomery. Here, more violence broke out. With the local police nowhere in sight, a mob of more than a thousand screaming "Get those niggers!" attacked them at the bus station. John Lewis suffered a brain concussion; an observer from the Justice Department was beaten unconscious and kicked as he lay on the pavement. Prodded by the publicity, JFK finally took decisive action, ordering four hundred U.S. marshals to Montgomery.

For decades, the white North had mostly ignored the terror that served as the ultimate enforcer of the South's caste system. But the assaults on the Freedom Riders received heavy media coverage. *Life* and other popular magazines published photographs and stories. Television news cameras caught rampaging whites brutalizing Freedom Riders. In publicizing these outrages, the media helped to push the black freedom struggle onto the national agenda.

On the evening of May 20, more than a thousand Montgomery blacks jammed into the Reverend Ralph Abernathy's First Baptist Church. Martin Luther King and others insisted that the Freedom Rides continue. Outside, a howling mob attacked blacks and hurled torches and stink bombs inside the sanctuary. At last the marshals moved in. For the first time since Little Rock in 1957, a president had protected black citizens exercising their constitutional rights.

The administration struggled to manage a social upheaval whose intensity it barely grasped. James Farmer later recalled his fury when Attorney General Robert Kennedy advised a cooling-off period. "We had been cooling off for a hundred years," wrote Farmer. "If we got any cooler we'd be in a deep freeze." The movement's new slogan, "Freedom Now," answered the calls for restraint by white liberals and conservative black leaders. When Robert Kennedy warned that civil-rights demonstrations would embarrass the president in his forthcoming meeting with Khrushchev, Martin Luther King responded tartly: "They don't understand the social revolution going on in the world."

On May 24, buses carrying Freedom Riders representing the major civil-rights organizations left Montgomery for Jackson, Mississippi. The tension was high. One rider later recalled: "[E]very blocked-off street, every back road taken, every change in speed caused our hearts to leap."

Robert Kennedy, still juggling conflicting political interests, struck a deal with the governors of Mississippi and Alabama: If they held off the white mobs, the administration would tolerate the arrest and jailing of Freedom Riders. The arrangement left Freedom Riders, male and female, at the mercy of racist prison guards far from the TV cameras.

More than 1,000 volunteers participated in the 1961 Freedom Rides, and over 350 went to jail. In late September, under Justice Department pressure, the Interstate Commerce Commission barred racial segregation in all facilities serving interstate travelers and ordered that signs announcing this policy be prominently posted by November 1. During the next year, segregation in interstate travel gradually ended.

Events again prodded the Kennedys to action in September 1962. When Mississippi governor Ross Barnett, a rabid segregationist, prevented James Meredith, a black air force veteran, from registering at the University of Mississippi, Attorney General Kennedy sent five hundred federal marshals to the university campus. "The eyes of the nation and all the world are upon you," President Kennedy reminded Mississippians. Nevertheless, on September 30, a mob incited by a Barnett radio harangue attacked the marshals, sparking a battle that left 2 dead and 375 injured. JFK ordered some thirty thousand regular army troops and federalized national guardsmen to restore order and ensure Meredith's safety. Barnett backed down, and Meredith enrolled.

FBI director J. Edgar Hoover, meanwhile, did all he could to discredit the black freedom struggle. Pandering to Cold War fears, Hoover portrayed movement leaders as communist dupes or worse. In September 1963, Hoover's assistant for domestic intelligence drafted a memo describing Martin Luther King as America's "most dangerous and effective Negro leader." Warning of "social revolution," the memo called on the FBI to document the Communist Party's supposed role in this upheaval. With Robert Kennedy's approval, the FBI wiretapped King's home and the SCLC's Atlanta headquarters. FBI snoopers compiled a file on King's private life, including extramarital affairs, that Hoover used to besmirch the movement. A 1963 FBI document, "Communism and the Negro Movement," full of half-truths and baseless innuendo, circulated through the government.

As Hoover pursued his vendetta and as the media highlighted the Freedom Rides and the Kennedys' maneuvering, a grassroots effort had arisen in rural Mississippi. In the summer of 1961, Robert Moses, a New York high-school teacher and SNCC volunteer, launched a voter registration drive centered in McComb, Mississippi, a Ku Klux Klan stronghold where only 5 percent of eligible blacks were registered. In many surrounding rural areas, not a single black voted. One volunteer, Charles Sherrod, later described conversations with local blacks in lunchrooms and pool halls: "We would tell them of how it feels to be . . . in jail for the cause. . . . We referred to the system that imprisons men's minds and robs them of creativity. We mocked the system that teaches men to be good Negroes instead of good men."

As the registration drive unfolded, whites struck back. When a white man murdered Herbert Lee, a black farmer who had endorsed the SNCC campaign, a jury acquitted him, accepting his claim of "self-defense." When a SNCC worker asked a local sheriff about jailed SNCC volunteers, the sheriff brutally assaulted him and then arrested him. One volunteer recalled, "[Fear] was always there, stretched like a tight steel wire between the pit of the stomach and the center of the brain."

This lonely struggle drew little national attention. Justice Department observers briefly visited McComb, but the administration took no action despite blatant civil-rights violations. Many local blacks also fearfully stood aside, but others responded to SNCC's challenge. A sixteen-year-old high-school student, jailed after joining a sit-in at a local Woolworth's, led her classmates in a march on the McComb city hall after her release.

As the McComb volunteers struggled on, setbacks elsewhere forced a reappraisal of civil-rights strategy. In the fall of 1961, SNCC, backed by King and SCLC, targeted Albany, Georgia, for a desegregation campaign that organizers hoped would attract Washington's attention. Month after month, Albany's black

Black Ministers
and the Black Church

The fact that Martin Luther King, Jr., and Malcolm X were religious leaders as well as prominent in the black freedom struggle underscores the importance of religion and of ministers in American black history. In slavery days, worship services provided spiritual comfort, strengthened slave communities, and offered a setting where the longing for freedom could be expressed. Free blacks in the antebellum North formed their own denominations, including the African Methodist Episcopal (AME) Church in 1816 and the AME Zion Church in 1821.

The black church remained strong after Emancipation, as many freedmen abandoned their ex-masters' churches and formed their own congregations. Commented one ex-slave (as recorded by a researcher): "Dat ole white preachin' wasn't nothin'. Old white preachers used to talk wid dey tongues widdout sayin' nothin', but Jesus told us slaves to talk wid our hearts." And ministers played a growing social role in African American life. AME bishop Daniel A. Payne was a prominent African American leader in the mid- and later nineteenth century. Another AME bishop, Henry M. Turner (1834–1915), gave up on racist America and advocated the creation of a Christian nation in Africa to which U.S. blacks could return. Turner visited Africa four times in the 1890s in pursuit of his dream.

In the rural South, the preaching, singing, baptisms, revivals, picnics, weddings, and funerals of the black church knit together the community. As W. E. B. Du Bois wrote in *The Souls of Black Folk* in 1903: "The Negro church of today is the social centre of Negro life in the United States, and the most characteristic expression of African character." At the heart of this social institution were the ministers, whose emotional call-and-response preaching style—a style that Martin Luther King, Jr., used to great effect—engaged their congregations powerfully.

In the urban South, black ministers exerted leadership in their own communities and functioned as brokers in dealings with the white power structure. The Reverend Martin Luther King, Sr. (whose photo appears above), father of the civil-rights leader and pastor of Atlanta's Ebenezer Baptist Church, was an influential figure in his own right long before his son achieved fame. Although much beloved figures, these charismatic black ministers could also be authoritarian, intensely moralistic, conservative in their social views, and jealous of their power. As Du Bois observed in 1903: "The Preacher is the most unique personality developed by the Negro on American soil. A leader, a politician, an orator, a 'boss,' an intriguer, an idealist—all these he is. . . . The combination of a certain adroitness with deep-seated earnestness, of tact with consummate ability, gave him his preeminence, and helps him maintain it."

As African Americans migrated north, they brought their faith with them. Every northern city had its black houses of worship, from large establishments like Harlem's Abyssinian Baptist Church to the storefront churches of the poor. The novelist James Baldwin, the son of a black preacher, himself preached as a teenager in a storefront church in Harlem. Baldwin's first book, *Go Tell It on the Mountain* (1953), drew upon his intimate knowledge of the black church.

The black minister continued to function in the larger arena as well. When racial violence erupted, he was at the center of the crisis, sometimes advising Christian forbearance, sometimes calling for resistance. As race riots raged in 1919, one black bishop urged blacks to "protect their homes at any cost."

Music, whether mournful sorrow songs or toe-tapping, hand-clapping gospel songs, sustained black religious life from the beginning. The slave songs, blending African and Christian influences, expressed both spiritual longings and a people's desire for liberation. Songs such as "Go Down, Moses" recounted familiar Bible stories while also protesting slavery. In the twentieth century, countless African American singers who became pop-music stars started out in black churches. Aretha Franklin, for example, the daughter of a famed black preacher, the Reverend C. L. Franklin, began her career as a singer in her father's New Bethel Baptist Church in Detroit.

When the freedom movement arose, black ministers (as well as many white religious leaders) inevitably became deeply involved. Some hesitated, perceiving a threat to their own role as power brokers. But others caught the vision and communicated it to their parishioners and to the larger community. None did so more effectively than Martin Luther King, Jr., whose strength lay in his roots in the black church. Another Baptist minister, the Reverend Jesse Jackson, a youthful King associate, would go on after King's assassination to build a career as a voice for the oppressed in America and abroad.

Perhaps no career better illustrates the prominent and complex social role of the minister in the African American community than that of the Reverend Benjamin Hooks. Born in 1925, Hooks served as pastor of a leading Baptist church in Memphis (1956–64) and then of Detroit's Greater New Mt. Moriah Baptist Church (1964–72). But he was also a lawyer, a criminal-court judge, the cofounder and director of a savings-and-loan association, and, from 1977 to 1993, executive director of the National Association for the Advancement of Colored People.

From the early nineteenth century to the end of the twentieth, the pulpit has been a highly effective launching pad for leadership in the black community. In the post-civil-rights era with its complex challenges, black ministers continued to provide community leadership. Though still mostly male, their ranks now also included gifted and charismatic women, including the Reverend Bernice Albertine King, the daughter of Martin Luther King, Jr., and Coretta Scott King.

residents marched for voting rights and to protest segregated schools, libraries, parks, and lunch counters. Hundreds were imprisoned, but local white leaders handled the demonstrations shrewdly. The police treated the arrestees well, avoiding the brutality that could rivet TV viewers and galvanize the White House. The police chief even prayed with the demonstrators prior to arresting them.

Organizational conflicts further weakened the Albany action. SNCC's youthful leaders ridiculed the NAACP as stodgy and timid, outraging leaders of the older organization. "We paid some of the expenses of the Albany movement," Roy Wilkins complained, "only to be insulted for being on the wrong side of the generation gap." Privately, Wilkins also attacked Martin Luther King, Jr., whose growing prominence rankled him. Some local black leaders viewed *all* outside organizations as interlopers.

Late that year, when white leaders in Albany orally accepted the demonstrators' demands, King proclaimed victory and left town. The white establishment quickly reneged, however, leaving Albany's walls of segregation firmly in place. This failure undermined the credibility of the civil-rights leadership and heightened blacks' frustration with the Kennedy administration, which had taken no steps to intervene.

Despite isolated successes, the movement seemed adrift as 1962 ended. Eight years after the *Brown* decision, most southern black children still attended segregated schools; most southern blacks could not vote; and segregation, although weakened, remained the rule across much of the South. In a strategy session that fall, SCLC leaders reached two sobering conclusions. First, the Albany outcome made plain that moral suasion alone would not suffice; new federal laws were needed. Second, the Kennedy administration would not push such legislation except in response to media-grabbing confrontations. These conclusions led directly to a showdown that riveted the nation's attention in May 1963.

1963: Victory in Birmingham, Action in Washington

Birmingham, Alabama, notorious as America's most segregated big city, displayed the full spectrum of southern views on race. The white elite, including the so-called "Big Mules" who controlled the city's steel mills, deplored crude racism and violent assaults on civil-rights activists. Yet most tacitly supported segregation and opposed the Supreme Court's 1954 *Brown* decision. Birmingham also had the Ku Klux Klan, Bull Connor, and thuggish white mobs.

The SCLC targeted Birmingham at the urging of Reverend Fred Shuttlesworth, a Baptist pastor and SCLC founder. To avoid the Albany mistakes, SCLC recruited 250 local black leaders to coordinate the drive. Intent on provoking encounters that would dramatize the city's institutionalized racism and prod Washington to action, SCLC set forth its strategy in a planning document labeled Project C—for *confrontation*. Along with marches, Project C included a boycott of Birmingham's department stores, which relied on African Americans' patronage while denying them equal employment opportunities.

On April 6, Shuttlesworth led a march on city hall and was arrested. King, with conscious symbolism, led a march on Good Friday and spent three days behind bars. Here he began "Letter from Birmingham Jail," a manifesto explaining the religious and philosophical underpinnings of the strategy of nonviolent civil disobedience. Blacks jailed for disobeying local statutes, he pointed out, had had no voice in framing those statutes. To those who criticized the timing of the Birmingham protests, he commented wryly, "Frankly, I have never yet engaged in a direct-action movement that was 'well timed.'" Articulating the anger spawned by segregation, he described his daughter's disappointment when he had explained that she could not go to an amusement park advertised on television, and his sorrow on seeing "the depressing clouds of inferiority begin to form in her little mental sky, and [to] see her . . . unconsciously developing a bitterness toward white people."

Introducing an economic theme that would loom large in the years ahead, King mentioned the "air-tight cage of poverty in the midst of an affluent society" that intensified black rage. If the moderate, religiously based movement failed, he wrote, chaotic upheavals could ensue. Many bitter and alienated blacks had already "lost faith in America," he warned, and were "perilously close" to violence.

Although "Letter from Birmingham Jail" drew worldwide attention, the local situation deteriorated. A series of marches, some by schoolchildren and students, provoked Bull Connor's police, who attacked the chanting demonstrators with clubs, cattle prods, police dogs, and fire hoses. Many suffered injuries or went to jail. King's warnings of explosive unrest in black America were soon confirmed.

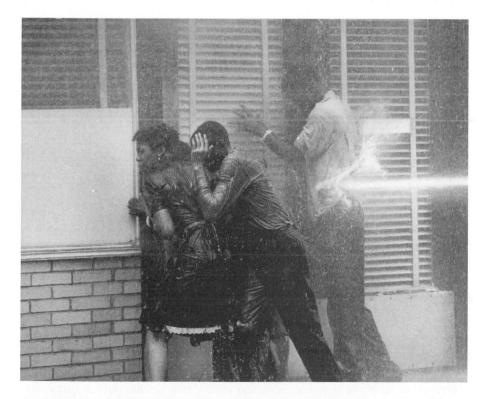

Birmingham, Alabama, 1963. Fire hoses batter young black marchers as the city's white power structure fights in vain to preserve racial segregation. (© *Charles Moore/ Black Star*)

When the Ku Klux Klan bombed SCLC's Birmingham headquarters in early May, gangs from the city's black slums roamed the streets for four days, assaulting police, throwing rocks and bottles, and burning white-owned businesses. Only urgent pleas by King and Shuttlesworth ended the rioting.

The climax came on Tuesday, May 7, as fire hoses ripped into four thousand black marchers assembled in a local park, tearing clothing from bruised bodies and knocking down adults and children as though hit by bullets. When Reverend Shuttlesworth was beaten and hospitalized, Bull Connor expressed regret that he had not been killed. Unlike McComb and Albany in 1962, the Birmingham violence attracted the media, and national outrage mounted. As the jails overflowed, marchers continued to pour from Shuttlesworth's Sixteenth Street Baptist Church, the movement's command center.

At last Birmingham's "Big Mules" had enough. Dismayed by the violence, the bad publicity, and the economic boycott and facing behind-the-scenes pressure from the Justice Department, the city's political and business leaders on May 10 granted the SCLC's demands: equal-opportunity hiring practices and a biracial council to dismantle Birmingham's segregated facilities on an agreed-upon timetable.

This outcome, hailed by Martin Luther King, Jr., as a "magnificent victory for justice," reverberated across the South. Some fifty southern cities desegregated in the summer of 1963. But change did not come painlessly. Bombings of homes and churches, police brutality, and even murders continued as white supremacists lashed out in impotent fury against the new order. Moreover, the locus of activism was shifting northward geographically and downward socially, into the ranks of the urban poor. As the uprising of Birmingham's black slum made clear, a struggle that had originated in the black middle class was now energizing a seething urban underclass trapped in poverty. Young ghetto blacks felt little patience with carefully planned campaigns or with King's doctrine of nonresistance.

As militancy rose, the civil-rights organization scrambled to keep up. "The arena of combat has shifted from the courtroom to direct mass action," warned an NAACP official in May 1963. King, speaking in Chicago that June, told a cheering throng of five thousand, "We're through with tokenism and gradualism and see-how-far-you've-comeism. . . . We can't wait any longer. Now is the time." After mid-decade, King shifted his focus from integration—a goal of the black middle class—to the economic plight of the urban poor.

A leader no less charismatic than King embodied the new militancy. Malcolm X, born Malcolm Little in 1925 in Omaha, was the son of a freelance Baptist preacher who had admired black nationalist leader Marcus Garvey. In 1941 Little drifted into the Boston urban underworld of narcotics, pimping, and burglary. Imprisoned in 1946, he converted to the Nation of Islam, or Black Muslims, an ascetic sect that brought discipline into the lives of its members, especially those in prison. Abandoning his "slave name," he became Malcolm X; the X stood for his lost African name.

Released in 1952, Malcolm X sought out Nation of Islam leader Elijah Muhammad, who assigned him to a temple in Harlem. His charisma soon helped to boost the national membership to some forty thousand. Sixty-nine Black Muslim temples, mostly in northern cities, and several dozen radio stations carried the word to the black masses. Black Muslims preached strict morality and black racial superiority. Like Garveyites in the 1920s, they rejected integration; denounced whites as "blue-eyed devils"; and called for black pride, black institutions, and, ultimately, a separate black nation.

Whereas King preached nonviolence, integration, and racial harmony, Malcolm X proclaimed a different and—to whites—frightening message. Confronted by a violent oppressor, he insisted, the oppressed must resist by "any means necessary." "[B]loodshed is a two-way street," he declared; "killing is a two-way street." By 1963 it was Malcolm, not Martin, who appeared most often on TV and in newspaper interviews and public forums. Flanked by stony-faced bodyguards, jabbing his finger to drive home his points, he made an unforgettable impression. Civil-rights leaders committed to integration deplored his separatist message. At a 1962 debate in Harlem, James Farmer challenged him: "[D]on't tell us any more about the disease—that is clear in our minds. Now, tell us, physician, what is thy cure?" In answer, Malcolm X simply reiterated the utopian dream of a separate black homeland.

Malcolm X's success roused jealousies within the Nation of Islam, and Elijah Muhammad expelled him in 1963. After a 1964 African tour and pilgrimage to Mecca, he rejected all varieties of racism and spoke of humanity's common bond. Again he took a new name, one denoting his Mecca pilgrimage: El-Hajj Malik el-Shabazz. On February 21, 1965, as he spoke in a Harlem ballroom, three Black Muslim thugs gunned him down.

Despite his evolving views, white America saw Malcolm X to the end as a fomenter of violence. Editorial writers contrasted his message of hatred and King's message of peace. Yet as theologian James H. Cone argues in *Martin and Malcolm and America* (1991), the two leaders' views were converging in 1964–65, with King growing more radical and Malcolm exploring the possibilities of racial reconciliation.

A generation after his death, Malcolm X would become a folk hero in the inner cities. Rap singers chanted his words; murals portraying his piercing gaze adorned building walls. Black filmmaker Spike Lee memorialized him in a 1992 movie. His enduring grip on the American imagination stemmed from the kaleidoscopic nature of his career: the early years as a street hustler; the fierce rhetoric of his Black Muslim days; the final, tentative message of racial understanding. In 1992 his widow Betty Shabazz offered her interpretation of his message:

> A lot of people . . . said "freedom by whatever means necessary" means violence. No, it's not violence. It's a comprehensive statement that says use more than one option. It could be political, social, education, or it could be self-defense.

With the rise of Malcolm X, civil-rights organizations such as the NAACP and the SCLC came to seem bastions of moderation. At a 1963 meeting in New York, corporate leaders and foundation heads raised more than a million dollars for the mainstream civil-rights groups. As the strategists of the Birmingham demonstrations had hoped, civil rights again dominated the national agenda. Fear as well as moral indignation rallied white support for decisive action. As the explosive buildup of racial tensions and sober warnings of worse to come spurred the administration to move from behind-the-scenes manipulation to forthright leadership, the White House prepared a tough new civil-rights bill.

Another showdown in Alabama triggered Kennedy's long-delayed action. On June 11, 1963, having pledged to "stand in the schoolhouse door" to prevent integration, Governor George Wallace physically blocked two black students seeking to enroll at the University of Alabama. But Wallace nimbly stepped aside when a Justice Department official read a court order mandating the students' admission. In contrast to the earlier violence at the University of Mississippi, integration at the University of Alabama proceeded peacefully.

On national television that night, JFK offered a plea for racial justice unprecedented from a U.S. president. Paraphrasing the Golden Rule, he declared, "Every American ought to have the right to be treated as he would wish to be treated, as one would wish his children to be treated." A century after the Emancipation Proclamation, African Americans still faced oppression, he went on, "and this nation . . . will not be fully free until all its citizens are free." Kennedy offered a stark choice: support civil-rights reform or face disaster. "The fires of frustration and discord are burning in every city, North and South," he warned. That very night, a stalker shot and killed Medgar Evers, president of the Mississippi NAACP.

On June 19, Kennedy sent his civil-rights bill to Congress. In sweeping language, it outlawed discrimination in all public places and empowered the Justice Department to sue school districts that delayed integration. To build support for the bill, two hundred thousand black and white civil-rights advocates from many organizations gathered in Washington on August 28. Kennedy initially opposed the march, fearing a backlash. But when the organizers held firm, the White House capitulated and worked closely with its planners.*

Under a late-summer sun, a sea of marchers assembled at the Lincoln Memorial. Joan Baez sang "We Shall Overcome," Bob Dylan performed a tribute to Medgar Evers, and black singers Odetta and Mahalia Jackson added their voices. The veteran activist A. Philip Randolph eloquently urged passage of the civil-rights bill. But it was Martin Luther King who transformed a lobbying event into a historic occasion. A master orator at his peak, King used vivid images and biblical language to make his point: "Now is the time to rise from the dark and desolate valley of segregation to the sunlit path of racial justice. . . . Now is the time to lift our nation from the quicksands of racial injustice to the solid rock of brotherhood. . . . We are not satisfied and we will not be satisfied until justice rolls down like the waters, and righteousness like a mighty stream."

In his now-famous extemporized conclusion, King in a few compelling phrases etched a vision of a society in which race did not matter:

> I have a dream that one day on the red hills of Georgia the sons of former slaves and the sons of former slaveowners will be able to sit down together at the table of brotherhood.
>
> I have a dream that one day even the State of Mississippi, a state sweltering with the heat of injustice, sweltering with the heat of oppression, will be transformed into an oasis of freedom and justice. I have a dream that my four

---

*The chief planner of the Washington march, Bayard Rustin, a gay Quaker pacifist, had earlier organized CORE's freedom rides after World War II. However, as John D'Emilio documents in *Lost Prophet: The Life and Times of Bayard Rustin* (2003), nervous civil-rights leaders downplayed Rustin's role in the 1963 march after the racist and homophobic South Carolina senator Strom Thurmond denounced him as a "sexual pervert."

Washington, D.C., August 1963. Expressing idealism and unity of purpose, thousands of black and white civil-rights marchers rallied at the Lincoln Memorial. Soon the movement would splinter as the focus moved northward and the demands grew more radical. *(UPI/Corbis-Bettmann)*

little children will one day live in a nation where they will not be judged by the color of their skin but by the content of their character. I have a dream today.

I have a dream that one day down in Alabama with its vicious racists, with its Governor having his lips dripping with the words of interposition and nullification—one day right there in Alabama, little black boys and black girls will be able to join hands with little white boys and white girls as sisters and brothers . . . .

When we let freedom ring, when we let it ring from every village and every hamlet, from every state and every city, we will be able to speed up that day when all God's children, black men and white men, Jews and Gentiles, Protestants and Catholics, will be able to join hands and sing in the words of that old Negro spiritual, "Free at last! Free at last! Thank God almighty, we are free at last."

Within two weeks, as if to mock King's eloquence, a bomb blast at Birmingham's Sixteenth Street Baptist Church killed four black girls. Furthermore, the movement's apparent unity masked widening rifts. Malcolm X, still in his separatist phase, ridiculed King's plea for harmony. A. Philip Randolph had wanted to focus the march on the economic and social crisis of the urban black poor, but this theme remained muted in favor of the more familiar message of integration. Even as King trained his oratorical guns on the Deep South, attention was shifting northward, where the issues would prove more complex and the modes of protest more divisive. The most prophetic words that day were those that the marchers did not hear. In the original version of his speech, omitted under pressure from more moderate leaders and administration officials, John Lewis of SNCC had written:

> In good conscience we cannot support the administration's civil rights bill, for it is too little and too late. . . . The revolution is at hand, and we must free ourselves of the chains of political and economic slavery. . . . Mr. Kennedy is trying to take the revolution out of the street and put it in the courts. . . . The black masses are on the march for jobs and freedom, and we must say to the politicians that there won't be a "cooling off" period.

Despite the Washington march, the administration's civil-rights bill languished in the Senate Judiciary Committee owing to James Eastland's stalling tactics. Despite the moral passion of Kennedy's June 1963 speech, he failed to translate his embrace of the cause into decisive legislative action. That task would fall to his successor.

1964: Breaking the Legislative Logjam

President Johnson took advantage of the nation's grief over Kennedy's assassination to push the stalled civil-rights bill. The mid-sixties brought a moment of near consensus in support of the black cause, and Johnson seized the opportunity.

As a Texas congressman, Johnson, fearful for his political career, had opposed President Truman's civil-rights proposals. At the same time, he attacked racism and deplored political race baiting. In 1957, now Senate majority leader and harboring presidential ambitions, Johnson shepherded Eisenhower's civil-rights bill through Congress, protecting his regional base by engineering some compromises favored by southern legislators.

As president, LBJ counted on his regional roots to overcome southern opposition to the Kennedy bill. To speechwriter Richard Goodwin, he confided, "Those Harvards [his term for the Kennedy team] think that a politician from Texas doesn't care about Negroes. . . . But I . . . always vowed that if I ever had the power I'd make sure every Negro had the same chance as every white man. Now I have it." Meeting with civil-rights leaders, he pledged quick action.

A coalition of civil-rights organizations, liberal labor unions, women's groups, and religious bodies rallied support. The National Council of Churches (NCC), an association of liberal Protestant denominations, lobbied, organized marches and letter-writing campaigns, and arranged speaking tours by civil-rights advocates. During the 1964 civil-rights debate, the NCC held daily services at a church near the Capitol. This religious involvement underscored the ethical dimension of the civil-rights cause. As James Reston of the *New York Times* wrote, "If there is no effective moral reaction out in the country, there will be no effective political reaction."

The civil-rights bill passed the House early in 1964. In the Senate, floor-leader Hubert Humphrey labored to overcome opposition. President Johnson sat on the phone, cajoling waverers. For seventy-five days, opponents filibustered against the bill. At last on June 10, 1964, the Senate voted to end the filibuster. Senator Clair Engle of California, unable to speak because of recent brain surgery, nodded his head "yes" from a wheelchair on the cloture vote. The next day, by a 73–27 tally, the Civil Rights Act of 1964 passed the Senate.

This historic measure targeted many expressions of racism in American life. The law made it easier for the attorney general to participate in private civil-rights cases and to prosecute segregated school districts and election officials who denied voting rights to blacks. Other sections forbade discrimination in hiring; in federally funded programs; and in public facilities such as restaurants, motels, theaters, and amusement parks. Finally, the law authorized the Equal Employment Opportunity Commission to enforce compliance with laws against workplace discrimination. The far-reaching act represented a big step toward eradicating racism's institutional manifestations.* The ban on racial discrimination in hiring had an immediate impact. As Timothy J. Minchin demonstrates in *Hiring the Black Worker* (1999), the work force of the southern textile industry, in which blacks appeared only as janitors or in other menial jobs before 1964, was 25 percent African American by 1978.

Out of the limelight, Robert Moses and other SNCC leaders continued their voter-registration campaign in rural Mississippi. Through Moses's efforts, SNCC and CORE joined forces to coordinate a major voter-registration drive in 1964, to be called Mississippi Freedom Summer. The question of whether to recruit northern white students proved divisive. Proponents argued that the presence of white volunteers would reduce the threat of violence and heighten media attention. Opponents warned that white volunteers would inhibit local blacks from developing their own leadership skills. Advocates of a biracial campaign won, and in June 1964, after a brief training period, nearly a thousand white northern student volunteers streamed into Mississippi.

The campaign roused murderous opposition. In mid-June, Michael Schwerner, a white CORE staff member; Andrew Goodman, a white summer volunteer from the North; and James Chaney, a local black volunteer, disappeared while investigating the burning of a black church. The FBI soon arrested twenty-one Ku Klux Klan members, plus the local sheriff and his deputy, on kidnapping charges. Six weeks later, the bodies of Schwerner, Goodman, and Chaney were discovered in shallow graves near Philadelphia, Mississippi. (*Mississippi Burning*, a 1988 Hollywood film about the case, not only presented an unrealistically heroic picture of the FBI, but also insultingly suggested that Mississippi blacks were so terrified of Klan violence as to be incapable of standing up for their rights.)

The summer also brought repeated bombings, arson, gunfire, and attacks on volunteers. Despite a beefed-up FBI presence in Mississippi, J. Edgar Hoover, deploring the "over-emphasis" on civil rights, did little to protect Freedom Summer volunteers. The violence further radicalized young black activists, hastening their turn to economic issues and deepening their skepticism of King's message of nonresistance. For white volunteers, the experience stirred distrust of Johnson-era liberalism. Many would soon emerge as critics of the Vietnam War. The summer also drove a wedge between white and black civil-rights workers, as some southern

---

*In an action little noticed at the time, Title VII of the Civil Rights Act of 1964 barred discrimination on the basis of sex as well as of race. Although introduced by a southern legislator in a frivolous effort to discredit the bill, Title VII would play an important role in feminists' efforts against job discrimination.

blacks criticized the white volunteers as liberal do-gooders who would soon return to their safe, affluent northern world.

In the end, Mississippi Freedom Summer yielded mixed results. Volunteers organized "Freedom Schools" where blacks studied not only academic subjects but also African American history and community-organizing strategies. Yet the goal of increasing blacks' political clout proved elusive: Confronted by hostile election officials, Freedom-Summer volunteers registered only about twelve hundred new voters.

Despite the numerically scant results, the Freedom Summer reverberated through the 1964 Democratic convention. Part of the project involved creating the Mississippi Freedom Democratic Party (MFDP) as an alternative to the all-white regular Democratic Party. The MFDP named forty-two delegates and twenty-two alternates, including maids, carpenters, farmers, ministers, and teachers of both races, to the Democratic convention in Atlantic City. Initially the project was mainly symbolic, but when influential Democratic liberals endorsed it, Freedom-Summer leaders worked to seat the MFDP delegation. Addressing the party's credentials committee, a parade of witnesses urged certification of the MFDP. The advocates included Martin Luther King, Jr.; Michael Schwerner's widow; and Fannie Lou Hamer, a sharecropper and MFDP delegate who recounted the persecution she had suffered for trying to vote.

President Johnson opposed seating the MFDP, fearful of jeopardizing his election chances and of angering the southern congressional leaders on whose support his Great Society reforms depended. Johnson worried, too, about Alabama governor George Wallace, whose appeal to the northern white working class had won him more than a third of the vote in Democratic primaries in Wisconsin, Indiana, and Maryland. Ever the compromiser, LBJ proposed that the MFDP delegates be designated as "honored guests" of the convention—with no voting rights. The MFDP delegates refused to yield, but after heavy negotiations most civil-rights leaders agreed to the seating of Mississippi's all-white delegation, provided two MFDP delegates were designated as at-large delegates with voting rights, the regular Mississippi delegation pledged to support the party ticket, and in the future no delegations from states that disfranchised blacks would be seated.

The deal deepened black activists' distrust of working within the system. A disillusioned Fannie Lou Hamer later recalled, "We learned the hard way that even though we had all the law and all the righteousness on our side—that white man is not going to give up his power to us." What young black activists saw as the sellout of the MFDP, coming after the frustrations and violence of the Mississippi Freedom Summer, contributed to the radicalization of U.S. politics in the later 1960s. As one SNCC leader later recalled, "After Atlantic City, our struggle was not for civil rights, but for liberation."

SNCC's turn toward militancy and "black liberation" intensified when eleven of its leaders visited Africa in September 1964 as guests of the Marxist government of Guinea. John Lewis and another SNCC leader also visited Kenya, where Malcolm X, on his own pilgrimage to the African homeland, lectured them on the need for black solidarity. Although SNCC did not embrace Malcolm X's ideology, his views influenced the movement. Lewis, as president of SNCC from 1963 to 1966, steered the organization toward increasingly radical goals.

1965: Selma and the Voting Rights Act

Having partially finessed the politics of race in the 1964 campaign, Johnson hoped to avoid another civil-rights battle and to give the South time to digest the Civil Rights Act of 1964. But as with Kennedy, events forced his hand. Demanding a stronger voting-rights law, civil-rights leaders took steps to gain their objective.

The Southern Christian Leadership Conference, relatively quiescent since the Birmingham campaign, again took the lead in 1965. Although still espousing nonviolence, King and other SCLC strategists increasingly saw it as a way to bring pressure on Washington. Repeating the Birmingham tactic of deliberate confrontation, SCLC formulated new strategies for drawing national attention and forcing federal action.

The target this time was Selma, Alabama, a bastion of white supremacy that had moved at a snail's pace to register black voters. Selma also had its own version of Bull Connor—Sheriff Jim Clark—who announced his sentiments with a large button asserting: "NEVER!" Asked by a reporter whether a jailed female demonstrator was married, Clark sneered, "She's a nigger woman and she hasn't got a Miss or a Mrs. in front of her name."

Selma's small group of local activists was led by Amelia and Samuel Boynton. When a SNCC voter-registration drive faltered, Amelia Boynton invited in SCLC. King's new militance emerged as he launched the campaign in January 1965: "We are not asking, we are demanding the ballot." Marchers besieged the courthouse, and soon more than two thousand sat in prison. Sheriff Clark, following the Albany playbook, at first avoided the brutality that attracted media attention. On February 17, however, a state trooper shot and killed civil-rights demonstrator Jimmy Lee Jackson. King announced a march from Selma to Montgomery, the state capital, to present a protest petition to Governor Wallace and demand action on voting rights. But when LBJ privately pressured King to call off the march, he and his lieutenants returned to Atlanta.

Other activists persisted, however. On March 7, soon dubbed "Bloody Sunday," the Reverend Hosea Williams of the SCLC field staff, together with SNCC's John Lewis and local supporters, proceeded with the march. As six hundred protesters approached the Edmund Pettus Bridge over the Alabama River, they met Sheriff Clark with two hundred deputies and state troopers. When the marchers refused to turn back, troopers and police, some on horseback, plowed into the throng, throwing tear gas, flailing nightsticks, and jabbing with electric cattle prods. Frightened and bloody, the marchers fell back. Fifty required hospital treatment.

Television once again carried the violent images to the nation and the world. Demands for presidential action and for a federal voting-rights law poured into Washington. Demonstrators attempted a White House sit-in as more paraded outside. Religious leaders descended on Selma to support the marchers.

As King and other civil-rights leaders hastened to Selma, pressure mounted to complete the march. As one SNCC leader recalled, "We were angry. And we wanted to show Governor Wallace, ... Sheriff Clark, Selma's whites, the federal government, and poor Southern blacks ... that we didn't intend to take any more shit. We would ram the march down the throat of anyone who tried to stop us." Nevertheless, a federal judge banned the march, and President Johnson warned King that further violence would jeopardize the voting-rights bill that he had now decided to introduce.

King had just won the Nobel Peace Prize and been named *Time*'s Man of the Year, but in the increasingly radicalized freedom movement, his leadership had come under challenge. Juggling conflicting pressures, he agreed to a symbolic gesture: The marchers would proceed to the Pettus Bridge, hold a prayer service, and return to Selma. But King failed to inform the marchers of the plan. With everyone primed for a trek to Montgomery, his instructions to return to Selma produced confusion and anger, deepening the rift in the movement.

Rabid segregationists, however, again displayed their ability to reenergize the campaign whenever it flagged. Shortly after King's controversial "Tuesday turnaround," several whites chanting "Nigger lover" brutally attacked three Unitarian ministers on the streets of Selma. One of the three, James Reeb, died a few days later. More protesters poured into Selma, now the focus of world attention, and more angry messages deluged the White House. On March 15, before a joint session of Congress, LBJ proposed a voting-rights bill.

Moving beyond details, Johnson defined racism as "a challenge . . . to the values and . . . the meaning" of America. "Should we defeat every enemy, and . . . double our wealth and conquer the stars, and still be unequal to this issue," he said, "then we will have failed as a people and a nation." Praising the Selma demonstrators for touching the nation's conscience, Johnson defined the immediate challenge: "Every American citizen must have an equal right to vote." He ended with the refrain of the civil-rights anthem: "We *shall* overcome." Martin Luther King, watching the speech with the family of the murdered Jimmy Lee Jackson, telephoned the president to offer his praise.

The speech broke the deadlock in Alabama. President Johnson pressured the local federal judge to permit the march and warned Governor Wallace against police brutality. On March 21, after a send-off sermon by King, eight thousand marchers set out from Selma. About three hundred continued all the way along Route 80, often in heavy rain but protected by a solicitous Alabama National Guard federalized by LBJ. Three thousand supporters joined them for a triumphant entry into Montgomery. Addressing the throng near the statehouse where the Confederacy was born in 1861, King not only demanded passage of the voting-rights bill but also defined the movement's broadening agenda, including de facto housing segregation and joblessness in the urban black slums.

As so often in these years, a stab of violence followed the moment of triumph. That evening, night-riding Klansmen shot and killed Viola Liuzzo, a volunteer from Detroit, as she drove marchers back to Selma.

The Voting Rights Act of 1965, passed in August, authorized federal officials to register voters and oversee elections in districts with a record of racial bias. It outlawed the devices long used in the South to exclude black voters. Together with the earlier voting-rights acts and the 1964 constitutional amendment outlawing the poll tax, this law at last gave real political power to southern blacks. By mid-1966, half a million blacks had joined the South's voting rolls; by 1968, nearly four hundred blacks held elective office in the region. While southern whites defected to the Republican banner, African Americans transformed the South's once all-white Democratic Party. Even in die-hard Mississippi, black registration rose from the single digits in 1960 to 59 percent by 1968. As blacks streamed to the polls, race-baiting politicians changed their tune. George Wallace, a politician first and a racist sec-

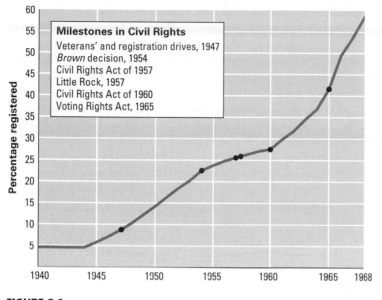

FIGURE 8.1

Percentage of Voting-Age Southern Blacks Registered, 1940–1968

ond, successfully courted black voters in a 1982 gubernatorial campaign. President Johnson acknowledged the altered climate in 1965 by naming the first black cabinet member, Robert C. Weaver, to head the new Department of Housing and Urban Development. In 1967 Johnson appointed NAACP lawyer Thurgood Marshall as the first black Supreme Court justice.

The year 1968 brought a final civil-rights measure: the Open Housing Act outlawing racial discrimination in the sale or rental of most housing units. By this time, however, one long cycle of civil-rights activism was over; new voices and new issues now held center stage.

The Civil-Rights Movement Reaches Hispanic Americans

The civil-rights movement resonated beyond black America. Mexican Americans, including 4 million farm workers and barrio dwellers in the Southwest, were one of the groups most immediately influenced. The black freedom struggle, coupled with the stimulus of the War on Poverty, had an electrifying effect on young Mexican Americans of the second or third generation facing discrimination, educational liabilities, and a lack of job opportunities. In 1963 in New Mexico, Reies López Tijerina started a movement to reclaim ancestral lands appropriated from Mexican Americans by white settlers or by the federal government. Like southern civil-rights activists, Tijerina and some of his followers spent time in prison for their militant tactics. In Delano, California, in 1965, a Mexican American labor leader, César Chávez, organized a strike of grape workers. This led to the formation of the United Farm Workers of

America, which attracted media attention and organized a national boycott of nonunion grapes. Chávez's nonviolent strategies, influenced by his Catholic faith, echoed Martin Luther King's approach. In 1967, students at St. Mary's College in San Antonio, Texas, formed the Mexican American Youth Organization (MAYO), which soon led to a national confederation of Mexican American student groups.

The new consciousness among younger Mexican Americans found expression in their preference for the term *Chicano* rather than *Mexican American, Latin American,* or the Census Bureau's clunky phrase *Spanish-surnamed American.* Difficult to define precisely, the word suggested pride in Mexican cultural identity and in Mexico's revolutionary tradition, as well as skepticism about the assimilationist goal. One of MAYO's founders, José Angel Gutiérrez, even founded a Chicano political party, the Partido Raza (Party of United People). Like SNCC, these proliferating student-led organizations sponsored voter-registration drives, publicized the social and economic problems of the barrios, and promoted group pride among Mexican Americans. As the sixties wore on, Mexican American communities across the Southwest and the West Coast bubbled with protest politics and organizational ferment rooted in the example of the African American freedom struggle.

Reflections on the Civil-Rights Struggle, 1960–1965

The black freedom struggle falls into two fairly distinct phases, with the demarcation line in 1965. The first stage, whose beginnings we examined in Chapter 5 and whose culmination we have just explored, focused on the southern caste system that denied most blacks the vote, excluded them from equal educational and job opportunities, and subjected them to a rigidly segregated social order.

This movement's immediate catalysts were the *Brown* decision of 1954, the Montgomery bus boycott, and the charismatic leadership of Martin Luther King, Jr. But with the sit-ins and Freedom Rides of 1960–61, the movement gained fresh energy and new leaders.

In this stage the leaders built a broad consensus by employing a vocabulary of individual rights and equality of opportunity enshrined in the American political tradition. With the end of legally enforced segregation across the South and the passage of the Civil Rights Act of 1964 and the Voting Rights Act of 1965, this phase of the struggle essentially closed. As historian J. Mills Thornton III has observed, it ended "for the same reason that World War II ended: the enemies had been defeated."

Yet like a mountaineering expedition in which conquering one peak reveals higher summits in the distance, the successes of the early 1960s exposed the next challenge: the social problems and economic marginality of the black masses in the inner cities—the alienated outsiders to whom Malcolm X appealed. After 1965, the focus shifted from voting rights and racial segregation to the complex problems of this black underclass. The rhetoric, often luridly embellished by fiery young radicals, centered not on constitutional rights and integration but on collective action to help the poorest and most desperate members of the African American community.

Although the first phase of the African American freedom struggle did not address every form of racism, its achievement was monumental: the overthrow of a southern caste system dating to slavery days and embedded in the South's culture, laws, and social structure. Demolishing this degrading system was an essential first step before more subtle forms of structural racism in the North as well as the South could be addressed.

This early phase of the civil-rights movement is also noteworthy for its decentralized, grassroots quality. If one looks only at the maneuverings of presidents, senators, governors, or national movement leaders such as Martin Luther King, Jr., one misses a key element of the story. Men and women like Robert Moses and Fannie Lou Hamer in Mississippi and Amelia Boynton and Fred Shuttlesworth in Alabama, no less than the better-known celebrities, are central to the story.

The early-sixties' movement unfolded in places like Greensboro, Anniston, McComb, Albany, and Selma. Its true heroes were not Washington politicians or national leaders, but ordinary Americans who found within themselves extraordinary reserves of courage. Identifying issues of immediate concern, they devised creative strategies for addressing them. Sometimes they called upon national organizations, but they were more than bit players in a drama directed by others. From this perspective, the movement dissolves into countless minidramas of personal empowerment and community action.

Nor was the movement a story of saints against villains. The civil-rights leaders were all too human, with their share of flaws and petty jealousies. They competed fiercely for contributions and media coverage, and sometimes demeaned their rivals. Although this competition offered activists a broad pallet of strategies, it took its toll in effectiveness. Internal struggles nearly immobilized the NAACP in the 1960s, as Gretchen Cassel Eick illustrates in *Dissent in Wichita* (2001), an account of the bitter conflict between Roy Wilkins and the cautious old guard at national headquarters and the more radical local branches, who rallied behind Chester Lewis, the assertive head of the Wichita, Kansas, branch.

Within white America, too, the freedom struggle elicited a full spectrum of responses, from murderous resistance to grudging acceptance to a deeply moral response to injustice. By a leap of imagination, one can even begin to understand the fears that motivated the whites who defied the African American drive for equality. Accustomed to a hierarchical social order and suddenly confronted by a mass uprising of the oppressed, some lashed out in fear and fury. The irony for them is that with every outbreak of violence, more supporters rallied to the civil-rights cause.

The mass media helped prepare the attitudinal change by which the denial of full citizenship and even full humanity to African Americans came to seem intolerable. Not only did TV bring the reality of racism into the nation's living rooms, but Hollywood, after years of crude racial stereotypes, also began to offer different images. Black actors like Sidney Poitier and Harry Belafonte portrayed characters who were sympathetic, if sometimes impossibly handsome, upright, and virtuous. In *The World, the Flesh, and the Devil* (1959), a movie that addressed several cultural preoccupations of the later 1950s, Belafonte, Mel Ferrer, and the Swedish actress Inger Stevens explored the possibilities of interracial cooperation as the only survivors of a global nuclear holocaust. Poitier played the saintly Porgy in the film version of *Porgy and Bess* (1959), and in *The Lilies of the Field* (1963) he portrayed a kindly handyman who helps a group of nuns build the chapel of their dreams.

The most revealing mass-culture product dealing with race in these years was Harper Lee's best-selling novel *To Kill a Mockingbird* (1960), made into an equally successful movie in 1962 starring Gregory Peck as a courageous southern lawyer who defends a black man (played by Brock Peters) falsely accused of rape. A fable of individual decency triumphing over racial hatred and the mob spirit, *To Kill a Mockingbird* captured an important part of the American mood in an early, idealistic stage of the civil-rights struggle, when the issues seemed clear and unambiguous to people of goodwill.

When all the complexities and ambiguities are recognized, the historical and moral significance of the African American freedom struggle shines through. Rejecting a status quo rooted in exploitation and injustice, thousands of black Americans, supported by many white Americans, took matters into their own hands and transformed a society.

For the civil-rights establishment, confronting the depth of African American frustration and the explosive potential in the urban black slums, these years spurred an effort to devise new strategies and formulate more radical goals. The early sixties taught militant black activists an important lesson as well: Aggressive confrontation—even the threat of violence—won attention in the media and in the centers of political power. This realization would give rise to more militant tactics consciously designed to elicit the kind of fierce and sometimes bloody encounters that brought results in 1960–65. Such a climate did not encourage strategies based on restraint, compromise, and turning the other cheek.

As the career of César Chávez and the rise of the Chicano movement made clear, the black civil-rights movement had a far-reaching impact. Lyndon Johnson's War on Poverty, for example, gained urgency from the heightened awareness of the economic plight of inner-city blacks that emerged from the freedom struggle. The antiwar movement of the later 1960s drew ideological and tactical inspiration from the civil-rights campaign.

Similarly, the women's movement of the 1970s owed a debt to the civil-rights cause. The earlier campaign drew on the talents of countless women—not only the relatively well known, such as Rosa Parks, Ella Baker, and Fannie Lou Hamer, but thousands more, black and white, who marched, joined sit-ins, and taught in Freedom Schools. The civil-rights campaign offered later feminists models of strong, committed women as well as a vocabulary for understanding oppression and strategies for confronting it. Still later, other activists, from Native Americans and persons with disabilities to homosexuals and environmental crusaders, would draw on the ideology and strategies of the civil-rights pioneers. Few other social movements in American history have had such a broad-ranging impact.

Conclusion

For all its transforming power, this phase of the civil-rights movement was losing momentum even at its apparent zenith in 1965, as the consensus that had taken shape over the preceding decade splintered. As the focus shifted from South to North, from individual rights to the politics of class conflict, from moderate leaders to fiery young radicals, and from carefully planned demonstrations to seemingly nihilistic explosions of violence, Middle America moved from sympathetic support to fearful uneasiness.

Divisions over the Vietnam War further undermined the civil-rights cause. Martin Luther King's rapport with Lyndon Johnson turned to hostility as King repudiated Johnson's war policies. Many who had cheered Johnson's stand on civil rights bitterly opposed his actions in Vietnam. White House speechwriter Richard Goodwin, recalling LBJ's eloquent voting-rights speech of March 1965, would reminisce years later: "God, how I loved Lyndon Johnson at that moment; how unimaginable it would have been to think that in two years' time I would—like many others who listened that night—go into the streets against him."

SELECTED READINGS

General Histories

Taylor Branch, *America in the King Years: Parting the Waters, 1954–1963* (1988) and *Pillar of Fire, 1963–1965* (1998); Claybourne Carson et al., *The Eyes on the Prize Civil Rights Reader* (1991); David Chalmers, *And the Crooked Places Made Straight: The Struggle for Social Changes in the 1960s* (1991); Charles W. Eagles, ed., *The Civil Rights Movement in America* (1986); James C. Hall, *Mercy, Mercy Me: African-American Culture and the American Sixties* (2001); Richard H. King, *Civil Rights and the Idea of Freedom* (1992); Fred Powledge, *Free at Last? The Civil Rights Movement and the People Who Made It* (1991); Harvard Sitkoff, *The Struggle for Black Equality, 1954–1992* (1993); Robert Weisbrot, *Freedom Bound: A History of America's Civil Rights Movement* (1991).

The Law, Politics, and Economics of Civil Rights

David L. Armor, *Forced Justice: School Desegregation and the Law* (1995); Jack Bloom, *Class, Race, and the Civil Rights Movement* (1987); Dan T. Carter, *The Politics of Rage* [George Wallace] (1995); Richard C. Cortner, *Civil Rights and Public Accommodations: The Heart of Atlanta Motel and McClung Cases* (2001); Chandler Davidson and Bernard Grofman, eds., *Quiet Revolution in the South: The Impact of the Voting Rights Act, 1965–1990* (1994); David Garrow, *Protest at Selma: Martin Luther King, Jr. and the Voting Rights Act of 1965* (1978) and *The FBI and Martin Luther King, Jr.* (1981); Richard Goodwin, *Remembering America: A Voice from the Sixties* (1988); Hugh Davis Graham, *The Civil Rights Era: Origins and Development of National Policy* (1990); Elizabeth Jacoway and David Colburn, eds., *Southern Businessmen and Desegregation* (1982); Timothy J. Minchin, *Hiring the Black Worker: The Racial Integration of the Southern Textile Industry, 1960–1980* (1999); Kenneth O'Reilly, *"Racial Matters": The FBI's Secret File on Black America, 1960–1972* (1989); Renee Romano, "No Diplomatic Immunity: African Diplomats, the State Department, and Civil Rights, 1961–1964," *Journal of American History* (September 2000); Mark Stern, *Calculating Visions: Kennedy, Johnson and Civil Rights* (1992); Charles Whalen and Barbara Whalen, *The Longest Debate: A Legislative History of the 1964 Civil Rights Act* (1985).

Civil-Rights Organizations; Specific Campaigns; Gender; White Resistance

S. Jonathan Bass, *Blessed Are the Peacemakers: Martin Luther King Jr., Eight White Religious Leaders, and the "Letter from Birmingham Jail"* (2001); Claybourne Carson, *In Struggle: SNCC and the Black Awakening of the 1960s* (1981); William H. Chafe, *Civilities and Civil*

Rights: Greensboro, North Carolina, and the Black Struggle for Freedom (1980); David L. Chappell, *Inside Agitators: White Southerners in the Civil Rights Movement* (1994); Daniel Crowe, *Prophets of Rage: The Black Freedom Struggle in San Francisco, 1945–1969* (2000); John Dittmer, *Local People: The Struggle for Civil Rights in Mississippi* (1994); Gretchen Cassel Eick, *Dissent in Wichita: The Civil Rights Movement in the Midwest, 1954–1972* (2001); Glenn T. Eskew, *But for Birmingham: The Local and National Movements in the Civil Rights Struggle* (1997); Sara M. Evans, *Personal Politics: The Roots of Women's Liberation in the Civil Rights Movement and the New Left* (1980); Adam Fairclough, *To Redeem the Soul of America: The Southern Christian Leadership Conference and Martin Luther King, Jr.* (1987); James F. Findlay, *Church People in the Struggle: The National Council of Churches and the Black Freedom Movement, 1950–1970* (1993); Herbert H. Haines, *Black Radicals and the Civil Rights Mainstream, 1954–1970* (1988); Elizabeth Higginbotham, *Too Much to Ask: Black Women in the Era of Integration* (2001); Doug McAdam, *Freedom Summer* (1988); Neil R. McMillen, *The Citizens' Councils: Organized Resistance to the Second Reconstruction, 1954–64* (1971); Nicolaus Mills, *Like a Holy Crusade: Mississippi 1964—The Turning of the Civil Rights Movement in America* (1992); Aldon D. Morris, *The Origins of the Civil Rights Movement: Black Communities Organizing for Change* (1984); Charles M. Payne, *I've Got the Light: The Organizing Tradition and the Mississippi Freedom Struggle* (1995); Belinda Robnett, *How Long? How Long? African-American Women in the Struggle for Civil Rights* (1997); Mary Aickin Rothschild, *A Case of Black and White: Northern Volunteers and the Southern Freedom Summers, 1964–1965* (1982); J. Mills Thornton III, *Dividing Lines: Municipal Politics and the Struggle for Civil Rights in Montgomery, Birmingham, and Selma* (2002); Stephen J. Whitfield, *A Death in the Delta: The Story of Emmett Till* (1989); Miles Wolff, *Lunch at the 5 & 10* (1990).

Leaders of the Civil-Rights and Black-Liberation Movements

Eric R. Burner, *And Gently Shall He Lead Them: Robert Moses and Civil Rights in Mississippi* (1994); Seth Cagin and Philip Dray, *We Are Not Afraid: The Story of Goodman, Schwerner, and Chaney and the Civil Rights Campaign for Mississippi* (1988); James H. Cone, *Martin and Malcolm and America: A Dream or a Nightmare* (1991); Michael Eric Dyson, *Making Malcolm: The Myth and Meaning of Malcolm X* (1995); John D'Emilio, *Lost Prophet: The Life and Times of Bayard Rustin* (2003); James Farmer, *Lay Bare the Heart: An Autobiography of the Civil Rights Movement* (1985); David J. Garrow, *Bearing the Cross: Martin Luther King, Jr., and the Southern Christian Leadership Conference, 1955–1968* (1986); Chana Kai Lee, *For Freedom's Sake: The Life of Fanny Lou Hamer* (1999); Malcolm X, with Alex Haley, *The Autobiography of Malcolm X* (1965); Kay Mills, *This Little Light of Mine: The Life of Fannie Lou Hamer* (1993); Bruce Perry, *Malcolm: The Life of a Man Who Changed Black America* (1991); Timothy B. Tyson, *Radio Free Dixie: Robert F. Williams & the Roots of Black Power* (1999).

Hispanic Americans and the Chicano Movement

Albert Camarillo, *Chicanos in California* (1984) and "Latin Americans" in Mary K. Cayton, Elliott J. Gorn, and Peter W. Williams, eds., *Encyclopedia of American Social History*, Vol. II (1993); John Chávez, *The Lost Land: The Chicano Image of the Southwest* (1984); Juan Gómez-Quinones, *Chicano Politics: Reality and Promise, 1940–1990* (1990); Richard A. Griswold del Castillo, *La Familia: Chicano Families in the Urban Southwest, 1848 to the Present* (1984); Richard Griswold del Castillo and Richard A. García, *César Chávez* (1995); John C. Hammerback and Richard J. Jensen, *The Rhetorical Career of César Chávez* (1998); Carlos Muñoz, *Youth, Identity, Power: The Chicano Generation* (1989); Armando Navarro, *Mexican American Youth Organization* (1995).

PART THREE

The Loss of Innocence

Between 1965 and 1974, American society reeled under a series of crises that pitted generation against generation, black against white, ethnic group against ethnic group, even women against men. The traumatic events of this period redirected and partially derailed the momentum for liberal reform that had taken shape in the late fifties and early sixties.

As this liberal momentum crested in 1964–65, Congress had enacted a remarkable body of legislation that attacked poverty and addressed such basic social issues as health care and environmental protection. Moreover, a broad national consensus had formed around the twin goals of ending racial segregation and transforming Lyndon Johnson's Great Society vision into reality. Johnson's sweeping electoral victory in November 1964 seemed a mandate to pursue this ambitious domestic agenda.

But the liberal consensus, always fragile, proved ephemeral. On the domestic front, growing cultural, social, and racial tensions foreshadowed conflict. Young black activists, rejecting the moderate leadership of Martin Luther King, Jr., espoused goals and strategies that alarmed white America. King himself adopted increasingly controversial positions, and northern cities erupted in racial violence. Simultaneously, as the affluent baby-boom generation reached college age, campus unrest and cultural rebellion intensified. Youthful radicals challenged their politically and now economically dominant parents, as well as the Old Left ideology of the 1930s and the Cold War liberalism personified by Kennedy and Johnson.

The liberal consensus might have survived had not President Johnson escalated the Vietnam War early in 1965. Just as the Berlin Wall once cut a city in half, the Vietnam experience bisects postwar American history. Johnson's decision to expand the conflict, rooted in twenty years of Cold War thinking and strategic calculations that seemed persuasive at the time, not only shattered a small Asian nation but exacerbated divisions at home. Although only a minority of Americans joined the antiwar movement, the drumfire of protest, heavily reported in the media, hastened the unraveling of the liberal dream. In 1968, with its street violence, political upheaval, and shocking assassinations, a torn nation reached its nadir of despair.

The chaos of 1965–68 pushed Americans powerfully to the right as citizens groped for stability and reassurance. The chief beneficiary of this shift was the durable Richard Nixon. Capitalizing on the conservative surge and building on the southern strategy that had become central to Republican planning, Nixon won the presidency in 1968 and laid the groundwork for a new political alignment that would wield influence for decades. Nixon's most pressing task was to grapple with the war in Vietnam that had destroyed his Democratic predecessor. While maneuvering to avoid a humiliating defeat in Southeast Asia, Nixon and his national security adviser, Henry Kissinger, plotted to muffle antiwar protest at home.

They succeeded; after a final outburst in the spring of 1970, the movement quietly expired. Nixon and Kissinger also initiated a reorientation of a U.S. foreign policy that seemed trapped in the straitjacket of Cold War platitudes. Adopting a strategy guided more by balance-of-power calculations than by anticommunist ideology, they pursued a policy of détente—lessening of tensions—with the Soviet Union and a diplomatic opening to the People's Republic of China. Riding the crest of his diplomatic successes, Nixon handily won reelection in 1972.

Meanwhile, new social and cultural trends growing from the conflicts of the 1960s caught the nation's attention in the early 1970s. A heightened ethnic awareness clearly owed a debt to the black-pride movement. Movements as diverse as environmentalism, feminism, gay rights, and so-called New Age self-awareness all had their roots in the 1960s. Just as Nixon transformed the political landscape, so the social and cultural trends of the Nixon years would shape American life for years to come.

Yet despite Nixon's larger-than-life role on the global stage, his presidency ended in dismal failure. If the social crisis of the late 1960s played itself out on city streets and college campuses, the political crisis of 1973–74 began in secrecy and unfolded in the press, the courts, and the halls of Congress. Seeking to destroy his political enemies and to discredit critics of his Vietnam policies, Nixon and his top advisers conducted illegal activities that violated Americans' constitutional rights. He committed further crimes as he and his aides tried to cover up their wrongdoing. In August 1974, amid a grave constitutional crisis, Nixon resigned.

The interlinked traumas of urban upheaval, generational conflict, political violence, divisions over Vietnam, and two failed presidencies shattered the self-assurance engendered by the Eisenhower era and the confident liberalism of the early Kennedy-Johnson years. An oil crisis in the mid-seventies worsened matters by triggering inflation and stirring anxieties about what had once seemed a limitless supply of energy. At home and abroad, American prospects in 1975 seemed far more clouded than they had in 1955 or even in 1965. The malaise that would shadow American life had its foundation in the years to which we now turn.

Radicalization: Black Power, the New Left, and the Counterculture

ON AUGUST 11, 1965, as civil-rights activists applauded the new voting-rights act, a Los Angeles police officer made a routine speeding arrest of an intoxicated young motorist. But the officer was white and the motorist was black, and race soon injected itself into the situation. As a crowd of blacks gathered, the mood turned ugly, and more patrolmen materialized. As the driver and his brother resisted, they were felled by a policeman's billy club. A young black woman accused of spitting at the police was arrested and taken away in a squad car. One onlooker screamed: "We've got no rights at all! It's just like Selma!"

The police soon left, but the crowd remained angry, inflamed by false rumors that the arrested woman was pregnant and had been brutally beaten. Residents lobbed rocks at passing cars, attacked white drivers, and overturned and torched vehicles. As the city sweltered in heat, street violence, looting, and arson swept through Watts, a crowded section of Los Angeles housing 250,000 black residents. Thousands of blacks, many of them teenagers, roamed the streets. Despite the eventual presence of over fifteen thousand police and national guardsmen, the uprising raged for thirty-six hours, leaving thirty-four dead, nine hundred injured, and $30 million in property damage that left the Watts business district a charred ruin. Over the next three years, each summer brought new waves of riots in the black ghettos of urban America.

As the sixties waned, young black radicals, some inspired by Black Muslim leader Malcolm X, spoke a vocabulary of resistance and separatism strikingly different from the rhetoric of Martin Luther King, Jr. As activists shouted the slogans of Black Power, city after city erupted in violence. A white backlash formed, splintering the already strained civil-rights coalition. The end of the 1960s found black America's anger—and white America's resentment—mounting. The gains of the 1950s and early 1960s in combating segregation seemed remote indeed.

As generational and ideological conflict divided the African American community, young white radicals, too, mostly on the college campuses, challenged their parents' political and cultural values. New Leftists dissected Kennedy-Johnson liberalism, and a growing counterculture expressed its rebelliousness in dress, music, and even hairstyle. Amid conflicts over the Vietnam War, hostility and divisiveness gripped American society. The upsurge of youthful radicalism that began in the mid-sixties would leave its stamp on the generation that experienced it. But many Americans recoiled from the protests and the counterculture, adding fuel to a conservative resurgence that would remain influential for decades.

Inner-City Upheavals and Black Power

A few days after the Watts riot, violence erupted in Chicago's black neighborhoods. The following summer, riots hit Chicago again, then Cleveland, Dayton, Milwaukee, and other midwestern cities. The cycle of inner-city turmoil climaxed in 1967, with outbreaks in more than twenty cities.

The most serious violence of 1967 struck Newark, New Jersey, and Detroit. Newark's black ghetto, beset by poverty and unemployment, exploded on July 12. As in Watts, reports of police beating a black motorist triggered the outburst. By nightfall, an angry, cursing mob surrounded the police station. As rioting and arson spread, New Jersey's governor called in the National Guard. When the crisis finally ebbed, twenty-five blacks had been killed.

Detroit's many antipoverty programs provided no shield against violence. On July 23, the arrest of patrons at an after-hours nightclub triggered six days of street fighting and burning that left the downtown area in ruin. In one incident, an arsonist tossed a Molotov cocktail through the window of a small business. Fanned by hot summer winds, the fire soon engulfed the entire block as residents tried to quench it with garden hoses. Oddly, an almost festive mood prevailed. "To riot and destroy appeared more and more to become ends in themselves," one observer reported. Other residents, by contrast, toured the riot district urging calm.

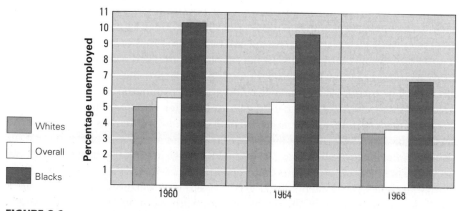

FIGURE 9.1

Unemployment Rates, 1960–1968

Source: *Historical Statistics of the United States, Colonial Times to 1970* (1975).

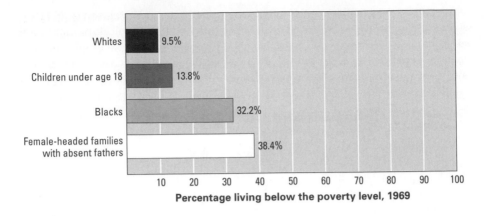

FIGURE 9.2

Poverty, 1969

SOURCE: U.S. Bureau of the Census, *Current Population Reports,* series P-60, No. 149, and unpublished data.

In retrospect, the 1965–68 riots might have been anticipated. For decades northern cities had lured southern blacks seeking a better life. From 1940 to 1960, the net migration of blacks from South to North totaled more than 3 million. Yet instead of greater opportunity, they more often confronted overcrowding and job discrimination. A far greater percentage of blacks than whites worked at the lowest-paid, unskilled ranks of the labor force, and many found no work at all. In 1966, more than 1 million nonwhite workers in the nation's central cities were unemployed or held only part-time jobs.

These urban black communities had their stable middle class and professional elite, strong families, churches, and other supportive institutions. But social disruption was widespread as well. High rates of infant mortality, alcoholism, crime, drug abuse, teenage pregnancy, and single-parent households spawned instability. The grim fact of poverty dominated all the statistics. In 1966, 42 percent of nonwhites living in urban America fell below the federal poverty line.

The civil-rights movement and the War on Poverty had roused hopes that federal laws could not meet; analysts spoke of a "crisis of rising expectations." Some black leaders tried to direct the anger into political action, but the pressure-cooker mood in many cities discouraged long-term strategies. Although the North did not have legally enforced segregation and the racism was often less blatant, subtle forms of prejudice affected not just the workplace but every facet of life. By various informal means, and sometimes by restrictive clauses in property deeds, residential segregation characterized all northern cities. Blacks who moved into white neighborhoods often faced silent hostility and even scrawled obscenities or a brick through a window at night. By the mid-sixties, with the suburbs 95 percent white, poverty and discriminatory real-estate practices left most blacks (and Hispanics) jammed in the inner city.

With an eroding tax base owing to the flight of businesses and middle-class taxpayers, urban services, from schools to parks to garbage collection, deteriorated. Worse still, the highway and urban-renewal programs of the 1950s had left many poor urban neighborhoods crisscrossed by freeways and access ramps, their residents warehoused in ugly high-rise housing projects. These conditions provided ample fodder for riots and unrest.

But despite the obvious catalysts (and precedents for urban disorder stretching back to the early nineteenth century), the riots stunned white America and official Washington, particularly since they came after a decade of apparent progress in race relations. Already grappling with Vietnam War critics, President Johnson now also confronted home-front threats to law and order. In July 1967, he created a National Advisory Commission on Civil Disorders. Its 1968 report rejected the charge that "outside agitators" or criminals had caused the upheavals. Moving beyond the immediate circumstances of specific riots, the study explored the larger pattern of white racism and rising black militance—combined with inner-city despair—that provided the breeding ground for violence. Noting that charges of police brutality had triggered many of the riots, the commission documented that most police forces remained overwhelmingly white, even in cities with large black populations. The report also observed that although the riots had broken out spontaneously, arsonists often targeted white-owned businesses and spared black-owned enterprises.

Concluding that "white racism is essentially responsible for the explosive mixture which has been accumulating in our cities," the commission warned, "Our nation is moving toward two societies, one black, one white—separate and unequal. . . . To pursue our present course will involve the continuing polarization of the American community and, ultimately, the destruction of basic democratic values."

While the urban black underclass seethed, some young blacks dismissed Martin Luther King's integrationist agenda and nonviolent strategies to call for an ill defined but militant Black Power. As the mainstream civil-rights movement lost steam, its original goals largely achieved, younger black radicals stepped in to fill the vacuum. SNCC led the way by electing as its head the firebrand Stokely Carmichael over the pacifist John Lewis. The militant Floyd McKissick replaced the more moderate James Farmer as director of CORE. On a march in Greenwood, Mississippi, in June 1966, Carmichael exhorted activists to "stop begging and take power—black power." When he hypnotically shouted "BLACK POWER! BLACK POWER! BLACK POWER!" and the crowd rhythmically responded, the media paid attention.

Black Power, Carmichael asserted, meant "smash[ing] everything Western civilization has created." At the 1966 CORE convention in Baltimore, he struck a separatist note: "We don't need white liberals. . . . We have to make integration irrelevant!" Early in 1967 he declared, "To hell with the laws of the United States. . . . If we don't get justice, we're going to tear this country apart."

The next head of SNCC, young H. Rap Brown of Louisiana, outdid even Carmichael in rhetorical overkill. Violence, he announced, "is as American as cherry pie." Speaking in Cambridge, Maryland, in July 1967 as flames engulfed Detroit, Brown harangued his volatile young audience with talk of guns and killing. A wave of arson soon devastated the city's black district. Soon after, Brown was arrested for inciting a riot. The moral idealism of the early civil-rights movement, and the apparent interracial unity at the 1963 March on Washington, were little in evidence by 1967.

In a West Coast manifestation of Black Power, Huey Newton and Bobby Seale, black college students in Oakland, California, founded the Black Panther Party in 1966. Their manifesto demanded decent housing, better education, an end to police brutality, and full employment for the black community. Their even more radical goals included exemption from military service for black males, all-black juries for blacks on trial, and "an end to the robbery by the capitalists of our Black Community." In their paramilitary uniforms of black leather jackets and black berets, the Panthers won local celebrity and national media attention. Newton became "Minister of Defense" and Eldridge Cleaver, recently released from prison, "Minister of Information." In May 1967, as the California legislature debated a bill banning the carrying of loaded guns, Black Panther Party members defiantly brought weapons into the capitol building. When the Panthers became the targets of FBI surveillance and of raids by local police that sometimes resulted in fatalities, their fearsome aura increased.

Lacking a clear-cut program, Black Power primarily was a riveting slogan expressing many young blacks' militant mood; impatience with the middle-class, church-based civil-rights movement; contempt for patronizing white liberals; and, above all, black pride. Martin Luther King, Jr., sought to end the racial power imbalance in America and the resulting exploitation of blacks by winning whites to the cause through appeals to a shared moral tradition. The Black Power radicals dismissed King's strategy and instead sought to forge a disciplined cadre that would achieve its goals through group solidarity, collective action, and intense racial consciousness.

The middle-class civil-rights organizations' strategy of building coalitions and working within the system held little appeal for Black Power devotees and their followers among the urban black poor. The oppressed should not collaborate with the oppressor, they insisted, or beg favors of the white enemy. Rather, some Black Power advocates espoused black political organizing, black business enterprises, black cultural institutions, and local control of schools and other institutions in black neighborhoods. This separatist vision had precedents in the mobilization of urban blacks by Marcus Garvey in the 1920s, but Black Power enthusiasts pushed the theme much further, lacing their prescriptions with apocalyptic visions of revolution and retaliation against a demonized white oppressor.

White and black critics alike dismissed this approach as a dangerous fantasy reflecting political naiveté and a failure of moral imagination. Yet the impulse that underlay the Black Power movement had roots not only in the Garvey movement but also in the smoldering anger, racial pride, and spirit of resistance bred by generations of white oppression. King downplayed these fierce impulses with his reassuring message of nonviolence, moral suasion, and integration, but they were an authentic part of the black experience. As historian Timothy Tyson has written:

> "[T]he civil rights movement" and "the Black Power movement," often portrayed in very different terms, grew out of the same soil, confronted the same predicaments, and reflected the same quest for African American freedom. . . . [V]irtually all the elements that we associate with "Black Power" were already present in the small towns and rural communities of the South where "the civil rights movement" was born.

Building on this tradition, the Black Power movement exerted its greatest impact in the realm of culture and consciousness. Historian William L. Van Deburg, in his 1992 history of the movement, *New Day in Babylon,* sees Black Power as essentially a ritual of cultural empowerment and racial assertiveness. In this sense, despite their repudiation of the civil-rights movement, Black Power champions shared basic goals with the earlier campaign. From the beginning, civil-rights leaders and local activists had focused on empowerment as well as on attacking Jim Crow and gaining voting rights. For them the word *freedom* encompassed racial pride, collective action, and breaking what historian David Chalmers has called "the white stranglehold on the black psyche." The call to Black Power intensified this concept of empowerment.

As Black Power enthusiasm spread among young urban blacks, the aesthetic summed up in the term *soul* became the test of racial authenticity. Artists and writers produced work rooted in the black experience that spoke to a black audience. Abandoning elaborate hair-processing techniques, young blacks adopted the natural "Afro" look. Some donned colorful African dashikis. Well-educated young blacks consciously employed black street slang. Black history courses sprang up on college campuses. In Detroit, the Reverend Albert Cleage opened his Shrine of the Black Madonna featuring a thirty-foot mural of a black Mary and baby Jesus.

In the sports world, some black athletes boycotted the 1968 Summer Olympics in Mexico City to protest racism—a strategy suggested by Harry Edwards, a young sociologist at San Jose State University. Runners Tommie Smith and John Carlos, both students at San Jose State, participated in the games but

Black Pride: Angela Davis Addresses a Street Rally.   Davis, a radical activist and supporter of the Black Panther Party, speaks in Raleigh, North Carolina, on July 4, 1974. *(© Bettmann/Corbis)*

chose a memorable form of protest. On the victory stand after winning the gold and bronze medals in the 200-meter sprint, they lowered their heads and raised black-gloved fists as the national anthem was played. Hailed by some, they also faced outrage and death threats. Both were expelled from the Olympic team and barred from the Olympic Village. (Smith went on to become a college professor and Carlos a high-school teacher.) Like Rosa Parks's refusal to give up her bus seat in Montgomery in 1955 or the 1960 Greensboro sit-ins, their gesture was a defining moment in the rapidly evolving black-liberation movement.

Soul music—Aretha Franklin's "Natural Woman" (1967), James Brown's "Say It Loud, I'm Black and I'm Proud" (1969), for example—epitomized the new racial consciousness. Nina Simone's bitter "Revolution" (1969) offered a musical salute to Black Power. Tony Clarke's "Ghetto Man" (1969) conveyed the psychological toll of slum life:

> I never knew my papa's name
> My ma scrubbed floors to keep me clad
> And me and three brothers had to share one bed
> When I was young I felt ashamed.

In one sense, the Black Power movement proved ephemeral. Entrepreneurs quickly cashed in on the vogue with such products as "politically correct" Afro wigs and "Soul Brother" T-shirts. By the mid-1970s, the leaders had scattered, some going

Olympic Protest. In a gesture that stirred both admiration and anger across America, track stars Tommie Smith and John Carlos raise black-gloved fists and bow their heads during the playing of the national anthem at the 1968 Summer Olympics in Mexico City. *(UPI/Corbis-Bettmann)*

to Africa (Stokely Carmichael), some embracing evangelical Christianity and Republican politics (Eldridge Cleaver), and at least one marketing barbecue sauce (Bobby Seale). Yet the cultural ferment summed up in the phrase *Black Power* exerted a profound long-range impact. For many African Americans, the movement both enhanced racial pride and heightened skepticism toward white America. Sinking deep roots into the black community, the assertive new outlook would be transmitted as a legacy to a younger generation of African Americans.

The movement also contained a misogynist strain that dismayed many black women. When a young woman presented a paper on the position of women in SNCC in 1964, Stokely Carmichael sneered, "The only position for women in SNCC is prone." Such offensive attitudes helped mobilize young African American women to form the National Black Feminist Organization in 1972. They noted the irony of Black Power advocates' rejecting everything white while retaining the most reactionary gender attitudes of 1950s America. Soon a group of black women writers, including Toni Morrison, Alice Walker, and Terry McMillan, would explore gender issues in the African American community. The issue would remain touchy a generation later, as black women protested the coarse sexist lyrics of some black male rap groups in the 1990s.

Although promulgated by individuals who in fact wielded little power, Black Power pronouncements terrified white America. After King's biblical cadences and uplifting vision of racial harmony, this rage-filled talk was alarming. The resulting white backlash would contribute to the rightward turn of U.S. politics and culture.

The Black Power movement repudiated the mainstream civil-rights organizations. Martin Luther King, Jr., and the SCLC tried for a time to maintain links to the radicalized SNCC and CORE, but with little success. The young radicals ridiculed King as "Reverend Dr. Chickenwing." The more conservative NAACP and Urban League rejected the Black Power theme entirely. Black Power radicals, in turn, jeered at the NAACP's Roy Wilkins as "a white man who somehow came out the wrong color."

Amid riots and calls for revolution, the efforts of the civil-rights organizations to address the problems of the urban black poor faltered. In 1966, seeking to mobilize Chicago's eight hundred thousand blacks, King moved into a poor black district of the city and announced a campaign for better housing and an end to real-estate discrimination. Meeting with black gang leaders, King aides preached political mobilization rather than crime and violence. But Mayor Richard J. Daley, while praising King's goals, shrewdly undercut him by mobilizing his powerful political machine, including local black politicians, and making superficial but popular gestures such as bringing portable swimming pools into the slums that hot summer.

As the SCLC campaign stumbled, Chicago blacks grew disillusioned. A "Freedom Sunday" march on city hall drew relatively few participants, and some black youths even heckled King as he spoke. Housing discrimination meant little to slum dwellers too poor to move to the suburbs, and the SCLC campaign alienated many Chicago blacks. As one complained, "We're sick and tired of middle-class people telling us what we want."

A rally in early August turned ugly as local whites, mostly second-generation European immigrants, threw bricks and shouted racial epithets. Late that month, Daley gave King a face-saving out, organizing a "summit conference" at which city officials and leading realtors made vague gestures toward open housing. Claiming victory, King left for Atlanta. In fact, little changed in Chicago. The hard realities of urban black poverty and white resistance did not yield to the techniques that had worked in Birmingham and Montgomery. In contrast to the South, writes historian Robert Weisbrot, "racism moved through Northern cities like Chicago in so many faceless, impersonal forms as to escape detection by a society inclined to ignore it." By the late 1960s, the earlier consensus on civil-rights goals had evaporated, and the movement lay in disarray. The cultural and psychological contributions of the Black Power campaign would later become apparent, but many at the time deemed it nihilistic and divisive.

The Personal Is Political: The New Left and the Counterculture

Adding to conservatives' anxiety levels, the unrest of the 1960s arose not only among young blacks alienated from the civil-rights establishment, but also among middle-class white college students who repudiated Cold War liberalism and their parents' cultural style. Indeed, the two movements were linked. Many of the white student activists had earlier participated in civil-rights demonstrations or the 1964 Mississippi Freedom Summer, and they looked to black movement leaders such as John Lewis, Robert Moses, and Fannie Lou Hamer as role models and cultural heroes.

The Peace Corps and the 1963 limited nuclear test ban treaty had encouraged the younger generation's faith in mainstream politics, but Kennedy's assassination and Johnson's succession eroded that faith. In contrast to the charismatic JFK, the crude and overbearing Johnson stirred little enthusiasm. His domestic reform program won grudging praise on campuses, but the Vietnam War rapidly eclipsed even that support.

Campus unrest had demographic sources as well. By the mid-1960s, the baby-boom generation had created a "nation within a nation" totaling more than 20 million young people. With some 3 million boomers reaching college age each year and more high-school graduates continuing their education,* college enrollment soared from 3.6 million in 1960 to almost 8 million in 1970.

The institutions that admitted these young people—particularly the large public universities—were ill equipped to handle their vast numbers. Forced to fill out forms, wait in lines, sit in jammed lecture halls, and endure crowded dorms, students protested. In *The Uses of the University* (1963), University of California president Clark Kerr praised the modern "multiversity" for its intellectual diversity, but his description of universities as "service stations" and "knowledge factories" hinted at what students found alienating.

Unrest first erupted in the fall of 1964 at Kerr's flagship campus, the sprawling University of California, Berkeley. When administrators banned recruitment tables for civil-rights organizations from a campus area traditionally open to political ac-

---

*The proportion of people eighteen to twenty-four years old who were enrolled in colleges or universities surged, from 12.5 percent in 1946 to 32 percent by 1970.

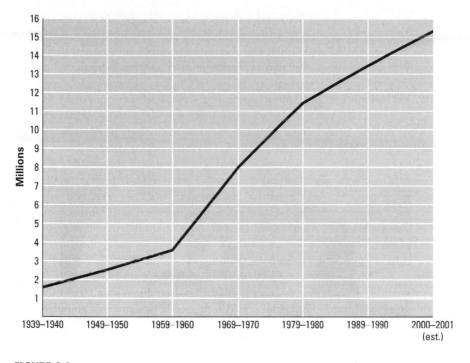

FIGURE 9.3

Total Enrollment in U.S. Colleges and Universities, 1939–2001

SOURCE: National Center for Education Statistics, U.S. Department of Education, in *World Almanac, 1998; The New York Times Almanac, 2003.*

tivity, a coalition of groups organized the Free Speech Movement (FSM). Police arrested a young man who challenged the ban, and masses of students mobbed the police car. Later, FSM backers occupied Berkeley's administration building.

Mario Savio, a philosophy graduate student just back from the Mississippi Freedom Summer, emerged as the voice of the FSM—the first of many 1960s student activists who railed against "the establishment." At one rally, Savio cried, "After a long period of apathy during the fifties, students have begun . . . to act. . . . There is a time when the operation of the machine becomes so odious . . . that . . . you've got to put your bodies upon the gears and upon the wheels [and] . . . make it stop."

As the demonstrations escalated, Berkeley officials eventually yielded on the specific point at issue. But the FSM foreshadowed a nationwide wave of campus protest as activists portrayed universities as cogs in a vast machine that was dehumanizing college students at home as it wreaked havoc in Vietnam.

A leader in harnessing the new mood politically was Students for a Democratic Society (SDS), an organization rooted in an earlier radical tradition. In the 1960s, children of leftists who had supported radical causes in the 1930s—the so-called red-diaper babies—launched a fresh critical assault on capitalist America. In 1960, trying to revive a struggling New York socialist group, the League for Industrial Democracy,

Sit-in at Berkeley.   Folksinger and antiwar activist Joan Baez joins students occupying an administration building at the University of California–Berkeley, December 1964. *(AP/Wide World Photos)*

Michael Harrington and others had formed a youth branch, the Students' League for Industrial Democracy, soon renamed Students for a Democratic Society. At a 1962 retreat in Port Huron, Michigan, some sixty SDS members issued *The Port Huron Statement,* a founding text of the so-called New Left. The principal author, Tom Hayden, of Detroit working-class origins, had just graduated from the University of Michigan. That summer, Hayden had been roughed up by local whites while visiting Robert Moses's voter-registration project in McComb, Mississippi.

The Port Huron Statement recounted the experiences that had shaped its authors' political outlook—nuclear fear, the civil-rights movement, and the vast disparity between America's wealth and power and conditions in much of the rest of the world. It deplored the world's lack of "revolutionary leadership," the U.S. electorate's supine passivity, and college students' "apathy and . . . alienation." Anticipating the Berkeley Free Speech Movement, the statement challenged universities' "cumbersome academic bureaucracy" and faculty links to big corporations and defense contractors.

Despite its critical edge, *The Port Huron Statement* reflected a Kennedy-era belief in liberal ideals and the promise of democracy. Rejecting doctrinaire ideology—"We have no sure formulas, no closed theories"—it proposed a strategy of "participatory democracy" by which young activists would pursue radical social and political change through grassroots organizing. As citizens discovered their collective strength, manipulative, business-dominated politics would give way to more authentic community-based democratic processes. (A more radical 1963 manifesto, *America and the New Era,* denounced the "corporate liberalism" of the Kennedy administration and called for resistance to it, domestically and in the Third World.) Targeting college students already politicized by the test-ban campaign and the civil-rights movement, SDS by 1964 had branches on some twenty campuses.

Emulating what Robert Moses and his SNCC coworkers had earlier done in Mississippi, idealistic young SDS members moved into working-class neighborhoods in industrial cities to promote local political action. By helping residents identify grievances and devise collective strategies for forcing change, they aimed to challenge society's basic power structure. Depression-era radicals had looked to oppressed workers as a force for change, as in Clifford Odets's 1935 play, *Waiting for Lefty,* and the early New Left to some extent continued to identify with the labor movement. Indeed, the United Auto Workers initially helped fund SDS's community-organizing efforts (as well as SNCC's grassroots campaign in the rural South).

However, with President Johnson's 1965 escalation of the Vietnam War (see Chapter 10), SDS shifted from organizing blue-collar workers and the poor to mobilizing college students. If not the working class, then the learning class, would be the engine of radical change! By the later 1960s, SDS was wholly committed to antiwar activism.

The New Left was more than manifestos and demonstrations, however; it blended the personal and the political. One early recruit, Todd Gitlin, later characterized his SDS colleagues: "They were ... analytically keen and politically committed, but ... [they also] cared about one another." In contrast to 1930s radicals, 1960s activists sought to change consciousness as well as the political system. As Tom Hayden put it, "[M]ost of the sixties generation ... were not interested in attaining office but in changing life-styles. They were not so interested in being opinion makers as in changing the climate of opinion."

Given this preoccupation with consciousness, some New Left activists developed a romantic identification with marginalized groups and social outcasts. Ken Kesey's novel *One Flew over the Cuckoo's Nest* (1962), later made into a movie starring Jack Nicholson, proved a favorite with campus radicals. It portrayed the inmates of a mental institution as victims of a repressive society. Persons labeled "insane," Kesey implied, were simply those who rebelled against a dehumanizing social order. New Left theorists did not literally view all mental illness as a rebellion against political repression, but on a metaphorical level, Kesey's novel epitomized their understanding of the links between the personal and the political.

As they explored the connections between the public and private realms, the New Left found certain social thinkers particularly relevant. Paul Goodman in *Growing Up Absurd* (1960) urged the young to move beyond conventional politics and to recover America's lost sense of community. Norman O. Brown, a classicist at Wesleyan University, advised young people to explore inner sources of awareness. In *Life Against Death: The Psychoanalytic Meaning of History* (1959), Brown argued for intuition rather than rationality as the truest source of knowledge, and he celebrated the erotic potential of human bodies freed from socially imposed inhibitions. Both academia and society at large, he argued, needed "more Eros and less strife."

In *Eros and Civilization* (1954), Herbert Marcuse, a German-born philosopher and refugee from Nazism, drew on both Marx and Freud to explore how elites manipulate sex to maintain their power. Extending Freud's theory of sexual repression, Marcuse argued that modern capitalist societies impose far more repression than is necessary to preserve order and then manipulate this "surplus repression" to promote consumption, through erotically charged advertising, for example. Marcuse, like Brown, offered a utopian vision of sensual freedom.

In *One-Dimensional Man* (1965), Marcuse examined further how marketers manipulate consumer desires so skillfully that people lose the capacity for political resistance, critical thought, or true sensual pleasure. Marcuse's apparent message—that rejecting needlessly repressive sexual taboos and the tyranny of the market is not only a revolutionary act but also an avenue to erotic fulfillment—appealed to campus radicals. They summed up his thesis in a potent slogan: "Make love, not war."

The quest for the true self beneath the false, socially imposed self, deeply rooted in the Romantic tradition, pervaded 1960s radicalism. The authors of *The Port Huron Statement* probed not only America's political and social inequities, but also their shifting psychic states—complacency, alienation, apathy, engagement—and dreamed of regaining emotional wholeness through "self cultivation, . . . self understanding, and creativity." Such introspection reflected a central New Left tenet: Consciousness and politics are inextricably connected; the personal is political.

Soon the media detected the emergence of a "counterculture" that not only challenged the political and economic system intellectually but also rejected the middle-class lifestyle. Not all radical activists joined the counterculture, but both movements rejected the repressive authority of the established order, political and cultural. As college students spurned their parents' lifestyles and outlook, SDS theorists predicted, radical political reform would inevitably follow. Even apolitical counterculture youths sensed that their preferences in music, dress, and hairstyle had political implications. As historian David Burner writes in *Making Peace with the Sixties* (1996), 1960s radicals firmly believed that social and political change must begin "with any number of personal decisions to live the transformed society."

The 1960s cultural rebels found inspiration in dissident voices from the 1950s. They admired Salinger, Ginsberg, and Kerouac; embraced rock-and-roll; and identified with movie rebels like Brando and Dean. But they politicized their rebellion. Joseph Heller's *Catch-22* (1960) anticipated the counterculture outlook. Set in World War II, Heller's novel captured war's inhumanity and irrationality and the bumbling of officials. At the end, the antihero Yossarian paddles off on a raft bound for neutral Sweden, a forerunner of thousands of Vietnam War draft resisters who would soon head for Canada or Scandinavia.

Counterculture youth imaginatively rejected bourgeois convention. They let their hair grow and eschewed makeup; burned incense and decorated their rooms with peace posters and Eastern symbols; and bought clothes from the Salvation Army or the Goodwill. Tie-dyed T-shirts, army fatigues, and long cotton dresses, sandals, and beads became their uniform. They unashamedly engaged in premarital sex, aided by the newly developed oral contraceptive ("the Pill") and, later in the decade, the intrauterine device (IUD). Although hardly the first to discover sex, they invested it with ideological meaning. To flout the dominant culture's sexual mores was also to reject its political ideology, its consumerism, and, eventually, its war in Southeast Asia.

The sexual revolution spread far beyond a narrowly circumscribed counterculture. As young women, particularly on college campuses, gained control of their sexual lives and reproductive behavior, full gender equality became a more realizable goal. As dating conventions and sexual taboos weakened, many young people discovered more rewarding and complex forms of intimacy beyond the constraints of engrained gender stereotypes. This, writes historian Beth Bailey in *Sex in the Heartland* (1999), a study of changing sexual mores in Lawrence, Kansas, "may be the most truly revolutionary part of the 'sexual revolution.'"

As the sixties wore on, drugs—mostly marijuana but also stronger substances such as lysergic acid diethylamide (LSD)—pervaded the youth culture as well as parts of the "straight" world. Marijuana and cocaine had been familiar in jazz circles for years, and in the 1950s the Beats had discovered peyote, a cactus-bud hallucinogen used in Native American religious rites. LSD, first synthesized in England, reached the United States in the early 1960s. For a time, marijuana and even LSD appeared as relatively harmless avenues to deeper levels of consciousness. Together with rock, long hair, and psychedelic posters, drugs became part of a counterculture scene that promoted a sense of community and demonstrated youthful alienation from the uptight adult world.

The high priest of LSD was Timothy Leary, a Harvard psychologist. Fired from Harvard in 1963, Leary promoted LSD through his *Psychedelic Review* and League for Spiritual Discovery. "Tune in, turn on, drop out," he counseled the young. Combining the sexual and pharmacological revolutions, Leary described LSD in a 1966 *Playboy* interview as "the most powerful aphrodisiac known to man."

Another drug-culture guru, novelist Ken Kesey, founded a commune near San Francisco in 1964 with a group of hangers-on called the Merry Pranksters. That spring Kesey and the Pranksters drove east in a psychedelically painted school bus wired for sound. The group visited Leary at a Hudson Valley estate provided by a well-heeled patron. They also conducted "acid tests": mixing LSD into foods or drinks, sometimes without recipients' knowledge, at rock concerts.

Above all, the counterculture defined itself through music—first folk, then rock. Joan Baez, a Boston folksinger and civil-rights activist, became the balladeer of social engagement. Bob Dylan, born Robert Zimmerman in Hibbing, Minnesota, joined the Greenwich Village folk scene in 1961. His hugely successful 1963 album *The Freewheelin' Bob Dylan* included political songs such as "A Hard Rain's Gonna Fall" and "Blowin' in the Wind." The last, with its call to political commitment— "How many times can a man turn his head/Pretending he just doesn't see?"—sold a million-plus copies in a version recorded by another popular group, Peter, Paul & Mary. Dylan's "The Times They Are A-Changin'" proved prophetic:

> There's a battle
> Outside and it's ragin'.
> It'll soon shake your windows
> And rattle your walls
> For the times they are a-changin'.

In the early sixties, Dylan's politics reflected the civil-rights movement and Kennedy liberalism, and his music remained in the folk vein. By 1965, with

IN PERSPECTIVE

The Politics of Music

The political and cultural up-heavals of the 1960s found expression through music. Arlo Guthrie's sardonic antiwar song "Alice's Restaurant" and the harsh dissonance of Jimi Hendrix's version of "The Star-Spangled Banner" at the 1969 Woodstock festival cap-tured the spirit of the countercul-ture better than any speech.

In articulating their protest musically, sixties activists were con-tinuing a long tradition of express-ing dissident political views and advocating change through the medium of song. In colonial Amer-ica, following ancient customs brought over from England, street hawkers in Boston, New York, and Philadelphia sold penny broadsides featuring song lyrics, set to well-known popular tunes, that commented on the political events of the day. As the Revolution approached, these broadsides took on a sharper edge and a dis-tinctly anti-British tone.

In antebellum United States, touring singing groups were enormously popular, and their performances often had a political and reformist aspect. Most famous of all were the Hutchinson Family Singers, Abby Hutchinson and her four brothers, who toured the North in the 1840s. Abby ("the sweet canary of New Hampshire") was the Joan Baez of her day. She joined her brothers to perform not only such sentimental fa-vorites as "The Snow Storm" and "My Mother's Bible," but also songs promoting an array of reform causes. "Cold Water" advocated temperance, "The Slave's Lament" championed abolitionism, and the ballad "There's a Good Time Coming" became the anthem of antebellum reformers. Even after the family group broke up following Abby's marriage in 1849, she continued to sing before women's-rights conventions in the 1850s and 1860s.

During the era of industrialization in the late nineteenth century, radicals and labor activists used music to protest the exploitation of workers. A song that circulated among the immigrant coal miners of northeastern Pennsylvania began:

> Come, listen, fellow-workingmen, my story,
>   I'll relate,
> How workers in the coal-mines fare in
>   Pennsylvania State;
> Come, hear a sad survivor, from beside his
>   children's graves,

And learn how free Americans are treated
now as slaves.

Communists and socialists joined voices in the "Internationale." The Swedish immigrant Joseph Hillstrom (Joe Hill), an itinerant laborer, songwriter, and activist, contributed many satirical songs, often set to popular hymn tunes, to the Industrial Workers of the World's *Little Red Songbook*. After Hill was convicted of murder in Salt Lake City and executed by a firing squad in 1915, in what many considered a gross miscarriage of justice, he himself was memorialized in the most famous song to emerge from the American labor movement, "The Ballad of Joe Hill."

Amid the Great Depression of the 1930s, songs again expressed the endurance and discontents of suffering Americans. Oklahoma's Woody Guthrie (1912–67), singer, songwriter, and radical, wrote what would become an anthem of the American Left, "This Land Is Your Land" (1940). America belongs to all its citizens, Guthrie's rousing ballad proclaimed, not just to the rich and powerful. Pete Seeger carried on the tradition of musical leftist politics in the Cold War era.

In the 1950s and early 1960s, Tom Lehrer's songs helped rouse opposition to the nuclear arms race. Stanley Kubrick sharpened the satirical edge of his antinuclear film *Dr. Strangelove* (1964) by staging his nuclear Armageddon to the accompaniment of such jaunty war songs as "When Johnny Comes Marching Home." The Australian folk song "Waltzing Matilda" echoes through another movie of nuclear annihilation, *On the Beach* (1959). Not only the speeches of antinuclear activists, but also music, helped mobilize public opinion against the bomb.

The civil-rights movement is inextricably identified with "We Shall Overcome," sung at countless rallies and protests as well as in jail cells. An African American gospel song, "We Shall Overcome" took on new meaning in the context of the black freedom struggle. Billie Holiday's rendition of "Strange Fruit" and Nina Simone's searing version of Kurt Weill's "Pirate Jenny" from *The Threepenny Opera* offered chilling commentary on lynching, racial injustice, and a coming day of reckoning.

Of course, music can be used not just to stir protest, but also to mobilize public opinion in support of government policies or to promote patriotism. During the Civil War, Julia Ward Howe's "Battle Hymn of the Republic," with its powerful biblical imagery, helped convince northerners of the righteousness of their cause. Confederate troops, meanwhile, marched off to war to the jaunty strains of "Dixie," their national anthem. In World War I, songs like "Over There" stirred Americans to support the war effort; in World War II an outpouring of patriotic songs such as "God Bless America" served the same purpose. Even during the 1960s, not all songs celebrated the counterculture or the antiwar cause. Merle Haggard's patriotic "Okie from Muskogee," for example, sharply attacked the pot-smoking, longhaired opponents of the war.

Although the tradition of political music diminished somewhat after the 1960s, it remained alive. The environmental movement spawned many songs lamenting the destruction of endangered species and rain forests. In the 1980s and 1990s, rap music, rooted in a long tradition of African American protest music and satirical verse recited orally, featured young ghetto blacks lashing out against a hostile social order. Some criticized rappers for misogyny, for antiwhite racism, or for advocating violence, but, like it or not, rap's raw power and unvarnished lyrics did carry on the centuries-old tradition of dissidents and outsiders using music to express their grievances, their seething anger, and sometimes their idealistic vision of a better world to come.

Kennedy's assassination, urban riots, Black Power rhetoric, and Vietnam as a backdrop, both Dylan's lyrics and his musical style grew more radical. At the Newport Folk Festival that summer, he dismayed purists by playing "folk rock" on an electric guitar. Songs like "Maggie's Farm" and "Desolation Row" sneered at the establishment and limned an apocalyptic vision of looming cataclysm.

Early in 1964, the Beatles jetted in from England sporting long hair and boyish smiles. After their TV debut on *The Ed Sullivan Show*, Beatlemania swept teenage America. As the Beatles outgrew their insipid early repertoire and became more creative musically and more politically engaged, they found a new audience on college campuses. Originally inspired by U.S. rock-and-roll performers and by African American rhythm-and-blues artists, and in turn shaping American popular music of the 1960s, the Beatles exemplified the cultural cross-fertilization made possible by the new technologies of LP records and global air travel.

As drug use swept the counterculture, groups such as San Francisco's Jefferson Airplane and The Grateful Dead incorporated LSD-inspired lyrics and encouraged the use of marijuana and other hallucinogens. Dylan's "Mr. Tambourine Man" and the Beatles's "Lucy in the Sky with Diamonds" (a thinly disguised allusion to LSD) testified to the role of drugs in the music scene. The "Human Be-In" held at San Francisco's Golden Gate Park in January 1967 became a daylong counterculture festival featuring psychedelic costumes, music making by bands and blissed-out participants, and the ubiquitous ingestion of mind-altering substances. A flower-bedecked Timothy Leary wandered about in white, proselytizing for LSD.

A few activists promoted radical politics at the Be-In, but by this time the New Left and the counterculture were on diverging trajectories. As New Leftists pursued theoretical disputes and protested U.S. imperialism, the counterculture succumbed to the lure of drugs, new varieties of rock, and the accoutrements of their alternative lifestyle. Leary spoke of his LSD crusade as "the Politics of the Nervous System," but his own career was orbiting into outer space. As historian William O'Neill has observed, "To 'turn on and drop out' did not weaken the state. Quite the contrary, it drained off potentially subversive energies. . . . [M]any adult Americans [were already] dependent on drugs like alcohol and tranquilizers. Now the young were doing the same thing."

For all its criticism of consumer capitalism, the counterculture flourished among the children of the well-to-do, and in fact depended on affluence. And for all the talk of linking the personal and the political, many young people, especially those seduced by mind-altering substances, turned from action to sensation. A narcissistic preoccupation with the self and its potential for gratification would prove to be one of the sixties' more enduring—and questionable—legacies.

The media loved the counterculture. San Francisco's "Human Be-In," gushed *Newsweek*, was "a psychedelic picnic, a hippie happening." *Time* pronounced San Francisco's Haight-Ashbury district the counterculture's "vibrant epicenter" as "flower children" converged there in 1967 for the "Summer of Love." By the early 1970s, however, the drug culture's darker side—its passivity, the "bad trips" (drug overdoses), the exploiters and psychotics lurking on the fringes—had given the entire counterculture the aura of a pleasant idyll turned sinister.

But one should be wary of reducing the counterculture to its drug-induced excesses. The counterculture challenged the tepid and conformist features of 1950s culture. In this respect its influence proved long-lasting. Long after the "Summer of Love" and the "Human Be-In" had faded in a haze of nostalgia, the underlying impulses of the counterculture and the New Left would continue to shape American life as 1960s young people moved into adulthood.

For example, the women's movement that would soon transform America (see Chapter 12) was influenced not only by the civil-rights campaign but also by the New Left and the counterculture. Civil-rights campaigns in the South and SDS's community-organizing efforts gave many young women invaluable political experience. Betty Friedan's feminist manifesto, *The Feminine Mystique,* appeared in 1963, the same year as SDS's *America and the New Era.* The National Organization for Women (NOW), founded in 1966, demanded the decriminalization of abortion and addressed other issues that would soon dominate the feminist agenda. Neither Friedan nor most of the early NOW activists were themselves New Leftists or counterculture devotees, but those movements created a climate that encouraged women to question repressive gender stereotypes.

New Leftists, like the Black Power advocates, also provoked the rise of feminism by their own gender attitudes. The young men who dominated SDS and other radical movements were initially dismissive when female activists questioned gender discrimination and *sexism* (a word coined as a direct analogue to *racism*) within the movement. When female SDS members raised gender issues at SDS's 1965 conference, male delegates, some barely past adolescence, shouted them down. But they persisted, laying the groundwork for their own movement. At a 1968 antiwar rally in Washington, D.C., five thousand women marched separately as the Jeanette Rankin Brigade, honoring a congresswoman who in 1917 had voted against America's entry into World War I.

Conclusion

The mid-1960s stands as a crucial transitional era in U.S. social history, as currents of protest and discontent erupted among young urban blacks, college students, and educated middle-class women. Although they pursued different goals, these groups collectively challenged the entrenched status quo. Building on the civil-rights movement and the promise of change in the Kennedy and early Johnson years, these movements unleashed yeasty activist energies that would remain potent long beyond the sixties.

The urban riots, the radicalism of the Black Power movement and the New Left, and the provocations of the counterculture were important, too, for the reaction they elicited. As many Americans recoiled from developments they found frightening and disturbing, a strong backlash developed, intensifying the conservative drift of U.S. politics. For years, playing upon such fears, conservative candidates, columnists, TV preachers, and radio commentators would rail against "the Sixties" as a shorthand symbol for social disorder and dangerously radical ideas.

Behind all the protest movements of the sixties lay the looming reality of Vietnam. The escalating war in Asia soon blotted out LBJ's domestic achievements and exacerbated the nation's internal conflicts. As the decade wore on, the war that began as a troubling distraction became an all-consuming obsession.

SELECTED READINGS

Inner-City Riots and the Black Power Movement

Alan I. Altschuler, *Community Control: The Black Demand for Participation in Large American Cities* (1970); Michal R. Belknap, ed., *Urban Race Riots* (1991); James Burton, *Black Violence: Political Impact of the 1960s Riots* (1978); Clayborne Carson, *In Struggle: SNCC and the Black Awakening of the 1960s* (1981); David Mark Chalmers, *And the Crooked Places Made Straight: The Struggle for Social Change in the 1960s* (1991); Robert Conont, *Rivers of Blood, Years of Darkness* [Watts riot] (1968); Theodore Draper, *The Rediscovery of Black Nationalism* (1970); James Forman, *The Making of Black Revolutionaries* (1985); Sylvia R. Frey, *Water from the Rock: Black Resistance in a Revolutionary Age* (1991); Herbert H. Haines, *Black Radicals and the Civil Rights Mainstream, 1954–1970* (1988); Manning Marable, *Race, Reform and Rebellion: The Second Reconstruction in Black America from 1945 to 1982* (1984); John T. McCartney, *Black Power Ideologies* (1992); James R. Ralph, Jr., *Northern Protest: Martin Luther King, Jr., Chicago, and the Civil Rights Movement* (1993) and *Report of the National Advisory Commission on Civil Unrest* (1968); Harvard Sitkoff, *The Struggle for Black Equality, 1954–1992* (1992); Timothy B. Tyson, "Robert F. Williams, 'Black Power,' and the Roots of the African American Freedom Struggle," *Journal of American History* (September 1998) (quoted passages, p. 541), and *Radio Free Dixie: Robert F. Williams and the Roots of Black Power* (1999); William L. Van Deburg, *New Day in Babylon: The Black Power Movement and American Culture, 1965–1975* (1992); Milton Viorst, *Fire in the Streets: America in the 1960s* (1979).

The Rise of the New Left and the Counterculture

David Allen, *Make Love, Not War: The Sexual Revolution, an Unfettered History* (2000); Terry H. Anderson, *The Movement and the Sixties* (1995); Beth Bailey, *Sex in the Heartland* (1999); John Borkima and Timothy L. Lukes, eds., *Marcuse: From the New Left to the Next Left* (1994); Wini Breines, *Community and Organization in the New Left* (1983); Howard Brick, *Age of Contradiction: American Thought and Culture in the 1960s* (2000); David Burner, *Making Peace with the Sixties* (1996); Dominick Cavallo, *A Fiction of the Past: The Sixties in American History* (1999); Sara Evans, *Personal Politics: The Roots of Women's Liberation in the Civil Rights Movement and the New Left* (1979); David Farber, *The Age of Great Dreams: America in the 1960s* (1994); David Farber, ed., *The Sixties: From Memory to History* (1994); Lewis Gann and Peter Duignan, *The New Left and the Cultural Revolution of the 1960s: A Reevaluation* (1995); Todd Gitlin, *The Sixties: Years of Hope, Days of Rage* (1987); Clinton Heylin, *Bob Dylan* (1991); Maurice Isserman, *If I Had a Hammer: The Death of the Old Left and the Birth of the New Left* (1989); Cyril Levitt, *Children of Privilege: Student Revolt in the Sixties* (1984); Peter B. Levy, *The New Left and Labor in the 1960s* (1994); Paul Lyons, *New Left, New Right, and the Legacy of the Sixties* (1996); Kevin Mattson, *Intellectuals in Action: The Origins of the New Left and Radical Liberalism* (2002); James Miller, *"Democracy Is in the Streets": From Port Huron to the Siege of Chicago* (1987); Edward P. Morgan, *The 60s Experience: Hard Lessons About Modern America* (1991); R. David Myers, ed., *Toward a History of the New Left: Essays from Within the Movement* (1989); Philip Norman, *Shout! The Beatles in Their Generation* (1981); William Novak, *High Culture: Marijuana in the Lives of Americans* (1980); Stanley Rothman and S. Robert Lichter, *Roots of Radicalism* (1982); Bob Spitz, *Dylan: A Biography* (1986).

Out of Control:
War in Vietnam,
Protest at Home

THEY COME BY the hundreds, walking slowly down the sloping path and gazing silently at the black marble wall on which are inscribed the names of more than 57,000 young Americans. Some visitors weep quietly; others leave a flower or a message; still others seek out the name of a son, a brother, or a friend.

This is Maya Lin's Vietnam Veterans Memorial in Washington, D.C., an intensely moving monument in a city filled with statuary honoring revered leaders or recalling proud events. This one commemorates the nation's longest and most controversial war—a conflict that devastated the people it sought to save and caused wrenching divisions at home. The war's end brought no celebrations, but only relief that a long ordeal was over. The Vietnam Veterans Memorial stands as a monument not only to dead youth but also to vast human suffering, misconceived strategies, the collapse of two presidencies, and a divided America. In 1580 the words of English playwright John Lyly foreshadowed the Vietnam War's ultimate meaning for the United States: "The wound that bleedeth inward is most dangerous."

The wound of Vietnam festered in a body politic already feverish. As the Vietnam struggle escalated in the later 1960s, the mood turned angrier in the African American community, and the New Left and the counterculture, already well entrenched, challenged the administration's war policies. The domestic turmoil that had first erupted in the mean streets of the nation's black ghettos now spread to college and university campuses. Less noticed at the time, millions of Americans dismayed by the unrest and the protests grew more conservative, laying the groundwork of a political shift that would prove enormously important in the future.

The Vietnam conflict, sometimes called "Johnson's War," was not entirely of his making. Its roots stretched back to decisions and actions of the Eisenhower and Kennedy administrations, and indeed to a whole nexus of entrenched Cold War assumptions. But Johnson's 1965 decision to commit U.S. power and prestige fully in Vietnam represented the decisive escalation. As a result, by 1968 not only the liberal consensus but also the American social fabric itself had been severely damaged.

Vietnam 1963–1967: The Years of Escalation

When Lyndon Johnson took office in November 1963, some 16,000 U.S. military personnel were in Vietnam as advisers to the South Vietnamese army. The White House was committed to maintaining a noncommunist government in Saigon, despite the recent overthrow and assassination of Ngo Dinh Diem. By 1967, 485,000 U.S. troops were in South Vietnam and U.S. bombers were raining death across much of the Vietnamese peninsula. But despite billions of dollars and a mighty military effort, the U.S. goal of a stable, popularly supported anticommunist government in South Vietnam remained out of reach.

The American commitment to a full-scale war in Vietnam had evolved gradually, through a series of decisions in Washington and Hanoi, the North Vietnamese capital. In March 1964, North Vietnam decided to escalate its military effort to unify the country under the rule of Hanoi and the Vietnamese Communist Party. Ho Chi Minh, General Vo Nguyen Giap, and other top leaders, having defeated the French in 1954, bitterly resented the United States' snatching national unification from their grasp. To carry out the plan, North Vietnamese soldiers slipped south to join the 23,000 Vietcong (VC), the military arm of South Vietnam's communist-led National Liberation Front. In addition to the VC, 50,000 local militia aligned with the VC stood ready. Regular North Vietnamese army units moved south as well. Hanoi improved and extended the Ho Chi Minh trail, a network of roads and paths linking north and south.

President Johnson, alerted to these moves by the U.S. ambassador in Saigon, Henry Cabot Lodge, fretted about becoming bogged down in the conflict. As he put it, he felt like a catfish that had swallowed "a big juicy worm with a right sharp hook in the middle of it." Underscoring South Vietnam's political instability, another coup in January 1964 brought to power yet another general.

Despite Johnson's doubts, many factors drove him deeper into Vietnam. Secretary of State Dean Rusk, Defense Secretary Robert McNamara, National Security Adviser McGeorge Bundy, Walt Rostow of the State Department policy planning staff, and the Joint Chiefs of Staff all warned that without a strong U.S. military response, South Vietnam would soon fall to the communists. This collapse, they cautioned, could weaken Japan's security and expand China's power in Asia, since Hanoi was siding with Beijing in the worsening Sino-Soviet dispute. Beijing's test of an atomic bomb in October 1964 deepened these fears. Invoking President Eisenhower's domino theory, they predicted that if South Vietnam fell, Laos, Cambodia, Malaysia, Burma, and even Indonesia could topple into the communist camp. Because these nations all had colonial pasts and ample reason to welcome indigenous radicals who championed national independence, the theory seemed plausible. Moreover, Indonesia's unstable ruler, Sukarno, was cozying up to the Indonesian Communist Party.

Johnson's advisers further believed that abandoning South Vietnam would cause America's allies to doubt Washington's reliability. If America allowed South Vietnam to fall, Dean Rusk asked rhetorically, how could the NATO allies trust Washington's pledge to defend West Berlin? More broadly, the situation in Vietnam appeared to fit the new Cold War paradigm that had evolved in the early 1960s. As we have seen, this conceptual framework focused less on preparation for all-out war with the Soviet Union and more on strategic maneuvering in Asia,

Latin America, and Africa. These developing regions, Washington planners concluded, represented the new Cold War battleground, involving local insurgents fighting "wars of national liberation" but inspired by Marxist ideology and equipped by Moscow or Beijing. The Sino-Soviet rivalry for dominance in the developing world, the pronouncements of Mao Zedong and other Chinese leaders encouraging local insurgencies, and Fidel Castro's success in Cuba lent credence to this analysis. Vietnam seemed the ideal opportunity to test America's ability to compete in this new arena.

This view of the Cold War derived from George Kennan's containment doctrine (see Chapter 2), but whereas Kennan in 1947 had focused on Europe and other key geopolitical regions, containment doctrine by the early 1960s was global in scope. In addition, Rostow and others continued to portray the Cold War struggle as more than military. Economic-development programs, they argued, would help Third World nations evolve into modern, prosperous democracies immune to the lure of communism. But such programs required political stability, so the suppression of guerrilla uprisings and leftist insurgencies—General Maxwell Taylor's "flexible response" capability—became the essential first step to achieving larger goals. Economic development, democratic nation building, and counterinsurgency efforts all fit into the overall strategic blueprint. As General Taylor put it, "We should have learned from our frontier forebears that there is little use planting corn outside the stockade if there are still Indians around in the woods outside." Once again, Vietnam seemed the perfect laboratory to test the new strategy.

For President Johnson in his more optimistic moods, the Vietnam effort and the Great Society program were two sides of the same coin. As historian Lloyd Gardner argues in *Pay Any Price* (1995), LBJ hoped that once the communist insurgency had been quelled, New Deal style reform could be exported to Vietnam. A liberal U.S. government would uplift Vietnamese peasants just as it was uplifting America's poor! Ultimately, Johnson paid a heavy price for this linkage: As the Vietnam War lost support, so did his Great Society reform agenda.

As Johnson weighed his Vietnam options, a crisis in the Caribbean seemed to underscore the Cold War issues at stake. In 1962, leftist Juan Bosch had won the presidency of the Dominican Republic in that island-nation's first free election since 1924, but a right-wing military coup soon overthrew him. When pro-Bosch forces rebelled against this military dictatorship in 1965, LBJ, fearing "another Cuba," sent in some thirty thousand marines and army troops to squelch the uprising.* In 1966, with nine thousand U.S. troops still present, a presidential candidate acceptable to Washington defeated Bosch in a second election. LBJ avowed, "We don't intend to sit here . . . with our hands folded and let communists set up any governments in the Western Hemisphere." Could similar boldness in Vietnam produce an equally satisfactory outcome?

America had long viewed Asia as its special province. After the Spanish-American War of 1898, the United States had occupied the Philippines and had ruled the islands until 1946. During World War II, thousands of GIs had given

---

*Other member nations of the Organization of American States, pressured by Washington, supplied an additional two thousand men.

their lives battling Japanese aggression. In the early 1950s, U.S. forces had prevented a takeover of South Korea by communist-led North Korea. This history, too, helped shape the administration's thinking about Vietnam.

Domestic political calculations also played a role. For years the Democrats had borne the onus of having "lost China," and Johnson, like Kennedy, dreaded becoming the president who "lost Vietnam." With an election looming, Johnson was determined not to appear weaker than Kennedy, who had stood tall during the Berlin and Cuban crises. Memories of the 1938 Munich Conference, when the British and French had caved in to Hitler's territorial demands, haunted the debate as well. Would a failure to resist "communist aggression" in Vietnam similarly whet the appetite of Moscow and Beijing for more?

In hindsight, of course, the case *against* escalation seems all too evident. The peasant society of Vietnam had little strategic or economic significance. The domino theory ignored the complexity of the various societies supposedly lined up ready to fall. And as Kennan himself often complained, advocates of the containment doctrine who spoke darkly of Russian or Chinese expansion worldwide ignored the caution that usually guided both nations' foreign policy and blurred the crucial distinction between vital and peripheral regions. As for China, the Vietnamese historically feared their giant neighbor, making it unlikely that Beijing could turn Vietnam into a puppet state. In general, broad-brush analyses by Washington's Cold War strategists missed the nuances of specific situations. They tended to ignore, for example, the importance of nationalism for Hanoi's leaders, viewing it as a rhetorical fig leaf masking ideological objectives orchestrated from abroad.

Still, the case against intervention was less clear-cut in 1964 than it would later appear. Johnson's decisions about Vietnam arose from strategic calculations that were at least plausible and that reflected a virtual consensus among foreign-policy experts and influential media voices. The wonder is not that Johnson chose escalation but that he proceeded so cautiously. While affirming America's commitment to a noncommunist South Vietnam, he initially rejected calls for a major buildup. Early in 1964, however, he did approve covert military action, including air raids against North Vietnamese and Pathet Lao (Laotian communist) bases in Laos and shelling of North Vietnamese installations by South Vietnamese gunboats. Even more ominously, with the Gulf of Tonkin Resolution of August 1964, Johnson laid the groundwork for a full-scale war.

The background of this resolution was murky, to say the least. On the night of August 1–2, 1964, North Vietnamese torpedo boats menaced the U.S. destroyer *Maddox* as it conducted espionage in the Gulf of Tonkin off North Vietnam. Earlier, South Vietnamese gunboats had shelled a North Vietnamese island, and Hanoi no doubt held the *Maddox* partially responsible for that attack. The *Maddox* drove off the torpedo boats and, on Johnson's orders, continued its spying mission, joined by another destroyer, the *Turner Joy*. Two nights later, in stormy seas and relying on radar and sonar rather than visual sightings, the two vessels reported another torpedo attack. Follow-up messages cast doubt on this report, and no firm evidence of an attack ever surfaced. ("For all I know the Navy was shooting at whales," Johnson conceded privately.) But the president used the incident to request from Congress blanket authorization to respond as he chose to any future aggression. As National Security Adviser McGeorge Bundy later commented, such incidents were like streetcars: If you missed one in the search for a pretext for a policy change, another would soon come along.

The Gulf of Tonkin Resolution, which passed the House unanimously after a half-hour's discussion, authorized Johnson

> to take all necessary measures to repel any armed attack against the armed forces of the United States and to prevent further aggression . . . [and] to take all necessary steps, including the use of armed force, to assist any member or protocol state of the Southeast Asia Collective Defense Treaty requesting assistance in defense of its freedom.*

The Senate passed the measure 88–2, with only Wayne Morse of Oregon and Alaska's Ernest Gruening in dissent. Later opponents of the war, including George McGovern of South Dakota and Wisconsin's Gaylord Nelson, harbored doubts but voted for the resolution nevertheless. The more typical response was that of Senator Richard Russell of Georgia, who proclaimed, "Our national honor is at stake. We cannot and will not shrink from defending it." In public-opinion polls, Johnson's approval ratings jumped 30 points, to 72 percent.

Johnson opted for a resolution of this sort rather than a formal declaration of war, which he feared might draw the Soviet Union or China directly into the conflict. Furthermore, as McGeorge Bundy advised him, a declaration of war would have "heavy domestic overtones." Adopting the useful fiction that South Vietnam was an independent nation, Bundy portrayed the planned action as simply an effort to help an ally defend itself. In *The Politics of Lying: Government Deception, Secrecy, and Power* (1973), Washington journalist David Wise called the Tonkin Gulf resolution "the most crucial and disgraceful episode in the modern history of government lying."

The Gulf of Tonkin Resolution, with later appropriations to pay for the conflict, provided the legal foundation for the Vietnam War. The resolution, as Johnson observed, was "like Grandma's nightshirt, it covers everything." In requesting it, Johnson concealed the operations already under way and the detailed war plans waiting in the Pentagon. In the 1964 election campaign, Johnson had declared reassuringly: "We seek no wider war. We don't want our American boys to do the fighting for Asian boys."

In 1965, however, the political instability in Saigon, combined with North Vietnam's stepped-up military campaign in the south, precipitated a series of decisions that moved the United States from a limited commitment to all-out war. In August 1964, Nguyen Khanh, South Vietnam's military ruler, had assumed near-dictatorial powers, sparking protests among Buddhists and other dissident groups. In February 1965, as protests flared in the streets of Saigon, Khanh fled the country.

Johnson's advisers had been advocating an air war against North Vietnam; with the Saigon government in crisis, their calls grew more urgent. General Maxwell Taylor, the new ambassador to South Vietnam, cautioned, "To take no positive action now is to accept defeat in the fairly near future." On February 24,

---

*The Southeast Asia Collective Defense Treaty was a 1954 mutual-defense treaty signed by the United States and various nations of Southeast Asia. A protocol attached to the treaty included Cambodia, Laos, and "the free territory under the jurisdiction of the State of Vietnam" within the area the signatories pledged to defend.

LBJ approved Operation Rolling Thunder, a large-scale bombing campaign. Soon U.S. bombers were conducting more than three thousand raids monthly north of the 17th parallel dividing North and South Vietnam. To justify this move, Johnson cited recent Vietcong attacks on U.S. military installations, including one at Pleiku that had killed nine Americans. He again concealed from Congress and the public the Pentagon's larger war plans. Instead, he presented his decision as merely a specific response to a particular incident. Thus, by "indirection and dissimulation," with no opportunity for full-scale debate, as historian George Herring has written, the nation edged closer to open war.

What was Johnson's objective as he took these fateful steps? What would have constituted "victory" in Vietnam? The goal was not North Vietnam's surrender or even the overthrow of the Hanoi government. Instead, U.S. war planners hoped to inflict enough damage through bombing (and later to kill enough Vietcong and North Vietnamese troops) to prevent Hanoi from unifying all Vietnam under its control. Sufficiently heavy attrition, they believed, would compel Hanoi to accept an independent, noncommunist government in the south. This goal, in turn, rested on two key assumptions: first, that a stable government could be established in Saigon; second, that the American people would support the war long enough for this goal to be achieved. Neither of these assumptions proved sound.

Each step up the escalation ladder led to the next. With the bombing campaign under way, General William C. Westmoreland, the U.S. military commander in Vietnam, asked for U.S. combat forces to defend the air base at Danang from VC attack. In March 1965, in a replay of legendary World War II Pacific invasions, thirty-five hundred U.S. marines sloshed ashore near the base. Greeting them were bouquet-bearing young Vietnamese women and a banner proclaiming, "Welcome to the Gallant Marines." Moving from an advisory to a ground-combat role, the United States had crossed a crucial threshold. Upping the ante in April, General Taylor and the Joint Chiefs asked that about forty thousand U.S. soldiers be assigned to Vietnam. In May, Congress approved Johnson's request for $700 million to pay for the expanded war.

Meanwhile, the revolving door in Saigon whirled on. In June, a cabal of junior South Vietnamese officers staged yet another coup. ("I'm sick and tired of this coup shit," an exasperated Johnson had earlier exploded.) Thirty-five-year-old Nguyen Cao Ky became premier. A French-trained pilot with a rakish mustache and a glamorous wife, Ky sported gold-rimmed sunglasses, black jumpsuits, and modish silk scarves.

Once more, political chaos led to further escalation. Westmoreland and the Joint Chiefs requested another 150,000 troops. Only a major enlargement of the war, McNamara claimed, could achieve America's goals in Vietnam. Walt Rostow supported the buildup, as did the "Wise Men," an informal group of senior counselors led by Dean Acheson. Privately, Johnson felt deep apprehension. In June 1965 he told Senator Birch Bayh of Indiana:

> I really believe [the Viet Cong will] last longer than we do. One of their boys gets down in a rut and he stays there for two days without water and without food and without anything and never moves, waiting to get up and ambush somebody. Now an American, he stays there about twenty minutes, and he's got to have him a cigarette.

In a conversation with Robert McNamara, Johnson prophetically foresaw worsening divisions at home and little hope for victory in Vietnam: "I'm very depressed about it. I don't believe [the North Vietnamese] are ever going to quit. And I don't see that we have any plan for victory militarily or diplomatically" (*The White House Tapes: Eavesdropping on the President* [2003], Minnesota Public Radio, Introductory CD, Track 2).

Nevertheless, Johnson in July 1965 ordered a vast expansion in both the air and ground war. When Operation Rolling Thunder had begun, Johnson had sharply limited the targets. "They can't even bomb an outhouse without my approval," he had boasted. Now he authorized expanded bombing of North Vietnam targets and of suspected enemy concentrations in South Vietnam. Monthly B-52 sorties soon increased to nearly five thousand. Johnson also approved sending one hundred thousand more GIs to Vietnam. Equally important, the president authorized a basic change in strategy. The combat troops sent earlier had served defensive duty, protecting the Danang air base and other U.S. installations. This was a variant of the enclave strategy advocated by James Gavin, a retired U.S. army general who urged that the United States defend only Saigon and other major South Vietnam cities. Americans, he reasoned, would support a defensive mission with minimal casualties long enough to force North Vietnam to the negotiating table.

But Westmoreland and the Joint Chiefs resisted Gavin's strategy. "No one ever won a battle sitting on his ass," jeered General Earle Wheeler, chairman of the Joint Chiefs. Under intense pressure, Johnson agreed to a more aggressive plan. After July 1965, the U.S. combat role in Vietnam shifted from defense to a search-and-destroy mission aimed at seeking out and killing Vietcong and North Vietnamese forces. Only Undersecretary of State George Ball continued to object. Ball warned Johnson, as he had Kennedy, of "an open-ended commitment of U.S. forces, mounting U.S. casualties, [and] no assurance of a satisfactory solution." "Once on the tiger's back," he added, "we cannot be sure of picking the place to dismount."

Johnson's July 1965 decisions fell short of what his generals recommended. He confined the bombing to the southern part of North Vietnam, and he scaled back Westmoreland's request for 150,000 troops. Nevertheless, this was a major escalation. By the end of 1965, 184,000 U.S. troops were amassed in South Vietnam. U.S. combat deaths had edged above six hundred, and the more aggressive strategy made heavier future losses inevitable. Yet Johnson, desperate to avoid jeopardizing his Great Society programs, hid the full magnitude of the escalation.

In 1966 and 1967, the air and ground war grew exponentially. Washington planners especially favored air strikes, for here the Americans dominated. Sorties against North Vietnam increased to more than a hundred thousand in 1967,* and the target range moved steadily north to include factories and oil tanks on the outskirts of Hanoi and the port of Haiphong. The civilian toll was heavy. All told, U.S. bombs killed an estimated one hundred thousand North Vietnamese civilians.

---

*The bombing was not constant throughout the year. It declined during Vietnam's rainy season (September to May) when visibility was poor, and it increased in other months.

MAP 10.1
The Vietnam War to 1968

Nevertheless, General Westmoreland in August 1966 saw "no indication that the resolve of the leadership in Hanoi has been reduced." A 1966 study ordered by Defense Secretary McNamara confirmed the air war's scant impact. As a Hanoi physician later recalled, "There was an extraordinary fervor then. . . . [T]he bombs heightened rather than dampened our spirits."

The North Vietnamese moved factories underground, built a network of tunnels and shelters, and quickly rebuilt bombed roads and bridges. By 1967 some six thousand tons of supplies arriving daily from China and the Soviet Union diluted the effects of the bombing. Soviet aid increased when Khrushchev's successor, Leonid Brezhnev, launched a drive to win Hanoi's allegiance.

From 1965 to 1968, North Vietnam's air defenses shot down nearly a thousand U.S. aircraft, valued at some $6 billion. Nearly six hundred captured pilots

Johnson Visits Wounded Vietnam Veterans, 1965.   LBJ dropped by this ward at Bethesda Naval Hospital near Washington following his own gall bladder surgery. *(LBJ Library Photo by Yoichi R. Okamoto)*

would serve the North Vietnamese as bargaining chips when peace talks began. One of these pilots, John McCain, a future U.S. senator, was shot down in 1967 and spent more than five years in prison.

The ground war in South Vietnam, too, exacted a high price. A major battle in la Drang Valley in Pleiku Province in November 1965 pitted a battalion of the U.S. Seventh Cavalry (the unit commanded by General Custer at the disastrous Battle of Little Big Horn in 1876) against a much larger North Vietnamese force. The battle left 230 American soldiers dead and 240 wounded. But the North Vietnamese toll of 3,000 dead implied a favorable "kill ratio," confirming Westmoreland's judgment that a war of attrition eventually would break Hanoi's will.*

Westmoreland requested ever more troops, and through 1966 Johnson complied. In June of that year, the president authorized 431,000 U.S. troops in Vietnam by the following summer. (One young American who went to Vietnam in 1966 was Yale graduate John Kerry, a future senator and Democratic presidential candidate.)

---

*The story of the battle of la Drang, *We Were Soldiers Once . . . and Young (1992),* by Harold G. Moore, a battalion commander, and Joseph L. Galloway, a journalist who was present, powerfully conveys the reality of the Vietnam combat experience.

Quang Ngai Province, 1967.   Having evacuated the inhabitants, a U.S. Army team nicknamed the "Zippo squad" (after a brand of cigarette lighter) burned down this village to deny its use by the Vietcong. Here a GI rests following the operation. *(© Photographer Philip J. Griffith/Magnum Photos)*

Nevertheless, the ground war continued to fare badly. Most search-and-destroy patrols proved futile. Operation Cedar Falls, a major search-and-destroy mission early in 1967 that sent thirty-five thousand troops to the so-called Iron Triangle region north of Saigon, illustrates the pattern. The soldiers destroyed entire villages identified as VC hideouts. In Ben Suc, U.S. military forcibly removed people to a refugee camp and flattened their village with earth-moving equipment. (During a similar operation in 1968 in the Mekong Delta, a U.S. officer memorably commented, "It became necessary to destroy the town in order to save it.") But most enemy troops simply withdrew into nearby Cambodia and returned when the operation ended.

Bombers augmented the ground war, pouring explosives on suspected enemy centers. In free-fire zones covering most of South Vietnam, B-52s could bomb at will. Ironically, South Vietnam, America's ally, absorbed more than double the bomb tonnage dropped on North Vietnam, at a fearful cost in civilian lives. C-47 transport planes converted into gunships rained deadly fire on VC forces. Helicopters deployed troops and picked up the wounded and dead. Napalm added to the toll. This gluelike flaming explosive, made of jellied petroleum and phosphorus, adheres to human skin. Over the course of the war, U.S. bombers dropped an estimated 400 million pounds of napalm.

U.S. technology backed the ground war. IBM computers in Saigon identified likely points of VC attack. Infrared viewing devices pinpointed enemy hideouts.

Marines bulldozed a twenty-five-mile-wide strip along the 17th parallel and created an electronic barrier against infiltration. In Operation Ranch Hand, the United States sprayed millions of gallons of herbicides and chemical defoliants such as Agent Orange over South Vietnam to deny the enemy concealment in the jungle. "Only you can prevent forests," joked the soldiers who handled the stuff. Johnson's policies brought environmental disaster to Vietnam while his wife preached beautification at home.

The North Vietnamese commander General Giap ridiculed the U.S. reliance on technology. The Americans "question the computers . . . and then go into action," he jeered. "But arithmetical strategy doesn't work . . . [w]hen a whole people rises up."

While strategists pored over their computer printouts, the ground war itself unfolded in the jungles, river deltas, and highlands of South Vietnam, with both sides paying a tremendous price. For American soldiers in the field, nicknamed "grunts," a yearlong tour of duty brought fatigue, psychological trauma, and the ever-present danger of death or injury from a sniper or land mine. The contrast between field conditions and the amenities of major bases like Danang added a surreal dimension to the war. These centers boasted bowling alleys, movie theaters, and PXs offering Cokes, hamburgers, beer, ice cream, and the latest magazines. Yet reminders of home offered only fleeting escape from the war's realities. Plucked from city streets, farms, and small towns, often possessing only a high-school education and little experience of the world, these young men found themselves in an alien environment facing a shadowy foe familiar with the land and its people. Set-piece battles were few. Days of boredom might explode in murderous fire from an unseen sniper during a reconnaissance mission or in a stealthy VC attack on a base camp.

For the thousands of women who served in Vietnam, the war brought its own traumas. As many as forty thousand worked for private organizations such as the Red Cross. Some eleven thousand served as army nurses or in other noncombat positions with the military. One army nurse recalled, "Our job was to look [wounded soldiers] in the eye and convince them that everything was all right. . . . [Y]ou finally built up a facade and could literally look at somebody dying and smile like Miss America or whatever we personified to them." Writes historian Marilyn Young: "The war gave many women responsibilities and a sense of power usually denied them in civilian life. But this new status too was confusing and even distressing in that there was no way to extricate it from the death and dehumanization that were its occasion."*

Individual moments perhaps best convey the war's reality. A journalist at the battle of Ia Drang in November 1965 recalled a seventeen-year-old's brush with death: "[A] kid wearing a white T-shirt stumbled out of the trees. . . . We all started yelling and waving to him to go back. . . . When he turned around we could see his back was shredded, the red blood startling against the white shirt."

---

*In 1993 a statue honoring the army nurses of Vietnam was erected near the Vietnam Veterans Memorial in Washington, D.C.

This youth survived, at least on that day; thousands did not. A veteran remembered a single death among many. On a search-and-destroy patrol, a shot rang out, hitting one of the men:

> The man . . . was writhing on the ground, his back arching up. He was gasping, hoarse, dragging air into his lungs. There was a perfect round hole about the size of a pencil, right in the middle of his sternum.
>   Then he stopped moving. . . . I looked at him—blond, All-American, crewcut with these pale ice-blue eyes. . . . Those eyes looked right through me. . . . I turned around and looked at the sky in the direction that his eyes were looking to see what he was staring at. I thought I was going to see something.
>   It ran through my mind for a moment, "Did his mother feel something, did his father feel something, did anybody? Was she reaching for a can of peas in the supermarket and feel a tug or a jolt and not know what it was? Does anybody close to him know that he just died?"

Many soldiers bitterly resented risking their lives in an increasingly futile conflict. In retrospect, one veteran angrily rejected the claim that the war could have been won if only Washington and the American people had supported it long enough. "The bureaucrats didn't push us into a winnable war and then tie our hands," he charged. "What they did was actually far worse. They put us into a war that was as unwinnable as it was immoral. They put us into a war that even they could not explain, and so, young men died for old men's pride."

Despite moments of courage and heroism, the war exacted a high price morally. Some GIs came to despise all Vietnamese, friend and foe alike, as "gooks." Napalmed bodies became "crispy critters." Some broke under the pressure. One recalled an incident in which a few GIs, after twenty days in a free-fire zone, stopped a Vietnamese man and his daughter riding a motorbike. After ripping up the man's identification papers so that he could be classified as Vietcong, they killed him and raped his daughter "like an animal pack," then shot and mutilated her. Recounting this incident, the veteran continued:

> I got back to [the United States], but . . . I did not fit into the real world any more. . . . When my mom came to see me, she was a different person. . . . I couldn't communicate with her. I just looked at her. . . . I would just sit in the room in the hospital and my mind would flash back. I would have dreams about the Nam and action. I could see myself fighting, when I'm actually sitting in a VA hospital on the bed.

Both sides committed atrocities. The VC and NLF forces shot wounded enemy soldiers, assassinated civilians who supported the Saigon government, devised ambushes that killed and maimed patrolling GIs, and held prisoners under terrible conditions. (For years after the war, some Americans remained convinced that North Vietnam still held GI prisoners of war.) Furthermore, North Vietnam's communist rulers proved ready to sacrifice hundreds of thousands of lives to achieve their goals. Nevertheless, the atrocities by U.S. forces, some of which gradually filtered out, received the heaviest attention in America, shaping home-front perceptions of the war.

Johnson's escalation only delayed the collapse of the Saigon regime, at enormous cost. The U.S. death toll reached 16,500 by the end of 1967—with almost 10,000 killed in that year alone. The monetary cost hit $21 billion in 1967. From

1961 on, 451,000 South Vietnamese civilians died as a result of the war, with more than twice that number wounded. Some 6.5 million were uprooted from their homes. U.S. officials sometimes portrayed this massive disruption as a strategic plus. As General Westmoreland responded when a reporter asked him about the refugee problem, "It does deprive the enemy of the population, doesn't it."

Despite the U.S. effort, the war failed in its central purpose: to force Hanoi to accept an independent, noncommunist South Vietnam. Ho Chi Minh matched the U.S. escalation step by step. Regardless of ghastly attrition rates, fresh waves of North Vietnamese troops arrived in the field as young boys came of age. By mid-1966, Hanoi commanded a force of more than 430,000 in South Vietnam, including North Vietnam regulars, VC, and local militia. When casualties reached prohibitive levels, the troops lay low awaiting reinforcements, regrouped in the north, or withdrew to jungle camps in nearby Laos and Cambodia. Hanoi counted on outlasting the invaders. As U.S. casualties mounted, predicted the astute General Giap, "their mothers will want to know why. The war will not long survive their questions."

The United States also launched pacification and nation-building programs in South Vietnam to build loyalty to the Saigon regime. To this end, Americans constructed schools and clinics in "pacified" areas. The New Life Hamlet Program moved villagers to new settlements in regions supposedly under Saigon's control. (When this program grew unpopular, a variant was introduced called *Ap Doi Moi,* or *"Really* New Life Hamlet Program.") Teams of South Vietnamese experts launched community-development programs in rural villages. But distrustful peasants remained leery of these emissaries from Saigon, and VC or North Vietnamese fighters often assassinated village leaders who cooperated.

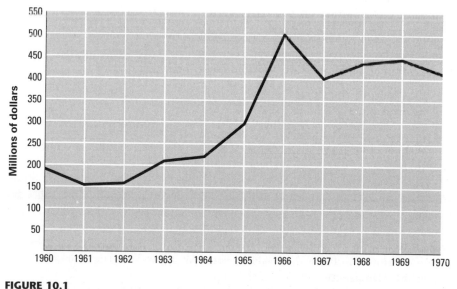

FIGURE 10.1

U.S. Government Grants and Credits to South Vietnam, 1960–1970

SOURCE: *Historical Statistics of the United States, Colonial Times to 1970* (1975).

Westmoreland's office gave priority to its military operations over the political goals of pacification and nation building, and the two programs bore little relation to each other. In fact, the military effort directly undermined the political goals. The bombing and search-and-destroy missions that shredded the fabric of life in South Vietnam eroded any hope of creating a viable nation. Every bombing raid was a propaganda gift to the Vietcong, allowing them to portray America as the outside aggressor devastating Vietnam. One U.S. official later bleakly observed, "It was as if we were trying to build a house with a bulldozer and wrecking crane."

In May 1967, to ease tensions between the military command and the pacification effort, Johnson placed the latter under Westmoreland's direct authority and chose an eager young National Security Council staffer to head it. Devising a computerized Hamlet Evaluation Survey, this official soon reported proudly that 67 percent of South Vietnam's peasants supported the Saigon government. This statistical precision roused suspicions, particularly because Westmoreland's predecessor, notorious for his unflagging optimism, had reported precisely the same percentage in 1963.

As Americans ran the war, they pushed the South Vietnamese aside and lost any prospect of a Vietnamese solution to the dispute. South Vietnam's forces stood at eight hundred thousand by 1967, but high desertion rates cast doubt on such figures. The U.S. presence also unleashed runaway inflation in South Vietnam, and the rural devastation drove refugees into crowded urban shantytowns. Once-lovely Saigon became a teeming warren of bars, brothels, and black markets. Even in remote villages, shacks made entirely of flattened beer cans cropped up—symbols of the American impact on Vietnamese society.

Saigon politics remained as muddled as ever. President Johnson lavishly feted Prime Minister Ky at a meeting in Honolulu early in 1966, but Ky's graft-ridden regime exercised little power and never won the trust of most South Vietnamese. In March 1966, when Buddhists in Hué and Danang demonstrated against the Ky regime, U.S. officials pressured him to modify his authoritarian rule. With much fanfare, the government adopted a constitution, complete with bill of rights. But U.S. officials shifted their support to Ky's less erratic sidekick, General Nguyen Van Thieu. In a September 1967 election marked by irregularities worthy of LBJ's 1948 Senate campaign, Thieu won a weak plurality and became president. Ky settled for the vice-presidency, but intrigue persisted.

The U.S. military, meanwhile, remained upbeat. Inflated enemy body counts ("If it's dead and Vietnamese, it's VC" was the rule in the field) ballooned still further as they rose through the chain of command. The flow of fanciful statistics not only lulled the U.S. public and official Washington but also seemingly mesmerized the generals themselves. Military historians harshly criticize Westmoreland's obsession with quantitative yardsticks of kill ratios, sorties run, bombs dropped, acres defoliated, and villages "pacified." The preoccupation with statistics, they argue, masked a failure of strategic vision and a blindness to the war's social and political context. In Washington, the Joint Chiefs, with a huge psychological and institutional investment in the war, mostly parroted Westmoreland's rose-tinted reports and rubber-stamped his calls for more troops.

But all the while, journalists filed stories and filmed scenes that belied the official briefings. As early as 1965, a reporter coined the term *credibility gap* to describe the growing distrust of the government's version of the war. As relations between the military and the press soured, some officers accused reporters of disloyalty. Acid rivulets of doubt—doubt that Lyndon Johnson had privately voiced from the beginning—began to corrode the facade of official optimism.

Gnawing Doubts at High Levels

The war persisted and so did Johnson's fundamental problems. The Saigon regime enjoyed little credibility; nation building in South Vietnam was stalled; Hanoi, despite punishing losses, remained committed to expelling the Americans and uniting Vietnam; and no one knew how long the American people would tolerate the war. To shore up support, LBJ initiated several "peace offensives." As early as April 1965 he offered Hanoi a development program for the Mekong River delta bigger than Franklin Roosevelt's TVA. A brief bombing halt accompanied this carrot, but to no avail. On Christmas Eve 1965, Johnson once more briefly stopped the bombing, largely for public-relations purposes. As Dean Rusk cabled Ambassador Lodge in Saigon, with a major escalation planned for 1966, Johnson had to convince the public that "we have explored fully every alternative but that the aggressor has left us no choice."

Outsiders attempted to mediate. In June 1966, professing to have positive signals from Hanoi, a Polish diplomat launched a peace initiative. Johnson refused even a temporary bombing halt to encourage this effort, however. Indeed, as low-level talks were set to begin in Warsaw, U.S. B-52s raided rail facilities near downtown Hanoi. Early in 1967, British prime minister Harold Wilson and Soviet leader Alexei Kosygin floated an initiative to bring the two sides to the negotiating table. This attempt failed as well, much to Wilson's annoyance.

As 1967 opened, General Westmoreland, as usual, reported progress on all fronts. Yet in March, he and the Joint Chiefs called for another big escalation: two hundred thousand more troops, mobilizing the reserves, expanding the war to VC staging areas in Cambodia and Laos, more bombing in the north, and mining the port of Haiphong. A top aide to Westmoreland summed up the plan: "The solution in Vietnam is more bombs, more shells, more napalm . . . till the other side cracks and gives up." Hard-liners in Congress ("hawks" in the lingo of the day) backed this request.

The appearance of military unanimity is misleading, however. As Robert Buzzanco shows in *Masters of War: Military Dissent and Politics in the Vietnam Era* (1996), midlevel Pentagon analysts had grave doubts about aspects of the war. Air force strategists documented the futility of the ground war; army analysts demonstrated that air power could not prevail against a guerrilla foe. These voices were not heard: President Johnson did not encourage diverse opinions, and the hierarchical nature of military decision making kept such differences out of public view.

But the steady escalation of the military's demands finally set off warning bells. "When we add divisions, can't the enemy add divisions?" Johnson queried Westmoreland. "And, if so, where does it all end?" Key Johnson advisers concluded that the military had lost sight of political reality in Vietnam and at home. George Ball, now out of the government, stepped up his criticism. President Johnson's press secretary, Bill Moyers, voiced skepticism and departed.

Even Defense Secretary McNamara, so closely identified with the conflict that antiwar activists derided "McNamara's War" and jeered his rare public appearances, was growing disillusioned. His quantitative techniques, including the 1966 study showing the air war's failure, offered little evidence that the U.S. strategy was paying off. In October 1966, on a trip to Vietnam, McNamara told Johnson that he saw "no reasonable way to bring the war to an end soon." The devastation that mighty America was wreaking on a small Asian country troubled him as well. In a May 1967 memo to Johnson, McNamara reflected, "The picture of the world's greatest superpower killing or seriously injuring 1,000 non-combatants a week, while trying to pound a tiny, backward nation into submission on an issue whose merits are hotly disputed, is not a pretty one." (In a 2003 documentary film, *The Fog of War,* the eighty-seven-year-old McNamara would again express his moral reservations about a war that he did so much to plan and implement.)

Meanwhile, opposition to the war was rising ominously on college campuses and among some legislators, religious leaders, and editors. Picketers targeted campus Reserve Officer Training Corps (ROTC) programs and recruiters for the Dow Chemical Company, the maker of napalm. An April 15, 1967, antiwar march in New York City sponsored by a coalition of peace and civil-rights groups attracted from 125,000 to 400,000 demonstrators. (Crowd estimates for 1960s antiwar rallies vary wildly, de-

Shaping Vietnam Strategy.   President Johnson, Defense Secretary Robert McNamara (at Johnson's left), and other advisers confer at LBJ's Texas ranch in early 1964. (© *LBJ Library photo by Yoichi R. Okamoto)*

pending on the source.) A San Francisco rally on the same day drew thousands more. Fighting back, the CIA launched an illegal domestic surveillance operation, code-named CHAOS, that compiled dossiers on antiwar organizations and leaders.

McNamara, now pressing for a scaling back of the war, argued for a bombing halt or cutback, a cap on force levels in Vietnam, and a shift from search-and-destroy missions to protection of South Vietnam's major cities—General Gavin's enclave plan. He also hinted that the United States might modify its rigid opposition to any National Liberation Front role in governing South Vietnam. In August 1967, the defense secretary told the Senate Armed Services Committee, "Enemy operations in the south cannot, on the basis of any report I have seen, be stopped by air bombardment—short, that is, of the virtual annihilation of North Vietnam and its people." In November, McNamara resigned. (LBJ saw his departure as a political double-cross engineered by Robert Kennedy.)

Endless White House meetings probed for a course that might hold promise. A bleary-eyed LBJ pored over the casualty reports and haunted the White House Situation Room at night, selecting the next day's bombing targets. George Ball's 1964 warnings about the difficulties of dismounting the tiger now seemed prophetic. With McNamara gone, the wagons circled tighter. Dean Rusk and Walt Rostow, who had become national-security adviser in 1966, still supported the war. So did McGeorge Bundy, now in private life, though with growing reservations.

While Johnson rejected McNamara's plan to scale back, he also dreaded the requests for further escalation. "Bomb, bomb, bomb, that's all they know," he complained of his generals. Another major buildup, the president feared, would require a tax increase that could further tilt U.S. public opinion against the conflict. On the other hand, withdrawal might trigger the dreaded accusation that he had "lost" Vietnam.

On November 1, Johnson reconvened the "Wise Men." Far gloomier than in 1965, they warned of eroding support for the war, a fact obvious to anyone who watched television or read newspapers, but advised Johnson to stay the course. Appalled by this advice, George Ball exploded at the panel of aging statesmen and bankers, "You're like a flock of buzzards sitting on a fence, sending the young men off to be killed. You ought to be ashamed of yourselves."

As congressional uneasiness mounted, Senator J. William Fulbright of Arkansas, chair of the Senate Foreign Relations Committee, emerged as a powerful critic of the war. As early as February 1966, Fulbright held special hearings on the war. Dean Rusk and other administration leaders faced a sharp grilling, and James Gavin, George Kennan, and others criticized the war's strategic assumptions. The hearings helped crystallize antiwar sentiment.

Although Johnson rejected Westmoreland's call for 200,000 more troops and an expanded air and sea war, he approved 55,000 additional men and continued high rates of bombing. Johnson presented his decision as a middle way between two extremes, but in fact it translated into a further substantial escalation. In 1965 he had expressed confidence (in public) that the expanded war would force Hanoi to yield. The 1967 escalation, by contrast, was the desperate action of a drained president and a defensive administration aware of its failure but fearful of the backlash that open acknowledgment of failure would trigger. The war's appalling toll had itself become the major rationale for slogging on.

Johnson tried to flog waning home-front support. Under a White House mandate to report good news, the flow of impressive body counts continued. In April 1967 Johnson brought General Westmoreland home to address a joint session of Congress. Standing stiffly at attention, the six-foot South Carolinian looked every inch the general as he smartly saluted the cheering legislators. But having defined Vietnam as a limited intervention to put down a guerrilla insurgency, LBJ could never mobilize the kind of support that President Roosevelt had been able to draw upon during World War II.

Behind the facade of unanimity, doubts increased among Johnson's inner circle. Even McGeorge Bundy, now one of the "Wise Men," advised LBJ that his generals' grasp on reality had slipped and warned of eroding home-front support. Geopolitical shifts in Asia also suggested the need for a policy reassessment. In 1966 an army coup had overthrown Indonesia's left-leaning president Sukarno, rendering the domino theory even less plausible. That same year, China turned inward in a spasm of ideological purification known as the Great Cultural Revolution, and its already peripheral role in Vietnam dwindled.

"The Wound That Bleedeth Inward . . . "

Despite Johnson's efforts, home-front opposition increased, fed by increasingly skeptical journalistic coverage. The Vietnam War did not create the New Left or the counterculture—both had got under way earlier—but after 1965, the war became the white-hot focus of campus unrest and radical organizing. The discontents roiling American society now centered on a single issue: Vietnam. To the war's opponents, the administration became first the object of suspicion, then of ridicule, and finally of scorn and hatred, as the idealism and reformist mood of the early sixties turned to bitter alienation. Simultaneously, millions of citizens appalled by the vehemence of the antiwar protests moved in an increasingly conservative direction politically.

The antiwar movement—or simply "the movement"—began in March 1965 with a "teach-in" at the University of Michigan after Johnson announced the bombing war against North Vietnam. Adapting the term from the civil-rights sit-ins, the organizers conducted an all-night round of lectures and discussions about the war. The idea soon spread to the University of Wisconsin, Harvard, and other schools. In April, SDS organized a march on Washington that drew twenty thousand protesters. That spring and fall, local antiwar groups from Berkeley to New York City initiated protests and marches. In January 1966, Johnson ended automatic draft deferments for college students, intensifying campus protest. From a small cadre of radical activists, SDS grew to a loosely knit national organization. Local chapters planned protest actions with minimal national supervision.

For all its intensity, the movement initially had a comparatively narrow base. Its early leaders, often veterans of the test-ban and civil-rights movements, mostly came from liberal, affluent, and politically active families. In some cases, as we have seen, their parents had been socialists or communists in the 1930s. Typically liberal-arts majors at elite schools, they viewed the college years as an opportunity for intellectual and cultural exploration rather than vocational training; protest proved a natural extension of this outlook. Few came from the sciences, engineering, or the professional schools. Fraternity and sorority members, religious and political conservatives, and the politically passive generally remained aloof. As the movement expanded, however, more campuses and a broader spectrum of students were drawn in.

Politically engaged writers joined the cause. The poet Robert Lowell, invited to a White House cultural festival in 1965, wrote a public letter to President Johnson refusing to attend because of the war. At the event itself, John Hersey read from his book *Hiroshima,* and critic Dwight Macdonald circulated an antiwar petition. (Actor Charlton Heston huffed, "Are you really accustomed to signing petitions against your host in his own home?") When the "festival" finally ended, President Johnson sighed, "At least nobody pissed in the punchbowl."

In 1966, dramatist Barbara Garson, a veteran of the Berkeley Free Speech Movement, dashed off *MacBird!* a parody of Shakespeare's *Macbeth* featuring a thinly disguised Lyndon and Lady Bird Johnson as the murderous Scottish monarchs. It sold more than one hundred thousand copies. Critic Mary McCarthy visited Vietnam in 1967 and in a series of essays in the *New York Review of Books* described B-52 Superfortresses roaming over an already shattered land, seeking new targets: "The Air Force seems inescapable, like the eye of God, and soon, you imagine . . . all will be razed, charred, defoliated by that terrible searching gaze."

With Bob Dylan's performance at the 1965 Newport folk festival and Barry Maguire's hit of that year, "Eve of Destruction," the music of the counterculture took on a sharp antiwar edge. Folksinger Pete Seeger, a link to an older protest generation, evoked the Vietnam quagmire in "Waist Deep in the Big Muddy" (1967), which he performed on *The Smothers Brothers Comedy Hour,* an iconoclastic TV show. A pop hit of 1966, Nancy Sinatra's "These Boots Were Made for Walking," expressed both the war's destructiveness and the homesickness of GIs in Vietnam.

The media crucially shaped perceptions of both the war and the home front protests. Although LBJ blamed an unpatriotic press for undercutting support for the war and glorifying the protesters, the reality was more complex. The media at first generally favored the war and endorsed the administration's justifications for it. But as time passed, doubts increased. By late 1966, the *New York Times* was exposing exaggeration in official reports of the bombing campaign. By 1968, media mistrust of the government's claims had reached a high level. Military spokespersons in Saigon and Washington remained doggedly upbeat, but as historian William M. Hammond writes in *Reporting Vietnam: Media and Military at War* (1998), the most skillful and optimistic military news briefings "could never hide the fact that the situation . . . was continuing its downward slide."

Shocking TV images of flaming villages, grievously injured GIs, children burned with napalm, and aged peasants fleeing U.S. bombs proved more potent than dubious statistics and earnest explanations of the administration's war aims.

The media's role in influencing attitudes toward the home-front protests was complicated as well. TV images and print accounts of campus protests and marches in New York and elsewhere publicized, and at times magnified, the opposition. Learning from the civil-rights movement, protesters displayed a vivid sense of theater: chanting demonstrators, flaming draft cards, symbolic coffins, and skull masks made for compelling television. But how individuals interpreted the images

IN PERSPECTIVE

The Imperial Presidency

The reaction against LBJ for waging war in Vietnam without explicit congressional approval—a reaction that culminated in the punitive War Powers Act of 1973—represented a particularly bitter phase in a debate that dates back to the founding of the nation. The framers of the Constitution, having repudiated the imperial claims of George III, feared that the presidency would evolve into a quasi-monarchical institution. They surrounded the office with many constraints, balancing the president's prerogatives by giving at least equal authority to the legislative branch, especially the power of the purse. In principle, no president can spend a penny that has not been appropriated by the people's representatives in Congress.

Although the Whigs of the 1830s professed to find monarchical tendencies in "King Andrew" Jackson, the presidency remained weak through most of the nineteenth century. (The major exception was Abraham Lincoln's exercise of sweeping powers during the Civil War.) Theodore Roosevelt (1901–9) and Woodrow Wilson (1913–21) significantly enlarged the office. Roosevelt pursued an activist approach in conservation, business regulation, and foreign affairs. ("I took Panama," he later boasted after wresting from Colombia the land on which the Panama Canal was built.) The Wilson administration assumed broad economic and censorship powers during the war years of 1917–18. Warren G. Harding and Calvin Coolidge in the 1920s, guided by their probusiness laissez-faire ideology, reverted to an earlier, narrower presidential role. Ironically, however, it was Coolidge who produced one of the more flowery characterizations of the presidency. The office, he mused, "does not yield to definition. Like the glory of the morning sunrise, it can only be experienced, it cannot be told."

With Franklin D. Roosevelt, the modern presidency took shape. Battling the depression, FDR proliferated agencies, built a deeply loyal personal following, and expanded the presidential office. Since his administration, presidents have been expected to set the national agenda and to introduce congressional programs that shape public discourse. Yet Roosevelt also stirred the old fears of a presidency slipping into dictatorship. When he tried to enlarge the Supreme Court in 1937 to give it a more liberal coloration, albeit by constitutional means, Congress slapped him down. Roosevelt broke tradition by seeking, and winning, a third term in 1940 and a fourth in 1944, but Congress retaliated posthumously with the Twenty-second Amendment (ratified in 1951), which limits presidents to two terms.

The postwar presidency continued to grow in size and influence. In 1973 historian Arthur Schlesinger, Jr., published a cautionary study, *The Imperial Presidency.* (Schlesinger had earlier written admiring studies of two presidents—Andrew Jackson and Franklin Roosevelt—who had contributed to the expansionary process, and he had served as a speechwriter for a third, John F. Kennedy.) Richard Nixon's gross abuses of the office, culminating in his forced resignation, produced a temporary reaction against strong chief executives. Yet despite periodic shifts in the balance of power, the general trend toward a stronger presidency continued under Republicans and Democrats alike. Ronald Reagan repeatedly insisted on the need to trim the federal government, and the presidency in particular, yet during his two terms, total civilian employment in the executive branch increased from 2.8 million to 3 million. Moreover, for all Reagan's railings against government power, the Iran-contra affair, one of the more flagrant abuses of executive power in American history, unfolded during his watch.

Students of the presidency such as historian Henry F. Graff attribute its growth in the modern era not to individual ambition but rather to trends largely beyond control. The end of World War II left the United States as the world's colossus, and the advent of the Cold War gave the president the grandiose title "leader of the Free World." The president literally took on the power to launch a world-destroying holocaust. Simultaneously, as social problems grew more complex and more national in scope, the programs, administrative tasks, and regulatory functions assigned to the executive branch expanded exponentially. Television contributed to the "imperial presidency" as well, turning the occupant of the White House into a media celebrity and granting him instant access to millions worldwide.

As the Cold War waned, some analysts foresaw a diminished presidency. In 1993, as President Bill Clinton took office, columnist Leslie H. Gelb of the *New York Times* wrote: "For 50 years, Presidents have defined themselves decisively and dramatically by their actions on the world stage. . . . Mr. Clinton is not likely to have such opportunities. . . . [He] faces mostly quicksand and mudholes."

As we shall see in Chapter 16, however, all of this changed after the terrorist attacks of September 11, 2001, early in the presidency of Clinton's Republican successor, George W. Bush. The USA Patriot Act, hastily passed in the hectic and fearful aftermath of the attacks, vastly expanded the powers of the executive branch, through the Department of Justice, to spy on citizens suspected of being security risks. President Bush asserted the federal government's right to hold suspected foreigners and even U.S. citizens without trial, indefinitely, as combatants in the "war on terrorism." Soon these sweeping claims faced court challenges as violations of the Constitution. In 2003, insisting that Iraq possessed weapons of mass destruction and that Iraqi strongman Saddam Hussein had supported Al Quaeda, the terrorist organization behind the 9/11 attacks, President Bush persuaded Congress to authorize a preemptive U.S. war to overthrow Saddam. As citizens recalled Lyndon Johnson, the Gulf of Tonkin Resolution, and the Vietnam War, warnings of an imperial presidency were once more heard in America.

depended on their politics. Scenes of mass protest that heartened the war's opponents dismayed many conservatives. Already upset by inner-city riots, conservatives saw a society sinking into chaos. Contributing to this reaction, as historian Melvin Small demonstrates in *Covering Dissent: The Media and the Anti-Vietnam War Movement* (1994), was the fact that the media, including the major news magazines and the TV networks, focused on scenes of violence and confrontation more than on peaceful demonstrations, and typically ignored the content of protest speeches or the substance of opponents' arguments against the war.

Responses to Vietnam: The Faces of Opposition and Support

Not only campus protesters, but many other Americans opposed the war. Leaders and members of liberal churches, already mobilized by the civil-rights campaign, passed antiwar resolutions and joined marches. As early as 1965, twenty-seven hundred ministers and rabbis, in a full-page *New York Times* ad, demanded, "Mr. President, In the name of God, stop it!" The differences among Hollywood celebrities epitomized the larger divisions within society. Whereas many stars, such as Gregory Peck, Dustin Hoffman, and Jane Fonda, opposed the war, others, including John Wayne, Bob Hope, Clint Eastwood, and Frank Sinatra, vigorously supported it.

Did social class determine attitudes toward the war? The evidence is mixed. George Meany, head of the AFL-CIO, backed Johnson's war policies. An AFL-CIO poll of some thirty-five hundred labor leaders in 1967 found some 80 percent in support of the war (with fully half of this group advocating further escalation), but about 20 percent favoring deescalation or withdrawal from Vietnam. A few highly publicized incidents of cursing construction workers assaulting antiwar marchers (see Chapter 11) buttressed the image of overwhelming blue-collar support for the war. But polls in 1964 and again in 1968 revealed nearly identical patterns of support for and opposition to the war among the working class, the lower middle class, and the upper middle class.

What about the role of religious belief in shaping attitudes toward the war? The evidence is similarly mixed. Eminent Protestants, such as Yale University chaplain William Sloane Coffin and Reinhold Niebuhr of Union Theological Seminary, opposed the war, as did leaders of the major liberal Protestant denominations. Naturally, pacifists like A. J. Muste and the historic peace churches—the Quakers, Mennonites, and Brethren—shared these views. Nevertheless, other influential Protestants supported the war. Paul Ramsey, a professor of religion at Princeton, argued in books and articles that the Vietnam War met Christianity's classic just-war criteria. Prowar sentiment flourished among fundamentalist and evangelical Protestants. *Christianity Today,* a leading evangelical journal, strongly supported the war. The evangelist Billy Graham proclaimed in 1965: "Communism has to be stopped somewhere, whether it is in Hawaii or on the West Coast. The President believes it should be stopped in Vietnam." Even in the liberal denominations, the leaders often opposed the conflict more strongly than did the laity. Despite the antiwar activism of a few high-visibility Catholics such as Philip and Daniel Berrigan, U.S. Roman Catholics, vigorously anticommunist and concerned about the fate of South Vietnam's many Catholics, generally backed the war. Jews were the first religious group to turn decisively against the war. As early as 1966, fully 63 percent of American Jews favored immediate withdrawal or a negotiated settlement in Vietnam, whereas only a minority of Protestants and Catholics embraced these dovish positions. Leading rabbis strongly condemned Johnson's escalation on moral grounds.

Gender was another significant variable. Opposition to the war among women at all educational and socioeconomic levels, and of all races and religions, ran about 10 percentage points higher than opposition among men.

Despite media images of youthful protesters, young people as a whole supported the war more strongly than any other age cohort. In 1965, 76 percent of Americans under thirty approved of the war, whereas only 51 percent of those aged forty-nine or older backed it. A mere 10 percent of eighteen- to twenty-two-year-olds, one study found, ever participated in any protest activity during the Vietnam War.

Further, despite the publicity given to campus protests, many college students supported the war. The nation's twenty five hundred institutions of higher learning in the 1960s were highly diverse, ranging from large state universities to conservative church colleges. Students and faculty on many of these campuses backed the war, and fewer than half of the schools ever witnessed any organized antiwar activism.

The stereotype of all campuses wracked by demonstrations and of college students united in opposition to the war had several sources. First, opposition to the war did emerge quickly and strongly at some of the nation's best-known universities, such as Harvard, Michigan, and Berkeley. Second, for brief intervals, notably the spring of 1970, campus protest did spread very widely. Third, as campus activists marched, demonstrated, and occupied buildings, they created images that pervaded the media from 1965 on. Finally, campus opponents of the war, even when in the minority, conveyed a passion and urgency typically lacking among those who supported the war or felt ambivalent about it.

No sectors of U.S. society opposed the war more strongly than the African American community. A few conservative black leaders—Roy Wilkins of the NAACP, Republican senator Edward Brooke of Massachusetts, UN diplomat Ralph Bunche—supported the war, or at least did not openly oppose it, but they were a tiny minority. The rising tempo of black militancy gained strength from a war that took a disproportionate toll among African Americans* and cut deeply into domestic social programs. Despite their support for LBJ's domestic programs, blacks turned quickly against his Vietnam policies. As early as March 1966, when most white Americans supported the war, a majority of blacks already opposed the conflict. Of all groups surveyed, African American women invariably showed the lowest levels of support for the war.

Opposition to the war linked African Americans who otherwise differed radically. The prizefighter Muhammad Ali, a Black Muslim, lost his heavyweight crown for refusing to register for the draft. The fiery orators of SNCC and CORE included the Vietnam War in their denunciations of white America, and Martin

---

*In the war's early stages, blacks accounted for 23 percent of U.S. fatalities. By 1969 the figure had dropped to 14 percent—still higher than blacks' 11 percent share of the population.

Luther King, Jr., broke with Johnson over the war as early as 1965, angering many Americans who still backed the president. Tirelessly, King pointed out the high proportion of young blacks fighting in Vietnam and deplored the war's devastating effect on social programs that benefited African Americans. As long as Vietnam drained the nation's human and economic resources, he asserted in 1967, the crisis in the inner cities would only worsen. Having lauded Johnson for his civil-rights stand two years earlier, King now denounced the administration as "the greatest purveyor of violence in the world today."

Despite the vocal opposition, however, Americans as a whole only slowly turned against the war, and never with anything approaching unanimity. A hefty 61 percent of Americans supported Johnson's escalation in 1965, and as late as mid-1967, a majority still backed Johnson's war policies. As peace advocates marched, hawks implored true patriots to rally 'round the flag. Senator Russell Long of Louisiana, launching a McCarthyite-like attack on activists "who encourage the Communists to prolong the war," orated, "I swell with pride when I see Old Glory flying from the Capitol. . . . My prayer is that there may never be a white flag of surrender up there." Many Americans endorsed such sentiments and gave LBJ the benefit of the doubt in the war's early stages. Certainly the families and friends of the young men and women in Vietnam felt little sympathy for critics who attacked the war as immoral or unwinnable.

Hostility toward campus demonstrators further influenced many citizens' view of the war. Many working-class and middle-class Americans saw the youthful protesters as pampered offspring of a privileged elite, reared too permissively, and now petulantly demanding their way in shaping national policy. The media's focus on confrontations between demonstrators and the police or other authority figures heightened these stereotyped perceptions. This gut-level aversion to campus demonstrators would crest in 1968–70, but it emerged even earlier. For many conservatives, distaste for the war's opponents proved stronger than their doubts about the war itself.

Indeed, in some respects the media missed the big story of 1965-67: the conservative turn in American politics. While some college students demonstrated against the war, other joined local chapters of Young Americans for Freedom (YAF), a conservative organization founded in 1960 on the Connecticut estate of William F. Buckley, Jr. The government's only duties, declared YAF's founding manifesto, were to preserve internal order, defend the nation, and administer justice. "[W]hen government ventures beyond these rightful functions," the statement went on, "it accumulates power, which tends to diminish order and liberty." Such a view radically challenged the ideology of FDR's New Deal, Truman's Fair Deal, and Johnson's Great Society. As social unrest increased in the 1960s, more and more Americans moved rightward politically. The conservative tide that would bring Richard Nixon to the White House in 1968 (see Chapter 11) and, still further in the future, propel Ronald Reagan to the presidency in 1980 and even George W. Bush in 2000, had its origins in the social and political turmoil of the 1960s.

As Vietnam and its domestic fallout dominated the news, numerous Americans tried to carry on as usual. Two bestsellers of 1966, amid the major escalation in Vietnam, were steamy sex novels: Jacqueline Susann's *Valley of the Dolls* and

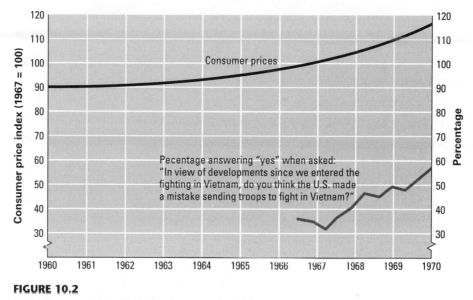

FIGURE 10.2

Inflation and Public Opinion on the Vietnam War, 1960–1970

SOURCE: *Historical Statistics of the United States, Colonial Times to 1970* (1975) and Gallup poll data.

Harold Robbins's *The Adventurers.* Popular movies of the early Vietnam War era included the escapist musical *The Sound of Music* (1965) and the 1930s true-crime tale *Bonnie and Clyde* (1967).

Yet even Americans who hated the protests grew restive as the war dragged on, casualties mounted, and victory seemed ever more remote. The war's economic costs, which soared to $20.6 billion in fiscal 1967, a year that saw the sharpest rise in the defense budget since 1943, worsened the doubts. Despite warnings from his economic advisers, Johnson wanted desperately to provide both "guns and butter"—that is, to finance the war in Vietnam *and* his Great Society programs—without a tax hike. This unwillingness to raise taxes underlay the overly optimistic projections of the war's cost and probable duration. In 1965 Defense Secretary McNamara predicted that hostilities would cease by June 30, 1967—not for any clear military reason but because that date marked the end of the fiscal year. In 1967 a congressional committee estimated that the war's costs in that year alone would exceed the administration's projections by as much as $6 billion. This juggling with figures and dates further undermined the administration's credibility.

Granted, the war fed the 1960s economic boom and stimulated employment. The jobless rate fell steadily in 1963–69, to an eventual low of 3.5 percent. But the conflict also increased federal deficits and fueled inflationary pressures, deepening Americans' uneasiness about the war's economic implications.

At last in August 1967, Johnson proposed a 10 percent surcharge on individual and corporate taxes, which Congress passed the following June. Immediately after the president's tax-increase proposal, with no dramatic worsening in the news from

Vietnam, a plurality of Americans for the first time turned against the war. In August 1967, 46 percent of those polled now viewed the war as a "mistake," with 44 percent still in support. This had ominous implications for Lyndon Johnson. Rising inflation and the threat of higher taxes stirred grave questions about the war even among Americans who did not oppose it on ideological or moral grounds.

Conclusion

Faced with stalemate in Vietnam and an eroding base at home, Johnson in a September 1967 speech modified the U.S. terms for peace talks and, like McNamara earlier, even hinted at a role for the National Liberation Front in ruling South Vietnam. Cautiously, the administration moved toward turning over more of the fighting to South Vietnam, a strategy of "Vietnamization" that President Richard Nixon would implement more fully.

Capitalizing on the shifting mood, a coalition of antiwar groups called a march on Washington for October 16, 1967. About one hundred thousand participants rallied on the Mall. Thirty-five thousand of them, chanting "End the War" and "Hell No, We Won't Go," proceeded to the Pentagon, where they faced a line of armed guards. Soon the flames from burning draft cards flickered in the darkness. Eventually military police cleared the demonstrators. Arresting 660 and clubbing many, they stirred memories of police violence against civil-rights activists. One young college student recalled:

> We were out on the grass, chanting, "Peace now. Peace now." [T]hen all of a sudden . . . people were being hit by soldiers. . . . I remember people falling on me, and I remember seeing blood. It was all kind of chaos. One minute was peaceful and fun, and then all of a sudden they're hitting.

Those arrested included the Jesuit peace activist Daniel Berrigan; pediatrician Benjamin Spock, a veteran of the nuclear-test-ban campaign; and novelist Norman Mailer, who described the march in *The Armies of the Night* (1968).

Johnson dragged Westmoreland home again in November for another round of optimistic speeches. "[Victory] lies within our grasp—the enemy's hopes are bankrupt," the general assured the National Press Club. But LBJ's edginess was apparent. "This is not Johnson's war," he shouted angrily to reporters that fall. "This is America's war."

At the same time, a major battle appeared about to erupt around Khe Sanh, in a remote corner of South Vietnam where the North Vietnamese reportedly had massed forty thousand troops. As Westmoreland urgently reinforced Khe Sanh's marine battalion, Johnson watched anxiously. Was this Dien Bien Phu all over again? Or would Khe Sanh at last provide the decisive victory that could turn the war around? In fact, Khe Sanh was a diversion. As 1968 opened, the enemy would strike not at an isolated outpost but at the very centers of American strength throughout South Vietnam. The Tet Offensive of January 1968 not only proved a pivotal point in the war but also became the overture to the bleakest, most divisive year in postwar American history.

SELECTED READINGS

The War in Vietnam

Christian G. Appy, *Working-Class War: American Combat Soldiers and Vietnam* (1983); William A. Buckingham, Jr., *Operation Ranch Hand: The United States Air Force and Herbicides in South East Asia, 1961–1971* (1982); Larry E. Cable, *Conflict of Myths: The Development of American Counterinsurgency Doctrine and the Vietnam War* (1986); Phillip Davidson, *Vietnam at War* (1991); George C. Herring, *America's Longest War: The United States and Vietnam* (3rd ed., 1996); Tom Holm, *Wounded Souls: Native American Veterans of the Vietnam War* (1996); A.J. Langguth, *Our Vietnam: The War, 1954–1975* (2000); Robert Mann, *A Grand Delusion: America's Descent into Vietnam* (2001); Richard Moser, *The New Winter Soldiers: GI and Veteran Dissent During the Vietnam Era* (1996); J. B. Neilands et al., *Harvest of Death: Chemical Warfare in Vietnam and Cambodia* (1972); James S. Olson and Randy Roberts, *Where the Domino Fell: America and Vietnam, 1945–1990* (2nd ed., 1996); Andrew J. Rotter, ed., *Light at the End of the Tunnel: A Vietnam War Anthology* (1991); Jonathan Schell, *The Village of Ben Suc* (1967) and *The Real War* (1987); Neil Sheehan, *The Bright and Shining Lie: John Paul Vann and America in Vietnam* (1988); Wallace Terry, ed., *Bloods: An Oral History of the Vietnam War by Black Veterans* (1984); James W. Westheider, *Fighting on Two Fronts. African Americans and the Vietnam War* (1997); Marilyn B. Young, *The Vietnam Wars: 1945–1990* (1991); Marilyn B. Young and Robert Buzzanco, eds., *A Companion to the Vietnam War* (2002).

Vietnam: The Strategic Planning Process;
Lyndon Johnson and the War

Loren Baritz, *Backfire: A History of How American Culture Led Us into Vietnam and Made Us Fight the Way We Did* (1985); Larry Berman, *Lyndon Johnson's War: The Road to Stalemate in Vietnam* (1989); Irving Bernstein, *Guns or Butter: The Presidency of Lyndon Johnson* (1996); Kai Bird, *The Color of Truth: McGeorge Bundy and William Bundy, Brothers in Arms* (1998); Anne E. Blair, *Lodge in Vietnam: A Patriot Abroad* (1995); H. W. Brands, *The Wages of Globalism: Lyndon Johnson and the Limits of American Power* (1995); Robert Buzzanco, *Masters of War: Military Dissent and Politics in the Vietnam Era* (1996); Warren I. Cohen and Nancy Bernkopf Tucker, eds., *Lyndon Johnson Confronts the World: American Foreign Policy, 1963–1968* (1994); Robert Dallek, *Flawed Giant: Lyndon Johnson and His Times, 1961–1973* (1998); John Ernst, *Forging a Fateful Alliance: Michigan State University and the Vietnam War* (1998); Lloyd C. Gardner, *Pay Any Price: Lyndon Johnson and the Wars for Vietnam* (1995); George C. Herring, *LBJ and Vietnam: A Different Kind of War* (1994); Michael H. Hunt, *Lyndon Johnson's War: America's Cold War Crusade in Vietnam* (1996); Richard A. Hunt, *Pacification: The American Struggle for Vietnam's Hearts and Minds* (1995); H. R. McMaster, *Dereliction of Duty: Lyndon Johnson, Robert McNamara, the Joint Chiefs of Staff, and the Lies That Led to Vietnam* (1997); Edward P. Metzner, *More Than a Soldier's War: Pacification in Vietnam* (1995); Minnesota Public Radio, *White House Tapes: Eavesdropping on the President* (9-CD set, 2003), Introductory CD and discs 4 and 5 (Lyndon Johnson telephone calls); Edwin Moïse, *Tonkin Gulf and the Escalation of the Vietnam War* (1997); John Prados, ed., *The White House Tapes: Eavesdropping on the President* (2003), pp. 151–213 (print transcriptions of Lyndon Johnson tapes); Jeffrey Record, *The Wrong War: Why We Lost in Vietnam* (1998).

The Domestic Response to the War;
1960s Thought and Culture

Some of the titles already listed cover home-front responses to the war as well. See also John A. Andrew III, *The Other Side of the Sixties: Young Americans for Freedom and the Rise of Conservative Politics* (1997); Peter Braunstein and Michael William Doyle, *Imagine Nation: The American Counterculture of the 1960s and 1970s* (2002); Howard Brick, *Age of Contradiction: American Thought and Culture in the 1960s* (1998); David Burner, *Making Peace with the Sixties* (1996); David Farber, ed., *The Sixties: From Memory to History* (1994); James J. Farrell, *The Spirit of the Sixties: The Making of Postwar Radicalism* (1997); William M. Hammond, *Reporting Vietnam: Media and Military at War* (1998); Maurice Isserman and Michael Kazin, *America Divided: The Civil War of the 1960s* (2000); Rebecca E. Klatch, *A Generation Divided: The New Left, the New Right, and the 1960s* (1999); David W. Levy, *The Debate over Vietnam* (1990); Thomas Powers, *Vietnam, the War at Home: The Antiwar Movement, 1964–1968* (1984); Doug Rossinow, *The Politics of Authenticity: Liberalism, Christianity, and the New Left in America* (1998); Melvin Small, *Covering Dissent: The Media and the Anti- Vietnam War Movement* (1994); Clyde Taylor, ed., *Vietnam and Black America: An Anthology of Protest and Resistance* (1973); Clarence R. Wyatt, *Paper Soldiers: The American Press and the Vietnam War* (1993); Nancy Zaroulis and Gerald Sullivan, *Who Spoke Up? American Protest Against the War in Vietnam, 1963–1975* (1984).

CHAPTER

1968 and the Nixon Years

ON MAY 17, 1968, nine antiwar activists led by two Catholic priests, the brothers Philip and Daniel Berrigan, entered a draft-board office in the Baltimore suburb of Catonsville. As a secretary screamed, "Don't you take my files!" the nine loaded several hundred file folders into baskets, carried them to the parking lot, and set them afire using homemade napalm. Encircling the blazing files, they recited the Lord's Prayer. Alerted beforehand, television crews crowded around. Both Berrigans went to prison for the action, which protested both the Vietnam War and the nuclear arms race. Shortly before his death in 2002, Philip Berrigan wrote: "I die with the conviction, held since 1968 and Catonsville, that nuclear weapons are the scourge of the earth . . . , a curse against God, the human family, and the earth itself."

The Berrigans were part of a rising swell of antiwar protest. After three years of mounting casualties and soaring costs, a majority of Americans finally had turned against "Johnson's War." But for many, this shift did not translate into support for the New Left or the counterculture. On the contrary, continued campus unrest, two shocking assassinations early in 1968, and violence at the Democratic convention that summer accelerated the conservative turn. Richard Nixon's victory that November began an era of Republican dominance of the White House that, with one four-year interlude, would continue until 1993.

Reversing course in Vietnam, Nixon and his national security adviser, Henry Kissinger, pursued negotiations and cut U.S. troop levels; the last U.S. combat units left South Vietnam in 1973. Within two years, the Saigon government collapsed, erasing Washington's twenty-year effort to maintain a noncommunist South Vietnam. Yet even amid peace talks, the war had persisted, and when Nixon expanded the ground war to Cambodia early in 1970, new protests erupted. By that time, however, the New Left and the counterculture were fading, victims of internal divisions and the nation's rightward shift. While withdrawing from Vietnam, Nixon and Kissinger reoriented U.S. foreign policy, crafting a strategy of détente— an easing of tensions—with China and the Soviet Union.

Domestically, Nixon displayed the same opportunism that characterized his foreign policy. In dealing with welfare policy and economic issues, he abandoned long-held Republican positions if it seemed politically expedient to do so. A consummate politician, he focused on building a new Republican majority among worried and angry white voters north and south.

1968: "The Center Cannot Hold"

Throughout the war, the two sides had observed an informal cease-fire during Tet, the Vietnamese New Year. In 1968, however, the National Liberation Front (NLF) and the North Vietnamese chose Tet—January 31—for a coordinated assault on cities, bases, and provincial capitals across South Vietnam. While the siege at Khe Sanh preoccupied the U.S. military command, eighty-four thousand NLF and North Vietnamese troops stealthily maneuvered into position. NLF sympathizers in the cities joined in the attack. In a particularly daring assault, nineteen NLF guerrillas penetrated the U.S. embassy compound in Saigon and held out for six hours before American soldiers finally gunned them down.

The NLF held Vietnam's ancient capital Hué for nearly four weeks, executing in cold blood as many as three thousand officials and others identified with the Saigon regime. U.S. officials pointed to this massacre as proof that a communist victory in South Vietnam would mean a bloodbath. After U.S. bombing and shelling pounded Hué to ruins, marines retook the city on February 25. The Tet Offensive pushed the war's savagery to new heights. Under the CIA's Phoenix Program and the related Provincial Reconnaissance Unit (PRU) program, U.S. and South Vietnamese assassination teams killed some sixty thousand South Vietnamese opponents of the Saigon regime, many of whom had revealed their loyalty to the North during Tet. Thousands more were jailed. The post-Tet phase also produced the worst American atrocity of the war. On March 16, 1968, a U.S. platoon commanded by Second Lieutenant William L. Calley, Jr., entered the village of My Lai in Quang Ngai Province on a search-and-destroy mission. Finding no Vietcong, Calley's men, under pressure to maintain the weekly "body count," systematically shot more than three hundred villagers—women, children, and old men. In the spasm of violence, they raped women, mutilated bodies, slaughtered domestic animals, and burned the village. A U.S. helicopter pilot, Hugh Thompson, saw what was happening, landed, and heroically tried to stop the massacre at the risk of his life. The story broke in 1969 despite official efforts to suppress it. As other veterans and journalists spoke up, an even more chilling realization emerged: My Lai was unique in its scale, but it was far from the only instance of the killing, rape, and torture of civilians.*

Having repelled the invaders and regained precarious control of South Vietnam's cities, U.S. authorities portrayed the Tet Offensive as a victory. The communists had gambled and lost. "The enemy is on the ropes," General Westmoreland crowed. The North Vietnamese, however, simply steeled themselves for more

---

*A military court in 1971 convicted Calley of premeditated murder of South Vietnamese civilians and sentenced him to life imprisonment. In fact, he went free in less than three years. Many felt that in singling out Calley, despite his proved complicity in the massacre, the army had failed to confront the larger pattern of atrocities against civilians in Vietnam.

MAP 11.1
The Tet Offensive

fighting. Whatever its military significance, Tet proved a propaganda disaster for the Johnson administration. Respected TV newsman Walter Cronkite asked, "What's going on here? I thought we were winning." If Tet was an NLF defeat, mused Senator George Aiken of Vermont, what would an NLF victory look like? Support for the war dropped to 41 percent, and Johnson's approval rating sank to 26 percent. Key periodicals, including *Time*, the *New York Times*, and the *Washington Post*, came out against the war.

Compounding Johnson's woes early in 1968, large-scale antiwar protests erupted on more than a hundred U.S. college and university campuses. The movement spread even into high schools, and to Paris and Berlin. Schools canceled classes as students flocked instead to hastily organized teach-ins and gathered in dorm lounges to discuss the war. At one such meeting at the University of Massachusetts, a young woman tearfully asked if her brother's death in Vietnam was meaningless. The question hung in the air, unanswerable.

At Columbia University, black militants and the local SDS joined forces to protest Columbia's ROTC program, campus recruitment by the military and Dow Chemical, and Columbia's plan to tear down some housing in nearby Harlem to build a gymnasium. Two mass sit-ins produced eight hundred arrests. For nearly a week, protesters occupied five campus buildings, including the president's office.

Across the nation, the antiwar speeches became angrier, the attacks on "the Establishment" more sweeping. Some protesters engaged in acts of civil disobedience. More than sixty performers recorded Dylan's antiwar "Blowin' in the Wind." Folksinger Phil Ochs declared in one song:

Call it "peace" or call it "treason,"
Call it "love" or call it "reason,"
But I ain't marchin' anymore.

The two sides eyed each other with deepening mistrust. Hounded by protesters, Johnson traveled only to military bases. The only difference between himself and John Kennedy, he complained, was that his assassination was more drawn out. The FBI stepped up surveillance of antiwar organizations. Paid informants spied on antiwar leaders and organizations, and even on elected officials who opposed the war.

Amid rising domestic discord, the reassessment of the war triggered by Westmoreland's 1967 request for 206,000 more troops proceeded urgently. Westmoreland himself was removed from active command and made army chief of staff. The new secretary of defense, Clark Clifford, the Democratic stalwart who had helped craft Harry Truman's 1948 election strategy, urged Johnson to scale back the war. Even Dean Acheson, at a gloomy meeting of the "Wise Men" in March 1968, counseled ending the conflict.

On the political front, Johnson faced rebellion in the ranks as Senator Eugene McCarthy of Minnesota, a devout Catholic and a poet, launched a campaign for the Democratic presidential nomination on an antiwar platform. Thousands of volunteers quickly responded. The "Dump Johnson" movement even lured student activists back to party politics. In preparation for door-to-door canvassing, young men shaved beards and got haircuts; young women made similar bows to conventionality, to be "neat and clean for Gene."

In the New Hampshire primary on March 12, McCarthy won a stunning 42 percent of the Democratic vote against Johnson, as even disillusioned hawks turned against the war. The New Hampshire outcome set the stage for an even more formidable challenge to Johnson by Robert Kennedy, now a U.S. senator from New York, who threw his hat into the ring on March 16. Remnants of John Kennedy's old team, along with many voters, rallied to the new Kennedy banner.

The third of four sons in a fiercely competitive family, nicknamed "the runt" for his small size, Robert Kennedy had a reputation for ruthlessness dating to his days as an aide of Senator Joseph McCarthy. As attorney general, he had pursued Jimmy Hoffa of the corrupt Teamsters' Union and authorized wiretaps on Martin Luther King, Jr. By 1967–68, however, he showed growing sensitivity to the alienated young and the poor. Lambasting LBJ for unleashing "the darker impulses of the American spirit," Kennedy linked the war to America's home-front crises, pledging "to end the bloodshed in Vietnam and in our cities, . . . to close the gap . . . between black and white, between rich and poor, between young and old, in this country and around the world."

In a televised address on March 31, 1968, as his political base crumbled, LBJ announced a partial bombing halt, called for negotiations, and concluded with the terse announcement: "I shall not seek, and I will not accept, the nomination of my party for another term as your President." He would devote his remaining time in office to the search for peace, he said. Johnson's withdrawal threw the campaign wide open. While McCarthy and Kennedy split the antiwar vote, Vice President Hubert Humphrey joined the race, hoping to rebuild the traditional Democratic coalition of farmers, blacks, Hispanics, union members, and white ethnic voters. Despite private doubts, Humphrey had publicly defended the war.

Alabama governor George Wallace also announced his candidacy on a third-party ticket, the American Independent Party. Having "stood in the schoolhouse door" in 1963 to oppose integration, Wallace appealed to southern and working-class whites resentful of black activists, campus demonstrators, and hippies. In rabble-rousing speeches, he denounced antiwar protesters and "pointy-headed intellectuals." With his running mate Curtis LeMay, a superhawkish former head of the Strategic Air Command, Wallace rose in the polls to 21 percent by September.

The angry mood reflected by the Wallace surge exploded in violence on April 4, 1968, as an assassin gunned down Martin Luther King, Jr., on a Memphis motel balcony. A white ex-convict, James Earl Ray, was convicted of the murder and sentenced to life imprisonment. Rumors circulated that he had hoped to collect a bounty for King's death posted by white supremacists.

In a sermon the night before his death, the thirty-nine-year-old King had mentioned death threats and ended, as he so often did, with a biblical allusion:

> Like anybody, I would like to live a long life. . . . But I'm not concerned about that now. I just want to do God's will. And He's allowed me to go up to the mountain. . . . I've seen the promised land. I may not get there with you. But I want you to know tonight, that we, as a people, will get to the promised land.

An assassin's gun had silenced not only a civil-rights leader but one who since 1965 had opposed the Vietnam War and championed the urban black poor. Despite the failure of his 1966 Chicago campaign, King had continued to stress economic issues. Indeed, he was in Memphis to support a strike by the city's mostly African American garbage collectors.

King's murder unleashed fresh inner-city violence. Rioting and arson in Chicago, Washington, D.C., and other cities left forty-three dead. In Washington, the area between the White House and the Capitol was partially devastated. In Chicago, Mayor Daley issued shoot-to-kill orders against arsonists.

Two months later, another assassination shocked the nation. Robert Kennedy had won the Indiana and Nebraska primaries, but McCarthy had triumphed in Oregon. The California primary on June 5 loomed as the crucial test. Kennedy won, but at a victory party in a Los Angeles hotel he was fatally shot by a Palestinian angered by his pro-Israel stand. Another Kennedy had been cut down, leaving the historians to speculate on what might have been. Against a backdrop of political turmoil and burning cities, the King and Kennedy assassinations sharpened the sense of a society unraveling and hastened the rightward shift of American politics, ending the brief mid-Sixties moment of resurgent liberalism.

At the Democrats' Chicago convention in August, Vice President Humphrey won a first-ballot nomination. In a weirdly inappropriate speech, he buoyantly proclaimed his campaign theme: "the politics of joy." Humphrey boasted a strong liberal record, but he bore the stigma of "Johnson's War." He first drafted a platform plank pledging greater efforts for peace, but when Johnson angrily protested, Humphrey embraced the administration's tougher position, further alienating antiwar Democrats. The New York delegation, filled with Robert Kennedy loyalists, defiantly sang "We Shall Overcome" on the convention floor.

Outside the convention hall, five thousand antiwar activists thronged the streets. Principled protesters mingled with publicity seekers from the counterculture's fringe. Abbie Hoffman and Jerry Rubin, cofounders of a parody political movement, the Youth International (Yippie) Party, presented a pig as their presidential nominee and issued fanciful threats to pour LSD into the city water supply. An unamused Mayor Daley vowed to restore order. On the night of Humphrey's nomination, as protesters jammed North Michigan Boulevard, helmeted Chicago police waded into the

Columbia University, 1968.   As the Vietnam War escalated, so did protests on the nation's campuses, such as this one in front of Columbia's Low Library. But the turbulence dismayed many Americans and gave rise to a powerful conservative backlash. *(Barton Silverman/New York Times Company/Archive Photos)*

throng, clubbing wildly. Many activists, as well as television crews and journalists, suffered beatings, some severe. Tear gas pervaded nearby hotel lobbies. TV images of rampaging police and bloody protesters reinforced fears of a society gone mad. An investigative panel later concluded that although the police were provoked, they had ignored citizens' rights and unleashed a "police riot."

The beneficiary of the chaos was Richard Nixon. Since his defeat in the 1962 California gubernatorial race, Nixon had patiently rebuilt his party credentials at gatherings of Republican faithful across the nation. In 1968 Nixon outmaneuvered several other contenders, including Governor Ronald Reagan of California, to win the nomination. The carefully staged GOP convention in Miami seemed a model of tranquility compared to Chicago.

Capitalizing on the growing antiwar mood, Nixon assured voters that he had a secret peace plan. Amid rising dismay over domestic turmoil, he assured the "forgotten Americans"—the white middle and working classes—that he would toughen law enforcement. "Law and order" became the code for cracking down on protesters and militants. Nixon's running mate, jut-jawed Spiro Agnew, governor of Maryland, echoed this theme. Nixon battled George Wallace for support in the South, where the lily-white Democratic Party had fallen into disarray as the black electorate had grown. Republican TV commercials linked Humphrey with violence and upheaval, and juxtaposed images of war and disorder with Nixon's soothing voice pledging peace and tranquility.*

Considering their initial liabilities, Humphrey and his running mate, Senator Edmund Muskie of Maine, ran strongly. Starting sixteen points behind Nixon in the polls, Humphrey by the end had pulled even. Had the campaign gone on a week longer, some analysts believe, he would have won. In late September Humphrey finally broke with Johnson, calling for a bombing halt and a shift of the fighting from U.S. to South Vietnamese forces.

The breakthrough toward peace that could have helped Humphrey never came. After Johnson's March 31 address, the North Vietnamese had agreed to talks in Paris. The United States was represented by W. Averell Harriman, and Hanoi sent a high official. But President Thieu of South Vietnam boycotted the talks, which quickly deadlocked. North Vietnam demanded a bombing halt; the United States insisted on concessions in return. By October, Hanoi had agreed to stop sending North Vietnamese units south and shelling South Vietnamese cities, and Johnson announced the bombing halt. In the campaign's final weeks, however, to undermine Humphrey's chances, Nixon's campaign manager, John Mitchell, discouraged Thieu from accepting a peace agreement until after the election.[†]

Nixon won six Deep South states and every state west of the Mississippi except Texas and Washington. He lost only eight states of the Upper South, Midwest, and Northeast to Humphrey. (Wallace carried five Deep South states.) The Electoral College tally, however, was the closest since 1916. Had Humphrey carried California

---

*Journalist Joe McGinniss, having won the confidence of top Republican campaign strategists, later produced a devastating account of this media campaign, *The Selling of the President* (1969).
[†]The full story is recounted in Jules Witcover, *The Year the Dream Died: Revisiting 1968 in America* (1997).

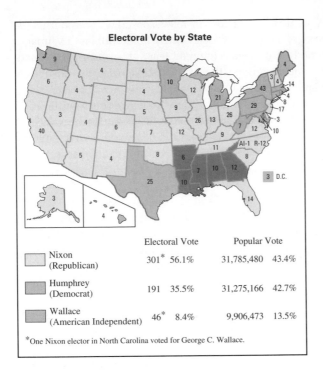

Electoral Vote by State

		Electoral Vote		Popular Vote	
	Nixon (Republican)	301*	56.1%	31,785,480	43.4%
	Humphrey (Democrat)	191	35.5%	31,275,166	42.7%
	Wallace (American Independent)	46*	8.4%	9,906,473	13.5%

*One Nixon elector in North Carolina voted for George C. Wallace.

MAP 11.2
Presidential Election of 1968

instead of narrowly losing it, Nixon would have fallen short of an Electoral College majority, and the House of Representatives would have decided the outcome.

Middle-class resentment of Johnson's antipoverty program contributed to Nixon's win, as did the New Right movement nurtured by conservative ideologues like William F. Buckley and his Young Americans for Freedom. Most important, however, was the Vietnam stalemate and the reaction against urban riots and campus protests.

George Wallace, showing surprising strength in the North, mobilized resentments that would soon drive mainstream politics. Populist politicians had once energized angry voters by railing against the rich and corporate elites. Wallace, by contrast, offered a new set of villains as a focus of working-class hostility: college students, intellectuals, the media, and Washington bureaucrats. The Alabama governor also exploited a growing white backlash against a decade of civil-rights activism and federal programs aimed at the inner-city poor.

As Mary C. Brennan argues in *Turning Right in the Sixties: The Conservative Capture of the GOP* (1995), this rightward thrust was long in preparation. Even in the 1950s, Buckley and other far-right conservatives had found the Eisenhower administration too easygoing toward communism and the welfare state. The conservative shift picked up steam in the 1960s, though often obscured by activism on the Left. With George Wallace at his heels, Richard Nixon successfully mobilized this emerging movement. Taken together, Nixon and Wallace won 57 percent of the votes, confirming the sharp right turn in American politics.

The most decisive loser in 1968 was Lyndon Johnson. His consensus style had served him well in the Senate and in his early years as president, but his preference for compromise over hard choices proved disastrous in Vietnam. His step-by-step escalation of the war never achieved its objectives, and in 1968 he paid the price. Back on his Texas ranch, LBJ let his graying hair grow long, conveying the odd impression of an aging hippie, and spoke wistfully of his Great Society. He died of a heart attack in 1973, at the age of sixty-four.

Nixon's War: Vietnam, 1969–1975

Richard Nixon, fascinated by foreign policy, welcomed the Vietnam dilemma that had proven too much for Johnson. The cabinet could handle domestic affairs; he would concentrate on global issues. Nixon's national security adviser, Henry Kissinger, emphatically agreed. The deep-voiced, owl-eyed Kissinger had lived in the United States since 1938 when his family had fled Nazi Germany. After serving in World War II and working with U.S. occupation forces in Germany, he had earned a B.A. and Ph.D. from Harvard and stayed on to teach government. In *Nuclear Weapons and Foreign Policy* (1957), Kissinger had advocated the deployment of tactical nuclear weapons, in addition to intercontinental ballistic missiles, to advance U.S. strategic interests. A foreign-policy adviser in the 1950s to Nelson Rockefeller, he filled various government positions in the 1960s. Now Nixon brought him to the White House.

The two men, although very different, shared a taste for strategic thinking. Both were secretive, and distrustful even of their own staff. Someone compared Kissinger's aides to mushrooms: "They're kept in the dark, get a lot of manure piled on them, and then get canned." With Kissinger at his side, Nixon functioned as his own secretary of state. The man who actually held that title, Wall Street lawyer William Rogers, had little knowledge of foreign affairs. "No secretary of state is really important," Nixon believed. "The President makes foreign policy."

Vietnam headed Nixon's agenda. The United States had 545,000 troops in that country, and nearly 31,000 Americans had already died there. In practice, Nixon's goal of "peace with honor" meant withdrawing most U.S. ground forces to reduce the casualties that fueled home-front protest, and turning the ground fighting over to U.S.-trained ARVN (Army of the Republic of Vietnam) forces. Through "Vietnamization" of the war, Nixon still hoped to secure a favorable outcome. After assuring President Thieu of Washington's continued support, Nixon in June 1969 announced the withdrawal of 25,000 U.S. troops. By the end of 1971, American troop strength in Vietnam had dropped to 140,000, half of them in noncombat roles.

The ARVN forces still relied on U.S. weapons, vehicles, communications, and air support. Moreover, Nixon escalated the bombing of suspected communist bases in Laos and stepped up both the pacification program and the CIA's Phoenix and PRU programs aimed at assassinating opponents of Thieu's regime. When confronted with proposals to cut these programs for budget reasons, Nixon protested:

"No. We got to have more of this. Assassinations. Killings" (quoted in Mark Moyar, *Phoenix and the Birds of Prey: The CIA's Secret Campaign to Destroy the Viet Cong* [1997], p. 167). In March 1969, amid a major North Vietnamese offensive, Nixon ordered the secret bombing of North Vietnamese bases and supply trails in neighboring Cambodia. By April 1970, B-52s had dumped 110,000 tons of bombs on the tiny country.

Journalists in Vietnam who reported developments accurately continued to be denounced as unpatriotic and dangerous, and often found themselves pressured to toe the line. At a National Security Council meeting in March 1971, when the discussion turned to an Associated Press reporter, Tammy Arbuckle, who had reported on the poor performance and heavy losses of South Vietnamese troops, Nixon burst out to General Al Haig, Kissinger's deputy: "I told you to watch that son of a bitch. . . . The AP has been responsible for most of the bad wire service and, of course, that gets on the TV, too" (quoted in John Prados, *The White House Tapes: Eavesdropping on the President* [2003], p. 234).

When the *New York Times* reported the Cambodian bombing, Kissinger ordered the FBI to wiretap the telephones of a National Security Council aide and other suspected leakers. Soon the wiretaps expanded to journalists and White House aides. The tangle of illegal activities that would drive Nixon from office in 1974 originated in this 1969 effort to conceal the Cambodian air war.

Nixon hoped to pressure Hanoi to accept U.S. terms even as American troop strength declined. As Kissinger commented, "I refuse to believe that a little fourth-rate power like North Vietnam does not have a breaking point." Nixon also intended the bombing to signal Hanoi that he was capable of any level of escalation. As he explained to his aide Robert Haldeman:

> I call it the madman theory, Bob. . . . I want the North Vietnamese to believe I've reached the point where I might do anything to stop the war. We'll just slip the word to them that, "For God sakes, you know Nixon is obsessed about Communists. We can't restrain him when he's angry—and he has his hand on the nuclear button"—and Ho Chi Minh himself will be in Paris in two days begging for peace.

In fact, the Paris cease-fire talks remained stalemated as Nixon continued to back the Thieu regime and insist that Hanoi withdraw its troops from South Vietnam. Hanoi, in turn, demanded full U.S. withdrawal and a government in Saigon that excluded Thieu. Kissinger met secretly with North Vietnamese negotiators in Paris in 1969 and 1970, but to little effect. When Ho Chi Minh died in 1969, Hanoi's new leaders vowed to carry on the struggle.

As the war dragged on, youthful alienation deepened. The counterculture crested in August 1969 when four hundred thousand young people gathered on a farm near Woodstock, New York, for a rain-drenched three-day festival featuring rock music, various hallucinogens, and communal good feeling. For decades after, participants would recall the festival as a defining moment of their youth. Although Woodstock was not an explicitly political event, antiwar and antigovernment themes pervaded the music, most memorably in Jimi Hendrix's sardonic, off-key version of "The Star Spangled Banner."

The organized antiwar movement, dormant since August 1968, also revived. Movement leaders designated October 15, 1969, as Vietnam Moratorium Day. Thousands of protesters rallied in Boston, New York, and other cities and college towns.

Coretta Scott King, carrying on her husband's cause, led a candlelight parade of 30,000 in Washington, D.C. The weekend of November 13–15 saw another mass rally in Washington, the March Against Death. As cold rain whipped the capital, 45,000 participants walked from Arlington National Cemetery to the Capitol, each carrying a placard bearing the name of a soldier killed in Vietnam. They called out the names as they passed the White House and, at the Capitol, deposited the placards in twelve wooden coffins. Several thousand of the more radical marchers descended on the Department of Justice shouting "Smash the state!" After ripping down and burning the U.S. flag, they raised an NLF flag in its place. On Saturday, from 250,000 to 800,000 demonstrators gathered on the Mall to decry the war. Nixon let it be known that he had spent the day watching football on TV. At about the same time, revelation of the My Lai massacre intensified revulsion against the war.

In South Vietnam, meanwhile, continued troop withdrawals eroded the morale of those who remained. Units openly evaded combat; two infantry units flatly refused orders. Among GIs, drug use and racial tension soared. The army reported more than two thousand cases of "fragging"—attacks on officers by their own men—in 1970. A marine colonel warned in the *Armed Forces Journal* in June 1971, "Our army that now remains in Vietnam is in a state approaching collapse, . . . drug-ridden and dispirited where not mutinous."

Still Nixon pressed on. On April 30, 1970, the president announced a joint U.S.–South Vietnamese ground attack on North Vietnamese bases in Cambodia. For Nixon and Kissinger, this operation had a twofold aim: to increase pressure on North Vietnam to settle the war on America's terms, and to support Cambodia's pro-Western ruler, a right-wing military officer who had recently overthrown the neutralist Prince Norodom Sihanouk. Sihanouk had managed to keep the worst of the war's ravages from Cambodia, but after 1970, as a result of U.S. involvement, Cambodia slipped into the maelstrom, with horrendous consequences for its people.

In announcing the Cambodian invasion, Nixon insisted that if his effort failed in Vietnam, the United States would become a "pitiful, helpless giant" respected by no one. Linking his foreign and domestic policies, the president warned of home-front radicals undermining America just as "small nations all over the world find themselves under attack from within and from without."

The Cambodian invasion further energized the antiwar cause. In a largely symbolic action, Congress rescinded the 1964 Gulf of Tonkin Resolution. The angry aftermath of Nixon's speech saw classes canceled at over a third of the nation's colleges and universities, including Kent State University in Ohio, where radicals had recently burned the ROTC building. Ohio's Republican governor, seeking his party's Senate nomination, ordered the Ohio National Guard to Kent State. On May 4, nervous guardsmen in gas masks—newly activated pharmacists, accountants, and salesmen—raked a crowd of students with M-1 rifle fire, killing two young men and two young women and injuring nine others. Apologists later claimed that the students had mortally threatened the troops, but insults and a few rocks hardly justified the murderous fusillade. One guardsman later confessed that he had taken off his glasses to don his gas mask and could see only a blur as he fired into the crowd. Ten days later, responding to campus protests at Jackson State College in Mississippi, state troopers sprayed a dormitory with gunfire, killing two women and wounding nine.

With the protests of May 1970, mass antiwar activism ended. Why did a movement that had roused such passion fade so quickly? The shock of campus killings certainly played a role. More broadly, so did Nixon's Vietnamization strategy and the decline in U.S. casualties. The weekly toll of U.S. combat deaths fell from nearly two hundred in 1969 to thirty-five by early 1971. Further, Congress in March 1969 limited the draft to nineteen-year-olds, to be chosen by lottery. Males twenty and older no longer faced military duty. In January 1972, Congress ended the draft entirely.

Government propaganda also weakened the movement. Nixon sneered at antiwar activists as "bums." Vice President Agnew, exploiting working-class resentment of college protesters, called them an "effete corps of impudent snobs." The FBI spied on SDS and other antiwar (and civil-rights) groups by bugging telephones, stealing mail, paying informants, and planting rumors to discredit the leaders. In October 1968, the FBI warned its field offices of protests planned by "the New Left with its anti-war and anti-draft entourage" and ordered a maximum effort "to destroy this insidious movement."

Nixon, his paranoid streak fed by media attacks, deep class resentments, and the skullduggery that he believed had cost him the presidency in 1960, became obsessed with silencing his critics. To this end, he approved an elaborate—and patently illegal—plan by a White House aide for discrediting antiwar groups and leaders. Although not implemented because it overlapped with the FBI's ongoing program, the plan underscored the White House's siege mentality.

Federal efforts to stifle protest found parallels in state and local action, including the Kent State killings. In May 1969, police fired on six thousand protesters in Berkeley, California, killing one and blinding another. The National Guard, ordered in by Governor Ronald Reagan, occupied Berkeley for over two weeks. As tensions flared again in April 1970, Reagan snapped, "If it takes a bloodbath, let's get it over with."

Through informants, agents provocateur, forged letters, and other means, the FBI also targeted the militant Black Panthers, described in 1968 by J. Edgar Hoover as "the greatest threat to . . . internal security" facing America. In a predawn raid on the headquarters of the Illinois Black Panthers in December 1969, Chicago police shot and killed two of the party's leaders, Fred Hampton and Mark Clark, and wounded four others. A federal court later awarded the survivors, and the families of Hampton and Clark, $1.85 million in damages.

Incited by alarming TV images and the government's inflammatory pronouncements, the public mood turned ugly. In opinion polls, most Americans rated campus unrest as a greater problem than the Vietnam War itself. Fearful of domestic turmoil, most Americans, particularly older citizens, sided with the authorities against "hippies," youthful radicals, and campus protesters. The anger had a class as well as a generational dimension. Working-class Americans resented affluent college students who protested at home while poorer, less well educated youth fought and died in Vietnam.

On May 8, 1970, four days after the Kent State shootings, construction workers at the New York World Trade Center attacked an antiwar march, injuring seventy. A similar demonstration by "hard hats" erupted in St. Louis. Soon after, President Nixon accepted a hard hat at a White House ceremony. On May 20, a hundred thousand

New Yorkers, mostly construction workers and longshoremen, staged a prowar march, waving flags and singing "God Bless America." Nixon's "silent majority" had found its voice, and it was a howl of rage against college youth and other privileged Americans who seemed so dismissive of military service and love of country.

But the movement also fell victim to internal conflicts. As frustration with the war mounted, many activists followed Timothy Leary's advice to drop out. SDS collapsed in 1969 in factional feuding between doctrinaire Maoists organized as the Progressive Labor Party and romantic activists who called themselves the Weathermen.* SDS itself, lamented Todd Gitlin, a leader in the organization's heady early days, "had degenerated into a caricature of everything idealists find alienating about politics-as-usual: cynicism, sloganeering, manipulation."

A few hundred Weathermen went underground to "bring the war home" to America and to foment the revolution they believed was imminent. They sought not U.S. withdrawal from Vietnam but U.S. *defeat* there. An NLF victory, they hoped, would hasten revolution at home and end U.S. imperialism worldwide. They thus embraced Nixon's view of the war: A loss in Vietnam would destroy America's credibility worldwide.

In October 1969, Weathermen organized the "Days of Rage" in Chicago, breaking store windows and battering parked cars. From September 1969 to May 1970, a handful of militants carried out some 250 bombings nationwide, including ROTC headquarters, draft boards, and other symbols of militarism or capitalism. One underground activist, arrested for bombing a Bank of America branch near Santa Barbara, explained, "It was the biggest capitalist thing around." On March 6, 1970, three Weathermen died when a blast rocked the Manhattan townhouse where they were making bombs. One night in August 1970, four radicals at the University of Wisconsin in Madison detonated a massive explosion near a campus building housing the Army Mathematics Research Center, killing a late-working student who was himself an opponent of the war.

On May 1, 1971, thirty thousand hard-core activists arrived in Washington intent on "shutting the government down." As some blocked traffic, others broke windows. A few days earlier, in a symbolic and wholly peaceful action, members of the recently formed Vietnam Veterans Against the War—among them the future U.S. senator John Kerry—had thrown away their medals and campaign ribbons in a ceremony at the Capitol. Yet neither street theater nor ventures in "smashing the state" had much apparent effect on the Nixon White House.

Some underground cells remained active for years. In October 1981, in Nyack, New York, a Weather Underground group murdered a Brinks security guard and two police officers in a botched robbery attempt. One of those convicted and imprisoned, Kathy Boudin, the daughter of a prominent left-wing New York lawyer, served for twenty-two years until her release in 2003, at age sixty.

Unable to stop the war, some activists focused on exposing the decision-making process underlying it. Secretary of Defense McNamara, before leaving office, had instructed his aides to compile from Pentagon files a history of the planning and

---

*The name came from a Bob Dylan line: "You don't need a weatherman to know which way the wind blows." This faction latter became known as the Weather Underground.

Vietnam Veterans Against the War.   Veterans protest the war at the Democratic National Convention in 1972. President Nixon, reelected in 1972, would defuse protests with his policy of "Vietnamization" of the war, which gradually reduced the number of U.S. ground troops in Vietnam. *(George Gardner/The Image Works)*

prosecution of the war. In March 1971, one of these aides, Daniel Ellsberg, having become an antiwar activist, gave the explosive documents to the *New York Times.* Nixon tried to halt publication, but the Supreme Court upheld the *Times*'s claim to First Amendment protection. The so-called *Pentagon Papers* revealed a disturbing pattern of official secrecy and deception.

The publication of the *Pentagon Papers* intensified Nixon and Kissinger's obsession with press leaks. On Nixon's orders, aides Robert Haldeman and John Ehrlichman recruited a team of former FBI and CIA operatives, appropriately code-named the Plumbers, to trace leaks by using wiretaps and other means. In their first extralegal project, the Plumbers broke into the office of Daniel Ellsberg's psychiatrist, seeking evidence that would discredit Ellsberg.

Meanwhile, the Paris peace talks continued. In May 1971, Kissinger offered a U.S. withdrawal after a cease-fire in exchange for the return of prisoners of war and Hanoi's pledge to stop sending troops to South Vietnam. When Hanoi and the NLF (now renamed the Provisional Revolutionary Government, or PRG) made a promising counteroffer, the negotiations took on new life. With South Vietnamese elections due in the fall, Hanoi's chief negotiator Le Duc Tho made the radical proposal that they be honest, confident that Thieu would lose. When Thieu instead rigged the outcome to give himself 94.3 percent of the vote, the Paris talks stalled.

Nixon and Kissinger were simultaneously pursuing improved relations with China and the Soviet Union (see page 307), and they informed both nations that peace in Vietnam would further that goal. Both Moscow and Beijing advised Hanoi to reach a settlement, but to no effect. In March 1972, hoping to deal a decisive blow as U.S. troop strength dwindled, Hanoi resumed full military operations in South Vietnam. As two hundred thousand North Vietnamese and PRG forces attacked, the ARVN troops fell back in panic.

Nixon, fearing a humiliating rout, ordered new bombing around Hanoi and Haiphong and on enemy-held territory in South Vietnam. "The bastards have never been bombed like they're going to be bombed this time," he vowed grimly. Land already pockmarked by years of bombing again endured incessant B-52 raids. In the heaviest air strikes of the war, the United States dropped 112,000 tons of explosives on North Vietnam in June alone. Nixon also approved the mining of Haiphong harbor to disrupt the flow of supplies to North Vietnam, a step the military had long urged.

Americans lulled by three years of Vietnamization suddenly confronted a newly raging war. Now, however, U.S. casualties were low. Of GIs remaining in Vietnam, only six thousand were assigned to combat duty. Although U.S. bombers and weapons remained crucial to the conflict, the protests had faded. As Senator George McGovern of South Dakota observed, when the corpses changed color, American interest diminished.

In October, Hanoi agreed to a cease-fire and accepted Thieu's regime as one of two "administrative entities" in South Vietnam, the other being the PRG. A commission made up of the PRG, the Thieu government, and neutralist elements, the negotiators agreed, would determine South Vietnam's political future. Kissinger, eager for a deal before the U.S. election, initialed a draft agreement on October 22. "Peace is at hand," he promised.

President Thieu denounced the accord, rightly fearing for his future once the Americans withdrew. Nixon himself opposed a settlement that all but abandoned the Saigon regime. Talks resumed, but Le Duc Tho rejected the changes that Thieu demanded in the agreement. Nixon, safely reelected, used the delay to transfer over $1 billion in military hardware to the Saigon government and promised Thieu "swift and severe" retaliation if Hanoi violated the agreement.

On December 18, with the Paris talks stalled, Nixon renewed bombing around Hanoi and Haiphong and further mining of Haiphong harbor. In twelve days of around-the-clock raids, thirty-six thousand tons of bombs fell, more than in the entire 1969–71 period. Amid worldwide denunciations of Nixon's "Christmas bombings," the antiwar movement again stirred to life. However, the Paris talks resumed, and on January 27, 1973, Kissinger and Le Duc Tho initialed a cease-fire accord, essentially the same one agreed to the previous October. Two months later, U.S. military operations ended in South Vietnam. Nineteen years after the 1954 Geneva Accords and eight years after the 1965 escalation, America's longest war had ended, at least in terms of U.S. casualties. During "Nixon's War," 20,553 more Americans had died, together with an estimated 107,000 ARVN forces and more than 500,000 North Vietnamese and PRG troops. The civilian toll ran into the hundreds of thousands. The U.S.-supported Saigon regime would struggle on for two more years (see Chapter 13), but by then most Americans had turned their attention elsewhere.

Vietnam stands as a watershed in postwar American history. Rooted in a Cold War mindset, it exacted a high price in life and resources, divided the populace, battered America's reputation abroad, and raised questions about the nation's world role. For years, Vietnam memories would fuel an aversion to any U.S. military involvement abroad. In 1991, when the first President Bush took the nation into war in the Persian Gulf, he did so in part, he asserted, to help Americans "kick the Vietnam syndrome once and for all."

The war also increased the power of the presidency. In pursuing the conflict, Nixon and Kissinger, like Kennedy and Johnson before them, had vastly enlarged the role of the White House and the National Security Council in implementing foreign policy. In a belated assertion of the legislative branch's constitutional role, Congress in November 1973, over Nixon's veto, passed the War Powers Act. This act requires the president to notify Congress "in every possible instance" before sending troops into combat or into situations where hostilities appear imminent, and to withdraw those troops within sixty days unless Congress approves further deployment. Had this law been in place in 1965, Lyndon Johnson would have found it difficult to escalate the war without broader congressional and public debate. But the basic tension between the executive and legislative branches over committing U.S. forces remained, and debate continued. After the terrorist attacks of September 11, 2001 (see Chapter 16), Congress again passed open-ended legislation under which President George W. Bush pursued a broad "war on terrorism," much as Johnson used the Gulf of Tonkin Resolution as the legal basis for the Vietnam War.

Above all, after Vietnam, Americans could no longer unquestioningly accept long-held certitudes about the nation's benign world role. Stanley Hoffmann, professor of government at Harvard, focusing particularly on the role of Nixon and Kissinger, would write in 1979: "At the root of this tree of evils one finds an extraordinary arrogance . . . , a self-intoxicating confidence in our capacity to manipulate other societies."

As Americans learned more about the war's human cost, the secretive means by which it was foisted on the nation, the dubious assumptions underlying it, and the shameful acts committed by some U.S. troops, the doubts deepened. A. J. Langguth, chief of the *New York Times*'s Saigon bureau during the war, reached a harsh judgment in his history of the conflict, *Our Vietnam: The War, 1954–1975* (2000): "American leaders, for thirty years, failed the people of the North, the people of the South, and the people of the United States."

Graham Greene's 1955 novel *The Quiet American*, though written years before full-scale U.S. involvement in Vietnam, would later seem prophetic in its portrayal of a naïve young CIA agent in Saigon who seeks to do good but ends by doing great harm. In 2002, a *Denver Post* film critic wrote of a newly released movie version of *The Quiet American*: "[T]here's an element of heartbreak to watching it now, . . . because we know what will happen after Greene's story ends."

As Shakespeare's Horatio comments at the end of *Hamlet*, written more than 360 years before the Vietnam War:

> [L]et me speak to th' yet unknowing world
> How these things came about. So shall you hear
> Of carnal, bloody, and unnatural acts,
> Of accidental judgments, casual slaughters,
> Of deaths put on by cunning and forc'd cause,
> And in this upshot, purposes mistook
> Fall'n on the inventors' heads. . . .

Realpolitik and Détente

For Nixon and Kissinger, extricating the United States from Vietnam constituted only one move in the chess game of global politics. Their overall goal, détente with the Soviet Union and China, served many functions. As we have seen, Nixon and Kissinger used the lure of improved relations to persuade Beijing and Moscow to pressure Hanoi to reach a settlement in Vietnam. And Nixon the politician realized that easing Cold War hostilities could raise his stock with moderates and liberals in the 1972 election.

At first glance, Nixon seems miscast in the role of either strategist or advocate of détente. He had made his reputation in the early Cold War as a strident anticommunist. But his thought had evolved. Shrewd, opportunistic, and highly intelligent, he adapted quickly to changed political realities, becoming more pragmatic and less ideologically rigid. His 1967 article in *Foreign Affairs*, "Asia After Viet Nam," had won notice for its strategic analysis and its early recognition that the Vietnam War might well reduce Americans' tolerance for acting as "world policeman." With Soviet nuclear parity and China's nuclear tests, he had further noted, the world power balance was shifting. Nixon remained wary of both nations, but he had concluded that normalizing relations with them would serve U.S. interests. As he mused to journalist Garry Wills in 1968, in coming years "a man who knows the world will be able to forge a whole new set of alliances."

Henry Kissinger—national security adviser and, after 1973, secretary of state—held an even more explicit realpolitik view in which power calculations, not moral judgments, shaped foreign policy. On occasion Kissinger quoted Goethe: "If I had to choose between justice and disorder, on the one hand, and injustice and order on the other, I would always choose the latter." His first book had analyzed the conservative statesmen who had reconfigured Europe after the Napoleonic wars. Kissinger shared Nixon's view that America must outgrow Cold War slogans and rethink international relations. Above all, the two men saw a historic opportunity to advance U.S. interests by exploiting the Sino-Soviet split.

Both men realized that the United States no longer dominated the world as it did after World War II. Not only were the Soviet Union and China nuclear powers, but Western Europe, too, had become a key player. On the economic front, Germany and Japan were emerging as major trading competitors. In 1971, for the first time since 1894, U.S. imports exceeded exports. For Nixon and Kissinger, strengthening America's world economic standing was crucial. In a 1971 speech, Nixon presciently declared, "Economic power will be the key to other kinds of power . . . in the last third of this century."

Nixon's quest for détente focused first on China. Ever since the Chinese communists' victory in 1949, the United States had treated this vast nation as a pariah. Clinging to the fiction that Jiang Jieshi's Taiwan regime was China's true government, Washington had refused to deal with Beijing and thwarted its efforts to join the UN. Now Nixon and Kissinger saw advantages in better relations with China. "Playing the China card," for example, might help extract concessions from the Soviet Union on arms control and other issues. The Chinese, eyeing the Soviet troops

IN PERSPECTIVE

The Nuclear Threat

The 1972 SALT I and ABM treaties brought a ray of hope to the long effort to restrain the nuclear arms race. At every stage from 1945 through the 1980s, powerful forces either propelled this effort forward or, more often, dragged it down. These forces included Cold War suspicions, periodic upsurges of popular nuclear fear, and advances in the technology of destruction.

Nothing thwarted nuclear arms control more than the harsh realities of the Cold War. U.S.-Soviet hostility repeatedly sabotaged efforts to regulate missile competition. The Limited Nuclear Test Ban Treaty of 1963 did not include underground tests because the mutually suspicious superpowers could not agree on verification procedures.

Grassroots fear of atomic war also influenced arms-control efforts, often in unexpected ways. As one example, after Hiroshima and Nagasaki, frightened U.S. scientists used terrifying descriptions of the bomb's effects to urge public demand for international control of atomic energy. In the long run, however, their campaign roused support not for disarmament but for keeping ahead of the Russians in nuclear competition. In the late fifties and early sixties, fear of radioactive fallout from nuclear tests led to strong popular support for a test-ban treaty. This grassroots movement helped to produce the 1963 ban on atmospheric tests. Nevertheless, with protests focused on fallout rather than on the larger nuclear threat, the activist momentum faded after 1963, even though the nuclear arms race continued unabated.

The ambiguous effects of nuclear fear and of antinuclear protest again became evident in 1981–83, when a campaign to freeze the nuclear arms race won broad backing. As in 1946, activists won recruits with graphic descriptions of thermonuclear annihilation. President Reagan, however, exploited the campaign for his own purposes. In a March 1983 TV address, Reagan professed his horror of nuclear war, but rather than suggest a freeze, he proposed a missile-defense system. As Americans debated Reagan's Strategic Defense Initiative (SDI), the freeze movement expired.

Technological advances complicated arms control as well. Moscow's testing of an atomic bomb in 1949, for example, led President Truman to launch a race for the hydrogen bomb—a race that physicist Edward Teller assured him the United States could win. The Soviets quickly developed their own H-bomb, upping the nuclear ante still higher. Another breakthrough that frustrated arms-control efforts came in the 1970s, when U.S.

technicians developed missiles that could carry multiple, independently targeted nuclear warheads or "reentry vehicles" (MIRVs). Although SALT I limited the number of *missiles,* it did not restrict the number of *warheads* that each missile could carry. Thus, thanks to MIRVing, the nuclear arms race roared on despite the 1972 accord.

With the Cold War's end, the superpowers' nuclear competition faded at last. In 1992 Washington and Moscow agreed upon a treaty imposing deep cuts in strategic missiles. In 1993, after soaking up $30 billion, the SDI program was put on the back burner. But a witches' brew of nuclear danger still simmered. The issue of safely stor-ing tons of radioactive waste from missiles and nuclear-power plants posed problems of enormous complexity, both technologically and politically. Moreover, dismantling the former Soviet Union's nuclear arsenal proved a tricky business. Newly independent Ukraine, for example, resisted giving up the missiles on its soil, not out of any inten-tion to use them but because of their value as economic bargaining chips.

Despite the easing of superpower tension, the threat of proliferation persisted, a part of the nuclear dilemma from the beginning. The 1968 Nuclear Nonproliferation Treaty (NPT), signed by 153 states, had failed to halt the spread of nuclear weapons. As Iraq, North Korea, and other nations ruled by authoritarian regimes pursued weapons research, the specter of nuclear terrorism stalked humanity. In 1993 North Korea withdrew from the NPT. India conducted five nuclear weapons tests in 1998. Pakistan responded with its own nuclear tests In 2002, raising the nightmarish threat of a nuclear exchange between two nations embroiled in a bitter border dispute.

Fear of nuclear proliferation intensified after the terrorist attacks of September 11, 2001, worsened by anxieties about chemical and biological weapons as well. Aban-doning the 1972 ABM Treaty, President George W. Bush pushed deployment of a missile-defense system in Alaska. This system was directed against North Korea, which continued to pursue nuclear-weapons research. The Bush administration also explored diplomatic efforts to persuade North Korea to halt its nuclear weapons program and supported UN efforts to monitor Iran's nuclear program. The Bush administration justi-fied its 2003 War in Iraq (see Chapter 16) in part on the grounds that Iraq was devel-oping weapons of mass destruction, including nuclear weapons. Although these claims later proved false, the larger risk of nuclear proliferation in an unstable world re-mained very real.

One group still haunted by the nuclear threat was the Americans exposed to radi-ation from weapons testing. In 1988 Congress permitted veterans who had served as human guinea pigs in nuclear tests to file service-related disability claims if they devel-oped one of thirteen types of cancer. In 1989, former civilian employees at the Nevada test site sued the U.S. government for failing to adopt adequate safety procedures. Many citizens exposed to windborne fallout in eastern Nevada and southern Utah lived in fear of developing cancer. In *American Ground Zero: The Secret Nuclear War* (1993), photojournalist Carole Gallagher offered a gripping memoir of this bitter legacy. Ironically, the most devastating effects of a program designed to protect American had been wrought on the American people themselves. Post–Cold War revelations made clear that Soviet testing, too, had exposed thousands of troops and civilians to highly dangerous radiation levels.

More than thirty years after SALT I, in short, the nuclear menace lives on. Americans who had hailed the atomic bomb in 1945 could scarcely have guessed what lay ahead.

massed along their border, discreetly welcomed closer ties with the United States, despite the two nations' contrasting ideologies.

Nixon signaled the shift in 1970 by speaking of "the People's Republic of China" rather than the usual "Red China" and by expressing curiosity about the distant land that no U.S. president had ever visited while in office.* Beijing responded by inviting a touring U.S. table tennis team to visit China. Practicing "Ping-Pong diplomacy," the Chinese players—the world's best—politely lost to the visitors or took care not to beat them too badly. In June 1971, Henry Kissinger secretly flew to Beijing to meet with Chinese leaders.

This laid the groundwork for Nixon's historic February 1972 trip to China. At the airport, the president shook hands with Premier Zhou Enlai, erasing John Foster Dulles's insulting refusal to greet Zhou at the 1954 Geneva Conference. Nixon drank toasts with Zhou and Mao Zedong as an orchestra played "America the Beautiful." At the Great Wall of China, he enthused, "This truly is a great wall." He attended a ballet choreographed by Mao's actress wife, who confided that her favorite movie was *Gone with the Wind*. The visit ended with a joint call for further contacts. Full diplomatic recognition came only in 1979, but Nixon laid the groundwork.

As for the Soviet Union, Nixon and Kissinger still embraced containment doctrine, and they maneuvered in many parts of the world to check Moscow's influence. But they viewed Russia simply as a major player in the global power game, not as an outlaw state. The Soviets—facing China on the east and NATO plus a restive group of satellites to the west, spending vast sums on armaments, and grappling with weak agricultural output and other economic problems—welcomed Washington's overtures. In 1971, at Nixon's initiative, the two nations, with the other World War II allies, signed an agreement guaranteeing Western access to Berlin in return for West Germany's pledge not to absorb the city into the Federal Republic. The issue that had sparked so many Cold War crises was thus neutralized.

Hard bargaining with the Kremlin led to another historic Nixon visit. In May 1972, fresh from Beijing, Nixon's entourage arrived in Moscow. Vietnam raised problems, but Nixon told the Soviet leaders, "There must be room in this world for two great nations with different systems to live together and work together."

Improved trade relations remained a prime goal of détente, and in Moscow Nixon completed a deal whereby the Soviets agreed to buy $750 million in American wheat, easing the U.S. trade deficit and earning Nixon points in the farm belt. Yet missiles, not wheat, dominated Nixon's Moscow agenda. The arms-control process had stalled after the 1963 test-ban treaty, as the two nations' nuclear arsenals had vastly increased. In 1969, however, U.S.-Soviet talks had begun in Geneva on a strategic arms limitation treaty, known by the acronym SALT I. Nixon and Kissinger secretly completed the SALT negotiations with Soviet ambassador Anatoly Dobrynin in Washington. (Typically, they concealed the meetings from both the Geneva negotiators and the State Department.) The treaty, signed by Nixon and Soviet leader Leonid Brezhnev in Moscow in 1972, froze each side's missile arsenals for five years. However, SALT I failed to address the latest technological advance: MIRVs, or multiple, independently targeted reentry vehicles. Through MIRVing,

---

*Former president Ulysses S. Grant had stopped in China on a world tour in 1879.

up to fourteen separately targeted warheads could be mounted on a single missile. MIRVs were highly destabilizing, for they increased the odds that a nuclear first strike could destroy all or most of the enemy's retaliatory missiles.

More important was the Anti-Ballistic Missile (ABM) Treaty, also signed in Moscow. Nuclear strategists had long insisted that fear of a decisive counterattack was the best deterrent to a nuclear first strike. But deterrence could work only if neither side possessed a defense against nuclear weapons. If one nation successfully deployed a full missile-defense system, that nation theoretically would be free to launch a nuclear attack, or try nuclear blackmail, without fear of reprisal. Such calculations underlay the ABM Treaty, by which both sides pledged not to develop nationwide missile-defense systems. Arms-control talks continued, as a key byproduct of Nixon's opening to the Soviet Union.

Nixon and Kissinger also addressed tensions in the volatile Middle East. As Israel's patron, Washington supplied the military and economic aid that ensured the Jewish state's survival. Yet Americans depended on oil from the Arab states. Complicating the picture, the Middle East had become a Cold War arena, where the United States and the Soviet Union vied for allies. In the Six-Day War of 1967, Israel had defeated its Arab foes and occupied the Golan Heights on its northern border with Syria, the Egyptian held Sinai peninsula and Gaza Strip, and the West Bank of the Jordan River and Jerusalem's historic Old City, hitherto controlled by Jordan. In October 1973, backed by Soviet arms, Egypt and Syria launched a war against Israel to redress their grievances. The attack came on Yom Kippur, the holiest day of the Jewish year. Israel, aided by an airlift of U.S. arms, fought off the attackers and pursued Egyptian troops across the Sinai. The war strained détente, as Brezhnev threatened to send troops to Egypt and the Pentagon went to a high level of nuclear alert. To halt Israel's counterattack, the United States withheld military supplies.

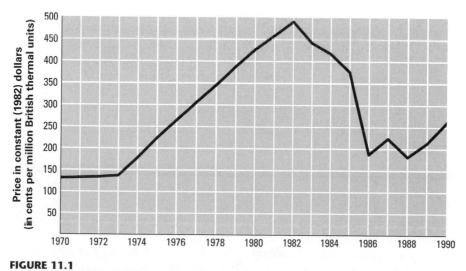

FIGURE 11.1

Crude Oil Prices, 1970–1990

SOURCE: U.S. Energy Information Administration, *Annual Energy Review.*

The Yom Kippur War illustrated the links between foreign policy and the domestic economy. Angered by U.S. support for Israel, the Arab states halted oil shipments to the United States from October 1973 to March 1974. Although the United States imported only 12 percent of its oil from the region, gasoline prices jumped from forty cents to a shocking fifty-five cents a gallon. Stock prices plummeted as inflation rose and the boycott's effects bit in. Hitting all sectors of the economy, the oil crisis contributed in 1974–75 to the worst recession since the 1930s.

The oil embargo focused attention on longer-term problems, including rising energy costs. Since OPEC's founding in 1960, oil prices had quadrupled. This increase was justified, the oil-producing nations insisted, because their oil reserves were finite, and inflation forced them to pay higher prices for imported manufactured goods. The crisis also underscored America's disproportionate consumption of the world's natural resources. Home to only 6 percent of the population, the United States gobbled 40 percent of the earth's resources.

For both strategic and economic reasons, Nixon and Kissinger concluded that the United States must mend fences with the Arabs. During two years of "shuttle diplomacy" on a plane dubbed the "yo-yo express" because it took off and landed so often, Kissinger jetted to Middle East capitals negotiating disputes, currying favor, and countering Soviet moves. Although the region's underlying animosities remained, Kissinger did make progress. In November 1973, he negotiated a cease-fire between Israel and Egypt and persuaded Israel to withdraw from Egyptian and Syrian land seized in the 1973 war. In return, the Arabs' oil boycott ended and Egypt's president, Anwar el-Sadat, having broken with the Soviets, warmed to the United States.

Oriented toward power, the Nixon-Kissinger team readily supported authoritarian and even dictatorial regimes that served U.S. strategic or economic interests. The administration gave military assistance and foreign aid to the autocratic shah of Iran; the corrupt Ferdinand Marcos of the Philippines; South Africa's white-supremacist government; and repressive regimes and military dictatorships in Argentina, South Korea, Brazil, Nigeria, and other nations. This approach allied the United States with rulers hated by many of their own people. When these despots fell, as they invariably did, the United States was reviled as well, making it difficult for Washington to build good relations with the new governments.

The administration's realpolitik manifested itself most brutally in Chile. In a 1970 presidential election, the Chileans gave Marxist Salvador Allende a plurality. The Nixon administration feared that Allende would jeopardize the Chilean investments of U.S. corporations such as International Telephone and Telegraph (ITT). Kissinger and Nixon also saw Allende as a potential Castro who would ally with Moscow. As Kissinger said, "I don't see why we need to stand by and watch a country go communist due to the irresponsibility of its own people." At Nixon's instructions, the CIA plotted a military coup to prevent Allende from taking office. When this failed, Nixon secretly channeled $10 million to the CIA to disrupt Allende's government and undermine the Chilean economy. He also cut off aid and pressured international monetary agencies to deny Chile development loans.

When Allende tried to break up Chile's large landholdings and nationalized nearly $1 billion in U.S. corporate investments, the campaign against him grew more urgent. In September 1973, a military junta seized power and killed Allende. Nixon recognized the new regime, and U.S. economic relations with Chile resumed. The CIA's role in the coup remains murky, but the administration clearly helped create the conditions that led to it. When Chile's new rulers resorted to such brutalities that even the U.S. ambassador protested, Kissinger snapped icily, "Cut out the political science lecture."

Richard Nixon and Henry Kissinger reshaped the conceptual foundations of postwar U.S. foreign policy.* In the 1950s and 1960s, the architects of U.S. diplomacy with their bipolar worldview had substituted crisis management and ideological formulas for strategic analysis. Nixon and Kissinger, by contrast, envisioned a multipolar world in which power arose not only from military might but also from economic and geopolitical realities. The emphasis on economic factors would prove especially important in laying the groundwork for the post–Cold War diplomacy of the 1990s.

Downplaying ideology, both men saw self-interest and long-term strategic calculations as the key to nations' behavior, and they molded U.S. policy accordingly. The important thing for them, as historian John Lewis Gaddis writes, was "the overall calculus of power . . . , not . . . defeats or victories . . . in isolated theaters of competition." Concentrating on areas they believed vital to U.S. interests, they disengaged from Vietnam, which Kissinger dismissed as "a small peninsula on a major continent." Instead, they pursued détente with China and Russia and cultivated better relations in the Middle East. Their strategy echoed the realist approach to foreign policy enunciated by George Kennan in the late 1940s. Downgrading ideology, Kennan, too, had stressed national interest. When Kissinger became secretary of state, Kennan observed, "Henry understands my views better than anyone at State ever has."

Nixon and Kissinger also responded to important long-term trends, notably the Sino-Soviet split, the nuclear balance of power, and problems plaguing the Soviet and U.S. economies. Tensions marked the partnership of this odd couple, once described by Nixon as "the grocer's son from Whittier and the refugee from Hitler's Germany, the politician and the academic." Yet with their shared worldviews, objectives, and secretive ways, they left their stamp on American diplomacy.

The duo had detractors. Cold Warriors such as Ronald Reagan criticized them for pursuing better relations with Moscow and Beijing and for supposedly weakening America's defenses through the SALT treaty and cuts in military spending.[†] Some liberal Democrats deplored the amorality and unconcern for human rights of their single-minded concentration on national interest and balance-of-power diplomacy. Unquestionably, their foreign policy had its brutal side, as the campaign against Allende revealed.

Nevertheless, détente with China and the Soviet Union represents Nixon's landmark achievement. The Cold War continued, but at a less dangerous level. And a veteran Cold Warrior accomplished this turnaround. As historian Stephen

---

*Although Nixon's role ended with his resignation in August 1974, Kissinger remained secretary of state until January 1977.

[†]Although advocates of U.S. strategic superiority favored plowing the savings gained through withdrawal from Vietnam back into other areas of military spending, U.S. outlays for defense declined at a steady annual rate of 4.5 percent from 1970 to 1975. Defense Secretary Melvin Laird, who presided over this cutback, became a target of conservative attack.

Ambrose observes, Nixon's key asset was that he did not have to contend with Nixon: "Had anyone but Nixon tried to promote détente, Nixon . . . would have rallied the right wing to kill it." As Nixon himself told the Chinese, "In America . . . those on the right can do what those on the left can only talk about."

In pursuing their grand strategy, Nixon and Kissinger centralized policymaking and resorted to secrecy and deception. Both looked askance at popular movements, such as the antiwar protests, that sought to influence foreign policy. Diplomacy, they believed, should be left to the experts (another link with the elitist Kennan). Both bypassed the State Department and used back channels to deal with foreign leaders. "Without secrecy," Nixon insisted, "there would have been no opening to China, no SALT agreement with the Soviet Union, and no peace treaty ending the Vietnam War." But the deviousness also fostered a climate of intrigue that ultimately would drag Nixon down.

Kissinger's reputation, too, fell after he left office. He had no role in the new Republican ascendancy that began in 1981, and his reputation for toadying to the powerful, his arrogance toward subordinates, and his contempt for the foreign-policy bureaucracy all cost him dearly. His self-serving memoirs did little to salvage his image, and Walter Isaacson's massive *Kissinger: A Biography* (1992) denigrated him with grim single-mindedness. But the reaction was as extreme as the earlier adulation, when cartoonists had portrayed him as a cape-wielding "Super-K." For all his flaws and the cold-blooded amorality of his worldview, Kissinger remains a towering figure. Emulating his heroes, the conservative statesmen of an earlier day, he set out to impose intellectual coherence on a foreign policy that had often substituted rhetoric and bluster for broad-gauge thinking. To a great extent he succeeded— although in history's ever-shifting terrain, success is often written in the sand.

Domestic Policy: New Departures, Conservative Affirmations

With his taste for foreign affairs, Nixon would have preferred to turn over domestic issues to his cabinet, but in the modern world, the two are inseparable. As Lyndon Johnson had learned, and as the 1973–74 Arab oil embargo underscored, events abroad resonated at home. Furthermore, Nixon's approaches to foreign affairs and domestic issues were remarkably similar. At home, too, he proved unexpectedly open to innovation. The same opportunism and even cynicism that led the one-time anticommunist zealot to Beijing and Moscow also gave him a nondogmatic adaptability on domestic issues. The fact that he had won only 43 percent of the vote in 1968 and faced Democratic majorities in both houses of Congress no doubt encouraged this flexibility.

Early in his term, Nixon adopted moderately progressive positions, adhering to Eisenhower's strategy of accepting reforms—the New Deal, the Fair Deal, and now the Great Society—while cutting costs and curbing their "excesses." He signed Democratic bills raising social security benefits, increased federal funds for low-income public housing, and even expanded the Job Corps. His first term saw increases in spending on mandated social-welfare programs, especially social security, Medicare, and Medicaid. Far from bucking this trend, Nixon in a 1971 TV interview sketched a vision of post-Vietnam America reminiscent of Lyndon John-son at his most expansive:

> If we can get this country thinking not of how to fight a war, but . . . of clean air, clean water, open spaces, of a welfare reform program that will provide a floor under the income of every family with children in America, . . . reform of educa-tion, reform of health . . . , then we will have the lift of a driving dream.

Nixon's most surprising departure from Republican orthodoxy came with his 1969 proposal to provide every U.S. family a guaranteed minimum income. The initial annual minimum, $1,600 for a family of four, represented about $11,500 in today's buying power. (Food stamps would have increased the total.) This so-called Family Assistance Plan (FAP) was the brainchild of Daniel Patrick Moynihan, head of Nixon's newly created Urban Affairs Council. Although a Kennedy Democrat, Moynihan had ideas that appealed to Nixon. Moynihan proposed to replace the nation's cumbersome welfare system, widely criticized for perpetuating a culture of dependence, with cash payments to bring society's poorest members up to an agreed-upon minimum without reducing their incentive to better themselves by working. As Moynihan put it in a TV interview: "The problem of the poor people is they don't have enough money. . . . Cold cash! It's a surprisingly good cure for a lot of social ills." Whereas Johnson's Great Society envisioned an array of federal programs to battle poverty, the FAP approach bypassed the welfare bureaucracy in favor of funneling money directly to the poor.

Winning approval in the House, the FAP failed in the Senate. Conservatives denounced it as socialistic, and liberals balked at the low payments. Although un-successful, the scheme reveals Nixon's capacity for innovation, and it anticipated an issue—welfare reform—that would gain momentum in the 1990s. Many leftists normally critical of Nixon cheered the FAP. Michael Harrington, the socialist whose *The Other America* had highlighted the problem of poverty in 1962, called it "the most radical idea since the New Deal."

Nixon's flexibility also emerged in his evolving response to the nation's eco-nomic problems. Johnson's effort to finance both the Vietnam War and domestic social programs without raising taxes had worsened inflation and the federal deficit. In response, the Democratic-led Congress in 1970 passed the Economic Sta-bilization Act, authorizing the president to freeze wages and prices. But Nixon in-sisted he would never use these powers; as a young lawyer in the World War II Office of Price Administration, he had developed a strong aversion to federal regu-lation of the economy.

Instead, Nixon tried to curb inflation by cutting government spending and prodding the Federal Reserve Board to tighten credit. This approach not only failed to halt inflation but also contributed to a business downturn. With produc-tion falling, the stock market weakening, and the jobless rate rising, the nation edged into recession. The economic fallout of Vietnamization—canceled defense contracts and returning veterans seeking jobs—worsened the problem. Boeing, the Seattle aircraft giant, slashed its work force from 101,000 to 44,000. As the economy sputtered, the Democrats gleefully attacked "Nixonomics" and widened their already formidable House majority by twelve seats in the 1970 midterm election.

In 1971, inflation continued, unemployment rose to 6 percent, the federal deficit exceeded $23 billion, and, as we have seen, America faced its first trade deficit in living memory. On the world's money markets, the dollar fell to its lowest point since 1949. In 1969 Americans had named Vietnam as the nation's most pressing problem; in 1971, economic worries topped the list.

In August 1971, after mulling over his party's losses in the 1970 midterm election, Nixon again demonstrated his pragmatic side. Abruptly reversing course, he announced a program of federal economic intervention such as he had rejected only months earlier. To combat inflation, the president slapped a ninety-day freeze on prices, wages, and rents. In November, he capped annual wage increases at 5.5 percent and price and rent increases at 2.5 percent. While urging voluntary compliance, Nixon nevertheless set up the Cost of Living Council empowered to enforce these restraints. As an economic stimulus, he proposed a 10 percent tax credit for corporate investment and other pump-priming steps.

To address the weak dollar and the trade deficit, Nixon imposed a 10 percent surcharge on imports. He also suspended the convertibility of the dollar into gold at the official price of $35 per ounce—an artificially high valuation that hurt America's export business. The dollar would now "float," finding its own value in the world currency market. As the dollar became cheaper in relation to other currencies, Nixon hoped, U.S. products would attract more foreign buyers.

Embracing Keynesian economics, with its advocacy of deficit spending as an economic stimulus, Nixon offered a "full employment" budget for 1972 that projected an $11.6 billion deficit. Fiscal conservatives protested, but the president responded in Rooseveltian terms that as long as U.S. workers lacked jobs, deficits were justified. Like most presidents, Nixon had shaped his economic program with one eye on the opinion polls and the election cycle. The whole story is well told in Allen J. Matusow's *Nixon's Economy: Booms, Busts, Dollars, and Votes* (1998).

By imposing wage-and-price controls and embracing deficit spending as a stimulus strategy, measures once anathema to Republicans, Nixon tacitly acknowledged the federal government's obligation to foster prosperity. This idea, a legacy of the New Deal and the Employment Act of 1946, had become entrenched in the nation's polity, no matter which party held power.

At first, the medicine seemed to help. Inflation slowed, and the trade gap narrowed. The stock exchange broke 1,000 for the first time late in 1971, a big psychological lift. But government welfare and health-care expenditures; rising imports, especially of fuel-efficient Japanese cars; and soaring gasoline and fuel costs caused by the Arab oil boycott all slowed recovery. The roller-coaster stock market dipped below 800 by late 1973; the trade deficit widened; and inflation spiraled upward, hitting 11 percent in 1974. Unemployment reached 8.5 percent by 1975.

The overall economic prospect looked bleak in the mid-seventies. In constant dollars, median family income, having risen steadily since World War II, stagnated between 1970 and 1975. The rate of increase of U.S. productivity, which averaged 3 percent annually from 1947 to 1965, fell to an anemic 1.4 percent in 1971–75. After three decades of rising productivity and economic expansion, Americans sensed that this downturn involved more than the usual pattern of a brief recession followed by a strong rebound. Severe structural problems had emerged. As the United States faced rising energy costs, growing trade competition from abroad, and a painful transition from a manufacturing-based economy to one driven by an expanding service sector, computerization, and new information technologies, economic worries further darkened the mood of a nation already rattled by domestic discord and a controversial war.

In his role as party leader, Nixon continued to woo the middle-class and blue-collar white vote so crucial to his 1968 victory. As Kevin Phillips explained in *The Emerging Republican Majority* (1969), Republican electoral success depended on reaching out to Democrats who had once revered Franklin Roosevelt but who had become alienated by antiwar demonstrations, urban riots, and proliferating government social programs for the poor and minorities. Political parties succeed, Phillips claimed, by understanding "who hates whom" and then exploiting those hatreds. In this spirit, Nixon courted disaffected voting blocs as the New Deal coalition splintered.

To this end, the president balanced heretical economic proposals such as FAP and deficit spending with more predictably conservative stands. He vetoed more than twenty spending bills passed by the Democratic Congress. In 1971, he refused to sign a bill providing daycare centers for working mothers. Such "communal approaches" to child rearing, he charged, would "sovietize" America's children. "Good public policy," he lectured, "requires that we enhance rather than diminish . . . parental involvement with children."

The president also exploited the middle-class reaction against Johnson's Great Society by calling for a less activist federal government. His 1972 budget proposed an annual rebate of $5 billion to the states, to be financed through cuts in federal social programs. Trolling for suburban votes, he predicted that with these rebates property taxes would fall by 30 percent.

In October 1972, two weeks before the election, Congress passed Nixon's revenue-sharing bill, distributing more than $30 billion in federal revenues over a five-year period to state, county, and local governments. At the same time, Congress capped federal welfare spending at $2.5 billion annually, expecting the states to pick up the slack. But big cities, grappling with poverty, crime, and a declining tax base, complained that state legislatures used the federal windfall to cover their own budget shortages and neglected urban needs.

Nixon's courting of the "hard hats" who attacked antiwar marchers reflected a calculated strategy to attract voters disturbed by campus unrest and street protests. In 1969, the Justice Department prosecuted eight antiwar activists and counterculture celebrities on charges arising from the demonstrations at the 1968 Democratic convention. This, too, served Nixon's purposes. The trial of the "Chicago Eight," before short-tempered judge Julius Hoffman, turned into a media circus as the defendants openly ridiculed Hoffman and otherwise disrupted the proceedings. Beneath the farcical surface, a serious political psychodrama unfolded as the counterculture flaunted its least attractive side while the Nixon administration ostentatiously displayed its commitment to law and order.

Kevin Phillips's "emerging Republican majority" included blue-collar workers, Catholic ethnics, white southerners, anti-Castro Cuban exiles, and upwardly mobile suburbanites. GOP strategists played on such groups' fears of social disorder and charged that the Democrats were more interested in minorities, welfare clients, and campus dissidents than in hardworking, patriotic citizens. The party of FDR, they told wavering Democrats, had been hijacked by antiwar protesters, New Left radicals, special interests, and entrenched federal bureaucrats.

With George Wallace planning another presidential run in 1972, Nixon avidly courted southern white voters. Attorney General John Mitchell, Nixon's erstwhile campaign manager, helped to implement the president's southern strategy. The mournful-looking, pipe-puffing Mitchell, a former partner in Nixon's New York law firm, opposed extension of the 1965 Voting Rights Act and thwarted enforcement of the 1968 Fair Housing Act. When he sued to delay school desegregation in Mississippi, even attorneys in his own Justice Department protested. The Supreme Court slapped down this effort, ordering that school desegregation proceed "at once."

When the Supreme Court in *Swann* v. *Charlotte-Mecklenburg Board of Education* (1971) approved school busing to achieve racial balance, Nixon found the kind of wedge issue on which he thrived. He denounced the decision and demanded that Congress outlaw the policy. When HEW officials and Justice Department civil-rights lawyers drew up integration plans involving busing for several cities, the president fired off an angry memo to Ehrlichman: *"Knock off this Crap.* I hold [HEW and the Justice Department] personally accountable to keep their left wingers in step with my express policy—Do what the law requires and not *one bit more."* Nixon offered a more sophisticated version of George Wallace's raw racism. As Dan T. Carter writes in *From George Wallace to Newt Gingrich: Race in the Conservative Counterrevolution, 1963–1994* (1996): "[I]n Richard Nixon's subtle manipulation of the busing issue . . . , the Wallace music played on."

Nixon's southern strategy emerged most blatantly in his Supreme Court nominations. When Chief Justice Earl Warren retired in 1969, Nixon nominated Warren Burger of Minnesota, a moderately conservative federal judge, as his successor. The Senate easily confirmed Burger. But when another vacancy opened in 1969, Nixon offered a nomination clearly intended to please southern whites: federal judge Clement F. Haynsworth of South Carolina, the home state of Senator Strom Thurmond, who had played a key role in Nixon's southern success in 1968. (The 1948 Dixiecrat candidate for president, Thurmond had later become a Republican.) A bitter opponent of the 1954 *Brown* school-integration decision, Thurmond favored jurists who believed in "strict construction" of the Constitution and avoided social issues.* Haynsworth, a strict constructionist, opposed labor unions and civil rights and also had a record of conflict-of-interest charges in cases he had handled. The Senate rejected him, 55–45, with seventeen Republicans joining in a stinging rebuke of Nixon.

---

*Strict constructionists hold that in interpreting the Constitution, the courts should follow the precise meaning intended by the framers; the other view, broad construction, sees the Constitution as a living document, adaptable to changing circumstances. The two approaches date to the time of Jefferson and Hamilton.

Nixon next proposed an even less qualified candidate, G. Harrold Carswell, a Florida judge. The American Bar Association and legal scholars deplored Carswell's nomination. As a candidate for the Georgia legislature in 1948, Carswell had declared, "Segregation of the races is proper and the only practical and correct way of life. . . . I have always so believed and I shall always so act." Carswell later renounced this statement, but he could not shake the charge of incompetence. Nixon's congressional liaison man advised the president: "[Most senators] think Carswell's a boob, a dummy. And what counter is there to that? He is." Republican senator Roman Hruska of Nebraska tried to turn Carswell's mediocrity into an asset. Many Americans were mediocre, Hruska pointed out; didn't they deserve a voice on the Supreme Court? Despite Hruska's argument, the Senate rejected Carswell, 51–45. Nixon denounced the vote as an insult to the South, enhancing his standing with white southerners.

Having made his gesture to the South, Nixon next nominated a moderate jurist, Harry Blackmun of Minnesota, who won easy confirmation. When two more Supreme Court vacancies occurred in 1971, Nixon nominated Lewis Powell and William Rehnquist. Powell, a Virginian, boasted a distinguished record, including presidency of the American Bar Association. Rehnquist, a classmate of Nixon's adviser John Ehrlichman at Stanford Law School, had been a Goldwater Republican in 1964. As an assistant attorney general under Mitchell, he was a hard-nosed "law-and-order" advocate, supporting secret wiretaps, for example, when the government judged them necessary. Both nominees won confirmation.

As reshaped by Nixon, the Supreme Court took a tough stand on issues of obscenity and law enforcement but avoided reversing the liberal rulings of the Warren era. On some issues, such as affirmative action, school busing, and abortion, the Court adopted positions unpopular with many conservatives. Blackmun, for example, wrote the majority decision in *Roe* v. *Wade,* the landmark 1973 decision upholding a woman's constitutional right to an abortion. William Rehnquist would eventually become chief justice, extending Nixon's influence for a full generation after his own departure from the White House in disgrace.

Conclusion

Richard Nixon's first term and the first year of his second brought landmark achievements: disengagement from Vietnam, détente with the Soviet Union and China, and resourceful diplomacy in the Middle East. Domestically, he moved beyond traditional Republican positions in several key areas. A consummate politician, Nixon capitalized on the country's rightward turn and rallied his "silent majority" of suburbanites, blue-collar voters, white southerners, and others unsettled by recent events. More than anyone else, he set the course of American politics for the coming decades.

But history's verdict on Nixon would prove far harsher than seemed possible in 1973. Behind the scenes, the president had conspired in illegalities that would produce the gravest crisis in the history of the presidency. As the nation grappled with social and cultural changes in the early 1970s, it also endured an ordeal summed up in a single word: Watergate.

SELECTED READINGS

The Vietnam War, from Tet to Cease-Fire; Domestic Responses

Many of the works listed in the Selected Readings of Chapters 9 and 10 are relevant to the first two sections of Chapter 11 as well. In addition, see David L. Anderson, ed., *Facing My Lai: Moving Beyond the Massacre* (1998); David Caute, *The Year of the Barricades: A Journey Through 1968* (1988); Todd Gitlin, *The Whole World Is Watching: Mass Media in the Making and Unmaking of the New Left* (1980) and *The Sixties: Years of Hope, Days of Rage* (1987); Lewis L. Gould, *1968: The Election That Changed America* (1993); James W. Hilty, *Robert Kennedy: Brother Protector* (1997); Andrew E. Hunt, *The Turning: A History of Vietnam Veterans Against the War* (1999); Jeffrey Kimball, *Nixon's Vietnam War* (1998); Peter Lowe, ed., *The Vietnam War* (1998); Timothy Miller, *The 60s Communes: Hippies and Beyond* (1999); Mark Moyar, *Phoenix and the Birds of Prey: The CIA's Secret Campaign to Destroy the Viet Cong* (1997); Keith W. Nolan, *Battle for Hué: Tet, 1968* (1983); James S. Olson and Randy Roberts, *My Lai: A Brief History with Documents* (1998); Joseph A. Palermo, *In His Own Right: The Political Odyssey of Senator Robert F. Kennedy* (2001); Murray Polner and Jim O'Grady, *Disarmed and Dangerous* [on the Berrigan brothers] (1997); W. J. Rorabaugh, *Berkeley at War: The 1960s* (1989); David Rudenstine, *The Day the Presses Stopped: A History of the Pentagon Papers Case* (1996); Herbert Y. Schandler, *The Unmaking of a President: Lyndon Johnson and Vietnam* (1977); William Shawcross, *Sideshow: Kissinger, Nixon and the Destruction of Cambodia* (1979); Melvin Small, *Johnson, Nixon, and the Doves* (1988); Ronald H. Spector, *After Tet: The Bloodiest Year in Vietnam* (1993); Irwin Unger and Debi Unger, *Turning Point, 1968* (1988).

Vietnam: The Long Aftermath

Michael A. Anderegg, *Inventing Vietnam: The War in Film and Television* (1991); Katherine Finney, *Friendly Fire: American Images of the Vietnam War* (2000); Kristin Ann Hass, *Carried to the Wall: American Memory and the Vietnam Veterans Memorial* (1998); Arnold R. Isaacs, *Vietnam Shadows: The War, Its Ghosts, and Its Legacy* (1997); Jim Neilson, *Warring Fictions: American Literary Culture and the Vietnam War Narrative* (1998); Charles E. Neu, ed., *After Vietnam: Legacies of a Lost War* (2000); Fred Turner, *Echoes of Combat: The Vietnam War in American Memory* (1996).

Nixon-Kissinger Foreign Policy

The general histories of the Cold War cited in the Chapter 2 Selected Readings are relevant to the Nixon-Kissinger years as well. See also Stephen E. Ambrose, *Nixon: Triumph of a Politician* (1987); Coit D. Blacker, *Reluctant Warriors: The United States, the Soviet Union, and Arms Control* (1987); Raymond L. Garthoff, *Détente and Confrontation: American-Soviet Relations from Nixon to Reagan* (1985); Stephen Green, *Living by the Sword: America and Israel in the Middle East, 1968–1987* (1988); Seymour M. Hersh, *The Price of Power: Kissinger in the Nixon White House* (1983); Walter Isaacson, *Kissinger: A Biography* (1992); Henry Kissinger, *White House Years* (1979) and *Years of Upheaval* (1983); Walter LaFeber, *Inevitable Revolutions: The United States in Central America* (1985); Robert S. Litwack, *Détente and the Nixon Doctrine: American Foreign Policy and the Pursuit of Stability* (1984); Keith L. Nelson, *The Making of Détente: Soviet-American Relations in the Shadow of*

Vietnam (1995); Herbert Parmet, *The World and Richard Nixon* (1990); Franz Schurman, *The Foreign Policies of Richard Nixon* (1987); William Slater, *Chile and the United* States (1990); Anthony Summers, *The Arrogance of Power: The Secret World of Richard* Nixon (2000); Daniel Yergin, *The Prize: The Epic Quest for Oil, Money, and Power* (1991).

Domestic Politics in the Early Nixon Years

William C. Berman, *America's Right Turn: From Nixon to Bush* (1994); Mary C. Brennan, *Turning Right in the Sixties: The Conservative Capture of the GOP* (1995); Dan T. Carter, *The Politics of Rage: George Wallace, the Origins of the New Conservatism, and the Transformation of American Politics* (1995) and *From George Wallace to Newt Gingrich: Race in the Conservative Counterrevolution, 1963–1994* (1996); Gareth Davies, *From Opportunity to Entitlement: The Transformation and Decline of Great Society Liberalism* (1996); Thomas Byrne Edsall with Mary D. Edsall, *Chain Reaction: The Impact of Race, Rights, and Taxes on American Politics* (1991); Dean J. Kotlowski, *Nixon's Civil Rights: Politics, Principle, and Policy* (2001); Allen J. Matusow, *Nixon's Economy: Booms, Busts, Dollars, and Votes* (1998); Richard M. Nixon, *RN: The Memoirs of Richard M. Nixon* (1978); Herbert Parmet, *Richard Nixon and His America* (1990); A. James Reichley, *Conservatives in an Age of Change: The Nixon and Ford Administrations* (1981), Melvin Small, *The Presidency of Richard Nixon* (1999); Tom Wicker, *One of Us: Richard Nixon and the American Dream* (1991); Garry Wills, *Nixon Agonistes: The Crisis of a Self-Made Man* (1970).

CHAPTER

Reform in the Nation, Crisis in Washington

ON THE AFTERNOON of August 7, 1974, facing the supreme crisis of his life, President Richard Nixon gathered his family in the White House solarium: wife Pat and daughters Tricia and Julie with their husbands Edward Cox and David Eisenhower, grandson of the revered Dwight Eisenhower. In a quintessentially Nixonian touch, the president summoned the White House photographer to record the moment "for history." In the photograph, Nixon's tightly clenched fists belie his smiling face. A moment after the staged shot, the photographer captured a sobbing Julie embracing her father as Tricia turns away weeping and Edward gamely smiles on. When the photographer departed, the family shared a grim, silent dinner. The next day, in a historic first for the history of the presidency, Nixon announced his resignation.

Nixon's efforts to conceal his role in a break-in at the Democratic Party headquarters during the 1972 campaign had spawned further crimes, and by the summer of 1974 he faced two choices: resign or be impeached. But the president's personal crisis paled in contrast to the nation's. Watergate stretched the fabric of constitutional government to the limit. Following the distrust that had dogged LBJ's final White House years, the scandal further weakened the presidency, and Americans' trust in government sank to all-time lows.

Watergate dominates the seventies, threatening to obscure the decade's larger contours. In part, the period was marked by reaction and passivity after the upheavals of the sixties. While Nixon rallied his "silent majority," some erstwhile activists and counterculture members bade farewell to radicalism and cultural protest and shifted their focus inward. Others, however, turned to new causes, including environmental protection, gay rights, and feminism. As in the sixties, this fresh wave of activism and challenges to the status quo stirred conservative opposition. The political and cultural reaction embodied in the Wallace movement and in Richard Nixon's election in 1968 intensified, laying the groundwork for the election of Ronald Reagan as the seventies ended.

The nation may have longed for a breather as the sixties ended, but history offers no time-outs. As we shall see in this chapter and the next, the seventies brought not only new movements and causes, but also political crises, economic worries, and deepening social and cultural divisions. A fascinating transitional era, the seventies posed issues and challenges that would occupy the nation for decades.

Escapism and the Collapse of the Counterculture

The culture and politics of the seventies unfolded amid the wreckage of the antiwar movement and the apparent collapse of the counterculture. Wracked by ideological disputes, the New Left faded as the political climate turned hostile and Nixon's policy of Vietnamization neutralized its most potent issue. The counterculture also suffered from commercial exploitation, drug abuse, and the actions of a few disturbed individuals hovering around its fringes. A more insidious force silently eroded these movements as well: time. With each passing year, more youthful activists and counterculture devotees started families, began professional training, entered the job market, or otherwise reached a truce with the society they had earlier dismissed.

As resourceful promoters co-opted the counterculture's music and fashions,* the movement itself took a lurid turn and then collapsed. In December 1969, Charles Manson, a psychotic drug cultist, and his "family" of young followers recruited in San Francisco's Haight-Ashbury district ritually murdered actress Sharon Tate and four others in Tate's Beverly Hills home. In 1970, the year the Beatles broke up, a rival British rock group, the Rolling Stones, set out to make a documentary movie like the profitable film version of the Woodstock festival. The Stones staged a free concert at Altamont Raceway near San Francisco and, cultivating their outlaw image, hired the Hell's Angels motorcycle gang to provide security in return for $500 worth of beer. The event proved a disaster: Concertgoers harassed physicians trying to treat drug-overdose victims, the Hell's Angels assaulted several people and fatally knifed a young man as he approached the stage, and three people died in drug-related accidents. The Manson murders and Altamont mocked the counterculture's avowals of peace and love and confirmed conservatives' worst nightmares about the counterculture.

In a post-Altamont article, "The End of the Age of Aquarius," Todd Gitlin criticized the movement's failure to confront the havoc of drugs. "Why doesn't this contaminated culture, many of whose claims are based on the virtues of drugs, help its own brothers and sisters?" he lamented. Would the youth culture "leave anything behind but a market?" Years later, Gitlin—by then a Berkeley sociologist—reflected on the movement's sad end: "The revolutionary mood had been fueled by the blindingly bright illusion that human history was beginning afresh because a graced generation had willed it so. Now there wasn't enough life left to mobilize against all the death raining down." As the counterculture disintegrated, a few loyalists preserved its verve and style in a kind of cultural time capsule. The Grateful Dead, a raffish counterculture musical group, retained a loyal following into the 1990s. For most, however, their season of youthful rebellion survived only in memory.

As the counterculture, urban riots, and massive antiwar protests receded into history, American society seemed momentarily disoriented. Except for Watergate, the 1970s struck many people as rather featureless. One early history of the decade bore the title *It Seemed Like Nothing Happened.* Indeed, the decade was generally free of the riots, assassinations, campus turmoil, bitter confrontations, and superheated

---

Hair, a musical celebrating the "Age of Aquarius" (also the title of a popular counterculture song) and featuring eye-popping nudity, opened on Broadway in 1968.

rhetoric that for many Americans defined the sixties. Profound changes were under way, but they became apparent only gradually, as a shell-shocked nation sought diversion in a bland mass culture. The antiwar, anti-Establishment, and drug-induced music of the late 1960s gave way to songs such as Don McLean's bittersweet and enigmatic 1971 hit "American Pie." John Denver's crooning "Rocky Mountain High" (1972) recommended unspoiled nature rather than LSD for spiritual transcendence. Groups like Led Zeppelin and The Who carried on the hard-rock tradition but without the overt political content of late-sixties rock.

Television fed the escapist mood. The three major networks—CBS, ABC, and NBC—tripled their revenues in the 1970s with forgettable situation comedies and police dramas, 1950s nostalgia *(Happy Days, Laverne and Shirley)*, and sexual titillation (*Charlie's Angels, Three's Company*). One bright spot, *M*A*S*H*, the long-running comedy-drama set in a Korean War medical unit, which premiered in 1972, upheld humane values and spoofed the idiocies of military authority. The show's implicit pacifist message suited the post-Vietnam mood. For the most part, however, 1970s TV, driven by ratings and marketing demographics, lived down to the "vast wasteland" label that an FCC chairman had applied to it in 1961.

It also only fitfully reflected America's diversity. The popular ABC miniseries *Roots* (1976) offered a panorama of the African American experience, but other series featuring blacks proved less impressive. George Jefferson on *The Jeffersons* was a weak buffoon, and the prancing teenager J. J. on *Good Times* perpetuated the grinning, blackface minstrel stereotype. Asians, Hispanics, and Native Americans rarely appeared.

Hollywood shared in the infantilization of mass culture in the 1970s, despite a few gripping movies such as *The Deerhunter* (1978), a portrayal of the psychological effects of Vietnam service. Typical escapist fare included Sylvester Stallone's *Rocky* (1976), *Superman* (1978), and Steven Spielberg and George Lucas's *Star Wars* (1977) with its comic-book storyline and computer-generated intergalactic warfare. These films transferred the sixties' sense of the clash of powerful forces from the real world of politics to the realm of fantasy.

A wave of ethnic awareness among Americans who traced their ancestry to various European nations, celebrated by Michael Novak in *The Rise of the Unmeltable Ethnics* (1973), similarly depoliticized an earlier cultural trend. In the sixties, calls for black pride had arisen as part of the larger African American freedom struggle. In the seventies, white ethnic groups asserted their pride with no overt political agenda. For blue-collar and middle-class white ethnics, allegiance to the Democratic Party had been a tradition since the 1930s. Now, as old party loyalties crumbled, a generalized affirmation of ethnic identity, freed of political implications, offered an alternative form of group identification.

Many early-twentieth-century immigrants had submerged their ethnicity in order to seize the opportunities that came with "Americanization." Now, with the transition successfully accomplished, the newly self-conscious "ethnics" of the 1970s could indulge in a sentimental journey into a semi-mythic past. But like most generalizations about the 1970s, this one must be qualified. Despite its ambiguous meanings and its silly side (like buttons reading "Kiss Me, I'm Italian"), the new ethnicity did challenge the homogenizing pressures of 1970s mass culture and the corporate world's tendency to reduce Americans to blocs of consumers living in "media markets."

The heightened awareness of race, class, and ethnicity underlay the decade's most popular TV show, *All in the Family*. The series starred Carroll O'Connor as Archie Bunker, a bigoted longshoreman and part-time taxi driver who spouted venom against blacks, radicals, feminists, Jews, and other groups. Archie's wife Edith, played by Jean Stapleton, gently challenged his prejudices and offered insights into the experiences that had shaped his worldview. "He'll never be more than what he is now," she says sadly in one show, "even though he had dreams once." The show's producer, liberal Democrat Norman Lear, intended to satirize bigotry, but audience surveys found that many viewers applauded Archie's diatribes and his scornful attacks on "Meathead," his liberal son-in-law.

Another portrayal of working-class frustration emerged in the 1979 film *Breaking Away*, which explored the lives of blue-collar youth in the university town of Bloomington, Indiana. With regional authenticity, *Breaking Away* conveyed the disorientation of post-Vietnam America as well as the class tensions and economic changes of the 1970s. Visiting the university campus, a displaced stonecutter reduced to selling used cars tells his son, "I cut the stone for this building. I was one fine stonecutter. I loved it. I was damned proud of my work." The hero, a recent high-school graduate who imagines himself an Italian bicycle racer, is devastated when a real-life, corporate-sponsored Italian racing team uses unfair tactics to prevent him from winning a race. "Everybody cheats," he surmises bitterly. "I just didn't know."

Novelists, too, examined ethnic sensibilities and tensions. Saul Bellow's *Mr. Sammler's Planet* (1970) and Bernard Malamud's *The Tenants* (1971) probed the uneasy relations between blacks and Jews. Toni Morrison's debut novel *The Bluest Eye* (1970) told of poverty-bound Pecola Breedlove, who dreams of having blue eyes like Dick and Jane in her school reader. Torn by conflicting aspirations, Pecola descends into madness.

A few ex-1960s activists, meanwhile, joined rural communes that proliferated across the country. Others, still suspicious of the modern technocratic order, embraced mysticism and the occult. Zen Buddhism and Indian gurus won followers; interest in astrology, Native American religion, and meditation techniques for heightening psychic awareness soared. One former SDS leader, writing in 1971, offered a snapshot of a radical in transit from public to private concerns:

> I am less involved in changing America. . . . This does not mean that I am less angry or upset or horrified by this country than before. If anything, I am more profoundly and intuitively aware, day-to-day, of what an ugly society this is and how desperately it needs change. But my information comes less and less from the papers—more and more from my own experience with it.

As ex-radicals embraced a "New Age" sensibility, cultural critic Edwin Schur captured the trend in the title of his 1976 book: *The Awareness Trap: Self-Absorption Instead of Social Change*.

As we shall see in Chapter 13, Christian evangelical and charismatic religious movements flourished, along with interest in Bible prophecies of the end times. For some in flight from 1960s activism, religion offered another avenue of retreat from social engagement; for many conservatives, by contrast, it provided a motivation for political involvement.

Other erstwhile activists, less mystically inclined, turned to physical fitness and material acquisitions. Many young, urban professionals (later dubbed Yuppies) whose acquisitive tastes would shape American life in the 1980s were veterans of the counterculture. In *The Greening of America* (1970), Charles Reich of Yale Law School, himself a late-blooming flower child, argued that a more peaceful and harmonious society would arise spontaneously as the counterculture's values spread by a kind of osmosis. Some movement dropouts welcomed Reich's reassuring message. Indeed, in 1976 journalist Tom Wolfe labeled the baby boomers the "Me Generation." The 1983 movie *The Big Chill* would later offer a sad image of cynical ex-sixties radicals in avid pursuit of money, sex, and power.

Historian Christopher Lasch in *The Culture of Narcissism* (1979) argued that the counterculture's dissident lifestyles and the New Left's politics of confrontation, initially undertaken to challenge suburban conformity and power-elite manipulation, had degenerated into "a politics . . . of style without substance." Citing psychiatrists' reports of patients needing immediate gratification and incapable of long-term planning, Lasch linked the turn toward narcissism to a post-sixties disillusionment with reform:

> Having no hope of improving their lives in any of the ways that matter, people have convinced themselves that what matters is psychic self-improvement: getting in touch with their feelings, eating health food, taking lessons in ballet or belly dancing, immersing themselves in the wisdom of the East, jogging, learning how to "relate," overcoming the "fear of pleasure."

New Activist Energies

Not all former radicals sold out; not all of the political activism and counterculture energies of the sixties degenerated into careerism or narcissism. Although the specific forms of protest and cultural alienation faded, a host of 1960s activists carried into the 1970s and beyond the left-liberal politics, social-justice commitments, and skepticism of consumer capitalism that they had acquired through civil-rights advocacy, antiwar protests, and the counterculture.

The environmental movement, for example, which arose in the early seventies, drew strength from the distrust of the technocratic order that had pervaded the New Left and the counterculture. As one counterculture theorist wrote apocalyptically in 1969, "[Our] primary project . . . is to proclaim a new heaven and a new earth so vast, so marvelous that the inordinate claims of technical expertise must of necessity withdraw to a subordinate and marginal status."

The U.S. moon landing of July 21, 1969, culminating a project launched by John F. Kennedy, ranks as a revealing cultural event. Television viewers thrilled as astronaut Neil Armstrong stepped on the lunar surface and delivered his prepared epigram: "That's one small step for [a] man, a giant leap for mankind." Yet many observers also voiced fears that the conquest of space would intensify America's long infatuation with technology, push the arms race to new levels, and eat up resources better directed to pressing social needs on earth.

Environmentalism and the related theme of energy conservation did not, however, simply arise from the ideological concerns of 1960s radicals. A series of

Earth Day in Milwaukee, 1970. Displaying an Earth Day poster, students paddle a homemade raft down the Milwaukee River to protest water pollution. *(© Bettmann/CORBIS)*

unsettling trends and events hastened their emergence. Down to the 1940s, America had produced more fossil fuels (coal, oil, natural gas) than it consumed. Yet as the long postwar boom got under way, consumption outran domestic supply. By the 1970s, with the gap steadily widening, Americans relied more heavily on imports and offshore drilling in the Gulf of Mexico and along the Pacific Coast. A stark reminder of the hazards of these operations came in 1969 as leaking drilling rigs in California's Santa Barbara channel turned seawater to oily scum, blackened beaches, and killed fish and shorebirds. As TV images of napalmed children in Vietnam gave way to oil-soaked cormorants flapping helplessly on the beach, a Santa Barbara citizens' group drafted the "Declaration of Environmental Rights." Echoing Rachel Carson's *Silent Spring,* the document implored Americans to pay more heed to the environmental cost of their profligate lifestyle:

> We need an ecological consciousness that recognizes man as member, not master, of the community of living things sharing his environment. . . . We must find the courage to take upon ourselves as individuals responsibility for the welfare of the whole environment. . . . We must redefine "progress" toward an emphasis on long term quality rather than immediate quantity.

On April 22, 1970, millions of Americans embraced an idea of Senator Gaylord Nelson of Wisconsin and observed the first Earth Day by cleaning up beaches and vacant lots and attending environmental teach-ins. The high-spirited mood reflected the early naiveté and deceptive harmony of a cause that would prove both divisive and complex, but Earth Day symbolically placed the environment on the public agenda for the seventies and beyond. Historian Samuel P. Hays has emphasized the distinctive features of post-1970 environmentalism. Whereas early-twentieth-century environmentalists had advocated the wise management of natural resources for productive use, the new environmentalists valued an unspoiled and pristine natural environment for the joy, aesthetic pleasure, and public-health benefits it could provide.

Two 1970 environmental laws, the Water Quality Improvement Act and the Clean Air Act, aimed at cleaning up the nation's air and waterways by regulating runoff to rivers and streams and setting emissions standards for auto exhausts. That year, President Nixon, attuned as always to voters' worries, signed bills creating the Environmental Protection Agency and the Occupational Safety and Health Administration with broad powers to enforce federal environmental and worker-safety regulations. Nixon also supported the Endangered Species Act (1973), which protected more than nine hundred plant and animal species whose survival was in jeopardy.

While the Nixon team recognized the political appeal of environmentalism, it viewed the movement with suspicion. Nixon's interior secretary chose Earth Day to approve an Alaska oil pipeline opposed by environmentalists. John Ehrlichman avowed, "Conservation is not the Republican ethic," no doubt making Theodore Roosevelt spin in his grave. On a 1971 Ehrlichman memo criticizing pollution controls, Nixon scribbled, "I completely agree—We have gone overboard on the environment." The head of the Atomic Energy Commission ridiculed critics of nuclear-reactor safety: "We can't live in a Garden of Eden and still have a technological society," he said.

The environmental movement continued to grow, however, influenced not only by oil spills but also by the more chronic problems of air and water pollution, shrinking wilderness areas, and declining resources. The media, having celebrated unbridled consumption in the 1950s, now struck a different note. Calls for a "sustainable economy" rather than heedless exploitation of nature's bounty found a receptive audience. Ecology, once a specialized academic field, became a fad. A cynical California politician called it "the political substitute for the word 'mother.'"

Products of a society enamored of technology and boundlessness, some Americans began to envision a less exploitive coexistence with the natural order. Books like Barry Commoner's *The Closing Circle* (1971), Frances Lappe's *Diet for a Small Planet* (1971), and E. F. Schumacher's *Small Is Beautiful* (1973) signaled the shift. The new consciousness also propelled the career of Ralph Nader, the young lawyer whose 1965 book *Unsafe at Any Speed*, an attack on the U.S. auto industry's poor safety record, had given rise to the National Traffic and Motor Vehicle Safety Act of 1966. By the early 1970s, advocacy groups nicknamed "Nader's Raiders" were lobbying against a wide range of dangerous products. Nader funded his operation in part with money won from General Motors in a legal battle.* Emulating Nader, many young lawyers turned to the field of public advocacy and environmental law.

―――――
*When GM hired detectives to spy on him, Nader sued for invasion of privacy. GM settled out of court for $425,000.

While environmental advocates appealed to all Americans, other groups drew inspiration from the civil-rights and Black Power movements to mount more narrowly targeted struggles against oppression. Thus, the early seventies also saw a sharp rise in activism by specific groups pursuing their own agendas. If the "new ethnicity" phenomenon was largely apolitical, the rising self-consciousness of Hispanics, Native Americans, gays, and feminists found intensely political outlets.

Among Mexican Americans, the new militancy that had arisen in the 1960s (see page 235) continued. Activist energies found outlets not only in national advocacy groups such as the Mexican American Legal Defense and Education Fund but also in numerous grassroots organizations addressing local issues. Cesar Chavez remained nationally prominent as leader of the United Farm Workers of America (UFWA), which he defined as a "cross between . . . a movement and . . . a union." It included Filipino and other farm workers as well as Mexican Americans. The UFWA settled its strike against grape-growing agribusinesses in 1970 and ended the five-year national grape boycott, but the struggle for better conditions continued. As UFWA leader Dolores Huerta declared in 1973: "[A]ll of the growers and right-wing elements . . . are trying to crush the farm workers. . . . [I]t's a real war."

The Hispanic population's rapid growth intensified its self-awareness. As a result of both immigration and natural increase, the Mexican American population grew from 4.5 million to 8.7 million in the 1970s. The 1980 federal census also recorded more than 330,000 residents from other Central American countries, especially El Salvador, Guatemala, and Nicaragua, of whom 61 percent had arrived within the past ten years.

Immigration from the Caribbean, especially Puerto Rico, increased as well. By 1980, New York's Puerto Rican population, mostly concentrated in New York City's East Harlem, approached 1 million, with 652,000 more in New Jersey, Pennsylvania, Illinois, Florida, and California. While battling poverty and lack of education, New York City's Puerto Ricans (nicknamed "nuyoricans") developed a vibrant culture rooted in the Catholic faith, in the island's distinctive dance rhythms (*bomba* and *plena*), and the popular salsa bands, which emerged in New York after World War II under the leadership of Tito Puente and others. (See Juan Flores, *From Bomba to Hip-Hop: Puerto Rican Culture and Latino Identity* [2000].)

With growing numbers came political activism. In the early 1970s, a militant Puerto Rican activist group called the Young Lords worked in East Harlem to uplift their fellow immigrants and protest inadequate city services. Emulating the Black Panthers, they wore berets and military fatigues. The Young Lords' young lawyer, Cesar Perales, became assistant secretary of health, education, and welfare in 1977 and, still later, president of the Puerto Rican Legal Defense and Education Fund.

Two Native American organizations, Indians of All Tribes (IAT) and the American Indian Movement (AIM), also took direct action in these years. In 1969 eighty young activists claimed Alcatraz Island in San Francisco Bay. Demanding that Alcatraz become an Indian cultural center, they occupied the island until 1971. In 1972 AIM occupied the Bureau of Indian Affairs in Washington, D.C., charging governmental violations of treaty obligations. A year later, AIM seized a trading post at Wounded Knee, South Dakota, where, in 1890, the U.S. Army had massacred three hundred Teton Sioux. After a ten-week siege, the occupation ended. Federal charges against the occupiers were dropped after revelations that the government had withheld evidence and used illegal wiretaps in building its case. These actions hastened the emergence of a new pantribal "Indian" ethnic identity and activist movement.

Native American protests spurred action. In 1970 the federal government restored forty-eight thousand acres to the Taos Pueblo of New Mexico, including the sacred Blue Lake region held by the U.S. Forest Service since 1906. In 1971 Congress restored 40 million acres to the native peoples of Alaska and granted over $960 million to tribal villages and associations in compensation for lands taken when Alaska became a state. In 1972 the federal government transferred to the Yakima Indians of Washington State some twenty-one thousand acres of the Mount Rainier Forest Reserve. Eight years later, the Supreme Court upheld a lower-court award of $107 million in damages to the Sioux of South Dakota and endorsed the Sioux claim that the Black Hills had been illegally seized from them during the 1870s gold rush. That same year, Congress granted $81.5 million to various Maine tribes to settle claims based on violations of a 1790 statute regulating the sale or disposal of Indian lands.

The Nixon administration also initiated a change in the legal status of Native Americans. In 1953, Congress had ended all federal benefits for Indians as a distinct category of citizens and had abolished the tribes' legal standing under federal law—a policy called termination. In the 1960s, responding to protests, Washington had modified this policy and made tribal governments eligible to participate in antipoverty and Great Society programs. President Nixon in 1970 urged Congress to abandon the termination policy altogether. The resultant Indian Self-Determination Act (1974) restored Indian tribes' legal status and granted them authority over federal programs on their reservations and more control of tribal schools and colleges.

Homosexuals, another group historically subject to discrimination, had also grown more assertive amid the cultural ferment of the late 1960s. A symbolic turning point came on June 29, 1969, when police raided the Stonewall Inn, a gay bar in Manhattan's Greenwich Village. Homosexuals had tolerated such harassment in the past, but now the patrons resisted, pelting the police with bottles and stones. Having formerly found precarious security in a shadowy subculture, growing numbers of gay men and lesbians "came out of the closet" in the 1970s. Embracing the "Gay Rights" banner, they proclaimed their sexual preference, formed organizations, founded newspapers, and protested discrimination. The National Gay Task Force,* founded in 1973, campaigned to include homosexuals as a protected class in civil-rights laws barring job or housing discrimination. Dade County (Miami), Florida, was among the jurisdictions to pass such legislation. Responding to pressure, the American Psychiatric Association in 1973 removed homosexuality from the list of mental disorders in its diagnostic manual.

---

*In 1986 the name was changed to the National Gay and Lesbian Task Force.

A Revived Women's Movement

Of all the movements to arise from the upheavals of the sixties, the most sweeping was the new feminism. After winning the vote in 1920, the women's movement had faded. The mass culture of the 1950s had reinforced strict gender distinctions: women in the home, men in the workplace; women as emotional, men as rational; women as sexual prey, men as predators. Yet even in the fifties, these polarities bore little resemblance to reality. For example, as we have seen, the percentage of women in the workplace actually rose in the decade. Instead, the stereotypes expressed the anxieties of a postwar society seeking stability in early marriage, family togetherness, and suburban domesticity.

Betty Friedan's *The Feminine Mystique* (1963), which had sold 1.3 million copies by 1967, challenged these images. Hardly the typical 1950s housewife, Friedan was a college graduate and political radical who had employed domestic help while launching her writing career. Still, *The Feminine Mystique* voiced the frustrations of many women as they confronted what Friedan called "the problem that has no name." She wrote, "Each suburban wife struggled with it alone. As she made the beds, shopped for groceries, matched slipcover material, ate peanut butter sandwiches with her children, chauffeured Cub Scouts and Brownies, lay beside her husband at night—she was afraid to ask of herself the silent question: 'Is this all?'" Friedan hit a nerve. Letters poured in revealing a reservoir of repressed anger. "I've seen too many women say they would 'do something' when the last children went to school," wrote one woman. "The something has usually been bridge, bowling or drinking." Diffuse discontent soon coalesced into a movement that, in Friedan's words, "spread like a nuclear chain reaction."

Post-1920 feminists had concentrated less on women's issues than on social justice and peace concerns. Their 1970s successors, by contrast, more closely resembled nineteenth-century women's-rights advocates, who had demanded not only the vote but access to higher education and the professions, married-women's property rights, fairer divorce laws, and other reforms. In the same spirit, the new feminists called for full gender equality. In time, the movement would divide into radical and moderate wings, but this initial phase was characterized by cohesiveness and confidence. In founding the National Organization for Women (NOW) in 1966 (see page 261), Friedan and others dedicated it to "equality of opportunity and freedom of choice" for all women and their "full participation in the mainstream of American society." This agenda, NOW made clear, embraced not only politics but also culture, including changes in the mass media's "false images of women" and "an equitable sharing of the responsibilities of home and children and of the economic burdens of their support." By 1977 NOW boasted sixty-five thousand members. The Women's Political Caucus, founded in 1971, lobbied both parties on behalf of women's issues. Despite changes since the 1950s, women still faced wage inequities and discrimination in politics, the media, higher education, most professions, and the managerial ranks of business.

The movement gained a sharper, more radical edge as it attracted young activists from the civil-rights and antiwar campaigns. As young women protesting southern racism or the Vietnam War had found themselves marginalized by male

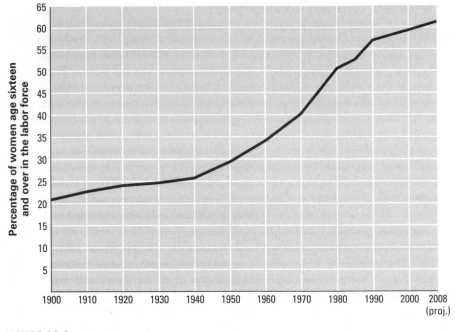

FIGURE 12.1

Women in the Labor Force, 1900–2008

SOURCE: *Historical Statistics of the United States, Colonial Times to 1970,* Part I (1975); *Statistical Abstract of the United States, 1997* (2001).

leaders, their resentment had built. The late-sixties climate of anti-Establishment protest encouraged the questioning of gender roles as well. Challenging the older liberals of NOW (as Black Power advocates were challenging the mainstream civil-rights groups), these younger feminists mounted a radical assault on the sexual status quo.

The civil-rights and antiwar campaigns equipped these new recruits to feminism with tactics, a vocabulary, and a taste of activism and also taught them how to attract media attention. They picketed the *Ladies Home Journal* offices just as antiwar protesters had picketed ROTC buildings. At Atlantic City in 1968, they paraded a sheep as Miss America, as the Yippies had nominated a pig for president. Emulating the draft-card burners, they immolated curlers, bras, and high-heeled shoes in "freedom trash cans." Students at an Iowa college echoed the southern sit-ins and staged a "nude-in" when a *Playboy* representative visited campus.

Robin Morgan's *Sisterhood Is Powerful* (1970) and Gloria Steinem's *Ms.* magazine (1972) captured the movement's early exuberance. Feminist writers explored issues ranging from wage inequities to media stereotypes to the merits of the clitoral orgasm. Feminist theologians challenged patriarchal religion. *Our Bodies, Ourselves* (1973), a women's health manual written by women, became a bestseller, appealing to women tired of being patronized by male physicians. Rape-crisis centers, battered-women shelters, and feminist "consciousness-raising" groups proliferated.

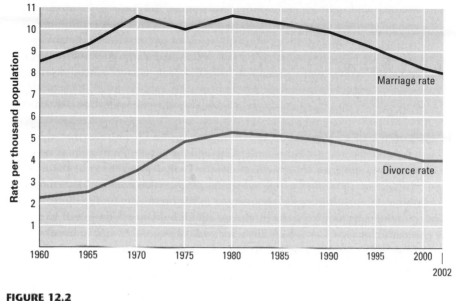

FIGURE 12.2
Marriage and Divorce Rates, 1960–2002
SOURCE: National Center for Health Statistics, reprinted in *World Almanac, 2004.*

Reviving a sexual revolution whose origins lay in the pre–World War I bohemian culture of Greenwich Village, many young women claimed as their due the sexual freedom long open to men. Aided by an array of contraceptive options and access to abortion, they experimented widely and postponed long-term commitments. As married women abandoned unsatisfying or abusive relationships, the divorce rate rose from 2.2 per 1,000 population in 1960 to 5.2 in 1980. The nation's lesbian community, emerging from furtive obscurity like its gay counterpart, grew more vocal.

Changes in women's employment status, under way since the fifties, provided the economic context of the new feminist consciousness. Women, married and single, poured into the workplace in the seventies; the percentage of gainfully employed women rose from 44 percent in 1970 to 51 percent by 1980. The reasons were often less ideological than economic. As inflation eroded families' income (see Chapter 13), women went to work to make up the gap. The changing patterns of women's work, in turn, affected marriage and birthrates. Many young working women chose to remain single, opting instead for relationships outside marriage. Many who were married delayed starting a family or chose to have only one or two children. The birthrate dropped from a postwar peak of 25.3 per 1,000 population in 1957 to 18.4 in 1970 and 14.8 by 1975. Again economic calculations played a role; as inflation increased, couples eager to maintain their accustomed standard of living limited the number of their offspring. Many women welcomed new possibilities for careers, higher education, and professional training. But the new openness could also stir uncertainty, as marriage and domesticity became only one of many options. And millions of working-class women and those living in inner-city slums remained little affected by the demographic shifts and feminist ferment.

The new feminist activism produced a series of political and judicial victories following on the Civil Rights Act of 1964, which had banned gender as well as racial discrimination in employment. In 1972 Congress barred gender discrimination in higher education and sent to the states for ratification the Equal Rights Amendment (ERA) to the Constitution outlawing discrimination on the basis of sex. By 1975 thirty-two states had ratified ERA, and final approval seemed certain. In 1973 the Equal Employment Opportunity Commission ordered the American Telephone and Telegraph Company to pay millions to women as well as minority employees to rectify past wage discrimination. That same year came *Roe* v. *Wade,* the Supreme Court's landmark decision upholding women's right to abortion.*

Gender discrimination and stereotyping did not suddenly disappear, of course. Men still tended to be promoted more rapidly than women, and to be paid more for comparable jobs. One female insurance broker wrote, "I just had this notion that I could pull myself up by my bootstraps. And my bootstraps kept breaking." In the 1970s, the proportion of women attorneys rose from 3 percent to 13 percent and of women physicians from 7 to 10 percent, evidence of progress but also of the long road to full equality. Gloria Steinem lamented at mid-decade, "We are triumphantly galloping toward tokenism."

TV portrayed a bright professional woman on *The Mary Tyler Moore Show,* but she reported to a male boss whom she invariably addressed as "Mr. Grant." Even this exception was more than matched by programs featuring sexual innuendo and exploitation. The head of ABC instructed the producers of *Three's Company* to make the show "the same kind of breakthrough in sexiness that 'All in the Family' was in bigotry." *Charlie's Angels* with its three female detectives claimed to celebrate women professionals, but it quickly degenerated into a voyeuristic show featuring revealing outfits and wet T-shirts.

As we shall see, an antifeminist backlash soon set in, fueled in part by male uneasiness about women's new assertiveness. In Woody Allen's 1972 movie *Play It Again Sam,* based on the classic *Casablanca* of 1942, the Humphrey Bogart character rasps through gritted teeth, "Dames are simple. I never met one who didn't understand a slap in the mouth or a slug from a forty-five."

But even women gave the new feminism a mixed reception. Many working-class women remained skeptical of the mostly middle-class, college-educated movement. (Working-class women did fight sexism in their trade unions, however, as Dennis A. Deslippe demonstrates in *"Rights Not Roses": Unions and the Rise of Working Class Feminism, 1945–80* [2000], and in some unions such as the International Union of Electrical Workers, they achieved notable success.) Although some black and Hispanic women responded, including writers like Alice Walker and Toni Morrison, many accused affluent white feminists of diverting attention from the more pressing

---

*"Jane Roe" (so called to protect her privacy) was a Dallas woman who in 1970 brought suit against the district attorney of Dallas County, Texas, an official named Wade, challenging the constitutionality of a Texas statute making it a crime to perform an abortion except to save the life of the mother. (Ironically, she emerged in the 1990s as an antiabortion activist.)

issues of racism and poverty. In 1971, *Essence,* a magazine for black women, called the new feminism "basically a family quarrel between white women and white men."

Catholic and evangelical Protestant women bristled when feminists welcomed lesbians and abortion-rights advocates to their ranks. Phyllis Schlafly, a conservative activist, formed a "Stop ERA" organization in 1972. Within the women's movement itself, conflict between moderate and radical wings, lesbians and heterosexuals, added further complications.* As with the civil-rights campaign, the women's movement's initial gains were undermined by internal divisions and growing resistance from the larger society.

In these early 1970s years, with the traumas of the sixties still raw and new reform energies stirring, America and its leaders urgently needed to address a broad range of domestic and international issues. Instead, a catastrophic political failure and a grave constitutional crisis distracted the nation.

The 1972 Election and Watergate: The Nation in Crisis

The term *Watergate,* like *Teapot Dome* from the 1920s, encompasses a complex tangle of events. Although stemming from criminal activities by the Nixon administration during the 1972 presidential campaign and the later attempts to cover up those crimes, the scandal had larger sources and implications. The specific crimes that ended Nixon's presidency revealed the no-holds-barred style of politics that he had practiced for years and exposed fundamental flaws in his character. The crisis, in turn, raised questions about presidential power and accountability that went to the heart of the U.S. system of governance.

The scandal began, appropriately, under cover of darkness on June 17, 1972, when a night watchman at the Watergate apartment complex in Washington, D.C., noticed a door lock taped open. He called the police, who arrested five burglars in the offices of the Democratic National Committee (DNC). One intruder was James W. McCord, Jr., a CIA veteran serving as security chief for Nixon's campaign organization, the Committee to Reelect the President (CRP, or, as many preferred, CREEP), headed by Attorney General John Mitchell. The others, Cuban exiles from Miami, had participated in the Bay of Pigs invasion.

The administration denied any knowledge of what White House spokesmen pooh-poohed as "a third-rate burglary attempt" and a bungled "caper" by overzealous underlings. The incident did indeed seem trivial compared to Nixon's recent trips to China and the Soviet Union. A few weeks after the incident, John Mitchell, citing family problems, resigned. Mitchell's successor as attorney general, Richard Kleindienst, promised a full investigation. Watergate sank to the back pages, and the presidential campaign moved forward.

---

*In *The World Split Open: How the Modern Women's Movement Changed America* (2000), historian Ruth Rosen argues that the radical/moderate split that divided some national feminist leaders was less evident at the local level, where cooperation on specific issues and goals, including "the problems of ordinary working women," tended to trump differences of ideology or sexual orientation.

Presidential Scandals
and Trust in Government

Though the Watergate scandal was unique in the scale of criminality involved and in its outcome—the resignation of a president—it was, in fact, simply one in a long series of scandals that have periodically swirled around the White House. Some involved sex, some money, and some the constitutional abuse of power, but all riveted the nation's attention as they unfolded.

One of the earliest presidential scandals involved Andrew Jackson. In the 1828 electoral campaign, opposition newspapers accused Jackson of adultery because he had married Rachel Robards in 1791 before her divorce had become final, even though both she and Jackson thought it had. (Jackson supporters responded by accusing his opponent, John Quincy Adams, of being an aristocrat who wore silk underwear.) Scandal tore at the Jackson administration itself in 1829 when the secretary of war, John H. Eaton, married Peggy O'Neale Timberlake, the daughter of a Washington tavern keeper. Vice President John C. Calhoun and his wife snubbed the Eatons, deeming Peggy to be socially inferior and of shady reputation. This infuriated Jackson, split the cabinet, and in 1830 contributed to Calhoun's resignation. As often happens, the scandal had a political dimension, since Jackson already suspected (correctly) that Calhoun had presidential ambitions himself.

The most scandal-ridden administration of the nineteenth century was Ulysses S. Grant's (1869–77). Though a brilliant Civil War general, Grant was a weak president, and his two terms produced an orgy of high-level corruption. His vice president profited from his connections with a fraudulent railroad-construction company, his private secretary took money from a ring of distillers who were cheating the government of whiskey taxes, and his secretary of war accepted bribes from persons seeking appointments to operate profitable Indian trading posts in Oklahoma. The degeneration of the presidency from Washington to Grant, wrote the historian Henry Adams, was alone enough to disprove all theories of inevitable progress.

Politics and sex again became entangled in 1884 when Republicans accused the Democratic presidential candidate Grover Cleveland of having fathered an illegitimate child years before. "Ma, Ma, Where's my Pa?" they chanted at Cleveland rallies. When Cleveland admitted the charge and made clear that he had supported the child, the voters overlooked his youthful indiscretion, electing him president not only in 1884 but again in 1892.

The worst pre-Watergate presidential scandal came during the administration of Warren G. Harding (1921–23). Like Grant's tarnished presidency, Harding's brief White House tenure (he died in office of a heart attack) was riddled with financial wrong-doing. His attorney general took bribes to fix cases, his director of veterans' affairs stole vast sums, and his interior secretary accepted payoffs from oil companies seeking access to oilfields that were part of the government's strategic oil reserve. One of these reserves was in Teapot Dome, Wyoming (so named because of the distinctive shape of a local geological formation), and the term *Teapot Dome* came to describe all the Harding financial scandals. Harding also had a mistress, Nan Britton, whom he occa-sionally invited for secret trysts in a White House cloakroom. But the full dimensions of the Harding scandals became known only later. In fact he was a popular president, and his death on August 2, 1923, was widely mourned.

Watergate was hardly the end of presidential scandals, as we shall see in later chapters. A major crisis gripped the Reagan White House when the press revealed that top Reagan advisers, if not Reagan himself, had approved the secret transfer of funds to the contras, insurgents fighting the leftist government of Nicaragua, despite Congress's explicit prohibition of such aid. The money came from another secret operation, the clandestine sale of U.S. arms to Iran, a nation widely and correctly viewed as deeply hostile to America. The popular Reagan rode out the storm, but for a time the "Iran-contra affair" held the public's fascinated attention nearly as fully as Watergate had earlier.

The administration of President Bill Clinton had its share of scandals, both finan-cial and sexual. The financial scandals involved charges of campaign finance irregulari-ties, and also the role of the Clintons in a failed real-estate venture, Whitewater, and a collapsed savings-and-loan association during his year as governor of Arkansas. The sexual scandals (which stirred considerably more public interest) involved a series of al-leged extramarital relationships or improper sexual advances by Clinton, the most spectacular one involving a young White House intern, Monica Lewinsky.

The presidency as an institution survived all these scandals, but they eroded pub-lic trust in government, particularly in recent decades. The Watergate crisis, coming after evidence of deceptions by the Johnson and Nixon administrations in their pursuit of the Vietnam War, severely jolted Americans' confidence in government and in elected officials. Indeed, *Watergate* sank so deeply into the public consciousness that subsequent scandals were often given nicknames that involved the suffix *-gate*, such as *Irangate*. (Some humorists even alluded to the Clinton-era sex scandals as "Forni-gate.") Much of the antigovernment mood that prevailed in the United States from the 1970s through the end of the century can be traced directly to Watergate and subsequent presidential scandals and attempted cover-ups. Presidents come and go, but the scandals in which they become involved, like the policies they initiate, have more long-lasting effects.

After the disastrous 1968 convention, the Democratic Party had adopted sweeping reforms. As one result, the delegates to the 1972 convention at Miami Beach included many more women, young people, blacks, Hispanics, and radical activists. The party's traditional power brokers, such as Chicago's Mayor Daley and union officials, exerted less influence. As one delegate quipped, convention visitors saw more hair and fewer cigars.

One potential candidate, Senator Edward M. Kennedy of Massachusetts, the surviving brother of the famous clan, had been tarred by scandal in July 1969 when a car he was driving had plunged into Nantucket Sound off Chappaquiddick Island after a late-night party, and his young female passenger had drowned. With Kennedy out of the running, Senator George McGovern of South Dakota, frontrunner in the primaries, won a first-ballot nomination. A historian and former Methodist minister, McGovern favored immediate U.S. withdrawal from Vietnam, amnesty for draft re-sisters, and broad domestic reforms. His running mate, Senator Thomas Eagleton of Missouri, withdrew after revelations that he had received electroshock therapy for depression. After several top Democrats turned him down, McGovern tapped Kennedy brother-in-law R. Sargent Shriver as Eagleton's replacement.

The Republican convention, also in Miami Beach, renominated Nixon and Agnew by acclamation. The party platform opposed school busing and amnesty for draft evaders. Already the strong favorite, Nixon gained additional ground in May when Governor George Wallace, again running as a third-party candidate, was shot by a deranged man at a rally in Maryland and left paralyzed. Nixon made

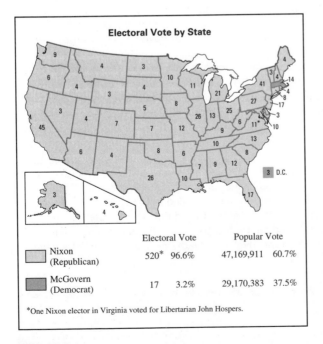

Electoral Vote by State

	Electoral Vote		Popular Vote	
Nixon (Republican)	520*	96.6%	47,169,911	60.7%
McGovern (Democrat)	17	3.2%	29,170,383	37.5%

*One Nixon elector in Virginia voted for Libertarian John Hospers.

MAP 12.1

Presidential Election of 1972

few appearances and refused to debate McGovern, relying on TV ads and on surrogate speechmakers.

Despite the administration's efforts, however, the Watergate break-in story refused to vanish. An address book carried by one of the burglars had linked the operation to E. Howard Hunt, who worked for Nixon aide Charles Colson. Also implicated was G. Gordon Liddy, a CREEP staffer. Both Hunt and Liddy had taken part in earlier clandestine operations by the White House Plumbers (see page 304). The FBI traced money in the burglars' possession to CREEP, and bit by bit the story emerged. Hunt and Liddy had planned the burglary, probably on orders from John Mitchell and deputy campaign director Jeb Stuart Magruder. In February 1972, Liddy had detailed the plan in a meeting with Mitchell, Magruder, and White House counsel John W. Dean III, who in turn had briefed the White House chief of staff, Bob Haldeman. Nixon himself had probably approved. As one investigator surmised, "If Haldeman knew, the President knew." (In a 2003 PBS special, Magruder, now a retired Presbyterian minister, recalled hearing Nixon on the phone specifically instruct Mitchell to proceed with the break-in.)

In an earlier break-in at the DNC late in May, the burglars had photographed documents and tapped the telephones of DNC chairman Lawrence O'Brien and another Democratic official. The second tap had worked well, and reports on the illegally recorded conversations went to Haldeman. But the O'Brien tap proved faulty, and the June 17 break-in was planned to correct the problem.

Why did the Nixon campaign attempt such a high-risk crime? FBI director J. Edgar Hoover had recently died, disrupting Nixon's normal channels of political intelligence. The immediate impetus was Nixon's urgent desire to learn how much O'Brien knew about corporate contributions to his campaign in exchange for preferential treatment, and about his shady financial dealings with billionaire Howard Hughes. More broadly, the operation continued a pattern of wiretaps and break-ins initiated by Nixon and Kissinger. Watergate, in short, was only part of a web of criminal activity spun in the Oval Office.

In September 1972, a grand jury indicted the five burglars, together with Hunt and Liddy—who became known as the "Watergate Seven." Soon after, Bob Woodward and Carl Bernstein of the *Washington Post* revealed that Mitchell, as attorney general, had managed a secret fund intended to gather information on Nixon's political enemies and potential challengers. Another fund, they reported, sought to sabotage Democratic presidential hopefuls by forging letters, planting spies, stealing campaign plans, and feeding false information to the media. The White House indignantly denied the *Post*'s charges. Outside Washington, however, the story still roused little interest. McGovern called the Nixon administration "the most corrupt ... in history," but few paid attention.

Despite Nixon's outward calm, the Watergate arrests had set off panic bells in the White House and triggered a massive effort to conceal the administration's complicity in the Hunt Liddy operation and other crimes. John Dean, hinting that national security was involved, pressured acting FBI director Patrick Gray to curb the Watergate investigation. Haldeman, drawing on a secret fund that he kept in his White House safe, gave $400,000 in cash to the Watergate defendants to ensure their silence. Magruder and other administration staffers lied to the FBI, the grand jury, and the press about the role of CREEP and the White House in the break-in.

Investigating Watergate.   Reporters Carl Bernstein (*left*) and Bob Woodward of the *Washington Post* probed the Watergate scandal, assisted by a shadowy source they dubbed "Deep Throat." *(AP/Wide World Photos)*

On Election Day Nixon won a landslide victory, carrying 49 states and garnering 49 million popular votes to McGovern's 29 million. McGovern, attracting mainly hard-core antiwar and liberal voters, carried only Massachusetts and Washington, D.C. The Democrats increased their Senate majority, however, and retained control of the House. In any showdown, Nixon would face a strongly Democratic Congress.

In January 1973, the trial of the Watergate Seven began before U.S. district court judge John Sirica, who grilled witnesses sharply. All seven were convicted. Facing a long prison term, James McCord wrote an explosive letter to Sirica revealing that the White House had paid him to keep quiet. The outraged judge called for further investigation.

On another front, Patrick Gray, testifying before the Senate Judiciary Committee on his nomination as permanent FBI director, had revealed John Dean's efforts to derail the FBI's investigation of Watergate. Meanwhile, the Senate created a Special Committee on Presidential Campaign Activities to investigate the spreading scandal. Seventy-seven-year-old Sam Ervin, a Democrat from North Carolina, chaired the committee. On March 21, Dean warned Nixon, "We have a cancer—within, close to the Presidency, that's . . . growing daily."

In a TV speech on April 30, Nixon counterattacked. Claiming that he had only just learned the full story of the burglary and the cover-up, he blamed everything on Dean, whom he fired. With lavish praise, he also announced the departure of his top aides Haldeman and Ehrlichman. Nixon then replaced Attorney General Kleindienst with Elliot Richardson, a Boston Brahmin of sterling reputation. On May 18, Richardson chose Archibald Cox, a Harvard law professor, as a special prosecutor to investigate the Watergate matter. The Cox investigation could involve criminal prosecution; the Ervin Committee's Senate hearings could lead to impeachment.

The Ervin Committee began televised hearings on May 17. For six months, Americans watched fascinated as witnesses uncovered the crimes hatched in the Nixon White House. The beetle-browed Senator Ervin, a self-described "simple country lawyer," possessed a razor-sharp mind and awesome legal expertise. Inexorably, the investigation circled closer to the Oval Office. Jeb Magruder conceded that he and Mitchell had helped plan the break-in. Nixon's lawyer admitted that he had raised $220,000 for the Watergate defendants and had managed a half-million-dollar fund earmarked for sabotage and espionage against Democrats. Mitchell, now in jeopardy himself, described what he called the "White House horrors." John Dean, demonized by Nixon, turned on his former boss and White House colleagues. Nixon himself, Dean testified, had directed the cover up from the start. Watergate, Dean made clear, was only part of a pattern of illegal and unethical activities carried out at the president's initiative against politicians, journalists, and others on the president's "Enemies List." Charles Colson, for example, had orchestrated the forging of State Department cables to make it appear that President John Kennedy had ordered the murder of Ngo Dien Diem in 1963. The aim was to damage Senator Edward Kennedy, whom Nixon feared as a potential rival.

The criminal goings-on, including the Watergate payoffs, had been financed by a vast pool of cash raised from corporate contributors in return for special treatment. The International Telephone and Telegraph Corporation, for example, paid much of the cost of the 1972 Republican convention after Nixon apparently intervened to help ITT in a 1971 antitrust case. The dairy industry contributed hugely after Nixon backed higher price supports for milk. The seamy record extended to Nixon's personal finances as well. Prodded by press reports, a congressional tax committee found that Nixon owed some $475,000 in back taxes and interest for 1969–72. The president's tax returns revealed a pattern of questionable deductions, including inflated valuations placed on presidential papers contributed to the National Archives.

Still, only Dean's testimony linked Nixon to criminal activity. Republican senator Howard Baker of Tennessee posed the key question of the Ervin hearings: "What did the President know, and when did he know it?" The big break came on July 16, 1973, when Nixon aide Alexander Butterfield testified that Nixon had secretly tape-recorded all Oval Office conversations. The Ervin Committee and special prosecutor Cox, seeking proof of Nixon's role in the cover-up, demanded that Nixon release the relevant tapes. But the president refused, invoking national security and "executive privilege." Instead, he offered to provide summaries of the requested tapes, their accuracy to be verified by Senator John Stennis (D., Mississippi), seventy-two years old, deeply conservative, and partially deaf. Cox rejected this offer.

When Cox secured a court order for the release of the tapes, Nixon instructed Attorney General Richardson to fire him. Richardson refused, and resigned. The deputy attorney general also refused, and was fired. Finally, the third-ranking

Justice Department official, Solicitor General Robert Bork, signed the order dismissing Cox. With this action, Richardson later wrote, Nixon abused his power "more blatantly than at any other stage in the whole sordid history of Watergate. A government of laws was on the verge of becoming a government of one man."

The Final Stage of the Crisis

Public reaction to Watergate built slowly. Nixon's policies had broad appeal, he had compiled an impressive diplomatic record, and he had just decisively won a second term. But his support was eroding, and with Cox's firing, impeachment demands mounted. Watergate now dominated the media. On NBC-TV, a commentator warned that America faced "what may be the most serious constitutional crisis in its history." Woodward and Bernstein of the *Washington Post* continued their revelations, relying heavily on an unnamed informant whom they nicknamed "Deep Throat." Under heavy pressure, Nixon appointed a new special prosecutor, Leon Jaworski, a Houston lawyer and former president of the American Bar Association.

Compounding Nixon's troubles, Vice President Spiro Agnew resigned in October 1973 after a grand jury found that he had accepted bribes while governor of Maryland and as vice president. In a negotiated settlement, Agnew pleaded *nolo contendere*—in effect a guilty plea—to a single tax-evasion charge. In exchange for the government's agreement not to prosecute, Agnew paid a $10,000 fine and re-

Democracy in the Streets.   Clad in prison garb and sporting a Nixon mask, a demonstrator in Washington, D.C., made his views clear as the Watergate cover-up unraveled. *(AP/Wide World Photos)*

ceived a three-year suspended sentence. As provided by the recently enacted Twenty-fifth Amendment, Nixon nominated as Agnew's successor House Minority Leader Gerald R. Ford, who won quick confirmation by the Senate and House.

Stories circulated of Nixon's heavy drinking. During the October 1973 Yom Kippur War, Henry Kissinger took control. Even the decision to declare a high state of nuclear alert was made by Kissinger, Secretary of Defense James Schlesinger, and a few other officials at a midnight White House meeting as Nixon slept.

On November 12, 1973, *Time* magazine called on Nixon to resign. Pressed at a gathering of newspaper editors to discuss his tax problems and other matters, the president finally exploded, "I am not a crook!" His approval rating sank to 27 percent, the sharpest one-year drop since polling began in the 1930s. In a defiant State of the Union address on January 30, 1974, he declared, "One year of Watergate is enough. . . . I have no intention . . . of ever walking away from the job that the people elected me to do."

Even as Nixon battled on, however, the House Judiciary Committee was gathering evidence for charges of impeachment. For the first time since 1868, the removal of a president by Congress, a procedure set forth in Articles I and II of the Constitution, seemed a real possibility. In February 1974, by an ominous 410–4 vote, the House granted the Judiciary Committee full subpoena powers to pursue its investigations.

On March 1, a grand jury convened by Judge Sirica indicted Haldeman, Ehrlichman, Mitchell, four other former White House and CREEP employees, and "other persons known and unknown" for conspiracy to obstruct justice. The charges included wiretapping, destroying documents, promising executive clemency, paying hush money, and lying to investigators. The indictments relied heavily on the testimony of John Dean, who had pleaded guilty to a single conspiracy charge and was cooperating with the grand jury. A few days later, Sirica turned over to the Judiciary Committee the grand jury's sealed report naming Nixon as an "unindicted co-conspirator" in the cover-up.

On a tour to shore up support, Nixon met mostly hostile crowds. Republican candidates in the upcoming midterm election distanced themselves from him. Even Vice President Ford denounced CREEP as "an arrogant elite guard of political adolescents."

On May 9, the Judiciary Committee began impeachment hearings. In June, Nixon toured the Middle East, where a million people cheered him in a Cairo motorcade, and made another trip to Moscow. But what should have been diplomatic triumphs now seemed mere diversions from the domestic crisis. The Ervin Committee's devastating final report, released in early July, a catalog of presidential wrongdoing, brought impeachment a step closer.

Meanwhile, the tussle over the Oval Office tapes had continued. In November 1973, Nixon had turned over to special prosecutor Jaworski some recordings that convinced him of Nixon's complicity in criminal activities. The tape for June 20, 1972, three days after the break-in, contained a gap of some eighteen minutes. Nixon's secretary loyally claimed to have erased this section by accident. Alexander Haig, Haldeman's successor as White House chief of staff, blamed some "sinister force of energy." Most Watergate scholars hold Nixon himself responsible.

In April, Sirica ordered Nixon to give tapes of sixty-four post-Watergate conversations to Jaworski. Instead, Nixon released his own edited version of forty-two taped conversations, with many cuts and alterations. In the Nixon version of one conversation, for example, he proposes "to get off the cover-up line." In the Judiciary Committee's later transcription of the same tape, the words are "to get on with the cover-up plan." Nixon entirely deleted his order to John Mitchell on March 22, 1973: "I want you to stonewall it, let them plead the Fifth Amendment, cover-up or anything else."

On May 20, Judge Sirica again ordered Nixon to release the subpoenaed tapes. Nixon's lawyers appealed Sirica's order to the Supreme Court. On July 24, in *United States* v. *Nixon,* Chief Justice Warren Burger read the Supreme Court's unanimous ruling: Nixon must obey Sirica's subpoena and turn over the tapes in the interests of "criminal justice." That same day, the House Judiciary Committee began debate on the impeachment resolutions. Upward of 35 million Americans followed the mesmerizing drama on TV or radio. Committee member Barbara Jordan from Texas declared, "My faith in the Constitution is whole, it is complete, it is total, and I am not going to sit here and be an idle spectator to the diminution, the subversion, the destruction of the Constitution."

On July 27, the Judiciary Committee approved, 27–11, the first article of impeachment, charging Nixon with obstruction of justice for attempting to impede the Watergate investigation and to "cover up, conceal, and protect those responsible." In committing these deeds, the article concluded, Nixon had "acted in a manner contrary to his trust as President and subversive of constitutional government." All twenty-one Democrats and six of the seventeen Republicans voted for this article. Two further articles, approved a few days later, cited Nixon's use of the FBI, Internal Revenue Service, and CIA to abuse "the constitutional rights of citizens" and his defiance of a congressional subpoena to release the tapes.*

On August 6, Nixon released the tapes. Here at last was the "smoking gun": conclusive proof of Nixon's direct role in the criminal obstruction of justice. On June 23, 1972, Haldeman had outlined to Nixon Mitchell's scheme for stopping the FBI investigation of the break-in by persuading the CIA to claim that the case involved sensitive national-security issues. Nixon had replied:

> All right. . . . Fine. . . . Play it tough. That's the way they [our enemies] play it and that's the way we're gonna play it. . . . Don't lie to them to the extent to say there is no involvement, but just say this is sort of a comedy of errors, bizarre, without getting into it. . . . [The CIA] should call the FBI in and say . . . , "[D]on't go any further into this case, period!" (John Prados, ed., *The White House Tapes: Eavesdropping on the President* [2003], pp. 264–268)

Other tapes proved damaging as well. In one meeting, for example, Nixon urged his aides to lie to the grand jury: "You can say I don't remember. You can say I can't recall."

Even before Nixon released the tapes, 66 percent of the American people had favored impeachment. With the tapes' release, even Nixon's last-ditch supporters

---

*The committee voted down two additional articles of impeachment. One accused Nixon of violating Congress's war-making powers with his secret bombing of Cambodia; the other accused him of demeaning the presidency by his handling of his personal finances, a reference to his massive underpayment of his federal income taxes.

jumped ship. At a meeting of Republican senators, Barry Goldwater growled, "There are only so many lies you can take and now there has been one too many. Nixon should get his ass out of the White House—today!" On August 7, GOP congressional leaders warned Nixon that impeachment and removal from office appeared certain.

On August 8, Nixon announced his resignation in a television address. Obliquely apologizing for "any injuries that may have been done in the course of the events that led to this decision," he barely mentioned Watergate and instead recited his foreign-policy triumphs. The next day, after an emotional farewell to his staff, he boarded a helicopter for the first leg of a flight to California. In his inaugural address, President Gerald Ford declared, "Our long national nightmare is over."

Nixon's reputation fell into deep eclipse following his resignation, worsened rather than salvaged by Ford's unconditional pardon of him a month later. But his ability to bounce back remained intact. Easing into the role of elder statesman, he revisited the scenes of his foreign triumphs and wrote extensively on global politics. By 1992, the twentieth anniversary of Watergate, he had regained a degree of grudging public respect.

Historians remained wary. Earlier presidential scandals had involved the all-too-human motive of greed. The Watergate crisis of 1972–74 jeopardized the most fundamental principles of constitutional government and citizens' rights under the rule of law. It arose from the intersection of long-term trends and Nixon's own character. Since the 1930s, the executive branch of the federal government had steadily expanded in power. The Truman-era loyalty program; the Kennedy-era FBI wiretaps on Martin Luther King, Jr.; Johnson's use of the Gulf of Tonkin Resolution to wage the Vietnam War; the secret bombing of Cambodia by Nixon and Kissinger, and other abuses of presidential power all paved the way for Watergate. As Nixon pointed out, every president since Franklin Roosevelt had authorized wiretaps. Lyndon Johnson, in fact, had approved a wiretap on Nixon's campaign plane in 1968.

But in the Nixon White House, isolated improprieties became commonplace. Nixon and Kissinger had operated at a rarefied level as they reshaped global alignments. Such power can breed a sense of immunity from the rules that govern others. In Nixon's case, the headiness of power combined with a strong paranoid streak. From his early days in politics, Nixon had conducted underhanded campaigns and attracted aides who shared his suspicious nature and his compulsion to annihilate opponents. Even as president he remained the suspicious outsider, seeing enemies everywhere. "Opponents are savage destroyers, haters, . . ." he noted in a personal memo early in 1974, as the Watergate crisis deepened. "Time to use full power of the President to fight overwhelming forces arrayed against us." The Watergate break-in and the subsequent cover-up, which Nixon orchestrated "from day one," as Bob Haldeman later conceded, fit a pattern characteristic of Nixon's entire political career. In superpower diplomacy, his ruthlessness and penchant for intrigue at times served him well; in the domestic arena, these traits proved fatal.

After Nixon resigned, editorial writers sighed in relief that "the system worked"—the rule of law had prevailed. But before Butterfield's revelation of the tapes, the outcome was by no means certain. In the last analysis, Nixon's own ingrained habits of distrust and deceit, which underlay his secret taping of even his closest advisers, undid him. As the conspirators turned on each other, the whole skein of illegality unraveled. Historian Stanley Kutler writes, "Lies became the quicksand that engulfed Nixon, estranged him from his natural political allies, and eventually snapped the fragile bond of trust . . . that binds government and the people."

"The system worked," but Watergate revealed its vulnerability to those intoxicated by power. Nixon's resignation offered no guarantee of the system's future invulnerability. The Iran-contra scandal of the 1980s, President Clinton's efforts to avoid the consequences of his misdeeds, and the Justice Department's assaults on civil liberties after the terrorist attacks of September 11, 2001 (see Chapters 14, 15, and 16) all offered reminders that no single crisis, even one as searing as Watergate, could grant permanent immunity against constitutional abuses by those in power.

"The system worked," but at a high price. Watergate obscured other urgent issues at the time, and in the long run it weakened public confidence in government. The crisis still haunts the nation with its legacy of unanswered questions—not only about details but, more profoundly, about the vulnerability of a constitutional system often taken for granted.

Watergate tainted scores of lives and derailed numerous careers. More than seventy persons were eventually convicted or pleaded guilty for their role in the scandal. Bob Haldeman, John Ehrlichman, and John Mitchell, along with eight other White House aides or campaign officials, all served time in prison. G. Gordon Liddy served the longest term, from January 1973 to September 1977. He later hosted a nationally syndicated conservative radio talk show.

Conclusion

Watergate tends to overshadow the 1970s, as does the man at the center of the crisis: Richard Nixon. Henry Kissinger's judgment on his former boss was harsh: "In destroying himself, Nixon had wrecked the lives of almost all who had come into contact with him." Nixon's darker side brought out the worst in others. John Ehrlichman confessed to Judge Sirica, "I abdicated my moral judgments and turned them over to someone else." More serious than the personal toll was Nixon's assault on the fabric of American government. That the fabric endured— however precariously—testifies to the farsighted wisdom of earlier, and finer, American statesmen.

But the larger changes in American society in this decade merit equal attention. The early seventies, in part a time of reaction and apathy, were also the radical energies of the 1960s channeled in new directions. The movements for environmental protection, gay rights, and gender equality, as well as the stirrings of activism in the Native American and Hispanic communities, all had roots in the political and cultural ferment of the sixties.

But, as in the sixties, these movements aroused opposition as well as support. Legalized abortion, activism by gays and lesbians, and feminist challenges to a familiar if inequitable gender order stirred intense reactions among Americans who found these developments threatening or offensive to their beliefs. The resulting controversies often translated into Republican votes and accelerated the nation's conservative turn as the decade wore on.

The politics of race, exploited so effectively by Richard Nixon, remained central as well. Although the black and Hispanic middle class was growing, the nation remained split between affluent, mostly white suburbs and poor, largely black and Hispanic inner cities. Unlike in the sixties, however, no Martin Luther King, Jr., or Lyndon Johnson arose to lead a renewed crusade against the inequities of American life. Instead, urban riots, growing welfare rolls, protests by minority groups, and the sometimes incendiary demands of radical activists alienated fearful white voters.

In the late nineteenth century, many native-born Americans had blamed the problems of an industrializing age on the immigrant newcomers. Similarly, the crime, drug abuse, housing deterioration, and other social problems of the inner cities, which had complex roots in an evolving economy, were blamed on the poor themselves, who often had little control over the larger forces shaping their lives. In such a setting, a racial backlash focused on such volatile issues as school busing.

As we shall see in the next chapter, runaway inflation, soaring energy costs, structural problems in the economy, and blows to American pride abroad in the later 1970s deepened the sense of unease and loss of direction, intensified the conservative turn culturally, and laid the groundwork for a resounding Republican victory as the 1970s ended.

SELECTED READINGS

Social Groups and Movements in 1970s America

Rodolfo F. Acuña, *Occupied America: A History of Chicanos* (3d ed., 1988); Lois Banner, *Women in Modern America* (1984); Albert Camarillo, *Chicanos in California: A History of Mexican Americans in California* (1984); Dudley Clendinen and Adam Nagourney, *Out for Good: The Struggle to Build a Gay Rights Movement in America* (1999); Stephen Cornell, *The Return of the Native: American Indian Political Resurgence* (1988); Barbara Hinkson Craig and David M. O'Brien, *Abortion and American Politics* (1993); Dennis A. Deslippe, *"Rights Not Roses": Unions and the Rise of Working-Class Feminism, 1945–80* (2000); Martin Duberman, *Stonewall* (1993); Alice Echols, *Daring to Be Bad: Radical Feminism in America, 1967–1975* (1989); Juan Flores, *From Bomba to Hip Hop: Puerto Rican Culture and Latino Identity* (2000); David J. Garrow, *Liberty and Sexuality: The Right to Privacy and the Making of Roe v. Wade* (1994); Susan M. Hartmann, *From Margin to Mainstream: American Women and Politics Since 1960* (1989); Bell Hooks, *Ain't I a Woman? Black Women and Feminism* (1981); Carolyn Johnson, *Sexual Power: Feminism and the Family in America* (1992); Troy R. Johnson, *The Occupation of Alcatraz Island* (1996); Jonathan Katz, *Gay American History: Lesbians and Gay Men in the U.S.A.: A Documentary History* (1992); Donald G. Mathews and Jane S. De Hart, *Sex, Gender, and the Politics of ERA* (1990); Miguel Meléndez, *We Took the Streets: Fighting for Latino Rights with the Young Lords* (2003); Joane Nagel, *American Indian Ethnic Renewal: Red Power and the Resurgence of Identity and Culture* (1996); Margaret Rose, "From the Fields to the Picket Line: Huelga Women and the Boycott, 1965–1975," *Labor History* (Summer 1990); Ruth Rosen, *The World Split Open: How the Modern Women's Movement Changed America* (2000); Leigh W. Rutledge, *The Gay Decades: From Stonewall to the Present* (1992); Guadalupe San Miguel Jr., *Brown, Not White: School Integration and the Chicano Movement in Houston* (2001); Lauri Umansky, *Motherhood Reconceived: Feminism and the Legacies of the Sixties* (1996); Melissa Walker, *Down from the Mountaintop: Black Women's Novels in the Wake of the Civil Rights Movement, 1966–1989* (1991).

Watergate

Stephen E. Ambrose, *Nixon* (1987); Congressional Quarterly, *Watergate: Chronology of a Crisis* (2 vols., 1973–74); John W. Dean III, *Blind Ambition: The White House Years* (1976); James Doyle, *Not Above the Law: The Battles of Watergate Prosecutors Cox and Jaworski* (1977); John Ehrlichman, *Witness to Power* (1982); David Greenberg, *Nixon's Shadow: The History of an Image* (2003); H. R. Haldeman, *The Ends of Power* (1978) and *The Haldeman Diaries: Inside the Nixon White House* (1994); Jim Houghan, *Secret Agenda: Watergate, Deep Throat, and the CIA* (1984); Leon Jaworski, *The Right and the Power: The Prosecution of Watergate* (1976); Stanley I. Kutler, *The Wars of Watergate: The Last Crisis of Richard Nixon* (1990) and *Abuse of Power: The New Nixon Tapes* (1998); J. Anthony Lucas, *Nightmare: The Underside of the Nixon Years* (1976); Jeb Stuart Magruder, *An American Life: One Man's Road to Watergate* (1974); Richard Oudes, ed., *From the President: Richard Nixon's Secret Files* (1989); John Prados, ed., *The White House Tapes: Eavesdropping on the President* (2003); Jonathan Schell, *The Time of Illusion* (1975) and *Observing the Nixon Years* (1989); John J. Sirica, *To Set the Record Straight* (1979); Melvin Small, *The Presidency of Richard Nixon* (1999); Bob Woodward and Carl Bernstein, *All the President's Men* (1974) and *The Final Days* (1976).

1970s Politics, Environmental Issues, and Cultural Trends

James L. Baughman, *The Republic of Mass Culture* (1992); Peter N. Carroll, *It Seemed Like Nothing Happened: America in the 1970s* (1982); Thomas Byrne Edsall with Mary D. Edsall, *Chain Reaction: The Impact of Race, Rights, and Taxes on American Politics* (1991); J. Brooks Flippin, *Nixon and the Environment* (2000); Robert Booth Fowler, *The Greening of Protestant Thought* (1995); Todd Gitlin, *Inside Prime Time* (1985); Samuel Hays, *Beauty, Health, and Permanence: Environmental Politics in the United States, 1955–1985* (1987) and *Explorations in Environmental History* (1998); Terence Kehoe, *Cleaning Up the Great Lakes* (1997); Christopher Lasch, *The Culture of Narcissism* (1979); Carolyn Merchant, *Major Problems in American Environmental History: Documents and Essays* (1993); Timothy Miller, *The Sixties Communes: Hippies and Beyond* (1999); Gregg Mitman, *Reel Nature: America's Romance with Wildlife on Film* (1999); Eva S. Moskowitz, *In Therapy We Trust: America's Obsession with Self-Fulfillment* (2001); Allan Schnaiberg, *The Environment: From Surplus to Scarcity* (1980); Bruce J. Schulman, *The Seventies: The Great Shift in American Culture, Society, and Politics* (2001); Donald Worster, *The Wealth of Nature: Environmental History and the Ecological Imagination* (1993).

PART FOUR

Setbacks, Achievements, New Dangers

T he contemporary era, from Watergate to the present, has seen profound changes at home and a radically altered international picture. In terms of presidential politics, these years have also witnessed a swing in the political pendulum, from conservatism to a cautious liberalism and back again, accompanied by a pervasive suspicion of government. Richard Nixon's disgrace intensified this revulsion against Washington, but its roots lay deeper, in Middle America's resentment of the Vietnam debacle, a costly welfare system, school busing, federal affirmative-action programs, and conflict over abortion and other issues. Inflation and other economic problems exacerbated the discontent. The immediate beneficiary, Jimmy Carter, rode the anti-Establishment wave to the White House in 1976. But Carter's frustrating one-term presidency suffered both from his personality traits and from factors beyond his control, including a humiliating hostage crisis in Iran.

Carter's perceived failure accelerated the electorate's rightward shift, and Ronald Reagan, a seasoned champion of conservative causes, capitalized on the insurgent mood. Reagan's program, featuring laissez-faire economics, Cold War militance, and a rollback of big government, won support from an electorate in full flight from Great Society-style liberalism. The "Reagan revolution" brought big tax cuts, business deregulation, slashes in social programs, and increased military spending. With inflation tamed and the affluent profiting from favorable tax and regulatory policies, the Reagan years saw a glow of prosperity, giddy real-estate speculation, high-stakes corporate takeovers, and a general aura of conspicuous consumption.

The Reagan political coalition survived long enough to send Vice President George Bush to the White House in 1988. But Bush had neither Reagan's charisma nor his clear-eyed domestic agenda, and his administration drifted despite military exploits in the Persian Gulf that earned him a brief spurt of popularity.

With the election of 1992, the baby boomers, now well into midlife, elevated one of their own—Bill Clinton—to the White House. Clinton shared the ideological allegiances of many members of this generation, including feminism and environmentalism. He appointed women to key posts and assigned his wife a central role in shaping health-care policy. His vice president, Al Gore, was admired by environmentalists.

Although heir to a liberal tradition extending from Franklin Roosevelt to Lyndon Johnson, Clinton himself adapted to the more conservative post-Reagan political climate. After a disastrous initial effort to promote a massive health-care program, Clinton shifted course. Intent on shedding the Democrats' reputation as a big-government "tax-and-spend" party, he called for spending cuts, a smaller government, and welfare reform. Sweeping Republican gains in the 1994 midterm election pulled him further to the right. He collaborated with Republicans on a budget-balancing plan and signed a historic welfare-reform bill involving a tough-minded, work-oriented, and decentralized approach. Aided by a booming economy, Clinton won a second term in 1996, but as he wrestled with a damaging sex scandal, neither he nor the Republican Congress seemed inclined to undertake bold new initiatives.

Despite the glow of prosperity, economic problems remained, especially those of the urban underclass. Millions in the inner cities, along with blue-collar workers displaced by industrial decline, found themselves marginalized in an emerging high-tech economy that required fewer and more highly trained workers.

As American society grew increasingly multiracial and multiethnic, gender roles, family structure, and even sexual identity seemed fluid and variable. Hispanics replaced African Americans as the largest minority, and the Asian American population grew rapidly. The political system, the cultural arena, and social institutions all bent before the winds of change. On the economic front, an agrarian society that had evolved into the world's industrial leader experienced an equally profound transformation. As the industrial base eroded, a new economic order based on global markets, electronic data processing, the delivery of services, and the transmittal of knowledge and information emerged. Simultaneously, a new world of mass entertainment based on giant corporate conglomerates and new electronic technologies loomed. While visionaries hailed these developments, others nervously pointed to the social and cultural tensions and economic hardship accompanying the transition. Cultural conservatives and evangelical Christians, dismayed by many of the changes they saw in America, became increasingly vocal.

The closing years of the old century and the opening years of the new brought world changes that were no less dramatic. The Cold War, which had shadowed so much of American history since 1945, ended abruptly in the late 1980s as the Soviet empire collapsed, a victim of military competition with the West and its own debilitating weaknesses. The United States now confronted a complex global reality in which the forces of consolidation and fragmentation warred for ascendancy. Islamic fundamentalism in the Middle East and Southeast Asia; ethnic conflicts in Eastern Europe; famine, disease, and warring tribal groups in Africa; and the longer-term scourges of poverty, illiteracy, overpopulation, and environmental deterioration all clamored for attention.

A razor-thin presidential election in 2000 brought to the White House George W. Bush, son of the former President Bush. Though he campaigned as a moderate, Bush presided over the most conservative administration since Ronald Reagan's, and perhaps even further back. The wealthy, corporate America, and religious conservatives generally applauded Bush's policies, but other Americans had a more mixed response. Even the surge of unity that followed the horrendous terrorist attacks of September 11, 2001, soon dissipated, as both the domestic and the international components of Bush's post-9/11 "war on terrorism" proved controversial. As the United States moved deeper into the twenty-first century, the victory celebrations of 1945 receded further into the past and the contours of a new era, one marked by novel challenges at home and abroad, slowly came into focus.

Nations, like individuals, in the words of Robert Frost, have promises to keep. For the United States, confronting a sometimes scary world, those promises involved honoring the values on which the Republic was founded: preserving the reality of democracy and not just its empty form, ensuring equality for all Americans, and tenaciously protecting the civil rights and personal freedoms embedded in the Bill of Rights.

Picking Up the Pieces: Post-Watergate America

IN 1976 THE United States threw a year-long party to celebrate the two-hundredth anniversary of the American Revolution. The American Revolution Bicentennial Commission sponsored a cornucopia of activities. The "American Freedom Train," laden with five hundred historic documents and funded by GM and other corporations, toured the nation. A VFW post in Ohio reenacted Washington's crossing of the Delaware. The Smithsonian Institution, with backing from General Foods, sponsored the "Festival of American Folklife." "The Bicentennial Wagon Train Pilgrimage," funded by Gulf Oil Company, lumbered across the nation from west to east and encamped at Valley Forge on July 4, 1976. That day, as President Ford delivered inspirational speeches, fireworks burst across the nation and a breathtaking flotilla of sailing vessels entranced New Yorkers.

Despite the hoopla, the United States was still unsettled by the aftershocks of an era marked by assassinations, riots, demonstrations, and the Watergate scandal. Economic problems exacerbated the edgy mood. As energy prices soared, a combination of inflation and recession that journalists dubbed "stagflation" struck. Gerald Ford, a Republican, and then Jimmy Carter, a Democrat, left the White House after brief presidencies that brought more frustration than achievement. Moreover, as the country moved to the right culturally and politically, a reactionary groundswell gained momentum. By 1980 it would startlingly alter the political landscape.

In 1941, the press tycoon Henry Luce had hailed "the American Century." By 1976 such soaring rhetoric was rare. Anxiety, not euphoria, marked the bicentennial year. Sociologist Daniel Bell discerned a "loss of faith in the nation's future." The nation's third century, Bell speculated, could well provide "yet another illustration of the trajectory of human illusions." To many Americans, such apprehensions seemed fully warranted.

A Ford, Not a Lincoln

Watergate left a diminished presidency. Gerald Ford, after completing Nixon's second term, failed to win election in his own right. Ford's Democratic successor, Jimmy Carter, served only one term. With mixed results, both leaders fought a hydra-headed array of economic problems that dominated the late seventies.

Gerald Ford's roots lay in the Middle America that Nixon had so avidly courted. His parents divorced when he was an infant, and he was adopted by his mother's second husband, a Grand Rapids businessman whose name he took. The tall, athletic Ford played football at the University of Michigan, earned a law degree from Yale, and practiced in Grand Rapids. In 1948 he won election to Congress, and in 1965 he became minority leader. With his friendly smile and reputation for honesty, Ford enjoyed wide respect. His integrity and modesty ("I'm a Ford, not a Lincoln") provided refreshing contrast to the scheming Nixon of the Watergate tapes.

But Ford's pardon of Richard Nixon in September 1974 "for all offenses against the United States which he . . . has committed or may have committed or taken part in" knocked his approval ratings from 72 to 49 percent. Ford argued that an indictment and possible imprisonment of the ex-president would have prolonged the agony of Watergate. But suspicions of an unsavory secret deal—the vice-presidency for Ford, pardon for Nixon—persisted. Ford's biographer John Robert Greene concludes that there was no deal: Ford's reasons for the pardon were those he stated. Greene goes on to argue, however, that Ford mishandled the pardon by failing to insist that Nixon apologize to the American people for his actions and give up his claim to his presidential papers and to the notorious Oval Office tapes.

Ford showed little of Nixon's openness to innovation. In Congress he had opposed most of Johnson's Great Society program, and in his first year in office he vetoed thirty-nine bills passed by the Democratic Congress, including one mandating increased regulation of strip-mining. Espousing a 1920s-style laissez-faire ideology, he called for "maximum freedom for private enterprise." In 1974, Ford vetoed the Freedom of Information Act, which, reflecting the post-Watergate mood, granted citizens access to their government files. Congress promptly overrode his veto.

Economic problems, and especially inflation, dogged Ford's presidency. Oil prices had risen 350 percent after the 1973 Yom Kippur War, and the 1973–74 Arab oil boycott pushed the inflation rate to a horrendous 11 percent. Taking office amid this price surge, Ford rejected Nixon's wage-and-price controls and instead grandly announced his "Whip Inflation Now" (WIN) program to persuade businesses to restrain prices voluntarily. When the effort fell flat, Ford conceded that it was "probably too gimmicky." With the oil boycott's end, inflation dropped, only to spike upward again in the late 1970s.

Compounding Ford's problems, the worst recession since the Great Depression struck in 1974–75. As business stagnated, the unemployment rate hit 8.3 percent in 1975. To stimulate recovery, Congress cut taxes by some $23 billion in 1975. The economy rallied, but the tax cut worsened the budget deficit, which in turn increased inflationary pressures. The recession battered the nation's cities, already floundering as businesses and middle-class taxpayers fled to the suburbs. By late 1975, New York City edged toward bankruptcy. When New Yorkers in Congress proposed a federal bailout, President Ford refused. "Ford to City: Drop Dead" headlined a Manhattan tabloid. Congress approved emergency loan guarantees, averting the immediate crisis, but urban America's long-term problems continued.

Exploiting the economic mess, the Democrats devised the "Discomfort Index" by combining the inflation and unemployment rates. From 1972 to 1975, this measure nearly doubled. In the 1974 midterm election, frustrated voters increased the Democratic majorities in both the House and Senate. Although some of the administration's inflation-fighting measures—spending cuts, the Federal Reserve Board's tightening of credit—had contributed to the recession, the downturn also had roots in economic changes beyond either party's control. Inflation, for example, stemmed mainly from the oil boycott and the resulting price hikes. Americans accustomed to paying thirty-five cents for a gallon of gas stared in disbelief as prices edged toward seventy cents a gallon. (Even with the price increases, gasoline cost far less in the United States than in Western Europe.) As an added irritant, U.S. oil-company profits more than doubled from 1972 to 1974 as domestic oil prices rose along with the cost of imported oil. Reacting to soaring gasoline prices, Congress in 1975 for the first time imposed fuel-efficiency standards on U.S. automobiles and set a national speed limit of 55 miles an hour.

Henry Kissinger, appointed secretary of state in 1973, remained in that post under Ford, but his brief tenure is mainly remembered for the final scenes of the Vietnam debacle. Nixon's policy of "Vietnamization" had not stopped the fighting, and the 1973 Paris agreement between the United States and the North Vietnamese proved less a formula for peace than a license for the war to proceed without U.S. ground troops. U.S. naval and air power remained on call, and President Thieu

Gas Shortages, March 1974. A citizen with a lawn mower joins car owners waiting to fill up at a San Jose, California, gas station. *(AP/Wide World Photos)*

hired six thousand hastily discharged U.S. army officers as "civilian" advisers. After the cease-fire ended U.S. bombing in Vietnam and Laos, Nixon had ordered a hundred additional B-52s to join the bombing raids on Cambodia, in a show of continued support for Thieu. "This was appalling," the secretary of the air force later wrote. "You couldn't even figure out where you were going to put them all." This bombing continued until August 15, 1973, when a congressional ban took effect. As B-52s rained 250,000 tons of bombs on Cambodia, ostensibly to destroy Khmer Rouge (Cambodian communist) strongholds, the devastation created 2 million refugees in a population of 7 million and hastened the collapse of Lon Nol's U.S.-backed regime. In April 1975, as Cambodia sank into chaos, the Khmer Rouge unseated Lon Nol and launched a reign of genocidal savagery. Before the Vietnamese overthrew the Khmer Rouge dictator Pol Pot in 1979, his regime had slaughtered as many as 2 million people—25 percent of the population. Recounting these events in his 1979 book *Sideshow,* British journalist William Shawcross wrote of Washington's role: "Cambodia was not a mistake; it was a crime."

In South Vietnam, President Thieu, relying on Nixon's pledge of U.S. support, pursued the war. Without U.S. ground forces, however, his cause was hopeless. Congress's rejection of Kissinger's urgent request for $1.5 billion in military aid to South Vietnam ended whatever slim chance Thieu might have had to cling to power a bit longer.

North Vietnamese forces captured Phuoc Long Province, north of Saigon, in January 1975. Pleiku and Danang soon fell, and Hué yielded without a fight despite Thieu's order to hold it at all costs. The retreat turned into a rout, and in late April,

War's Human Toll: Cambodia, 1975. As fighting related to the Vietnam War overwhelmed Cambodia, refugees fled the capital, Phnom Penh. *(© Bettmann/CORBIS)*

after denouncing the United States for reneging on its pledges, Thieu fled to Taiwan with fifteen tons of luggage.* Saigon fell on May 1 and was promptly renamed Ho Chi Minh City. In a final humiliating scene, South Vietnamese who had worked for U.S. officials frantically scrambled aboard helicopters atop the U.S. embassy roof as North Vietnamese forces closed in.

Vietnam memories would long haunt the American psyche and influence the nation's approach to global politics. On one hand, Americans were determined to avoid another Vietnam. On the other, they feared lest the world discount U.S. resolve. In this context, minor incidents took on special significance. For example, in May 1975, when Cambodia's communist regime seized a U.S. merchant vessel, the *Mayaguez,* Ford spurned negotiations and ordered a military rescue by two thousand U.S. marines. The thirty-nine *Mayaguez* crewmembers were "rescued"—at a cost of forty-one marines' lives. (In fact, the Cambodians had released the crew before the operation began.) The symbolic value of Ford's macho display weeks after the Saigon evacuation was clear. *Newsweek* hailed his "daring show of nerve and steel." The families of the dead marines were left to count the cost of this fleeting boost to American self-esteem.

Yet post-Vietnam reluctance to engage U.S. power underlay Congress's refusal to sanction U.S. intervention in the African nation of Angola, which became a cockpit of Cold War conflict after gaining its independence from Portugal in 1974. As civil war erupted, the United States and China backed one faction, Moscow another. When the Soviets flew in Cuban troops in 1975, Kissinger proposed massive aid to the U.S.-backed faction. Gripped by the "no more Vietnams" spirit, Congress refused. Kissinger disgustedly concluded that a traumatized nation was embracing isolationism.

Détente, another Nixon legacy, advanced haltingly. At a 1974 meeting in Vladivostok, Ford and Soviet leader Leonid Brezhnev made some progress on SALT II, an arms-control treaty, but final agreement eluded them. A 1975 summit conference in Helsinki, Finland, constituted the foreign-policy highlight of the Ford years. At this meeting, the nations of Europe, including the Soviet Union and its satellites, agreed to stabilize their national boundaries and the East-West power balance. Equally important, they also adopted a set of accords on human rights and freedom of travel that strengthened reform pressures behind the Iron Curtain. U.S. Cold Warriors and many Americans of Eastern European origin denounced the agreement for conceding Russian hegemony in Eastern Europe, but the Helsinki Accords contributed to the Soviet Union's eventual collapse.

A Sea of Troubles: The Carter Years

As the recession dragged on, the 1976 Democratic presidential nomination tempted several potential candidates, including senators Lloyd Bentsen of Texas and Henry Jackson of Washington (dubbed "the senator from Boeing" for his links to the Seattle

---

*Thieu eventually settled in Great Britain. His vice president, the flamboyant Nguyen Cao Ky, became a prosperous liquor-store operator in California.

aerospace giant). California's maverick governor Jerry Brown, something of a New Age mystic, and James Earl (Jimmy) Carter, Jr., of Georgia, a former governor now running the family's peanut business, also entered the race.

Like George McGovern in 1972, Carter benefited from the post-1968 Democratic Party reforms that had increased the role of primaries and grassroots activists in the choice of candidates. He also was helped by television, which allowed obscure candidates to gain national visibility almost overnight. Supporters of Carter's better-known opponents jeered "Jimmy who?" but he won the Iowa and New Hampshire primaries and soon had the nomination sewn up. As his running mate, he chose Senator Walter Mondale of Minnesota, a leading northern liberal.

Carter offered a pledge of simple honesty ("I will never lie to you") that before Nixon would have sounded ridiculous. A devout Baptist whose sister was an evangelist and faith healer, Carter proclaimed himself a "born-again" Christian who strove to apply his faith in daily life. This open avowal of faith mirrored a larger religious resurgence in American life and politics in the 1970s. Carter's 1976 speechwriter Patrick Anderson later described Carter's evangelical religion as "basic to the idealism and decency that made him attractive to millions who didn't otherwise share his . . . beliefs." Anderson added, however, that this same piety contributed to an aura of self-righteousness that many people eventually found grating.

Gerald Ford withstood a challenge by former governor Ronald Reagan of California to win the Republican nomination. On taking office, Ford had chosen as his vice president former governor Nelson Rockefeller of New York, a prominent lib-

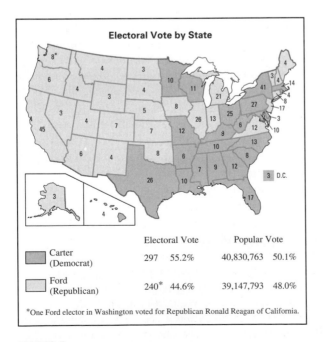

MAP 13.1

Presidential Election of 1976

eral. Now, however, seeking conservative support, he named Senator Robert Dole of Kansas as his running mate.

Carter eked out a victory, winning a scant 50.1 percent of the popular vote. The stricken economy, Watergate memories, and the Nixon pardon had cost Ford the victory. As a pro-civil-rights southerner, Carter won 94 percent of the black vote, which provided his victory margin in thirteen states. Revealing the depth of post-Watergate voter alienation, fewer than 55 percent of those eligible had bothered to cast a ballot. Apathy, it seemed, was the true winner in 1976, summed up in a cynical bumper sticker: DON'T VOTE, IT ONLY ENCOURAGES THEM.

On Inauguration Day, highlighting the contrast with Nixon's imperial presidency, Carter walked from the Capitol to the White House with his wife, Rosalynn, and daughter, Amy. Throughout his term, Carter would project a populist image, favoring blue denims and sports shirts and carrying his own garment bag aboard Air Force One. Fulfilling a campaign pledge, he pardoned some ten thousand Vietnam War draft resisters. Veterans' organizations protested, but most Americans welcomed this gesture of reconciliation.

On domestic issues, Carter built a modest but creditable record. His civil-service reform bill, passed in 1978, introduced a merit-pay system and made it easier to fire incompetents. Honoring a platform promise to the teachers' union, a power in Democratic politics, he created the Department of Education in 1979. At Carter's behest, Congress created a $1.6 billion environmental "Superfund" to clean up the nation's worst pollution sites. The new president set aside over 100 million acres in Alaska, eyed by developers, as parkland, forest reserves, and wildlife areas. Carter appointed a record number of women and minorities to federal office, including three women cabinet members. Civil-rights veteran Andrew Young became UN ambassador.

Carter's political skills proved lame, however, and he failed to achieve such major domestic goals as welfare reform, a stronger social security system, and a national health-insurance system—a liberal objective since Truman's day. Despite Democratic majorities in both houses, his relations with Congress remained prickly. Commented TV journalist Eric Sevareid in 1977: "[Carter] has the mind of an engineer. . . . He's got a lot of little filing cabinets in his mind that he seems able to use as needed. But he doesn't . . . have much stylistic change of pace, and I fear he will become less and less stimulating." Good at analyzing issues and devising paper solutions, he lacked Lyndon Johnson's talent for political deal making. The outsider's role and the aura of rectitude that had helped him win the election also soured his relations with Congress. As his popularity fell, he became more withdrawn, relying on a tight circle of advisers he had brought from Georgia.

The same economic problems that had bedeviled Ford—inflation, recession, rising energy costs—haunted Carter as well. In October 1978, with inflation at 9 percent, Carter announced a program of voluntary wage-and-price restraints. But inflation only worsened, and by 1980 the dollar was worth forty cents compared to 1967. Unemployment crept up as well, reaching 7 percent in 1980, and double that among black and Hispanic workers. The recession erased the gains of the War on Poverty. By 1978, 29 percent of black families and 23 percent of Hispanic families fell below the poverty line, more than three times the rate for whites.

Remedies for one part of the economic crisis worsened another. For example, to fight the recession, Congress, at Carter's request, cut taxes by $34 billion in 1977 and appropriated $4 billion for public-works spending. But the stimulus came too late and only intensified inflationary pressure. Conversely, as the Federal Reserve Board tightened credit—the classic remedy to cool an overheated economy—interest rates soared as high as 20 percent, pushing home mortgages and business loans out of reach and deepening the recession. Carter never devised a coherent economic plan to unravel these dilemmas.

The president's attempt to address energy issues, his top domestic priority, proved equally frustrating. A graduate of the U.S. Naval Academy, he applied his considerable analytic skills to the problem. In April 1977 a sweater-clad Carter sat by a fireplace in the White House library and addressed the nation on energy. Borrowing a phrase from William James, he called the issue the "moral equivalent of war." Soon Congress created a Department of Energy to enforce energy legislation and to formulate national energy policy.

Carter sought to force Americans to conserve by raising the cost of energy. Moreover, he aimed to reduce America's oil imports, which grew from 35 percent of total consumption in 1973 to nearly 50 percent in 1977. In an energy bill presented before a joint session of Congress, Carter proposed phasing out the price controls that kept the cost of domestic oil and natural gas artificially low, while taxing domestic oil production to prevent windfall profits by oil and gas companies. He also called for stiffer federal taxes on gasoline, tax penalties on cars that violated federal fuel-efficiency standards, tax credits for conservation measures, and other measures.

The bill met strong opposition from oil and gas companies, which favored ending price controls but opposed heavier taxes and federal regulation. Political ideology shaped the debate as well. Free-market advocates favored easing environmental regulations and lifting price controls on oil and natural gas, to encourage drilling for new reserves. Liberals emphasized conservation and environmental protection. The energy law that finally passed in October 1978 contained elements of both positions. It lifted price controls on natural gas in phased steps and penalized gas-guzzling cars. It also provided incentives for coal use by industry and energy-saving measures by consumers, including solar heating units. The law fell short of Carter's dream of a "national energy policy," but it was a step in that direction. The public remained skeptical, however, fearful of higher energy costs and unconvinced that the situation was as dire as Carter claimed.

The energy crisis took on new urgency in 1979–80 when OPEC instituted a second round of price increases. A revolution had unseated Iran's pro-U.S. government, and Iran's new regime, together with Iraq, Libya, and Algeria, pushed the cartel to raise prices. Soon Saudi Arabian light crude, the industry benchmark, was selling for over thirty dollars a barrel, ten times the pre-1973 price. Long queues again formed at service stations, and gasoline prices broke the dollar-a-gallon barrier. Rising energy costs rippled through the economy, from producing and transporting consumer goods to college tuition and hospital fees. Americans paid over $16 billion in higher prices in these years, directly related to OPEC's price hikes. U.S. oil companies, by contrast, boomed as energy prices rose. Exxon's first-quarter profits in 1980, $1.9 billion, ranked the highest of any corporation in history.

Capitalizing on the drive to conserve energy, the nuclear-power industry promoted this panacea as the obvious way to conserve fossil fuels, cut pollution, and reduce U.S. reliance on imported oil. The industry had a case: Since it used water-power, nuclear energy was renewable. Under normal operations, nuclear plants, unlike coal-burning generators, did not pollute. President Carter, who had served aboard nuclear submarines in the navy, supported this option.

But environmentalists, already dubious about nuclear power, warned of accidents and the hazards of radioactive-waste disposal. In 1974, a 500-foot tower marking the site of a planned nuclear-power plant in Massachusetts crashed to the ground after an antinuclear activist loosened the bolts. Turning himself in, he explained his gesture as an act of conscience against a project he considered dangerous. As the antinuclear movement gathered momentum, led by such groups as New Hampshire's Clamshell Alliance and California's Abalone Alliance, the activist spirit of the 1960s, and even the test-ban fervor of the 1950s, revived. The 1970s anti-nuclear-power movement anticipated an anti-nuclear-weapons campaign in the early 1980s.

An accident at Pennsylvania's Three Mile Island nuclear power plant in March 1979 bore out the critics' warnings. Some eight hundred thousand gallons of radioactive water burst from a cooling unit, threatening nearby Harrisburg. As tension mounted, Jimmy Carter toured the plant to reassure the public, but his toothy smile seemed forced. In an odd convergence of mass culture and reality, the 1979 movie *China Syndrome*, starring the 1960s antiwar activist Jane Fonda, dramatized the kind of accident that had actually occurred a few weeks earlier. The double whammy of Three Mile Island and *China Syndrome* dealt the nuclear-energy industry a heavy blow. More than thirty planned plants were canceled, and new orders fell to zero. President Nixon had once predicted that by the year 2000 nuclear power would supply half the nation's electricity. In fact, after 1979 the figure stalled at about 20 percent.

Doggedly pursuing his battle for a comprehensive energy policy, Carter again targeted the federal price controls that kept domestic oil prices artificially low. Price controls were already scheduled to end in 1981, but in 1979 Carter announced an immediate, phased decontrol. Again he called for a windfall-profits tax on the oil companies, with the revenue to go for public transportation, alternative-energy development, and heating-bill assistance for the poor. He also proposed a freeze on imported oil and a government program to produce synthetic fuels from coal and shale. When Congress took no action, the president geared up for yet another energy speech.

The public's weariness with Carter's lectures on these complex issues deepened. As he wrote in his memoirs, "My repeated calls for action on energy . . . were . . . falling on deaf ears." Furthermore, his pollster convinced him that the basic problem was not public resistance to energy conservation but a crisis of morale and loss of confidence in Carter himself. This led to one of the more unusual episodes in presidential history. Canceling his scheduled speech, Carter retreated to Camp David with Rosalynn and a few close advisers for ten days of introspection about his and the nation's problems. Scores of pundits from various fields shuttled in and out to conduct a seminar for one student: the president. As Carter and his wife scribbled notes, economists, preachers, journalists, and historians offered their opinions.

After the retreat, Carter gave his postponed speech, in which he diagnosed a national "malaise." America's inability to confront its energy problems, he insisted, reflected "a moral and spiritual crisis . . . a loss of a unity of purpose." In sermon-like tones, he upbraided citizens for abandoning the old values:

> In a nation that was proud of hard work, strong families, close-knit communities, and our faith in God, too many of us now tend to worship self-indulgence and consumption. . . . But . . . piling up material goods cannot fill the emptiness of lives which have no confidence or purpose.

Citing Vietnam, Watergate, inflation, and other reasons for the erosion of civic spirit, Carter nevertheless ended on a cautiously hopeful note:

> There are two paths to choose. One . . . leads to fragmentation and self-interest. . . . All the traditions of our past [and] . . . all the promises of our future point to another path, the path of common purpose and the restoration of American values.

Many agreed that the nation had suffered a failure of nerve, often blamed on the aftershock of Vietnam, which some compared to Great Britain's loss of empire. Opinion polls showed increases in feelings of alienation and powerlessness. But although Carter's call for a renewal of national purpose had a certain eloquence, people had wearied of White House sermonizing. In fact, Americans castigated Carter himself for a failure of leadership and a tendency to blame others for his own deficiencies. The president's firing of three cabinet members, including the secretary of energy, after his "malaise" speech and the resignation of two others highlighted this pattern of blame shifting and underscored Carter's failure to resolve the problems to which he himself had given top priority.

Defining energy policy as the test of whether "we can seize control again of our national destiny," Carter sent to Congress a ten-year, $140 billion energy plan that encompassed research on synthetic fuels, higher oil and natural-gas taxes, and tougher automobile fuel-efficiency standards. Except for funding synthetic-fuel research and imposing a windfall-profits tax on oil companies, Congress once more took little action. Carter's four-year battle for a national energy policy had produced a few victories, much acrimony, and many frustrating setbacks.

By 1979 nearly 75 percent of the American people disapproved of Carter's performance—worse than Nixon's lowest ratings. At the *Boston Globe,* a joke title for an editorial on a Carter speech accidentally slipped into print: "More Mush from the Wimp." In August 1980, as mounting problems battered the White House, a *Time* magazine columnist pronounced Carter "a political cripple" and went on:

> [T]he larger issues have swamped him. . . . In his own inexperience and uncertainty, the President could not define a mission for his Government [or] a purpose for the country. . . . Carter's mind fixed on the small parts of the effort and not the whole.

No one doubted Carter's honesty, intelligence, or sense of duty, but the traits that make for a successful presidency eluded him. Lacking the charisma of a Franklin Roosevelt or a Jack Kennedy, the manipulative genius of a Johnson, or even the cynicism of a Nixon, Carter gamely soldiered on. After Johnson's and Nixon's involuntary departures and Ford's caretaker term, yet another failed presidency loomed. On NBC's popular *Saturday Night Live* TV show, comedians made their reputations by successively parodying Richard Nixon, Gerald Ford, and Jimmy Carter.

But the economic problems of the seventies would have challenged even the ablest leader. No president had the power, short of war, to stop OPEC's oil-price increases, the driving force behind the inflationary spiral. The U.S. economy generated more than 26 million new jobs in the seventies, but unemployment rates still went up as baby boomers flooded the labor market. The combination of recession and inflation added to the economic conundrum. The classic Keynesian solution to recession, adopted by both Democrats and Republicans in the postwar years, featured increased federal spending, tax cuts, and eased credit to stimulate recovery. But as these measures made money and credit more plentiful, inflation worsened. Thus, the Carter administration vacillated between mutually contradictory strategies.

Lobbying by special-interest groups further complicated decision making. These pressures increased, ironically, after passage of a campaign-finance reform law in 1974. This post-Watergate measure provided for public financing of presidential campaigns through a check-off system on federal income-tax forms but permitted political-action committees (PACs) to contribute up to five thousand dollars to any one candidate. By contributing to an array of PACs, a corporation or lobbying group could multiply its influence. By 1980, some three thousand PACs were shoveling money to candidates to promote their legislative agenda. Union PACs, blaming unemployment on imports, pushed for higher tariffs and trade restrictions; corporate PACs blamed the recession on excessive federal regulation. Carter reacted by deregulating the airline, trucking, and railroad industries and persuading Congress to ease banking controls, thereby launching a wave of deregulation that President Reagan would pursue enthusiastically in the 1980s.

Conservative critics also attacked the welfare system. Massive welfare spending, they charged, fed the federal deficits, which in turn worsened the recession. Social-welfare spending, although proportionately modest when compared to that of Sweden and other Western democracies, did climb sharply in the recession-prone 1970s. Adjusted for inflation, public assistance, including welfare, jumped by 47 percent; the food-stamp program by 546 percent; and Medicaid and other health services by 186 percent. Overall, this sector of the federal budget, adjusted for inflation, more than doubled from 1970 to 1979.

As welfare costs mounted and entitlement programs like social security expanded, the federal deficit ballooned. The government borrowed heavily to cover the shortfall and to service the national debt—the legacy of past deficits—driving up commercial interest rates. This in turn inhibited home buying, consumer-credit buying, and business borrowing for expansion. Few professed to have answers to the worsening dilemmas.

A Changing Economy

Beneath the inflation and unemployment that helped to torpedo Carter's presidency lay deeper, more ominous trends. The nation's industrial infrastructure, based in gritty midwestern cities like Pittsburgh, Buffalo, Cleveland, and Detroit,

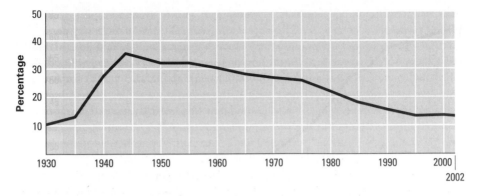

FIGURE 13.1

Percentage of Labor Force Belonging to Unions, 1930–2002

SOURCE: Bureau of Labor Statistics, U.S. Department of Labor, in *World Almanac, 2004*.

was crumbling. Cleveland made unwelcome history in 1978 by becoming the first U.S. city since the 1930s to default on its bonds. Plagued by foreign competition, aging equipment, rising labor costs, and shifting consumer tastes, the factories that had made America the world's industrial leader from the 1880s through World War II limped along or closed their gates. Journalists labeled the region the "Rust Belt." With the industrial decline, union membership in the nonagricultural labor force fell from about 28 percent in 1970 to 23 percent by 1980. The erosion of organized labor in turn weakened a central prop of the Democratic Party and contributed to the conservative turn of American politics.

Two core industries, automobiles and steel, typified the trend. In the 1950s and 1960s, U.S. automakers had ruled the domestic market. True, in these years Americans had bought 4 million Volkswagen "Beetles," an ungainly German import, and other imports had edged into the market, but as late as 1970, the Big Three—General Motors, Ford, and Chrysler—still accounted for 89 percent of U.S. auto sales. All this changed in the seventies. As gasoline prices soared and inflation bit deeper, car buyers welcomed affordable, more fuel-efficient imports like Japan's Toyota and Datsun. Ad campaigns stressing economy—summed up in the slogan "Datsun Saves"—challenged Detroit's traditional emphasis on glamour and style. Domestic automakers with their bulky six-passenger sedans saw their market drift away. By 1980, imports had grabbed 34 percent of the U.S. auto market. The United States now imported 3.2 million foreign cars annually, about 60 percent of them from Japan. Detroit's automotive giants, once America's pride, seemed to have become lumbering dinosaurs.

As the decade ended, conditions worsened. GM ran a deficit in 1980 for the first time since 1921. Ford lost $1.2 billion that year. Only $1.5 billion in federal loan guarantees saved Chrysler, the weakest of the Big Three, from bankrupcy.*

---

*The controversial bailout worked, at least in the short run. Chrysler returned to profitability in 1982 and the following year repaid the loans in full, including $23.4 million in interest.

The Chrysler bailout illustrated how quickly laissez-faire ideology can fade when corporate survival is at stake. Chrysler's chairman Lee Iacocca later wrote, "[T]he last thing in the world I wanted to do was turn to the government. . . . I've always been a free enterpriser, a believer in survival of the fittest. Once the decision was made, however, I went at it with all flags flying."

The auto industry's troubles aggravated the recession. GM, Ford, and Chrysler laid off more than 225,000 workers in 1974 alone. Thousands more faced lengthy "temporary leaves." Skilled workers anticipating a comfortable retirement instead haunted employment offices. With 17 percent of the U.S. labor force linked to auto production, Detroit's problems rippled across the economy.

The steel industry presented a similarly bleak picture. In earlier times, the steel mills of Pittsburgh, Youngstown, Wheeling, and other cities had provided jobs for millions of immigrants. As late as 1950, the United States produced 97 million tons of steel—nearly half the world's total. In 1959, with the steel industry plagued by a long strike, steel imports exceeded exports for the first time in the century. By 1980 U.S. steel output accounted for only 14 percent of total world production. In that year the Soviet Union, Japan, and the twelve-nation European Community all exceeded the United States in steel production, with Canada and Brazil offering strong challenges as well. An industry that had been a bedrock of U.S. industrial might since the 1880s was faltering badly.

Although the auto industry's troubles contributed to steel's decline, the crisis also reflected management's failure to adapt to new technologies, including the basic oxygen furnace, which replaced the old open-hearth system, and the production of steel in continuous sheets rather than in separate ingots. Foreign steelmakers such as Japan's giant Nippon Steel embraced these innovations, abandoning old mills and building new ones. The U.S. steel industry, by contrast, heavily invested in older mills, resisted. By 1980 Japan could make a ton of steel for one-third less than U.S. producers. Even more telling, Japanese steel companies plowed profits back into research and development (R&D) at twice the rate of U.S. companies.

The U.S. companies' behavior contrasted with the boldness that had once characterized American steelmakers. "Well, what shall we throw away this year?" Andrew Carnegie once demanded of his directors. Now, instead of investing in new technologies to ensure future competitiveness, steelmakers, answerable to dividend-hungry stockholders, chose to maximize short-run profits. Furthermore, despite the myth of open competition, the U.S. steel industry was a largely noncompetitive oligopoly of big companies, each with its established market share, charging uniform prices. This, too, discouraged innovation.

The overall U.S. productivity rate (that is, total output divided by total hours of work) lagged as well. During the long postwar boom from 1947 to the mid-1960s, the United States enjoyed average annual productivity increases of 3.2 percent. From 1965 to 1973, the average annual rate increase fell to 2.4 percent. By 1978–80, productivity was declining in absolute terms. With inflation raging, workers' wage raises, which were tied to cost-of-living increases mandated by union contracts, far outstripped productivity.

In explaining declining productivity, analysts reflected their ideological bias. Conservatives pinpointed government regulations, soaring worker-benefit packages, and an overpaid unionized labor force. Liberals stressed short-term profit taking, poor schools and job-training programs, and the lack of a governmental strategy for nurturing new technologies. All agreed on weak investment in R&D as a key problem. Not only the steel industry but also many other corporations shied away from the costly long-term research investment essential to better productivity.

As U.S. productivity declined, that of the nation's trade competitors surged. This was especially true of Japan and West Germany, the World War II foes whose economies, ironically, had rebounded with American aid. In 1980, Toyota produced five times as many cars per worker as did Detroit automakers. As foreign-made cars, TVs, appliances, shoes, clothing, and other products flooded in, U.S. imports far out-ran exports. The 1971 trade deficit, the first since 1888, amounted to $2.3 billion. By 1981 the figure had climbed to $28 billion; soon it would rise far higher.

Despite these difficulties, the U.S. economy remained the world's largest. As we have seen, millions of new jobs were created in the 1970s. Although the trade deficit widened, U.S. exports more than doubled in the decade. For all its problems, America still enjoyed an overall standard of living unmatched in the rest of the world.

Some analysts saw an economy not in decline but in transition. In any dynamic economy, they pointed out, some sectors erode as others expand. They noted U.S. dominance in aerospace, electronics, information processing, and other high-tech fields and the success of companies such as Rochester's Xerox Corporation, a leader in the photocopying industry. The computer field struck many as a beacon of promise. The earliest bulky computers, such as IBM's 360 Series, introduced in 1965, were affordable only by the government and large corporations. Miniaturization came in the 1970s, transforming the industry. First, transistors replaced bulky vacuum tubes. Then sophisticated integrated circuitry made possible desktop computers as powerful as the behemoths of a decade earlier. By the mid-1970s, as computer sales edged upward, more and more people found employment in the growing industry.

Personal-computer (PC) sales took off as the decade ended. In 1976 two college dropouts in Cupertino, California—Steven Jobs and Stephen Wozniak—built a prototype in the Jobs's family garage. (Like Henry Ford tinkering in his garage in the 1890s, the story would become the stuff of legend.) After selling early models to local hobbyists, Jobs and Wozniak founded Apple Computer in 1977. By 1980, sales soared to $118 million. The "Cupertino comet" made *Fortune* magazine's list of the nation's top 500 corporations faster than any other company in history. IBM introduced its first PC in 1981, and other companies rushed into the market. The computer revolution was under way.

Thus, signs of renewal as well as decline marked the economy. As the industrial work force fell, jobs in the service sector increased. In fact, every decade since 1900 had seen increases in the service-sector work force and declines in the percentage of farmers, manual laborers, factory operatives, and other blue-collar workers. This long-term trend accelerated in the 1970s as basic industries faltered. The United States of 1980 more closely resembled the middle-class consumer-and-service society portrayed in Edward Bellamy's 1888 utopian novel *Looking Backward* than it did Karl Marx's vision of a vast industrial proletariat mired in misery.

Along with white-collar professionals, however, the growing service sector also included low-paying jobs: domestic service, motel-room cleaning, car washing, supermarket checkout, Wal-Mart clerking, hamburger flipping at McDonald's, and so on. Laid-off factory employees sometimes found work only in the lower ranks of the service sector. Some economists spoke of the "de-skilling" of the work force. Others warned of a bimodal labor force with highly paid professionals and technicians at one end, unskilled service workers (often minorities and recent immigrants) at the other, and little in between. For better or worse, they argued, the economic trends of the 1970s offered a preview of the future.

The economy thus presented a mixed picture in the 1970s. While the southwestern oil belt, the necklace of high-tech industries encircling Boston, and California's "Silicon Valley"* south of San Francisco boomed, the industrial heartland stagnated. In the inner cities, minority youths and recent immigrants confronted an economy that increasingly demanded specialized skills and advanced education.

With billions going for defense and for mandated entitlement programs, and with the recession driving down tax revenues, the federal deficit soared from $8.7 billion in 1970 to a whopping $72.7 billion in 1980, and the total national debt approached $1 trillion. Worse lay ahead, but in the seventies the tide of federal red ink was already rising ominously.

To many, the nation's best years lay in the past. Eighty years after historian Frederick Jackson Turner had explored the meaning of the closing of the geographic frontier, the end of the industrial frontier and the can-do spirit associated with it seemed at hand. Worry and resentments rooted in economic problems increasingly seeped into the cultural and political climate.

Backlash: Culture and Politics in the Later Seventies

The 1970s defy easy categorization. Self-absorbed narcissism coexisted alongside movements for social change. Environmentalism, feminism, gay-rights protests, and activism by older Americans (including an organizations called "Gray Panthers") and persons with disabilities all remained strong, winning legislative and legal victories, yet the public sphere as a whole seemed diminished. Amid the crosscurrents, one trend emerged with clarity: The liberalism that had peaked in 1964–65 steadily lost support, laying the groundwork for a conservative resurgence.

Tom Wolfe's "Me Generation" continued to display narcissistic self-absorption. "Americans have retreated to purely personal preoccupations," observed historian Christopher Lasch in 1979. Faced with gnawing economic problems and a series of disgraced or weak presidents, many Americans gave up on civic engagement and, like Voltaire's Candide, cultivated their own gardens instead. The years following the Civil War and both world wars had witnessed a retreat to private concerns, and the aftermath of Vietnam brought a similar reaction.

The evidence for this shift was everywhere. Escapist novels like Erich Segal's *Love Story* (1970) and Peter Benchley's *Jaws* (1974) spawned hit movies. In the blockbuster film *Saturday Night Fever* (1977), John Travolta pushed narcissism to

---

*The nickname came from the silicon chip, a key component in the new integrated circuitry that made possible the miniaturized personal computer.

new heights, preening before the mirror, devoting loving attention to his hair styling, and only fully coming alive as he dances in his white suit at a Brooklyn disco club. Richard Bach's *Jonathan Livingston Seagull* (1970), a dreamy New Age allegory of self-realization, tells of a seagull that withdraws from the flock to pursue its lonely dream of flying more gracefully than any seagull has ever flown before. (By 2004, amazon.com was offering hundreds of used copies of the book, with prices beginning at $0.01.)

Baby boomers "gentrified" decaying urban neighborhoods, creating islands of trendy sophistication amid inner-city blight. A jogging fad swept the middle class, inspiring a 1978 *Newsweek* story that began with the Whitmanesque line "I hear America puffing." James Fixx's *The Complete Book of Running* sold eight hundred thousand copies. (Sales fell after Fixx died of a heart attack while jogging.) The fitness vogue heightened interest in natural foods and healthy diets. Beef sales declined; fish and chicken consumption rose. Low-calorie "lite" foods and beverages filled supermarket shelves. The sexual liberation that in the 1960s had been linked to radical protest now proceeded on its own, unencumbered by ideology. The lavishly illustrated *Joy of Sex* by the aptly named Alex Comfort became another 1970s bestseller.

As two-career households proliferated, often because of economic necessity, couples postponed having children or placed their offspring in daycare facilities. In 1977, 35 percent of all children under age five spent their days with a nonrelative or in a childcare center. Semimythic stories told of middle-class parents' scrambling to place their children in prestigious nursery schools to enhance the little ones' chances of gaining admission to a top college.

The activist energies of the 1970s often found conservative, even reactionary, outlets, as the national mood tacked to the right. This conservative impulse took many forms and found many targets. "Liberals" and "secular humanists" were demonized as threats to religion and "traditional values," a catch-all term for the supposed moral and cultural unity of an earlier time. Some leftists and liberals of the older generation, repelled by the excesses of the 1960s, moved rightward. Warning against left-wing utopianism and naiveté and invoking absolutist moral principles, these neoconservatives praised the free-enterprise system and preached a militant anticommunism. The conservative movement flourished outside the electoral arena, as George Wallace's political eclipse and Nixon's resignation stymied its natural political expression. As Thomas and Mary Edsall later wrote, "Watergate . . . effectively choked off the growth of conservatism from 1973 through 1976. . . . [I]nstead of finding an outlet within the political system, rightward pressure built throughout the decade to explosive levels. . . . Watergate resulted in a political system out of sync with larger trends."

This disjunction between politics and the national mood produced striking anomalies. For example, while the Supreme Court issued rulings protecting the rights of arrested persons and convicts, and even for a time abolished the death penalty, many Americans, alarmed by rising crime rates, demanded a crackdown on criminals.* Similarly, as the Equal Employment Opportunity Commission and

---

*According to FBI statistics, the number of reported violent crimes (murder, robbery, assault, and rape) rose from 738,000 in 1970 to 1,345,000 in 1980.

other federal agencies promoted minority rights and developed affirmative-action programs, many whites turned against what they labeled "reverse discrimination."

The conservatism of the 1970s had economic as well as cultural sources. Oil shocks, recessions, inflation, and industrial decline hit millions of families. In three successive years (1973–75), for the first time since World War II, the median income of the average U.S. family, adjusted for inflation, actually fell. Regular increases in social security taxes voted by Congress in these years further reduced workers' after-tax income. Millions of Americans also experienced "bracket creep." As cost-of-living clauses in union contracts pushed their wages up (with no increase in buying power because of inflation), they moved into higher tax brackets, forking over a larger share of their earnings to Uncle Sam.

Nagging economic worries fueled a grassroots tax revolt. In 1978 California voters overwhelmingly passed Proposition 13. This measure slashed real-estate taxes, creating havoc for the state's education and welfare systems. Similar referenda soon appeared on ballots across the nation. Declared one pollster, "This isn't just a tax revolt. It's a revolution against government." Economic anxieties also intensified a reaction against Johnson-style liberalism with its emphasis on helping disadvantaged groups, sometimes through preferential programs. In a time of prosperity, the majority had supported such programs. But as Middle America saw its own status eroding, sympathy for such reforms gave way to hostility against welfare recipients, minorities, and other groups that seemed to enjoy special attention.

The women's movement became a prime target of this backlash. As the economy weakened, the flow of women into the workplace stirred resentment among men fearful of losing their own jobs. Conservatives attacked "radical feminism" as pro-abortion, antifamily, and a threat to traditional values. Illustrating how social class can trump gender, many working-class women rejected the feminist movement, sensing that its agenda mainly concerned college-educated and professional women. Marabel Morgan's *The Total Woman* (1975) appealed to such resentments, urging women to discover new meaning in traditional roles. "A total woman caters to her man's special needs," she wrote, "whether it be in salads, sex or sports." Formulaic romance novels (sometimes called "bodice rippers") set in distant times and exotic locales and featuring dreamy women ravished by domineering males, evoking the gender stereotypes of the 1950s, sold 20 million copies in the 1970s.

In 1978, when twenty thousand feminists gathered in Houston for a National Women's Conference, eight thousand conservative women at a counter-rally cheered Phyllis Schlafly, who proclaimed, "The American people do not want the ERA [Equal Rights Amendment], and they do not want government-funded abortion, lesbian privileges, or [federally funded] . . . universal child care."

Schlafly's conservative Eagle Forum fought the ERA as a radical assault on traditional gender roles that would force women into combat and even require unisex toilets! One anti-ERA Missouri housewife baked and sold 450 coconut cakes and sent the proceeds to Schlafly. In 1979, with only three more states needed for ratification, Congress granted a three-year extension. But the climate had changed since ERA was first proposed, and the amendment failed.

The battle over *Roe* v. *Wade,* the 1973 Supreme Court decision establishing women's right to terminate pregnancy, proved even more emotion laden. As legal abortions rose from 18,000 in 1968 to 1.3 million in 1977, public opinion remained polarized, with an uncertain middle group hesitant to criminalize the procedure, but doubtful about its ethics. This opened the way for a well-organized antiabortion "Right to Live" movement, led by the Roman Catholic Church with support from Protestant evangelicals and Orthodox Jews.

In 1976, Congress barred the use of Medicare funds to finance abortions. To the dismay of pro-choice forces, the Supreme Court upheld this ban. In 1978 Congress extended the ban on federally funded abortions to military personnel and their families and to Peace Corps volunteers. By 1980, abortion had become a defining issue in American political culture.

As thousands of gays and lesbians "came out," marching in Gay Pride parades and protesting discrimination, this movement, too, drew hostile attention. Beginning around 1973, under pressure from gay activists, states and municipalities adopted ordinances barring discrimination on the basis of sexual orientation. But a reaction soon set in. Conservative religious leaders denounced homosexuality as contrary to God's law and a sign of national degeneracy. Right-wing politicians deplored the movement as an example of 1960s-style liberalism run amok. When Miami adopted a gay-rights statute in 1977, pop singer Anita Bryant mounted a protest campaign. If God had favored homosexuality, she pointed out, "[He] would have created Adam and Bruce." In a referendum, Miamians repealed the statute by a two-to-one margin. Voters rejected similar measures in other cities.

The conservative backlash also focused on issues of race. In the 1950s and early 1960s, a consensus had supported civil rights and antipoverty programs aimed at uplifting inner-city minorities. In the 1970s, that consensus collapsed. Goodwill gave way to resentment, and cities torn by racial violence elected get-tough "law-and-order" candidates. As the struggle against racial discrimination shifted northward, it sparked complex reactions involving not only race but also social class. Two issues catalyzed the tensions: school busing to achieve racial balance and affirmative-action plans to compensate for past discrimination.

Busing plans ignited angry white protest in many cities. Critics denounced busing as federal meddling with a local issue to promote an abstract social ideal. The fact that the officials who mandated school busing often lived in affluent suburbs unaffected by the plans added a class dimension to the resentment. The most heated dispute erupted in Boston, where the school committee had resisted black pressure to propose a school-integration plan. In 1974 federal Judge W. Arthur Garrity, finding systematic racial segregation in Boston's schools, ordered the school committee to develop a desegregation plan that included busing. Irish American and other ethnic neighborhoods of South Boston and Charlestown—insular, conservative, and hurting economically—exploded at the meddling of affluent "limousine liberals" like Garrity. That fall, white students boycotted "Southie" (South Boston High School), and their supporters stoned black students bused from nearby Roxbury. When a white youth was stabbed, a mob trapped 135 black students in the school for four hours. Eerily echoing Little Rock in 1957, white parents marched under banners such as ROAR (Restore Our Alienated Rights). Young white thugs, one of them wielding a flagpole bearing an American flag, beat a young black lawyer outside Boston City Hall. President Ford, following Nixon's script, fueled the protests by denouncing school busing to achieve racial integration.

The seventies also saw bitter fighting over programs to increase blacks' access to skilled jobs, education, and the professions. The issue reached the courts when Allan Bakke, a white, sued the medical school of the University of California at Davis, charging that his rejected application was stronger than that of others who had been admitted under a racial quota system. In 1978 the Supreme Court, by a 5–4 vote, upheld Bakke's claim and ordered the school to enroll him. Ruling that admissions offices might consider race as one factor in their decisions, the Court forbade the setting of specific quotas for minorities. Justice Thurgood Marshall, veteran black civil-rights activist who as an NAACP attorney had argued the *Brown v. Board of Education* case in 1954, angrily dissented, citing the nation's history of discrimination. Affirmative-action programs, even quotas, he declared, were an appropriate minimal response by white America to centuries of racial injustice.*

The spirit of unity that had pervaded the 1963 March on Washington seemed distant in the later 1970s as race-related issues spawned acrimony. Jimmy Carter, who owed his election to African American voters, appointed a number of blacks to office but did not place race high on his agenda. Issues that had appeared clear-cut in the sixties now seemed riddled with ambiguity. Even some black leaders criticized busing to achieve integration, urging more attention to upgrading black schools. In *The Declining Significance of Race* (1978), William Julius Wilson, a black sociologist, argued that the central division in modern America was no longer between the races but between middle-class, upwardly mobile Americans—white and black—and the inner city underclass cut off from jobs, education, and hope.

The backlash hit other minorities as well, including the more than 12 million Hispanics, 60 percent of Mexican origin. The Hispanic jobless rate far exceeded the national average, and the wages of male Hispanic workers averaged only 70 percent of white male earnings. One and a half million job-seeking Hispanics entered the United States legally in the 1970s, mostly from Mexico and the Caribbean. Many more came clandestinely. Yet in this anxious decade, the Hispanic poor, viewed as competitors in a tight labor market, stirred more resentment than solicitude.

The Asian population also rose sharply in the 1970s, as 1.8 million immigrants arrived from the Philippines, Korea, China, Vietnam, India, and other nations. Fueled by immigration, the ranks of Asian Americans grew to 3.7 million by 1980, further diversifying the American demographic palette. Again, however, economic stress produced an edge of hostility toward these newcomers, intensifying the decade's broader conservative trend.

Some social observers foresaw an America splintered into separate groups, each preoccupied with its own concerns. Channeled positively, such heightened group consciousness encouraged a quest for new sources of community, as expressed in ethnic pride and interest in ancestral roots. But social fragmentation also expressed itself as a retreat from civic engagement and hostility to those outside one's immediate circle of identity.

---

*In 2003, in two cases involving the University of Michigan, the Supreme Court, by a 5–4 vote, upheld the Bakke ruling, holding that public universities may consider race as one factor in admissions, provided they do not use racial quotas or adopt mechanical, point-based admissions procedures.

Both the search for community and the new conservatism found an outlet in religion. A fifteen-year trend of declining church attendance reversed in the 1970s, owing mainly to an upsurge in evangelicalism. In the 1950s, despite the popularity of revivalist Billy Graham, the mainstream liberal denominations had set the tone of American Protestantism. Observers of religious trends had long assumed that Protestantism's theologically conservative evangelical wing, and its even stricter variant, fundamentalism, would gradually fade away, leaving the field to the theologically liberal and socially progressive mainstream denominations and their organizational voice, the National Council of Churches. Yet evangelicalism not only survived but flourished, sustained by a network of local congregations, church colleges, regional leaders, publications such as *Christianity Today*, and the National Association of Evangelicals, an umbrella organization.

In the 1970s, the liberal denominations hemorrhaged members while evangelical bodies like the Southern Baptists and the Assemblies of God burgeoned. Americans troubled by the fragmentation and impersonality of modern life welcomed the sense of community offered by evangelical congregations. In *Why Conservative Churches Are Growing* (1972), Dean M. Kelley accused the liberal denominations of neglecting their own members in their fervor for social action, while evangelical churches more fully met parishioners' spiritual and psychological needs. In a 1978 survey, 22 percent of Americans identified themselves as evangelicals; other polls put the total as high as one-third. Although strongest in the South, with its high concentration of Protestants, evangelicalism flourished in all regions and at all socioeconomic levels. "Born-again" celebrities included Bob Dylan (briefly) and Watergate conspirator Charles Colson. Jimmy Carter saturated his speeches with the language and moral outlook of evangelicalism. The decade also saw a surge in Christian schools founded by evangelicals dismayed by the public schools' "secularism" and by such social realities as teenage sex, alcohol abuse, and drug use.

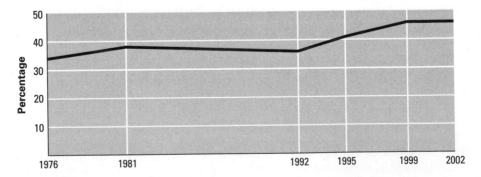

FIGURE 13.2

Percentage of Americans Identifying Themselves as Evangelical or "Born-Again" Christians, 1976–2002

SOURCE: Data from John C. LaRue, "Myths We Tell Ourselves," *Christianity Today,* May/June 2001; Nicholas D. Kristof, "Born-Again Christians Surge in Influence," *International Herald Tribune,* March 5, 2003.

TV preachers led the evangelical resurgence. Oklahoma's Oral Roberts built a vast TV ministry based on evangelical preaching and divine healing. Jimmy Swaggart of Louisiana, Jack Van Impe of Michigan, Jim and Tammy Bakker of South Carolina, and many others reached worldwide audiences via satellite. Pat Robertson's Christian Broadcasting Network (CBN) aired many of these programs. Robertson's own *700 Club* featured talk-show-style interviews with evangelical leaders. The "pope" of the electronic church, Jerry Falwell of Lynchburg, Virginia, broadcast his weekly *Old Time Gospel Hour* on 325 TV stations and 300 radio stations. Televangelists reached millions each week and raked in contributions from what they fondly called their "television family." By the decade's end, they had become a major force not only in religion but also in politics.

As the political culture became more conservative, evangelical churches, with their biblical literalism and clear-cut moral codes, were well positioned to benefit. Energized by the TV preachers and reinforced by conservative Catholics, Mormons, and Jews, Protestant evangelicals wielded potent influence in the 1970s as they engaged political and cultural issues. Via television, magazines, paperbacks, and local pulpits, they called for action to reverse the nation's moral breakdown.

Best-selling religious paperbacks promulgated the evangelical perspective on modern society. The Reverend Tim LaHaye, writing in 1980, cited an array of trends, including divorce, pornography, abortion, gay rights, and "militant feminism," that threatened to make America a modern Sodom and Gomorrah. One popular genre used Bible prophecy to explain world events. The nonfiction bestseller of the 1970s, Hal Lindsey's *The Late Great Planet Earth* (1970), found America's moral decline, the Cold War, the nuclear arms race, Russia's destruction, and the emerging global economy all foretold in scripture. Soon, he predicted, all true believers will be spirited from the Earth in the Rapture, and the Antichrist, a demonic figure portended in the Bible, will rule the world by means of giant computers and orbiting TV satellites.

The political mobilization of the Christian Right, initially directed against federal efforts to deny tax-exempt status to Christian schools, quickly gained momentum and a broader focus. The Moral Majority, an organization founded by Falwell in 1979 to spearhead America's spiritual regeneration at the ballot box, attracted numerous adherents and intense media attention. Politicized evangelicals mobilized against rock music, sex magazines like *Playboy,* and offensive movies and TV shows. The Reverend Don Wildmon's National Federation for Decency organized boycotts of advertisers that sponsored sexually suggestive TV shows. Evangelicals favored prayer in the schools and denounced "secular humanism" in textbooks. Strongly patriotic, they urged morality in government, denounced the Soviet Union, and called for increased military spending to fight "godless communism."

The evangelical upsurge underscored the longing for connectedness and moral clarity spawned by the cultural disarray, economic troubles, and political failures of the 1970s. In Robert Altman's 1975 movie *Nashville,* lonely, unfulfilled people hover like moths around Nashville's glamorous country music stars while a sound truck for a mysterious, unseen presidential candidate blares endlessly in the city's streets. Nostalgia for a sense of community lost somewhere in the past surfaced in cultural products as diverse as the Bicentennial projects of 1976, the 1977 *Roots* miniseries, and Woody Allen's chronicling of a failed relationship in *Annie*

IN PERSPECTIVE

That Old-Time Religion

The election of a born-again Christian, Jimmy Carter, as president in 1976 focused attention on the continued vitality of evangelical Protestantism, a surprise to many who long ago had written its obituary.

In nineteenth-century America, evangelicalism was a powerful force. From the revivals on the Kentucky frontier in 1801 to a long series of urban revivals led by Charles Finney, Dwight L. Moody, and others, evangelical piety pervaded American life. While missions, Sunday schools, and tract societies spread the faith in the cities, Methodist circuit riders and missionaries carried the Word to isolated interior settlements. Evangelicals led many nineteenth-century reforms; Harriet Beecher Stowe, author of the antislavery bestseller *Uncle Tom's Cabin* (1852), was the daughter of a prominent evangelical minister, Lyman Beecher.

By the end of the century, however, evangelicalism seemed on the wane. From the 1890s through the 1920s, the liberal Social Gospel dominated mainstream Protestantism. Evangelicals fought back, battling "modernism" and codifying the fundamentals of their faith, including the verbatim inspiration of the Bible and the resurrection and Second Coming of Jesus Christ. In the interwar years, regional leaders such as Aimee Semple McPherson of Los Angeles attracted large congregations and employed the new medium of radio to spread the message.

The faith continued to make steady gains after World War II, thanks to evangelists like Billy Graham (shown in photo) and organizations such as Youth for Christ. The Assemblies of God church and other charismatic or "pentecostal" groups that featured divine healing and emotional worship grew rapidly. In the 1970s and 1980s, with mainstream Protestantism in decline, evangelicalism attracted waves of new adherents. Evangelical paperbacks sold by the millions; "Bible-believing" independent churches proliferated across the land; TV preachers entered countless homes via cable and satellite; and evangelical missionaries made dramatic inroads among the Catholic populations of Latin America.

Long ignored, evangelicalism drew increasing scholarly notice. In *American Evangelicalism: Conservative Religion and the Quandary of Modernity* (1983), sociologist James Davison Hunter examined how evangelicals both resist and accommodate contemporary trends in a process that he called "cognitive bargaining." For example, evangelical authors published many self-help books offering techniques for achieving personal happiness and emotional well-being—popular themes in the general culture—but written from a specifically evangelical theological perspective. Returning to the theme in *Culture Wars: The Struggle to Define America* (1991), Hunter portrayed religious conservatives as key players in a battle for the nation's soul. "America," he wrote, "is in the midst of a culture war that [reverberates] . . . not only within public policy but within the lives of ordinary Americans everywhere."

What were the political implications of this struggle? Some believers repudiated the wicked world and withdrew into their own spiritual realm. At its most extreme, this separatist impulse produced phenomena such as David Koresh's Branch Davidian sect, whose members barricaded themselves in a heavily armed compound near Waco, Texas, to await the end. In April 1993, after a long standoff with the FBI, Koresh and most of his followers perished in a fiery holocaust that tragically fulfilled their prophecies of a final Armageddon-like confrontation.

More typically, however, religious conservatives turned to politics to realize their moral vision. In the 1980s, the Moral Majority led by televangelist Jerry Falwell enthusiastically supported the Reagan movement. In the 1990s, Pat Robertson's Christian Coalition mobilized conservative activists who ran for school board, city council, and other local offices, building a righteous nation at the grassroots level. Founded in 1989, the Christian Coalition boasted 350,000 members in 750 chapters by 1993. In many states and communities, well-organized religious conservatives maneuvered for control of the Republican Party.

Scholars observing this trend saw a decline in traditional denominational loyalties and a rise in special-agenda groups—the Christian Action Council, the Christian Heritage Center, the National Pro-Family Coalition, and scores of others—that pursued specific agendas while sharing a common goal. Nineteenth-century evangelicals had formed single-issue organizations such as the Anti-Saloon League (1895) but had lacked the computer-based direct-mail techniques available to their modern-day successors. Mobilizing around what they saw as defining moral issues, politically active religious conservatives embraced symbolic causes such as creationism, school prayer, and "family values" and battled abortion, pornography, homosexuality, radical feminism, sexual permissiveness in the media, sex education in the schools, government support for "obscene" art, and the worldview that they denounced as "secular humanism." One skeptic defined the latter term as "a label used by the Far Right to attack virtually everything that they disagree with about the schools and society at large."

Mark Twain once dismissed reports of his death as "greatly exaggerated," and the same might be said of evangelical religion in modern America. Amid turbulent world events and unsettling social changes at home, millions of Americans still find meaning and reassurance in religious beliefs and folkways. As they enter the public arena to apply their religious vision to public policy, they demonstrate once again evangelicalism's central role in U.S. history and life.

Hall (1977). It emerged, too, in the pop-culture mythologizing of America's past offered in John Jakes's *Kent Family Chronicles,* which sold 30 million copies between 1974 and 1980.

Right-wing political movements exploited this volatile stew of economic worries and white backlash, evangelical moralism and traditionalist longings. Conservative think tanks such as Washington's Heritage Foundation (1973), financed by Colorado beer baron Joseph Coors, funded New Right intellectuals. William F. Buckley's venerable *National Review* flourished. Mass-mail specialist Richard Viguerie, a Louisiana-born Roman Catholic, marshaled computerized lists of names to raise funds for conservative causes and candidates by focusing on such emotion-laden themes as gun control, abortion, gay rights, the death penalty, and school prayer. The American Conservative Union in 1978 boasted three hundred thousand members and contributions of $3 million. Jerry Falwell summed up the ultimate political objective of all this organizational effort: "We have enough votes to run the country. And when the people say, 'We've had enough,' we are going to take over."

As the Watergate trauma faded, the New Right found its political legs. In 1976 candidate Jimmy Carter moved to the right, downplaying his party's traditional championing of the underdog and emphasizing instead such themes as fiscal restraint, governmental efficiency, and tax-code revision. Even so, working-class whites abandoned the Democratic ticket in ominous numbers that year. In 1960, 61 percent of blue-collar whites had voted for John F. Kennedy; in 1976, only 53 percent of the voters in this category cast their ballots for Carter.

By the 1978 midterm election, the political realignment was fully under way. Much of the $17.3 million spent by PACs that year came from conservative sources. Using computerized mailings lists, right-wing PACs targeted liberal legislators for defeat and conservatives for support. With an overall voter turnout of under 38 percent, such motivational tactics proved effective: Targeted liberals fell, while New Right favorites such as Jesse Helms, seeking a second term in North Carolina, sailed to victory. Antiabortion candidates backed by the National Right-to-Life Committee won elections across the nation, Proposition 13 passed in California, and Republicans enjoyed a net gain of nearly three hundred seats in state legislatures.

The rightward drift affected both parties—conservative Democratic mayors in Los Angeles and Philadelphia capitalized on the white backlash—but the main beneficiary was the GOP. Arising from the ashes of Watergate, the Republicans reinvented themselves. Historically the party of privilege, the GOP now redefined itself as the vehicle of grassroots resentments and fears. The successes of 1978 portended an even more dramatic triumph two years later. With inflation raging, unemployment rising, and family income continuing to sag, the anger surging throughout Middle America intensified.

In the 1960s, liberalism had come under attack from the Left; now it faced a far stronger assault from the Right. Political conservatism had once been the domain of corporate America and the moneyed class, who had denounced high taxes, big government, and federal regulation. These issues remained alive, but the New Right democratized conservatism, reaching out to the grassroots not only with political and economic appeals but also with potent cultural and religious themes.

One last crisis, centered in distant Iran, drove the final nail into Jimmy Carter's political coffin and buoyed conservative Republican hopes as the 1980 election neared.

Carter Diplomacy and the Middle East Hostage Crisis

As in the Ford years, Richard Nixon's agenda continued to shape U.S. foreign policy during Carter's term. In 1979, Carter formalized full diplomatic relations with the People's Republic of China, completing the process that Nixon and Kissinger had initiated a decade earlier. Carter also set out to apply his problem-solving skills to international issues, but forces beyond his control ultimately thwarted his ambitions abroad, just as they did at home.

In assembling his foreign-policy team, Carter drew on his contacts as a member of the Trilateral Commission, a private organization started in 1972 by David Rockefeller, head of Chase Manhattan Bank, and by Zbigniew Brzezinski, professor of international relations at Columbia University. The commission brought together political, economic, and strategic leaders of the United States, Western Europe, and Japan to address issues of global concern. As secretary of state, Carter named Cyrus Vance, a New York lawyer and pillar of the foreign-policy establishment. As national security adviser, he chose Brzezinski. The son of a pre–World War II Polish diplomat, Brzezinski, like Kissinger, had immigrated to America as a youth. A confirmed Cold Warrior, he deeply distrusted Moscow. U.S. foreign policy in the late 1970s reflected the personalities and ideology of Carter, Vance, and Brzezinski.

Like Woodrow Wilson, Jimmy Carter believed that morality had an important role in foreign policy. Committed to expanding human rights around the world, he rejected Kissinger's realpolitik approach, which largely ignored the internal policies of nations friendly to U.S. interests. Cyrus Vance found Carter's goals congenial. Using U.S. influence, along with threats to cut off foreign aid, he prodded Chile, Argentina, Ethiopia, South Africa, and other nations to improve their human-rights record. Carter and Vance focused more on Africa and Latin America than had Nixon and Kissinger, who had viewed these regions simply as arenas for pursuing the superpower game.

Carter hoped to make Latin America a showcase of his human-rights policy, yet when leftists rebelled against Nicaragua's right-wing dictator, Anastasio Somoza, in 1977, Carter showed more concern about the spread of communism than about Somoza's brutal suppression of the insurgency. When the rebel Sandinistas (named for an earlier revolutionary hero, Augusto Sandino) overthrew Somoza in 1979, Carter recognized the new regime but gave it little attention. In El Salvador, terrorist "death squads" supported by the ruling junta assassinated thousands, including the archbishop of El Salvador and four American Roman Catholic missionaries in 1980. Washington's protests proved ineffectual. When Carter's term ended, he left festering problems in both countries.

In Panama, by contrast, Carter's moralism and U.S. strategic interests converged. In the 1960s, alarmed by anti-American demonstrations in Panama, President Johnson had begun talks to renegotiate the one-sided 1903 treaty by which the United States owned and operated the Panama Canal. Under Carter, the two nations agreed on treaties by which the United States restored Panamanian sovereignty to the Canal Zone and pledged to transfer canal operations to Panama by 1999. The Senate approved the treaties by the bare two-thirds necessary. Although the agreements safeguarded U.S. security interests, the New Right seized upon them as another symbol of the failure of American will.

Extending another Nixon initiative, Carter at first pursued détente with Moscow. Meeting in Vienna in June 1979, Carter and Leonid Brezhnev initialed the SALT II Treaty limiting each nation to 2,250 missile launchers. When Carter submitted the treaty to the Senate for ratification, conservatives denounced it for accepting the principle of nuclear parity instead of U.S. superiority. Hawkish neoconservative Democrats formed a lobbying group, the Committee on the Present Danger, to fight the treaty. To reassure the critics and in response to hard-line pressure from Brzezinski, Carter approved a new nuclear missile system, the MX, to replace the older Minuteman ICBMs. He also sanctioned a new missile-launching submarine, the Trident, ratcheting up the nuclear arms race even as he tried to push SALT II through the Senate.

Prospects for the ratification of SALT II collapsed in December 1979 when the Soviets invaded Afghanistan, on their southern border, to squelch a militant Islamic fundamentalist movement that jeopardized the pro-Soviet regime in Kabul and threatened to spread to the Soviet Union itself. For Americans convinced of Moscow's desire to rule the world, the action confirmed their worst fears. National Security Adviser Brzezinski, already suspicious of détente, pushed Carter toward a tough anti-Soviet stance. Under his influence, Carter's human-rights policy became mainly a club for bludgeoning Moscow. Amid rising anti-Soviet sentiment, Carter withdrew SALT II from the Senate. Pronouncing Russia's Afghan invasion "the most serious threat to world peace since World War II," he canceled trade agreements with the Soviets and even pulled the United States out of the 1980 Moscow Olympics.

Early in 1980, addressing a joint session of Congress, Carter warned that the Soviet invasion of Afghanistan had brought them within three hundred miles of the Persian Gulf and menaced the flow of oil to the West. Echoing the 1947 Truman Doctrine, the president enunciated the Carter Doctrine: any "attempt by an outside force to gain control of the Persian Gulf" would be deemed a grave threat to the United States. Détente lay in shambles. The harshly anti-Soviet tone of the early Reagan years was set by Jimmy Carter in 1980.

Carter's greatest foreign-policy achievement and his costliest failure both came in the Middle East. In the Nixon-Ford years, Henry Kissinger had worked in vain for a comprehensive peace settlement in this tempestuous region. President Carter avidly pursued this goal, impelled in part by his evangelical beliefs, which gave special meaning to Israel and its history. Carter's peacemaking impulse gained a boost in November 1977 when Egyptian leader Anwar el-Sadat initiated peace talks with the Israelis.

In September 1978 Carter invited Sadat and Israeli prime minister Menachem Begin to Camp David. After thirteen days of negotiations, the president announced that a framework of peace had been agreed on. The following March, Sadat and

Begin signed a peace treaty at the White House. Egypt recognized Israel, and Israel agreed to return the Sinai peninsula to Egypt. Peace in the Middle East remained a distant vision, but Carter had facilitated an important first step, in the process scoring a rare success for his embattled presidency.

But events in the Middle East also brought Carter's administration to its nadir. Since 1953, Iran had been ruled by Shah Reza Pahlavi, a strong U.S. ally since 1953, when the CIA had helped him crush his domestic opponents (see page 111). Yet the shah proved no match for the fundamentalist energies roiling the Islamic world. In January 1979, he fled Iran in the face of a revolutionary uprising led by the Ayatollah Ruhollah Khomeini, a leader of Islam's intensely militant Islamic Shiite sect that hated the shah's secular, Westernizing regime.

When Carter admitted the shah to the United States for cancer treatment in November 1979, Iran's Shiites exploded. With the blessings of Khomeini, who regularly denounced the United States as "the Great Satan," Shiite militants occupied the U.S. embassy in Tehran and seized seventy-six American hostages. Six escaped unseen, and the kidnappers soon released thirteen black or female embassy employees. The Carter administration expelled Iranian students and froze Iranian assets in the United States but seemed powerless to break the impasse.

The hostage crisis, reported daily in the media, dominated the rest of Carter's term. The Khomeini regime took full advantage of America's obsession with the prisoners. The nightly news brought images of blindfolded hostages paraded by their captors and of kidnappers using American flags to carry out garbage. The more the U.S. media focused on the hostages, the greater their propaganda value became for Iran.

In April 1980, an attempted U.S. rescue operation failed as three helicopters broke down in dust storms in the Iranian desert. During the evacuation, a helicopter and a C-130 transport collided, killing eight Americans and further humiliating the United States. Secretary of State Vance, who had opposed the operation, resigned. Carter's approval ratings, already feeble, sank even further. The ordeal consumed him. Recalling the crisis in his memoirs, Carter admitted, "The release of the American hostages had become almost an obsession with me."

As the hostage crisis dragged on and the inflation-recession cycle continued, a weakened Jimmy Carter faced the 1980 electoral campaign. Responding to conservative critics, he called for cuts in federal welfare spending, an approach that upset liberal Democrats without winning back the alienated white working class. He fended off a challenge for the Democratic nomination by Senator Edward Kennedy, inheritor of the Kennedy legacy but still dogged by the Chappaquiddick incident. In the general election, however, Carter was roundly trounced.

Returning to private life, he founded the Carter Presidential Center at Atlanta's Emory University, where he organized conferences aimed at the peaceful resolution of regional conflicts. For the next quarter century he would play a constructive role in various world trouble spots. He also worked with Habitat for Humanity, a volunteer group that rehabilitated slum housing. But although Carter eventually regained the nation's esteem, few Americans in 1981 regretted seeing him leave the White House that he had entered so confidently four years earlier.

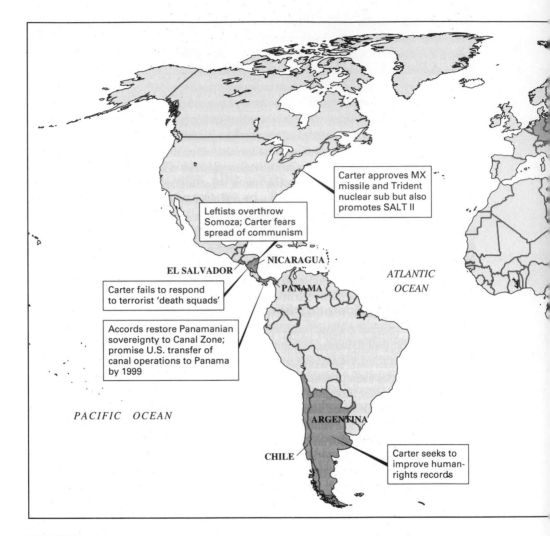

MAP 13.2
Carter Diplomacy

Conclusion

The decade that had begun with the invasion of Cambodia and the killings at Kent State at last dragged to a close. "Nobody is apt to look back on the 1970s as the good old days," *Time* magazine observed. After the turmoil of the 1960s and the political scandals, economic troubles, and international setbacks of the 1970s, it is small wonder that Americans seemed drained by psychic fatigue. Giving up on the public sphere, many pursued purely personal goals or devoted their energies to groups

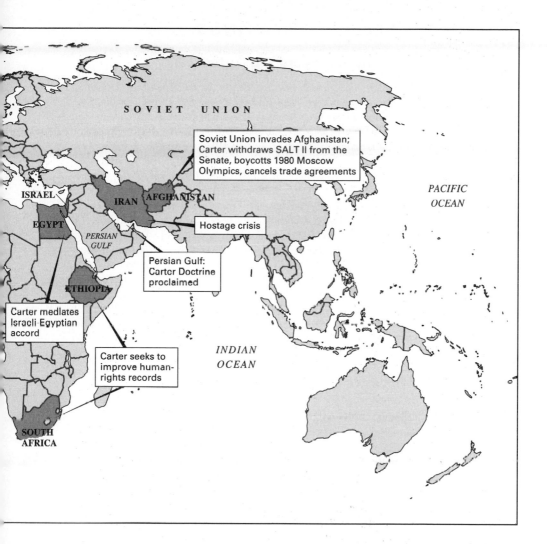

Soviet Union invades Afghanistan; Carter withdraws SALT II from the Senate, boycotts 1980 Moscow Olympics, cancels trade agreements

Hostage crisis

Persian Gulf: Carter Doctrine proclaimed

Carter mediates Israeli-Egyptian accord

Carter seeks to improve human-rights records

SOVIET UNION

ISRAEL

EGYPT

PERSIAN GULF

IRAN AFGHANISTAN

ETHIOPIA

SOUTH AFRICA

PACIFIC OCEAN

INDIAN OCEAN

based on ethnicity, gender, age, sexual orientation, or religious belief. As a conservative reaction spread through the culture, others embraced campaigns to restore traditional values or to eradicate one or another evil from American life. Jimmy Carter correctly identified a national "malaise" in his much-maligned speech of 1979, but he proved unable to lead the United States out of its collective funk.

By 1980 the nation clearly craved fresh leadership and a new infusion of political energy. Eager to oblige, the Republican Party delivered its messiah: Ronald Reagan.

SELECTED READINGS

Politics and the Economy in the Ford and Carter Years

Carl Abbott, *The New Urban America: Growth and Politics in the Sunbelt Cities* (1981); Patrick Anderson, *Electing Jimmy Carter: The Campaign of 1976* (1994); William C. Berman, *America's Right Turn: From Nixon to Bush* (1994); Michael A. Bernstein and David E. Adler, eds., *Understanding American Economic Decline* (1994); Barry Bluestone and Bennett Harrison, *The Deindustrialization of America* (1982); Douglas Brinkley, *The Unfinished Presidency: Jimmy Carter's Journey Beyond the White House* (1998); James Cannon, *Time and Chance: Gerald Ford's Appointment with History: 1913–1974* (1993); Jimmy Carter, *Keeping Faith* (1982); Robert J. Duffy, *Nuclear Power in America* (1997); Thomas Byrne Edsall with Mary D. Edsall, *Chain Reaction: The Impact of Race, Rights, and Taxes on American Politics* (1991); Gerald R. Ford, *A Time to Heal* (1979); John Robert Greene, *The Presidency of Gerald R. Ford* (1995); David Halberstam, *The Reckoning* [decline of the U.S. auto industry] (1986); John P. Hoerr, *And the Wolf Finally Came: The Decline of the American Steel Industry* (1988); Burton I. Kaufman, *The Presidency of James Earl Carter, Jr.* (1993); David P. McCaffrey, *The Politics of Nuclear Power* (1991); Lisa McGirr, *Suburban Warriors: The Origins of the New American Right* (2002); A. James Riechley, *Conservatives in an Age of Change* (1980); J. Harvey Wilkerson, *From Brown to Bakke* (1979); William Julius Wilson, *The Truly Disadvantaged: The Inner City, the Underclass, and Public Policy* (1987); Jules Witcover, *Marathon* [1976 election] (1977).

Social and Cultural Trends in the Seventies

Paul Boyer, *When Time Shall Be No More: Prophecy Belief in Modern American Culture* (1992); Peter Carroll, *It Seemed Like Nothing Happened: America in the 1970s* (2d ed., 1990); John Crewden, *The Tarnished Door: The New Immigrants and the Transformation of America* (1983); Donald W. Dayton and Robert K. Johnston, eds., *The Variety of American Evangelicalism* (1991); Editors of Rolling Stone, *The Seventies: A Tumultuous Decade Reconsidered* (2000); Ethics and Public Policy Center, *No Longer Exiles: The Religious New Right in American Politics* (1993); Jo Freeman, *The Politics of Women's Liberation* (1979); Paul Freiberger, *Fire in the Valley: The Making of the Personal Computer* (2d ed., 1999); Douglas Glasgow, *The Black Underclass* (1980); Elsebeth Hurup, ed., *The Lost Decade: America in the Seventies* (1996); Christopher Lasch, *The Culture of Narcissism* (1978); Michael Lienesch, *Redeeming America: Piety and Politics in the New Christian Right* (1993); Kristen Luker, *Abortion and the Politics of Motherhood* (1984); Michael Moritz, *The Little Kingdom: The Private Story of Apple Computer* (1984); Maureen Muldoon, *The Abortion Debate in the United States and Canada: A Source Book* (1991); Mark Noll, *One Nation Under God: Christian Faith and Political Action in America* (1988); Timothy J. O'Neill, *Bakke and the Politics of Equality* (1985); Jerome Price, *The Antinuclear Movement* (1982); Bruce J. Schulman, *The Seventies: The Great Shift in American Culture, Society, and Politics* (2001); Quentin J. Schultze, *Televangelism and American Culture* (1991); Edwin Schur, *The Awareness Trap: Self-Absorption Instead of Social Change* (1976); Suzanne Staggenborg, *The Pro-Choice Movement* (1991); John R. Stone, *On the Boundaries of American Evangelicalism: The Postwar Evangelical Coalition* (1997); Winnifrid D. Wandersee, *On the Move: American Women in the 1970s* (1988); William J. Wilson, *The Declining Significance of Race* (1978); Mark Royden Winchell, *Neoconservative Criticism* (1991).

America and the World in the Seventies

Zbigniew Brzezinski, *Power and Principle* (1983); Alan Dawson, *55 Days: The Fall of South Vietnam* (1977); Raymond L. Garthoff, *Détente and Confrontation: American-Soviet Relations from Nixon to Reagan* (1987); Arnold R. Isaacs, *Without Honor: Defeat in Vietnam and Cambodia* (1983); George D. Moffett III, *The Limits of Victory: The Ratification of the Panama Canal Treaties* (1985); William B. Quandt, *Camp David* (1987); Barry Rubin, *Paved with Good Intentions* [U.S.-Iranian relations] (1983); David Schoenbaum, *The United States and the State of Israel* (1993); Lars Schoultz, *Human Rights and U.S. Policy Toward Latin America* (1981); William Shawcross, *Sideshow: Kissinger, Nixon, and the Destruction of Cambodia* (1979); Gary Sick, *All Fall Down: America's Tragic Encounter with Iran* (1986); Gaddis Smith, *Morality, Reason and Power: American Diplomacy in the Carter Years* (1986); Robert A. Strong, *Working in the World: Jimmy Carter and the Making of American Foreign Policy* (2000); Strobe Talbott, *Endgame* [SALT II] (1979); Cyrus Vance, *Hard Choices* (1983); Daniel Yergin, *The Prize* [the world petroleum industry] (1999).

Prime-Time Politics:
The Reagan-Bush Years

JIMMY CARTER PACED the White House all night on January 19, 1981, hoping to announce, as his final presidential act, that Iran had released the U.S. hostages. Even as he rode to the inaugural ceremony on January 20, his eyes puffy from lack of sleep, Carter was on the phone, seeking word of the hostages' release. But this final balm eluded him. Not until a few minutes after Ronald Reagan took the oath of office did Iran, after 444 days, at last free the Americans.

Reagan set about enacting the political agenda of the New Right, whose advocates had gained ground steadily in the 1970s. Although his policies won broad support, Reagan's two terms saw grave economic problems ignored or worsened. The federal deficit and trade gap widened, and the industrial infrastructure crumbled even further. As corporate profits soared, the nation's inner cities decayed.

Avidly pursuing the Cold War, Reagan accelerated the military-spending increases and rhetorical assaults on Moscow that had begun during Carter's administration. He particularly focused on battling communism in Africa and Latin America. Indeed, the latter campaign spawned a major scandal, the Iran-contra affair. Yet by the end of his watch, sweeping changes within the Soviet Union heralded the Cold War's end and the final, improbable act of Reagan's long career: a warm embrace of the world's top communist in Moscow's Red Square.

The Reagan revolution mobilized the conservative mood that had gripped Middle America in the troubled 1970s. The individualistic and acquisitive outlook that Reagan personified had cultural as well as political manifestations, and the decade of the 1980s remains indelibly the Reagan era. Despite the scandals and long-term economic problems, Reagan remained personally popular. Envious Democrats dubbed him the "Teflon president."

In 1988, Vice President George Bush won the presidency. As when William Howard Taft succeeded the larger-than-life Theodore Roosevelt in 1909, Bush's single term seemed pale after eight years of Reagan, even though these years did see a momentous event: the end of the Cold War. Bush's leadership in the Persian Gulf War pushed up his approval ratings, but even that conflict would later seem a less clear-cut triumph that it did at the time.

The New Right Takes Charge: 1980–1984

In electing Richard Nixon in 1968, frustrated voters had rejected radicalism of the Left, redistributive liberalism, and affirmative action in favor of stability and the status quo. New Right activism, intensified in the 1970s by economic worries and white backlash, crested in 1980, a watershed year in American political history.

On the Democratic side, Senator Edward Kennedy's convention speech evoking the party's reformist tradition won a nostalgic ovation. But in the end, the dispirited Democrats renominated Carter, realizing he had little hope of reelection. The Republicans turned to Ronald Reagan, who had easily bested five challengers in the Republican primaries. The most liberal of the five, Illinois congressman John Anderson, later ran in the general election as an independent. Reagan chose as his running mate one of his erstwhile rivals, George Bush, a party stalwart who had held various government posts, most recently as head of the CIA.

The GOP platform attacked abortion and the Equal Rights Amendment, criticized SALT II, and demanded higher military spending. On the economy, the platform embraced two seemingly contradictory goals: major tax cuts and a balanced budget. Reagan's acceptance speech praised "family values" and the free enterprise system and called for lower taxes, less government regulation, and a beefed up national defense.

Reagan's acting skills shone in a televised debate with Carter. His rhetorical query, "Are you better off today than you were four years ago?" resonated with voters battered by inflation. When Carter warned of the dire consequences of Reagan's policies, Reagan smiled benevolently and sighed, "There you go again." On voting day, Reagan won a narrow 51 percent of the popular vote. Carter trailed with 41 percent, and Anderson picked up 7 percent. The Republicans won control of the Senate for the first time since 1954 and cut the Democrats' majority in the House from 119 to 50.

The oldest president ever elected, Reagan was sixty nine when he took office. Yet aided by his Hollywood training and his skillfully dyed hair, he projected a sprightly image. Of Irish immigrant stock (the name was originally O'Regan), he grew up in Dixon, Illinois, where his alcoholic father supported the family during the Depression as a local New Deal relief administrator. A pious mother left him a legacy of fundamentalist religious beliefs.

In 1937, then a radio sports announcer in Des Moines, Reagan took a screen test arranged by a friend. Signing a contract with Warner Brothers, he played supporting roles in a series of forgettable movies. His best-known role, as the dying football player George Gipp in *Knute Rockne—All American* (1940), gave rise to his nickname, the Gipper.

Reagan voted for Roosevelt in 1932, but as a postwar president of the Screen Actors Guild amid investigation of communist influence in Hollywood, he had turned to the right. In 1954 he began hosting TV's "General Electric Theatre" and became GE's corporate voice. A ceaseless round of speechmaking in these years fixed his palette of political ideas. Reagan's second marriage in 1952, to actress Nancy Davis, a staunch conservative, deepened his right-wing political bent. A Reagan TV speech for Barry Goldwater in 1964 won national attention. As governor of

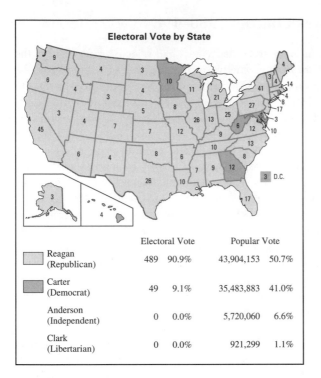

Electoral Vote by State

	Electoral Vote		Popular Vote	
Reagan (Republican)	489	90.9%	43,904,153	50.7%
Carter (Democrat)	49	9.1%	35,483,883	41.0%
Anderson (Independent)	0	0.0%	5,720,060	6.6%
Clark (Libertarian)	0	0.0%	921,299	1.1%

MAP 14.1
Presidential Election of 1980

California (1966–75), he denounced campus antiwar protests. Resuming his speechmaking after leaving the governorship, he expanded his national following.

A seasoned conservative politician, Reagan was also a creature of the media. Observers marveled at the gap between the media image molded by scripted TV speeches and staged appearances and the person behind the image. The former was charismatic and eloquent and seemed deeply thoughtful about politics and the human condition. The latter was detached, bored by details, and fairly inarticulate except when recounting an anecdote that supported his conservative ideology.

In his upbeat inaugural address, Reagan lauded private initiative as the key to renewal. "Government is not the solution to our problem," he insisted. "Government *is* the problem." The inaugural became a festival of privilege, as private jets shuttled in Hollywood stars and the Reagans' rich friends. At Washington's elegant Union Station, scene of one inaugural party, street people mingled with invited guests to filch hors d'oeuvres.

Reagan's presidency nearly ended on March 30, 1981, when a deranged young man shot at Reagan as he emerged from a Washington hotel. One bullet hit presidential press secretary James Brady, inflicting brain damage. (Brady and his wife would later champion the cause of gun control.) Another punctured Reagan's lung. He survived after surgery, although in graver condition than the public realized. Borrowing a movie line, he quipped, "I forgot to duck." His already high approval ratings soared.

An early defining moment came in August 1981 when the 11,600-member Professional Air Traffic Controllers Organization (PATCO) called a strike. The president fired the strikers when they defied a back-to-work order. Some found his action callous, but many Americans, judging PATCO workers arrogant and overpaid, applauded his tough stance. The failed PATCO strike symbolized the weakening clout of organized labor. By 1987 only 17 percent of American workers belonged to unions, down from 23 percent in 1980.

Reagan's domestic program featured five key elements: tax cuts, less federal regulation, a tacit downgrading of civil-rights and affirmative-action programs, increased military spending, and—somewhat improbably—a balanced budget in three years.

Reduced taxes, Reagan claimed, would jump-start the economy by encouraging consumer spending and businesses investment in plants and equipment. The resulting boom would increase tax revenues even at lower rates. This theory, called supply-side economics, had found an easy convert in Reagan, long convinced that high taxes served as socialism's entering wedge. Despite endorsements from the *Wall Street Journal* and some corporate leaders, most economists viewed it as wishful thinking. George Bush during the 1980 primary campaign had called it "voodoo economics." (Once on the ticket, Bush quickly reversed himself, reinforcing his reputation for opportunism.)

Reagan's youthful budget director, David Stockman, shared his boss's tax-cutting fervor. Stockman had joined SDS in the sixties, but in 1976 he went to Congress as a Republican. For him, as he revealed in a candid *Atlantic Monthly* interview, tax cuts were part of a larger project: to dismantle the welfare state and move toward a "minimalist" government. Supply-side economics, he conceded, was simply the old "trickle-down" theory: If the rich get richer, the benefits will seep down to the rest of society. In May 1981, only slightly modifying the administration's proposed 30 percent tax cut, Congress approved a 25 percent cut: 5 percent in 1981 and 10 percent in 1982 and 1983.

Conservative southern Democrats called "boll weevils" joined Republicans in supporting the call for spending cuts. The list of slashed social programs included food stamps, child nutrition, job training, and Aid to Families with Dependent Children. Ironically, despite cuts of $45 billion in specific programs, total federal welfare spending, including entitlement programs such as social security and Medicare, rose by 70 percent from 1980 to 1988. Yet the slashes in social spending were significant, reflecting both a budget-balancing impulse and fears of welfare dependency—a concern that would produce a sweeping welfare-reform law in 1996.

In simplest terms, these tax and spending cuts redistributed income from the poor to the wealthy. In 1980–85, the proportion of total after-tax income that went to the poorest one-fifth of U.S. households fell slightly, while the proportion going to the wealthiest 20 percent rose by 2 percent, reaching the highest level since World War II. In actual buying power, the inflation-adjusted income of the poorest 10 percent of American families fell by 10.5 percent in 1980–85. By contrast, the very richest Americans, the top 1 percent, saw their taxable income from salaries and investments spurt upward.

The income decline among the poor cannot be blamed entirely on Reagan's economic policies. The loss of factory jobs also depressed income statistics, as did rising immigration. The Hispanic population, fed by a steady flow of newcomers from Mexico and the Caribbean, grew by 53 percent in the 1980s. As immigrants continued to flood in from the Philippines, China, Korea, and Vietnam, the Asian population doubled. Although some of the new arrivals were well educated and moved quickly into good jobs, most began their life in America at the bottom of the economic ladder.

Although the administration insisted that a "safety net" protected the truly needy, cuts in social spending made life harder for the poor. In 1987 one of five American children lived in poverty, up by 24 percent from 1979. A few activists still championed the cause of the poor. The Children's Defense Fund calculated that the money spent annually on the secretary of defense's private dining room would restore morning snacks for 1 million low-income schoolchildren, one of many Reagan-era budget cuts. In *Rachel and Her Children: Homeless Families in America* (1988), Jonathan Kozol described life in a New York City welfare hotel:

> There are families in this building [who] . . . , like refugees . . . in the midst of war, cling to each other and establish a small zone of safety. . . . Chaos and disorder alternate with lethargy and nearly absolute bewilderment in face of regulations they cannot observe or do not understand.

Reaganomics struck even at Americans who had jobs. In 1988, *U.S. News and World Report* found that some 9 million working adults earned incomes below the poverty level, including "people like Glen Witbeck, a short-order cook whose $8,000 annual salary doesn't stretch to cover his two little girls' medical bills. . . . Or Pamela Kelley, a onetime airline-passenger screener who shifted to canned food at home because pot roast was too expensive for her and her two-year-old daughter." An advanced degree offered no guarantee of security in the spotty Reagan economy. In 1988 the Ambassador Cab Company of Cambridge, Massachusetts, reported six Ph.D.s among its drivers.

Not even the middle class particularly benefited from the tax cuts. State taxes and fees rose to cover new costs caused by cuts in federal spending. Overall, the average family's total tax burden remained about the same or rose slightly in these years. And although Reagan justifiably boasted of 20 million new jobs created in the 1980s, these were often service-sector positions with low pay, few benefits, and little prospect of advancement. As in the 1970s, skilled workers in declining industries found their wages cut as they left the factory for unskilled work in the service sector.

Reagan's first term did see the end of the raging inflation of the 1970s. Owing to the Federal Reserve's tight-money policy and a drop in world oil prices, the inflation rate fell from 13.5 percent in 1980 to 1.9 percent by 1986. But the other component of the 1970s economic crisis, the recession, initially worsened as the Fed's credit policies, designed to starve inflation, impeded business recovery. The unemployment rate for 1982 and 1983 remained stuck at 9.5 percent, the highest since 1941. Bank failures and business bankruptcies soared. The recession gradually bottomed out, however, and in November 1982 the stock market began a five-year rise. The later Reagan years would bring better times.

Implementing another New Right goal, the administration also set out to deregulate the economy. Jimmy Carter had moved in this direction, but Reagan carried it much further. Indeed, many Reagan appointees scorned the entire concept of federal regulation. Secretary of the Interior James Watt of Colorado, a leader of the "Sagebrush Rebellion" promoting private development of public lands, did his best to reduce federal control and to open these lands to exploitation. Watt's religious beliefs reinforced his laissez-faire ideology. Asked at his confirmation hearing about preserving the environment for future generations, he responded that he did not know how many generations remained before Christ's return. Watt's bigotry (he characterized one advisory panel as "a black, a woman, two Jews, and a cripple") soon made him a liability, and Reagan dumped him in 1983. But the antiregulatory ideology lived on. The budget of the Environmental Protection Agency was slashed. The head of EPA, in charge of the $1.4 billion Superfund to clean up hazardous sites, showed favoritism toward polluters, with whom she had close links. The head of the Securities and Exchange Commission (SEC), a deregulation enthusiast, radically reduced the SEC's oversight of the stock market.

A similar laxity at the federal agency responsible for overseeing the savings and loan (S&L) industry led to a wave of risky speculation and outright fraud that left many S&Ls in ruins. A multibillion-dollar federal program set up in 1989 to salvage failed S&Ls and to reimburse depositors (who were federally insured up to $100,000) became part of the price of the deregulation mania.

The head of the Federal Communications Commission, another disciple of deregulation, ridiculed the notion that TV had a public-service role. "Television is just another appliance," he insisted. "[It is] time to . . . treat [broadcasting] the way almost everyone else in society does . . . as a business." Under his chairmanship the FCC increased the amount of time television stations could air commercials and dropped the rule requiring a minimal amount of public-service programming.

The Federal Trade Commission, the Occupational Safety and Health Administration, and other agencies similarly sabotaged the regulatory laws that they existed to uphold. In his inaugural address Reagan had joked, "It's not my intention to do away with government," yet many of his appointees seemed intent on doing just that.

Attuned to the white backlash that had fueled the New Right, Reagan had opposed the civil-rights acts of 1964 and 1965 and in private told stories of a mythic "welfare queen" who had amassed a fortune by defrauding the welfare system. Emulating the Nixon-Ford foot-dragging approach to civil rights, the Reagan White House encouraged school boards to resist court-ordered school busing and slashed the budgets of the Equal Employment Opportunity Commission and the Office of Federal Contract Compliance. The head of the Justice Department's civil rights division, a Reagan appointee with no background in civil rights, openly proclaimed his goal of reversing the division's support for affirmative-action programs.

Acting on the GOP platform pledge to beef up the military, Reagan and his allies in Congress launched the largest military expansion in peacetime history. Secretary of Defense Casper Weinberger presided over this buildup. As President

Nixon's budget director, Weinberger had fought wasteful spending. Now at the Pentagon, warning of a "dangerous slide" in military preparedness, he persuaded Congress to open the tap wide. In 1981–86, U.S. military spending increased more than 70 percent. The administration's enthusiasm for reactivating battleships illustrated the symbolic component of the military buildup. These dinosaurs had little utility, and indeed were sitting ducks in an era of missiles, nuclear submarines, and communications satellites, but Reaganites' nostalgia for the glory days of World War II, when battleships had symbolized U.S. power, ignored such realities.

Reagan's admirers would later claim that the military-spending binge drove the Soviet system into crisis by forcing Moscow into a foolhardy effort to keep pace. This argument has some merit, but political and economic conditions within the Soviet sphere itself probably played the major role in the U.S.S.R.'s collapse. Whatever its Cold War impact, Reagan's military expansion had profound effects at home. It benefited defense contractors and buttressed their political clout, and it generated thousands of jobs, especially in the heavily Republican Sun Belt. Glamorous high-tech weapons systems proliferated on the drawing boards. But ballooning defense budgets also worsened the federal deficit, worrying even conservatives. A 1987 *Business Week* article on the Pentagon's budget was entitled "Defense Spending: The Wild Blue Yonder."

The arms expansion met resistance among some religious leaders, college students, peace advocates, antinuclear activists, Democrats who resisted the lure of Reaganism, and even some conservatives alarmed by soaring deficits. Environmentalists and advocates for the poor and minorities criticized Reagan's spending priorities as well. But many conservative, patriotic blue-collar and middle-class citizens—Richard Nixon's "silent majority"—cheered Reagan's martial emphasis. Smarting over the Vietnam defeat, taught to fear the Soviet Union, and angered by OPEC's manipulation of oil prices and Iran's anti-Americanism, they welcomed the morale boost that came from displays of U.S. military might.

Antinuclear activism, already stirring in the late 1970s (see page 361), intensified in the early 1980s, aroused by the plans of the Federal Emergency Management Agency (FEMA) to disperse city dwellers to rural areas if nuclear war threatened and by President Reagan's failure to take any arms-control initiatives. Events in Europe fed nuclear worries as well. To counter Soviet missiles in Eastern Europe, NATO and the Carter administration had agreed in 1979 to deploy 572 U.S. missiles in Great Britain and West Germany. NATO also affirmed its "first-use" policy on nuclear weapons: A Soviet attack on Western Europe could trigger a nuclear response. Reagan's first secretary of state, Alexander Haig, described the utility of "nuclear warning shots" in conventional war situations.

As antinuclear marches in Great Britain and Germany appeared on American television, protests stirred in the United States as well, reaching levels not seen since the test-ban campaign of a quarter century before. The movement coalesced around the "nuclear freeze" idea, which proposed that the nuclear powers, while pursuing arms-reduction talks, should declare a mutual freeze on building, testing, and deploying nuclear weapons. In June 1982, eight hundred thousand nuclear protesters—the largest political rally in U.S. history—gathered in New York's Central Park. That fall, voters in nine states, including California and Wisconsin, approved nuclear-freeze resolutions.

In *The Challenge of Peace* (1983), the U.S. Catholic bishops raised grave doubts about U.S. nuclear policies. College students, writers, artists, and filmmakers joined the campaign. In the 1983 movie *WarGames,* an out-of-control Defense Department computer nearly obliterates the world. Jonathan Schell's *The Fate of the Earth* (1984) warned of a nuclear holocaust that could leave a silent planet inhabited only by insects. *The Day After,* a 1984 ABC-TV special, portrayed the devastating effects of nuclear war.

Reagan responded to the freeze campaign with a TV speech in March 1983. Conceding the horror of nuclear war, the president offered his remedy: not a nuclear freeze but the Strategic Defense Initiative (SDI), a space-based missile-defense system involving lasers, a computerized command system, and other high-tech weaponry. Reagan's proposal, a surprise to the Pentagon, was the brainchild of physicist Edward Teller, "the father of the H-bomb," whom Reagan much admired.

Dubbed "Star Wars" by the media, SDI drew criticism from scientists skeptical of its futuristic technology, including computer programs that could never be fully tested before an actual attack. Others warned that SDI would violate the 1972 Anti-Ballistic Missile Treaty, which had outlawed missile-defense systems that might tempt a nation to deliver a first-strike attack. Nonetheless, legislators fearful of challenging Reagan on a defense issue voted billions for SDI research. In 1993 the *New York Times* revealed that key SDI tests had been rigged, not only to deceive the Soviets but also to ensure continued funding. Despite many vicissitudes, the missile-defense dream survived, and in 2002 the George W. Bush administration would repudiate the ABM treaty and actively pursue antimissile research and even deployment of an operational system. In 1984, SDI served Reagan's immediate political purpose: As people debated the practicality of missile defense, the nuclear-freeze movement faded.

Tax cuts and increased military spending drove the federal deficit from $74 billion in 1981 to $185 billion in 1984, and tripled the national debt. This did not surprise budget director Stockman. In his 1981 *Atlantic Monthly* interview, Stockman admitted that he had gambled that Congress, faced with soaring deficits, would radically cut domestic spending, thereby severing Americans' "umbilical cords of dependency" on the federal government. In short, the administration deliberately induced budget deficits to starve spending on social programs.

New Anticommunist Militance: Reagan and Foreign Policy

If Reagan's domestic policy repudiated governmental activism, his foreign policy was highly activist, battling communism and leftism in the Third World, especially in Latin America. Sharpening the anti-Soviet tone of Jimmy Carter's final year in office, Reagan adopted a highly belligerent stance toward the Soviet Union.

But Reagan also faced foreign challenges that lay outside the stark polarities of Cold War ideology, especially in the Middle East. Attention initially centered on Lebanon, an unstable nation prey to its powerful neighbors Syria and Israel, and home to thousands of displaced Palestinians living in squalid refugee camps. The

Palestine Liberation Organization (PLO) had its headquarters in Beirut, Lebanon's capital. In June 1982, countering a terrorist faction within the PLO, Israel attacked PLO strongholds and established an Israeli-controlled "security zone" in southern Lebanon. This invasion led to a horrendous massacre of Palestinian refugees by Lebanese militia linked to Israel. The PLO leadership, expelled from Lebanon, shifted to Tunisia. President Reagan ordered 2,000 U.S. marines to Lebanon as part of an international force overseeing the PLO withdrawal and mediating among Lebanon's warring factions. Because of America's ties to Israel, radical Shiite Muslim groups reviled the marines. In October 1983 a Shiite terrorist drove a truck loaded with explosives into the lightly guarded U.S. barracks. The shattering blast

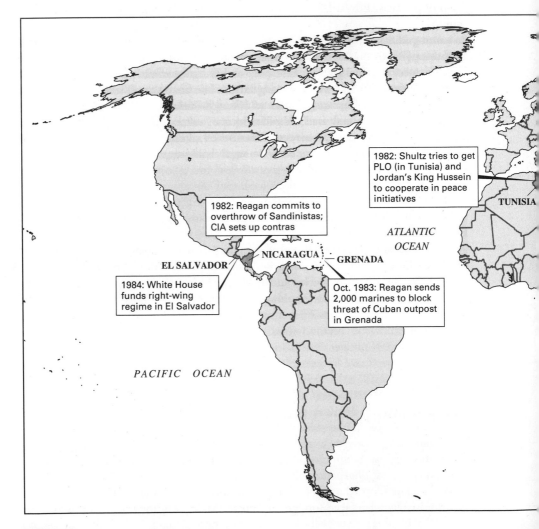

MAP 14.2
Reagan and the World, 1980–1984

killed 239 marines, and 50 French troops died in a related attack. Reagan soon withdrew the U.S. force.

A wave of political kidnappings also hit Beirut. In 1982–85, nine Americans were seized. One, the head of the CIA bureau in Beirut, died in captivity, probably under torture. European hostages were taken as well. Although Reagan agonized less publicly over the hostages than had Carter, he was equally preoccupied with winning their freedom.

Secretary of State George Shultz, who replaced Alexander Haig in 1982, tried in vain to revive the Middle East peace process. Deeming the PLO a key to this effort, Shultz sought to bring PLO leader Yasir Arafat and Jordan's King Hussein

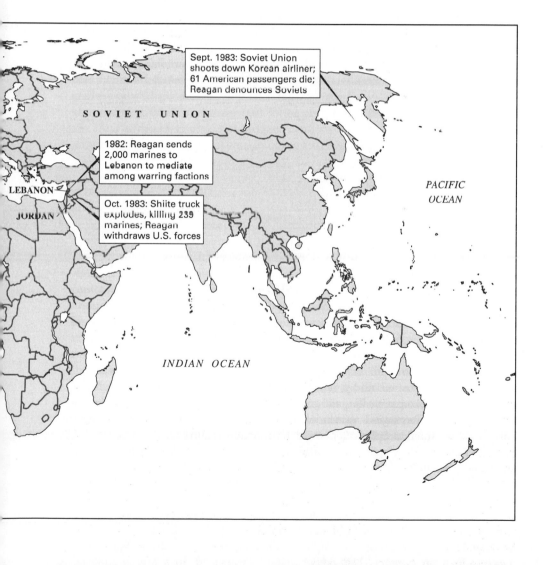

Sept. 1983: Soviet Union shoots down Korean airliner; 61 American passengers die; Reagan denounces Soviets

SOVIET UNION

1982: Reagan sends 2,000 marines to Lebanon to mediate among warring factions

PACIFIC OCEAN

LEBANON

JORDAN

Oct. 1983: Shiite truck explodes, killing 239 marines; Reagan withdraws U.S. forces

INDIAN OCEAN

into the negotiations. Yet Israeli security fears, Syria's intransigence, and PLO suspicions of Hussein all undermined Shultz's efforts. So, too, did expanding Jewish settlements in the Palestinian West Bank territories seized by Israel in the 1967 war.

Closer to home, the Reagan administration fought radical insurgencies in Latin America, a region buffeted by rapid population growth, disparities of wealth and poverty, military coups, and guerrilla violence. Reagan, ever the Cold Warrior, saw in all these complexities the hand of Moscow. Here was an opportunity to resume the anticommunist struggle abandoned in Vietnam. In El Salvador, the White House funded a right-wing military government fighting guerrillas backed by Nicaragua and Castro's Cuba. Aware that a less brutal regime was more likely to win popular support, the State Department backed the moderate José Napoleon Duarte in a 1984 presidential election. Duarte won, but death squads linked to the army continued to murder civilians suspected of opposing the regime.

In Nicaragua, President Reagan not only reversed Carter's policy of recognizing the Marxist-led Sandinistas but also committed the United States to the Sandinistas' overthrow. Moscow, he charged, wanted to turn Nicaragua into another communist enclave like Cuba. Beginning in 1982, the CIA organized, trained, and financed the contras, an anti-Sandinista guerrilla army. Some top contra leaders had links to the discredited Somoza dictatorship, overthrown in 1979. Infiltrating Nicaragua from Honduras and Costa Rica, the contras conducted raids, carried out sabotage, and used a CIA manual that explained how to "neutralize" local Sandinista officials. Civilians suffered heavily in this CIA-funded guerrilla war, but Reagan praised the contras as "the moral equivalent of our Founding Fathers."

Critics of the CIA-run contra war accused the administration of perpetuating the old practice of backing corrupt Latin American elites. Others feared a repeat of the Vietnam disaster. In December 1982, Congress banned military aid to the contras for one year. Early in 1984, the *Wall Street Journal* reported that CIA agents, with President Reagan's approval, had mined Nicaragua's harbors, running the risk of an international incident. Members of the Senate Intelligence Committee, charged with overseeing the CIA, exploded in anger, for CIA head William Casey had concealed the operation from them. That October the House passed a bill introduced by Edward Boland of Massachusetts imposing a two-year ban on contra aid. The Sandinistas and the contras reached a truce in 1988, but Reagan never abandoned hope for a contra victory.

Reagan's anticommunist campaign in Latin America unfolded on many fronts. In October 1983, U.S. marines invaded the tiny Caribbean island of Grenada, where Cuban-backed radicals had seized power, and evacuated some American students. The real purpose was to prevent another outpost of Cuban-Soviet power and to show America's post-Vietnam determination to protect its interests. Expelling Cuban workers building an airfield, the marines installed a pro-U.S. government in Grenada.

In Afghanistan, the CIA supplied funds and military equipment to Muslim fundamentalists battling a regime supported by Moscow. (A leader in this Muslim jihad, or holy war, was Osama bin Laden of Saudi Arabia, who would later be implicated in the September 11, 2001, attacks on the World Trade Center and the Pentagon.) With Russian troops in Afghanistan, and Reagan accusing Moscow of mischief in Latin America, U.S.-Soviet relations worsened. In a March 1983 address to evangelical leaders, Reagan lambasted the Soviet Union as an "evil empire." Relations further deteriorated that September when the Russians shot down a Korean airliner that had entered Soviet air space because of a navigational error, killing 269 passengers, including 61 Americans. Rejecting Moscow's claim that the plane had been conducting espionage, the White House and right-wing political groups stepped up their denunciations of Soviet perfidy. Détente, already floundering as Carter's term had ended, now seemed moribund.

In summary, Reagan's first term saw increased military spending, the neglect of arms control, and heightened Cold War hostility. Vigorous support of anticommunist regimes and guerrilla campaigns in Latin America and Afghanistan won applause from the New Right, as proof that America's post-Vietnam funk had lifted. But Reagan's ideologically driven initiatives failed to sustain Nixon's détente strategy. Nor did they acknowledge the indigenous sources of the conflicts raging in the poverty-wracked nations south of the U.S. border or the unpredictable power of Islamic fundamentalism.

Buoyed by its aggressive militance in foreign affairs, Reaganism crested in the 1984 election year. Most Americans, impressed by Reagan's unabashed patriotism, rated his first term a success. Flag-waving fans chanting "We're Number One" at the 1984 Summer Olympics in Los Angeles summed up the expansive mood.

Although the Democrats had gained twenty-six House seats in the 1982 midterm election, Reagan's popularity posed a serious hurdle for Democratic presidential hopefuls, including Senator Gary Hart of Colorado and Chicago's Jesse Jackson, a former aide of Martin Luther King, Jr., who was backed by many

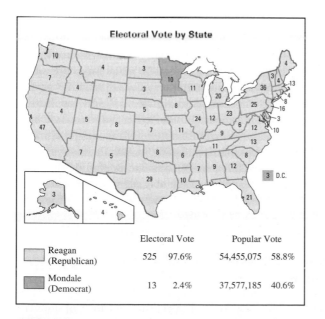

	Electoral Vote		Popular Vote	
Reagan (Republican)	525	97.6%	54,455,075	58.8%
Mondale (Democrat)	13	2.4%	37,577,185	40.6%

MAP 14.3

Presidential Election of 1984

African Americans. In the end, Walter Mondale of Minnesota, Carter's vice president and a prominent liberal supported by party leaders, teachers, labor unions, women's organizations, and other interest groups, won the nomination. Criticizing Reagan's military buildup and belligerent rhetoric, Mondale pleased union backers by calling for import quotas on manufactured goods from abroad.

Mondale's running mate, Congresswoman Geraldine Ferraro of New York, became the first woman to appear on a major-party presidential ticket. Hoping to win points for candor, Mondale announced in his acceptance speech that as president he would be forced to raise taxes to combat Reagan's soaring deficits. To many voters, however, this simply confirmed GOP charges that Democrats were the "tax-and-spend" party.

Despite eye-popping deficits, Reagan again promised a balanced budget and blamed free-spending Democrats for sabotaging this goal. In a TV debate, the seventy-four-year-old president jokingly pledged not to make a campaign issue of his fifty-six-year-old opponent's "youth and inexperience." The Reagan-Bush ticket triumphed in a landslide. Without a third-party challenge to siphon off support, Reagan garnered 59 percent of the popular vote and won every state but Mondale's Minnesota and the District of Columbia. Even with Ferraro on the ticket, Mondale lost New York and won only a minority of women voters. Blacks and Hispanics (except for pro-Reagan Cuban exiles in Florida) voted heavily Democratic but could not stem the Reagan tide. Portraying Mondale as a captive of "special interests," Reagan ran well in white working-class neighborhoods.

The election revealed the scope of the post-1964 shift in U.S. politics. In place of the liberal consensus stood a new conservative coalition forged in the economic stresses and cultural upheavals of the later 1960s and 1970s. This unlikely but potent alliance of wealthy Americans, corporate leaders, evangelicals, Catholic ethnics, suburbanites, and white blue-collar workers shared a patriotic and individualistic ethic and an antipathy to intrusive federal regulations and cultural trends that threatened "traditional values." They decried policies that favored minorities, welfare recipients, feminists, homosexuals, and others who seemed to seek preferential treatment.

The election outcome also reflected the population shifts of these years. Whereas the Northeast and Midwest grew only slightly in 1970–90, the South's population exploded from 63 million to 87 million; the Pacific states, from 27 million to 39 million. California, having already passed New York as the most populous state in the 1960s, grew still more in the 1980s, from 24 million to 30 million. These changes contributed to the 1984 Reagan landslide as the South and West, enjoying the lion's share of Reagan-era military spending, voted solidly Republican. In the onetime Democratic bastion of Texas, 64 percent of the voters chose Reagan. Across the Sun Belt, a similar story unfolded.

Iran-Contra Scandal and a Waning Cold War: Reagan's Second Term

Reagan's second inaugural address again exuded optimism and love of country, but the underlying themes—individualism, acquisitiveness, and competition—offered no unifying vision other than jingoistic patriotism. A rising cycle of Middle

East terrorism and the Iran-contra affair marred Reagan's second term. The most momentous developments of Reagan's final White House years, however, unfolded in Moscow, where dramatic events portended nothing less than the collapse of the Soviet Union and the end of the Cold War.

Three Supreme Court retirements enabled Reagan to place his stamp on the judicial branch. In 1981 he nominated Sandra Day O'Connor of Arizona, the first woman to serve on the high court. When Chief Justice Warren Burger retired in 1986, Reagan elevated William Rehnquist, a Nixon appointee, to the chief justiceship and named to the vacancy the conservative Antonin Scalia, a federal judge and former University of Chicago Law School professor. Scalia soon emerged as a doctrinaire advocate of presidential power. The third opening, in 1987, sparked a fight. The Senate rejected Reagan's first nominee, Robert Bork, a critic of judicial activism who struck many as unsuited by temperament and judicial philosophy for the Supreme Court. Reagan's next choice withdrew after revelations that he had smoked marijuana while a law-school professor. Reagan finally turned to Anthony M. Kennedy of San Francisco, who gained easy confirmation. Although chosen for their conservative credentials, O'Connor and Kennedy would emerge in the 1990s as centrists in contrast to the Court's more doctrinaire right-wingers.

On the economic front, inflation remained low and unemployment declined in the later 1980s. Yet in Washington the red ink gushed on. The federal deficit soared to $238 billion in 1986. Washington borrowed billions merely to pay interest on the ever-rising $3 trillion national debt, which threatened to push up interest rates and bring back recession. Only heavy purchases of U.S. government bonds by foreign investors staved off this disaster.

Reagan did achieve one goal that had eluded Jimmy Carter. The tax-reform law of 1986 plugged some loopholes and exempted millions of poor Americans from paying taxes. But it also extended the regressive feature of Reaganomics, cutting tax rates for the wealthiest Americans. As the deficit grew and Cold War tensions eased, Congress at last slowed the rate of increase in defense spending, from nearly 9 percent in 1985 to under 1 percent in 1988.

The United States' international economic position weakened in Reagan's second term as the trade gap widened. In 1987, U.S. imports, mostly from Japan and other Asian nations, exceeded imports by $160 billion. Alarmed, the administration pressured Japan to open its domestic market to more U.S. imports and to stop "dumping," or selling exports below cost, to maintain market dominance. In 1987, retaliating for Japan's dumping of microchips, Reagan slapped duties on Japanese electronic products. The White House rejected calls for more protectionism from industries hurt by imports, however, and in 1988 signed a free-trade pact with Canada.

While the defense industry, the service sector, and high-tech businesses prospered in the eighties, other sectors of the economy languished. Inner-city joblessness remained high. As Americans caught the acquisitive spirit, total consumer debt exploded from $302 billion in 1980 to $671 billion by 1988. All of these problems—the deficit, the trade gap, the uneven economy, the upsurge in credit buying—fostered uneasiness. In October 1987, the five-year stock-market boom crashed with a 500-point plunge, shrinking total stock values by 20 percent. The market slowly recovered, but the 1987 collapse exposed the nagging doubts induced by six years of Reaganomics.

World events and their domestic fallout dominated Reagan's second term. In 1988, George Shultz launched a final Middle East peace effort based on a "land for peace" formula: Israel would give up the occupied territories in Gaza and the West Bank in return for security guarantees. Under U.S. pressure, PLO head Yasir Arafat renounced terrorism and conceded Israel's right to exist. But Israel's government, now headed by the right-wing Likud Party, which favored continued Jewish settlements on the West Bank, rejected Shultz's efforts.

Terrorism, not peace hopes, more typically preoccupied the White House in these years. The 1983 bombing of the U.S. marine barracks in Beirut heralded a larger campaign of fear launched by shadowy groups linked to the PLO, Iran's Hezbollah (Party of God), Libya's ruler Muammar el-Qaddafi, and groups demanding the release of Israeli-held Palestinians. In June 1985, passengers on a TWA flight hijacked over Greece endured seventeen nightmarish days of captivity. That October, PLO agents seized an Italian cruise ship and murdered a wheelchair-bound Jewish American passenger. In April 1986, when Libyan terrorists bombed a Berlin discotheque popular with GIs, Reagan ordered a bombing raid on military sites around Tripoli. In the deadliest incident, a Pan Am jet en route from London to New York crashed over Scotland in December 1988, killing all 259 aboard, including many Americans, after a bomb exploded in the baggage section. In 1991 the U.S. and British governments accused two Libyan officials of masterminding the bombing. A decade later, a Scottish court acquitted one of the accused but found the other guilty of murder and imposed a life sentence.

Two administration goals—release of the U.S. hostages in Beirut and support for the U.S.-funded contras seeking to overthrow Nicaragua's Marxist government—led to the web of misdeeds known as the Iran-contra affair. In August 1985, President Reagan had secretly approved the sale of antitank missiles to Iran, then at war with Iraq. In return, officials hoped that Iran would use its influence to secure the release of the U.S. hostages in Beirut, Lebanon. In all, the United States sold 2,004 antitank missiles and 18 antiaircraft missiles to Iran. The effort failed: Three hostages in Lebanon were freed, but three more were seized, and Iran remained stridently anti-American. The deal mocked Reagan's pledge never to negotiate with terrorists and his pressure on other nations to boycott Iran. It also violated the Arms Control Export Act and an arms embargo against Iran imposed by Congress in 1979. In November 1986, a Beirut newspaper broke the story of these arms shipments and added startling details. In May 1986, the paper said, Reagan's former national-security adviser Robert McFarlane had flown with a shipment of antiaircraft-missile parts to Tehran, bearing a Bible autographed by Reagan for presentation to the Ayatollah Khomeini. Other evidence soon confirmed that Washington had indeed sold arms to and curried favor with the same U.S.-hating Iranian regime that had perpetrated the hostage ordeal of 1979–81.

Soon came still more explosive news: A National Security Council aide stationed in the White House, marine colonel Oliver North, had funneled millions of dollars from the Iranian arms sales to the contras at a time when Congress had explicitly forbidden such aid. Further circumventing the law, North had raised some $37 million for the contras from Saudi Arabia and other governments, as well as from wealthy U.S. conservatives. North's operation, with its own airplanes, pilots, ships, and communications system, had unfolded in deep secrecy, with no account-ability to Congress or the public.

When this story broke, North and his secretary shredded key documents and erased computer files just before FBI investigators arrived. Some files survived, however, and provided crucial evidence of North's activities. President Reagan praised North as "a national hero" but dismissed him nevertheless. John Poindexter, McFarlane's successor as national security adviser, resigned. In March 1987 an investigative panel appointed by Reagan criticized the president's lax management style but blamed the Iran-contra debacle mainly on Chief of Staff Donald Regan, who also resigned. On TV, Reagan denied knowing of any illegalities but admitted "mistakes."

In May–July 1987, a joint House-Senate committee investigating the scandal heard 250 hours of testimony, much of it televised to a fascinated nation. Oliver North, ramrod straight in full-dress uniform, admitted lying under oath, destroying documents, and falsifying records to conceal the White House role in the arms-for-hostages and contra-diversion schemes. Love of country, he insisted, had motivated his every action. He claimed that he had kept his superiors informed and that he had worked closely with CIA director William Casey (who had died in May 1987) to develop a covert-operations network beyond the reach of Congress. Many people found North mawkish and self-serving, but others thought his patriotism inspiring. John Poindexter admitted that he had approved North's plan to divert funds to the contras but loyally insisted that he had not told Reagan, in order to give him "plausible deniability." Poindexter also revealed that he had destroyed Reagan's written approval of the initial arms sale to Iran, to spare him future political embarrassment.

In its report, the joint committee cited a litany of illegal acts, including failure to notify Congress of the arms sales, destroying and altering official documents, and violating Congress's ban on aid to the contras. The committee also noted a pervasive contempt for the law by North and others. While finding no evidence of Reagan's direct knowledge of criminal activity, the committee sharply criticized lax White House procedures. The scandal, the report concluded, had not only strained relations between the White House and Congress but also diminished the international credibility of the presidency and, indeed, of the United States.

Attorney General Edwin Meese, after a casual initial investigation, had appointed a special prosecutor to handle the criminal aspects of the case. In 1988, a federal grand jury indicted North, Poindexter, and two of North's intermediaries on various charges. Robert McFarlane pleaded guilty to misleading Congress (a misdemeanor) and cooperated with the prosecution. In 1989, North was convicted of destroying evidence and other offenses. A federal judge fined him $150,000 and ordered him to perform twelve hundred hours of community service. (By this time North was earning up to $200,000 a month on the lecture circuit.) In 1990, a jury found Poindexter guilty on five felony charges. He received a six-month jail term, but a federal appeals court reversed both convictions on a legal technicality.

In contrast to Richard Nixon's fate, the Iran-contra scandal left Reagan relatively unscathed. Not only did he enjoy a deeper reserve of goodwill, but also no "smoking gun" comparable to the Nixon tapes linked him directly to illegal activities. Many

Americans agreed that the operation, however misguided, arose from patriotic motives. Yet the affair again underscored the vulnerability of constitutional government to executive abuse. When North's secretary justified her shredding and concealing of documents by asserting that "sometimes you have to go above the written law," the arrogance of power became apparent.

The Cold War Thaws

As the Iran-contra affair receded, events on the main Cold War stage seized the limelight. Under President Mikhail Gorbachev, who came to power in 1985, the Soviet Union changed profoundly. Decades of Communist Party control had stifled the Soviet economy and led to massive shortages in food and consumer goods. In addition, unrest simmered in Eastern Europe and in the Soviet republics, including Latvia, Estonia, and Lithuania, swallowed up by Moscow in 1940. To foster his twin goals of *glasnost* (openness) and *perestroika* (restructuring), Gorbachev urgently sought improved relations with the West.

A hint of the new order came during arms-control talks between Reagan and Gorbachev at Geneva in 1985 and Reykjavik, Iceland, in 1986. Although differences over inspection procedures and Reagan's Strategic Defense Initiative (see page 391) derailed the Reykjavik summit, the two nations in 1987 agreed on the INF (Intermediate Nuclear Forces) Treaty withdrawing some twenty-five hundred missiles from Europe and, for the first time, eliminating an entire category of nuclear weapons. Gorbachev also announced a reduction in Soviet military forces and troop withdrawals from Eastern Europe and Afghanistan.

As Americans contemplated the unthinkable, the end of the Cold War, Ronald Reagan, despite his years of anti-Soviet rhetoric, responded imaginatively. In May 1988, the Senate having approved the INF Treaty, the president flew to Moscow for the signing. Talks also continued on a strategic-arms reduction (START) treaty. For several days the two leaders socialized and posed for the media.

Reagan's cordiality with Gorbachev dismayed the Far Right, but most Americans sighed in relief as the Cold War crumbled. Diplomatic historian John Lewis Gaddis wrote early in 1989: "[D]uring his eight years as president, Ronald Reagan has presided over the most dramatic improvement in U.S.-Soviet relations—and the most solid progress in arms control—since the Cold War began. History has often produced unexpected results, but this one surely sets some kind of record."

Reagan's farewell address, delivered on January 11, 1989, proved a vintage performance. Highlighting achievements and gliding over failures, he concluded with a lump-in-the-throat call for a rebirth of patriotism. His popularity had remained high throughout his two terms, enhanced by prosperity and the sudden outbreak of peace. Insiders, however, depicted a remote, uninvolved figure. In part, these traits reflected the infirmities of age and perhaps the early onset of the Alzheimer's disease that would darken his final years. But essentially Reagan was a performer—the "Great Communicator"—smiling on cue and reading speeches with consummate skill. Unconcerned with details and most at ease in front of the camera, he seemed more a master of ceremonies than a president. Tom Shales of the *Washington Post* commented, "Historians can decide if Ronald Reagan was a

Such Good Friends. Soviet premier Mikhail Gorbachev and his wife Raisa visit former president Ronald Reagan and his wife Nancy at the Reagans' Santa Barbara, California, ranch in 1992. *(Blake Sell, © Reuters/CORBIS)*

great president, but any TV viewer can see he has been a great leading man." At White House briefings, Reagan displayed a weak grasp of details and fell back on generalities. Supporters contended that he preferred to sketch broad goals while leaving details to others.

The most damaging picture of the Reagan presidency came from insiders. Donald Regan, forced out during the Iran-contra scandal, got his revenge in *For the Record* (1988), a book that portrayed his boss as a puppet controlled by his handlers: "He listened, acquiesced, played his role, and waited for the next act to be written." A daily schedule leaked to the press showed that Reagan's every public word was scripted, down to the most trivial small talk. Regan also described the behind-the-scenes power of Nancy Reagan, who planned her husband's trips on the basis of astrological advice. He wrote:

> The president's schedule is the single most potent tool in the White House. . . . By humoring Mrs. Reagan we gave her this tool, or, more accurately, gave it to an unknown woman in San Francisco who believed that the zodiac controls events and human behavior.

Mrs. Reagan epitomized the materialism of the era as well, wearing high-fashion gowns loaned by New York couturiers delighted by the free advertising.

To his admirers, Reagan had restored patriotism, rebuilt the military, ended inflation, stimulated the economy, and reaffirmed the verities of individualism and self-reliance. Great Britain's conservative prime minister Margaret Thatcher

IN PERSPECTIVE

Politicians, the Media, and Campaign-Finance Reform

No matter how people differed about Ronald Reagan's political ideology, on one point everyone agreed: He was a master of television. And small wonder—Reagan was, after all, a trained actor. As one staff member later recalled, whenever the cameras focused on Reagan and he began to speak, they could relax: The master was in control.

In one sense, this was nothing new. American politicians have loved (or loved to hate) the media for two centuries. In the earliest days of the Republic, long before CNN or Larry King, newspapers left no doubt about their political allegiance. As early as the 1790s, some newspapers tirelessly promoted the Federalist Party of John Adams and Alexander Hamilton; other papers just as vigorously championed the emerging Republican Party of Thomas Jefferson.

By the campaign of 1840, when the Whig William Henry Harrison ran against the Democrat Martin Van Buren, the politics of media image-making were in full swing. Serious issues faced the nation, but the campaign mainly involved mudslinging newspaper editorials and raucous torch-light parades at which Harrison supporters carried miniature log cabins and swigged hard cider, symbolizing their candidate's allegedly humble western origins. In fact, Harrison was of aristocratic Virginia stock, and the Whigs were the party of the well-to-do, but in the arena of media manipulation, facts have never been a serious impediment. No president was above the allure of the media. When John Wilkes Booth shot Abraham Lincoln at Ford's Theater in April 1865, Lincoln was carrying in his pocket a well-thumbed packet of press clippings.

By the early twentieth century the media had expanded beyond newspapers to include radio and film, and politicians quickly adapted. Just as contemporary presidents invite sports heroes and celebrities to the White House to bask in their reflected glory, so did earlier chief executives. When Charles A. Lindbergh became an instant celebrity in 1927 for his solo flight across the Atlantic, President Calvin Coolidge quickly invited him to Washington for a joint press appearance.

President Franklin D. Roosevelt was a legendary master of radio, and the media fully cooperated in concealing Roosevelt's inability to walk: Movie newsreels and newspaper photos invariably showed a jaunty, vigorous Roosevelt seated at his desk, relaxing in a comfortable chair, riding in a car, or occasionally standing at a podium, but never in a wheelchair or painfully walking with crutches, dragging the heavy steel of his leg braces.

Both John F. Kennedy and Richard Nixon played the media like a violin. At the height of Kennedy mania in the early 1960s, the media vied to publish photographs or transmit TV images of the handsome young president with his beautiful, adoring, whispery-voiced wife and their two sweet children. Nary a hint of Kennedy's incessant philandering—including romps with young women in the White House swimming pool when Jackie went traveling—reached the public until long after his death. As for Nixon, aficionados of media manipulation still speak in awed tones of the 1952 "Checkers" speech, in which he tearfully dragged in the family dog as he wheedled his way back into public favor after revelations of a secret campaign fund contributed by wealthy backers.

But although the symbiotic relationship between politics and the media has been a part of American public life from the beginning, there is also no question that the advent of television raised the stakes immeasurably. The dominance of the catchy sound bite, the attack ad, and the soft-focus image of family togetherness—with its inevitable corollary, the decline of serious discussion of complex issues—increased enormously in the decades after 1950.

So, too, did the price tag of running for office in an era when the key to victory was no longer the public forum where serious matters were discussed, but the professionally crafted media campaign. At all levels, from the presidency down to judgeships and mayoral races, television added enormously to the cost of campaigning, turning politicians into nonstop fundraisers and leading to endless discussions of—but little action on—campaign-finance reform. Some proposed much shorter campaigns, in the British manner; others suggested that TV stations be required to provide free time to all candidates to debate the issues on a regular basis, as an alternative to paid commercials and evening-news sound bites.

But campaign-finance reform, too, has been around for a long time. In 1883, after President James A. Garfield was shot by a disappointed (and insane) office seeker, Congress passed the Pendleton Act, which, among other provisions, forbade political candidates from soliciting contributions from federal workers. In 1939, disgruntled congressional Republicans, suspecting that WPA relief funds and New Deal arts and theater programs had been manipulated to influence the 1938 congressional elections, passed the Hatch Act forbidding federal employees from participating in electoral campaigns.

Whether the latest drive for campaign-finance reform will succeed remains to be seen. So, too, does the question of whether American politicians can ever wean themselves from the fifteen-second sound bite and the manipulative TV commercial to once again address the electorate in a thoughtful way, as Abraham Lincoln and Stephen A. Douglas did in 1858, when they conducted a senatorial campaign by debating the vital issues of the day in long, grueling face-to-face debates up and down the state of Illinois. What a concept!

affirmed, "He has left America stronger, prouder, greater than ever before." But skeptics saw him as substituting rhetoric for policy analysis and, with his ridicule of "the government," contributing to cynicism about politics. Reagan responded to individual need with impulsive warmth, but the ideology he so artfully championed revealed an impoverished social vision.

Yet his popularity was certified by two sweeping electoral victories to which millions of "Reagan Democrats" contributed. Of the old New Deal coalition, only black Americans resisted the lure of Reaganism; the white working class defected in droves. Journalist Garry Wills in *Reagan's America* (1987) saw Reagan's serene confidence as a key to his appeal: "Self-assurance reassures others, and that has not been the least of Reagan's gifts to us, at a time when the nation needed some reassuring."

In 1994, five years after leaving the White House, Reagan announced that he was suffering from Alzheimer's disease and withdrew from public life. His death a decade later, at ninety-three, produced an outpouring of tributes at home and abroad. His eulogists stressed his jaunty mood, his perennial optimism, and his role in ending the Cold War and restoring American pride and confidence. Some even ranked him with Franklin Roosevelt among the greatest of twentieth-century presidents.

Ultimately, however, the issue is not Reagan's personality but his policies. Whether his belligerent Cold War rhetoric, military build-up, and costly missile-defense program were indeed the crucial factors in the Soviet collapse continues to be debated. Domestically, the "Reagan revolution" cut social services while emasculating federal regulatory agencies and diverting resources from the neediest Americans. Reagan barely mentioned such grave national issues as the AIDS epidemic. Celebrators of the top-down prosperity of the mid- and later 1980s ignored the ballooning trade gap and federal deficit. They also overlooked the plight of the poor and urban minorities, as well as displaced industrial workers and even struggling members of the middle class.

Individualism Rampant: American Life in the 1980s

Reagan's contempt for government and his glorification of self-interest helped spawn a series of Washington scandals in which officials placed personal gain above the public interest. The so-called Wedtech affair is typical. For years, this small Bronx machine shop founded by Puerto Rican immigrants had tried to win government contracts set aside for minority-owned companies. Its fortunes rose dramatically when it hired E. Bob Wallach, a close friend of Attorney General Meese, and retained a Washington public-relations firm headed by Reagan's former political director. With these patrons, Wedtech won $250 million in no-bid minority Pentagon contracts. In 1986, shortly before the Small Business Administration cut Wedtech from its minority-business program, the insiders who had aided the corporation's rise sold their stock for $10 million. Clouded in scandal, Wedtech went bankrupt. Wallach and others were indicted on a variety of criminal charges.

Deceptive pricing, inflated labor costs, and other Pentagon-procurement abuses proliferated in this era of runaway military spending. Defense contractors practiced what one reporter called "plunder in the name of patriotism." Arkansas senator David Pryor spoke of "an eight-year feeding frenzy at the Department of Defense." By 1985 nearly fifty Pentagon contractors had come under investigation.

The most unsavory of all federal agencies was the Department of Housing and Urban Development (HUD), where top officials funneled millions in contracts to builders and consultants with political connections. James Watt, for example, back in the private sector after his brief tenure as secretary of the interior, earned $420,000 by making a few telephone calls to HUD for friends. As the HUD scandals unfolded, even Reaganites held their noses. Conservative columnist James J. Kilpatrick wrote, "The more one hears of this rotten affair, the worse it gets."

A cloud of opportunism and greed hung over the capital. By 1989, 138 administration officials had run afoul of the law. Among Reagan's inner circle, deputy chief of staff Michael Deaver received a three-year suspended sentence for perjury related to influence-peddling charges. Edwin Meese underwent a criminal investigation on charges including bribe taking, falsified income-tax returns, and conflict of interest in his actions as attorney general. In 1988 Meese's two top aides resigned, disgusted by his official conduct. In the end, Meese escaped indictment.

The individualism and shriveled social vision of the Reagan presidency infected the larger culture. As in the Gilded Age and the 1920s, amassing wealth became a national obsession. President Reagan declared in 1983, "What I want to see above all is that this remains a country where someone can get rich." The 1960s had honored John Kennedy and Martin Luther King, Jr., as heroes; the eighties idolized entrepreneurs who flaunted their wealth. Donald Trump, a New York real-estate tycoon, became a celebrity for his flamboyant lifestyle and a 1987 book on deal making. Chrysler head Lee Iacocca revealed his success formulas in *Iacocca* (1985). Some pushed him for president. Leona Helmsley, wife of another New York real-estate baron, posed as the regal "Queen" in ads for one of her husband's hotels, the Helmsley Palace.

High-flying deal makers ruled Wall Street. The years 1985–87 saw twenty-one corporate mergers involving stock transfers of over $1 billion each. The torrent of mergers often involved hostile takeovers by raiders seeking a quick kill. T. Boone Pickens, Ivan Boesky, and other raiders became household names. Having acquired a company, they wrote off weaker divisions as tax losses and sold the remaining units at huge profits, with a devastating impact on workers and local communities.

So-called junk bonds (high-risk stocks offered to speculators attracted by possible vast profits) financed this wave of corporate takeovers, and young Michael Milken reigned as the junk-bond king. Displaying a genius for complex takeover deals, Milken directed the junk-bond division of the Drexel Burnham Lambert firm from his luxurious office in Beverly Hills. Using the telephone like a bodily appendage, he worked around the clock to set up intricate deals. His 1987 income exceeded $1 billion. Milken's annual High Yield Bond Conference in Los Angeles earned a revealing nickname: the Predators' Ball.

The turbulent history of the savings-and-loan (S&L) industry exemplified the decade's go-go economic climate. S&Ls had traditionally given small investors a

A Decade of Excess. Leona Helmsley after a 1990 court appearance on tax-evasion charges. Featured as "Queen" in 1980s ads for her husband's luxury hotel, the Helmsley Palace, Helmsley once told an aide: "Taxes are for little people." *(David Cantor, AP/Wide World Photos)*

modest but secure return on home-mortgage loans. The high interest rates of the late 1970s, however, had impelled S&Ls to raise *their* rates to attract deposits, even though their capital was tied up in low-interest mortgages. In the deregulated climate of the 1980s, many S&Ls resorted to risky investments and high-pressure marketing tactics, including full-page newspaper ads promising fantastic returns, to lure new depositors, some of whom invested their life savings. Congress increased federal insurance on S&L deposits from $20,000 to $100,000, attracting still more funds. Many S&Ls, especially in the Southwest, used this infusion of capital to made loans on high-risk commercial ventures such as malls, apartment complexes, and office towers.

When the economy turned sour (see Chapter 15), hundreds of S&Ls went bankrupt, and some S&L officials faced criminal indictments. In the most notorious case, the head of California's Lincoln Savings & Loan was convicted in 1991 for securities fraud after inducing 23,000 investors to buy $250 million worth of essentially worthless bonds. He spent five years in prison.

The era of corporate takeovers, highly leveraged buyouts, and junk-bond millionaires soon faded. Ivan Boesky, Michael Milken, Leona Helmsley, and others went to jail for various white-collar crimes. Jerry Sterner's 1989 play, *Other People's Money,* dissected the era's get-rich-quick mania as it chronicled the destruction of a venerable New England firm by corporate raiders. Commented Sterner:

> There hasn't been a more selfish generation in the United States since this country was founded. . . . We suffer from a disease. . . . It's called instant gratification. We expect it from our politicians, our investments, . . . even our wars. We've come from an era of "What can I do for my country?" to "What's in it for me?" to "What's in it for me TODAY?"

Other writers captured the decade's mood. Mystery writer Sara Paretsky examined the sleazy world of Yuppie lawyers and white-collar lawbreakers in 1980s Chicago in *Guardian Angel* (1992). Tom Wolfe's *Bonfire of the Vanities* (1987) did for the eighties what F. Scott Fitzgerald had done for the twenties in *The Great Gatsby.* The novel offered a panorama of New York City life, from stockbrokers' Park Avenue penthouses to the mean streets of Brooklyn and the South Bronx.

Amid rampant individualism, the sense of community waned. In *Habits of the Heart: Individualism and Commitment in American Life* (1985), the sociologist Robert Bellah and four colleagues offered a disturbing picture of America at the high noon of Reaganism. The title echoed Alexis de Tocqueville's warning in *Democracy in America* (1835) of an individualism so powerful that each citizen would be "shut up in the solitude of his own heart." In modern America, the authors speculated, this extreme individualism had been severed from a balancing social vision. Their interviews revealed a longing for stronger communal bonds. The search for an alternative to radical individualism, they suggested, could lead to a rediscovery of classical republican political thought, with its stress on the common good and the balance of individual rights and civic obligation. "We are beginning to understand," they concluded, "that our common life requires more than an exclusive concern for material accumulation."

The decade's media-dominated politics and socially barren ideology added immediacy to these perennial questions. Political theorist Benjamin Barber, writing in *Harper's* magazine, criticized the unalloyed individualism celebrated in Reagan's second inaugural address. Wrote Barber:

> [T]he great American dream has always been *a public* dream. . . . Entrepreneurs may make money, but only citizens can make justice. The struggle for common goods—clean air, justice, peace—is a common struggle in which democratic government is our only ally. President Reagan . . . burdens the market with demands for progress and prosperity, but of the community and the government that is the community's instrument he asks nothing.

Mass Culture in the 1980s

The mass media became more consolidated in the 1980s as conglomerates swallowed up one company after another. By 1990 one such conglomerate, controlled by S. I. Newhouse, owned twenty-seven newspapers, several upscale magazines including the *New Yorker,* and the publishing behemoth Random House. Foreign investors transformed the world of book publishing. The German corporation

Bertelsmann, the Australian-born tycoon Rupert Murdoch, and the British press lord Robert Maxwell all acquired major U.S. publishing firms in the 1980s.

The consolidating process extended to newspapers as well. By 1986 twelve newspaper chains accounted for nearly half of total U.S. circulation. The ultimate generic newspaper, *USA Today,* designed for mass circulation, had appeared in 1978, with little regional flavor or editorial distinctiveness. This concentration of media ownership muffled the intellectual diversity and clash of opinion on which a healthy democracy and vibrant culture depend.

A wave of corporate takeovers also hit the movie industry. Gulf + Western Corporation acquired Paramount Studios. Time Inc. bought Warner Communications, already an entertainment octopus, for $13 billion in 1989. At the same time, the movie studios moved into other entertainment fields. The Disney Corporation, for example, not only made movies but also produced TV series, owned a record company, and ran theme parks in Florida and California. By the late eighties, the mass-culture industry had become so interconnected that the tangled relationships nearly defied sorting out.

Foreign capital poured into the entertainment industry in the 1980s. Japan's SONY Corporation acquired Columbia Pictures. The Matsushita Corporation, a consumer electronics firm, snapped up the media conglomerate MCA-Universal for $7 billion. Bertelsmann bought RCA Records, and Murdoch gained control of 20th Century Fox. By 1990, four of the five top U.S. record companies were foreign owned. Sustained by multinational investment and multibillion-dollar deals, U.S. mass culture in the 1980s extended its reach to every realm of national life. The inner cities might be decaying, the schools in crisis, and class divisions widening, but the juggernaut of commercial entertainment rumbled on.

Ironically, an increasingly consolidated mass media targeted a more and more segmented market, further diminishing the common culture and the outlets for civic discourse. While general-interest periodicals such as *Harper's* and the *Atlantic Monthly* limped along, specialized periodicals focused on narrow market niches, targeting readers interested in everything from golf, stock car racing, and the Civil War to antiques, computers, and physical fitness.

Radio grew more segmented as well. Some stations featured news; others offered nonstop call-in programs or catered to musical tastes ranging from "Top 40" and "Easy Listening" to country, religious, and rock. Stations for black and Hispanic listeners proliferated. National Public Radio (NPR) had begun in 1971 with federal funding and listener contributions. By the eighties, some three hundred NPR stations offered classical music, jazz, and in-depth news coverage.

Technology promoted the segmentation and the privatization of popular culture. The rise of cable TV, for example, splintered the viewing audience among an array of channels. By 1989 the three major networks' audience share had shrunk to 61 percent. Many viewers now watched channels specializing in religion, business, black interests, history, the weather, sports, old TV series, and much else. Viewers could catch first-run movies on Home Box Office, news on CNN, erotica on the Playboy Channel, and gavel-to-gavel coverage of Congress on C-Span. The home-shopping channel hawked jewelry, cosmetics, fashions, and kitchenware.

Other new technologies promoted privatized leisure as well. The videocassette recorder (VCR) enabled people to watch rented movies at home rather than go out to a theater. Introduced in the 1960s, VCRs were in 70 percent of American homes by 1985. The Walkman—a radio and tape cassette unit played through earphones, muting the sounds of the outside world—symbolized the turn to privatized pleasure and away from social engagement. The social critics of the 1950s had feared a homogeneous, standardized culture. By the 1980s, the question had shifted: Could a highly segmented populace caught up in socially isolating patterns of consumption and mass-media diversion sustain a common public discourse or even a sense of community?

The mass-culture industry itself occasionally critiqued its own manipulative techniques. In the movie *Network* (1976), a TV network desperate for higher ratings hypes a mentally unbalanced newscaster (Peter Finch) as "the mad prophet of the airwaves." In *Broadcast News* (1987), a cynical TV news anchor (William Hurt) resorts to deception to further his career. Despite such exposés of the media's strategies to expand their audience (and thereby charge higher advertising rates), the public seemed passively to accept more of the same.

One mass-culture trend remained glaringly obvious: television's dominance. In his 1953 novel *Fahrenheit 451*, Ray Bradbury had imagined a citizenry for whom TV became the only reality; by the 1980s, some found Bradbury's nightmare all too real. Average daily viewing time crept to nearly seven hours by 1990, up from about six hours in 1970. In a 1976 survey, 51 percent of Americans rated television their "most believable" news source. Ironically, the big general-magazine success of the postwar era was *TV Guide*, founded in 1952. With rare exceptions, the masters of TV continued to aim abysmally low, relying on escapism, violence, and sexual innuendo. The popular *A-Team* featured cartoon cutout crime fighters. *Miami Vice* offered music videos and fashion statements in the guise of a limp police drama.

The FCC's lax regulation made television more than ever a vehicle for commerce. By 1990 annual TV ad revenues surpassed $26 billion. Enormous talent and technical expertise went into producing commercials for cars, breakfast cereals, pet food, breath fresheners, and hemorrhoid remedies. A parade of Saturday morning children's cartoons peddled plastic toys and sugared breakfast cereals. Even public TV's award-winning educational program *Sesame Street* sparked criticism for mimicking commercial TV. "Commercials" for "the letter R" or "the number 7," for example, softened children up for actual TV ads and their underlying consumerist ethos.

The link between television and professional sports tightened in the 1980s. A thirty-second commercial during football's Super Bowl could cost as much as $675,000. By 1990 the Super Bowl accounted for eight of the ten largest audiences in TV history. The National Basketball Association (NBA) went big time as well. Millions followed the exploits of Isiah Thomas and the flamboyant Dennis Rodman of the Detroit Pistons; Larry Bird of the Boston Celtics; and Magic Johnson and Kareem Abdul-Jabbar, who in 1980–90 led the Los Angeles Lakers to five NBA championships. (The greatest superstar of all, Michael Jordan, would drive the Chicago Bulls to six NBA titles in the 1990s.) Contract negotiations between the professional sports leagues and the networks became major corporate events. Details of superstars' multimillion-dollar salaries and product endorsements—and occasional run-ins with the law—filled the sports pages.

Because the big-money professional sports were male dominated, television sharpened the disparity in the attention given to men's and women's sports. But this was changing as well. Title IX of a 1972 federal law relating to education had prohibited gender discrimination by educational institutions receiving federal aid. In response, colleges and universities devoted more resources to women's athletics. Women's basketball, soccer, swimming, and other sports received more attention and drew more fans. In 1982 the National Collegiate Athletic Association (NCAA) held the first national women's basketball championship. (Louisiana Tech defeated Cheyney College, 76–62.)

Critics deplored television's effects on politics. In *Amusing Ourselves to Death* (1985), Neil Postman contrasted manipulative TV campaigns with the serious public discourse of earlier times, as exemplified by the 1858 Lincoln-Douglas debates. Indeed, from 1968 to 1988, the average TV "sound bite" by presidential candidates shrank from 42 to 10 seconds.* TV's role in the electoral process, already great, increased in the 1980s. As Haynes Johnson of the *Washington Post* perceptively wrote, "Ronald Reagan and television fitted into American society like a plug into a socket. . . . He was the Sun King, presiding over the new national celebration from the White House."

In one example of the power of visual images, ABC News during the 1984 campaign showed scenes of Reagan's visit to the Special Olympics (an event for physically impaired competitors), while a reporter cited statistics documenting the administration's spending cuts on programs for the handicapped. To the reporter's surprise, a Reagan media adviser called to thank her for the wonderful story. When she reminded him of her negative commentary, he taunted her, "Nobody heard what you said. They just saw the five minutes of beautiful pictures of Ronald Reagan. They saw the balloons, they saw the flags, they saw the red, white, and blue. Haven't you people figured out yet that the picture always overrides what you say?"

The Reagan-era ethos found its TV apotheosis in the prime-time soap opera *Dallas,* which chronicled the business deals and torrid sex life of oilman J. R. Ewing. Another show explored *Lifestyles of the Rich and Famous.* Reagan's first wife, Jane Wyman, starred in *Falcon Crest,* another TV drama of intrigue among the wealthy. By contrast, America's minorities, migrant workers, and others left behind in the glitzy 1980s rarely appeared on TV. The *Cosby Show,* a domestic sitcom, portrayed an affluent African American family but ignored the larger portion of the black population: the inner-city poor.

The differences over Vietnam that in the 1960s had raged in the streets were replayed in the 1980s on the cultural front. While films such as *The Deer Hunter* (1978), *Platoon* (1986), and *Born on the Fourth of July* (1989) explored combat experience and the war's psychological toll, Sylvester Stallone's *Rambo* (1985) offered a comic-strip version of the war in which America triumphs. Even Maya Lin's design for the Vietnam Veterans Memorial raised angry disputes. Some found the listing of the dead on a black marble wall somber and defeatist and demanded a monument emphasizing military valor. Texas billionaire Ross Perot campaigned for a more conventionally patriotic memorial. In the end, a group statue was erected

---

*A sound bite is a catchy phrase uttered by a politician in hopes that it will be shown on TV.

near the memorial wall, but its three young soldiers look more fatigued and un-comprehending than heroic.

The most successful 1980s movies provided fantasy and diversion. Stephen Spielberg's fairy tale *E.T.* (1982), recounting the friendship between a small boy and a little green space alien, won praise as a parable of cross-cultural understanding, but a wave of escapist movies with no apparent social significance soon followed. In a series of cartoonlike *Rocky* movies, Sylvester Stallone played a washed-up prizefighter who prevails over various fearsome opponents. Apart from some Vietnam and antinuclear films, Hollywood rarely addressed real-world issues, even in fictional form. In one notable exception, the 1987 hit *Wall Street,* Michael Douglas plays a corporate buccaneer who gets his comeuppance. Douglas also costarred in *Fatal Attraction* (1987), in which a psychotic career woman (Glenn Close) stalks him and nearly destroys his marriage after a casual sexual fling. To some critics, the movie tapped into a rising antifeminist backlash.

Pop music increasingly involved the high-tech marketing of images. On MTV, a pop-music channel, rock groups and singers lip-synched their hits in minidramas called music videos. Michael Jackson, a global superstar, became a reclusive eccentric whose androgynous and racially ambiguous image heightened his mystique. Madonna (Madonna Louise Veronica Ciccone) blatantly flaunted her sexuality as she branched out from popular music to movies, TV videos, and concert tours.

Recording technology continued to evolve with the advent of the compact disc (CD) in 1982. The CD, in which laser beams "read" information molded into concentric circles on a metallic disk, provided remarkable fidelity, although some found the sound, like the decade, a bit sterile. On Broadway, the 1980s saw the rise of gaudy sound-and-light shows whose flashy production outshone the music or the story. The most successful of these high-tech musicals, *Les Misérables,* derived, ironically, from Victor Hugo's tale of the poor of Paris.

Personal computers, the hot new data-processing technology of the 1970s, proliferated in the 1980s. By 1988 some 45 million Americans owned PCs. Students took PCs to college, small businesses did their record keeping by computer, and library research speeded up enormously as electronic databases replaced card catalogs and bulky multivolume indexes. The number of public schools using PCs in instruction more than doubled from 1985 to 1990.

Critics worried that the new technologies would produce a generation that experienced life vicariously as computer bytes, TV images, or aural messages emanating from a CD player. In a media-dominated world, they feared, the capacity to respond to direct experience and the sense of social connectedness would atrophy.

As in earlier decades, TV roused criticism for producing a nation of "couch potatoes" passively absorbing an endless stream of images in the isolation of their living rooms. A car bomb in Beirut, starving children in Somalia, upheavals in Eastern Europe, a drive-by shooting, a fashion show at a suburban mall, reports of the AIDS epidemic, commercials for perfumes and weight-loss products—all flickered on the tube, creating a mishmash of unconnected impressions. One critic described Americans as "metaphorically chained to their TV screen and, like Plato's cave dwellers, blind to the real world behind them, unable to differentiate between shadow and substance." Such judgments overstated the passivity of mass-culture consumers and understated the degree to which Americans remained engaged with the real world through family, church, neighborhood, and work. Nevertheless, the media's dominance raised legitimate concerns.

Mass culture remained America's hottest export. The *Economist* of London summed matters up in 1989: "America is to entertainment what South Africa is to gold and Saudi Arabia is to oil." By the late 1980s, the U.S. entertainment industry earned $5.5 billion annually in foreign exchange. The U.S. music industry, mainly rock and other pop genres, garnered 70 percent of its revenues from overseas sales. One show-business executive commented, "Hollywood, unlike Detroit, has found a product that the Japanese can't improve on."

The world's image of America increasingly derived from mass-culture exports. A Jamaican journalist bitterly noted, "Because of what they see on television, everyone in Jamaica thinks . . . that everything in America is wonderful. . . . It makes people think that money and material wealth are the only ways to be rich in this world." American democracy continued to inspire other peoples, particularly in regions breaking free of communism, but the mass media exported another image of the United States: a society of self-seeking individuals absorbed in the pursuit of money, amusement, and material possessions.

Campaign '88

In 1988, Vice President George Bush claimed his chance at the top spot. As Bush won a string of primaries, challengers including televangelist Pat Robertson fell by the wayside, and the nomination was his. Bush's acceptance speech evoked a psychological mood rather than a program as he called for "a kinder, and gentler nation" and pledged "Read my lips: No new taxes." Bush tapped Indiana senator Dan Quayle, son of a conservative newspaper publisher, as his running mate. Few discerned presidential qualities in Quayle, and doubts about him deepened with revelations that during the Vietnam War, which his family's newspapers had supported, he had pulled strings to avoid the draft.

Among the Democratic aspirants, Jesse Jackson, the favorite among African Americans, bettered his 1984 showing with white voters in several state primaries. But the field quickly thinned. Colorado senator Gary Hart withdrew after the *Miami Herald* revealed his affair with a Florida model. The ultimate victor was Governor Michael Dukakis of Massachusetts, a Greek American. As his running mate, he chose Senator Lloyd Bentsen of Texas. Dukakis initially surged to a wide lead in the polls. Democrats saw Bush, with his penchant for malapropisms, as an easy target. "Poor George," gibed one Democratic leader, "he was born with a silver foot in his mouth."

But Dukakis's lead soon faded. An inept campaigner, he bored even fellow Democrats. He refused to challenge the Reagan-Bush ideology and instead stressed his administrative skills. By contrast, Bush pointed to the new jobs, reduced world tensions, and low inflation of the 1980s, ignoring the budget and trade deficits, the Iran-contra scandal, and other embarrassments. The Bush forces further damaged Dukakis with insidious TV commercials. The most notorious of these featured a black convict who had committed rape and murder while on a weekend pass under Massachusetts' prisoner-furlough program. Implying that Dukakis was soft

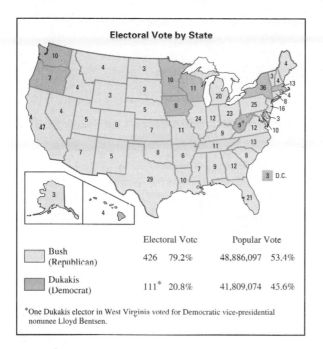

Electoral Vote by State

	Electoral Vote	Popular Vote
Bush (Republican)	426 79.2%	48,886,097 53.4%
Dukakis (Democrat)	111* 20.8%	41,809,074 45.6%

*One Dukakis elector in West Virginia voted for Democratic vice-presidential nominee Lloyd Bentsen.

MAP 14.4
Presidential Election of 1988

on crime, the commercial also subtly exploited racial stereotypes. Both sides pandered to the TV cameras: Bush visited flag factories; Dukakis posed in a tank. With the candidates marketed like soap or deodorants, serious debate rarely interrupted the sound bites and photo opportunities.

Aided by prosperity and Dukakis's weak campaign, Bush grabbed 53 percent of the popular vote. Carrying forty states, including vital California and Texas, he dominated the electoral tally. Dukakis claimed only ten states plus the District of Columbia. Except for West Virginia, he lost every southern and border state. Yet voters returned Democratic majorities to Congress. This outcome reflected the advantage of incumbency in good times, reinforced by heavy PAC contributions. With the White House controlled by one party and Congress by the other, and neither inclined to cooperate, the resulting impasse contributed to four years of legislative gridlock.

Bush and the World:
End of the Cold War, Desert Storm, NAFTA

George Herbert Walker Bush, the son of a Connecticut senator, epitomized New England's WASP elite. An Episcopalian and sportsman, he attended Yale, where he led the baseball team and was elected to the elite secret society Skull and Bones. A bomber pilot in World War II, he won the Distinguished Flying Cross. Marrying

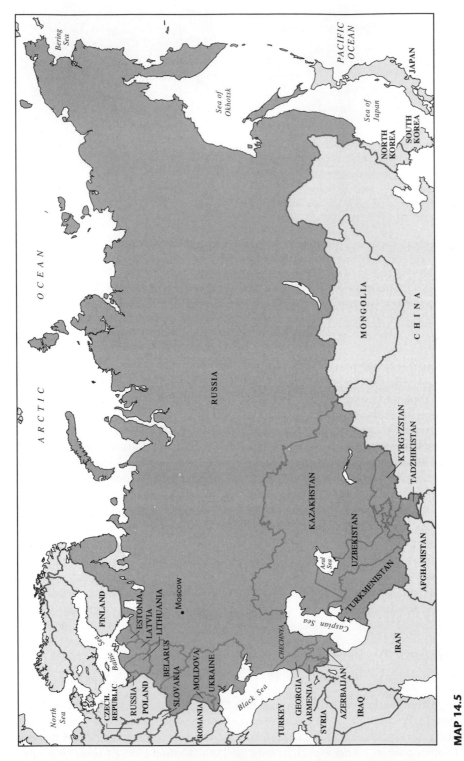

MAP 14.5
The Former Soviet Union

Barbara Pierce, of a prominent magazine publishing family, he moved to Texas and entered the oil business. He won election to Congress in 1966 but lost a 1970 Senate race. His close Texas friend James Baker III became his secretary of state.

As vice president, Bush had avoided entanglement in the Iran-contra affair but also gained a reputation for opportunism. On abortion, for example, he abandoned a long-held pro-choice position and courted the antiabortion vote. His gauzy inaugural address called on Americans to ignite "a thousand points of light" and to view the future as "a door you can walk right through into a room called tomorrow."

As Bush uttered these banalities, stunning events unfolded abroad—events that cumulatively spelled nothing less than the end of the Cold War. In 1989, as East European communist regimes long propped up by Soviet power collapsed, Lech Walesa of Poland's independent labor movement Solidarity and Václav Havel, a Czech playwright and former political prisoner, were elected presidents of their nations. In Romania, the dictatorship of Nicolae Ceausescu ended bloodily as he and his wife were hunted down and shot.

Unrest also rumbled across East Germany, as demonstrators protested the oppressive rule of the aging hard-line communist Erich Honecker, who resigned in October 1989. On November 9, Honecker's successor ordered the opening of the Berlin Wall. As the world watched on television, jubilant Berliners flocked to the squat gray barrier that had long stood as the Cold War's most visible and hated symbol. The celebration continued far into the night. At the historic Brandenburg Gate, near what had once been Hitler's Reichstag, young people danced atop the wall. Others hammered off chunks of the wall as souvenirs.

The next day, East Berliners poured through once heavily guarded checkpoints for their first view of life beyond the wall. One woman, overwhelmed by the shops along West Berlin's glittering and elegant Kurfürstendamm, murmured, "There is so much color, so much light. It's incredible." Another East Berliner returned several books to a West Berlin library that he had borrowed twenty-eight years earlier, the day before the wall went up in 1961. Soon after, Leonard Bernstein conducted a gala performance of Beethoven's Ninth Symphony in the reunited city, restoring *Freiheit* ("Freedom") for *Freude* ("Joy") in the choral movement. East Germany's communist regime soon collapsed, and in October 1990 the division of Germany, a legacy of World War II, ended as the Bonn government assumed power over all Germany.

Soon the Soviet Union itself fragmented. Mikhail Gorbachev had hoped to introduce democratic socialism while preserving the Soviet Union and reforming the Communist Party. But in 1991 the forces he had unleashed overwhelmed him. As the party's grip weakened, nationalism swept over the Soviet republics. The Baltic republics of Estonia, Latvia, and Lithuania regained their independence. In August, Soviet military officers alarmed by the pace of change briefly took Gorbachev captive, but President Boris Yeltsin of the Russian Republic, backed by a mass outpouring of Muscovites, defied the coup leaders' tanks and restored Gorbachev to freedom. Late in 1991 the Soviet Union formally disbanded, its fifteen republics joined only in an amorphous Commonwealth of Independent States, and Gorbachev found himself a private citizen. Europe's last great empire had dissolved into a jumble of new nations torn by ethnic turmoil, border disputes, and economic problems and united only in their repudiation of communism. Statues of communist leaders toppled; Leningrad resumed its ancient name of St. Petersburg. In May 1992, speaking at Westminister College in Missouri, the scene of Churchill's "Iron Curtain" address of 1946, Gorbachev declared the Cold War over.

Americans reared on "the Soviet threat" felt a mixture of relief, disorientation, and residual mistrust. In John Updike's *Rabbit at Rest* (1990) the lead character reflects: "It's like nobody's in charge of the other side any more. I miss it, the cold war. It gave you a reason to get up in the morning." For Russia and the other former Soviet republics, the transition from a state-run economy to a free-market system on the Western model proved monumentally difficult. As Russia's economy foundered, Boris Yeltsin urgently sought Western help. The Bush administration dragged its feet, but in 1992, prodded by Richard Nixon, Bush proposed a $35 billion aid package.

The Cold War's end accelerated the arms-control process. In August 1991, in Moscow, President Bush signed the START Treaty cutting the two nations' nuclear arsenals by one-quarter. In 1992 Yeltsin, in Washington seeking aid, accepted still deeper cuts. Tacitly conceding the altered balance of power, Yeltsin agreed to give up all of Russia's land-based MIRV missiles, whereas the United States would cut its submarine missile force only by half. The Russian president also pledged to deactivate all missiles targeted on the United States.

With the Soviet Union's collapse, NATO announced a 50 percent troop reduction. For decades, the existence of a common foe had cemented the Western alliance. With the Soviet threat gone and Western Europe forging a single economic bloc, America's future relationship with Europe remained uncertain. Indeed, the end of the Cold War disoriented U.S. foreign policy. From Truman to Reagan, anti-communism and containment of the U.S.S.R. had given coherence to American diplomacy. Suddenly the old formulas seemed irrelevant. Like Nixon and Kissinger, Bush savored the role of world leader, but unlike them, he had no grand strategy and simply reacted to events as they occurred. Although he served in stirring times, he did little to put his personal imprint on U.S. foreign relations.

The new era also rattled the Pentagon. Bush's secretary of defense, Dick Cheney, proposed a 20 percent reduction in military spending over five years. Leading Democrats urged far deeper cuts. Whatever the levels, job losses and other economic disruptions were inevitable. At the peak of the Reagan buildup, annual military spending had neared $375 billion, and 1.4 million Americans had worked in military-related jobs. By 1992 military spending had fallen below $300 billion, and defense jobs declined by some two hundred thousand.

In mid-1990, as world attention focused on the collapsing communist regimes of Eastern Europe, a crisis suddenly erupted in the Middle East—an early warning of things to come. On August 2, Iraq invaded its neighbor, the tiny but oil-rich Kuwait, with which it had a long-running dispute over control of the vast Rumaila oilfield. Iraqi dictator Saddam Hussein, eager to gain access to the Persian Gulf, claimed that historically Iraq had ruled Kuwait. Even before the attack, Saddam had roused fears with his anti-Israel threats, his hostility to other Arab states, and his nuclear- and chemical-weapons research. Nevertheless, during Iraq's war with Iran (1980–88), the CIA had secretly supplied Saddam with weapons, electronics, and satellite intelligence to aid his battle against Tehran's anti-American Shiites. The flow of aid and military hardware had increased under George Bush, even though the Iran-Iraq war had ended and Iran had softened its anti-American tone after Ayatollah Khomeini's death in 1989.

With Saddam's invasion of Kuwait, Bush suddenly shifted gears. Comparing Saddam to Hitler, Bush denounced the attack as a threat to regional stability and a violation of international law. Perhaps most important, Saddam's action jeopardized two major oil producers with close ties to the West, Kuwait and neighboring Saudi Arabia.

The UN Security Council slapped trade sanctions on Iraq, ordered its withdrawal from Kuwait by January 15, 1991, and authorized member states to use "all means necessary" to achieve this end. The Pentagon rushed U.S. air and sea power to the Persian Gulf and deployed four hundred thousand ground forces in Saudi Arabia. Bush assembled a coalition of nations led by the Saudis, Great Britain, Egypt, and France. Avoiding LBJ's mistake in Vietnam, he cultivated home-front backing by defining the issues starkly: resisting aggression and protecting U.S. strategic interests.

On January 12, 1991, overriding Democratic calls for more time to allow the sanctions to take effect, both houses of Congress authorized military action. Four days later, the Allies launched Operation Desert Storm under U.S. General H. Norman Schwarzkopf. For a week, two thousand Allied warplanes rained

The Reality of War: Kuwait, 1991. In a scene from the Persian Gulf War that did not appear on prime-time television, three GIs impassively consider the body of an Iraqi soldier incinerated by American firepower. (© 1991 Peter Turnley/Black Star)

bombs on Iraqi forces in Kuwait, military targets in Iraq, and strategic sites in Baghdad itself. On February 23, after U.S. marines feinted an amphibious assault, 200,000 ground forces moved across the desert into Kuwait. What Saddam called "the mother of all battles" proved pitiably one-sided. U.S. forces destroyed 3,700 Iraqi tanks, while losing only 3. The United States suffered 467 wounded and 148 dead, including 35 killed accidentally by U.S. fire. The number of Iraqi dead, military and civilian, while heavy, remains unknown, with estimates ranging from 25,000 to 85,000.

The war's most dramatic moments came when Iraq, trying to provoke another Arab-Israeli war, fired Soviet-made Scud missiles against Tel Aviv and other Israeli targets and at U.S. staging areas in Saudi Arabia. U.S. Patriot missiles destroyed most incoming Scuds or threw them off course. Americans watched fascinated as CNN broadcast the aerial fireworks.

Indeed, the whole war played well on TV. Death or suffering rarely intruded on the images of abandoned tanks and surrendering Iraqis. Having learned the lesson of Vietnam, the Pentagon restricted press access to the war. Skillfully edited shots of bombs exploding on distant targets, some filmed through the bombsights of U.S. aircraft, resembled the simulated combat of video games.

As Americans savored the media-enhanced victory, Bush gloated, "By God, we've licked the Vietnam syndrome once and for all." Before a wildly cheering Congress, Bush proclaimed: "We hear so often about our young people in turmoil; how our children fall short; how our schools fail us; how American products and American workers are second-class. Well, don't you believe it. The America we saw in Desert Storm was first-class talent." Bush's approval rating spurted to 89 percent; Schwarzkopf enjoyed a hero's welcome. In contrast to the Vietnam era, citizens hailed the returning troops. The untelevised war, including the heavy toll of Iraqi lives, hardly impinged on the American consciousness.

The euphoria soon faded, however. Iraq had left Kuwait, but Saddam remained in power. The cease-fire provided for the UN-supervised ending of Baghdad's nuclear- and chemical-weapons programs, but Saddam raised many roadblocks. Washington's earlier role in arming Saddam further complicated the picture. The political bonus to Bush of the Desert Storm triumph soon dissipated.

Amid stirring events in Europe and the Middle East, events elsewhere also demanded attention. In China, an aging communist oligarchy clung to power while edging toward a freer economy and pursuing trade with the West. In 1989, when Chinese students calling for democracy occupied Beijing's Tiananmen Square, the government ordered a tank assault that left hundreds dead. A subsequent crackdown on dissidents included arrests and public executions. Bush condemned the brutality and proposed economic sanctions, but he resisted congressional demands that he sever trade and diplomatic relations with Beijing.

Dramatic changes in South Africa also unfolded on Bush's watch. In 1986, overriding a Reagan veto, Congress had barred all U.S. trade or corporate investment in South Africa with its white-only government and its system of apartheid. These sanctions and other countries' efforts induced South Africa to moderate its racial stance. A breakthrough came in 1990 when the government released Nelson Mandela, leader of the African National Congress (ANC), the major political organization of black South Africans, after years of detention. When the government dismantled apartheid in 1991, Bush lifted U.S. sanctions. In South Africa's first universal election, in 1994, the ANC won 63 percent of the vote, and ex-prisoner Mandela became president of his country.

Elsewhere in Africa, a severe drought in 1992 threatened 40 million people with famine, especially in war-torn Somalia. Relief agencies stepped in, and the United States, under UN auspices, supplied emergency food shipments. When warring factions diverted relief shipments to the black market, President Bush sent thirty thousand U.S. troops to protect food deliveries. His action reflected less a strategic decision than a response to TV images of famished Somalis. His intervention would soon generate controversy as the American forces suffered casualties (see Chapter 15), but at the time the nation supported it. As one citizen put it, "You see these starving kids on T.V., and you think how could we not do this?"

In Latin America, the Soviet collapse reoriented U.S. policy. Bush and Baker abandoned Reagan's failed contra policy in Nicaragua and backed efforts to reintegrate the contras into the country's politics. A 1990 election brought an anti-Sandinista coalition to power. In neighboring El Salvador, U.S.-promoted peace talks bore fruit in 1992 as the right-wing government agreed to various reforms, and the twelve-year civil war ended. Foreign policy and domestic concerns interacted in Panama in 1989 when U.S. troops captured strongman Manuel Noriega, accused of aiding the flow of cocaine from Colombia and Peru to U.S. cities. The action cost five hundred Panamanian and twenty-three U.S. lives, but it won applause in America and from Panamanians relieved to be rid of Noriega, who went to prison after a federal trial in Miami. As with U.S.-Iraqi relations, however, the story proved complex. Noriega had long been on the CIA payroll, and only after his drug trafficking became too blatant to ignore did Washington move against him.

If the Cold War's end eased some regional conflicts, it worsened others. In the former Soviet Union and Eastern Europe, long-suppressed ethnic and religious hatreds erupted, perplexing U.S. diplomats accustomed to dealing with a unified Soviet bloc. In 1992 Czechoslovakia split into the Czech Republic and Slovakia. Old animosities turned murderous in the Balkans when Yugoslavia's communist state splintered in 1991. The region was historically unstable, with its mix of Muslims, Catholic Croatians, and Orthodox Serbs. As Yugoslavia's western provinces of Slovenia, Croatia, and Bosnia-Herzegovina proclaimed their independence, the Serb-dominated federal government in Belgrade launched military operations against Croats and Muslims in areas dominated by ethnic Serbs. Serbian guerrillas besieged Sarajevo and other Bosnian cities, killing residents, cutting off food and medicine, and leaving many thousands homeless. Troops loyal to Serbian president Slobodan Milosević murdered, raped, imprisoned, and deported Muslims and other non-Serbs in a campaign of "ethnic cleansing" reminiscent of the Nazis. (In World War II, by contrast, Croatian fascists allied with Hitler had brutalized the Serbs.) Despite urgent calls for Western military intervention to stop the slaughter, President Bush confined the U.S. role to safeguarding UN convoys bringing food and relief to Bosnia. (As we shall see, the United States would play a more active role in the Balkans under Bush's successor Bill Clinton.).

The administration's most solid diplomatic achievement, significantly, came on the economic front, underscoring Washington's shifting post–Cold War priorities. In 1992, U.S., Canadian, and Mexican trade representatives completed the

North American Free Trade Agreement (NAFTA), joining the three nations into a single trading bloc containing more people and more production than the European Community.* Hailing the agreement, Bush declared: "The Cold War is over. The principal challenge now facing the United States is to compete in a rapidly changing, expanding global marketplace."

But the path to a successful foreign-trade policy proved rocky. The annual trade deficit hovered at around $40 billion in the early nineties. In 1992, on a Bush-led trade mission to Japan, the heads of GM, Ford, and Chrysler ham-handedly pressured the Japanese to buy more U.S. cars. When a flu attack caused Bush to collapse and vomit on Japan's prime minister at a state dinner, the mishap seemed symbolic of America's foreign-trade woes.

Beyond the NAFTA accord and its role in coordinating the international response to Iraqi aggression, the Bush administration groped uncertainly toward what the president hopefully called a "new world order." As historian Stephen Graubard observed, "Like many Americans of his generation, Bush had become so habituated to living with the Cold War . . . that he lacked any moral or political compass to guide him when he wished to turn away from its simple and brutal verities." As Graubard noted, Bush was hardly alone in this uncertainty.

Marking Time: Bush's Domestic Record

At home, Bush floundered as the nation grappled with a tangle of economic problems. The federal budget deficit continued to rise under the lingering impact of Reagan's tax cuts and increased military spending, together with the cost of ever-growing entitlement programs. In 1990, in a rare moment of accord, Congress and the president agreed on a five-year deficit-reduction package. Breaking Bush's "read my lips" pledge, the plan increased a variety of taxes. Yet the deficit persisted, reaching $290 billion in 1992. So did interest payments on the $4 trillion national debt, which by 1992 amounted to $200 billion annually, 15 percent of all federal spending.

If the trade gap and budget deficits remained abstract to many citizens, a recession that hit in 1990 proved all too real. By mid-1992, despite some hopeful trends, consumer confidence remained depressed, and the jobless rate stood at nearly 8 percent. The GDP, which had grown robustly under Reagan, increased only an anemic 2.2 percent in the recession-battered Bush years. The problem had several sources, including reduced defense spending and a collapse of the overextended commercial real-estate market. Further, Americans had plunged heavily into debt in the 1980s to sustain high levels of consumption. The bill came due in the early 1990s, contributing to the economic downturn.

The recession hit the poor most severely, but it also brought bad news for the middle class and exacerbated a long-term economic erosion. From 1989 to 1991, median household income (adjusted for inflation) fell from $31,750 to $31,125. In *Boiling Point: Republicans, Democrats and the Decline of Middle Class Prosperity* (1993),

---

*NAFTA was ratified by Congress in 1993, after Bush left office.

Kevin Phillips documented that the real income of the middle class had been falling since 1973, worsened by the tax cuts of the 1980s that had redistributed income from the lower and middle ranks to the wealthy. The postwar baby-boom generation, observed anthropologist Katherine Newman in *Declining Fortunes: The Withering of the American Dream* (1993), was "the first . . . since the Great Depression that can expect to have a *lower* standard of living than its parents." Middle-class economic worries played a pivotal role in the 1992 presidential election.

Although Bush proclaimed himself both "the environmental president" and "the education president," he won scant praise on either front. He did sign the 1990 Clean Air bill intended to reduce smog, acid rain, and industrial pollution, but he also appointed environmental officials who undercut the rules they were pledged to enforce, advocating expanded logging on public lands, more oil exploration in Alaska, and the commercial development of protected wetlands. A "Competitiveness Council" headed by Vice President Quayle attacked environmental laws for supposedly stifling business growth. Bush's petulant speech at the Earth Summit, a 1992 environmental conference in Rio de Janeiro, boasting of his environmental record and attacking his critics, further alienated environmental activists.

Bush's education agenda proposed national student testing, competency exams for teachers, and a system by which students could attend private or church-run schools at public expense. While private-school administrators praised the "school choice" idea, most educators criticized the proposals for doing little to help a public-school system battered by recession and neglect.

Two Supreme Court justices retired during Bush's term. His first nominee, Judge David Souter of New Hampshire, proved thoughtful and open in his confirmation hearings and won easy confirmation. With Sandra Day O'Connor and Anthony Kennedy, Souter would emerge as a centrist on abortion and other volatile issues.

Bush's choice of Clarence Thomas to replace Thurgood Marshall proved more divisive. Both African American, the two men had little else in common. Marshall, an NAACP attorney before joining the high court, had long upheld liberal and civil-rights causes. Thomas, a rigidly ideological conservative, had risen from a poor Georgia boyhood to attend Yale Law School. Head of the Equal Employment Opportunity Commission (EEOC) under President Reagan, he had been appointed a federal judge only in 1990. Thomas refused to discuss his legal views in his confirmation hearings. But the hearings took a startling turn when a former associate at EEOC, Anita Hill, accused Thomas of sexual harassment. Thomas angrily denied the charges, and Republican committee members angered feminists by harshly grilling Hill. In the end, Thomas narrowly won Senate confirmation, 52–48. Once on the bench, he consistently took the most conservative position, holding that judges must try to discern the "original intent" of every law, including the Constitution and the Bill of Rights, and not twist laws to "address all [the] ills of our society."

The crisis in the inner cities got only sporadic federal attention in the Bush years. Jack Kemp, a former pro football player who headed the Department of Housing and Urban Development, urged tax incentives to encourage inner-city job creation by private capital, but the White House showed scant interest. After rioting erupted in an African American district of Los Angeles in 1992 over a case involving alleged police brutality (see page 455), Bush and Congress agreed on a $5 billion urban aid package, but Washington's attention soon waned.

Addressing the nation's $50 billion illegal drug traffic, Bush urged a doubling of the federal anti-drug budget and named William Bennett, a former secretary of education, as "drug czar." Under Bennett's get-tough policy, drug-related arrests rose to a million each year, but the problem persisted, and Bennett soon departed in frustration.

Conclusion

Presided over by a benign but often vague chief executive, the Bush administration increasingly seemed a kind of postscript tacked onto the Reagan era. Marked by short bursts of energy, the Bush presidency lacked sharp focus, sustained momentum, or clear objectives. A twelve-year presidential cycle that had begun with the excitement and ideological fervor of Reagan's 1981 inaugural address ended with a sense of diminishing energy and lost opportunities.

Reagan did not single-handedly cause the materialism, selfishness, and vulgarity of the 1980s, but his endless praise of unrestrained individualism encouraged some of the era's less appealing features. Urgent national issues—from inner-city joblessness, troubled schools, and drug abuse to environmental threats, the AIDS epidemic, and health care—suffered neglect as the celebration of business values and material success set the political and cultural tone. Despite Reagan's personal decency and kindly manner, the decade to which he gave his name offered little by way of inspiration or guidance to the future. Instead, Reagan and Bush primarily bequeathed to their successors an array of festering problems at home and abroad.

SELECTED READINGS

Ronald Reagan and Reagan-Era Politics

Sidney Blumenthal, *The Rise of the Counter Establishment: From Conservative Ideology to Political Power* (1988); Sidney Blumenthal and Thomas Byrne Edsall, eds., *The Reagan Legacy* (1988); Paul Boyer, ed., *Reagan as President: Contemporary Views of the Man, His Politics, and His Policies* (1990); William J. Broad, *Teller's War: The Top-Secret Story Behind the Star Wars Deception* (1992); W. Elliot Brownlee and Hugh Davis Graham, *The Reagan Presidency: Pragmatic Conservatism and Its Legacy* (2003); Robert Busby, *Reagan and the Iran-Contra Scandal: The Politics of Presidential Recovery* (1999); Lou Cannon, *Governor Reagan: His Rise to Power* (2003) and *President Reagan* (1991); Thomas Byrne Edsall with Mary D. Edsall, *Chain Reaction: The Impact of Race, Rights, and Taxes on American Politics* (1991); Haynes Johnson, *Sleepwalking Through History: America in the Reagan Years* (1991); Peter Kornbluth, ed., *The Iran-Contra Scandal: The Declassified History* (1993); Jonathan Lash, *A Season of Spoils: The Story of the Reagan Administration's Attack on the Environment* (1984); Peggy Noonan, *What I Saw at the Revolution: A Political Life in the Reagan Era* (1990); Kevin Phillips, *The Politics of Rich and Poor* (1990); Donald T. Regan, *For the Record: From Wall Street to Washington* (1988); Bob Schieffer and Gary Paul Gates, *The*

Acting President (1989); C. Brant Short, *Ronald Reagan and the Public Lands: America's Conservation Debate, 1979–1984* (1989); David A. Stockman, *The Triumph of Politics: How the Reagan Revolution Failed* (1986); Walter Williams, *Reaganism and the Death of Representative Democracy* (2003); Garry Wills, *Reagan's America* (1987).

U.S. Foreign Policy, 1981–1988

Dana H. Allin, *Cold War Illusions: America, Europe, and Soviet Power, 1969–1989* (1998); Michael R. Beschloss and Strobe Talbott, *At the Highest Levels: The Inside Story of the End of the Cold War* (1994); Seweryn Bialer and Michael Mandelbaum, eds., *Gorbachev's Russia and American Foreign Policy* (1988); Thomas Crothers, *In the Name of Democracy; U.S. Foreign Policy Toward Latin America in the Reagan Years* (1991); John Lewis Gaddis, *The United States and the End of the Cold War* (1992); Raymond L. Garthoff, *The Great Transition: American-Soviet Relations and the End of the Cold War* (1994); Patrick Glynn, *Closing Pandora's Box: Arms Races, Arms Control, and the History of the Cold War* (1992); Roy Gutman, *Banana Diplomacy* (1988); David E. Kyvig, ed., *Reagan and the World* (1990); Michael Mandelbaum and Strobe Talbott, *Reagan and Gorbachev* (1987); Constantine Menges, *Inside the National Security Council* (1988); Morris H. Morley, *Washington, Somoza, and the Sandinistas* (1994); Kenneth Oye et al., *Eagle Resurgent? The Reagan Era in American Foreign Policy* (1987); Ronald E. Powaski, *Return to Armageddon: The United States and the Nuclear Arms Race, 1981–1999* (2003); David Schoenbaum, *The United States and the State of Israel* (1993); Lawrence Wittner, *Toward Nuclear Abolition: A History of the World Nuclear Disarmament Movement: 1971 to the Present* (2003); Joann Wypijewski, *Blue Skies and Broken Hearts: A Tour Across the Political Geography of Star Wars* (2003).

Economic Trends, Protest, and Social Thought in the Eighties

Carl Abbott, *The New Urban America: Growth and Politics in the Sunbelt Cities* (1981); Robert Bellah et al., *Habits of the Heart* (1985) and *The Good Society* (1991); Connie Bruck, *The Predators' Ball: The Inside Story of Drexel Burnham and the Rise of the Junk Bond Raiders* (1989); Kathleen Day, *S&L Hell: The People and Politics Behind the $1 Trillion Savings & Loan Scandal* (1993); Paul S. Dempsey, *The Social and Economic Consequences of Deregulation* (1988); Barbara Ehrenreich, *Fear of Falling: The Inner Life of the Middle Class* (1989) and *The Worst Years of Our Lives* (1990); Benjamin Friedman, *Day of Reckoning: The Consequences of American Economic Policy Under Reagan and After* (1988); Larry N. Gerston et al., *The Deregulated Society* (1988); J. David Hoeveler, *Watch on the Right: Conservative Intellectuals in the Reagan Era* (1991); Daniel Horowitz, *The Anxieties of Affluence: Critiques of American Consumer Culture, 1939–1979* (2004); Harry Hurt, *The Lost Tycoon: The Many Lives of Donald J. Trump* (1993); J. Anthony Lukas, *Common Ground: A Turbulent Decade in the Lives of Three American Families* (1986); Frances Fox Piven and Richard A. Cloward, *The New Class War: Reagan's Attack on the Welfare State and Its Consequences* (1982), Patricia Cayo Sexton, *The War on Labor and the Left: Understanding America's Unique Conservatism* (1991); James B. Stewart, *Den of Thieves* [Wall Street trading scandals] (1991); Sidney Weintraub and Marvin Goodstein, eds., *Reaganomics in the Stagflation Economy* (1983); William J. Wilson, *The Truly Disadvantaged: The Inner City, the Underclass and Public Policy* (1987).

Popular Culture in the Eighties

"America's Hottest Export: Pop Culture," *Fortune,* December 31, 1990; Michael A. Anderegg, *Inventing Vietnam: The War in Film and Television* (1991); Bob Carroll et al., *The Hidden Game of Football* (1988); Richard M. Clurman, *To the End of Time: The Seduction and Conquest of a Media Empire* [merger of Time, Inc. and Warner Communications] (1992); Stuart Ewen and Elizabeth Ewen, *Channels of Desire: Mass Images and the Shaping of American Consciousness* (2d ed., 1992); "Fancy Free: A Survey of the [U.S.] Entertainment Industry," *Economist* London, December 23, 1989; Jane Feuer, *Seeing Through the Eighties: Television and Reaganism* (1995); Todd Gitlin, *Inside Prime Time* (1985) and *Watching Television* (1986); Ron Grover, *The Disney Touch* (1991); Nicholas Mills, ed., *Culture in an Age of Money* (1991); Edward Palmer, *Television and America's Children: A Crisis of Neglect* (1988); Brian L. Porto, *A New Season: Using Title IX to Reform College Sports* (2003); Neil Postman, *Amusing Ourselves to Death* (1985); Randy Roberts and James S. Olson, *Winning Is the Only Thing: Sports in America Since 1945* (1989); Michael Sorkin, ed., *Variations on a Theme Park: The New American City and the End of Public Space* (1993); Michael Winship, *Television* (1988).

George Bush and the Bush Presidency

Philip John Davies, ed., *An American Quarter Century: U.S. Politics from Vietnam to Clinton* (1995); Michael Duffy, *Marching in Place: The Status Quo Presidency of George Bush* (1992); Jack W. Germond and Jules Witcover, *Whose Broad Stripes and Bright Stars: The Trivial Pursuit of the Presidency, 1988* (1989); David Mervin, *George Bush and the Guardianship Presidency* (1996); Kevin P. Phillips, *The Politics of Rich and Poor: Wealth and the American Electorate in the Reagan Aftermath* (1990); John Podhoretz, *Hell of a Ride: Backstage at the White House Follies, 1989–1993* (1993); Richard Rose, *The Post-Modern President: George Bush Meets the World* (1991).

Bush and the World: Foreign Affairs, Trade, the Persian Gulf War

Rick Atkinson, *Crusade: The Untold Story of the Persian Gulf War* (1993); George Bush and Brent Scowcroft, *A World Transformed* (1999); Maxwell A. Cameron and Brian W. Tomlin, *The Making of NAFTA* (2002); Alan Friedman, *Spider's Web: The Secret History of How the White House Illegally Armed Iraq* (1993); Stephen R. Graubard, *Mr. Bush's War: Adventures in the Politics of Illusion* (1992); Bradley S. Greenberg and Walter Gantz, *Desert Storm and the Mass Media* (1993); Richard Hallion, *Storm over Iraq: Air Power and the Gulf War* (1992); Roger Hilsman, *George Bush vs. Saddam Hussein* (1992); Kim R. Holmes and Burton Yale Pines, *George Bush's New World Order* (1991); Gary C. Hufbauer, Jeffrey J. Schott, and Diana Orejas, *NAFTA: A Seven-Year Appraisal* (2004); Allen Hunter, ed., *Rethinking the Cold War* (1998); Robert D. Kaplan, *Balkan Ghosts: A Journey Through History* (1993); Stephen Kotkin, *Armageddon Averted: The Soviet Collapse, 1970–2000* (2001); John D. Martz, *United States Policy in Latin America: A Decade of Crisis and Challenge* (1995); Jack F. Matlock, Jr., *Autopsy on an Empire: The American Ambassador's Account of the Collapse of the Soviet Union* (1995); Gale Stokes, *The Walls Came Tumbling Down: The Collapse of Communism in Eastern Europe* (1993); U.S. News and World Report, *Triumph Without Victory: The Unreported History of the Persian Gulf War* (1992).

15

America at the Turn of the Century: Prosperity, Scandal, a Changing Society

IN 1992, WITH the economy stagnant, a frustrated electorate vented its discontent at the polls. After twelve years of Republican rule, voters ushered Democrat Bill Clinton into the White House. Domestically, Clinton began by proposing a sweeping national health-care plan reminiscent of Johnson's Great Society at its most expansive. When it failed, the pliant Clinton scaled back his ambitious domestic program. When the 1994 midterm election produced Republican majorities in both houses of Congress, Clinton moved further to the right and joined Congress in crafting a welfare-reform program that partially dismantled a federal welfare system whose origins dated to the 1930s. Though Clinton won re-election in 1996, both he and the Republican Congress proceeded cautiously, avoiding high-visibility initiatives.

World trends continued to flow America's way in the nineties, but devising a coherent post–Cold War foreign policy proved no easier for Clinton than it had for Bush. The Soviet Union's collapse reduced fears of nuclear war, but new world realities posed novel challenges. As the global economy became more integrated, trade issues increasingly dominated—and complicated—the diplomatic process.

In 1998 a Clinton sex scandal led to a Republican effort to remove him from office. The impeachment campaign, though ultimately unsuccessful, brought his presidency to an inglorious conclusion. A booming economy muted economic anxieties in the Clinton years (and helped him survive the impeachment effort), but despite the rosy statistics, nagging problems remained, including excessive stock-market speculation, wage depression, and chronic problems and poverty in the inner cities.

The late twentieth and early twenty-first centuries brought demographic and social changes with profound import for the future. As Americans struggled to define a common national purpose amid rampant consumerism and interest-group politics, debate swirled around such diverse issues as abortion, affirmative action, the environment, and an aging population's health-care needs.

The new global economy, the rise of megacorporations and media conglomerates, and new communications technologies—especially personal computers and the Internet—made clear that twenty-first-century America would be very different from the America of 1950 or even of 1980. The pace of social and technological change proved both exhilarating and unsettling. Nostalgia, religious piety, suspicion of government, and a politically aggressive conservative movement all loomed large as Americans uneasily contemplated their future on the eve of a new millennium.

Campaign '92

George Bush had made extravagant promises in 1988. In addition to the "Read My Lips: No New Taxes" pledge, broken in 1990, he had spoken glibly of 30 million new jobs. His call for a "kinder, gentler America" had suggested concern for those left behind in the 1980s. In fact, Bush disdained what he called "the vision thing" and largely ignored domestic issues. Apart from a law barring discrimination against persons with disabilities, even Bush's admirers had trouble identifying domestic achievements. Bush boasted of ending the Cold War and standing up to Iraq, but his flip-flop on taxes and his neglect of economic issues amid a recession weakened him. By mid-1992 his approval rating had sagged to 34 percent, and fewer than 20 percent of Americans approved his handling of the economy.

Bush's post–Persian Gulf popularity had led top Democrats to opt out of the 1992 presidential race. Into the vacuum stepped Arkansas governor Bill Clinton. The personable Clinton battled rumors of extramarital affairs, Vietnam-era draft dodging, and an opportunistic streak summed up in the epithet "Slick Willy."

Public cynicism about politics-as-usual emerged on many fronts in 1992. The movie *JFK* postulated a bizarre conspiracy theory to explain Kennedy's assassination. The PAC (political-action committee) money that showered down on Washington intensified the anti-incumbency mood. In 1992 House Speaker Tom Foley received $401,000 in PAC contributions, and majority leader Richard Gephardt raked in a whopping $1.2 million.

The insurgent mood inspired the third-party candidacy of Ross Perot, a billionaire Texan who headed EDS Corporation, a data-processing firm. Perot's politics remained obscure apart from a deficit-cutting obsession, but he enjoyed a reputation for can-do activism. Above all, he was an outsider, untainted by old-style politics. Millions flocked to Perot's banner, stirring fears that the election, for the first time since 1824, might be thrown into the House of Representatives.* But the mercurial Perot, angered by media scrutiny and tripped up by his off-the-cuff style, withdrew from the race in July. He reentered to participate in the televised presidential debates but never regained his momentum.

Bill Clinton easily won the Democratic nomination. Born in 1946, he battled an abusive stepfather, adored Elvis Presley, and briefly contemplated a career as a saxophonist. Instead, he attended Georgetown University, Oxford University as a Rhodes scholar, and Yale Law School. In 1978, at thirty-two, he won election in Arkansas as the nation's youngest governor.

---

*If no presidential candidate receives an Electoral College majority, the Constitution authorizes the House of Representatives to make the decision, with each state delegation casting a single vote.

Clinton's acceptance speech, focused on health care, education, jobs, and programs to promote economic growth, earned him a spurt in the polls. So did his choice of Senator Al Gore of Tennessee as running mate. To attract younger voters, Clinton appeared on MTV, sporting sunglasses and saxophone. Hillary Clinton, also a Yale Law graduate, initially struck many voters as too aggressive, but she softened her image—challenging Barbara Bush to a cookie-recipe contest, for example—and emerged as an asset to her husband's cause.

Both Clinton and Gore belonged to the Democratic Leadership Council (DLC), a group intent on wooing back "Reagan Democrats" by shedding the Democrats' reputation as a "tax-and-spend" party beholden to minorities and special interests. Clinton thus distanced himself from Jesse Jackson and from union leaders. His acceptance speech praised hardworking Americans and included tough talk on welfare. The party platform echoed the theme, describing welfare as "a second chance, not a way of life." Clinton called for a two-year limit on welfare payments, coupled with various programs to help recipients find work. He demanded tough laws to compel delinquent fathers, or "deadbeat dads," to support their offspring.

Bush never offered a coherent second-term agenda, and Vice President Quayle, already a butt of humor, drew more ridicule when he misspelled *potato* while presiding over a school spelling bee. The unstable Republican coalition that had twice elected Richard Nixon and Ronald Reagan comprised an uneasy alliance of laissez-faire ideologues who hated "big government" and of corporate

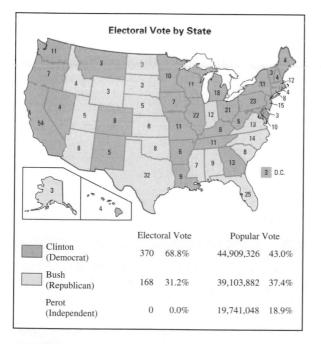

		Electoral Vote		Popular Vote	
	Clinton (Democrat)	370	68.8%	44,909,326	43.0%
	Bush (Republican)	168	31.2%	39,103,882	37.4%
	Perot (Independent)	0	0.0%	19,741,048	18.9%

MAP 15.1
Presidential Election of 1992

executives and wealthy citizens who favored lower taxes but often took a liberal stand on social issues. The coalition also accommodated millions of white working-class and middle-class Americans, frequently Protestant evangelicals or Catholic ethnics, concerned with such cultural issues as abortion, pornography, school prayer, and the encouragement of traditional family life. This bloc of voters also deplored what they perceived as favoritism to ethnic minorities and special-interest groups. Through the 1980s, anticommunism and prosperity, together with Reagan's charisma, had held the coalition together. But by 1992 the Cold War had ended, the economy was stalled, and the lackluster Bush had replaced Reagan.

As the GOP splintered, the party's right wing flexed its muscle. In early primaries, Bush faced a strong challenge by conservative columnist Pat Buchanan. The party platform adopted the New Right's cultural agenda. The convention celebrated Barbara Bush and Marilyn Quayle as traditional wives and attacked Hillary Clinton as a "radical feminist." Delegates representing Pat Robertson's Christian Coalition cheered a slashing speech by Buchanan vowing all-out ideological war on a variety of cultural and moral issues.

Bush's campaign strategist James Baker sketched a high-minded theme: President Bush, having devoted his first term to global issues, would now focus on domestic problems. Yet the campaign quickly sank to the low level that now seemed the rule. Issues were reduced to TV sound bites; innuendo and stereotypes substituted for serious discussion. Clinton blamed Bush for economic problems that had complex causes. When Bush denounced the Democratic platform for omitting "three simple letters, G-O-D," even jaded political observers groaned.

Election Day 1992 thrilled victory-starved Democrats. Clinton won 43 percent of the vote to Bush's 38 percent, with Perot garnering an impressive 19 percent. Economic worries won "Reagan Democrats" back to the fold and cut into Republican strongholds in the South and West. African Americans voted overwhelmingly Democratic. Both houses of Congress went Democratic, placing the legislative and executive branches under the same party for the first time in twelve years. Still, the outcome sent a cautionary signal to Clinton: Perot's tally was the best third-party showing since Theodore Roosevelt's in 1912. As for Bush, the *New York Times* summed up a prevailing view in a postelection editorial, "The Half-Way Man." The *Times* conceded Bush's foreign-policy achievements but observed that on domestic policy he "created the disquieting and ultimately fatal impression that he didn't know what to do, and worse, didn't much care."

Liberalism Lite: Clinton at the Helm

As in 1960, the 1992 election brought both a change of party and a generational shift. George Bush would be the last president to have fought in World War II and to have lived through the entire Cold War as an adult. With Clinton and Gore and the new Congress, the baby boomers took the helm. This generation's memories were not of Pearl Harbor, Stalin, and Bing Crosby, but of the Peace Corps, civil-rights marches, antiwar protests, JFK, and the Beatles. The Clintons' daughter, Chelsea, was even named for a popular sixties ballad, Joni Mitchell's "Chelsea Morning."

The election dramatized the new gender dynamics of U.S. politics. Voters sent six women to the Senate and forty-eight to the House of Representatives. California became the first state to elect two women senators—Barbara Boxer and Dianne Feinstein. Women still remained a small minority in Congress, but the men's-club atmosphere was fading. Clinton appointed women to head three departments—justice, energy, and health and human services—as well as the Environmental Protection Agency, the Council of Economic Advisers, and the UN delegation. To fill a Supreme Court vacancy in 1993, he chose Ruth Bader Ginsburg, a federal appeals court judge. Making clear that Hillary Clinton would be more than a ceremonial First Lady, he gave her an office in the White House West Wing—the official side—and named her to head the Task Force on National Health-Care Reform.

Fulfilling a campaign call for "a government that looks like America," Clinton chose Ron Brown, an African American, as secretary of commerce, and two Hispanics, Henry Cisneros and Federico Peña, to head Housing and Urban Development (HUD) and the Department of Transportation, respectively. The new Congress included thirty-eight African Americans (up from twenty-five); seventeen Hispanics (up from ten); the first Korean American; and the first American Indian senator, Ben Nighthorse Campbell of Colorado.

Clinton soon learned some hard lessons in Washington politics. Fulfilling a campaign pledge, he called for an end to the exclusion of homosexuals from military

Clinton and Gore. President Bill Clinton and Vice President Al Gore confer at an Oregon environmental conference in April 1993. (© Wally McNamee/CORBIS)

service. The move proved controversial, and in the end Clinton endorsed a watered-down "don't ask, don't tell" policy. Clinton's first two choices as attorney general withdrew after allegations that they had hired illegal aliens for childcare services or had failed to pay social security taxes for domestic employees. The media feasted on "Nanny-gate."

As he shaped his domestic program, Clinton faced conflicting advice. Moderate DLC Democrats and budget hawks at the Bureau of the Budget, eager to prove the party's fiscal responsibility, gave highest priority to deficit reduction. Democrats attuned to the party's blue-collar contingent urged new federal programs to create jobs. And social-activist Democrats such as the Clintons' friend Marian Wright Edelman of the Children's Defense Fund wanted substantial spending on social programs.

Clinton eventually settled on an amalgam of these different viewpoints. To reduce the deficit, he proposed an array of tax increases and spending cuts, including a further tightening of military outlays, a one-year freeze on federal salaries, and elimination of one hundred thousand federal jobs through attrition. The plan capped Medicare and Medicaid payments to doctors and hospitals and reduced funding for such big-ticket projects as the space station. Clinton's proposed tax hikes hit the richest Americans hardest, went easier on the middle class, and spared families earning under $30,000 a year.

To promote job creation and economic growth, while also assisting the disadvantaged, Clinton proposed more spending on worker-training programs and Head Start, tax credits for small-business investment, and a national service corps by which college students could pay off federal education loans through community work. To avoid the familiar Republican charge that the Democrats favored "big government," Clinton insisted that he would trim government fat and make the private sector principally responsible for economic growth. He would, he pledged, "show the American people that we can limit [government programs], that we can not only start things but we can actually stop things."

Mixed economic signals complicated the debate over the need for a stimulus. The Gross Domestic Product, adjusted for inflation, rose by 2 percent in 1992, but unemployment remained stuck at around 7 percent through 1993. In parts of the country, notably California, the jobless rate remained as high as 10 percent. Thirty-six million Americans struggled below the poverty line. Large-scale layoffs by GM, IBM, Sears, aerospace companies Boeing and McDonnell-Douglas, and other top corporations further weakened the job market. Many displaced skilled workers took jobs in the service sector at much lower wages. A 1993 study of two thousand workers fired by RJR-Nabisco Corporation, for example, revealed that those who found employment elsewhere earned on average less than half their former pay. When the Defense Department in 1993 announced the closing of thirty-one military bases and cutbacks at others, Clinton proposed a program to retrain displaced workers, aid the affected communities, and help defense industries convert to civilian production.

In August 1993, after long debate, Congress by razor-thin margins enacted a five-year economic plan quite different from Clinton's original proposal. The president's requested tax increase survived more or less intact, but with the economy improving, Congress appropriated only a fraction of what Clinton had sought for education, retraining, and apprenticeship programs. The bill's spending cuts had scant deficit-cutting potential because they spared the mushrooming entitlement programs such as Medicare and social security. The bill passed without a single Republican vote and with many Democratic defections, but the adoption of even a modified economic plan spared Clinton a major early embarrassment.

The controversial North American Free Trade Agreement (NAFTA) negotiated by the Bush administration, which incorporated Mexico into the free-trade zone already created by the United States and Canada, posed tricky political challenges for Clinton. Union leaders and their political friends, including House majority leader Richard Gephardt, warned of job losses to Mexico—a result feared by the blue-collar workers whom the Democrats hoped to win back. NAFTA's supporters, including most economists, conceded that low-wage jobs in labor-intensive industries might be lost, but insisted that NAFTA would create more high-wage jobs by opening the Mexican market to U.S. machinery and other products.

In the end Clinton supported NAFTA; in November 1993 Congress approved the agreement by a comfortable margin, handing Clinton another political victory. The administration followed up this success with a campaign for expanded U.S. trade opportunities in Asia and lower trade barriers worldwide.

As for NAFTA, the treaty initially had little effect on the U.S. economy. By 1997 some 117,000 U.S. citizens had applied for the benefits offered to workers displaced by the treaty, but in a booming economy this was negligible. The treaty's principal effects were felt in Mexico, since it promoted not only trade but also economic reform, U.S. investment, joint Mexican-U.S. business ventures, and other ties between the two nations. As one Clinton administration official candidly put it: "We bought ourselves an ally with NAFTA." A healthier Mexican economy, it was hoped, would also reduce illegal immigration and drug smuggling.

Next on Clinton's agenda came health-care reform, a goal of liberals since the 1930s. The problem had two elements: coverage and cost. Some 37 million Americans, most of them poor, lacked medical insurance. And costs continued to soar as patients demanded the latest treatments and technologies and as physicians prescribed expensive tests and procedures to forestall malpractice suits. In 1980–92, Medicare and Medicaid payments had ballooned from 8 percent to 14 percent of the total federal budget.

Hillary Clinton's health-care task force set out to devise a program to extend coverage and control costs. In October 1993, the administration unveiled a plan that would guarantee universal medical and dental coverage and various preventive services. All Americans would carry a "health security card" modeled on the social-security card that had reassured Depression-era Americans.

The plan's cost-containment provisions included caps on Medicare and Medicaid reimbursements and fostering competition among providers by enrolling all Americans into large regional purchasing groups, called health alliances, to negotiate fees with health-care providers. Individuals could join either a fee-for-service plan, enabling them to choose their own physicians, or a less expensive health maintenance organization (HMO). To cover the plan's estimated $100 billion in start-up costs, Clinton proposed stiff new taxes on tobacco. With tobacco-related illnesses killing 418,000 Americans annually, adding massively to health-care costs, this proposal won general support.

Hillary Clinton defended the plan in congressional testimony, but critics warned of government meddling, bloated bureaucracies, and a decline in health-care quality and ease of access. The American Medical Association, the physicians' organization, long a foe of "socialized medicine" and armed with a $7 million lobbying budget, attacked key parts of the plan.

Other critics focused on the secretive process by which the plan had been formulated and the central role of Hillary Clinton, who held no elective office. In September 1994, facing heavy lobbying attacks and a drumfire of criticism, the administration dropped its efforts to bring the measure to a vote in the Senate. The health-care debacle represented a turning point for the administration. Hillary Clinton thereafter played a much less visible public role, and President Clinton limited himself to modest, noncontroversial initiatives.

Although Clinton drew on New Deal symbolism and occasionally echoed LBJ's expansive vision of government's role in addressing social problems, his version of liberalism—even before the health-care defeat—differed markedly from the past. Recognizing the nation's rightward shift and the collapse of the liberal consensus, he more typically stressed such classic conservative themes as individual responsibility, free enterprise, and the dangers of big government. Even his health plan had rejected Canada's centralized, government-run system in favor of a decentralized plan of "managed competition" that mixed private enterprise and public oversight. Clintonian liberalism still embodied concern for the poor and notions of entitlement—such as the right of all citizens to health care. But he also stressed fiscal restraint, managerial efficiency, the importance of the private sector, and the economic anxieties of the middle class.

Clinton's post-1993 approach reflected not only the electorate's rejection of 1960s-style liberalism but also the pervasive cynicism about government that Perot had exploited. Tellingly, even while Clinton had pushed for health-care reform, Vice President Gore had led a task force for "reinventing government" by cutting paperwork and tightening management controls. The Clinton administration, in short, reflecting shifting political and economic realities, offered a bargain-basement vision of government's role.

The conservative coalition that had captured the White House in 1980 remained a potent force. Pat Robertson's Christian Coalition, having shown its muscle at the 1992 GOP convention, focused on the grassroots, electing candidates to school boards and town councils. Robertson's organization rallied the Christian Right not only on such cultural matters as abortion, school prayer, and pornography but also on political issues such as economic policy and health care. Neoconservative intellectual William Kristol, Dan Quayle's former chief of staff, derided Clinton's program as the product of a decayed liberalism that had "lost its force, its real conviction, and its real confidence in itself."

With the failure of the Clintons' health-care plan, Republicans eagerly awaited the 1994 midterm election. In an ominous prelude to scandals ahead, Clinton was further weakened by allegations of wrongdoing when he was governor of Arkansas, including illegalities associated with a complex real-estate deal and a sexual harassment suit filed by a female state employee. The 1993 suicide of Vincent Foster, Clinton's deputy White House counsel, created more rumors. Seizing the moment, Georgia congressman Newt Gingrich drafted a Republican "Contract with America." Amid much hoopla, several hundred GOP candidates signed it, turning the midterm election, normally dominated by local issues, into an ideological referendum. On Election Day, Republicans won control of both houses of Congress.

When the new Congress convened early in 1995, jubilant Republicans in the House of Representatives elected Newt Gingrich as Speaker; conferred honorary membership on Rush Limbaugh, a conservative radio commentator; and set about enacting the "Contract with America" agenda. One early measure prohibited "unfunded mandates," that is, federal requirements imposed on the states without money to carry them out. The House also passed a constitutional amendment requiring a balanced federal budget. Criticized by economists as a simplistic panacea, this measure died in the Senate. Tackling an issue much on voters' minds, Congress passed, and Clinton signed, a crime bill that included tougher sentencing provisions and other measures aimed at "getting tough on criminals." Another measure targeted Internet pornography.

Major attention focused on welfare reform. Americans across the political spectrum agreed that parts of the federal welfare system encouraged long-term dependency rather than preparation for gainful employment. The number of women and children receiving benefits under the largest program, Aid to Families with Dependent Children (AFDC), grew from 8 million in 1970 to 12.6 million in 1996. And since welfare benefits increased with the number of children, the system appeared to reward out-of-wedlock pregnancies. With unmarried women accounting for one third of all births, and 14 percent of American children on welfare, this issue hit home. Candidate Clinton had pledged to "end welfare as we know it," but it was congressional Republicans and GOP governors such as Wisconsin's Tommy Thompson who actively pushed the issue.

In August 1996, Clinton signed a historic welfare-reform bill passed by the Republican Congress. Sharply curtailing Washington's sixty-year role in welfare, the new law ended AFDC and empowered the states to devise their own welfare programs, partially funded by federal block grants under tough guidelines. The law limited able-bodied welfare recipients to two years of continuous benefits, with a five-year lifetime maximum. It also cut the food-stamp program, slashed benefits to immigrants, and authorized states to deny Medicaid to persons dropped from the welfare rolls.

Supporters of the hard-edged new law praised it for addressing the abuses of a bloated program that had outlived its original purpose. By ending long-term dependency, they claimed, it would encourage self-reliance. "[P]eople who are able-bodied are actually going to have to get trained to go to work," declared the chair of the House Budget Committee, "because they can't be on welfare all of their lives." Critics, however, charged that it would push vast numbers of women and children into poverty and that it reflected an attack by the well-to-do on the poor. Since blacks and Hispanics were heavily represented on the welfare rolls, some argued that in some cases the enthusiasm for "welfare reform" reflected subtle racist attitudes.

The new law's long-term impact remained unknown. Would fifty state welfare systems succeed any better than the discarded federal system? Would states fund the job training, counseling, childcare, and public-sector employment essential to meaningful welfare reform? And how would the tough new system fare in times of recession? Such questions went unanswered amid broad public approval of "welfare reform."

Clinton's signature on the Republican welfare bill, marking his decisive break with the liberal tradition, split the Democratic Party. Half of the Democrats in the House and twenty-one Senate Democrats, including such liberal stalwarts as Edward Kennedy of Massachusetts, voted against the bill. Labor unions, advocacy groups for immigrants and the poor, and organizations representing African Americans, Latinos, and women—traditional Democratic strongholds—opposed it. Clinton, with his eye on the polls and on America's middle class with its rich harvest of votes, ignored the protests. He did, however, promise to work for more funding of training programs to help welfare recipients find jobs.

Clinton's first Supreme Court appointee, Ruth Bader Ginsburg, joined Sandra Day O'Connor to become the second woman justice. To fill another vacancy in 1994, Clinton named Stephen Breyer of Harvard Law School. Less social activist than the Warren Court, the Clinton-era Supreme Court was more libertarian, often championing individual rights against government infringement. In one 1997 ruling, for example, the Supreme Court extended First Amendment protection to the Internet, overturning a portion of the Communications Decency Act of 1996, the first of several legislative efforts to protect the nation's mouse-wielding juveniles from pornography. In another 1997 ruling, the Court overturned part of a 1993 federal gun-control law as an infringement of states' rights.

Clinton's Second Term: Chastened Liberalism

The GOP sweep in 1994 did not, as Republicans had hoped, translate into a presidential victory two years later. House Speaker Gingrich attracted a firestorm of criticism in 1995 when he permitted two partial shutdowns of the government as a tactical maneuver in budget negotiations with the White House. President Clinton, meanwhile, bouncing back from the health-care defeat, benefited from a booming economy as the 1996 election neared.

Republicans initially placed their hopes in General Colin Powell, an African American and a much-admired former chairman of the Joint Chiefs of Staff. But Powell declined to run, and the nomination went to seventy-three-year-old Senator Bob Dole, with Jack Kemp as his running mate. A plainspoken Kansan who had been severely wounded in World War II, Dole was a long-time power in the Senate, most recently as majority leader. He campaigned gamely but ineptly, and the Clinton-Gore ticket handily gained a second term, carrying thirty-one states plus the District of Columbia. Clinton won 49 percent of the popular vote to Dole's 41 percent, while a die-hard 8 percent went for Ross Perot. Although the Republicans retained control of Congress, the predicted conservative revolution did not materialize.

The 1996 election send a message of moderation, not extremism, and Clinton hewed so closely to a centrist position in his second term that he seemed more a moderate Republican than a classic liberal Democrat. His preferred stance, observed historian Allan Brinkley, was to be "moderate, responsible, and nonfright-

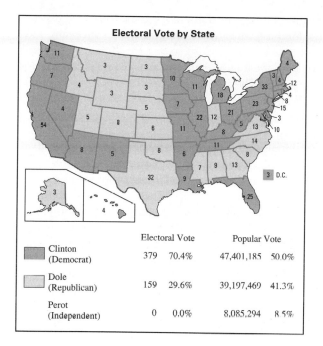

Electoral Vote by State

	Electoral Vote		Popular Vote	
▓ Clinton (Democrat)	379	70.4%	47,401,185	50.0%
☐ Dole (Republican)	159	29.6%	39,197,469	41.3%
Perot (Independent)	0	0.0%	8,085,294	8.5%

MAP 15.2
Presidential Election of 1996

ening, but marginally more progressive than the Republicans." The Democratic Party of FDR in 1936, LBJ in 1964, or George McGovern in 1972 was but a fading memory in the later 1990s.

Embracing a cherished Republican goal—a balanced budget—Clinton in 1997, after long negotiation, signed an omnibus bill that mandated a balanced budget by 2002 while providing $94 billion in tax cuts. The measure slashed the capital gains tax (another long-time GOP objective), raised to $1.2 million the portion of estates exempted from death taxes, and created numerous tax loopholes for the wealthy. Fulfilling a pledge in Gingrich's 1994 Contract with America, it included a $500 tax credit for each child. The spending cuts included caps on what health-care providers could charge to Medicare and Medicaid. While Republicans and Clinton-Gore "New Democrats" praised the bill, a dwindling band of Democratic liberals charged that it favored the rich. The act did reflect some of Clinton's social concerns, including $24 billion over five years for health care for children without health insurance and Medicaid and disability benefits for legal immigrants, cut off in the 1996 welfare-reform law.

In fact, a booming economy and cuts in military spending soon achieved the law's budget-balancing goal. The federal deficit, after peaking in 1992 at $290 billion, fell steadily thereafter, and 1998 saw a surplus of $70 billion, the first in nearly three decades.

On another front, the hazards of tobacco smoking took on increasing public-health and economic implications. Since 1965, cigarettes had carried a mandated health warning, but more victims of lung cancer and other tobacco-related diseases sued the tobacco companies for misleading advertising and for concealing their product's hazards. Some states sued as well, seeking to recover the costs of providing health care to smokers. In 1998 the tobacco industry reached a landmark $368 billion settlement with forty-six states. The companies agreed to pay $50 billion in punitive damages and $318 billion to settle liability claims and to reimburse states for tobacco-related medical costs. The agreement restricted tobacco advertising, set heavy fines if teenage smoking did not decline by 60 percent in ten years, and authorized the Food and Drug Administration to regulate tobacco as a lethal and addictive substance. In return, the tobacco industry received protection from lawsuits and immunity from further penalties for past actions. Three more states reached separate settlements.

Antitobacco crusaders and public-health officials criticized the agreement for not going far enough. President Clinton expressed fear that tobacco companies would deduct the settlement costs as a business expense, reducing their tax payments and jeopardizing his budget-balancing efforts. Clinton also called for stiffer penalties on tobacco companies if teenage smoking did not decline. Warned C. Everett Koop, a former surgeon general: "[R]emember, the tobacco companies are a sleazy bunch . . . who misled us . . . and lied to us for three decades. Under this settlement . . . , the tobacco lobby will still be there, and they will never stop." With the industry allocating $30 million to influence Congress, bankroll protobacco politicians, and recruit former senators and governors as lobbyists, Koop's warning seemed well taken.

The role of money in politics, vividly on display in the tobacco wars, was highlighted by a 1997 Senate inquiry into charges of illegal Democratic fundraising in 1996, including hundreds of thousands of dollars in laundered money allegedly contributed by corporate sources in China and other Asian nations. The hearings publicized such episodes as Vice President Gore's appearance at a fundraiser at a California Buddhist temple where monks vowed to poverty had miraculously raised $140,000 for the Democratic cause. Two Chinese immigrant housewives of modest means explained to the committee how they happened to contribute $25,000 to the Democratic National Committee. Big contributors were rewarded with rounds of golf with President Clinton, nights in the White House Lincoln bedroom—and possibly special treatment on sensitive trade and export issues.

Democrats dismissed the charges as politically motivated, pointing out that both parties had scrambled for money in the 1996 campaign, which had cost a staggering $2.2 billion. Campaign-finance reform, they argued, like balanced-budget legislation, should be a nonpartisan issue. The hearings ended inconclusively, but they underscored the forbidding cost of running for office in the era of television and encouraged the cynical view that America had the best government money could buy. When the Senate in 1997 buried a campaign-finance bill proposed by Republican John McCain of Arizona and Democrat Russ Feingold of Wisconsin, the cynicism deepened. But McCain and Feingold continued the battle, and California voters in 1996 approved a ballot proposition setting the strictest campaign-finance rules in the nation.

With Clinton ineligible for reelection and increasingly viewed as a lame duck, the administration seemed adrift on the domestic front as Clinton's second term wore on. Preoccupied with his place in history, he announced one lofty but amorphous goal after another. He appointed a commission to lead a national dialogue on race. He urged measures to protect the environment, combat global warming, promote literacy, encourage volunteerism, improve children's health, get more computers in schools, and reform the Internal Revenue Service. For a while he focused on uniforms for schoolchildren. Clinton's enthusiasms proved fleeting, however, as his notoriously short attention span propelled him to one issue after another in quest of the precise center of the road at any given moment.

Despite his favorable approval ratings, Clinton's support seemed tepid rather than passionate. Continued investigations of alleged financial and sexual improprieties took their toll. (In 1996 the media reported that Clinton's third-grade teacher had given him a C for conduct.) In 1997 a Labrador retriever, Buddy, joined Socks, the Clintons' cat, in the White House, but despite many winsome photographs, the political payoff proved disappointing.

In October 1996 essayist Josef Joffe, writing in *Time* magazine, had offered an intriguing assessment: "Clinton is both right and left. He is the first postmodern President, the first to turn 'anything goes' into a political creed." Reflecting on how such a mercurial leader could enjoy such electoral success, Joffe wrote: "[Voters] who have traditionally heeded the call of class, religion, or ethnicity have become nimble-footed shoppers in the market of political goodies." The leader and the era, it appeared, were well matched.

America and a Changing World: The 1990s

The end of the Cold War opened exciting possibilities, yet U.S. foreign policy in the 1990s seemed curiously unfocused. Reversing his predecessor's priorities, Clinton initially ignored foreign affairs, leaving matters to his taciturn secretary of state, Warren Christopher, who was succeeded in 1996 by the more feisty and outspoken Madeleine Albright, the U.S. ambassador to the UN. Born in 1937 into a Czech Jewish family that soon fled to escape the Nazis, Albright was reared as a Catholic. As secretary of state, she became the highest-ranking woman ever to serve in a U.S. presidential administration.

Clinton retained the U.S. troops in Somalia that President Bush had sent to protect food intended for famine victims, but this humanitarian mission soon gave way to an effort to restore order in Somalia's anarchic capital, Mogadishu. The U.S. force was part of a UN peacekeeping army, and UN secretary general Boutros Boutros-Ghali had played a central role in directing the Americans' mission. As U.S. casualties mounted, eventually reaching forty-four, so did home-front calls for U.S. withdrawal. Political cartoonists drew Somalia in the shape of Vietnam. TV scenes of starving children gave way to images of dead GIs. Clinton withdrew the U.S. troops in 1994, and in March 1995 the last UN peacekeepers left.

The ill-starred Somalia intervention illustrated a larger problem in defining America's global role in the 1990s. During the Cold War, U.S. policy in the Third World had been shaped by strategic calculations. Somalia's ports, for example, were important to control of the Indian Ocean. The Cold War's end reduced the Third World's strategic importance, and the administration seemed unsure how far it wished to commit U.S. power and prestige in situations that did not involve vital American interests.

Later evidence suggested that the attacks on GIs in Somalia, including a 1993 gun battle that killed eighteen Americans, were conducted by radical Islamic fighters loyal to Osama bin Laden, who would later plan the deadly attacks of September 11, 2001 (see Chapter 16). Bin Laden was then living in nearby Sudan. In August 1998, simultaneous bombings of the U.S. embassies in Kenya and Tanzania, also linked to bin Laden, killed 226, including 12 Americans, and wounded thousands. Clinton ordered missile attacks on training camps and other facilities in Afghanistan financed by bin Laden, as well as on a Sudan factory thought to be used for chemical-weapons production. The administration froze all bin Laden assets in the United States, and the FBI placed him on its "Ten Most Wanted" list. Bin Laden vowed retaliation.

In Bosnia, meanwhile, ongoing fighting among warring ethnic groups, and murderous "ethnic cleansing" campaigns to expel Muslims from areas controlled by ethnic Serbs, had left one hundred thousand dead by early 1993, created 3.6 million refugees, and wrought untold suffering. Clinton ordered the U.S. Air Force to drop food and relief supplies to besieged Bosnian Muslims. In 1995 the administration brought leaders of the warring factions to a conference in Dayton, Ohio, where they signed an accord ending the war and providing for separate Serbian and Muslim-Croatian jurisdictions under the umbrella of a coalition government. President Clinton sent twenty thousand U.S. troops to Bosnia as part of a NATO force to monitor the cease-fire and implement the Dayton accords. As Clinton left office, forty-six hundred U.S. troops remained in Bosnia, and the fragile cease-fire generally held.

In 1998, Serbia invaded its southern region of Kosovo, where ethnic Albanians had declared independence. More killings of civilians resulted, and "ethnic cleansing" drove thousands of ethnic Albanians from their homes. Once again NATO intervened, with U.S. cooperation, bombing Serbian military installations in Kosovo and in Serbia itself, including the capital, Belgrade. In 1999 fifty thousand NATO troops, including a U.S. contingent, occupied Kosovo to subdue the rampaging Serbs and enable refugees to return. In 2001, Serbian president Slobodan Milosevic, whom many blamed for the atrocities in Bosnia and Kosovo, resigned under pressure and was taken to the Netherlands for trial as a war criminal before a UN tribunal.

Many observers viewed the Clinton administration's role in these crises as a high point of post–Cold War U.S. diplomacy. Critics of the later U.S. war in Iraq (see Chapter 16) would cite America's role in the Balkans as an example of cooperating with allies rather than adopting a go-it-alone approach.

Meanwhile, conditions in Russia and elsewhere in the former Soviet sphere remained volatile. In 1993, as falling productivity and hyperinflation battered the Russian economy, right-wing nationalists and former communists in the parliament tried to unseat President Boris Yeltsin. Visions of Russia in anarchy or even of a renewed Cold War haunted Washington. The crisis peaked in October, as Yeltsin's opponents occupied the parliament building. After several tense days, Yeltsin crushed the resistance. In parliamentary elections later that year, Russian voters backed a constitution proposed by Yeltsin but gave surprising support to the party of Vladimir Zhirinovsky, a rabid Russian nationalist and neofascist. Washington responded with renewed expression of support for Yeltsin. To help Russia's rocky transition to democracy and capitalism, President Clinton backed Russia's membership in the World Trade Organization and Moscow's participation in the annual gatherings of the leading industrialized nations (the so-called Group of Seven, or G7), renamed the Group of Eight in 1998.

Battling economic problems, political instability, organized crime, and periodic alcoholic binges, Yeltsin resigned in 1999 after passing power to Vladimir Putin, a former agent of the KGB, Russia's security agency. At a Moscow meeting with Putin in 2000, Clinton was restrained, a cautious and businesslike approach replacing his close rapport with Yeltsin. One area of disagreement was a U.S. plan to respond to a possible North Korean nuclear threat by deploying an antiballistic missile (ABM) system in Alaska, in violation of the 1972 ABM treaty. The two leaders did agree to dispose of sixty-eight tons of plutonium, used in making nuclear bombs.

Europe's new power realities were underscored in 1999 when Hungary, Poland, and the Czech Republic, all former Soviet satellites, joined NATO. To ease Moscow's objections, NATO gave Russia a voice in shaping NATO policy and agreed not to introduce nuclear weapons into the new members' territory. The function of the post–Cold-War NATO remained unclear. While some NATO officials envisioned a rapid-deployment force to deal with local crises as in the Balkans, the Clinton administration emphasized NATO's political role in promoting democracy and good relations among the new Eastern European members.

Airline hijackings abated in the early 1990s, but in February 1993 a massive bomb exploded in a parking garage under one of the twin 110-story towers of New York's World Trade Center. The blast killed six people, left hundreds injured, and forced thousands of office workers and tourists to grope their way down smoke-filled stairs. In 1994, four Muslim Shiite fundamentalists, followers of a militant Egyptian sheik, were convicted of the bombing. In 1997 the mastermind of the plot, Ramzi Ahmed Yousef, who had fled the country, was extradited, convicted, and given life imprisonment.

In 2000, twelve U.S. sailors died when terrorists exploded a bomb near the U.S.S. *Cole* as it refueled at the port of Aden in Yemen. Though far worse lay ahead, these attacks offered a sobering reminder that danger still stalked the world despite the easing of superpower tensions.

In the Middle East, the Cold War's end initially appeared to reduce tensions. Cut adrift by their former patron Moscow, hard-line Arab leaders like Syria's Hafez-al Assad grew more flexible. The Bush administration had nudged the Arabs toward talks with Israel while pressuring Israel to halt Jewish settlement in the occupied West Bank. Bush had added to the pressure by withholding loan guarantees urgently sought by Israel to settle 360,000 Jewish immigrants from the former Soviet Union. Israel's right wing Likud Party showed little interest in peace talks, but Yitzhak Rabin of the Labor Party, who became prime minister in 1992, proved more receptive. When Rabin curbed Jewish settlements in the West Bank and proposed limited Palestinian self-government, Bush approved the loan guarantees.

In 1993, at meetings in Oslo, Norway, Israel and the Palestinians agreed on a six-year peace plan leading to the creation of a Palestinian state, the withdrawal of

Israeli troops from the West Bank and Gaza, and continued talks on other disputed issues, such as the future status of Jerusalem. In return, PLO leader Yasir Arafat agreed to renounce terrorism and recognize Israel. As Clinton looked on, Rabin and Arafat signed the accord at the White House. Hard-liners on both sides rejected the accord, however, and the terms were not implemented.

The cycle of violence continued. In 1994, an Israeli gunman killed twenty-nine worshippers at a mosque in the predominantly Palestinian city of Hebron. In 1995, an Israeli youth fanatically opposed to the peace process assassinated Rabin. In 1996–97, with the Likud Party back in power, tensions flared as the Israelis conducted excavations near a Muslim holy site on Jerusalem's Temple Mount and built a Jewish settlement in a Palestinian district of East Jerusalem. The UN General Assembly condemned this action by a vote of 130–2, but more killings of Israeli civilians by Hamas suicide bombers strengthened the hand of Israeli hard-liners.

In 1998, under pressure from President Clinton, Likud prime minister Benjamin Netanyahu announced a partial withdrawal from Hebron, but Likud hard-liners objected, leading to more Palestinian protests and more Hamas-inspired terrorist attacks. Peace prospects briefly brightened in 1999 when an Israeli election restored the Labor Party to power and Ehud Barak became prime minister. But talks in Washington between Arafat and Barak failed, and the Palestinians in 2000 launched a new intifada (uprising against Israeli occupation of Palestinian territories). As the Clinton presidency ended and yet another Israeli election brought Likud hard-liner Ariel Sharon to power, peace prospects looked bleak. Despite more than $3 billion in U.S. military and economic aid to Israel each year; millions more to Egypt and Jordan; and some $100 million in humanitarian and development aid to the Palestinians, Washington's ability to promote peace between Israel and its neighbors seemed endlessly thwarted.

On another Middle East front, Iraqi strongman Saddam Hussein, defeated in the Persian Gulf War, remained under tough UN sanctions, including an embargo on Iraqi oil exports, no-fly zones in northern and southern Iraq, and a UN inspection team assigned to dismantle Saddam's stockpile of chemical-biological weapons (sometimes called "the poor man's atomic bomb") and to prevent further development of weapons of mass destruction. With France and Russia eager to resume trade with Iraq, Saddam hoped to exploit divisions in the alliance against him. In 1997, he tried to bar Americans from the inspection team. The UN rejected this demand, and for a time all of the inspectors left. The alliance remained firm, and in 1998 U.S. and British warplanes bombed Iraqi military targets. Saddam backed down, and the inspectors returned. In neighboring Iran, the landslide election of a somewhat more moderate Shiite leader, Mohammed Khatami, as Iran's president in 1997 suggested that Iran's hard-line position might be softening. While still denouncing the U.S. government, Khatami expressed goodwill toward the American people. The more moderate forces in Iran continued to clash with hard-line Islamic fundamentalists, but in 2000 the reformers gained a parliamentary majority. The Clinton administration responded to these encouraging developments by easing some trade sanctions imposed on Iran after the hostage crisis of 1979–81.

Asia—and especially trade with Asia—loomed large on Clinton's foreign-policy agenda. And small wonder: In 1996, the United States ran up trade deficits of $47 billion with Japan and $37 billion with China. The trade deficit with all the

Pacific Rim nations together soared to $102 billion. Given such numbers, the administration pressured Japan, China, and other Asian nations to open their doors to more U.S. products. Pursuing this goal, the administration in 1996 organized an eighteen-nation Asian-U.S. trade conference that agreed on a phased elimination of all tariffs on computers and electronic equipment by 2000.

Trade calculations threatened to override other diplomatic goals in U.S. relations with China, where the ruling Communist Party encouraged free-market experimentation while stifling democracy, imprisoning political dissidents, and harassing members of a popular religious movement called Fulan Gong. Despite these provocations, the Clinton administration in 1996 granted "most favored nation" trading status to China (that is, China received as favorable trading privileges as America accorded to any other nation). In 1997, as top U.S. officials, including Secretary of State Albright and Vice President Gore, visited Beijing, China signed trade agreements with the U.S. corporations Boeing and General Motors. Meanwhile, Chinese exiles in America and human-rights organizations—and, much more cautiously, the Clinton administration—pressed China to democratize its political system and improve its human-rights record.

Chinese president Jiang Zemin visited the United States in 1997, but except for a few symbolic gestures, Beijing ignored demands for reform. Critics in Congress complained of China's human-rights abuses, exploitation of workers, use of prison labor, and pirating of U.S. records and films. Nevertheless, in 1999 the two nations signed a trade agreement by which China pledged to lower its tariff barriers on U.S. goods. The United States, in turn, agreed to support China's admission to the World Trade Organization (WTO), which occurred in 2002.

Looming over all these negotiations were the awesome statistics of U.S.-Chinese trade, which reached $147 billion in 2002. Most of this total represented U.S. imports from China, creating a massive trade deficit with China of $103 billion. As trade issues loomed ever larger, economic considerations were clearly driving America's China policy.

After the abortive Somalia intervention, Washington had generally neglected Africa. President Clinton sought to rectify this neglect (and woo black voters) with a 1998 swing through sub-Saharan Africa, a region of poverty, indebtedness, and authoritarian rule, but with signs of political and economic progress as well. In South Africa Clinton honored President Nelson Mandela; in Uganda, Botswana, Rwanda, and Senegal he praised movements toward democracy, wildlife protection, and economic development. Again emphasizing U.S. commercial interests, Clinton preached the message of "trade not aid."

At times, the administration seemed out of step with the rest of the world, as in its resistance to a humanitarian campaign to ban land mines. Nearly 100 million land mines deployed worldwide, many left over from past conflicts, annually killed or wounded some twenty-five thousand people, often children. In 1997, citing military considerations in Korea, the United States refused to join nearly one hundred nations in signing a treaty outlawing land mines. When the American Jody Williams won the 1997 Nobel Peace Prize for her leadership in the campaign against land mines, she strongly condemned the U.S. position.

Many Americans of the 1990s, including some powerful politicians, criticized even the cautious internationalism of the Clinton administration. This neoisolationist "go it alone" attitude often focused on the United Nations. In 1996, under U.S. pressure, the UN denied a second term to UN Secretary General Boutros Boutros-Ghali, a target of right-wing attack in America, and instead chose the U.S.-educated Kofi Annan of Ghana. Despite this concession, conservatives in Congress continued to withhold over $1 billion in dues owed by the United States to the UN, charging that the world organization was overstaffed and poorly administered. Senator Jesse Helms, chair of the Senate Foreign Relations Committee, when not defending the tobacco industry, battled the United Nations and other international organizations.

With the Cold War over, no single, overarching goal gave clarity and coherence to American foreign policy. Instead, many different problems had to be addressed as they arose in different parts of the world. Television's short attention span and oversimplification of complex issues further complicated the effort to set coherent long-term foreign-policy goals.

From the days of Woodrow Wilson through the Carter and Reagan administrations, a concern for democracy, freedom, and human rights had at least episodically suffused American foreign policy. Initially, President Clinton appeared to share this outlook, pledging to oppose dictatorships "from Baghdad to Beijing." But as trade considerations increasingly dominated the administration's approach to the world, human rights received little but lip service.

In general, Clinton sought to preserve U.S. national security, advance U.S. economic interests, build up a framework of international order, and to some extent promote America's tradition of upholding democracy and human rights. When these goals conflicted, as in American relations with China, or when they stirred domestic opposition, as in policy toward the United Nations, problems arose.

Although these aspects of America's world role merited criticism, they are perhaps understandable in light of the fact that diplomats and strategists in the 1990s confronted a breathtakingly transformed world. An American of 1980 suddenly propelled forward two decades would scarcely have believed his or her eyes. The Cold War was over; America's long-time antagonist the Soviet Union was no more. With capitalism triumphant, nearly 90 percent of the world's population was linked by common trading agreements, in contrast to some 25 percent in 1980.

Further, the threat of global thermonuclear war had radically diminished. The 1991 START Treaty (see page 416), was approved by the Senate in 1991, and by Russia in 1994. As part of this approval process, Ukraine and Kazakhstan, with nuclear arsenals dating from the Soviet era, agreed to return their weapons to Russia. The START II Treaty, signed in Moscow in 1993, reduced the nuclear arsenals of the United States and Russia still further and dismantled their missile-launching systems. This treaty was ratified by the Senate in 1996 and by the Russian Duma (legislature) in 2000. Although both sides' nuclear arsenals remained awesome by 1945 standards, they were much smaller than they had been at the Cold War's height.

But nuclear dangers remained, with nuclear weapons already in the hands of China, India, Pakistan, and Israel; Russia's nuclear materials and know-how vulnerable to theft; and the potential spread of weapons to many other countries, including Iran and North Korea, or even into the hands of terrorist organizations.

Indeed, as we shall see, weapons of mass destruction, including not only nuclear bombs but also chemical and biological weapons, would soon become a source of grave concern.

Adjusted for inflation, the U.S. military budget fell by some 23 percent between 1985 and 2000. As late as 1988, some 6 percent of America's gross domestic product went for military purposes; a decade later, the figure had fallen to just over 3 percent. This process stirred controversy. Some argued that the cuts should go much further, while others hawkishly insisted that the reductions were dangerously weakening the nation.

Amid the complex calculus of developments, the underlying reality stood out boldly, however: Although the world remained a dangerous place as the 1990s ended, and although the United States had fumbled some of the challenges of the post–Cold War era, the world seemed less threatening, and America a far less militarized society, than had been true a decade earlier. Within months of the end of Clinton's term, however, terrifying events would once again drive up military spending and shatter any sense of complacency about the trend of world events.

A Booming Economy, Soaring Stocks, and Growing Economic Disparities

Central to many developments of the later 1990s, from welfare reform and budget surpluses to Clinton's high approval ratings, was the prosperity of these years. The benefits of this prosperity were not evenly distributed, and warning signals accompanied the good times. But the prosperity was real, and particularly impressive as the economies of Germany and Japan, as well as of "Asian tigers" such as Thailand, Indonesia, and South Korea, the pacesetters of the seventies and eighties, fell into recession.

The beginning of the decade had given little hint of good times ahead. After a dismal sales year in 1991, GM announced twenty-one plant closings and a reduction in its labor force by seventy thousand. Reports that top management at the Big Three automakers had received fat raises and stock benefits as their firms lost billions and fired workers stirred bitter resentment. IBM lost nearly $5 billion in 1992 and, despite a proud record of never laying off employees, revealed plans to shed twenty-five thousand workers. IBM stock plunged to half its value.

But some economic indicators had already improved in 1991, and by 1993 the turnaround was clear. The resulting boom roared on into 2001. The gross domestic product, which measures aggregate economic growth, rose from $5.5 trillion in 1990 to $7.5 trillion in 2000. Corporate profits, adjusted for inflation, surged from $313 billion to nearly $1 trillion in the decade. Corporate mergers and acquisitions hit record levels. The years 1996–2000 saw thirty-four corporate mergers involving acquisition costs of $20 billion or more—in many cases far more. In 1997 the telecommunications giant WorldCom swallowed up its rival MCI for $41 billion. The pharmaceutical company Pfizer acquired Warner-Lambert for $89 billion in 2000.

The South enjoyed the most rapid growth, but nearly all regions basked in the glow of prosperity. The Midwest, dismissed in the 1980s as "the Rust Belt," bounced back as industries downsized and retooled, and as exports surged. Thanks to microprocessing and other new technologies, marveled the *Economist,* American industry had "reinvented manufacturing." California, earlier battered by defense-industry cuts, created four hundred thousand new jobs in 1996–97 alone. Los Angeles's economy, once heavily dependent on aerospace industries, became more diversified.

Americans rushed into the stock market, often by investing in mutual funds, creating one of the longest bull markets in U.S. history. The Dow Jones Industrial Average, a key stock-market indicator, which stood at 2,679 in 1990, hit 11,497 at the end of 1999. In the feverish year 1998 alone, the Dow rose by 25 percent. WorldCom stock soared so high that by 2000 the company's paper value stood at $180 billion. Enron, a Texas-based energy company, also proved extremely popular with investors for its phenomenal profit record. Corporations lavishly rewarded their chief executive officers (CEOs) with multimillion salaries and stock options, permitting them to profit handsomely as speculators pushed stock prices higher. In 1999, the one hundred top CEOs earned an average of $37.5 million, more than a thousand times the pay of the average worker. Jack Welch, the CEO of General Electric, was paid $123 million in 2000, mostly in stocks and stock options.

As the decade wore on, a giddy euphoria gripped investors and the stock market displayed all the signs of a classic speculative bubble, reminiscent of the mood before the crash of 1929. "Is this a wonder economy or what?" crowed *Business Week* in mid-1997; "On Top of the World," gushed *Newsweek.* The market's recent performance, agreed the *New York Times* in 1998, was "nothing short of amazing."

Leading the boom were computer software and information-processing companies, many based in California's Silicon Valley, south of San Francisco. Investors snapped up the initial stock offerings of many small start-up companies, making instant millionaires of young people still in their twenties. In 1997, the stock price of Yahoo, an Internet search engine company that had yet to show a profit, increased by 500 percent. The stock of Amazon.com, an Internet bookseller, similarly profitless, soared as well.

Alan Greenspan, head of the Federal Reserve Board, warned investors of "irrational exuberance" and even "infectious greed." Economists cautioned that many stocks were selling for vastly more than their earnings record justified. But the boom surged on. As in the S&L bubble of the 1980s, many new investors poured their life savings into the market. Retirement funds rose dramatically as the stock market spiraled upward.

Corporate executives; white-collar professionals such as lawyers, accountants, and stock brokers; workers in the surging information-technology sector; and citizens with inherited wealth or accumulated savings to invest did very well in the boom years of the 1990s, as the paper value of their holdings soared. Also on the plus side, the inflation rate remained low in the 1990s. Consumer prices rose by only 1.6 percent in 1998 and 2.8 percent in 2001.

The economy added 18 million jobs as businesses hired more workers to meet production demands and fill positions in the expanding service sector. United Parcel Service and Federal Express, two private companies competing with the U.S. Postal Service for parcel delivery, grew rapidly in these years, as did Wal-Mart, the giant retailer. Silicon Valley data processing companies such as Hewlett Packard and Intel took on thousands of new employees as well (see Table 15.1.) Seattle's Microsoft Corporation, with 128 employees in 1981, had a workforce of 50,500 by 2002.

The welfare rolls shrank by almost 10 percent in 1996, even before the welfare-reform law took effect, as marginal workers found jobs. In 2000 the jobless rate stood at 4 percent, the lowest since the early 1970s. Economists and journalists became almost euphoric over such statistics. Commenting on the "stunning job growth," President Clinton's chief economic adviser exulted in 1997: "We're in the best of all possible worlds." The 1990s, said the *New Republic* that year, "will be seen in future decades as a golden age in American history."

Some observers spotted warnings signals. The job gains were unevenly distributed, as many manufacturing corporations, such as General Motors, Kodak, Xerox, DuPont, and Goodyear laid off workers. While Wal-Mart boomed, the workforce at Sears Roebuck, the marketing giant of an earlier era, shrank by one-quarter from 1980 to 2002.

TABLE 15.1

Percentage Increase or Decrease of Persons on Payroll of Selected U.S. Corporations, 1980–2002

Reynolds Tobacco	–90.2%
Exxon + Mobil*	–72.2
General Motors	–53.1
Chevron + Texaco*	–50.5
Kodak	–46.0
Xerox	–44.3
Bristol Myers + Squibb*	–43.9
CSX Railroad	–43.0
DuPont	–41.9
Goodyear	–36.3
Campbell Soups	–34.2
Sears	–25.9
Boeing	+55.3%
Procter & Gamble	+67.2
Pfizer	+137.9
American Airlines	+144.2
Hewlett-Packard	+147.4%
United Parcel Service	+224.3%
McDonald's	+253.0%
Intel	+395.0%
Federal Express	+2,620.6%
Wal-Mart	+4,714.8%
Microsoft	+39,453%

*Decrease in employment after mergers.

Source: *New York Review of Books,* February 12, 2000; Microsoft Annual Report, 2002.

Economists worried about the low rate of savings and the continued high levels of consumer debt, which reached $1.5 trillion by 2000. Despite the budget surplus, they warned of renewed deficits as the baby boomers retired, placing heavy demands on Medicare and an underfunded social-security system. Others noted that while the total volume of goods and services was growing, the annual increase in the productivity *rate* (that is, output per worker) remained stuck at around 1 percent, in contrast to the 1945–73 era of economic growth, when the productivity rate had risen dramatically. More optimistic analysts argued, however, that older methods of calculating productivity underestimated the new forms of economic growth, in which intangibles such as electronic communications and information processing loomed large. They spoke glowingly of a "new economy" to which the old rules did not apply.

Still other observers cautioned that the benefits of prosperity were very unevenly distributed. Employment rates for all groups improved in the 1990s, but while the jobless rate among white workers dropped to 3.8 percent by 1997, for Hispanic workers it stood at around 7 percent, and for African Americans, nearly 10 percent. Among black teenagers, it approached 30 percent. Lack of education and of the skills demanded by a high-tech economy were severe liabilities in the job market. The poverty rate fell, but in 2000 it was still 11.5 percent. In many inner-city neighborhoods, it rose far higher.

In contrast to unprecedented corporate profits and soaring stock prices, inflation-adjusted wages remained flat for most of the 1990s (although by 1997, as businesses competed for a dwindling pool of workers, real wages did rise somewhat). Indeed, from 1991 through 1997, the average income of the lower 60 percent of American families, adjusted for inflation, actually declined slightly. This wage stagnation had various causes, including the flood of imports from Asian nations with lower wage scales, workers' job anxieties about "downsizing" and high-tech automation, and the continued decline of labor unions. By 2000 only 13.5 percent of U.S. workers were unionized, compared to 35.5 percent in 1945. Lacking the clout of collective bargaining, most workers had to accept the wages they were offered.

Almost 20 percent of the U.S. labor force held part-time or temporary positions in the 1990s, at lower wages and often without health coverage or other benefits. Although some part-timers preferred this option, the pattern was troubling. Significantly, the nation's largest employer in the decade was Manpower, Inc., a clearinghouse for temporary workers. Many big companies had a two-tier labor force, with trained, well-paid workers in one category and less skilled, lower-paid part-timers in another. The 1990s also saw a surge in the number of part-time college teachers who earned less, enjoyed fewer benefits, and lacked job security.

An extreme example of the part-time phenomenon was the sprawling United Parcel Service with its familiar brown trucks. Of UPS's 185,000 employees in 1997, 60 percent were part-timers earning less than half the hourly rate of the company's full-time employees. Facing a strike that year, UPS agreed to shift more part-timers to full-time status.

The trend toward corporate giantism and mass marketing was typified by the Wal-Mart Corporation, launched in 1962 by Sam Walton. Wal-Mart grew rapidly in the 1990s and beyond, with some 3,500 stores, 1.2 million "associates" (employees), and sales of $244 billion in the United States in 2003, plus vast operations abroad. Wal-Mart fought unionization and paid low wages with few benefits, and its relentless price cutting forced small businesses across America to close their doors. Wal-Mart claimed that its low prices benefited low-income consumers, including recent immigrants, and that its stores proved an economic boon rather than blight for many communities. However, in 2003, federal agents raided sixty Wal-Mart stores across the country and arrested janitorial workers as illegal aliens. The government charged that Wal-Mart had broken the law by contracting its janitorial services to companies that hired illegal immigrants, who earned even less and enjoyed fewer benefits than regular Wal-Mart employees.

The boom years of the 1980s and 1990s widened the gap between the prosperous and the poor, and between the upper class and the middle class, leaving society more polarized economically than at any time since the late nineteenth century. Many Americans prospered thanks to their social connections, stock holdings, or the education and skills they possessed. Outside this charmed circle, however, were not only the poor but also the millions lacking advanced job skills, holding only a high-school diploma at best, and earning low wages in marginal, part time, or temporary jobs. In 1997, after six years of sustained growth, the top 20 percent (quintile) of U.S. families enjoyed an average income of $117,489—almost thirteen times the average income of the bottom quintile ($9,254). In New York State, the income of the top quintile was nearly *twenty times* that of the lowest. As with the employment data, these numbers also reflected racial and ethnic differentials: The average income of Hispanic and African American families was only 58 percent that of white, non-Hispanic families. At the very top, the total income of America's thirteen thousand richest families in 1998 fell only slightly below that of the 20 *million* poorest families.

While an auto dealer in Wichita, Kansas, reported selling twenty-two $35,000 BMW luxury cars in six weeks in 1997, millions struggled at the economic margins. Robert Reich, former secretary of labor in the Clinton administration, summed up the consequences of this situation vividly: "For all its riches, the United States now has a greater percentage of its citizens in prisons or on the streets, and more neglected children, than any other advanced nation." Princeton economist Paul Krugman offered an even more devastating analysis in 2002:

> The concentration of income at the top is a key reason that the United States, for all its economic achievements, has more poverty and lower life expectancy than any other major advanced nation. Above all, the growing concentration of wealth has reshaped our political system: it is at the root both of a general shift to the right and of an extreme polarization of our politics.

President Clinton, congressional Republicans, and corporate America all took credit for the boom while downplaying its uneven effects. Commenting on the pattern of wage stagnation, a *New York Times* business writer noted in 1997: "Corporate success in global competition has become an overriding goal, even at the price of greater wage inequality." Those who called attention to the vast disparities of income were accused of "fomenting class warfare." As for the victims of that disparity, resignation rather than anger seemed to prevail. A 1997 study found a high correlation between wealth and voting: The well-to-do protected their interests at the polls; the disadvantaged, apparently having lost faith in politics, took little interest in elections. Representative John Conyers of Michigan said in 1996: "I

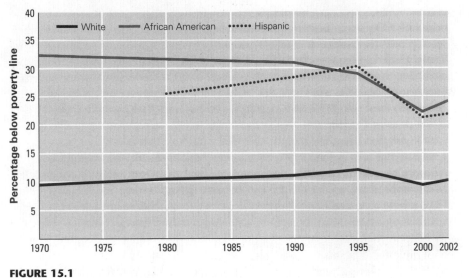

FIGURE 15.1

Poverty, Race, and Ethnicity in America, 1970–2002

SOURCE: Bureau of the Census, in *World Almanac, 2004.*

have never heard . . . more complaints about the government's insensitivity to what people need in this country . . . , [but] instead of . . . angry protests at the polls, it turns into a whimper."

In short, although the prosperity of the 1990s was real and important, it came hedged with reservations. This helps explain why the national mood remained edgy and uncertain, not expansive as in the 1950s. With the recessions, hyperinflation, downsizing, and other economic problems of the 1973–91 years fresh in memory, and with the income of most workers flat or rising only slightly, Americans welcomed the prosperity but did not assume—as many had in the more innocent fifties—that it would last forever. The average workweek lengthened, as employees worked longer, and took overtime, to salt away as much as they could against a possible downturn.

Scandal and Impeachment: The Final Years of Clinton's Presidency

By 1997, with the economy booming; the struggles over health care, NAFTA, and welfare-reform behind him; and a record of at least modest foreign-policy achievements, Bill Clinton seemed on track for a successful second term. In fact, however, he was soon mired in a scandal that would threaten his presidency and undermine his historical standing.

Rumors of extramarital affairs had long dogged Clinton. In an extraordinary TV appearance with his wife Hillary during the 1992 campaign, he had obliquely acknowledged past philandering but had insisted that his marriage was now strong and secure. But Paula Jones, a former Arkansas state employee, encouraged by conservative groups, filed a sexual-harassment lawsuit. The Supreme Court helped Jones's cause by permitting lawsuits against incumbent presidents to go forward. (Clinton eventually settled out of court, paying Jones $850,000.)

In January 1998, Jones's lawyers, trying to establish a pattern of behavior, asked Clinton under oath about rumors of an affair with a White House intern, Monica Lewinsky. Clinton denied having had sexual relations with Lewinsky, and she backed up his story in a sworn affidavit. Hillary Clinton spoke darkly of "a vast right-wing conspiracy" to discredit her husband.

Their denials unraveled, however, when Linda Tripp, a former White House employee who had befriended Lewinsky, secretly recorded telephone conversations in which Lewinsky discussed in graphic detail her sexual encounters with Clinton in the Oval Office from 1995, when she was twenty-one, through early 1997. Early in 1998, Tripp passed the recordings to Kenneth Starr, a lawyer who had been appointed as an independent counsel by a three-judge panel to investigate the so-called Whitewater affair, involving allegations of illegalities by the Clintons in an Arkansas real estate development. Starr now obtained permission to investigate whether Clinton had committed perjury in denying the Lewinsky affair and had persuaded Lewinsky to lie as well. Starr secured further incriminating evidence by arranging for Tripp to meet Lewinsky while wearing a hidden recording device. Confronted with this evidence and threatened with long imprisonment, Lewinsky appeared before Starr's grand jury in August, with a grant of immunity, to acknowledge the affair. She even provided a blue dress containing physical evidence of a sexual encounter with the president.

Summoned by the grand jury, Clinton now admitted "conduct that was wrong" with Lewinsky, but again denied a "sexual relationship." In a brief TV address to the American people, he acknowledged wrongdoing but insisted that his testimony had been legally accurate. (Clinton's definition of "sexual relationship" was considerably narrower than most people's.) Clinton further accused Starr, a Republican, of pursuing a vendetta against him.

Matters now moved forward rapidly. In September 1998, Starr presented to the House Judiciary Committee evidence of Clinton's perjury, together with much lurid detail about his furtive Oval Office encounters with Lewinsky. Starr also documented Clinton's efforts to persuade Lewinsky to conceal the affair. As the media feasted on the scandal, the Judiciary Committee, controlled by Republicans, narrowly voted four articles of impeachment against Clinton. They did so under the constitutional provision that impeachment of federal officials must begin in the House, with the Senate conducting the trial. In December, the full House, by close margins, approved and forwarded to the Senate two articles of impeachment accusing Clinton of perjury and obstruction of justice.

The outcome was hardly in doubt, since the Constitution requires a two-thirds vote of the Senate to remove a president, and the Republicans, with fifty-five seats, fell far short of that total. But the process gave Republicans ample opportunity to prolong the scandal and further embarrass Clinton, and they exploited it to the full. At the trial, conducted early in 1999 with Chief Justice Rehnquist presiding, Republican members of the House Judiciary Committee presented the case for impeachment, while White House lawyers denied that the charges met the constitutional impeachment standard of "high crimes and misdemeanors." In early February, by a predictably partisan vote, the Senate rejected the charges, and the impeachment failed. (The only other presidential impeachment, of Andrew Johnson in 1868, similarly failed.)

Said Clinton: "I want to say again to the American people how profoundly sorry I am for what I said and did to trigger these events." Said Lewinsky, when asked what she would say about the affair to any future children: "Mommy made a big mistake." Her TV interview with Barbara Walters attracted 70 million viewers.

Significantly, Clinton's approval ratings remained high throughout the entire process. Indeed, the Republicans lost House seats in the 1998 midterm elections, as the impeachment drama unfolded. Most Americans, it appeared, while disapproving of Clinton's personal behavior, drew a distinction between that and his actions as president. The scandal clearly hurt Clinton, however, and what might have been a dignified, even triumphant, exodus from the White House turned into a muted and embarrassed one. Still under a perjury indictment by an Arkansas court, he admitted the charges, paid a $25,000 fine, and had his lawyer's license revoked for five years. Even in his final days in office, Clinton reinforced his "Slick Willy" reputation by pardoning a major Democratic Party contributor who had fled to Switzerland to escape prosecution for fraudulent business practices. It was a sorry end to a presidency that had begun with high hopes.

A Diverse People: Contemporary Social Trends

As the twentieth century gave way to the twenty-first, and as the Democrat Bill Clinton gave way to the Republican George W. Bush in the White House, America experienced demographic and social trends that would mold U.S. life far into the future. The nation's population of some 288 million in 2002 comprised a mosaic of immigrants and native-born citizens, Native Americans, blacks, Asians, whites, and Hispanics. The population also included many persons of mixed race who resisted checking one box or another on the census forms. Each of these groups, in turn, included many subgroups differentiated by geography, religion, cultural roots, and economic status.

Immigration in these years approached or exceeded a million a year, the highest levels since the early twentieth century. The 2002 total of 1,063,732, supplemented by thousands of illegal immigrants who entered from Mexico, was typical. This influx produced a population that by 2002 was nearly 12 percent foreign born, up from 4.7 percent in 1970; in California, the foreign-born figure was 27 percent. In the 1950s, the media had portrayed America as blandly homogenous. Unrealistic even then, the stereotype collapsed a generation later as diversity, not uniformity, became the rule. By 2050, the Census Bureau predicted, non-Hispanic whites would make up barely half of the population.

For Native Americans, these years brought quickened ethnic pride. Nearly 2.5 million persons identified themselves as American Indians in the 2000 census, three times the 1970 total. These figures reflected not only natural increase but also the growing numbers of Indians eager to affirm their ethnic roots. Under a 1961 law permitting tribes to buy or develop land for commercial purposes, Indians pursued business ventures ranging from vacation resorts to gambling casinos. The lat-

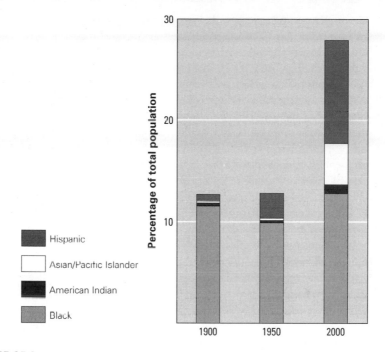

FIGURE 15.2

Minority Groups as a Percentage of Total U.S. Population, 1900–2000

SOURCE: Theodore Caplow, Louis Hicks, and Ben J. Wattenberg, *The First Measured Century: An Illustrated Guide to Trends in America, 1900–2000* (Washington, D.C.: The American Enterprise Institute, 2001), p. 19.

ter generated vast revenue for some tribes, but they also led to intratribal disputes and conflicts with opponents of commercialized gambling. Yet Indians remained among the nation's poorest citizens. Both on the reservations and in the cities, joblessness, alcoholism, and poor health care took their toll.

Some Native American communities fought back. A number of tribes, including the Oneida of Wisconsin, used casino earnings to fund alcohol-treatment centers. The treatment center at the Pine Ridge Indian Reservation in South Dakota used traditional methods such as the sweat lodge to help young people overcome alcoholism. Said Tim Giago, the editor of the newspaper *Indian Country Today,* in 1997: "Our people are becoming more aware of our traditional ways and culture. And they're realizing that drunkenness was not part of it."

The Asian American population continued to grow, fed by immigration from the Philippines, Korea, and Vietnam and by well-established Chinese American and Japanese American communities. In 2000 Los Angeles County was more than 12 percent Asian, up from 5 percent in 1980. With their strong family culture and emphasis on academics, Asian Americans showed high rates of college attendance and upward mobility. As in most other immigrant groups, however, generational tensions arose as young people wavered between traditional ways and the lure of the mass culture.

The Multiculturalism Debate

"*Epluribus unum,*" the nation's motto proclaims: "Out of many, one." Yet in the post-1960 decades, the ideal of a common national culture proved elusive. As U.S. society grew more fragmented, with an array of groups clamoring for cultural as well as political equality, debate raged over how literature and history should be taught.

The so-called multiculturalism controversy took many forms. Advocates for women, African Americans, Native Americans, Hispanics, Asian Americans, gays and lesbians, and other groups protested the way in which traditional pedagogy had ignored or marginalized them. Even evangelical Christians, once the dominant cultural group, complained that the academic world ignored and devalued their beliefs. In English departments, academics argued over whether to reconstruct a canon dominated by works of "dead white European males." Instructors devised new courses that privileged works by women, persons of color, and Third World writers. History textbook writers and publishers scrambled to give more space to nonelites.

Some observers, however, saw in these efforts an erosion of any sense of common American identity: The *pluribus* seemed triumphant, the *unum* in retreat. In *Cultural Literacy: What Every American Needs to Know* (1987), E. D. Hirsch, Jr., cautioned that American culture was becoming a "tower of Babel." Yet many judged Hirsch's own effort to define a common culture traditionalistic and exclusionary. The University of Chicago classicist Alan Bloom, an unabashed elitist, defined culture more narrowly still. In his best-selling polemic, *The Closing of the American Mind* (1987), Bloom lamented the erosion of standards and called for an intellectual elite that would disdain the ephemera of politics, social conflict, and mass culture to ponder the great themes of Western civilization. Historian Arthur Schlesinger, Jr., in *The Disuniting of America* (1991), urged a renewed effort to define a common core of American citizenship and culture. Finally, historians warned that the impulse to enhance the self-esteem of minority groups might encourage shoddy history.

The dispute spilled over into politics. Cities such as Miami with large Hispanic populations debated resolutions making English the official language. President Reagan's choice to head the National Endowment for the Humanities, Lynn Cheney (spouse of Defense Secretary Dick Cheney), battled multiculturalism and lauded the classical tradition. Pat Buchanan, the conservative columnist who briefly ran for president in 1992, rallied the forces of the Right at the Republican convention, stridently summoning cheering supporters to take back "our cities, our culture, and our country." These critics often idealized the past's cultural unity and intellectual harmony in contrast to today's fragmentation and raucous conflicts. In fact, a close look at history from ancient Greece onward shows not harmony but conflict and a disputatiousness remarkably similar to our own.

It is not surprising that the "multicultural" demand eventually became so vehement. Up to the very recent era, courses in history and literature did focus on the exploits and writings of white male elites of European origin. In U.S. history courses, Indians appeared solely as a quickly vanquished foe, blacks mainly as victims of slavery, and Hispanics and Asian Americans hardly at all. Absent, too, was working-class culture, of whatever ethnic character. A few women merited notice, but the historical experience of women as a whole—half the population—was ignored. As these groups asserted themselves politically, the corresponding demand to rectify decades of cultural distortion soon followed.

Some proponents of "multiculturalism" and "politically correct" speech dismissed their critics as expressing the bigotry and xenophobia that have always existed in America. Indeed, as early as the 1740s, Benjamin Franklin warned of the German immigrants who were "polluting" Pennsylvania's Anglo society with their alien ways and language. Throughout American history, prejudice against newcomers and minorities has led to periodic demands for exclusion and control.

Yet the contemporary debate involves more than just covert prejudice and has unfolded in a unique cultural setting. In the past, minorities were either powerless or had far less power than the dominant elite. In modern America, advocates for the underdog occupy powerful positions in government, the media, and academia. When demands for the redress of minority grievances in the cultural realm come from such quarters, they can be accompanied by credible threats to impose sanctions that will enforce acceptable standards of conduct and expression. This potential for abuse raises legitimate concerns about "Big Brother" and the repression of individual freedom. It also can encourage a culture of victimization, in which individuals and groups demand legal redress for insensitive behavior or speech that, however deplorable, may be the price of a free society. Conflicts once fought out in private now land in the courts. Furthermore, the obsession with "political correctness" can stifle discussion in the classroom and elsewhere, as people become so fearful of giving offense that they choose to remain silent rather than express potentially unpopular views. Thus, the debate over multiculturalism and "political correctness" can inhibit the vigorous give-and-take on which democracy thrives.

Some observers have tried to move the controversy off dead center. In *Beyond the Culture Wars* (1992), Gerald Graff of the University of Chicago viewed the debate as evidence not of disintegration but of cultural renewal. Passivity over issues of cultural meaning is far more to be feared than discord, Graff contended. He urged teachers to incorporate the cultural debate into the curriculum as a way of bringing texts alive for students. Despite occasional excesses, the multiculturalism debate has in fact pumped new energy into education. Textbooks and course syllabi now more closely reflect the ethnic and gender realities of the larger society. Students vigorously debate issues of gender, race, and social class in canonical works that they once accepted without question.

One champion of multiculturalism, the Japanese American historian Ronald Takaki, insists that only by recognizing the reality of cultural diversity can the "E pluribus unum" dream ever be realized. Hopes for a genuinely inclusive culture, Takaki wrote in *A Different Mirror* (1993), lie in "'unlearning' much of what we have been told about America's past and substituting a more inclusive and accurate history of all the peoples of America." Takaki's point is well taken, but the risks remain: Intolerance in pursuit of multiculturalist or "politically correct" goals can lead to new forms of prejudice, pressures toward a sterile conformity, and the prospect of a backlash damaging to all concerned. Clearly this complex debate is far from resolved as a new century begins.

The African American population remained divided along economic lines. A growing professional and upper middle class enjoyed good incomes, stable families, and advanced degrees. In 2000, nearly one-third of blacks aged eighteen to twenty-four were enrolled in college. From 1967 to 2001, the proportion of black households earning more than $50,000 (in constant 1990 dollars) more than tripled, rising from 9 percent to 28 percent. Communities like Cranwood in Cleveland, Chicago's Auburn Park, and Baldwin Hills in Los Angeles featured the attractive homes of this black professional and middle class. By 2000, there were more than eight hundred thousand black-owned businesses, from small local enterprises to large insurance, publishing, and advertising firms and car dealerships. In 2001, fifty-seven black-owned businesses had revenues in excess of $100 million.

Black scholars and writers participated in the nation's intellectual and cultural life. Thousands of African Americans, including the television talk-show celebrity Oprah Winfrey, were prominent in the music, sports, and entertainment fields. Growing numbers of blacks held elective and appointive office at all levels of government. Prominent African Americans in the George W. Bush administration (see Chapter 16) included Secretary of State Colin Powell and National Security Adviser Condoleezza Rice. Below this elite, millions of middle-class and blue-collar African Americans earned steady wages, owned their own homes, were pillars of black churches, and enjoyed stable family lives.

At the lower end of the scale were the impoverished inner-city blacks, perhaps a quarter of all African Americans in 2000. From this battered group, whose education often ended before high-school graduation, came the blacks who accounted for 55 percent of all murder arrests and 69 percent of all arrests for robbery. Although strong families, thriving churches, and vigorous social institutions existed in the inner city, the social pathologies were powerful. Among black youngsters aged fifteen to nineteen, the death rate by homicide stood at nearly ten times the rate for white youths in the early 1990s. In a trend for which analysts offered various explanations, pregnancy rates among black teenagers spiked upward beginning in the 1970s. In 2001, 68 percent of all black births were to single women, in contrast to 18 percent in 1950. Often barely beyond childhood themselves, these new mothers frequently had no means of support. As a result, more than two-thirds of all black children were on welfare by their eighteenth birthday.

Lacking the training for skilled jobs that in any event were often located in distant suburbs, inner-city youths faced life on the streets or marginal service-sector jobs in car washes or fast-food establishments. Inner-city crime, welfare dependency, and teenage pregnancy were inseparable from the problem of joblessness. For the unskilled, one economist observed, the America of the early 1990s had become "a harder, rougher place."

Illegal drug use reached epidemic proportions in the 1990s in poor inner-city neighborhoods. In many urban areas, drug gangs battled over the lucrative cocaine and heroin trade. In many communities, children lured by drug dealers' gold jewelry and flashy cars acted as lookouts or made deliveries. The drug of choice in the inner cities was crack, an extrapotent form of cocaine. Public-health officials estimated that from thirty thousand to fifty thousand "crack babies" came into the world annually, addicted at birth.

To be sure, drug use, including cocaine, was found at all socioeconomic levels. In the late 1990s, the amphetamine-like pill Ecstacy was widely used by young people at parties, rock concerts, and "raves" (mass dancing events), sometimes with fatal consequences. In 2003 the conservative radio commentator Rush Limbaugh admitted an addiction to prescription pain pills. But the drug problem was especially severe in the inner cities. Of those arrested for drug violations (nearly 1.6 million in 2001), some 35 percent were African American. Of the 880,000 blacks in prison in 2002 (constituting some 40 percent of the 2 million prison population), many were young males convicted on drug charges.

Caught in the coils of joblessness, welfare dependence, and destructive behavior, millions in the inner cities seemed in the 1990s at risk of becoming a permanent undercaste. Books such as Alex Kotlowitz's *There Are No Children Here* (1991) and movies like John Singleton's *Boyz 'N the Hood* (1991), with its portrayal of young Los Angeles blacks devastated by drugs and gang warfare, evoked the human tragedies behind the aggregate statistics.

Inner-city tensions exploded into violence in Los Angeles in 1992. On March 3, 1991, L.A. police had arrested Rodney King, a young black man, after a high-speed chase. Though unarmed, the intoxicated King resisted arrest. After zapping him with a 50,000-volt stun gun, the police forced King to the ground, and four officers took turns kicking and clubbing him, causing serious injury, as eleven other policemen stood by. Unknown to the police, a nearby resident had captured the mayhem on videotape. Four policemen faced trial, but despite the videotape, a jury acquitted them in April 1992. As word of the verdict spread, violence erupted in South Central Los Angeles, a black and Hispanic district. For thirty-six hours, gangs roamed the streets, burning and looting. Black youths viciously beat a white truck driver. Rioters especially targeted the shops of Korean merchants. In scenes unhappily reminiscent of the 1960s, entire blocks went up in flames. "Can't we all get along?" pleaded Rodney King in a televised call for calm. When an uneasy quiet returned, Los Angeles counted 44 dead, nearly 1,800 injured, 6,345 arrests, and $500 million in property damage. The "Rodney King riots" underscored the pressure-cooker environment of many inner-city neighborhoods.

Even for the blacks most at risk, however, the 1990s and beyond saw signs of improved conditions. The African American poverty rate fell from 31 percent in 1986 to 24 percent in 2002. In contrast to the general population, median black family income rose significantly in the later 1990s, with the strongest gains among the poor. The inner-city murder rate—often linked to drugs and gang warfare—also declined, contributing to a drop of some 25 percent in the overall violent-crime rate from 1992 to 2001, a decline experts attributed to better job prospects, tougher law enforcement, and stricter sentencing laws. By the late 1990s the high-school graduation rate for young African Americans was about the same as for whites. The Office of National Drug Control Policy reported a decline in occasional and hard-core cocaine users from nearly 10 million in 1988 to 5.6 million in 2000. Problems remained, but statistical indicators were encouraging. As a Washington think tank that studies trends in the black community observed in 1996: " [B]y virtually every measure of well-being, African Americans have been on a significant uptrend during the '90s." In the "Million Man March" of 1995, thousands of black males gathered in Washington, D.C., to affirm their family responsibilities. Though sponsored by the small Nation of Islam sect, the event's larger symbolism was encouraging.

The 1996 welfare-reform law significantly impacted the African American community, since some 40 percent of the women and children receiving AFDC benefits were black. From a peak of 14 million in 1994, the welfare rolls fell to 5.5 million by 2001. While some ex-welfare recipients sank deeper into poverty, early data suggested that at least half went to work, many with the help of state-funded job-training, placement, and childcare programs. In New Jersey, out-of-wedlock births fell sharply after a 1992 law barred increased welfare payments to women who bore more children. Welfare-reform advocates hoped to see a similar trend nationwide as the ideology of "work not welfare" took hold.

In 2003, as the nation's Hispanic population reached 39 million—nearly four times the 1970 total—the Census Bureau reported that Hispanics had supplanted blacks as the nation's largest minority. By 2050, demographers predicted, Hispanics would make up one-quarter of the U.S. population. In 2000, Hispanics constituted 40.5 percent of the population of southern California, making them the region's largest ethnic group, ahead of non-Hispanic whites (39 percent).

The Hispanic population included more than 26 million Mexican Americans centered in California and the Southwest; Cuban Americans living in Florida; and

Hispanic American Family, 2001. The nation's Hispanic population grew from 22.3 million in 1990 to 35.3 million in 2000. (© *Rob Lewine/CORBIS*)

immigrants from the Caribbean and Central America residing along the East Coast. Puerto Ricans, who are U.S. citizens, arrived in great numbers as well. Like earlier immigrants, Hispanics came to America seeking a better life, especially as falling oil prices rocked the Mexican economy.

The 1986 immigration law tightened border controls and imposed tougher restrictions on hiring undocumented aliens. Nevertheless, the Census Bureau estimated 7 million illegal aliens, most of them Mexicans, in the United States in 2000. (Others placed the figure as high as 13 million.) Some found this alarming. "America has lost control of its borders," warned the head of an organization favoring tighter immigration laws in 2003.

Illegal or not, these Hispanic immigrants played a vital role in the economy as agricultural laborers and urban workers in the economy's custodial, manual-labor, garment-making, manufacturing, and service sectors. With few health benefits or other protections, many worked long hours for low wages. Hispanic families, churches, and cultural institutions provided support, but life was often harsh, scourged by drugs, crime, school dropouts, and teenage pregnancy. Although Hispanics benefited from the economic boom of the 1990s, 22 percent still lived below the poverty line in 2002, compared to 8 percent of non-Hispanic whites.

Ironically, economic deprivation often pitted minority groups against each other. Inner-city blacks resented Asian American shopkeepers. Friction arose as blacks and Hispanics competed for the same low-wage jobs. Hispanics who moved from inner cities to outlying suburbs often faced discrimination. When they moved into the working-class Chicago suburb of Addison, the white ethnics from earlier waves of immigration who ran the town reacted with hostility, bulldozing housing in Hispanic neighborhoods for alleged building code violations. When the displaced Hispanics filed a class-action lawsuit in 1997 supported by the U.S. Justice Department, the town backed down, pledging to construct affordable housing to replace the demolished residences, to pay moving costs and compensation to the families, and to construct parks and a community center in Hispanic neighborhoods.

But the Hispanic American story was more than poverty and problems. The Hispanic middle class grew by 25 percent in the 1990s. By 2003, some 12 percent of Hispanic full-time workers earned $50,000 or more per year. The more than 1.2 million Hispanic-owned businesses in 2000 ranged from one-person shops selling herbs and incense to giant enterprises such as Albuquerque's Garcia Automotive Group, New Mexico's second-largest dealership, and Miami's Brightstar Corporation, a provider of wireless communications products and services, with 2002 revenues of $849 million.

America's rich diversity at the turn of the century found religious expression as well, with some 800,000 Buddhists, 900,000 Hindus, more than 5 million Muslims, and thousands of adherents of other non-Western religions contributing to the tapestry of faith. The Muslim community included not only immigrants from Muslim countries but also some 2 million African Americans, most of whom followed the mainstream Sunni Islamic faith. For some, this was a return to an ancestral faith, since at least 20 percent of the Africans transported to America as slaves were Muslims. By 2020, demographers predicted, Islam will replace Judaism as the nation's largest religion after Christianity. The U.S. military added its first Muslim chaplains in the 1990s, and in 1996 the Clintons celebrated the end of Ramadan (the Islamic holy month) with a group of Muslim children at the White House. The terrorist attacks of September 11, 2001, led to backlash against Muslims, but U.S. Muslims vigorously challenged stereotypes about their faith, insisting that terrorism against the innocent in pursuit of political goals violates Islamic belief and is repudiated by all but a tiny fringe of fanatics.

As a new century dawned, the changing status of women continued to shape American society. Women writers, artists, and scholars, moving rapidly toward full equality with their male colleagues, energized the cultural and intellectual scene. Black literature, once largely a male domain, now boasted women such as Alice Walker, Maya Angelou, and Toni Morrison, who won the 1993 Nobel Prize for literature.

Impressive statistics documented women's rising status. In 1999, 64 percent of female high-school graduates went on to college, in contrast to 61 percent of male graduates. In 1970, 8 percent of women over twenty-five had college degrees; in 2000, 24 percent did. In 1982, the entering class in U.S. medical schools was 32 percent female; in 2002, the figure was 49 percent.

Employment patterns changed as well. In 1950, fewer than 40 percent of women aged twenty-four to fifty-four worked outside the home; by 1998, more than 75 percent did. Women worked in all positions, from motel maids, firefighters, dental technicians, and carpenters to white-collar positions. By 1998 some 30 percent of working women held executive and managerial positions. In 1999 Carly Fiorina became CEO of the computer giant Hewlett-Packard. Nevertheless, the top

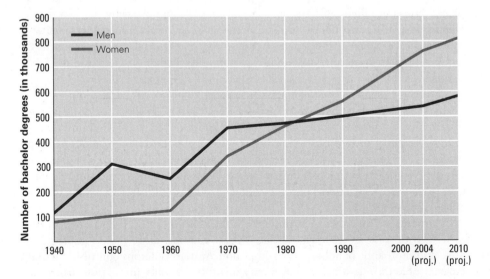

FIGURE 15.3

Number of Bachelor (B.A.) Degrees Awarded, 1940–2010 (Actual and Projected), by Gender

SOURCE: National Center for Education Statistics, U.S. Department of Education, in *World Almanac, 2004.*

ranks of business remained male bastions, reflecting subtle but entrenched patterns of discrimination that became known as the "glass ceiling."

Shifting marital and family patterns shaped women's lives as well. With births to unmarried women still at high levels and nearly half of all marriages ending in divorce, single-parent families, usually headed by a female, grew steadily. The proportion of children living in traditional, two-parent families fell from 85 percent in 1970 to around 70 percent in 2000. (For Hispanic children, the figure was 65 percent, and for black children, only 38 percent.) The overall birthrate remained low, with couples opting for one or two children or none at all. The median age at first marriage rose from around twenty-three for men and twenty for women in 1950 to twenty-seven for men and twenty-five for women in 2002. The number of unmarried couples living together rose sharply in these years as well All these trends directly influenced women's life choices. As the journal *Public Interest* noted in 1993, "In a long-life-expectancy, low-birth-rate society, there really is no serious alternative to major lifelong working careers for most women. The career of full-time wife, mother and homemaker has simply ceased to be an adequate life project."

Abortion, viewed as a central right by most feminists, continued to stir emotions long after the 1973 *Roe* v. *Wade* decision. Books such as *Life Itself: Abortion in the American Mind* (1992) by Roger Rosenblatt sought a middle ground but failed to sway the committed partisans of either camp. While advocates defended unrestricted access to abortion, the antiabortion forces, mostly Catholics, evangelical Protestants, and conservative Republicans, denounced the procedure as immoral. In 2003, the thirtieth anniversary of *Roe* v. *Wade*, thousands of antiabortion demonstrators held a "March for Life" in Washington. With thirty Catholic bishops and sympathetic politicians on hand, they chanted slogans, brandished signs, and

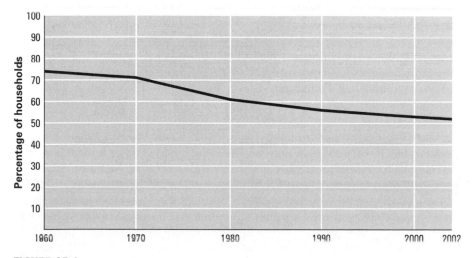

FIGURE 15.4

Percentage of U.S. Households Headed by a Male-Female Couple, 1960–2002

SOURCE: Bureau of the Census, U.S. Department of Commerce.

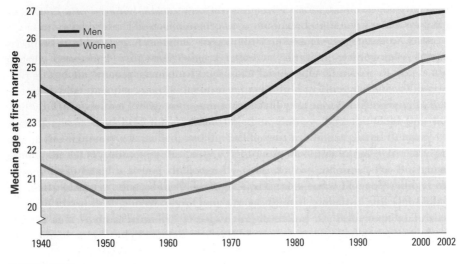

FIGURE 15.5

Median Age at First Marriage for U.S. Men and Women, 1940–2002

SOURCE: Bureau of the Census, U.S. Department of Commerce.

carried small white coffins to symbolize abortion's toll. President George W. Bush expressed his support by telephone.

Civil disobedience, once employed by antiwar and civil-rights activists, now became a technique of antiabortion groups like Operation Rescue, whose members courted arrest as they picketed clinics and even the homes of individual physicians. Some activists crossed the line into violence. From 1977 to 2000, extremists carried out 2,400 acts of violence against abortion clinics. In 1993, an antiabortion activist in Pensacola, Florida, shot and killed a physician whose photograph had earlier appeared on a "Wanted" poster circulated by Operation Rescue. In 1994, a young man on the fringe of the antiabortion movement fatally shot the receptionists at two Boston-area abortion clinics. In 1997, bombs damaged abortion clinics in Tulsa and Atlanta. A Buffalo gynecologist was slain in 1998. Nearly all "pro-life" leaders condemned such tactics, but they revealed the passions that swirled around the issue.

State legislatures, Congress, and the courts continued to address the abortion issue. In 1992 the Supreme Court by a 5–4 vote upheld parts of a Pennsylvania law imposing various procedural requirements on women seeking abortions, including a mandatory waiting period, an informed-consent form, and parental consent for minors. The majority, however, explicitly affirmed *Roe* v. *Wade*, declaring: "[A]n entire generation has come of age free to assume *Roe*'s concept of liberty in defining the capacity of women . . . to make reproductive decisions. . . . To overrule *Roe* . . . [would cause] profound and unnecessary damage to the Court's legitimacy, and to the Nation's commitment to the rule of law." In 2000, the Food and Drug Administration approved RU-486, a pill that induces abortion.

Opinion polls consistently find a clear majority of Americans in support of the basic principle of *Roe* (a constitutional right of abortion in the first trimester of pregnancy), but with a substantial minority opposed. In a 2003 NBC/*Wall Street Journal* poll, for example, 59 percent said that abortion decisions should be left to women and their physicians. Other data, however, also showed substantial support for procedural restrictions such as counseling, a waiting period (typically twenty-four hours), and parental notification (or even parental consent) for minors.

Late-term abortions, called "partial-birth" abortions by opponents, were far more controversial. In 1996, President Clinton vetoed a Republican bill to ban late-term abortions, arguing that this should be a medical decision, not a political one. In 2003, however, President George W. Bush signed into law a bill banning late-term abortions, even when the woman's life or health was in jeopardy. Meanwhile, the actual abortion rate, after rising steadily from 1974 to a 1990 peak of 27.4 per 1,000 women aged fifteen to forty-four, slowly declined thereafter, to 21.3 in 2000.

As the abortion controversy raged, the women's movement itself, after registering dramatic gains, came under assault from conservatives who deplored feminists' emphasis on autonomy and careers as "antifamily" and a threat to "traditional values." In *Backlash: The Undeclared War Against American Women* (1991), Susan Faludi saw a systematic drive in politics, fashion, and advertising to reassert stereotypes of women as subordinate, deferential sex objects.

The movement also entered a period of self-scrutiny, as feminists questioned their assumptions and strategies. In *The Second Stage* (1981), Betty Friedan criticized feminists who focused exclusively on career goals and women's rights and left family issues to conservatives. She called for more family-friendly business practices, such as flextime schedules and corporate-sponsored daycare centers. From a conservative perspective, Sylvia Ann Hewlett criticized the feminist movement in *When the Bough Breaks: The Cost of Neglecting Our Children* (1991) and *Creating a Life: Professional Women and the Quest for Children* (2002).

As the nation grew more conservative, feminists found themselves on the defensive. In a 1997 poll, fewer than 20 percent of U.S. women described themselves as "feminists," down from around 35 percent in 1989. Even more revealingly, the women who said they would prefer an outside job to full-time homemaking fell from about 70 percent in 1974 to about 40 percent in 1997. "People are saying that all feminism ever got us is more work," reported the director of a research organization on women's issues in 1997.

The Environmental Movement in the 1990s and Beyond

Environmentalism, another legacy of the 1970s, remained strong through the 1990s, but like the woman's movement, it, too, experienced a backlash amid controversies over complex issues. Environmental concerns sharpened in 1989 when the giant oil tanker *Exxon Valdez* ran aground in Prince William Sound, Alaska. The ship dumped 10.8 million gallons of crude oil that blackened miles of coastline; killed sea otters, bald eagles, and shorebirds; and endangered Alaska's fisheries. President Bush deplored the disaster but insisted that America's energy needs required continued oil drilling in Alaska. In a similar clash of economic and environmental interests, the campaign to preserve the Pacific Northwest's last old-growth forests and their delicate ecosystem, including the northern spotted owl, angered loggers and timber companies worried about jobs and profits.

The environmental movement took on fresh urgency as new threats emerged. Scientists warned of acid rain, a product of atmospheric pollution that kills plant and animal life in lakes and forests. They also cautioned that chlorofluorocarbon gases from spray cans and other sources were eroding the Earth's ozone layer, which filters out cancer-causing solar radiation. The threat of global warming, as pollution prevented the Earth's heat from escaping, built support for the Clean Air Act of 1990 (see Chapter 14). At the local level, cities established recycling programs to conserve resources and to avoid choking on their own refuse, which reached more than 200 million tons per year by 2000.

In *Earth in the Balance* (1992), then-senator Al Gore of Tennessee spotlighted aspects of the environmental crisis. While the industrialized world gobbled up dwindling natural resources and fossil fuels, poor nations such as Egypt, India, and Brazil, with its ecologically vulnerable rain forests, pursued economic development at the expense of environmental concerns. Recognizing the global dimensions of the crisis, the UN in 1992 convened Earth Summit in Rio de Janeiro, attracting thirty-five thousand participants. The delegates signed treaties related to biodiversity and global warming and endorsed "Agenda 21," a sweeping, although nonbinding, manifesto.

The success of the Clinton-Gore ticket in 1992 heartened environmentalists, but Clinton initially focused on other matters. However, when the Republican Congress elected in 1994 tried to roll back years of environmental regulation, the administration was prodded into action and in 1996–98 played a more active environmental role. In 1996, Clinton secured passage of a bill strengthening pesticide regulation. In 1997, despite fierce industrial lobbying, Clinton approved tough new EPA regulations on the emissions of pollutants that caused respiratory problems (particularly for children, the elderly, and asthmatics) and contributed to global warming.

Clinton's belated environmental activism played well politically. In a 1996 poll, 57 percent of Americans favored environmental protection even if job losses resulted. The GOP's opposition to environmental laws proved deeply unpopular. The administration also had the weight of scientific evidence on its side, especially on global warming. The year 1998 was the hottest ever recorded, and nine of the ten hottest years occurred in the 1990s. In 1998 the National Oceanographic and Atmospheric Administration reported that average temperatures worldwide had risen by a degree since 1900, with the warming trend increasing, and pinpointed pollutant emissions as a likely culprit. The United States' per capita pollutant emissions of some twenty metric tons per year sharply contrasts with Europe's average of around eight metric tons per capita. The long-range consequences of global warming, scientists warned, could include agricultural disruptions, the inundation of coastal cities from melting polar icecaps, and malaria epidemics as malaria-carrying mosquitoes expanded their range

In 1997, delegates from 150 nations gathered in Kyoto, Japan, for a UN conference to negotiate a treaty to reduce the emissions of the heat-trapping gases implicated in global warming. The conference threatened to bog down in disputes between developing nations and industrialized nations over the rates of reduction. Lobbyists for the automobile, steel, petroleum, and other industries warned that strict emissions standards could spell economic disaster. When Vice President Gore flew to Kyoto to push the negotiations forward, the delegates agreed on a draft treaty. It required the United States to reduce its emissions of greenhouse gases 9 percent below 1990 levels by 2012. The United States signed the agreement, but President Clinton did not submit it for Senate ratification. In 2001 President George W. Bush announced that the United States would neither accept the treaty nor participate in ongoing negotiations aimed at meeting U.S. concerns (see Chapter 16). By late 2003, 116 nations had ratified the Kyoto Protocol, including the European Union and Japan, but the United States continued to boycott the process.

Another troubling environmental problem was the disposal of tons of deadly radioactive waste from decades of nuclear-power and nuclear-weapons production. In 1997, scientists reported a higher-than-expected rate of water seepage in the government's designated waste-disposal site, a man-made cavern deep under Nevada's Yucca Mountain. Experts foresaw years of study before any nuclear waste was permanently stored.

The early twenty-first century saw a decline of environmental awareness. Not only did the George W. Bush administration prove generally indifferent to environmental concerns, but gas-guzzling sport-utility vehicles (SUVs), exempt from fuel-efficiency laws, increased their market share from 14 percent of all new vehicles purchased in 1996 to 27 percent in 2000, with continued surging sales thereafter.

And as a recession and terrorist attacks preoccupied voters, environmental awareness diminished. A 2003 poll of New Jersey residents found a sharp decline in those who considered environmentalism a "very serious" issue, from 52 percent in 2000 to 32 percent in 2003. Given the accumulating scientific evidence, however, environmental issues were clearly destined to remain high on the national—and global—agenda.

Health Care and AIDS, a Wired Nation, Mass-Culture Trends

Just as uncertainty marked U.S. foreign relations in the 1990s despite the Cold War's end, so Americans grappled with domestic concerns and unsettling changes despite the booming economy. Complex biomedical issues, soaring medical costs, the AIDS crisis, mass-culture changes, and the ongoing computer and information-technology revolution all made the turn of the century an edgy and uneasy time.

On the biomedical front, as the U.S. population aged, Americans confronted an array of ethical issues, including assisted suicide for the terminally ill, the soaring cost of nursing-home care, and the challenge of maintaining the quality of life for the old. Feminist pioneer Betty Friedan, now in her seventies, addressed this issue in *The Fountain of Age* (1993). "Grey power" received a boost in 1998 when NASA sent seventy-seven-year-old Senator John Glenn, who in 1962 had become the first American to orbit the earth, on a ten-day space mission. "[C]hildren will look at their grandparents differently," predicted a NASA official.

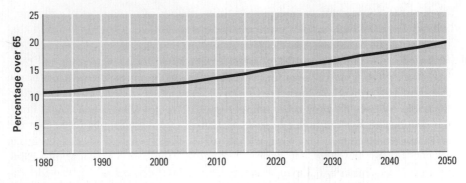

FIGURE 15.6

Percentage of U.S. Population Aged 65 or Older, 1980–2050 (Actual and Projected)

SOURCE: Bureau of the Census, Statistical Abstract of the United States, 1997.

The beginnings of life raised thorny issues as well, not all related to abortion. As childless couples sought help from science, problems of medical ethics arose. Fertility drugs sometimes produced multiple births ranging from twins to sextuplets, and the science-fiction prospect of human cloning moved a step closer to reality in 1997 when scientists in Scotland cloned a sheep, called Dolly.

A stark reminder of a health crisis related to corporate behavior came in 1998 with the release of tobacco-industry documents revealing deliberate targeting of children and young people. President Clinton again urged tougher controls on cigarette advertising and sales to minors. In 2002, after years of health warnings, 26 percent of Americans still smoked, including 17 percent of high-school seniors.

The nation also continued to face the scourge of AIDS (acquired immunodeficiency syndrome), the fatal disease first identified in 1981. AIDS spreads by the direct transmission of body fluids. The most vulnerable populations are sexually active homosexuals or bisexuals, persons having unprotected sex with infected individuals, drug users sharing needles, and babies born to infected mothers. Early in the epidemic, blood transfusions also spread the virus. With no cure in sight, public-health agencies urgently advised protective measures, including the use of condoms. By 2002, 486,000 Americans had died of AIDS. The U.S. picture brightened somewhat at the end of the 1990s, thanks to improved therapies and prevention education. Nevertheless, 45,000 new cases were reported in North America in 2002, swelling the total to nearly 1 million persons infected with AIDS or HIV, a virus that is a precursor of AIDS.

While some religious fundamentalists viewed the disease as God's "punishment" of homosexuals, AIDS activists called for expanded research budgets and quicker testing of experimental drugs. Hospice organizations and support networks helped sufferers, and a giant AIDS quilt made of panels crafted by victims' friends and relatives toured the nation.

The AIDS epidemic took a heavy toll in the arts and entertainment worlds. Actor Rock Hudson, a closet homosexual during his movie career, died of AIDS in 1985. The popular pianist Liberace succumbed in 1987. In the early 1990s basket-

The AIDS Quilt. With the Washington Monument as a backdrop, the 20,000 panels of the quilt commemorating AIDS victims cover the mall in Washington, D.C., October 1992. *(© Vanessa Vick/Photo Researchers, Inc.)*

ball superstar Earvin "Magic" Johnson and tennis pro Arthur Ashe announced that they were HIV positive. Ashe, infected from a blood transfusion, died in 1993, the same year as ballet dancer Rudolf Nureyev, another AIDS victim. Plays such as Larry Kramer's *The Normal Heart* (1985) and Tony Kushner's epic *Angels in America* (1993), Jonathan Larson's musical *Rent* (1996), and movies such as *Philadelphia* (1993), starring Tom Hanks, explored the devastation of AIDS and the courage it could call forth.

As the AIDS epidemic peaked in America, its global toll worsened. Total HIV/AIDS cases worldwide reached 42 million in 2002, with sub-Saharan Africa being the hardest hit, along with regions of Asia and Eastern Europe. From 1986 through 2001, the United States contributed nearly $1.6 billion to multinational and UN efforts to combat AIDS/HIV, malaria, and tuberculosis in the developing world.

The defeat of the Clinton health-care plan in 1993 did not end governmental involvement in health issues. The soaring cost of Medicare, the 1965 program to cover health services to the elderly and severely disabled, caused deepening worry. In 2003, with 41 million beneficiaries, Medicare cost $255 billion, surpassed only by social security and military spending. (The $159 billion spent on Medicaid, the program that provides medical services to the poor, pushed the total federal health-care bill still higher.)

Total U.S. health-care spending of $1.3 trillion in 2000 represented more than 13 percent of the gross domestic product (up from 7 percent in 1970). As the nation's 75 million baby boomers retire after 2010, annual Medicare costs will soar still higher, threatening massive budget deficits. Charges of waste, inefficiency, and government overpayments to hospitals, physicians, and other health-care providers have added to concerns about runaway costs.

With Medicare threatening to spiral out of control, Congress moved to rein in costs. In 1997 the Senate approved raising the age of Medicare eligibility from sixty-five to sixty-seven and increasing premiums for the well-to-do. The House demurred, but the trend was clear as Congress set up an advisory panel to address the problem. Congress also capped Medicare payments to health maintenance organizations (HMOs), causing many of them to raise monthly premiums and co-payment fees for prescription drugs.

Nevertheless, the spread of HMOs—private, for-profit, managed-care providers—did moderate the inflationary increases in health-care costs. By 2000, 26 percent of Americans were enrolled in HMOs, in contrast to 4 percent in 1980, and an ever-growing percentage of the nation's doctors worked full-time or part-time for an HMO. The consolidation sweeping corporate America and the mass media was transforming U.S. health care as well.

The benefits of HMOs were partially offset by the fact that sometimes HMOs cut costs at patients' expense. As stories mounted of patients denied needed treatment by their HMO or rushed from the hospital after surgery, anger grew and regulatory measures were proposed at both the state and federal levels, including a Clinton administration plan for a "bill of rights for health-care consumers" setting mandatory HMO guidelines and requiring HMOs to inform consumers about their policies.

Health-care worries and other pressing issues did not impede Americans' quest for entertainment, as the mass-culture trends of the 1980s (see Chapter 14) continued in the 1990s and beyond. Movies, television, theme parks, professional sports, gambling casinos, video games, and the pop-music industry all provided leisure-time diversion. In 2001, some six hundred thousand visitors—second only to the number of visitors to the White House—toured Graceland, Elvis Presley's garish mansion in Memphis. As in the past, escapist fare dominated the mass media. The two top-grossing movies of 1996, *Independence Day* and *Twister,* both loaded with special effects, dealt, respectively, with invading aliens and killer tornadoes. *Titanic,* a 1997 Hollywood spectacular, retold the story of that ill-fated vessel's 1912 sinking. As computer-animation technology grew more sophisticated, real and simulated action in movies became barely distinguishable. The top-grossing film of 2002, *Spider-Man,* full of computerized special effects, was based on a comic-strip character.

Seinfeld, the top TV comedy of the 1990s, involved a cast of self-absorbed New Yorkers who confronted in wildly bizarre ways the petty irritations of everyday life and tried, with little success, to hold jobs and sustain long-term relationships. In 1994, network TV news programs devoted 491 stories to O. J. Simpson, a football star and media celebrity on trial for murdering his ex-wife and a friend, and only 409 stories about that year's pivotal midterm elections. Still, TV continued to influence politics profoundly. Campaigns became hardly distinguishable from toothpaste promotions, as advertising agencies "packaged" candidates and commercials featured manipulative visual images, superficial sound bites, and "attack ads" discrediting the opponent.

Influenced by the popularity of confessional TV talk shows, politicians told heart-tugging stories of parental abuse, injured children, and other traumas that had shaped their outlook. Ronald Reagan's patented catch-in-the-throat was legendary, and although Bill Clinton's easy emotion ("I feel your pain") provoked ridicule, it was effective. The line between politics and entertainment blurred in 1998 when Minnesotans elected a professional wrestler, Jesse Ventura, as governor, and again in 2003 when Californians threw out Governor Gray Davis in a recall campaign and sent bodybuilder and Hollywood action hero Arnold Schwarzenegger to the governor's mansion.

The year 2000 saw the onset of low-budget TV "reality" shows. In *Survivor,* a group of men and women on a remote island voted each week to expel one of their number. *Joe Millionaire* featured young women competing for the favor of a wealthy bachelor. In *American Idol,* amateur pop singers competed for stardom. *The Simple Life* sent two rich young socialites to live on a farm—or "from the penthouse to the outhouse," as the show's website elegantly put it. "Does Wal-Mart sell walls?" one asked. Another show featured aging rock star Ozzy Osbourne and his family as they went about their everyday life.

Meeting Americans' voracious appetite for entertainment involved mind-boggling sums of money. The 2002 sales of CDs (which in the 1990s largely replaced cassette tapes in popularity) reached 624 million. (Even that staggering total was lower than in the preceding two years, as more young people shared music on the Internet, a practice the music industry combated in the courts.) *Seinfeld* generated $200 million a year for NBC. In high-level negotiations in 1998, ABC paid $4.4 billion to televise *Monday Night Football* for eight years and ESPN acquired the cable rights to National Football League (NFL) games for $4.8 billion. The total contract negotiations produced $18 billion for the NFL over eight years and made the league the major supplier of TV programming.

Corporate conglomerates increasingly dominated the mass culture. The Disney Corporation, with 2002 revenues of $25 billion, counted ABC, ESPN, a movie studio, and theme parks among its crown jewels. Disney's 2000–2001 toy sales alone reached $2 billion. The media giant Viacom (also $25 billion in 2002 revenues) controlled Paramount Pictures; Blockbuster video rental; fifteen book-publishing companies, including the Free Press and Simon & Schuster; 28 TV stations; 140 radio stations; and the Showtime, Nickelodeon, and MTV television channels (the latter with affiliates in fourteen foreign markets), along with many other holdings.

Monarch of the media moguls was the politically conservative Australian Rupert Murdoch, who became a U.S. citizen in 1985. In 1997, after decades of acquisitions, Murdoch's parent corporation owned 789 businesses in fifty-two countries. His U.S. holdings included Fox movie studios and TV network, twenty-two television stations, the *New York Post, TV Guide,* and the Los Angeles Dodgers baseball team, and much more. What the *Washington Post* called Murdoch's "planet-girdling ring of satellite TV systems" could theoretically broadcast simultaneously to 75 percent of Earth's population.

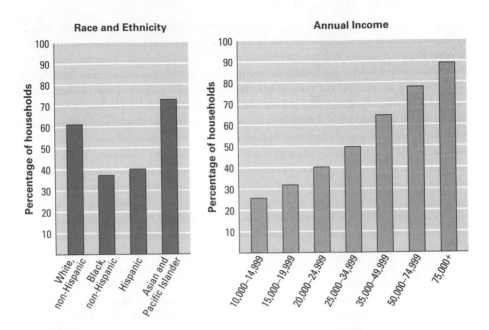

FIGURE 15.7

Percentage of U.S. Households with a Computer, 2001, by Selected Characteristics

SOURCE: National Telecommunications and Information Administration.

Some critics deplored the ever-growing commercialization and consolidation of mass entertainment and longed for a simpler time. In October 2003, *Time* magazine columnist Michael Elliott noted that Americans spent nearly $7 billion celebrating Halloween, including schlocky plastic pumpkins that moaned ominously when someone walked by. Halloween Express, a franchise operation selling such products, had some seventy stores in twenty-one states. The marketers, Elliott complained, "have turned an innocent night of excitement for children into something run by and for adults." He continued:

> Halloween, for me, is the gaudiest example of the infantilization of American culture. It's up there with . . . McDonald's Happy Meals or Hollywood's . . . decision to concentrate on making kids' films for grownups. . . . In time, infantile societies become degraded, unable to meet the realities that face them.

Meanwhile, the personal-computer revolution roared on. By 2001, 56.5 percent of U.S. households had personal computers, in contrast to 41 percent only four years earlier. In addition to the desktop PC, laptop and even smaller versions proliferated. As in the entertainment industry, giant corporations dominated the computer-software business. Biggest of all was Seattle's Microsoft, founded by Harvard dropout Bill Gates III. By the late 1990s, Gates was the richest person in America. With $9 billion in cash and a stock-market valuation of $160 billion (three times that of General Motors), Microsoft in 1997 absorbed its onetime rival, Apple Computer, founded by Steve Jobs and Steve Wozniak in the 1970s. After years of largely unregulated operation, Microsoft in 1997 faced a Justice Department antitrust suit charging unfair competitive practices such as installing its own Internet browser, Explorer, in its Windows 95 operating system. Like Standard Oil earlier, the Microsoft juggernaut crushed or bought out weaker competitors through its sheer size, wealth, and ruthlessness. In a 2001 settlement, Microsoft accepted a number of restrictions that the Justice Department claimed would "stop Microsoft's unlawful conduct . . . [and] restore competition in the software industry."

The computer made possible the multibillion-dollar video-game industry; revolutionized personal communications through an electronic message system (e-mail); and opened a vast world of information exchange and discussion through the Internet. Developed in rudimentary form by the Department of Defense in 1969, the Internet soon took on a life of its own. By 2001, more than half of U.S. households had Internet access. The World Wide Web, developed in Geneva in the early 1990s and featuring images, movement, and sound, offered an even richer Internet environment.

In contrast to the corporate consolidation typified by Microsoft, the Internet was initially decentralized to the point of anarchy, a condition that infused it with a heady excitement but that also gave rise to calls for censorship, leading to the Communications Decency Act of 1996. The Supreme Court ruled this law unconstitutional in 1997, shifting from the government to parents the responsibility for shielding minors from the Internet's proliferating pornographic websites. Civil libertarians cheered, but antipornography groups bemoaned this further blow to morality. A follow-up measure, the Children's Internet Protection Act (2000), requiring libraries to install antipornography filters on their public computers, passed Supreme Court muster in 2003.

The Internet soon tempted the marketers. Mail-order distributors like L.L. Bean and Victoria's Secret sold their goods through websites. Amazon.com marketed books, CDs, and other products. A national flea market sprang up as people bid for everything from baseball cards to marimbas on eBay. Internet users also battled a deluge of unsolicited commercial messages, dubbed "spam." Trying to stem the tide, New York State and Microsoft filed suit against one of the largest spammers in 2003.

The computer revolution inspired both utopian visions and hand-wringing warnings. Critics claimed that computer-based teaching programs encouraged rote memorization and stifled creativity. On the other hand, Seymour Papert, a learning researcher at the Massachusetts Institute of Technology, argued in *The Children's Machine: Rethinking School in the Age of the Computer* (1993) that imaginative, interactive programs could stretch pupils' imaginations.

Other critics warned of numbed moral sensibilities in a generation reared on computer games that often featured extreme violence without consequences. In *War of the Worlds: Cyberspace and the High-Tech Assault on Reality* (1995), Mark Sloutka offered a broader critique, contending that the virtual reality of the computer can become more "real" for users than the actual world around them. Underscoring such fears, teachers reported that school kids were bonding emotionally with their digital "pets" (a fad of the late 1990s) and grieving when they "died" from lack of "feeding." Sociologist Sherry Turkle, in *Life on the Screen: Identity in the Age of the Internet* (1995), saw a weakening of fixed identity as people assumed different roles in the anonymity of Internet chat rooms. For Turkle, the Internet was the ultimate "postmodern" phenomenon, foreshadowing the dissolution of any stable reality.

Others noted the uneven distribution of access to computers. In 2001, when 61 percent of white, non-Hispanic households owned personal computers, only 37 percent of black households and 40 percent of Hispanic households did. A similar disparity emerged along income lines. Nearly 90 percent of families with annual incomes above $75,000 had computers in 2001, but computer access fell off sharply further down the income scale. Sometimes praised as a great leveler, the computer revolution in some ways simply reinforced the divisions of American society along lines of class, race, and ethnicity.

Other new communications technologies further transformed American life. DVDs (digital video disks), with more capacity and sharper images than videocassettes, became increasingly popular, as more people rented films for home viewing. Television itself evolved rapidly, with the advent of large-screen, high-definition LED (light-emitting diode) sets. The larger TVs with their vaguely ominous flat black screens literally overwhelmed the living room, dwarfing the human inhabitants. Ray Bradbury's vision of a TV-dominated society in *Fahrenheit 451* (1953) seemed about to be realized.

The mobile cellular telephone, meanwhile, freed users from a fixed telephone and allowed them to make calls from the car, the gym, the airport waiting room, or anywhere they chose. In 1990, 5 percent of households had cell phones; in 2002, 66 percent did, with the number increasing daily. The largest of the new telecommunications companies, Verizon, chalked up revenues of $67.6 billion in 2002. But telecommunications, too, was awash with marketers, who invariably called at dinnertime. The Federal Trade Commission set up a "Do Not Call" registry in 2003 to curb this annoying invasion of privacy, but its success remained uncertain, particularly since it exempted political and philanthropic calls.

The new electronic world was changing fast. The dinosaur-like computers of the late 1940s, a byproduct of World War II, had by the 1990s spawned a vast progeny of personal computers that, together with cell phones, DVD players, digital cameras, pagers, and other innovations, were creating a wired society of instant communication and nonstop entertainment.

Beyond the technological wizardry, how would these changes affect American life? Would computers and manipulative TV lead to ever-greater concentrations of governmental and corporate power? Would the Internet, computerized learning, and instant global communication have the positive effects that some foresaw? Or would the future confirm the apprehensions of those who feared a society of isolated individuals addicted to the mass culture's endless distractions, for whom the electronic world seemed more "real" that the actual world? The actual world included not only human intimacy and the unspoiled wilderness, but also suffering, poverty, injustice, and conflict. Would the wired world allow for moments of privacy, quiet reflection, and simple, spontaneous pleasure, apart from the insistent allure of the CD, the DVD, the LED, and the quick cell-phone exchange?

An Apprehensive Mood as a New Millennium Dawns

As Americans of the 1990s anticipated not only a new century but also a new millennium, the national mood, upbeat in some ways, was also uneasy and uncertain. Certainly Americans welcomed prosperity, the Cold War's end, and the lowered threat of nuclear war. They applauded in 1997 when NASA's *Pathfinder* space probe sent back stunning photos of Mars, and when the orbiting Hubbell telescope returned breathtaking images of distant star systems.

But for many Americans, the pace of social, cultural, and technological change also proved disorienting. One expression of the edginess was the preoccupation with the "Y2K" phenomenon: the fear of a mass computer failure at midnight on December 31, 1999, as computers' internal clocks, not programmed to function beyond that date, went dead. Another sign of the times was a mood of nostalgia for a supposedly simpler past that sometimes edged over into near paranoia. Too much was changing too fast.

Some saw the anxiety as a lingering aftereffect of the Cold War. As New York senator Daniel Moynihan observed in 1997: "Perceptions lag. It takes time for a culture that was deeply pessimistic about the future and deeply anxious . . . during the Cold War to come out of that." Economist Robert J. Samuelson offered a different explanation in *The Good Life and Its Discontents* (1995), arguing that the long cycle of post-1945 economic growth had created unrealistic expectations of endless expansion and personal entitlement, leaving Americans in an "almost permanent state of public grumpiness."

Whatever the reasons, the unease and anger coursing through the nation's political and cultural life surfaced in unexpected ways. When the Smithsonian Institution announced an exhibit in 1995 marking the fiftieth anniversary of the atomic bombing of Japan that included a range of historical judgments regarding Truman's decision, as well as information on the bombs' human toll, veterans' groups, patriotic organizations, and sympathetic politicians protested noisily, and the exhibit was canceled. Historian John Dower noted the irony of "demanding a pristine, heroic, official version of a war that presumably was fought to protect . . . the free play of ideas."

Some native-born Americans found the nation's increasingly multiethnic, multicultural profile upsetting. As newcomers arrived from Latin America and Asia, they sometimes encountered hostility. Stricter rules imposed in 1997 raised the economic barrier for immigration and made it harder for recent immigrants to bring in relatives. The notoriously porous U.S.-Mexican border was more heavily fortified. In 1997, U.S. marines patrolling for drug smugglers shot and killed a Mexican youth herding sheep along the border.

But the anti-immigrant sentiment was muted, since the newcomers supplied crucial agricultural labor in the West and took low-paying jobs that native-born workers often spurned. As a Texas woman observed: "We may vote against immigration, but we still want a cheap gardener." Noting this paradox, the *Economist* of London commented in 1997: "Americans' bouts of anti-immigrant fervor tend to be ambivalent, hypocritical . . . , and futile."

The 1990s also saw a reaction against affirmative-action programs that granted preferences to minorities. The Supreme Court in 1995 restricted the use of race as a consideration in awarding federal contracts, and in 1996 California voters passed Proposition 209, ending racial or ethnic preferences in any state agency, including the University of California. Minority enrollment at the University of California Law School at Berkeley fell sharply, and set-asides for minority businesses in state-contract competitions ended. Other states considered similar initiatives. Critics of affirmative action insisted that they were simply upholding the principle of equality for all. Others, however, including Andrew Hacker in *Two Nations Black and White: Separate, Hostile and Unequal* (1995), saw subtle racism in the anti-affirmative-action backlash. But a 1997 opinion poll found that although most whites opposed legally mandated racial or ethnic preferences in academia or the workplace, they did support other programs designed to increase minority access. The poll also revealed more support for affirmative-action programs based on economic need rather than on race or ethnicity.

As these debates unfolded, Americans wrestled with the problem of how to preserve a common sense of civic loyalty within a context of multiculturalism and interest-group politics. In *Democracy's Discontent: America in Search of a Public Philosophy* (1996), government professor Michael Sandel discussed strategies for reversing the erosion of America's political culture, which he called "civic republicanism." In *Bowling Alone: The Collapse and Revival of American Community*, political scientist Robert Putnam cited an array of evidence, from the decline of bowling leagues and family dinners to a drop in volunteerism and voter turnout, suggesting a weakened social consciousness in favor of self-centered pursuits.

The cultural wars of the 1970s and 1980s, featuring a conservative backlash against multiculturalism, "political correctness," and the alleged decline of academic standards, continued in the 1990s. Conservative critics like William Bennett and Lynne Cheney, Republican officials in the Reagan and first Bush administrations, lamented the erosion of intellectual rigor in the schools and the decline of a shared civic culture as society splintered into separate camps, each pursuing its own objectives.

Other observers took a more hopeful view. In *Post-Ethnic America: Beyond Multiculturalism* (1995), historian David Hollinger argued for a cosmopolitan society in which individuals could choose their affinity group on the basis of their interests, talents, and preferences rather than remain locked into a fixed cultural-political identity determined by gender, ethnicity, race, or income. Historian Lawrence Levine, in *The Opening of the American Mind* (1996), rejected the romantic idea of a lost Eden of social homogeneity and cultural consensus. Cultural diversity and contentious disagreements, he insisted, have characterized America from the beginning. In *One Nation, After All* (1998), sociologist Alan Wolfe found a broad middle ground of agreement on many volatile social issues, despite the inflamed rhetoric at the extremes.

The evangelical revival remained strong at century's end. Evangelical churches flourished, the nation's twenty-five hundred Christian bookstores racked up $3 billion in annual sales, Christian music groups proliferated, and bumper sticks proclaimed "Praise the Lord" and "Real Men Love Jesus." From the evangelical perspective, modern America was a degenerate society where academic postmodernists dismissed timeless verities; the mass-culture denigrated religion, marketed indecency, and celebrated homosexuality; and the government upheld abortion, defended pornography, and banned prayer in the schools. In such a situation, troubled believers found assurance in a God-given moral code and the clarity of their "Bible-based" faith. Evangelicalism's quarrel with America was highlighted in 1997 when Southern Baptist leaders urged the church's 15 million members to boycott Disney theme parks for sponsoring "Gay Pride" days and granting benefits to the partners of homosexual employees.

In 1991, a former University of Colorado football coach, Bill McCartney, founded Promise Keepers, a religious movement that called upon American males to love Jesus, remain faithful to their wives, and fulfill their God-ordained role as strong husbands and attentive fathers. Featuring mass rallies at football stadiums, the movement attracted mostly white, middle-class young males of evangelical backgrounds. In October 1997, thousands of Promise Keepers rallied in Washington, D.C., for a day of prayer, hymn singing, and tearful male bonding. Some feminists criticized the movement as a reactionary reassertion of patriarchal authority.

Evangelical Christians continued to make their voices heard in politics. Jerry Falwell disbanded the Moral Majority, but Pat Robertson's Christian Coalition, founded in 1989, continued to thrive. Under executive director Ralph Reed, a savvy young political operative, the Christian Coalition perfected its "stealth" strategy of electing conservative Christians to local committees and school boards. *U.S. News and World Report*, praising Reed's organizing skills, said: "He looks like a choir boy and acts like a ward boss." Calling for a return to traditional morality and "family values," the Religious Right stressed such hot-button issues as abortion, creationism, school prayer, lewd pop music lyrics, Internet pornography, sex education in the schools, and suggestive movies and TV programs. Evangelicals overwhelmingly backed conservative Republican candidates. Bill Clinton's sexual escapades confirmed their darkest fears of the nation's moral collapse.

The nostalgia for a simpler era often took a benign form: Civil War battle reenactments; revivals of Broadway musicals; biographies of the Founding Fathers; David McCullough's affectionate *Truman* (1993); sepia-tinted TV documentaries on the Civil War, jazz, and baseball. Sometimes, however, the reaction against modernity took a more unsettling turn. For many citizens, Washington, D.C., embodied all that had gone wrong in America. Right-wing radio commentators like Rush Limbaugh tirelessly ridiculed the government. A freshly hatched Wyoming congresswoman in 1995 denounced the Internal Revenue Service as "the Gestapo." In 1964, 76 percent of Americans had told pollsters that the government could be trusted "always" or "most of the time." By 1994, the figure had fallen to 19 percent. (Interestingly, most respondents saw their own legislators as exceptions to the general rule.)

The paranoia seeped into the mass culture. The popular 1990s TV series *The X-Files* featured two FBI agents battling weird, sometimes paranormal conspiracies hatched by government agencies and other shadowy powers. The series' motto, "Trust No One," summed up the mood. Cultural historian Ruth Rosen noted the program's ability to tap into "a deep and abiding distrust of our government . . . that has been powerfully reinforced during the past three decades." The 1998 film *Wag the Dog* offered a deeply cynical view of political manipulation of public opinion. In another 1998 movie, *The Truman Show,* Jim Carrey gradually realizes that his life is actually an elaborately staged TV soap opera. In *The Matrix* (1999), Keanu Reeves learns that his world is in fact a virtual reality controlled by a powerful computer program. Wrote the *New Yorker* critic of a 2003 *Matrix* sequel: "[I]n a period in which gigantic corporations and entire governments devote themselves to promoting made-up realities, people may genuinely wonder what world they are living in."

Some observers saw the distrust of government as another Cold War legacy. For decades, Americans had been conditioned to view the world in black-and-white terms: the Soviet Union evil, America wholly virtuous. With the end of the Cold War, these observers suggested, many citizens simply transferred this black-and-white worldview to the domestic sphere, with Washington replacing Moscow as the heart of darkness.

When combined with religious fundamentalism, this outlook could lead to a view of the federal government as, quite literally, satanic. Pat Robertson's best-selling *The New World Order* (1991) portrayed U.S. history as a vast conspiracy that will culminate in the rule of the Antichrist. Another Bible-prophecy believer with a conspiratorial turn of mind, David Koresh, isolated his followers in a compound near Waco, Texas, warning them that satanic powers, in the form of government authorities, were arrayed against them. When the authorities sought to arrest Koresh for gun-law violations, his prophecies were tragically fulfilled. Ten persons died early in 1993 when federal agents stormed the Waco compound. Then, on April 19, after a two-month standoff, the FBI launched a second assault. As the tanks rumbled in, fires broke out inside the compound; Koresh and some eighty of his followers, including seventeen children, perished in the flames.

In its most extreme form, the antigovernment ideology led some Americans (estimates ranged from ten thousand to sixty thousand) to form heavily armed "militias" or retreat to survivalist communes in remote corners of the Northwest, preparing for the final battle against the forces of evil. Often racist, anti-Semitic, and obsessed with conspiracy theories, these groups used the latest technologies, including faxes and the Internet, to spread their message of hate.

On April 19, 1995, the second anniversary of the Waco disaster, a bomb hidden in a truck destroyed the Murrah Federal Building in Oklahoma City, killing 168 men, women, and children. (A daycare center in the building was hard hit.) Police soon arrested Timothy McVeigh, a decorated Gulf War veteran with a fierce hatred of government. Convicted of murder, McVeigh died by lethal injection in 2001. A co-conspirator, Terry Nichols, convicted on lesser charges, escaped the death penalty. Both had tenuous links to the militia movement. Many wondered what America was coming to.

In another instance of ideologically motivated violence, numerous package bombs were mailed from 1978 to 1995 to individuals whose activities could be interpreted as protechnology or antienvironment. Three died and others were injured when the packages were opened. The perpetrator, dubbed the "Unabomber," sent long manifestoes to the press denouncing modern technology. In 1996, authorities arrested Theodore Kaczynski, a mathematician and Harvard graduate, in his remote Montana cabin and charged him with the bombings. Convicted in 1998, he was sentenced to life imprisonment.

A series of multiple shootings, several of them in schools, added to the edgy national mood. In the most horrendous incident, in 1999, two male students at Columbine High School in Littleton, Colorado, shot and killed twelve students and a teacher before killing themselves. Advocates of gun control, critics of violent video games, and conservatives convinced of America's moral decline or the erosion of social connectedness all found evidence for their cause in the tragedy.

Although clearly the work of a few disturbed individuals, these isolated acts of antisocial violence contributed to the nagging sense of unease, suggesting the psychic toll that rapid social and technological change can take on a society, particularly on those who feel marginalized, disinherited, and powerless.

Americans celebrated New Year's Eve 1999 in a muted mood, despite the added excitement of a new millennium. The feared computer meltdown associated with Y2K (the year 2000) did not materialize, but vague apprehension hovered around the edges of the celebrations.

Conclusion

In retrospect, the 1990s does not rank as the golden age some perceived at the time. The prosperity and the surging stock market reflected not only genuine economic advances but also speculative greed and wishful thinking. Within months of the decade's end, the stock market would collapse and a series of spectacular corporate failures would shatter the reputations of some of America's best-known business leaders.

Politically the Clinton presidency began with the failure of a major health care initiative, signaling the collapse of the kind of liberalism that had inspired the social initiatives of the New Deal and the Great Society. The 1995 Welfare Reform Act, which ended federal welfare programs dating to the 1930s and shifted welfare responsibility to the states, further underscored the nation's conservative shift.

Internationally, the Clinton administration cooperated with the nation's allies and with the world community as it intervened militarily and diplomatically to end the murderous conflict in the Balkans and helped develop the Kyoto Protocol, a multinational response to global environmental problems. U.S. support for the NAFTA Treaty and for the World Trade Organization, as well as its policies toward a major trading partner, China, underscored the importance of trade considerations in shaping the nation's foreign policy. The bombing of the World Trade Center in 1993 and of U.S. embassies in Africa in 1998 highlighted the dangers lurking in the post–Cold War world—dangers that would soon become a major preoccupation.

Not all the terrorism came from abroad. The bombing of the Oklahoma City federal building in 1995 and a series of multiple killings by disturbed individuals, most terribly at Columbine High School in 1999, bore witness to internal problems facing the nation as it looked to a new millennium.

As politics and the economic boom dominated the headlines, demographic and technological changes were creating a new society. The America of the future would be a multicultural, multiethnic nation. It would also be a society in which multinational corporations and new electronic technologies would play a role whose full dimensions could only be imagined from the perspective of the early twenty-first century.

Like the nation's own mixed record in the 1990s, the president who presided over most of the decade left a legacy of both achievement and failure. With high intelligence, impressive political skills, and an obvious desire to succeed as president, Bill Clinton also had a notoriously short attention span, a casual way with the truth, and a serious inability to control impulses of momentary self-gratification whatever the long-term consequences. Although these character flaws did not destroy him politically, as his political opponents hoped, they diminished his reputation and seriously tarnished what might have been a far more memorable and distinguished presidency.

SELECTED READINGS

For contemporary trends and issues, the *New York Times, Washington Post,* and other major newspapers can provide background and perspective. So, too, can leading news magazines and journals of opinion such as the *Atlantic, Business Week, Christian Century, Christianity Today,* the *Economist* (London), *Foreign Affairs, Harper's, Ms.,* the *Nation, National Review,* the *New Republic,* the *New York Review of Books, Newsweek,* the *Progressive,* the *Public Interest, Science, Time, Variety,* and *U.S. News and World Report.*

Clinton Biographies, Clinton-Era Politics, Welfare Reform, Impeachment

Peter Baker, *The Breach: Inside the Impeachment and Trial of William Jefferson Clinton* (2000); Sidney Blumenthal, *The Clinton Wars (2003);* Hillary Rodham Clinton, *Living History* (2003); E. J. Dionne, *They Only Look Dead: Why Progressives Will Dominate the Next Political Era* (1996); Jack W. Germond and Jules Witcover, *Mad as Hell: Revolt at the Ballot Box: 1992* (1993); Mark Gerson, *The Neoconservative Vision* (1996); Jacob S. Hacker, *The Road to Nowhere: The Genesis of President Clinton's Plan for Health Security* (1997); Nigel Hamilton, *Bill Clinton: An American Journey* (2003); Kathleen Hall Jamieson, *Packaging the Presidency: A History and Criticism of Presidential Campaign Advertising* (3d ed., 1996); Michael B. Katz, *The Price of Citizenship: Redefining the American Welfare State* (2001); Joe Klein, *The Natural: The Misunderstood Presidency of Bill Clinton* (2003); David Maraniss, *First in His Class: A Biography of Bill Clinton* (1995); Robert A. Moffitt and Michelle Ver Ploeg, eds., *Evaluating Welfare Reform in an Era of Transition* (2001); Carrick Mollenkamp et al., *The People v. Big Tobacco* (1998); Charles Noble, *Welfare as We Knew It: A Political History of the American Welfare State* (1997); Richard A. Posner, *An Affair of State: The Investigation, Impeachment, and Trial of President Clinton* (2000); Robert B. Reich, *Locked in the Cabinet* (1997); Tom Rosenstiel, *Strange Bedfellows: How Television and the Presidential Candidates Changed American Politics, 1992* (1993); Michael J. Sandel, *Democracy's Discontent: America in Search of a Public Philosophy* (1996); Isabel V. Sawhill et al., *Welfare Reform and Beyond: The Future of the Safety Net* (2002); James B. Stewart, *Blood Sport: The President and His Adversaries* (1996); Jacob Weisberg, *In Defense of Government: The Fall and Rise of Public Trust* (1996); Bob Woodward, *The Choice: How Clinton Won* (1996).

America and the World at Century's End

Benjamin R. Barber, *Jihad vs. McWorld* (1996); Wesley K. Clark, *Waging Modern War: Bosnia, Kosovo, and the Future of Combat* (2002); Ivo H. Daalder, *Getting to Dayton: The Making of American Bosnia Policy* (2000); Herbert Druks, *The Uncertain Alliance: The U.S. and Israel from Kennedy to the Peace Process* (2001); Thomas L. Friedman, *The Lexus and the Olive Tree: Understanding Globalization* (2000); David C. Gompert and F. Stephen Larrabee, *America and Europe: A Partnership for a New Era* (1997), Richard Holbrooke, *To End a War* [U.S. role in Bosnia] (1999); Susan Hunter, *Black Death: AIDS in Africa* (2003); William G. Hyland, *Clinton's World: Remaking American Foreign Policy* (1999); David M. Lampman, *Same Bed, Different Dreams: Managing U.S.-China Relations, 1989–2000* (2001); Thomas W. Lippman, *Madeleine Albright and the New American Diplomacy* (2000); Stansfield Turner, *Caging the Nuclear Genie* (1997).

Economic Trends, Wealth and Poverty, the Communications Revolution

Ken Auletta, *World War 3.0: Microsoft and Its Enemies* (2001); Thomas D. Boston and Catherine L. Ross, eds., *The Inner City: Urban Poverty and Economic Development in the Next Century* (1997); Francis Cairncross, *The Death of Distance: How the Communications Revolution Will Change Our Lives* (1997); Richard E. Fogelsong, *Married to the Mouse: Walt Disney World and Orlando* (2003); Joshua B. Freedman, *Working-Class New York: Life and Labor Since World War II* (2000); Louis Galambos and Eric John Abrahamson, *Anytime, Anywhere: Entrepreneurship and the Creation of a Wireless World* (2002); Katie Hafner and Matthew Lyon, *Where Wizards Stay Up Late: The Origins of the Internet* (1996); Daniel Ichbiah, *The Making of Microsoft* (1991); Haynes Johnson, *The Best of Times: The Boom and Bust Years of America Before Everything Changed* (2002); Christopher Lasch, *The Revolt of the Elites and the Betrayal of Democracy* (1995); Kevin Phillips, *Wealth and Democracy: A Political History of the American Rich* (2003); Robert Slater, *The Wal-Mart Decade* (2003); Don Tapscott, *Growing Up Digital: The Rise of the Net Generation* (1998); James Wallace, *Overdrive: Bill Gates and the Race to Control Cyberspace* (1997), Sam Walton, *Made in America* (1993); William Julius Wilson, *When Work Disappears: The World of the New Urban Poor* (1996).

Social and Demographic Trends in the 1990s and Beyond

Peter Arno, *Against the Odds* (1992) [AIDS research and politics]; Francis J. Beckwith and Todd E. Jones, eds., *Affirmative Action: Social Justice or Reverse Discrimination?* (1997); Jeff Benedict, *Without Reservation: The Making of America's Most Powerful Indian Tribe and Foxwoods, the World's Largest Casino* (2000); Arthur L. Caplan, *Am I My Brother's Keeper? The Ethical Frontiers of Biomedicine* (1997); Philip E. Devine and Celia Wolf-Devine, *Sex and Gender: A Spectrum of Views* (2003); Geoffrey Fox, *Hispanic Nation: Culture, Politics, and the Constructing of Identity* (1996); Juan Gonzáles, *Harvest of Empire: A History of Latinos in America* (2000); Jong-deuk Jung, *A Study of Korean Immigration in America* (1991); Richard Kluger, *Ashes to Ashes* [cigarettes and public health] (1996); Gina Kolata, *Clone: The Road to Dolly, and the Path Ahead* (1997); Alex Kotlowitz, *There Are No Children Here: The Story of Two Boys Growing Up in the Other America* (1991); Jonathan Kozol, *Amazing Grace: The Lives of Children and the Conscience of a Nation* (1995); Walter Benn Michaels, *Our America: Nativism, Modernism, and Pluralism* (1995); Joel Millman, *The Other Americans: How Immigrants Renew Our Country, Our Economy, and Our Values* (1997); Richard

Moe and Carter Wilkie, *Changing Places: Rebuilding Community in the Age of Sprawl* (1997); Joseph Nevins, *Operation Gatekeeper: The Rise of the 'Illegal Alien' and the Making of the U.S.-Mexico Boundary* (2002); David N. Pellow, *Garbage Wars: The Struggle for Environmental Justice in Chicago* (2002); Joan K. Peters, *When Mothers Work: Loving Our Children Without Sacrificing Ourselves* (1997); James Risen and Judy Thomas, *Wrath of Angels: The American Abortion Wars* (1998); Roger Rosenblatt, *Life Itself: Abortion in the American Mind* (1992); William A. Rushing, *The AIDS Epidemic: Social Dimensions of an Infectious Disease* (1995); Randy Shilts, *And the Band Played On: Politics, People, and the AIDS Epidemic* (1987); Peter Skerry, *Mexican Americans: The Ambivalent Minority* (1993); Robert C. Smith, *Racism in the Post–Civil Rights Era: Now You See It, Now You Don't* (1995); Rickie Solinger, *Abortion Wars: A Half Century of Struggle, 1950–2000* (1997); Joseph E. Stiglitz, *The Roaring Nineties: A New History of the World's Most Prosperous Decade* (2003); Rodolfo D. Torres, *Latino Metropolis* [Los Angeles] (2000); William Wei, *The Asian American Movement* (1993).

Cultural Issues, Religious Trends, Alienated Americans

Michael Barkun, *A Culture of Conspiracy: Apocalyptic Visions in Contemporary America* (2003); Paul Boyer, *When Time Shall Be No More: Prophecy Belief in Modern American Culture* (1992); Joel A. Carpenter, *Revive Us Again: The Reawakening of American Fundamentalism* (1997); Stephen L. Carter, *The Culture of Disbelief: How American Law and Politics Trivialize Religious Devotion* (1993); James L. Guth et al., *The Bully Pulpit: The Politics of Protestant Clergy* (1997); Martin Harwit, *An Exhibit Denied* [the Enola Gay controversy] (1996); Robert Hughes, *Culture of Complaint: The Fraying of America* (1993); Gilles Kepel, *Allah in the West: Islamic Movements in America and Europe* (1997); Philip Lamy, *Millennium Rage: Survivalists, White Supremacists, and the Doomsday Prophecy* (1996); Edward T. Linenthal, *The Unfinished Bombing: Oklahoma City in American Memory* (2001); Edward T. Linenthal and Tom Engelhardt, eds., *History Wars: The Enola Gay and Other Battles for the American Past* (1996); William Martin, *With God on Our Side: The Rise of the Religious Right in America* (1996); Joseph S. Nye et al., *Why People Don't Trust Government* (1997); Robert Putnam, *Bowling Alone: The Collapse and Revival of American Community* (2001); Ralph Reed, *Active Faith: How Christians Are Changing the Soul of American Politics* (1996); Robert J. Samuelson, *The Good Life and Its Discontents: The American Dream in an Age of Entitlement, 1945–1995* (1995); James D. Tabor and Eugene V. Gallagher, *Why Waco? Cults and the Battle for Religious Freedom in America* (1995); Justin Watson, *The Christian Coalition: Dreams of Restoration, Demands for Recognition* (1997).

CHAPTER

16

A Sea of Troubles, Glimmers of Promise, as a New Century Dawns

As Americans celebrated New Year's Eve 1999, they looked to the new century, and the new millennium, with a mixture of excitement and apprehension. (In fact, neither the new century nor the new millennium would officially begin until January 1, 2001, but most people viewed January 1, 2000, with its satisfying row of zeroes, as the date of the historic transition.)

The apprehension proved well justified, as Americans soon confronted events that ranged from unsettling to catastrophically traumatic. The bitterly contested presidential election of 2000 was finally resolved by a divided Supreme Court, but not without a residue of bitterness. The long boom of the 1990s ended in 2001 as a stock-market collapse ushered in two years of business stagnation, wrenching job losses, and high-profile corporate scandals. Less visible but no less important demographic trends—the aging of the population, continued growth in the South and West fueled in part by immigration from Asia and Latin America, the rise of Hispanic Americans as the nation's largest minority group—were changing America as well. (See the section "A Diverse People: Contemporary Social Trends" in Chapter 15.)

All this paled, however, on September 11, 2001, when a horrendous terrorist attack shocked the nation and brought unprecedented changes at home and in America's role abroad. The date "9/11" soon took its place with December 7, 1941, and other dates marking fateful turning points in American history.

Five Judges Choose a President: The Disputed Election of 2000

As the Clinton presidency dragged to its conclusion amid scandal and acrimony, the 2000 election offered an opportunity for a fresh start. The two parties had been evenly balanced through the 1990s, so most observers assumed that the 2000 outcome would be close. Few imagined how close, however.

The Democrats nominated Clinton's heir apparent, Vice President Al Gore. The son and namesake of a once-prominent Tennessee senator, Gore had grown

479

up in Washington and attended elite schools and Harvard College. Some called him "Prince Albert." As a senator from Tennessee he had supported the Democratic Leadership Council, a group of moderates intent on winning back Democrats who had defected to Ronald Reagan. In the Senate, Gore had supported a strong national defense and a tough U.S. foreign policy. Environmentalists admired his 1992 book *Earth in the Balance.* As vice president, Gore had headed a commission charged with making government leaner and more efficient and had been involved in trade and environmental issues. Apart from some dubious fundraising in the 1996 campaign, he had generally stayed free of scandal. His wife Tipper, author of a book called *Raising PG Kids in an X-Rated Society*, was known for her campaign against sex and violence in pop music.

As his running mate, Gore tapped Senator Joseph Lieberman of Connecticut, who thus became the first Jew to run on a major party ticket. (Barry Goldwater, the 1964 Republican nominee, although of Jewish background, was himself an Episcopalian.) Lieberman, known for his moral rectitude, had sharply criticized Bill Clinton's affair with Monica Lewinsky, and this figured in Gore's decision to add him to the ticket.

On the Republican side, the Bush family with its extensive political network remained powerful, and George W. Bush, the eldest son and namesake of ex-president Bush, announced his candidacy. Fending off a challenge by Senator John McCain of Arizona, Bush won the nomination. He tapped Dick Cheney, secretary of defense in his father's administration, as his vice-presidential running mate.

A graduate of Yale University and Harvard Business School, Bush had a record of business failures and alcohol dependence, but he stopped drinking after a 1986 religious conversion. He later credited his wife Laura, a former school librarian, for his turnaround. In his father's 1988 presidential race he had overseen relations with the religious Right. In 1989 he purchased the Texas Rangers baseball team with a group of wealthy associates. Elected governor of Texas in 1994, he backed efforts to make public education more rigorous and gained national attention by upholding the death sentence of a woman convicted of murder who had become an evangelical Christian.

The environmentalist Green Party nominated consumer activist Ralph Nader, while conservative pundit Pat Buchanan won the nomination of Ross Perot's Reform Party. Seemingly little more than historical footnotes, the candidacies of Nader and Buchanan would prove fateful for the outcome of the race.

Each major candidate had strengths and liabilities. The booming economy helped Gore, as did his reputation for integrity and competence. But voters found him wooden—an impression he combated at the Democratic convention by fervently kissing Tipper. Mindful of the Lewinsky scandal, Gore kept Clinton at arm's length during the campaign. In retrospect, many Democrats criticized Gore for not exploiting Clinton's political charisma more fully.

Bush's major liability was his reputation as a bumbling lightweight who owed his political career to his famous father. Democrats gleefully tabulated his verbal gaffes. (One favorite: "Teach a child to read and he or her will be able to pass a literacy test.") But he seemed sincere, if no oratorical Churchill, and many found him likeable. In oblique allusions to Clinton's impeachment, he promised to restore integrity to the White House. In the TV debates, now a standard feature of presidential campaigns, Gore rattled off names, dates, and facts while Bush spoke in generalities in an easy conversational manner reminiscent of Ronald Reagan.

On Election Day the Republicans retained control of Congress.* The presidential race, however, proved extremely close. Gore received some 540,000 more popular votes, but the Electoral College tally seesawed. The networks declared first Gore and then Bush the winner, finally ruling the outcome too close to call. Several states had contested results, but Florida became the focus of attention. Whoever won Florida's twenty-five electoral votes would be president. For five weeks the battle raged. With fewer than 2,000 votes separating the two candidates, flaws in Florida's balloting process made it nearly impossible to get an accurate count. Some poorly designed ballots misled Gore supporters into voting for Buchanan. Mechanically operated voting machines rejected many ballots because of "dangling chads" or "pregnant chads." (A chad, as Americans quickly learned, is the small tab sliced from a ballot or any piece of paper by a punch.)

As election officials floundered, both parties sent high-powered lawyers to promote their candidate's cause. Lawsuits and counterlawsuits sought to force recounts or prevent recounts. As the controversy raged, Florida's secretary of state, Katherine Harris, a Republican, insisted on observing the deadline for certifying the outcome. Democrats protested that since the Electoral College would not convene until mid-December, ample time remained to resolve the dispute. (When George Bush finally won, some Democrats suggested that he appoint Harris ambassador to the African nation of Chad.) Suspicious Democrats suspected Florida's governor Jeb Bush, George Bush's brother, of maneuvering to help the family cause.

Florida's Supreme Court, composed mostly of Democrats, ruled on November 21 that official certification should await a recount of all disputed ballots. Bush's lawyers appealed to the U.S. Supreme Court, which returned the case for clarification. On November 26, Harris declared Bush the winner in Florida by 537 votes, but the Florida Supreme Court ordered the recount to continue. On December 12, however, the U.S. Supreme Court, by a 5–4 vote, overruled the Florida court's order and, in effect, declared George Bush president.

Although states normally resolve electoral disputes, the Supreme Court had decisively intervened. Four of the five pro-Bush justices had been appointed by Ronald Reagan or the elder George Bush. (The fifth, Chief Justice Rehnquist, was a Nixon appointee.) Democrats cried foul, but Gore urged people to accept the Court's ruling. Bumper stickers soon appeared proclaiming "RE-ELECT GORE IN 2004." Others angrily criticized Ralph Nader. Had he not been on the ballot, most of his 97,488 Florida votes would have gone for Gore, giving him the presidency. The outcome illustrated the classic dilemma of third-party voters, who can, in fact, indirectly help elect the candidate they most oppose. The chaotic struggle also revived calls to abolish the Electoral College and choose presidents by popular vote. But the movement won little support, and the Electoral College remained, with its quirky ability to produce unexpected results.

---

*Fifty Democrats and fifty Republicans won election to the Senate, but in such cases the vice president casts the deciding vote, so Republicans retained control. In May 2001, however, Republican senator James Jeffords, a moderate from Vermont, left the Republican Party, giving the Democrats control of the Senate until the Republicans regained control in the 2002 midterm elections.

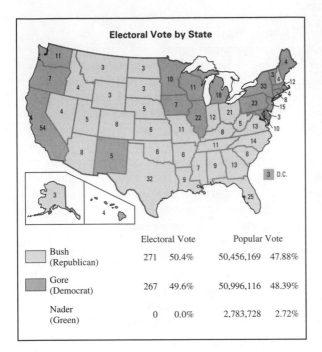

MAP 16.1
Presidential Election of 2000

Assured of the presidency, George Bush quickly named his cabinet, including Colin Powell, a former chair of the Joint Chiefs of Staff, as secretary of state; Donald Rumsfeld, a veteran of various posts in past Republican administrations, as secretary of defense; and John Ashcroft, an archconservative who had just lost a Senate race in Missouri, as attorney general. All three would soon face daunting challenges.

September 11, 2001:
A Day That Changed America

Monday, September 10, 2001, seemed a day much like any other. Newspapers reported a slowing economy. On Geraldo Rivera's TV show, the talk was of a congressman who had admitted an affair with a young intern who later disappeared. The *Stanford University Cardinal* provided information on an upcoming women's volleyball game with Washington State. A *New York Times* story discussed schoolsucks.com, a website offering free term papers and book reports. At Big Sky, Montana, a Federal Emergency Management Agency team was meeting with emergency-response officials from all fifty states. One of the topics: preparation for terrorist attacks.

In the space of a few minutes the following morning, September 11, all else was swept aside by the most appalling acts of terrorism ever to strike the nation. At

8:48 A.M., a Boeing 767 loaded with fuel and bound for Los Angeles from Boston's Logan Airport slammed into the north tower of New York's World Trade Center. Eighteen minutes later, a United Airlines plane, also en route to Los Angeles from Logan, struck the south tower. As flames engulfed both structures, police and fire-fighters rushed into the buildings, intent on rescuing those trapped inside. But as television viewers and those on the scene watched in horror, both towers soon collapsed, entombing those inside in a smoldering pyre.

Meanwhile, a third hijacked commercial aircraft had crashed into the Pentagon, and a fourth went down in western Pennsylvania, its hijackers most likely foiled by courageous passengers as they tried to reach another target, perhaps the Capitol or the White House. Government buildings, including the White House, were hastily evacuated. All civilian flights were grounded as military aircraft roamed the skies. "The world just changed today," said Democratic presidential adviser James Carville, reached by a reporter on his cell phone as he drove his children home from school. "Everything . . . is going to be different tomorrow."

As the nation reeled in horror, people struggled to comprehend the human toll. The final tally, though lower than initially feared, was appalling. In addition to 19 hijackers, 246 passengers and crew died on the four planes. On the ground, 125

September 11, 2001. Onlookers react in horror as an inferno envelops the World Trade Center towers following a terrorist attack by means of hijacked airplanes. *(Ernesto Mora, AP/Wide World Photos)*

perished at the Pentagon, and some 2,600 at the World Trade Center, including 343 New York City firefighters. For days, the nation mourned the dead in public and private ceremonies. At a memorial service in New York, actor James Earl Jones said: "Our spirit is unbroken. . . . Today we reaffirm our faith in the essential dignity of every individual. What we share as Americans and as human beings is far greater than what divides us."

Expressions of sympathy poured in from around the world. *Le Monde,* France's leading newspaper, declared: *"Nous sommes tous Americains"* ("We are all Americans"). Said German chancellor Gerhard Schroeder: "This is not only an attack on the United States, but an attack on the civilized world."

Political differences faded in a wave of national solidarity. Older Americans recalled the 1941 Japanese attack on Pearl Harbor as a comparable moment of national unity in the face of crisis. Stores sold out their stock of U.S. flags. Citizens displayed flag-becked banners and bumper stickers proclaiming "United We Stand" or "These Colors Don't Run."

As the hijackers' Middle Eastern identity became known, isolated incidents of anti-Arab prejudice occurred. Some Muslim mosques were attacked and a few of America's 5 to 6 million Muslims were harassed. In Phoenix, an elderly Indian Sikh was shot and killed, evidently because he was wearing a turban. Some religious leaders fanned the flames of prejudice. The Reverend Franklin Graham, Billy Graham's son, denounced Islam as "an evil religion." However, President Bush, insisting that the enemy was not Islam, but terrorism, met with U.S. Muslim leaders. The televangelist Jerry Falwell stirred controversy by describing the attacks as a manifestation of God's anger with feminists, gays, abortion-rights defenders, the American Civil Liberties Union, and People for the American Way.

A New Kind of War: Mobilizing Against Terrorism

Addressing the nation on September 12, a somber President Bush pledged that those behind the attacks would be punished. "We will make no distinction between the terrorists who committed these acts and those who harbored them," he said. At a prayer breakfast, Bush laid out a breathtaking agenda for the nation: "Our responsibility to history is already clear: to answer these attacks and rid the world of evil." Addressing a joint session of Congress on September 20, the president identified the nineteen hijackers as members of Al Qaeda, a shadowy association of anti-Western Muslim fundamentalists led by Osama bin Laden, an expatriate Saudi Arabian based in Afghanistan. He enjoyed the protection of the Taliban, a Pakistan-based Islamic political movement that had ruled Afghanistan since 1996. Proclaiming an open-ended war on terrorism, Bush announced two major goals: tightening domestic security and eradicating terrorist networks worldwide. Congress authorized the use of "all necessary and proper force" to combat terrorism. Bush's approval ratings, which had been hovering at around 50 percent, surged to a high of 90 percent in October 2001.

September 11 did, indeed, transform the domestic landscape, as James Carville had predicted. Nearly a thousand recent immigrants, mostly Middle Easterners, were detained and questioned. The national jitters worsened in late September when letters infected with deadly anthrax bacteria were mailed to government leaders and journalists. Five persons died, mostly postal workers. The Hart Senate Office Building and a mail-distribution center in Washington were closed for decontamination. Investigators failed to find the perpetrator but suspected a domestic source, perhaps someone involved with U.S. biological weapons research, rather than Al Qaeda.

In October 2001, with 9/11 memories still vivid, Congress rushed through the administration's USA-PATRIOT Act (an acronym for "Uniting and Strengthening America by Providing Appropriate Tools Required to Intercept and Obstruct Terrorism"). This omnibus measure had many provisions. It authorized the Justice Department to pursue suspected terrorists by secretly tapping telephone calls, eavesdropping on conversations between prisoners and their attorneys, seizing financial and medical records, and monitoring suspects' e-mail. The FBI was authorized to seize library records, including patrons' computer use. Attorney General Ashcroft vowed to utilize these new powers to the fullest.

In May 2002, the FBI arrested young José Padilla, a U.S. citizen and former Florida gang member, as he arrived at Chicago's O'Hare Airport, claiming that he had conspired with Al Qaeda to commit terrorist acts. Designated an "enemy combatant" by President Bush, Padilla was held in a navy brig in Charleston, South Carolina, with no access to a lawyer. Also held in Charleston was Yaser Esam Hamdi, a U.S.-born Saudi American seized in Afghanistan. By 2004 some 660 prisoners, mostly men of Middle Eastern origin, including many Afghans and Pakistanis, were imprisoned at Guantánamo, the U.S. base in Cuba, without legal representation. The authorities refused even to release their names, on the grounds that this could aid Al Qaeda. The president's authority as commander in chief, claimed Attorney General Ashcroft, granted him unlimited power in the treatment of these prisoners.

Soon after 9/11, 47 percent of Americans told pollsters that they were willing to sacrifice civil liberties to make America safer. But by August 2002, as the implications of the government's actions sank in, the figure fell to 29 percent. Richard Falk, a Princeton professor of international law, warned of "an unprecedented assault on our liberties as a free people since September 11." Supreme Court justice Stephen Breyer told the New York Bar Association early in 2003: "The Constitution always matters, perhaps particularly so in times of emergency." That July, Congress repealed a key PATRIOT Act provision that permitted authorities to obtain secret search warrants without informing the target of the search. "We moved too far, too fast," commented Idaho Republican congressman C. L. Otter. Over 150 communities passed resolutions criticizing the PATRIOT Act's "Big Brother" aspects. The International Red Cross and Amnesty International deplored the indefinite detention of prisoners at Guantánamo. Ashcroft fought back. Any weakening of the PATRIOT Act "would senselessly imperil American lives," he warned. Critics of the law, he implied, condoned terrorism.

In December 2003, a federal appeals court in New York ruled that José Padilla's continued imprisonment without legal counsel and with no charges filed against him violated his Fifth Amendment rights to due process. At the same time, a California appeals court, in a case involving prisoners at Guantánamo, ordered that they either be released or turned over to the civil courts for trial. Giving no ground, the Justice Department appealed these rulings to the Supreme Court.

In a stinging rebuke to Ashcroft's position, the Supreme Court in June 2004 ruled that the Guantánamo prisoners, and U.S. citizens such as Hamdi designated as "enemy combatants," must be granted access to the courts to present their case. "[A] state of war is not a blank check for the president," the majority held; the "essential constitutional promises [of due process] may not be eroded."*

In another post-9/11 antiterrorism measure, President Bush created an Office of Homeland Security under former Pennsylvania governor Tom Ridge. In November 2002, Congress upgraded Ridge's office to departmental rank. This megadepartment merged 22 government agencies that collectively had 170,000 employees. Its activities included a color-code system to indicate the level of security risk. In December 2003, Ridge raised the alert level from yellow to orange, the next-to-highest level of danger. Additional FBI agents were mobilized; airport security was tightened; and armed guards patrolled bridges, national monuments, power plants, and government buildings.

The alert system and other Homeland Security advisories could be confusing. Even with the code level at orange, President Bush urged Americans to continue all planned holiday activities, including mall shopping and air travel, and simply "be alert." Homeland Security's recommendation that families stock bottled water, canned food, and duct tape to seal windows seemed eerily reminiscent of widely discredited Cold War civil-defense advice on how to survive nuclear war.

The new security measures hit air travelers hard. The Transportation Safety Administration increased the number of security personnel, tightened job requirements for these individuals, and imposed strict procedures for checking passengers and their baggage. As passengers endured long lines at security checkpoints, even such seemingly innocuous objects as nail clippers were confiscated. Armed U.S. marshals flew on some flights, and in 2003 immigration officers began photographing and fingerprinting passengers arriving from abroad.

Although Americans understood the need for heightened security, many found the Bush administration's cavalier view of the Bill of Rights disturbing. Some accused the administration of exploiting public fears to sweep aside constitutional protections. Even conservative Republicans, historically suspicious of big government, raised questions. In December 2002, under pressure from the families of 9/11 victims, President Bush appointed a ten-member bipartisan commission to investigate circumstances surrounding the attacks.

Like the domestic response to 9/11, the international component of the "war on terrorism" enjoyed broad initial support but stirred controversy as time went by. The administration's military response first focused on Osama bin Laden's Al Qaeda organization ("the Base," in Arabic) centered in Afghanistan. Bin Laden, the son of a wealthy Saudi Arabian contractor, had fallen under the influence of radical Islamists who hated the "infidel" West, and especially the United States, for violating Islamic law by encouraging alcohol consumption, a sexually permissive

---

*On procedural grounds, the justices did not rule on Padilla's appeal, which had been filed in New York, holding that it should be refiled in South Carolina. But the court's ruling in Hamdi's case, guaranteeing the right of a trial, clearly applied to Padilla as well.

popular culture, freedom for women, and so forth. Bin Laden's message of hate and his catalog of grievances resonated powerfully among the poor of the Arab street, some of whom embraced his call for *jihad*, or holy war. Although many Muslim leaders and theologians denounced bin Laden for perverting Muslim principles with his readiness to use terrorism, a core of fanatical followers and a network of locally based groups loosely affiliated with Al Qaeda looked to him for inspiration. Bin Laden was implicated in the 1998 bombing of U.S. embassies in Kenya and Tanzania. Indeed, after these attacks he had appeared on the FBI's Most Wanted list and President Clinton had ordered the bombing of Al Qaeda camps in Afghanistan.

After 9/11, the campaign against bin Laden escalated dramatically. Beginning on October 7, U.S. and British planes bombed Al Qaeda strongholds in Afghanistan and Taliban-held buildings in Kabul, the nation's capital. Upon seizing power, the Taliban had imposed a repressive version of *Sharia* (Islamic law), forcing women to be completely veiled and denying education to girls, and had incurred world censure for dynamiting ancient Buddhist stone carvings. In the 1980s, when Soviet troops had invaded Afghanistan, the United States had supplied arms to the Taliban and even to Osama bin Laden, to help them drive out the Soviet invaders. But now all was different, and the Taliban and Al Qaeda had become the enemy. In cooperation with the Northern Alliance, a loose coalition of anti Taliban forces inside Afghanistan, some one thousand U.S. troops, with small units from other nations, killed or captured many Al Qaeda fighters and overran the major centers of Al Qaeda power. But many Al Qaeda fighters and Taliban supporters escaped, hiding in the mountains or slipping across the border into Pakistan.

Ordinary Afghanis suffered heavily. The U.S. command boasted of its sophisticated targeting, but hundreds of villagers were killed or wounded in misplaced bombing attacks. When villagers at a wedding party fired shots in the air, a traditional form of celebration, U.S. planes dropped seven 2,000-pound bombs on them, killing at least thirty.

After expelling the rag-tag Taliban regime from Kabul in mid-November, U.S. officials convened a grand assembly, or *loya jirga,* of Afghan leaders to form a new government. This conclave chose an interim president, Harmid Karzai, who gained the blessing of Afghanistan's eighty-seven-year-old former king, Mohammad Hahir Shah, who had returned after twenty-nine years of exile in Italy. Bitter disputes erupted between Afghanistan's two major ethnic groups, the majority Pashtuns, to which President Karzai belonged, and the Tajiks, centered in the north. But early in 2004, thanks to the negotiating skills of a UN envoy, a seventy-year-old Algerian diplomat, the *loya jirga* adopted a constitution. While proclaiming Afghanistan an Islamic republic, it provided for democratic elections and a division of powers among a president, a legislature, and an independent judiciary. It also expanded women's rights and bridged Pashtun and Tajik differences over language and other issues.

Afghanistan remained turbulent and dangerous, however, underscoring the challenges facing Bush's "war on terrorism," not to mention his pledge to eradicate "evil" from the world. Al Qaeda insurgents and Taliban remnants attacked U.S. forces, spread disruption, and targeted government officials. Regional warlords and

IN PERSPECTIVE

Balancing Freedom and Security

The dilemma of tightening security while safeguarding civil liberties was not a new one. In fact, the nation has confronted this issue at many times of crisis in the past. In 1798, as the ruling Federalist Party worried about a possible war with France, the opposition of Jeffersonian Republicans, and the loyalty of pro-French Irish immigrants, Congress passed the Alien and Sedition Acts. Under these laws, any alien could be expelled, without a hearing, if found to be "dangerous to the peace and safety" of the nation. The especially draconian Sedition Act made it a crime to defame the government or the president. Jeffersonian critics of President John Adams soon found themselves hauled before Federalist judges. Thomas Jefferson and James Madison thought these laws so dangerous that they drafted resolutions, adopted by the legislatures of Virginia and Kentucky, denouncing them for disrupting the constitutional balance of powers between the branches of government and for violating the free-speech guarantees of the Bill of Rights.

In 1836, as abolitionists deluged Congress with antislavery petitions, a committee headed by South Carolina congressman Henry Pinckney offered a resolution declaring that all such resolutions would "be laid on the table," that is, ignored. Congress adopted Pinckney's "gag resolution" by a vote of 117–68. One of the dissenters, former president John Quincy Adams, now a Massachusetts congressman, denounced the resolution as "a direct violation of the Constitution . . . , of the rules of this House, and of the rights of my constituents."

During the Civil War, as President Lincoln faced secessionist sentiment in the North, he supported measures barring all "treasonable correspondence" from the mails. Lincoln also suspended the writ of habeas corpus (guaranteeing all prisoners the right to a trial) in border states such as Maryland and Missouri, where secessionist feeling ran strong. The goal of saving the Union, Lincoln argued, justified jailing secessionists without a trial.

During World War I, when superpatriotism gripped the nation and suspicion fixed on German Americans, socialists, and pacifists, opposition to the war became a crime. Under the Espionage and Sedition Acts of 1917–18 and similar state laws, authorities banned socialist and antiwar publications and arrested individuals for speaking out against the war. Among those imprisoned was the socialist leader Eugene V. Debs, who spent two years in a federal penitentiary before President Warren Harding pardoned him in 1921. (In a dramatic protest gesture, nearly 920,000 people voted for Debs for president in 1920.)

Another citizen who ran afoul of this wartime legislation was the socialist leader Charles Schenck, convicted for mailing a pamphlet opposing the draft. Schenck appealed to the Supreme Court (*Schenck* v. *United States,* 1919) on First Amendment grounds. The High Court rejected Schenck's appeal, however, ruling that his pamphlet had posed a "clear and present danger" to the nation in wartime.

In 1919, amidst a postwar Red Scare, hundreds of suspected communists and radicals were arrested. The New York legislature expelled seven socialist members, and Congress refused to seat the socialist Victor Berger, who had been duly elected by the voters of Milwaukee. On January 2, 1920, in a series of nationwide raids coordinated by Attorney General A. Mitchell Palmer and the young J. Edgar Hoover, later head of the Federal Bureau of Investigation, more than four thousand alleged radicals, both aliens and U.S. citizens, were rounded up and imprisoned. Organizational headquarters and private houses were broken into without search warrants and papers and records seized. Many of the arrestees eventually faced deportation.

As we saw in Chapter 1, the worst violation of civil liberties in the name of national security came in 1942, at the outset of World War II, when some 120,000 Japanese Americans, most of them native-born citizens, were arrested by the U.S. Army and shipped to internment camps in remote parts of the West. This action, authorized by President Franklin D. Roosevelt, was upheld by the Supreme Court in *Korematsu* v. *United States* (1944) on national-security grounds. Forty years later, in 1982, a congressional committee concluded that the internments had resulted from "race prejudice, war hysteria, and a failure of political leadership." In 1988, some 62,000 surviving internees received an official apology and a payment of $20,000 each.

During the early Cold War, the communist threat became the rationale for restricting First Amendment freedoms. The House Un-American Activities Committee and Senator Joseph McCarthy (shown in photo with chief counsel Roy Cohn) investigated alleged communists and radicals in Hollywood, higher education, and even the clergy. In *Dennis* v. *United States* (1951), the Supreme Court upheld the conviction and imprisonment of U.S. Communist Party leaders, even though no specific act of violence or espionage was charged against them, solely because of the ideas they espoused. In a by-now familiar refrain, the Court insisted that in times of danger national security trumped the Bill of Rights.

In short, as Justice Breyer observed in 2003, civil liberties are most at risk in times of war and stress. In the fearful aftermath of 9/11, Americans again confronted the challenge of preserving U.S. security while safeguarding the freedoms that make the nation worth preserving.

their heavily armed forces controlled most of the country. Early in 2004, when an explosion in the Taliban stronghold of Kandahar killed thirteen children and two adults, a pro-Taliban group apologized: their actual target had been a nearby U.S. barracks. The United States struck back, sometimes with tragic results. When U.S. jets strafed two buildings thought to house Al Qaeda and Taliban leaders, they succeeded only in killing fifteen children playing nearby. Promised international aid for long-term development projects such as better roads often failed to materialize. And Osama bin Laden remained at large, periodically issuing anti-American diatribes broadcast throughout the Arab world. Whether Afghanistan would evolve into a modern, democratic, and peaceful state, as Washington planners hoped, or sink into chaos remained unclear.

War in Iraq

The assault on Al Qaeda in Afghanistan enjoyed broad international support as an appropriate response to the 9/11 attacks. The next phase of Bush's antiterrorism campaign proved more controversial, however. In his January 2002 State of the Union address, Bush pinpointed three nations as an "Axis of Evil": Iraq, Iran, and North Korea. The phrase, contributed by a young White House speechwriter, David Frum, evoked World War II, when Germany, Japan, and Italy were "the Axis Powers." (When Frum's wife boasted in e-mail messages to friends that her husband had coined the phrase, the White House suggested that he apply his creative talents elsewhere.)

Of this triumvirate of evil, Iraq topped the list. The United States had had a complex relationship with Iraq since Saddam Hussein seized power in 1979. In the 1980s, during a long war between Iraq and Iran, Washington had aided Iraq. In 1983, Donald Rumsfeld, representing President Reagan, had met with Saddam and shaken hands with him. With the Iran hostage crisis fresh in memory and the violently anti-American Ayatollah Khomeini ruling Iran, this policy had made sense. Further, Iraq had vast oil reserves. So the Reagan administration had held its nose and aided Saddam, despite the well-documented brutality of his regime.

In 1990, however, when Saddam invaded neighboring Kuwait and seized its oilfields, the first President Bush had mobilized a multinational force to expel the invaders. But he had rejected the advice of those who wished to invade Iraq itself and overthrow Saddam. Such an action, he had concluded, could end in a long occupation with unknown consequences. But key Republicans remained convinced that the elder Bush had missed an opportunity to unseat Saddam. With George W. Bush's election, they saw their opportunity. This view was particularly strong among neoconservatives: former liberals who had become increasingly hawkish and right wing. Prominent advocates of overthrowing Saddam included Vice President Cheney; Defense Secretary Rumsfeld and his deputy Paul Wolfowitz; Richard Perle, chair of the Defense Policy Board; Kenneth Adelman, an official in the Ford and Reagan administrations; and others throughout the administration.

These officials offered a seductive vision of America's post–Cold War mission, rooted in what had once been called the nation's "manifest destiny." As the sole remaining superpower, they believed, the United States should mobilize that power to promote democracy, modernity, and free-enterprise capitalism worldwide. And where better to begin than in the Middle East? Replacing Saddam's backward and repressive regime with a modern, progressive, and democratic government, they argued, could transform the region. In a kind of reverse domino effect, reminiscent of the arguments for the Vietnam War, they predicted that decisive action in Iraq would lead to reform in Saudi Arabia, Syria, Iran, and the region's various autocratic sheikdoms and principalities. Further, they hoped, a decisive display of U.S. power would make Arab leaders more receptive to U.S. proposals for resolving the conflict between Israel and the Palestinians. Post-Saddam business opportunities in Iraq and assured access to Iraqi oil added a hard-nosed practical component to the case for getting rid of Saddam.

This vision was essentially a unilateralist one. The support of the UN and America's allies would be welcome, but was not crucial. The important thing was for America to act decisively and use its vast power for good, while simultaneously promoting U.S. strategic and economic interests. In a 2004 "tell all" book, a disgruntled former insider, Bush's first treasury secretary, Paul O'Neill, claimed that active planning for an Iraq invasion began as soon as Bush took office in January 2001. A top government antiterrorism expert, Richard A. Clarke, made the same point in his 2004 book *Against All Enemies*. The 9/11 attacks provided an occasion to incorporate this goal within the larger war on terrorism.

Soon the nation faced a barrage of administration propaganda insisting that Saddam had played a key role in the 9/11 attacks and that he possessed weapons of mass destruction (WMDs) that posed an imminent danger to the United States. Both claims proved highly controversial. Osama bin Laden hated Saddam's secularist regime, and no credible evidence linked Saddam to 9/11. As for WMDs, Saddam had earlier shown an interest in chemical, biological, and even nuclear weapons and a willingness to use them. A 1988 chemical attack on Halabja, a center of Kurdish resistance in northern Iraq, had killed at least five thousand people. But scant evidence existed for a current WMD programs. After Saddam's defeat in the 1991 Persian Gulf War, a UN Security Council resolution required Iraq to end all WMD programs and to admit UN weapons inspectors. To promote compliance, the UN also slapped tough import-export sanctions on Iraq. Despite Saddam's disruptive efforts, UN inspections continued though 1998. Inspectors visited many sites and destroyed stocks of biological and chemical weapons. Iraqi compliance remained erratic, as Iraqi officials demanded modifications in the trade sanctions in return for Iraq's cooperation, but the inspectors generally concluded that Iraq's WMD programs had ended. The UN called for even more rigorous international inspections, but the Bush administration rejected this approach, arguing that Saddam could too easily conceal his WMD stockpiles and programs.

Throughout 2002, Bush, Cheney, Rumsfeld, National Security Adviser Condoleezza Rice, and other leading Republicans focused on Iraq. Citing intelligence data, Bush asserted unequivocally that Iraq possessed chemical and biological weapons and would soon have nuclear weapons. Further, the war advocates insisted, Iraqis would welcome American troops. "[D]emolishing Hussein's military power and liberating Iraq would be a cakewalk," wrote Kenneth Adelman in the *Washington Post* in February 2002, and "would constitute the greatest victory in America's war on terrorism." A few months later, speaking at West Point, Bush embraced the doctrine of preemptive war, generally considered a violation of international law except when an imminent attack by a foreign power is absolutely certain. In an age of terrorism and WMDs, he said, America must be prepared to strike first against nations that posed a threat.

As a U.S. attack on Iraq became more likely, world opposition increased. NATO allies France and Germany expressed strong opposition. So did China, Russia, and, closer to home, Canada and Mexico. As the post-9/11 outpouring of goodwill evaporated, hostile editorials appeared in the world press; polls showed a growing distrust of the Bush administration; and massive antiwar marches were held in Rome, Paris, London, and other capitals.

In a belated appeal for international support, Bush addressed the UN in September 2002. Describing Saddam's foot-dragging on weapons inspection despite UN resolutions, he exhorted the world body to back its demands with action. "Are Security Council resolutions to be honored and enforced," he asked rhetorically, "or cast aside without consequences?" UN Secretary General Kofi Annan summed up member states' reservations about a war to overthrow Saddam: "The question is the morning after. What sort of Iraq do we wake up to after the bombing?" Four days after Bush's UN appearance, Saddam invited UN inspectors to return "without condition." They did so, and reported better cooperation. The Bush administration dismissed this as last-minute propaganda, however, and war plans went forward. Kofi Annan pled with Washington not to act on its own: "If . . . nations discount the legitimacy provided by the UN, and . . . use force unilaterally and pre-emptively, the world will become even more dangerous."

Some nations backed the American position, including Spain, Italy, Poland, and Great Britain. British prime minister Tony Blair supported the United States so enthusiastically, despite domestic opposition, that cartoonists portrayed him as Bush's lap dog. The administration welcomed this makeshift alliance as "the coalition of the willing." Donald Rumsfeld, noting Eastern European support for the U.S. position, contemptuously dismissed France and Germany as "old Europe."

Bush's move toward war proved equally divisive at home. Launching a preemptive war against a nation that had not attacked America, critics argued, would violate international law and long-standing U.S. policy. The administration's claims that Saddam had helped plan 9/11 and that he possessed an arsenal of WMDs faced increasing scrutiny. Still others deplored the administration's go-it-alone spirit. To invade Iraq without strong international support verged on the reckless, they charged. In a series of widely quoted Senate speeches, West Virginia's venerable Democratic senator Richard Byrd accused the administration of pursuing a vendetta against Saddam Hussein, with unknown long-term consequences, under the guise of conducting a war on terrorism.

Nevertheless, on October 10–11, 2002, as midterm elections approached, Congress authorized Bush to use U.S. armed forces "as he determines to be necessary and appropriate" in response to "the continuing threat" posed by Iraq. Essentially a blank check for war, this resolution passed the House by 296–133 and the Senate by 77–23. Democratic presidential hopefuls John Kerry, Joseph Lieberman, John Edwards, and Richard Gephardt all voted for it. (So did a possible future candidate, Senator Hillary Clinton of New York.) As with the 1964 Gulf of Tonkin Resolution, under which Lyndon Johnson waged the Vietnam War, most legislators hesitated to oppose the president on a national-security matter, whatever their private reservations. Secretary of State Powell, addressing the UN in early February 2003, again insisted that Iraq possessed WMDs, but few minds were changed. Domestically, public opinion was divided, with some 60 percent of voters supporting Bush's position and 40 percent opposing it.

Despite back-channel Iraqi offers to admit U.S. troops and weapons specialists to confirm that Iraq had no WMDs, war planning went forward. Indeed, in late 2002 and early 2003, in preparation for the ground war, U.S. planes had dropped over six hundred bombs on 391 Iraqi military command centers, communications complexes, and radar installations. (The official rationale for these attacks was that they were a response to alleged Iraqi violations of a "no-fly zone" in southern Iraq imposed by the UN after the Persian Gulf War.)

After the long buildup, the actual war seemed almost anticlimactic. In a night raid on March 19, 2003, U.S. bombers hit a Baghdad building where senior Iraqi officials, possibly including Saddam Hussein, were meeting. If Saddam was present, he escaped. The ground war began the next day with more bombing and a joint U.S.-British invasion of Iraq from the south. U.S. forces totaled some 130,000, including regular troops and Special Operations units, plus a British contingent of about 10,000. (Some thirty other nations eventually sent small numbers of soldiers, totaling some 14,000, for occupation duty.) In this high-tech conflict, laser range-finders guided missiles to distant targets and analysts 6,300 miles away at Langley Air Force Base in Virginia directed operations on the basis of live video images transmitted from reconnaissance aircraft.

The war's combat phase unfolded with deceptive speed. While the British secured Basra, an oil-production center, the Americans advanced on Baghdad, Iraq's capital, which fell on April 5. In ensuing weeks GIs occupied government buildings and Saddam's ostentatious palaces, pulled down a giant statue of the dictator, publicized mass burial sites testifying to the regime's brutality, and seized military leaders and government officials. Saddam himself initially eluded capture. Although opposition had been light, this stage of the war cost the lives of 103 Americans.

In the war's murkiest episode, Iraqi troops ambushed a U.S. convoy that became lost near the town of Nasiriya on March 23. Iraqi troops killed several members of the convoy, including Pvt. Lori Piestewa, a Hopi Indian and a single mother of two, the first Native American woman to die in combat in a U.S. war. Pvt. Jessica Lynch of Palestine, West Virginia, who suffered broken legs and head wounds when her vehicle overturned, was taken by local Iraqis to a nearby hospital. Eight days later, a U.S. Special Forces team, accompanied by military photographers, staged a nighttime raid on the hospital and evacuated Lynch by helicopter. Soon gripping scenes of the operation dominated TV screens and newsmagazine covers. The Pentagon hailed the daring rescue and Lynch's valiant, gunblazing heroism in resisting capture.

The heartwarming story soon unraveled, however. When she eventually met the press, Lynch insisted that she had never fired her weapon. An Iraqi physician at the hospital reported that after treating Lynch he had tried to arrange for her safe return days before the "daring" rescue, only to be rebuffed. Lynch was annoyed at the way the military and the media had hyped her story. "They used me . . . ," she told a TV interviewer. "It's wrong." A BBC investigative team called

the episode "one of the most stunning pieces of news management ever con-
ceived." Some recalled the 1998 movie *Wag the Dog,* in which the government
manufactures heart-tugging stories to justify an unpopular war. Others remembered the 1944 Preston Sturges film *Hail the Conquering Hero,* in which a Marine
Corps reject is idolized for his supposed military exploits. Meanwhile, Lynch
signed a $1 million book contract with Knopf, and the Iraqi physician, granted asy-
lum in the United States, signed a $300,000 book deal with HarperCollins.

On May 1, President Bush, wearing a bulky Air Force flight suit, flew to the
aircraft carrier *Abraham Lincoln* as it returned to San Diego from war duty. Before a
large banner proclaiming "Mission Accomplished," Bush declared that the war's
major combat phase was over. "In the battle of Iraq," he said, "the United States
and our Allies have prevailed." Unfortunately, the battle of Iraq had only begun.

Reconstruction and Resistance in Iraq, Uneasiness at Home

With Saddam overthrown, the United States turned to what the war's advocates
had pictured as an easy task: setting up a government and restoring Iraq's infrastructure—including the oil industry—after years of war, repression, and neglect.
Bush appointed L. Paul Bremer III, a U.S. diplomat and crisis-management specialist, to oversee these goals. Neither proved easy.

Bremer set up a Governing Council representing Iraq's major ethnoreligious
groups: the Shiite Muslim majority in southern Iraq, the Sunni Muslims in the
north (the core supporters of Saddam's Baathist Party), and the fiercely independent Kurds in the northeast. The Kurds had enjoyed autonomy since the Persian
Gulf War, shielded from Saddam by a "no-fly zone" enforced by U.S. and British
air power. Each group had firm ideas about Iraq's future. The majority Shiites demanded general elections, which would maximize their power. The Sunnis favored
a legislature chosen by provincial caucuses, which would increase their influence.
The Kurds sought continued autonomy and even independence—a prospect that
alarmed neighboring Turkey and Iran with their large Kurdish minorities. Apart
from abolishing the national holiday marking Saddam's birthday, the Governing
Council initially expended most of its energy on internal bickering.

Lucrative reconstruction contracts went to U.S. corporations to rebuild Iraq's
antiquated oil industry and restore electricity, telephones, sewers, health care, mail
delivery, and other vital services. Some of these corporations, such as Halliburton
and Bechtel, had strong Republican ties. Vice President Cheney had formerly
headed Halliburton; George P. Shultz, Ronald Reagan's secretary of state, was a
Bechtel director. Executives and employees of the seventy companies awarded reconstruction contracts had collectively contributed $500,000 to the Bush campaign.

In September 2003, Bush asked Congress for $87 billion to cover reconstruction
and occupation costs in Iraq. Many legislators, including conservative Republicans,
gasped at the total. Wisconsin congressman David Obey calculated that the cost of
upgrading Iraq's electrical grid alone would average $225 for every Iraqi, whereas
proposed spending on a much-needed upgrade of the U.S. electrical system averaged 71 cents per person. And $87 billion was only a down payment; the total cost

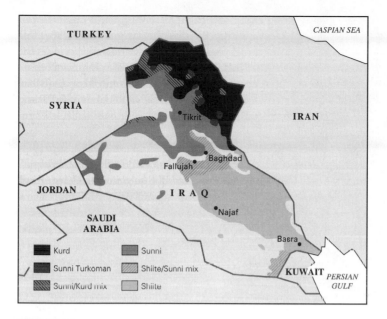

MAP 16.2
Iraq, with Major Ethnic Groups and Key Cities

of reconstructing Iraq, Paul Bremer warned, was "almost impossible to exaggerate." Most of these billions, of course, would go to U.S. corporations holding reconstruction contracts. Some argued that the appropriation should be a loan against Iraq's future oil earnings, but the administration said no, and Congress voted the requested funds. Economists warned of a deepening federal deficit, already about $450 billion in 2003. Bush urged other nations to share the reconstruction costs, but most declined unless the United Nations were involved. The administration's effort to persuade Iraq's major creditors, including France, Germany, and Russia, to cancel or stretch out Iraq's $350 billion in foreign debt was undercut when the Pentagon announced that only nations that had supported the war could bid on reconstruction contracts.

Ambassador Bremer boasted of steady progress on reconstruction, and conditions did improve for many Iraqis. But continuing violence undermined the effort. Vice President Cheney and others had predicted that Iraqis would greet the Americans with open arms, and indeed, apart from Saddam's hard-core supporters, most Iraqis did welcome his overthrow. Quickly, however, U.S. and coalition forces faced growing hostility, especially in the so-called Sunni Triangle north of Baghdad. Insurgents targeted GIs on patrol, mined roads traveled by military vehicles, and shot down helicopters. Through August 2004, more than 900 American soldiers had died in Iraq-related operations, most of them after Bush declared major hostilities ended on May 1, 2003. In the same period nine helicopters had been shot down, with a loss of forty-nine lives. More than five thousand were injured, many seriously. Each of these casualties spread shock waves of loss and grief at

Baghdad, December 2003. An abaya-clad Iraqi woman with two small children passes a patrol of U.S. soldiers and members of the U.S.-sponsored Iraqi Civil Defense Corps. *(Mario Tama/Getty Images)*

home. Said Birgit Smith of Holiday, Florida, whose husband Paul was among the dead: "I'm living . . . like a zombie. I'm hoping I'll wake up one day and it won't be true." British and Italian troops suffered casualties as well.

Insurgents bombed railroads, oil facilities, and even busy streets to disrupt the nation-building process. An Iraqi woman on the Governing Council was assassinated. The UN's Baghdad headquarters was bombed in August 2003, killing seventeen, including the UN's top envoy in Iraq, and wounding scores. Kofi Annan, citing security risks, withdrew the UN mission. Soon after, a revered Shiite mosque in Najaf was bombed, killing 125, including a leading cleric whose brother sat on the Governing Council. In addition to the insurgency, ordinary criminals flourished amid the general breakdown of law and order. In the chaos following Baghdad's fall, looters had ransacked Iraq's national museum and national library, stealing priceless treasures.

As conditions worsened, President Bush's approval ratings fell, editorial criticism mounted, and home-front grumbling increased ominously. Summoning Bremer to Washington in November 2003, Bush instructed him to turn over power to an Iraqi government by June 30, 2004. (Further seeking to counter the downbeat mood, Bush made a surprise Thanksgiving visit to Baghdad and was photographed serving a turkey to the troops.) Prospects for meeting Bush's accelerated timetable for transferring power to an Iraqi government darkened as disputes among the country's disparate groups intensified. In January 2004 Iraq's Shiite leader, Grand Ayatollah Ali al-Sistani, rejected the Governing Council's proposal for regional caucuses and insisted on general elections.

The Bush Administration and the United Nations. After invading Iraq in 2003 without Security Council authorization, the Bush administration sought the help of the United Nations in 2004 to facilitate the transfer of power to an Iraqi authority and arrange national elections. *(By permission of Mike Luckovich and Creators Syndicate, Inc.)*

Having hitherto bypassed the United Nations, the Bush administration now asked for UN help in establishing a workable government in postwar Iraq. Supporters of the world organization cautiously welcomed this development. Said David Malone, a former Canadian ambassador to the UN: "The positive feature is that the U.S. belatedly, but importantly, is realizing what its friends have told it all along—that the UN can be useful in these situations."

The administration's justifications for the war came in for heavy scrutiny as U.S. casualties mounted. A UN investigation found no links between Saddam Hussein and Al Qaeda. As for WMDs, the administration sent 1,200 U.S. inspectors into Iraq to search for them. In October 2003, the team's leader, David Kay, told the Senate Intelligence Committee that no WMDs had been discovered. Kay's report made clear, said the *New York Times,* that "whatever threat Iraq posed did not require an immediate invasion without international support." Democrats accused the White House of manipulating intelligence data. Senator Carl Levin of Michigan criticized the "questionable statements and exaggerations by the intelligence community and administration officials" before the war. A study by the Carnegie Endowment for International Peace faulted the administration for overstating the WMD threat and for pressuring intelligence agencies to shape their findings to fit administration plans. Bush's specific claim in his 2003 State of the Union address that Saddam had tried to import weapons-grade uranium from Africa had been included despite two CIA warnings that it was unsubstantiated. Responding to the critics, Vice President Cheney insisted that it would have been irresponsible for the administration to ignore the WMD threat. President Bush blithely told a TV interviewer that it really made no difference whether Saddam actually possessed WMDs or only had the *potential* to develop such weapons.

World opinion remained deeply hostile. A September 2003 poll, reported the German Marshall Fund, found Europeans "increasingly dismayed by U.S. leadership and the use of U.S. force." A Bush visit to London in November spurred fresh protests. In contrast to the post-9/11 sympathy, the United States was increasingly viewed abroad as an imperialistic bully unconcerned with world opinion.

Saddam Hussein's two sons died resisting capture in July 2003, and in December Saddam himself was finally captured, hiding in a hole beneath a house near his hometown, Tikrit. Emaciated and unkempt, he scarcely resembled the notorious "Butcher of Baghdad." Others, however, argued for a trial under UN auspices, to give the full weight of international law to his ultimate punishment. Bush's approval rating, having fallen to 37 percent, rose to 52 percent. But did finding Saddam increase U.S. security and make the Middle East more peaceful? One *Time* magazine reader remained skeptical. "Now that Saddam Hussein has been captured . . . ," he wrote, "can we get back to fighting terrorism?" In July 2004, however, beginning their trials, Saddam and eleven top leaders of his regime were arraigned before an Iraqi judge in a heavily guarded Baghdad courtroom on charges of mass murder and other crimes.

Despite Saddam's capture, conditions in Iraq worsened. When U.S. authorities shut down the anti-American newspaper of a young Shiite cleric, Moqtada Sadr, in March 2004, his supporters unleashed a bloody uprising as Sadr took refuge in the holy city of Najaf. Farther north, in the so-called Sunni Triangle, insurgents in Fallujah ambushed four American civilian contract workers in late March, burned their truck, and brutalized their bodies. As fighting raged around Najaf and Fallujah, and attacks continued in Baghdad, the situation looked grim. The same month, Islamic terrorists planted bombs on crowded commuter trains in Madrid, killing 191 and injuring 1800. Three days later, Spanish voters elected a socialist government that soon withdrew all Spanish troops from Iraq.

A fresh crisis arose in May 2004 with the release of graphic photographs of the torture and sexual humiliation of Iraqi prisoners held in U.S. custody in Baghdad's notorious Abu Ghraib prison, scene of earlier torture and killings by Saddam Hussein's regime. As the International Red Cross reported widespread U.S. abuse of prisoners in Iraq and Afghanistan, Americans reacted in disgust and disbelief, anti-Americanism in the Arab world and in Europe intensified, and Iraqis demanded ever more vehemently that the Americans leave their country.

With the formal transfer of sovereignty in Iraq in late June, an interim prime minister and other government officials took office, and they spoke hopefully of conducting national elections in 2005. But 135,000 U.S. troops remained, along with 27,000 British and other coalition forces. To maintain army strength, the Pentagon extended GIs' tours of duty and called up more reservists. GI casualties continued, and the Iraqi death toll mounted. A July 2004 suicide bombing by insurgents in Baquba, north of Baghdad, targeting police recruits, killed some seventy Iraqis.

The Insurgents targeted officials of the new government for assassination, and began kidnapping foreign truck drivers and other workers and threatening them with death unless their companies left Iraq. Some were eventually released, but others were killed. To spare the life of a kidnapped Filipino worker, the government of the Philippines withdrew its small occupation force from Iraq. U.S. officials insisted that a stable and democratic Iraq would eventually emerge, but amid continuing bloodshed and disorder, the final outcome of a war launched so confidently remained deeply uncertain.

Battling Terrorism Worldwide

Terrorists struck in many countries. Pakistan's president Pervez Musharraf, who allied himself with the United States after 9/11, narrowly survived two assassination attempts in 2003. Daniel Pearl, a reporter for the *Wall Street Journal,* was kidnapped and murdered by Islamic extremists in Karachi, Pakistan's capital. In Indonesia, a predominantly Muslim nation, an October 2002 bombing at a Bali nightclub killed more than 200, including many Australian tourists. In 2003, 10 died and 150 were injured when a bomb destroyed a Marriott Hotel in Indonesia's capital, Djakarta. Soon after, in Ankara, Turkey, terrorists linked to Al Qaeda bombed two synagogues, the British embassy, and a British bank. Al Qaeda was also implicated in bombings in Saudi Arabia, Morocco, and elsewhere.

The effort to combat terrorism was global as well. Middle Easterners with ties to Al Qaeda were tracked down and arrested in Germany, England, and other countries. The Bali bomber was arrested and sentenced to death. Turkish authorities seized the perpetrators of the Ankara bombings. U.S. Navy Seals in cooperation with Philippine marines attacked a Muslim extremist group in the Philippines in 2002, killing the leader. In 2003, an alleged mastermind of the 9/11 attacks, Khalid Sheikh Mohammed, was seized in Pakistan, and a top lieutenant of Osama bin Laden, implicated in the Marriott Hotel bombing and the 2000 attack on the U.S.S. *Cole,* was captured in Indonesia. The administration also pursued the terrorists' money supply. A philanthropic foundation was shut down because its funds were allegedly reaching terrorist groups.

As for the other nations in Bush's "Axis of Evil," Iran and North Korea, the administration adopted a more conciliatory approach than toward Iraq. In 2003 Washington assured Iran that it had no plans to attack. Soon after, Iran accepted intensive UN inspections of its nuclear facilities. The administration welcomed this initiative and prepared to deal with Tehran through diplomatic channels.

North Korea, an isolated and impoverished communist nation ruled by a capricious despot, Kim Jong Il, openly boasted of its nuclear program, even though it had signed the 1970 nuclear nonproliferation treaty. U.S. strategists feared that North Korean nuclear weapons or nuclear know-how might fall into terrorists' hands. Bush's "Axis of Evil" speech had understandably stirred fear in North Korea, and its nuclear bluster seemed in part a diplomatic ploy aimed at winning security guarantees. In cooperation with Japan, China, and South Korea, the United States pursued negotiations, offering North Korea economic aid and security guarantees in return for an end to its nuclear-weapons program, verified by inspection. Although the outcome remained uncertain, this approach seemed to hold out promise.

In December 2003, Libya's ruler Mu'ammar Ghadhafi agreed to UN inspections to verify that Libya had no weapons of mass destruction. Ghadhafi was notorious for sponsoring international terrorism, including an attack on GIs in a Berlin nightclub and the devastating crash of Pan Am flight 103 over Scotland in 1988. Supporters of Bush's war policy pointed to Ghadhafi's apparent change of heart as a direct consequence of Saddam Hussein's overthrow.

When defining the threat facing America, Bush spoke in broad-brush generalizations with religious overtones. The nation's mission, he asserted, was to battle "evildoers" worldwide and track down terrorists who disliked the United States for no apparent reason except that they "hated freedom." Such rhetoric rallied support, but it also limited Americans' ability to understand the terrorists' motivations. However despicable their actions, they did cite specific grievances beyond a general hostility to the wickedness of Western culture. The stationing of U.S. troops in Saudi Arabia, home of Islam's most sacred shrines, outraged Osama bin Laden and his followers. They also denounced America's support of Israel, and especially the apparent inability of successive U.S. administrations, despite billions in annual aid to Israel, to halt the expansion of Jewish settlements in Palestinian lands in the West Bank. Such matters obviously did not justify slaughtering innocent people, but clarity about the specific grievances that fed the terrorists' anger seemed a first step toward combating the consequences of that anger.

Amid the confusion and frustrations of the war on terrorism, one thing was certain: The initiatives undertaken by the Bush administration after the attacks of September 11, 2001, both at home and abroad, had thrust the nation on a new course whose end no one could predict.

Recession and Corporate Scandals

Along with their other effects, the 9/11 attacks jolted American business. The airlines lost millions as many people stopped flying. Several carriers declared bankruptcy. The New York Stock Exchange, damaged in the attacks, closed for several days. When it reopened, stock prices plunged.

Even before 9/11, however, the stock market had begun a long downward slide from the giddy heights of the late 1990s. From its peak of 11,723 on January 14, 2000, the Dow Jones stock average slid to a low of 7,286 on October 9, 2002. In one week in March 2001, the market fell by 6 percent. Investors lured into a market that had seemed to go only upward felt they had been plunged into a cold shower.

Technology stocks, the darlings of the market during the boom, suffered the most. Some became practically worthless as the stock prices of many Silicon Valley start-up companies collapsed. From December 2000 to May 2003, 38 percent of all workers in computer-systems companies lost their jobs. The celebrated "new economy" proved to be vulnerable to the same market rules as the old economy.

The downturn ripped across the economy. Corporations cut production and investment. Unemployment spiked upward, reaching almost 6 percent by late 2001 as companies laid off workers or stopped hiring. The downturn hit not only wealthy investors and dot.com millionaires but also persons with modest incomes, retirees who had invested in mutual funds, and low-wage workers in the service sector. Toward the end of 2001, service-sector employment sank at the fastest rate in more than fifty years. Persons thrust into the labor market by the Welfare Reform Act of 1996 found tough going.

The Federal Reserve Board tried to stimulate recovery by a series of interest-rate cuts, making business and personal loans and mortgages easier to finance. By November 2002, after eleven successive cuts, the rate stood at .75 percent, a forty-year low. Automobile manufacturers tried to jump-start sales by offering interest-free financing. The combination of a recession plus Bush administration tax cuts (see below) once again plunged the federal budget into deficit, after the surpluses of the Clinton years.

The year 2002 brought some recovery, but the recession's effects hung on into 2003, as the stock market remained depressed, business investment stagnated, and unemployment remained high. By early 2004 the market had partially rebounded and corporate earnings and investment were reviving. Even the battered computer-technology sector showed signs of life. But new job creation stagnated, in part because of the outsourcing of jobs to Asia and Latin America. "[W]e are still stuck in a jobless recovery," observed one economist. The job picture improved as 2004 wore on, though many of the new jobs were in the bottom rungs of the service sector, where employees earned low wages and enjoyed few benefits.

The recession triggered a wave of corporate scandals as some of the nation's largest businesses, whose stock had soared in the 1990s, collapsed amid charges of deception and fraud. The first to fall was Houston's Enron Corporation, a natural-gas company that in the 1990s had expanded rapidly as an energy broker and telecommunications giant. In 2000 Enron claimed assets of more than $60 billion, placing it seventh on *Fortune* magazine's ranking of America's largest corporations. Enron seemed a model of the new economy, surfing the opportunities offered by new technologies, deregulation, and the sizzling market climate of the 1990s. Mutual fund managers and individual investors poured billions into Enron, driving its stock prices ever higher.

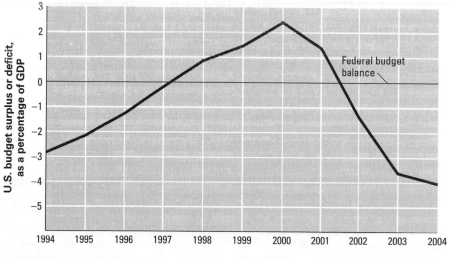

FIGURE 16.1

Federal Budget Surpluses and Deficits as a Percentage of Gross Domestic Product, 1994–2004

Source: *The World in 2004* (The Economist Magazine, London, 2004), p. 26.

In fact, Enron was an empty shell, kept afloat by debt, fraud, and off-the-books partnerships. The market decline exposed the charade, and Enron filed for bankruptcy in December 2001. Shortly before, CEO Kenneth Lay had sold millions in Enron stock while urging his employees to buy more stock. Enron's gleaming corporate headquarters (with its ironically appropriate logo, a crooked E) stood nearly empty as thousands of employees lost their jobs. Enron Stadium, home of the Houston Astros, changed its name to Minute Maid Stadium, after an orange juice company. Investors lost billions in stock holdings. Federal investigators pored over Enron's tangled records, and several of its top executives, including Kenneth Lay, faced indictments and possible prison terms.

A collateral victim of Enron's collapse was Chicago's Arthur Andersen Company, a giant accounting firm. Investigators found that Andersen auditors had routinely certified the accuracy of Enron's deceptive annual reports, sometimes to their own personal gain. Andersen, too, soon collapsed.

The Enron scandal drew special attention because Kenneth Lay and President George W. Bush were good friends. Enron was the Bush campaign's largest single contributor, kicking in over $600,000, and Lay helped shape the administration's energy policy (see page 504). Bush quickly distanced himself from Lay, and Bush's post-9/11 surge in popularity partially blunted the scandal's political fallout.

Other scandals soon followed, particularly in the glamorous telecommunications industry, whose new technologies and expanding markets lured investors. The most high-visibility collapse was WorldCom, the nation's second-largest long-distance and data-service provider, with 85,000 employees in sixty-five countries, headed by a charismatic Mississippean, Bernard Ebbers. In the summer of 2002, a team of auditors (replacing WorldCom's regular accountants, Arthur Andersen) found that some $7 billion in assets claimed by WorldCom did not exist. WorldCom soon filed for bankruptcy, the largest in history. The Securities and Exchange Commission launched an investigation, and Ebbers resigned. In May 2003 WorldCom (having resumed an earlier name, MCI) received a no-bid contract to build a cellular phone network in Iraq.

The telecommunications giant Global Crossing, with a book value of $50 billion two years earlier, filed for bankruptcy in 2002. As at Enron, top executives had unloaded hundreds of millions in company stock just before the collapse. Even Xerox, the respected photocopier company, allegedly concealed billions in losses through deceptive accounting practices. The scandals hurt not only accounting companies like Arthur Andersen but also brokerage firms and credit-rating agencies, where analysts who knew about the problems continued to give the troubled companies high ratings, misleading ordinary investors.

Samuel Waksal, the head of ImClone, a company specializing in biopharmaceutical research, was arrested in 2002 for insider trading. When one of ImClone's experimental cancer drugs failed a crucial test, Waksal had alerted family and friends, enabling them to sell their stock before the report was released. One friend Waksal allegedly tipped off, the home-decor guru Martha Stewart, was convicted of obstruction of justice and lying to investigators, and sentenced to five months in prison. These corporate scandals worsened the stock market decline.

In 2003 scandal hit the mutual-fund industry, as government investigators accused top firms of various illegal practices, such as after-hours trading, that favored large clients at the expense of smaller investors. New York's attorney general Elliot Spitzer, a bulldog in unearthing corporate wrongdoing, played a key role in this investigation. In a particularly glaring instance of out-of-control greed, the chairman of the New York Stock Exchange (NYSE), Dick Grasso, resigned in September 2003 after revelations that the NYSE board had approved a pay package for him of $187 million. The board members, dependent on Grasso for their well-paid positions, had OK'd this sum with little apparent question. As the embarrassing story unfolded, the NYSE radically reformed its management structure.

The corporate scandals unfolded in a Wild West business environment in which regulatory agencies such as the Federal Trade Commission, the Federal Communications Commission, and the Securities and Exchange Commission were underfunded and understaffed, or run by political appointees hostile to their basic purpose. Investors paid a heavy price for a prevailing assumption that capitalism works best when largely free of oversight or restraint. In the aftermath of the scandals, Congress passed legislation making corporate CEOs personally liable for the accuracy of their firm's financial statements. Whether this and other reforms were sufficient to ensure corporate good behavior when the next economic boom arrived remained to be seen.

The Bush Presidency: Serving God and Big Business

In the 2000 campaign, George W. Bush, a self-proclaimed "compassionate conservative," had positioned himself as a moderate who would reach out to all Americans. He appeared likely to seek the middle of the road, as Bill Clinton had done with such success until he hit a speed bump in the form of Monica Lewinsky. Instead, once in office, Bush primarily served two constituencies: the religious Right and big business.

A born-again Christian himself, President Bush targeted evangelicals in the campaign—for example, by answering "Jesus Christ" when asked in a TV debate to name his favorite philosopher—and they responded. Forty percent of his votes came from white evangelicals. In office, he catered to evangelical interests and sprinkled his speeches with evangelical language. In his January 2003 State of the Union address, for example, he observed that "there's power, wonder working power, in the goodness, idealism, and faith of the American people," borrowing the phrase from a gospel song beloved by evangelicals. Under Bush, National Park Service officials upheld the right of religious zealots to affix biblical mottos to rocks in Grand Canyon National Park.

Bush supported school-voucher programs, by which students in underperforming public schools could receive scholarships to attend church-sponsored schools. He soon dropped the idea in the face of congressional opposition, however. Bush also set up a White House office to push his "faith-based initiative" by which churches and religious organizations would receive federal funds to provide social services. The program faced criticism as a violation of the constitutional separation of church and state, but in 2002 televangelist Pat Robertson received a large grant to fund social programs run by various religious organizations.

Bush also spoke out on cultural issues important to religious conservatives. His administration cut off funds for family-planning groups in poor countries if they countenanced abortion. He promoted the campaign to stop the international trafficking in women for prostitution, a key issue with evangelicals. He addressed antiabortion rallies and in 2003 signed a bill banning late-term abortions. When a Massachusetts court in 2003 upheld the right of gay marriage, Bush called for a constitutional amendment banning same-sex marriage, and proposed spending $1.2 billion on a program to promote (heterosexual) marriage. In May 2004, Bush's top political strategist, Karl Rove, was graduation speaker at Jerry Falwell's Liberty University.

On education, Bush also responded to conservatives who criticized public schools for lacking academic rigor. His showcase education bill, the No Child Left Behind Act, passed by Congress in January 2002, required that every teacher be "highly qualified" and mandated annual standardized testing of all pupils from grades three through eight in reading, math, and science. The law aimed to promote academic rigor and to identify "failing schools," but critics charged that it ignored such problems as overcrowded classrooms and low teachers' salaries; provided few resources to enhance teachers' qualifications; and represented an unprecedented level of federal meddling in education, historically a state and local matter. Teachers would "teach to the test," critics warned, encouraging rote memorization. Some called the program "No Child Left Untested."

Bush's secretary of education, Rod Paige, had supposedly achieved dramatic improvements in test scores and dropout rates as Houston's superintendent of schools. However, a *New York Times* investigation found that the "Houston Miracle" resulted mostly from the manipulation of data, analogous to the fantastic profits claimed by Enron in the 1990s. Houston's educational record was in fact about the same as the national average. Rosa Arevelo, a Houston high-school graduate who had been designated a "Texas Scholar" for her academic achievements, found herself unable to do college-level work and soon dropped out. "I thought I was getting a good education," she said. "I was shocked."

President Bush also catered to the interests of the wealthy and of corporate America. Taking a leaf from Ronald Reagan's playbook, he proposed a $1.6 trillion tax cut, stretched over a ten-year period, that was particularly generous to corporations and the wealthy. The tax bill passed by Congress in May 2001 slashed taxes by $1.35 billion and somewhat reduced the cuts for the rich that Bush had proposed. As the economy faltered, the tax cuts contributed to the growing federal deficit. Economists calculated that the full ten years of the cuts would reduce federal revenues by $4 trillion. This, combined with rising Medicare and social-security costs, threatened future deficits of staggering proportions. The portion of the tax cut that went to middle-income and lower-income families did encourage spending and helped stimulate economic recovery.

Bush's energy proposals similarly reflected corporate interests. Vice President Cheney assembled a group of oil executives, including Enron's Kenneth Lay, who secretly drafted an energy bill focused on subsidies, incentives, and tax breaks to boost coal, oil, and natural gas production. Conservation, alternative energy sources, and environmental protection received scant attention. The bill authorized oil drilling in Alaska's Arctic National Wildlife Refuge, an ecologically sensitive area dismissed by Interior Secretary Gale Norton as "a flat white nothingness."

The Republican-dominated House enacted a bill that the White House approved, but early in 2002 a closely divided Senate passed a quite different bill stressing conservation and environmental protection. The bill that finally emerged from a Senate-House conference committee in November 2003 was close to the administration's original bill, though without the provision allowing drilling in the Arctic National Wildlife Refuge. Bush insisted that his bill was essential to national security, but the conservative British publication the *Economist* called it "a costly law that does little for America's energy problems, but piles subsidies and tax breaks in the lap of every conceivable business connected to energy." One provision tacked on to the bill by a Louisiana congressman authorized tax-free bonds for the construction of an energy-efficient Hooter's Restaurant in his district. Democrats ridiculed the "Hooters and polluters" energy program. The Senate blocked the bill, but backers vowed to keep trying.

Early in 2004, Bush proposed immigration-law reform granting temporary visas to the nation's 8 to 10 million illegal immigrants, mostly from Mexico, working in the United States. These workers played a crucial economic role, holding low-wage jobs that others spurned, and Bush won praise in some quarters for addressing their precarious situation. Others, however, saw it as a sop to companies employing illegal aliens, or as an election-year ploy to gain Hispanic votes. Groups seeking stricter enforcement of immigration laws also criticized the proposal.

On the environmental front, the administration sought to reverse regulations that corporations found oppressive, from logging in national forests to snowmobiles in national parks. Among other actions, the administration tripled the mercury emissions allowed from power plants, revoked regulations requiring power plants and refineries to install pollution controls when they upgraded their factories, dropped investigations of more than 140 refineries and industrials sites suspected of Clean Air Act violations, and exempted giant hog farms from laws regulating toxic air and water pollution. The administration also withdrew from negotiations over the final terms of the 1997 Kyoto Protocol, a UN-sponsored agreement, approved by 178 other nations, to reduce emissions contributing to global warming. Continued cooperation with this effort, said a State Department official, would put the United States in an "ever-tightening regulatory straitjacket."

Declared the Sierra Club's director, Carl Pope: "The Bush administration is systematically turning back thirty years of environmental progress. You really have to go back to the McKinley administration in the late nineteenth century to find so many gratuitous giveaways to special interests looking to exploit our air, water and natural areas." A few radical environmentalists resorted to terrorism. In August 2003, a group calling itself the Earth Liberation Front torched a car dealership in West Covina, California, destroying twenty Hummers, giant gas-guzzling dinosaurs.

In 2003, Congress passed the administration's Medicare reform bill providing limited prescription-drug benefits for seniors, a goal of the American Association of Retired Persons, a potent lobbying organization. Critics charged that the new entitlement, with estimated costs of $400 billion in the first decade alone and lacking any provision for regulating drug costs, would vastly worsen the federal deficit and jeopardize drug benefits that many seniors already enjoyed. Critics also asserted that the bill undermined Medicare by allowing seniors to choose private health-care providers instead. Here was another example, they charged, of the administration's readiness to pander to special interests and serve corporate America even at the price of fiscal irresponsibility.

On the international front, the Bush administration's go-it-alone tendency, already evident in the Iraq War and the abandonment of the Kyoto Protocol, emerged in other areas as well. The administration refused to join the International Criminal Court (ICC), created in 1998 to prosecute individuals charged with war crimes, genocide, and crimes against humanity, on the grounds that U.S. officials might be wrongly prosecuted. The administration also threatened other nations with reprisals if they joined the ICC. Responding to pressure from the tobacco industry and the National Rifle Association, the administration opposed an international treaty aimed at curbing smoking and denounced a proposed UN pact limiting the worldwide trade in small arms, including handguns and shoulder-launched rockets.

Updating Ronald Reagan's 1983 Star Wars proposal, the Bush administration pushed the testing and deployment of a missile-defense system—described by skeptics as hitting a bullet with a bullet. This meant repudiating the 1972 Anti-Ballistic Missile Treaty, long opposed by neoconservatives. Russia and other nations protested, as did arms-control specialists. But the administration proceeded to develop launch sites in California and Alaska, with deployment of the first ten missiles scheduled for 2004 and a much larger system envisioned for the future. With the cost for the first five years estimated at nearly $50 billion, Democrats and even many Republicans objected, but to no avail.

In 2003, despite its worries about nuclear proliferation, the administration requested funds to research a new generation of nuclear weapons capable of penetrating underground command centers. The Senate approved but the House did not, temporarily derailing the project. Said Republican congressman David Hobson of Ohio: "Before we go blindly into new areas, we have to think about where we are and what we are doing with what we've got."

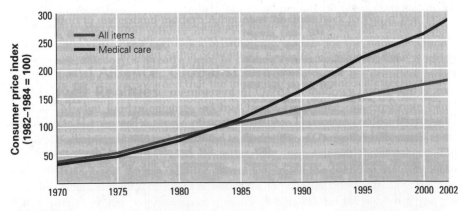

FIGURE 16.2

U.S. Consumer Price Index for All Items and for Medical Care, 1970–2002

SOURCE: Bureau of Labor Statistics, U.S. Department of Labor.

As the 2004 presidential race approached, the early Democratic frontrunner was Howard Dean, a feisty former Vermont governor who roundly criticized the Iraq War and mobilized the Internet to raise funds and energize his supporters. But party elders like Senator Ted Kennedy backed the more moderate Senator John Kerry of Massachusetts, who emphasized his Washington experience, leadership qualities, and heroic Vietnam War record. Defeating Dean and other contenders in the early primaries, Kerry won the nomination. As his running mate, he chose the charismatic Senator John Edwards of North Carolina, who had risen from humble beginnings to become a successful trial lawyer specializing in medical malpractice suits. At the Democratic convention in Boston, Kerry, Edwards, and most other speakers courted undecided voters by avoiding direct criticism of Bush and stressing patriotism, national unity, and positive goals for the future.

The Bush-Cheney campaign emphasized the president's leadership in battling terrorism, highlighted the cultural "wedge issues" important to Bush's conservative base, and dismissed Kerry as a product of "the far liberal wing" of his party and a politician who had flip-flopped on many issues. With Bush's approval ratings standing at 45–50 percent in various polls, political emotions running high, and the nation deeply polarized, all signs pointed to another close election.

While Kerry built a war chest of $200 million, President Bush, amassed an even larger campaign fund of some $250 million. Each candidate also received $75 million in taxpayer contributed campaign funds, and both parties raised millions more to spend on state races and voter-registration drives. Clearly the 2004 campaign would be among the most expensive in history.

The politics of big money hit a speed bump in 2002 with the passage of a campaign-finance law that blended the McCain-Feingold bill (see page 436) with a House bill sponsored by a Massachusetts Democrat and a Connecticut Republican. Upheld by the Supreme Court in 2003, the campaign-finance law restricted bogus TV "issue ads" aimed at influencing elections and limited so-called soft-money contributions given to national parties but typically redirected to specific candidates. (In 2000, the two parties raised nearly $500 million in soft money, 60 percent of it from only eight hundred donors.) Whether this law would reform campaign financing remained uncertain, as wealthy individuals and lobbying organizations worked to circumvent it.

Republican voters tuned in to conservative radio talk shows and right-wing political commentary on Rupert Murdoch's Fox TV channel, and they devoured paperbacks such as Ann Coulter's *Treason: Liberal Treachery from the Cold War to the War on Terrorism* (2003). Democrats, in turn, snapped up Al Franken's *Lies and the Lying Liars Who Tell Them: A Fair and Balanced Look at the Right,* Molly Ivins' *Bushwhacked: Life in George W. Bush's America,* and Michael Moore's *Dude, Where's My Country?* all published in 2003. Moore's anti-Bush documentary film *Fahrenheit 9/11* packed theaters in 2004.

Amid the political pyrotechnics, the bipartisan 9/11 commission (see page 486) issued its report in July 2004. Led by Republican Thomas Kean, a former governor of New Jersey, and Democrat Lee Hamilton, a former member of Congress, the commission had held hours of hearings and supervised a large investigative staff. The unanimous report identified many failures, from slipshod immigration procedures and airport security checks to intelligence lapses and inaction in both the

Clinton and Bush administrations. (Bush, for example, spent much of the summer of 2001 vacationing on his Texas ranch despite increasingly explicit warnings of Al Qaeda terrorist plans, including an August intelligence briefing captioned "Bin Laden Determined to Attack Inside the U.S." that reported "patterns of suspicious activity in this country consistent with preparation for hijackings"). "[N]one of the measures adopted by the U.S. government from 1998 to 2001 disturbed or even delayed the progress of the Al Qaeda plot," the commissioners damningly concluded.

The report did not dwell on scapegoating individuals, however, and it sidestepped such divisive issues as whether the Iraq War had advanced or impeded the war on terrorism. Rather, it focused on the systemic failure of the nation's airdefense and intelligence agencies, notably the CIA and FBI, to put together critical bits of intelligence data or to share their findings with other agencies. Overextended and underfunded, the intelligence agencies were hobbled by their "outmoded structure and bureaucratic rivalries." (CIA head George Tenet resigned shortly before the report appeared.)

Warning of possible future terrorist attacks of even greater severity, the report grimly observed: "We believe we are safer today. But we are not safe." It proposed many reforms, including the creation of a National Counterterrorism Center (NCTC), to monitor and assemble information from the government's fifteen intelligence agencies. The NCTC head, in turn, would report to the National Intelligence Director, a new cabinet-level official charged with detecting terrorist plots. While emphasizing that "[t]he enemy is not Islam, a great world faith," the report called for an integrated global strategy against Islamist terrorism, "a minority strain of Islam that does not distinguish politics from religion, and distorts both." This worldwide effort, the commissioners added, should utilize "all elements of national power: diplomacy, intelligence, covert action, law enforcement, economic policy, foreign aid, . . . and homeland defense."

The report concluded: "We call on the American people to remember how we all felt on 9/11, . . . how we came together as a nation—one nation. Unity of purpose and unity of effort are the way we will defeat this enemy and make America safer for our children and grandchildren." As they digested the somber report, Americans relived the horror that had unfolded on that tranquil autumn morning three years earlier and were again reminded how fundamentally the events of 9/11 had changed the course of the nation's history.

Conclusion

The opening years of the twenty-first century proved more eventful than the celebrators on New Year's Eve 1999 had anticipated. The economic boom suddenly collapsed, and the Bush administration proved more conservative and hard-edged than most observers had predicted. Above all, the terrorist attacks of September 11, 2001, brought profound changes at home and in America's world role.

Domestically, the quest for security led to a significant expansion of the federal government's power to control and monitor citizens' activities. Indeed, the Bush team had transformed the Republican Party from one favoring individualism and restraints on federal power to one that championed an unprecedented level of federal intrusion into American life, from the surveillance powers of the PATRIOT Act to the school testing of the No Child Left Behind Act to the regulation of personal morality. The one group exempted from this newly intrusive government was corporate America. The Bush administration worked assiduously to serve corporate interests, undercut environmental laws, and reduce business regulation. In sharp contrast to the traditional Republican concern for fiscal responsibility, Bush's economic initiatives, from massive tax cuts to new Medicare entitlements, seemed to be undertaken with little concern for the mountainous debt they bequeathed to future generations.

Internationally, the convergence of 9/11 with an administration intent on asserting U.S. power with scant regard for the United Nations and the emerging multinational world order it represented, or even for America's historic allies, produced the most unilateralist U.S. foreign policy since World War II, expressed most dramatically in the go-it-alone preemptive war in Iraq.

In January 2004, after years of preparation, NASA landed two highly sophisticated 400-pound solar-powered robotic vehicles on Mars on a three-month scientific mission to determine the possible presence of water, the essential ingredient of life, at some point in the past. Named *Spirit* and *Opportunity,* they beamed back photographs of remarkable clarity as they moved about on the Martian surface, guided by Earth-bound computers. Scientists and engineers at NASA's Jet Propulsion Laboratory in California cheered the success of the $800 million mission.

Back on Earth, humanity continued to be wracked by wars, conflicts, atrocities, surging religious fanaticism, and terrorist attacks whose principal victims were often innocent men, women, and children. And the world community remained divided between a minority enjoying rising levels of health, longevity, and physical comfort and a vast majority battling for survival amid poverty, malnutrition, disease, illiteracy, and high rates of infant mortality.

The stark contrast between the shining achievement of NASA's Mars mission and the problems afflicting the human family back home underscored both the promise and challenges Americans confronted as they moved into the new century.

SELECTED READINGS

The periodicals listed in the Chapter 15 selected readings are valuable sources for the period covered in this chapter as well.

The 2000 Election, the George W. Bush Administration

Frank Bruni, *Ambling into History: The Unlikely Odyssey of George W. Bush* (2002); James W. Caesar and Andrew E. Busch, *The Perfect Tie: The True Story of the 2000 Presidential Election* (2001); Sue E. S. Crawford and Laura R. Olson, eds., *Christian Clergy and American Politics* (2001); Alan M. Dershowitz, *Supreme Injustice: How the High Court Hijacked Election 2000* (2001); David Frum, *The Right Man: The Surprise Presidency of George W. Bush* (2003); Todd Gitlin, *Letters to a Young Activist* (2003); Fred I. Greenstein, ed., *The George W. Bush Presidency: An Early Assessment* (2003); Molly Ivins and Lou Dubose, *Bushwhacked: Life in George W. Bush's America* (2003); Paul Krugman, *The Great Unraveling:*

Losing Our Way in the New Century (2003); Stephen Mansfield, *The Faith of George W. Bush* (2003); Kevin Phillips, *American Dynasty: Aristocracy, Fortune, and the Politics of Deceit in the House of Bush* (2004); Jack N. Rakove, ed., *The Unfinished Election of 2000* (2001); Cass R. Sunstein and Richard A. Epstein, eds., *The Vote: Bush, Gore, and the Supreme Court* (2001); Ron Suskind, *The Price of Loyalty: George W. Bush, The White House, and the Education of Paul O'Neill* (2004); Spencer R. Weart, *The Discovery of Global Warming* (2003).

Recession, Corporate Scandals, Economic Trends

John Cassidy, *Dot.con: The Greatest Story Ever Sold* (2002); Kenneth W. Dam, *The Rules of the Global Game* (2001); Peter C. Fusaro and Ross M. Miller, *What Went Wrong at Enron* (2002); Kevin Phillips, *Wealth and Democracy* (2002); Michael Rowbotham, *Goodbye America: Globalization, Debt, and the Dollar Empire* (2001); Richard J. Schroth and A. Larry Elliott, *How Companies Lie: Why Enron Is Just the Tip of the Iceberg* (2002); Rebecca Smith and John R. Emshwiller, *24 Days: How Two Wall Street Journal Reporters Uncovered the Lies That Destroyed Faith in Corporate America* (2003).

9/11 and After, Homeland Security, Iraq War

Greg Anrig, Jr., and Richard C. Leone, eds., *The War on Our Freedoms: Civil Liberties in an Age of Terrorism* (2003); Peter L. Bergen, *Holy War, Inc: Inside the Secret World of Osama bin Laden* (2001); Cynthia Brown, ed., *Lost Liberties: Ashcroft and the Assault on Personal Freedom* (2003); Craig Calhoun, Paul Price, and Ashley Timmer, eds., *Understanding September 11* (2002); Carnegie Endowment for International Peace, *WMD in Iraq: Evidence and Implications* (2004); Richard A. Clarke, *Against All Enemies* (2004); Alan M. Dershowitz, *Why Terrorism Works: Understanding the Threat, Responding to the Challenge* (2003); Anne Garrels, *Naked in Baghdad: The Iraq War as seen by NPR's Correspondent Anne Garrels* (2003); Fawaz A. Gerges, *America and Political Islam: Clash of Cultures or Clash of Interests?* (2001); M. J. Gohari, *The Taliban: Ascent to Power* (2000); Fred Halliday, *Two Hours That Shook the World: September 11, 2001: Causes and Consequences* (2001); James Mann, *Rise of the Vulcans: The History of Bush's War Cabinet* (2004); Joanne Meyerowitz, ed., *History and September 11* (2003); Judith Miller, Steven Engelberg, and William Broad, *Germs, Biological Weapons and America's Secret War* (2001); National Commission on Terrorist Attacks Upon the United States, *The 9/11 Report* (2004); Salam Pax, *The Clandestine* [Internet] *Diary of an Ordinary Iraqi* (2003); Todd S. Purdum, *A Time of Our Choosing: America's War in Iraq* (2004); Ahmed Rashid, *Jihad: The Rise of Militant Islam in Central Asia* (2002); Strobe Talbott and Nayan Chanda, eds., *The Age of Terror: America and the World after September 11* (2001); Bob Woodward, *Plan of Attack* (2004).

Contemporary America and the Global Community

Victor D. Cha and David C. Kang, *Nuclear North Korea: A Debate on Engagement Strategies* (2003); Ivo H. Daalder and James M. Lindsay, *America Unbound: The Bush Revolution in Foreign Policy* (2003); Chalmers Johnson, *Blowback: The Costs and Consequences of American Empire* (2001); Anthony Lake, *Six Nightmares: Real Threats in a Dangerous World and How America Can Meet Them* (2001); John Newhouse, *Imperial America: The Bush Assault on the World Order* (2003); Richard Perle and David Frum, *An End to Evil* (2004); Paul Pillar, *Terrorism and U.S. Foreign Policy* (2001); Clyde Prestowitz, *Rogue Nation: American Unilateralism and the Failure of Good Intentions* (2003); Bernard Wasserstein, *Israelis and Palestinians: Why Do They Fight? Can They Stop?* (2003).

Index

Credits

Photographs

Page 1: Archive Photos/Getty Images. Page 24: © CORBIS. Page 44: UPI/CORBIS-Bettmann. Page 82: CORBIS-Bettmann. Page 104: UPI/CORBIS-Bettmann. Page 129: Hulton Archive, John Kobal Foundation/Getty Images. Page 140: Hulton Archive/Getty Images. Page 172: UPI/CORBIS-Bettmann. Page 200: AP/Wide World Photos. Page 222: © Bettmann/CORBIS. Page 241: © Bettmann Archive/CORBIS. Page 258: Dan McCoy/ Rainbow/The Image Works. Page 282: LBJ Library photo by Yoichi R. Okamoto. Page 308: Photograph by Bernard Gotfryd/Getty Images. Page 336: © CORBIS. Page 349: © Rob Howard/CORBIS. Page 374: © Photographer Elliott Erwit/Magnum Photos. Page 402: © 2004 Rick Friedman/CORBIS. Page 452: © Jean-Claude Lejeune. Page 488: AP/Wide World Photos.

Text

"Blowin' in the Wind": Copyright © 1962 by Warner Bros. Music, Inc. Copyright renewed © 1990 by Special Rider Music. All rights reserved. International copyright secured. Reprinted by permission.

Robert Frost, "Stopping by Woods on a Snowy Evening": From *The Poetry of Robert Frost,* edited by Edward Connery Lathem. Copyright 1951 by Robert Frost. Copyright 1923, 1969 by Henry Holt and Company, Inc. Copyright 1997 by Edward Connery Lathem. Reprinted by permission of Henry Holt and Company, Inc.

Allen Ginsberg, "Howl": Four lines from "Howl" from *Collected Poems 1947–1980* by Allen Ginsberg. Copyright © 1955 by Allen Ginsberg. Reprinted by permission of HarperCollins Publishers, Inc.

Randall Jarrell, "Losses": Excerpt from *The Complete Poems* by Randall Jarrell. Copyright 1969 by Mrs. Randall Jarell, renewed 1997 by Mary von S. Jarrell. Reprinted by permission of Farrar, Straus & Giroux, Inc.

Martin Luther King, "I Have a Dream": Excerpt reprinted by arrangement with the Estate of Martin Luther King, Jr., c/o Writers House, Inc. as agents for the proprietor, New York, N.Y. Copyright 1963 by Martin Luther King, Jr., copyright renewed 1991 by Coretta Scott King.

Phil Ochs: **I Ain't Marchin' Anymore,** Words and Music by Phil Ochs. Copyright © 1964 BARRICADE MUSIC INC. Copyright renewed. All Rights Controlled and Administered by ALMO MUSIC CORP. All Rights Reserved. Used by Permission.

"The Times They Are A-Changin'": Copyright © 1963 by Warner Bros. Music, Inc. Copyright renewed 1991 by Special Rider Music. All rights reserved. International copyright secured. Reprinted by permission.